MEDICINE

FOR MOUNTAINEERING
& Other Wilderness Activities

5TH EDITION

EDITED BY

JAMES A. WILKERSON, M.D.
Merced Pathology Laboratory
Merced, California

THE
MOUNTAINEERS
BOOKS

Published by
The Mountaineers Books
1001 SW Klickitat Way, Suite 201
Seattle, WA 98134

First edition 1967. Second edition 1975. Third edition 1985. Fourth edition 1992. Fifth edition: first printing, 2001.

Published simultaneously in Great Britain by Cordee, 3a DeMontfort Street, Leicester, England, LE1 7HD

Manufactured in the United States of America

Project Editor: Christine Ummel Hosler
Copyeditor: Chris DeVito
Cover and Book Designer: Dottie Martin
Layout Artist: Dottie Martin
Illustrators: Marjorie Domenowske, Dana Peick

Front cover photograph: *Silhouette of mountain climber at crest* © Cheyenne Rouse/ImageState, Inc.
Back cover photograph: *A mountaineer crosses a ridge during an ascent of Mount Fitz Roy, Patagonia, Argentina.* © Galen Rowell/Corbis

Library of Congress Cataloging-in-Publication Data
Medicine for mountaineering & other wilderness activities / edited by James A. Wilkerson.— 5th ed. [fully updated].
    p. cm.
Includes index.
 ISBN 0-89886-799-1
 1. Mountaineering injuries. 2. Outdoor medical emergencies. 3. First aid in illness and injury. I. Title: Medicine for mountaineering and other wilderness activities. II. Wilkerson, James A., 1934–
  RC1220.M6 M4 2001
  617.1'027—dc21

2001002230

CONTENTS

CONTRIBUTORS

▼ **C. KIRK AVENT, M.D.,** Professor of Medicine, Infectious Disease Division, The School of Medicine, The University of Alabama at Birmingham, Birmingham, Alabama

▼ **FRED T. DARVILL, M.D.,** Diagnosis and Internal Medicine, Mount Vernon, Washington; Clinical Assistant Professor of Medicine, University of Washington School of Medicine, Seattle, Washington

▼ **BEN EISEMAN, M.D.,** Emeritus Professor of Surgery, University of Colorado School of Medicine and Veterans Administration Hospital, Denver, Colorado

▼ **BLAIR D. ERB, M.D.,** Internal Medicine and Cardiology; Past President, Wilderness Medical Society, Jackson, Tennessee

▼ **COLIN K. GRISSOM, M.D.,** Internist and Pulmonologist, LDS Hospital, Salt Lake City, Utah

▼ **CHARLES S. HOUSTON, M.D.,** Internist and Cardiologist, Burlington, Vermont; formerly Professor of Medicine, The University of Vermont College of Medicine, Burlington, Vermont

▼ **EUGENE E. MOORE, M.D.,** Chairman, Department of Surgery, Denver Health Hospital, Denver, Colorado

▼ **BRUCE B. PATON, M.D.,** Emeritus Professor of Clinical Surgery, University of Colorado Health Sciences Center; Past President, Wilderness Medical Society, Denver, Colorado

▼ **LAWRENCE C. SALVESEN, M.D.,** Psychiatrist; Staff Psychiatrist, Outpatient Stress Unit, Veterans Administration Hospital, Togus, Maine; Mental Health Member, Southern Maine and Tri-County Stress Debriefing Teams, Pownal, Maine

▼ **JOSEPH B. SERRA, M.D.,** Orthopedist, Stockton, California; Assistant Clinical Professor of Orthopedics, University of California at Davis, School of Medicine, Davis, California

▼ **JAMES A. WILKERSON, M.D.,** Pathologist, Merced, California

FOREWORD

Mountaineering: The Freedom of the Hills had been off the press scarcely long enough for copies to traverse the continent to the shores of the Atlantic Ocean when I received a letter from there commenting on a serious imbalance. The writer, a climber completing his medical education at Johns Hopkins, commented that while the chapters on snowcraft and geology were admirably thorough, the chapter on first aid, though expertly written by climber-physicians, was the barest of elementary outlines. The book told more about the snow under climbers' boots and the rocks in their hands than it did about their bodies.

Given this level of instruction, what could the average wilderness traveler do about pyelonephritis, a pulmonary embolism, a retinal hemorrhage? Could he or she cope with snakebite, a flail chest, a "cafe coronary"? Or, for that matter, with a swollen wisdom tooth, fecal impaction, poison oak?

In The Mountaineers' climbing course and in a companion course in mountaineering first aid, we went a considerable distance into second aid and urged students to enroll, as well, in a Red Cross program. Still, the unspoken rule was: Don't get badly hurt or seriously ill at any distance from civilization unless you have an M.D. in the party. Or, to paraphrase an old Alpine maxim, "When a climber on a weekend trip comes down with the flu or breaks an ankle, he apologizes to his friends. When he gets acute appendicitis three days from the road, his friends apologize for him."

Halfway and more through the twentieth century, wilderness mountaineers were recapitulating the frontiering of their nineteenth-century ancestors, settlers of lonesome lands where in emergencies they could turn only to themselves and God, and where, ministers and physicians being equally rare visitors, the family library like as not consisted of two volumes—the Bible and the "doctor book."

Our ancestors were better off than we, because they *had* a doctor book. Jim Wilkerson's offer to prepare one was welcomed enthusiastically by those of us who had produced *Freedom of the Hills* yet never in the wildlands been free from submerged anxieties (Does that sudden stabbing pain in the abdomen emanate from the appendix? Or the salami?), anxieties that erupted as panic when a companion took a hard hit on the head (Is it a fracture? A concussion? Is blood coming out of the ears? Or flowing into them from a cut in the scalp?).

As a nonprofit publisher we had no need to consider the potential sales, if any; we expected to sell fewer copies than we gave away to indigent expeditions unable to recruit an M.D. We were content— if on one climb in one mountain range of the world the book ever saved one life, it was worth doing. We were certain there would be, over the years, many more than one.

Supposing, though, all the wilderness travelers who ever owned copies were guarded by an incredibly lucky star and never experienced or witnessed mortal peril? Even so, the book would be a blessing, for the confidence it gave in "copeability." To be sure, it could not help a layman remove an inflamed appendix, but it could help him distinguish a dozen feel-alikes from the real thing, and that would be a comfort. Those travelers under the incredible star might never turn the pages, yet in all their lucky years would gain peace of mind from having the book in their rucksack.

In the early 1960s, we of The Mountaineers book-publishing program took great satisfaction and pride in encouraging Dr. Wilkerson to proceed, and we knew the discriminating few would be grateful. What surprised us was that, far from the pages yellowing on the shelves, the book soon was moving out of our warehouse at a rate exceeded only by that of *Freedom* itself. That it has continued to do so, and now, after these thirty-four years, comes forth in a state-of-the-art fifth edition, shows how wrong publishers can be. Plainly, the merit of the volume has been recognized by the discriminating many.

Harvey Manning

ACKNOWLEDGMENTS

The fifth edition of *Medicine for Mountaineering* has provided an opportunity to include some new contributors—and to make a few unwanted changes. Herb Hultgren, an original contributor who performed so many of the initial, astute studies of high altitude disorders—one of the smartest, and one of the nicest, most considerate people I have known—has succumbed to leukemia. We feel the loss of this man deeply.

Drummond Rennie, who played an active role in many of the later altitude investigations—and who is also one of the smartest people I have known—is so swamped with his editorial responsibilities for the *Journal of the American Medical Association* that he has been unable to revise his chapter.

Blair Erb, a former President of the Wilderness Medical Society, has taken on Herb's chapter on cardiac disorders. Charles Houston has rewritten the chapter on altitude illnesses. Colin Grissom, a pulmonologist at the LDS Hospital in Salt Lake City, Utah, has accepted the responsibility for reviewing Houston's chapter on pulmonary problems.

Kirk Avent, Professor of Medicine in the Division of Infectious Diseases at the University of Alabama at Birmingham School of Medicine, is not only the principal contributor for the chapter on infections but also reviewed much of the discussion of infections and their treatment in other portions of the book.

Peter Hackett, who was a co-investigator with Drummond Rennie in many studies—they were the first to clearly identify the syndrome of acute mountain sickness and described many of the features of high altitude cerebral edema—is another new contributor. He has allowed his chapter, "Altitude and Common Medical Disorders," which has been published in a book for physicians and altitude investigators edited by Thomas F. Hornbein (a former contributor) and Robert B. Schoene, to be converted to a format suitable for nonphysicians and to be included in this edition. I am grateful for the opportunity to include this material, which is one of the most significant additions since *Medicine for Mountaineering* was first published.

In previous editions, contributors' names have not been listed with their chapters because all chapters were edited, some extensively, to conform to a uniform format, which is considered essential for a text of this type. In this edition, contributor's names are listed with the chapters, but as principal contributors, not as authors, because the text has once again been edited for uniformity.

Since the first edition of *Medicine for Mountaineering* appeared, interest in wilderness medicine has grown exponentially. The Wilderness Medical Society has been founded and continues to grow. It provides a number of educational programs for physicians, other medical professionals, and other individuals. It supports the publication of the *Wilderness Medicine Letter* and *Journal of Wilderness and Environmental Medicine,* a peer-reviewed journal listed in the *Index Medicus.* Individuals wanting to learn more about wilderness medicine and to keep abreast of new developments are urged to join that society. Its web address is *www.wms.org.* Email can be sent to *membership@wms.org.* Alternatively, inquiries can be addressed to: Wilderness Medical Society, Suite A-1, 3595 East Fountain Boulevard, Colorado Springs, CO 80910; telephone: 719-572-9255.

Jim Wilkerson
Merced, California

INTRODUCTION

Anyone who partakes in wilderness activities that demand skill, knowledge, strength, and stamina, such as mountaineering, cross-country skiing, or white-water kayaking and rafting, must expect sooner or later to be involved in misfortune—if not his own, then someone else's. The outcome of such misfortune often depends on the medical care the victims receive. For accidents or illnesses that occur at a considerable distance from a physician or hospital, ordinary first aid often does not suffice. If the individuals are to recover with minimal permanent disability, the admonition "Don't do any harm until the doctor comes!" is not adequate. In many wilderness situations, the doctor is not coming.

In addition to injuries resulting from falls or similar accidents, members of wilderness outings must cope with the problems presented by high terrestrial altitudes and extremes of heat and cold. They must be prepared to provide immediate, appropriate treatment for anaphylactic reactions to insect stings, or to institute cardiopulmonary resuscitation for victims of drowning or lightning strikes. They must avoid the infectious and parasitic disorders that are a constant threat in developing countries. And they must be prepared to deal with a variety of medical problems usually cared for by physicians. Infectious diseases such as hepatitis and poliomyelitis, noninfectious disorders such as thrombophlebitis and strokes, and surgical problems such as appendicitis have all occurred on wilderness outings.

The ability to rationally analyze a problem or situation and select and pursue a direct, logical course to a solution is a rare talent known as "common sense." No ability is more important in caring for individuals with medical disorders in wilderness situations. However, the body's functions and the intricacies of its varied disorders are highly complex, and only those knowledgeable about the principles of diagnosis and therapy can provide optimal medical care for the victims of injury or disease, particularly in remote situations.

Medicine for Mountaineering has been compiled by physicians who actively pursue a variety of wilderness interests, and is intended to be a source for the information needed to care for medical problems that may be encountered in such circumstances. It is a handbook of medicine—not first aid. The treatment described for some conditions includes potent medications or sophisticated therapeutic procedures. Such remedies are necessary to care for many disorders, but they could lead to disaster if used incorrectly. In the more than thirty years since the publication of the first edition of this book, wilderness enthusiasts who are not medical professionals have demonstrated an ability to assimilate such information and use it appropriately.

To reduce potential complications from the use of medications, the doses of drugs usually are provided only in appendix A, along with contraindications and side effects. By this expedient, a warning of the precautions that must be observed whenever a drug is used has been provided without undue repetition. (Most of the medications can be obtained only by prescription from a physician, who should make certain the person obtaining the drugs knows their proper use.)

Because no alternative methods for treating some disorders are available, a few procedures have been included that would be impractical or impossible in many wilderness circumstances. Intravenous fluid therapy is an example. A small wilderness party would almost never carry intravenous fluids and the equipment for administering them. Even a large expedition might have difficulty keeping such materials in locations where they could be obtained quickly. However, intravenous fluids are the only means for keeping alive individuals with some disorders, and instructions for their use have been included. (Large expeditions have left behind a considerable quantity of medical supplies on some popular routes and a significant supply of items such as intravenous fluids is available.)

The members of wilderness outings should know how to provide basic medical care and should be prepared to administer any treatment that may be needed. The knowledge and medical equipment required depends upon the location and duration of the outing. Traumatic disorders—the injuries produced by physical forces such as falls or falling objects—are most common in wilderness situations, particularly on outings of only a few days. Signs and symptoms of nontraumatic disorders, such as infections or diseases of the heart or lungs, usually develop gradually over a period of several days and often do not become apparent during short trips. On longer trips, the slower onset may permit the victim to be evacuated under his own power before he is incapacitated. Additionally, wilderness enthusiasts tend to be young and healthy and are less susceptible to nontraumatic disorders.

Members of any wilderness outing, regardless of its location or duration, should be capable of:
- ▼ Caring for soft-tissue injuries, including anticipating and treating hemorrhagic shock
- ▼ Anticipating and treating anaphylactic shock, particularly after insect stings
- ▼ Recognizing and caring for fractures
- ▼ Diagnosing and treating head injuries, including maintaining an airway while evacuating an unconscious individual
- ▼ Diagnosing and treating thoracic and abdominal injuries
- ▼ Recognizing a need for, and performing, cardiopulmonary resuscitation

Potentially threatening environments may call for the capabilities of:
- ▼ Recognizing and treating heat or cold injuries
- ▼ Recognizing and treating altitude disorders

Members of extended expeditions should, in addition, develop:
- ▼ The ability to take a simple medical history and perform a physical examination
- ▼ Familiarity with the techniques of patient care, particularly administration of medications
- ▼ Knowledge of the medical disorders, particularly infectious disorders, likely to be encountered on that specific expedition

Every participant in wilderness activities should have regular examinations by a physician knowledgeable about and sympathetic with his interests. Wilderness organizations probably should require such examinations before anyone participates in an outing. (Medical disorders that a physician would recognize during his examination and subsequently treat are too complex for inclusion in a handbook such as this.) For prolonged expeditions into isolated areas, a prior medical examination is essential. Individuals with a peptic ulcer, gallstones, hernia, pregnancy (particularly in the first and third trimesters), a history of intestinal obstruction following an abdominal operation, or chronic malaria and an enlarged spleen must be aware of the risk in prolonged isolation where surgical help is not available.

GENERAL PRINCIPLES

CHAPTER 1

DIAGNOSIS

"Disease manifests itself by abnormal sensations and events (symptoms), and by changes in structure or function (signs). Symptoms, being subjective, must be described by the patient. Signs are objective and these the physician discovers by means of physical examination, laboratory studies, and special methods of investigation."[1]

This statement succinctly describes the way medical disorders are diagnosed. Injuries resulting from physical forces (trauma) are identified primarily by physical examination. Symptoms play a greater role in the recognition of nontraumatic disorders. The absence of laboratories, diagnostic radiology, or other facilities should not prevent identification of disorders in the wilderness. Most common disorders have to be diagnosed—or at least suspected—before appropriate investigative studies can be ordered.

Diagnosis is usually the most difficult aspect of care for a person with a nontraumatic disorder. Physicians commonly expend more effort identifying problems than treating them. Outlines are provided to help caregivers recognize the organs that are the site of a disorder. Later chapters contain diagnostic features of the common disorders of specific organs. These sources should be consulted repeatedly. "Mistakes are just as often caused by lack of thoroughness as by lack of knowledge."[2]

Effectively examining someone with a medical disorder is not an easy, straightforward procedure. A calm, understanding, and sympathetic manner is essential. The ability to judge the subject's personality and to adopt an approach that instills confidence is vital. A seriously ill or injured person can not be expected to be cheerful and understanding or, on some occasions, even cooperative.

If an individual has traumatic injuries, an initial cursory examination should identify problems that require immediate attention, such as bleeding, an obstructed airway, or fractures. However, a complete, unhurried, and uninterrupted examination should be carried out as soon as possible, although evacuation from a position of imminent danger such as rockfall may be necessary first.

THE MEDICAL HISTORY

The individual should be encouraged to describe symptoms in his own words. Leading questions should be avoided, although some prompting or direct inquiries are almost always necessary. A person's failure to describe a symptom must not be considered a reliable indication that the symptom is not present.

The time and circumstances in which symptoms appear and their chronological sequence are significant. The precise location of pain, the time it began, whether the onset was gradual or sudden, the severity of the pain, and the quality of the pain—cramping, stabbing, burning, or other—should be ascertained. Whether symptoms are continuous or intermittent, how they are aggravated or relieved, how they are related to each other, and how they are affected by position, eating, defecation, exertion, sleep, or other activities must be determined. Nonpainful symptoms such as tiredness, weakness, dizziness, nausea—or their absence—may be highly significant, particularly at high altitude.

An account of any past illnesses must always be obtained, even though in the wilderness the current illness is usually the most significant part of the history. If the person's illness is a recurrence of a previous disease, awareness of that disorder can provide the key to its recognition. Additionally, preexisting diseases, such as diabetes or epilepsy, must be brought to light so that necessary treatment can be continued. Even the victims of trauma can have such disorders and should be carefully questioned about them.

MEDICAL HISTORY
Past History

Previous illnesses: Bronchitis, asthma, pneumonia, pleurisy, tuberculosis, rheumatic fever; any other heart or lung disease; malaria, diabetes, epilepsy, anemia; any other severe or chronic illnesses.

Operations: Date, nature of operation, complications.

Injuries: Date, nature of injury, residual disability; wilderness-related injuries, particularly cold injury or altitude illness.

Medications: Any medications taken regularly, currently or in the past.

Exposure: Recent exposure to infection or an epidemic.

Immunizations: When administered, boosters.

Allergies: Allergy to food, insect stings, or drugs, particularly penicillin and sulfa drugs.

Review of Systems (including present and past illnesses)

Head: Headache, dizziness, hallucinations, confusion, or fainting.

Eyes: Inflammation, pain, double vision, loss of vision.

Nose: Colds, sinus trouble, postnasal drip, bleeding, obstruction.

Teeth: General condition, abscesses, dentures.

Mouth: Pain, bleeding, sores, dryness.

Throat: Sore throat, tonsillitis, hoarseness, difficulty swallowing or talking.

Ears: Pain, discharge, ringing or buzzing, hearing loss.

Neck: Stiffness, pain, swelling, or masses.

Heart and lungs: Chest pain, palpitations, shortness of breath (greater than that experienced by others during similar exercise at the same altitude), cough, amount and character of material that is coughed up, coughing up blood.

Gastrointestinal: Loss of appetite, nausea, vomiting, vomiting blood or "coffee ground" material, indigestion, gas, pain; constipation, use of laxatives, diarrhea, bloody or tarry black stools, pale or clay-colored stools, hemorrhoids; jaundice.

Genitourinary: Increase or decrease in frequency of voiding, color of urine (light yellow, orange), back pain, pain with voiding; passage of blood, gravel, or stones; sores, purulent discharge, venereal disease or sexual contact; menstrual abnormalities such as irregular periods, increased bleeding with periods, bleeding between periods, cramps.

Neuromuscular: Fainting, whether total or incomplete (see chapter 9, "Heart and Blood Vessel Disorders"), unconsciousness from other causes, dizziness or vertigo, twitching, convulsions; muscle cramps, shooting pains, muscular or joint pain; anesthesia, tingling sensations, weakness, incoordination, or paralysis.

Skin: Rashes, abscesses, or boils.

General: Fever, chills, weakness, easy fatigability, dizziness, weight loss.

THE PHYSICAL EXAMINATION

If a physical examination is to provide useful information, the examiner must have some prior experience, particularly examining the chest and abdomen. For the inexperienced, comparison with a normal individual may be helpful, but nothing can substitute for tutelage by a physician.

A thorough physical examination is essential in the evaluation of anyone with a medical disorder. Even a person with traumatic injuries must be completely examined to ensure that no wounds are overlooked, particularly in the presence of an obvious injury. For the examination, the subject should be made comfortable and protected from wind and cold. The examiner's hands should be warm, and the examiner must be gentle. Any roughness makes obtaining diagnostic information more difficult and could aggravate the individual's disorder.

To ensure that all areas of the body are examined, a definite routine should always be followed. The following outline is relatively complete and is adequate for both traumatic and nontraumatic disorders. The examination of some anatomical areas, particularly the chest and abdomen, is described in more detail in the chapters dealing with those areas.

PHYSICAL EXAMINATION

General (vital signs): Pulse rate, respiratory rate, temperature, blood pressure, general appearance.

Skin: Color, texture; rashes, abscesses, or boils.

Head

Eyes: Eyebrows and eyelids, eye movements, vision, pupil size and equality, reaction of pupils to light, inflammation.

Nose: Appearance, discharge, bleeding.

Mouth: Sores, bleeding, dryness.

Throat: Inflammation, purulent exudates.

Ears: Appearance, discharge, bleeding.

Neck: Limitation of movement, enlarged lymph nodes.

Lungs: Respiratory movements, breath sounds, voice sounds, bubbling.

Heart: Pulse rate, regularity, blood pressure.

Abdomen: General appearance, tenderness, rebound and referred pain, spasm of muscles, masses.

Genitalia: Tenderness, masses.

Rectum: Hemorrhoids, impacted feces, abscesses.

Back: Tenderness, muscle spasm, limitation of movement.

Extremities: Pain or tenderness, limitation of movement, deformities, unequal length, swelling, ulcers, soft-tissue injuries, lymph node enlargement, sensitivity to pin prick and light touch, muscle spasm.

EXAMINING TRAUMA VICTIMS

Individuals with traumatic injuries may have respiratory impairment or severe bleeding that must be cared for immediately. After these emergencies have received attention, however, the care provider must pause and essentially start over from the beginning. An account of the accident and the time and circumstances in which it occurred should be obtained. Frequently the nature of the accident provides clues to injuries that should be anticipated. If the person is unconscious, witnesses must be asked whether unconsciousness caused the accident or resulted from the accident. Witnesses and companions also should be asked whether the individual had any preexisting medical conditions that may have contributed to the accident or that may require treatment.

The subject's pulse and respiratory rate (and blood pressure, if possible) should be measured and recorded immediately and every ten to fifteen minutes until they are clearly stable. If the person is moved, the vital signs should be rechecked immediately; an increase in pulse rate or fall in blood pressure at such times is often an early sign of shock.

Although a few injuries, such as fractures, may have to be cared for first, the person must be completely and thoroughly examined. Concealed injuries must be carefully sought. Injuries of the back are most frequently overlooked, even in hospital emergency rooms. If the individual is lying on his stomach, his back should be examined before he is turned over. At some point his back must be examined, unless suspected fractures of the vertebral column—and the absence of bleeding or other evidence of injury—dictate that the examination be postponed.

A systematic routine must be followed so that no areas of the body are overlooked. Chest injuries are unquestionably more threatening than hand injuries and deserve prior attention, but failure to recognize and care for a hand injury can result in a permanent deformity. "Many errors in care are due to incomplete diagnosis, to overlooking some serious injury while concentrating on the obvious. A systematic method of examination will obviate such errors."[3]

If evacuation requires more than one day, examinations must be repeated to monitor the subject's condition and to ensure that all injuries have been found. If the individual is unconscious at the time of the initial examination, he must be reexamined as soon as he regains consciousness.

THE MEDICAL RECORD

For disabling diseases or injuries, a written account of the history and examination findings is an essential element in the person's medical care, particularly when a physician's help is more than a few hours away. In the confusion associated with an accident and subsequent evacuation, a medical attendant may be unable to remember whether a symptom was present or physical changes were detectable, even a few hours after the examination. Memory is not a dependable record of numerical data such as pulse and respiratory rates, temperature, and blood pressure. If any medications have been administered, a written account of the doses and times they were given is essential. Any other treatment must be recorded.

For individuals with nontraumatic illnesses, a written record allows the examiner to systematically review his findings while trying to arrive at a diagnosis. Written records are much easier to use when trying to obtain help by such means as radio or cellular telephone.

Written records of the vital signs (pulse, respiratory rate, blood pressure, and temperature) and other features of the person's illness allow small changes in these signs to be detected. Such changes usually precede more obvious indications that the individual's condition is worsening and allow treatment to be instituted earlier, when it often is more effective. These changes may also indicate a response to treatment and presage more obvious improvement in the subject's overall condition, perhaps allowing a difficult evacuation to be delayed until circumstances are more favorable.

When evacuation is prolonged, written records allow more than one person to share in the individual's care. Because all can determine what the signs or symptoms were at any time, all can recognize changes and initiate any therapy that is needed. Written records are also essential for administering medications without omitting or duplicating doses.

If the subject is evacuated, written records are essential for the physician who is to care for him, particularly when his attendants are unable to accompany him. If evacuation has required several days and more than one person has been involved in the subject's care, a written record is the physician's only source of accurate information about the individual's original condition, how that has changed, and the treatment that has been given—particularly medications that have been administered.

Medical records play such a vital role in medical care they are begun immediately when someone enters a hospital emergency room or physician's office. Such records are subpoenaed at the beginning of any medically related litigation, and omissions are often damaging to the physician's defense, which might be a significant consideration for nonphysicians in an increasingly litigious society.

The outlines provided for the medical history and the physical examination are entirely appropriate for the medical record. Obviously, all abnormalities should be recorded, but the absence of abnormalities is frequently of equal importance, particularly for nontraumatic disorders. Without a specific statement that a sign or symptom was not present, a physician subsequently caring for the individual may be unable to determine whether that change was really absent or simply was not noticed.

For traumatic injuries, an account of the accident should be recorded at the earliest opportunity. All injuries should be carefully described. The absence of injuries, or signs such as swelling or discoloration that are suggestive of injury over major areas of the body—chest, abdomen, head, arms, or legs—should also be noted. The vital signs should be recorded every thirty to sixty minutes for at least four hours, but for longer if these signs are not stable. After stabilization, vital signs need to be recorded only about every four hours until the person is well on his way to recovery. Any preexisting medical conditions should be described. The dosage, route, and time of administration of all medications must be accurately logged. Notes about any other treatment or changes in the subject's condition must include the time.

The written record must be accessible, not buried in a pack. Notations of changes in the individual's condition or the administration of medications must be made immediately and not recorded from memory at a later time.

REFERENCES

1. Adams FD: *Cabot and Adams Physical Diagnosis,* 14th ed. Baltimore, The Williams & Wilkins Co., 1958. (Quoted by permission of the author and publishers.)
2. Ibid.
3. Kennedy RH in Committee on Trauma, American College of Surgeons: *Early Care of Acute Soft Tissue Injuries.* Chicago, 1957. (Quoted by permission of the publishers.)

2 BASIC MEDICAL CARE AND EVACUATION

Most individuals injured in accidents or contracting an illness in the wilderness are evacuated within hours or, at the most, one to two days. Occasionally, however, bad weather, difficult terrain, distance from a hospital or transportation (particularly on an expedition), insufficient personnel for evacuation, or other problems may force an individual to remain in a remote situation. Some persons may not need evacuation if they are expected to recover enough to walk out or resume activity within a relatively short time.

NURSING CARE

Anyone confined to bed (or sleeping bag) by illness or injury has certain needs that require attention. Ministering to those needs is most readily identifiable as "nursing care." The objective of this care is simple: to allow the body to heal itself.

Comfort and Understanding

Comfort and understanding—the essence of nursing—are needed by all, regardless of the nature or severity of their medical problems. Some have a greater need than others; some, particularly young men, try to deny their need. Regardless of the situation, the medical supplies on hand, or the sophistication of available medical knowledge, interest and concern, sympathy and understanding can always be shown; comfort and reassurance can always be provided. All are essential.

Rest

Rest promotes healing in several ways. Exertional and emotional stress are reduced; additional injury to damaged tissues is avoided. Rest can allow improved nutrition, and the nutrients are used for healing instead of muscular effort. Individuals with heart or lung disease and individuals with severe injuries, particularly fractures, may need to be immobilized, but most do not need such confinement. Often, remaining in camp rather than hiking or climbing is all that is required to hasten recovery.

Sedation

In the absence of brain injury or disease, medications that promote sleep may be given at altitudes below 10,000 feet (3,000 m). At higher elevations, sleeping medications should not be administered because they reduce blood oxygenation during sleep, which often aggravates symptoms of altitude sickness. The sleeplessness and irregular breathing associated with high altitude can be relieved safely with acetazolamide. (See chapter 21, "Disorders Caused by Altitude.")

Analgesia

Analgesics should be supplied liberally, but judiciously, in wilderness situations. The risk of narcotic addiction for individuals with painful injuries or illnesses is essentially nonexistent, particularly when the agents are administered for a week or less.

The hazard of strong analgesics consists largely of further depressing cerebral activity in a person whose central nervous system function is already impaired as the result of a head injury or an illness. Depressed cerebral function is typically manifested by impaired respiration—breathing is slower and shallower. Further depression of respiration by narcotics can lead to significant hypoxia, particularly at high elevations. A person with a severe head injury might stop breathing altogether, which usually is catastrophic.

For individuals who do not have a head injury, analgesics can relieve severe discomfort and the associated emotional distress. For many subjects with traumatic injuries, control of pain reduces the severity of shock. Analgesia promotes healing by allowing people with painful injuries or illnesses to sleep restfully. Many individuals are more aware of pain at night when nothing is diverting their attention. For three or four days after a major injury—sometimes even longer—strong analgesia may be needed.

Major analgesics have so much sedative effect that a sleeping medication is not needed. Administering a sleeping medication with a major analgesic would be hazardous.

Warmth

Individuals who are ill or injured must be kept warm. At low environmental temperatures, persons with severe illnesses or injuries may not be able to generate enough heat to maintain body temperature, even in a sleeping bag, and like victims of hypothermia, may require external sources of heat. (See chapter 23, "Cold Injuries.")

Lower Altitude

Evacuation from altitudes above 15,000 feet (4,600 m) promotes recovery. Individuals with diseases of the lungs or heart should be taken as low as possible, preferably below 8,000 feet (2,400 m), and provided with supplemental oxygen if it is available.

Coughing

People who are immobilized with a severe injury or illness usually do not breathe deeply, particularly if breathing is painful. As a result of diminished respiratory excursions, their lungs are not fully expanded and fluid accumulates in the immobile segments. These collections are an ideal medium for bacterial growth, which leads to pneumonia. (Such infections are the most common cause of death for elderly persons confined to bed with fractured hips or similar injuries.)

To eliminate the fluid, expand the lungs, and reduce the danger of infection, individuals must be encouraged—or forced—to breathe deeply and to cough at frequent intervals. Coughing may be difficult for someone who is very ill, or very painful for someone with a chest or abdominal injury, but these individuals are the most prone to pulmonary infections and most need to clear their lungs. The practice in most hospitals is to have the person sit up, hold his sides, and cough deeply—not just clear his throat—at least every two hours. A similar routine should be adopted in wilderness circumstances, particularly at higher altitudes where any compromise in pulmonary function could be disastrous.

Elimination of fluid from the lungs can also be increased by postural drainage. If the head and chest are slightly lower than the rest of the body, gravity helps get rid of the fluid. In a tent, such positioning can best be achieved by elevating the abdomen, pelvis, and legs. After the person has recovered to the extent that he is able to be up and walking around, forced coughing or postural drainage are usually no longer necessary.

Ambulation

Anyone confined to bed as a result of illness or injury should be encouraged to get up and walk around several times a day. Such exercise increases the circulation in the legs and helps prevent thrombophlebitis. (See chapter 10, "Respiratory Disorders.") The only major exceptions to this rule are individuals with injuries that prevent walking and individuals who have already developed thrombophlebitis and should remain as immobile as possible until the disorder has resolved.

Diet

Food is not as important during the acute stages of an illness as adequate fluid intake. Unless a specific disorder dictates a particular diet, such as the bland diet for peptic ulcer, the person should eat whatever he desires. During convalescence, more attention can be given to a nutritionally adequate diet, perhaps with extra protein.

Bowel Care

Difficulties with bowel evacuation are common for persons confined to bed, who repress the urge to defecate, have a low food intake, and become dehydrated. If not corrected, fecal impaction often results. (See chapter 12, "Gastrointestinal Disorders.") Even though stool volume is reduced in the absence of solid food in the diet, bowel movements should occur every three to four days. The best way to ensure normal elimination is to make certain fluid intake is adequate; roughage or fiber in the diet increases stool bulk and is helpful. Laxatives or enemas should rarely be needed to prevent impaction in a bedridden individual.

Convalescence

Although physical activity should be encouraged during convalescence, strenuous exercise too early may delay recovery, particularly at high altitudes. In addition, individuals are more susceptible to other injuries during convalescence. To be certain that recovery is complete, delaying a return to full activity for two or three extra days may be desirable.

FLUID BALANCE

An adequate fluid intake is essential. A person can live for weeks without food, but only for a few days without water. Fluid balance implies equilibrium between losses (through the kidneys, skin, and lungs—or other routes) and gains (from fluids and foods that have been ingested). During an illness that increases fluid losses and makes fluid intake difficult or impossible, fluid balance can become critical. Dehydration from massive diarrheal fluid loss kills two to three million children annually in developing countries.

An adult of average size normally loses 1,500 cc to 2,000 cc of water from his body each day. The "sensible loss" excreted by the kidneys ranges from one to two liters per day. The "insensible loss" through perspiration (even in cold climates) and evaporation from the lungs (to moisten air that is inhaled) is one-half to one liter per day in temperate climates and at low altitudes. In hot climates or with high fever, several liters of water may be lost daily through perspiration (which is no longer insensible). At high altitudes, up to four liters of water can be lost through the lungs each day.

Salt (sodium chloride), potassium, and bicarbonate, known collectively as electrolytes, are vital constituents of body fluids. As with water, a balance between intake and loss must be maintained. The daily salt requirement for an average adult is three grams. When large amounts of salt are lost through perspiration, needs may be considerably higher.

Normally functioning kidneys are very sensitive to changes in the body's fluid balance and react immediately to conserve or eliminate water. The urine volume and color are highly reliable indicators of fluid status. A twenty-four-hour volume of less than 500 cc, or urine that has a deep yellow or orange color, is indicative of fluid depletion; a volume of 2,000 cc of very lightly colored urine is typical of a high fluid intake.

These water and electrolyte requirements represent the needs of a healthy adult. Individuals with heart or kidney disease may be unable to get rid of excess salt and water and can have quite different requirements. The administration of normal quantities of electrolytes and water, particularly salt, to persons with one of these disorders may have serious consequences.

When an illness, such as dysentery or cholera, causes high fluid losses by vomiting and watery stools, the volume of fluid lost should be estimated to stay abreast of the person's fluid status. Insensible losses must be estimated also, taking into consideration fever, environmental temperature, and altitude. The volume of fluid ingested must be recorded to ensure that enough is consumed. These measurements and estimates must be written down so the individual's fluid needs can be calculated.

Urine volume and color are good indicators of a subject's fluid balance, but they tend to reflect what has already happened. Measuring losses and gains as they occur provides more immediate insight into the condition of someone with a fluid-losing disorder.

Dehydration at Altitude

Higher altitudes tend to cause dehydration, and this tendency becomes progressively greater as the elevation increases and the environment becomes colder. Almost all trekkers or climbers are dehydrated above 18,000 feet (5,500 m). Some investigators have suggested that the depression, impaired judgement, and other psychologic and intellectual changes that commonly occur at high altitudes—and have been blamed on hypoxia—may actually be the result of dehydration.

The principal cause of dehydration at high altitude is the increased fluid loss associated with more rapid and deeper breathing of cold air. Air is warmed to body temperature and is saturated with water as it passes through the upper air passages; it has a relative humidity of one hundred percent when it reaches the lungs. Because cold air contains essentially no moisture (at 5°F [-15°C] the vapor pressure of water is 1.24 mm Hg), it requires more water for humidification. Most of this moisture, and the heat expended to warm the air to body temperature, is lost when the air is exhaled. (Some of the water may be regained during expiration by condensation in cool upper air passages, but mouth breathing bypasses the air passages where most condensation occurs.) In addition, loss of heat through evaporation of water and through warming inhaled cold air is a significant contributor to hypothermia at high altitudes.

If individuals are not careful about managing clothing to minimize sweating, particularly with the bulky clothing required to keep warm during periods of immobility at high altitude, fluid loss from this source may not be held to the lowest levels possible.

Decreased fluid consumption often contributes to dehydration at high elevations. Both the need to carry fuel and melt snow to obtain water for drinking or cooking, and dulling of the sensation of thirst that accompanies the loss of appetite, nausea, or even vomiting of acute mountain sickness, tend to reduce fluid intake.

Individuals who are active at high altitudes must consciously force themselves to drink large volumes of fluid. Thirst alone is not a reliable indicator of the need for water. Above 15,000 to 16,000 feet (4,600 to 4,900 m), fluid requirements often exceed four liters per day. Urine color and volume indicate the adequacy of fluid intake. Darkly colored urine—orange snow flowers instead of light yellow—and the absence of a need to void upon awakening from a night's sleep are indicators of significant dehydration.

Fluid Replacement

The easiest and most reliable method for replacing fluids is to drink more. Almost any nonalcoholic liquid is suitable, but because water contains no electrolytes, fruit juices, soft drinks, soups, and similar liquids should be encouraged. (Coffee, tea, and hot chocolate are not as satisfactory because they contain caffeine, a diuretic that increases renal fluid loss.)

Seriously ill individuals with very little appetite often refuse liquids as well as solid foods. However, they can usually be persuaded to drink small quantities, just two or three sips, at intervals of fifteen to twenty minutes. With tenacity, patience, and gentle encouragement, such persons can be coaxed to drink several liters of fluid over a twenty-four hour period.

Some individuals, particularly those with intractable vomiting or in coma, are unable to take fluids orally. If medical attention can be obtained within one or two days and fluid losses are not increased, the intervening fluid depletion is usually not too severe. However, longer periods without fluid, and disorders that increase fluid loss, can produce severe dehydration. If rectal suppositories that control vomiting—Compazine® or Phenergan®—are not available, fluids must be administered intravenously.

Only knowledgeable persons experienced with such therapy should attempt administering fluids intravenously. Fluids suitable for intravenous administration can not be improvised and would be carried only by a well-equipped expedition, although such fluids might be obtained by airdrop. Such fluids are often left behind by expeditions, and in some popular areas a significant supply has accumulated. These fluids come from many nations and their labels are printed in many languages, but the contents are usually in standard chemical symbols or in English.

The volume of fluids to be given intravenously must be determined each day. Fluids are required to replace both normal and abnormal losses. Two liters of five percent glucose and one-half liter of a salt-containing electrolyte solution (preferably a balanced salt solution, but normal saline if only that is available) usually satisfy the body's daily needs when no abnormal losses are occurring. Fluids lost through vomiting, diarrhea, or excessive perspiration should be replaced with an electrolyte solution. Excessive fluid loss through the lungs due to high altitude should be replaced by glucose because no electrolytes are lost with the moisture in expired air.

Most electrolyte solutions contain little potassium. Individuals with poor kidney function can not rid themselves of excessive potassium, which may rapidly accumulate to lethal levels. However, persons with normal renal function excrete potassium in the urine. As a result, blood potassium concentrations can fall to dangerously low levels during prolonged intravenous fluid therapy if the potassium is not replaced. Therefore, individuals receiving intravenous fluids for more than two to three days, or losing large volumes of fluid with diarrhea, who have a normal urine volume, should receive an extra 15 to 20 mEq of potassium per liter of electrolyte. (The occasions when such potassium supplements are available in wilderness circumstances must be rare. When available, the supplements are usually supplied in a solution that can be added directly to the electrolyte solution.)

If a person with a healthy heart and normally functioning kidneys is provided with an adequate intake of water (as glucose) and electrolytes (balanced salt solution), the kidneys compensate for any imbalance. The inevitable inaccuracies inherent in measuring fluid intake and output are fully corrected. However, an individual with preexisting heart disease, particularly congestive heart failure, a person with kidney disease, or someone with acute renal failure as a result of disease or injury requires much more precise therapy, which can only be provided with hospital facilities. For such individuals, any error in administering fluids must be on the side of not giving enough.

CARE FOR TRAUMA VICTIMS

Traumatic injuries are by far the most common medical problems encountered in the wilderness.

Emergencies

True medical emergencies in which a delay of a few minutes in providing care can significantly affect the outcome are rare. In wilderness accidents, the opportunity to provide such treatment may pass before anyone is able to get to the individual. Nonetheless, wilderness users must be familiar with the procedures for treating traumatic medical emergencies if they are to deal with them successfully when the rare opportunities do occur. True emergencies do not allow time for referral to a textbook.

If immediate action is necessary to prevent loss of life following an accident, the order in which problems should receive attention is as follows:

1. **Cardiopulmonary resuscitation (CPR).** An open airway must be established first; interference with breathing by chest wounds must be quickly corrected. If needed, CPR should be

started. Emergency rescue personnel approaching an unconscious person follow the algorithm *ABC*, which stands for *airway, breathing,* and *circulation.*

2. **Bleeding.** After the subject is breathing or being resuscitated, bleeding should be controlled by direct pressure at bleeding sites, not by tourniquets or pressure points.

3. **Shock.** After cardiac and respiratory function have been established and bleeding has been controlled, attention should be directed to treating or preventing shock. Treatment given in anticipation of shock is more effective than treatment instituted after shock has developed.

Although the order of the first two problems may appear reversed because control of severe bleeding should take only seconds but CPR can be prolonged, in reality they are not. Anyone whose heart has stopped does not bleed. Therefore, CPR must take first priority. Furthermore, anyone who has bled so severely that his heart has stopped can not be resuscitated. The combination of cardiac arrest and severe hemorrhage is essentially always lethal.

Other Injuries

All injuries should be treated as completely as possible before the person is moved. Open wounds are always contaminated to some extent; further contamination should be avoided. Soft-tissue wounds should be covered with voluminous dressings that apply pressure to control bleeding, provide immobilization, minimize swelling, and control infection. Even when no fractures are present, severely injured extremities should be immobilized and elevated slightly to aid blood circulation. If the lower extremities are injured and evacuation requires the person to walk or climb, he should stop periodically to lie down and elevate his feet. Splinting fractures before the subject is moved is particularly important. "Splint 'em where they lie" is a time-proven adage.

The equipment necessary for the treatment of some injuries, such as injuries of the chest, is not available on most short outings. However, this equipment should always be available in popular wilderness recreation areas and should be a part of the emergency gear of all wilderness rescue organizations.

SPECIFIC ACCIDENTS

Avalanches

Most avalanche victims are killed by the impact of large blocks of hard-packed snow or ice. Others are suffocated by densely packed snow. Almost no one buried more than three feet below the surface by an avalanche survives. Avoiding avalanches and finding avalanche victims is beyond the scope of this publication, but the following outline can be followed in caring for individuals caught in an avalanche immediately after they have been found:

1. Obviously lethal injuries should be sought so that attention can be directed to the living. Evacuation of a body can be delayed until the hazard of additional avalanches has passed.

2. If the subject is unconscious and no lethal injuries can be found, he should be assumed to have a broken neck. Appropriate splinting must be continued as long as he remains comatose.

3. An open airway must be established, chest injuries must be covered, and resuscitation must be initiated if the person is not breathing. Movement of his neck must still be avoided, which is not easy.

4. After the individual is breathing, his injuries should be treated rapidly so he can be protected from cold and moved out of the avalanche path at the earliest possible moment.

Lightning

In the United States, between 150 and 300 persons die from lightning strikes every year; in 1943, 430 lightning deaths occurred. However, the number who die is less than one-third of those who are struck. Because only the individuals with severe lightning injuries are reported, the true fatality rate is probably between ten and twenty percent. Most survivors have no significant residual disabilities.

Because the voltage in a bolt of lightning is so high (200 million to 2 billion volts of direct current), it typically "flashes" over the outside of the body, particularly if the body is wet. Electricity does penetrate the body enough to disrupt the electrical functions of the brain and heart, but lightning injuries are not usually associated with the extensive burns produced by man-made voltages (up to 200,000 volts of alternating current, usually less than 30,000 volts). Because the current from a lightning bolt flows around the outside of the body (just as electricity tends to flow along the outside of a conductor), the electrical energy can instantly vaporize moisture on the body surface and blow away the person's clothing, resulting in unusual incidents.

The most significant effects of lightning are on the brain. The electricity does shock the heart, causing it to arrest, but the heart's intrinsic tendency to contract rhythmically causes it to resume beating, just as it sometimes does after being shocked to stop ventricular fibrillation. However, the brain requires significantly longer to recover from the effects of the electrical current, and because the brain controls respiration, the person does not breathe. Although the heart has resumed beating, it can not function without oxygen and subsequently goes into ventricular fibrillation, resulting in death.

Clearly, the emergency treatment for someone struck by lightning consists of immediate, and sometimes prolonged, artificial respiration. (Cardiac resuscitation should be given only if needed; the heart most often resumes beating on its own.) More than seventy percent of the individuals struck by lightning have enough disruption of brain function to lose consciousness. Recovery of enough function to resume breathing commonly takes as long as twenty to thirty minutes, and rarely takes hours.

If more than one person has been struck, which commonly occurs, attention should be directed first to the ones who are not breathing and appear dead. Those who are groaning or moving, although unconscious, are breathing and do not require immediate attention. (An airway must be maintained.)

After the subject is breathing on his own, he should be evacuated to a hospital. Other problems are common. Occasionally and unpredictably, heart failure, which requires intensive care, develops several hours later, apparently as the result of electrical damage to the heart muscle. Most individuals who have been struck by lightning lose their short-term memory for two to five days and can never recall the circumstances of the accident. Emotional or psychiatric problems are common but usually clear up with time and appropriate treatment. Various types of paralysis appear but are usually transient. The extremities may appear blue and pulseless, as if the arteries were obstructed. This change usually is the result of intense spasm of the muscles in the walls of the arteries and passes after a few hours. More than fifty percent of the people struck by lightning have one or both eardrums ruptured, possibly as the result of incredibly loud thunder. Superficial burns are common and typically have a feathery or fernlike pattern.

Delayed problems sometimes occur. Neurologic problems have developed three to twelve months after injury. Cataracts can appear as long as two years later.

Drowning

Drowning is by far the most common fatal accident among participants in outdoor activities, even though relatively few drownings occur in situations that would be considered wilderness, and most of the victims are children. In the United States, more than 8,000 deaths occur annually. Drowning is the second most common cause (after motor vehicle accidents) of accidental death in children between ages one and fourteen years, and the third most common cause of accidental death overall. Forty to fifty percent of drowning victims are four years old or younger; the only other large group is teenage males.

Alcohol plays a major role in many adult drownings by causing the accident that results in submersion and by impairing the individual's ability to get out of the water or contrive some type of flotation device. (The term "near-drowning" has been used for submersion incidents survived for at least twenty-four hours. It is most appropriate for incidents in which resuscitation is not required, but it has also been defined as "two fishermen in a flat-bottomed boat with a case of beer.")

Some drowning victims, such as white-water boaters and kayakers, get pinned or trapped underwater. A few people dive into shallow water, strike their heads on the bottom or on submerged objects, and are knocked unconscious or suffer cervical fractures. Individuals competing to determine who can stay underwater the longest or swim the greatest distance underwater may lose consciousness, particularly if they have hyperventilated beforehand and lowered their blood carbon dioxide concentration, a major component of the drive to breathe.

The mechanism of death for others is less obvious. Many drowning victims dive or jump into cold water and simply do not come up. No struggle of any kind is witnessed. In many accidents of this type, the sudden contact with cold water apparently prompts a sudden, uncontrollable gasp that results in aspiration of water. This response has been labeled the "gasp reflex" and is essentially universal, although it usually can be controlled. Many have observed a similar response upon stepping into a cold shower.

Many individuals temporarily trapped underwater have experienced an overwhelming compulsion to breathe. (The length of time anyone can hold his breath when submerged in cold water is much shorter than when submerged in warm water or while on land—usually one-fourth to one-third as long.) Apparently, some individuals give in to this urge, perhaps thinking they can safely take a single breath to relieve the respiratory drive until they reach the surface.

One inhalation or gasp of water may stop all efforts to reach the surface; complete asphyxia apparently is not necessary. Possibly the water passes without delay through the lungs into the blood, and the reduced osmotic pressure or some other altered characteristic of the diluted blood has an immediate effect on the brain. Individuals who have been resuscitated after drowning have described the sensation as enjoyable, even using such terms as "orgasmic." This hypothetical mechanism would explain the drowning of individuals after water washes over their head in a turbulent stream or ocean surf, but it does not explain the deaths of individuals who suffer laryngeal spasm and can not inhale any water, approximately fifteen percent of all drownings.

Reviving drowned individuals requires cardiopulmonary resuscitation, which does not differ significantly from CPR given for other disorders. If the subject has entered the water head first, particularly by diving, measures to splint a cervical fracture should be instituted before he is removed from the water. CPR should be initiated without delay as soon as the individual is out of the water. Attempts at chest compression while the person is still in the water are ineffective and delay extraction. Any effort to remove water from the lungs, particularly with the Heimlich maneuver, is a waste of time. Water in the lungs passes immediately into the blood, even after salt water drowning, can not be removed, and can not interfere with oxygen transport. Efforts to relieve laryngeal spasm in that fifteen percent of drowning victims are not needed.

No other specific treatment can be administered outside of a hospital, although some individuals require treatment for immersion hypothermia. Distinguishing drowning from severe hypothermia following cold water immersion may be difficult. Awareness of the need for this distinction appears limited. However, initiation of CPR on a severely hypothermic individual whose heart is beating, but very slowly—twelve to fifteen beats per minute—would essentially always precipitate ventricular fibrillation, which often would be disastrous. In situations where this distinction is needed, an electrocardiograph (ECG) should be used to determine whether the heart is beating, if possible. (See chapter 23, "Cold Injuries.")

Therapy for pulmonary and other complications produced by the aspirated water is often needed, but it can be administered only in a hospital. Although dissimilar effects from drowning in fresh water and salt water, due to their chemical and osmotic differences, have been anticipated, little substantive variation has been found.

A few individuals, mostly children but some adults, have been successfully resuscitated after prolonged submersion. Most have been submerged less than thirty minutes in water colder than 50°F (10°C). The longest submersion followed by successful resuscitation was sixty-six minutes. CPR was started for that two-and-a-half-year-old girl by an experienced, professional rescue team as soon as she was retrieved from 41°F (5°C) water. She was transported in minutes to a hospital that was prepared for her arrival and was immediately rewarmed with cardiopulmonary bypass.

Apparently, when some submerged individuals aspirate cold water, the cooled blood is selectively transported to the brain, which begins to cool immediately and can tolerate oxygen deprivation that would be disastrous at normal temperature. Animal studies have demonstrated such immediate cooling, but not all investigators are willing to accept this explanation for the well-documented survival of a few individuals following prolonged submersion.

Such successes are uncommon. Relaxation of surveillance or other protective measures for individuals engaged in water sports can not be justified. Submerged individuals should be located and retrieved as quickly as possible; if submersion has lasted less than thirty minutes, CPR should be attempted. However, unjustifiable expectations of success can lead only to frustration, anger with no suitable target, and the emotional consequences of such responses.

EVACUATION

An effective wilderness rescue requires a good stretcher and enough people to carry it without further injury to the subject or the rescuers—four dozen, one writer has asserted in jest. Basket stretchers are the best available in most areas. Leg dividers interfere with splinting broken legs and packaging of the subject and should be removed if that can be accomplished without destroying the structural integrity of the stretcher. Better stretchers have been developed but are rarely found in wilderness areas within the United States. The McInnes stretcher can transported by just two people over the roughest terrain.

Few circumstances can justify rolling someone with fractures of the legs, pelvis, back, or neck onto a makeshift stretcher and bouncing him along over a rough descent simply because a rigid support, such as a basket stretcher or a body board, and enough people to carry it are not immediately available.

If bad weather makes evacuation urgent, the person rarely needs to be carried very far below tree line before personnel and equipment are obtained to complete the evacuation with minimal risk of further injury. The rescue may be easier and the outcome better if equipment and supplies for an overnight stay are carried to the party and the evacuation is delayed until the following morning or even until the weather improves.

"Four dozen" stretcher-bearers are essential too. Transporting an injured person over rugged terrain is physically demanding. A basket stretcher containing an adult is heavy. Fewer than six ordinary individuals can not readily lift or carry one. Maneuvering the heavy stretcher in a manner that is not painful for the injured individual being transported is so tiring that rest stops—or replacement of stretcher-bearers—must be frequent.

If the party is small, deciding who should go for help and who should stay with the injured may be a problem. If the group has signed out with a park ranger or similar official, the wisest course may be to wait until search efforts locate the entire party. A fire may be built to attract attention and to provide warmth. Because at least one person must stay with an injured individual, small parties should always register.

The safety rules for wilderness activities are the same after an accident as before. Further injuries or loss of life as the result of ignoring these rules simply because one accident has occurred can not be justified. One person must not go for help alone over terrain such as a snow-covered glacier that he would not cross by himself under normal circumstances. The fundamental soundness of this policy was pointed out in a Pacific Northwest accident in which a climber died from hypothermia while attempting to go for help, but a search party subsequently rescued the accident victim and an uninjured climber who remained with him.

Helicopters

The use of helicopters for wilderness rescues has greatly reduced the time needed to get an injured or ill individual to medical care. It has also reduced the number of stretcher-bearers to four or six, most of whom can be brought in by the helicopter along with a stretcher. In addition, helicopters routinely used for rescue are typically equipped with sophisticated medical equipment that can not be backpacked to a wilderness site, such as ECG monitors, defibrillators, oxygen, endotracheal intubation equipment, suction apparatus, intravenous fluids, and emergency drugs. (See Fig. 2-1.)

In many areas, helicopter pilots are notified of the need for their help and directed to the site by the local sheriff's dispatcher. Rescuers should know the procedures for obtaining helicopter aid and should notify helicopter operators before they initiate a rescue.

Working effectively with helicopters requires knowledge of their capabilities and limitations. Although landings have been made at altitudes above 20,000 feet (6,100 m) by turbine (jet) helicopters, most helicopters can not land or take off above 8,000 to 10,000 feet (2,400 to 3,000 m). The maximum altitude at which a helicopter can operate is determined by air density. Cold air is more dense and a helicopter can operate at higher altitudes at lower temperatures. Conversely, the altitude at which a helicopter can land or take off can be reduced several thousand feet by high air temperatures.

Helicopters usually can not operate in bad weather. Small helicopters are rarely equipped with instruments that allow them to fly in clouds or when clouds obscure the ground (instrument flight regulations, or IFR). Strong or gusty winds also make helicopter operations difficult or unsafe.

Most helicopters can not make absolutely vertical ascents or descents. Space for an approach and departure is needed, particularly when a significant wind is blowing. A space approximately 300 by 150 feet (90 by 45 meters) is ideal. (Such a large landing area is not only safer, it gives the pilot space in which to land if he has an engine failure on takeoff, the time at which the engine is under greatest stress.) The most level spot that is free of obstructions, particularly electrical or telephone wires, which are difficult to see from the air, should be selected. Snowfields can make excellent landing areas, but one or more people, or identifiable items such as packs, must be placed at the edge of the area to give the pilot a sense of scale so he can judge his height above the featureless snow.

One member of the party or rescue team—the parking tender—must direct the helicopter to the landing, preferably using standard arm signals. Waving to the pilot to attract attention must be avoided. Waving is the universal signal not to land—the "wave-off" signal.

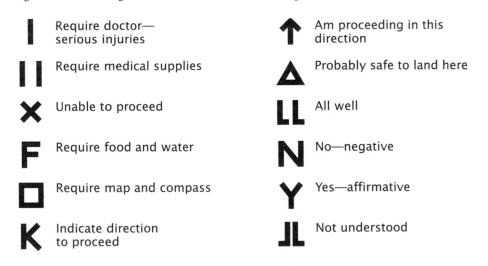

I Require doctor—serious injuries

II Require medical supplies

X Unable to proceed

F Require food and water

□ Require map and compass

K Indicate direction to proceed

↑ Am proceeding in this direction

△ Probably safe to land here

LL All well

N No—negative

Y Yes—affirmative

JL Not understood

FIGURE 2-1. Standard symbols for ground-to-air communication

As the helicopter makes its final overhead pass and begins its final approach, the parking tender should stand with his back to the wind to indicate its direction and point with both arms outstretched to the site at which he expects the helicopter to land. The inexperienced parking tender should signal the moment when the skids touch the ground by holding his arms outward at a forty-five-degree angle with his thumbs pointing to the ground. Experienced tenders know other signals that are useful for the helicopter pilot.

Helicopters can be hazardous. The downward thrust from the main rotors can produce winds ranging from 60 to 120 miles per hour. Obviously a person helping to guide a helicopter to a landing should not be standing on the edge of a sheer drop. Eyes must be protected from flying dirt and debris. Personal equipment must be stored where it can not be blown away. Strong rotor winds can tumble full packs over the ground and over a drop or into a crevasse. Burning embers from fires can be blown about, causing injuries to rescuers or starting fires in surrounding brush or forests.

The danger from the tail and main rotors would seem to be obvious, but a surprising number of people walk into spinning rotors. While spinning, tail rotors may be invisible. When the helicopter is on the ground, the main rotors may be higher than a person's head, but a sudden gust of wind or slowing of their speed can bend them downward to an amazing extent. No one should stand beneath the tips of the rotors.

Rescue personnel should approach a helicopter only after they receive a "thumbs-up" signal from the pilot indicating he is expecting them to approach, and only from the front, where they can be seen by the pilot. (The single exception to this rule is approaching large Chinook helicopters. The front rotors of these craft can tilt so far that a frontal approach is hazardous. Additionally, the loading ramp is in the back; it should be approached at a sixty-degree angle.) To avoid rotors that may be deflected by a gust of wind, anyone approaching beneath them should be in a crouched position. Any equipment being carried, particularly skis, should be held in front of the body parallel with the ground, not slung over a shoulder where they could strike a rotor.

In terrain where no appropriate helicopter landing sites are available, hovering or one-skid landings may be attempted. Anyone on board, getting on, or departing a helicopter in such a situation must not move until the pilot is fully aware of his intentions. Any movements he makes must be slow and deliberate. In such conditions, even small movements change the helicopter's center of gravity. If the pilot is not prepared to compensate for that change, his corrections may come too late, resulting in damage to the craft and possibly injury to those on board.

When the helicopter has landed at a heliport, even one at a hospital, experienced individuals—who are available in most such locations—should be recruited to help with unloading injured persons.

3

SPECIAL PROBLEMS

Fever and chills are signs of infections, as well as other illnesses. Shock and unconsciousness are associated with widely varying disorders. These problems are discussed in this chapter only instead of with all of the disorders with which they might occur.

FEVER

Normal body temperature averages 98.6°F (37°C) when measured orally, ranges from 96.5°F (35.8°C) to 100°F (37.8°C), and usually varies 1.25° to 3.75°F (0.7° to 2.1°C) daily. The lowest temperature occurs between 3:00 and 5:00 A.M. and the highest in the late afternoon or early evening in individuals who are active during the day and sleep at night. The temperatures of women of childbearing age rise about 1.0°F (0.5°C) at the time of ovulation and remain elevated until menstruation begins. During vigorous exercise, a healthy, well-conditioned athlete's temperature can climb to 104°F (40°C) or higher if he is generating heat faster than it can be lost.

In a moderate or hot wilderness environment, a person should not be considered to have a fever until his temperature at rest exceeds 100°F (38°C) orally or 101°F (38.5°C) rectally. In a cold environment, hypothermia can mask a fever, sometimes a very high fever, by reducing the body's temperature to normal or subnormal levels.

Oral temperatures are easier to measure but are affected by recently consumed food or beverages, smoking, or mouth breathing and talking. Oral temperatures should not be taken for at least ten minutes after eating or smoking, and the person should preferably have been sitting or lying quietly. Rectal temperatures are more reliable and usually are about 1.0°F (0.5°C) higher than the oral temperature. If rectal measurements are necessary, a rectal thermometer is preferable. It should be lubricated, gently inserted about one and one-half inches into the rectum, and left for three minutes.

If the subject is delirious or thrashing about, he must be watched carefully and perhaps restrained to prevent breaking the thermometer and injuring himself, regardless of where the temperature is measured. Taking the temperature may have to be postponed until he is calmer.

As long as an illness persists, the temperature and pulse rate should be recorded every four hours. Fevers sometimes follow specific patterns that are diagnostically helpful. The temperature may go up and stay up, gradually coming down at the termination of the illness, or it may spike to high levels and then fall to normal or below normal every day or every second or third day. A record is essential for such patterns to be recognized. (A soundly sleeping individual rarely needs to be awakened just to have his temperature taken.)

A moderate fever, although it may make the person uncomfortable, does not produce lasting harmful effects. In contrast, temperatures above 106°F (41°C) can cause irreversible damage to several organs if not promptly lowered. In hot or temperate climates, such high fevers should be lowered. Covering the individual's body and extremities with wet cloths (or wetting the clothes he is wearing) and fanning him to increase evaporation and cooling is the technique used in many emergency rooms. A person with a life-threatening fever in an ice and snow environment may only require removal of a portion of his clothing.

Cooling should be continued until the temperature is below 103°F (39.5°C). If the fever is not the result of heat stroke, antipyretic drugs may be given orally if the individual is fully conscious or rectally if he is stuporous or comatose. Ibuprofen (Advil®), acetaminophen (Tylenol®), and aspirin are all effective for reducing fever. The temperature must be watched very carefully until the individual is clearly recovering because high fevers frequently recur quite rapidly.

Although his fever must be lowered, the subject must be protected from environmental extremes of heat or cold. He must be dressed in clothing similar to that being worn by everyone else. He should not be closed up in a sleeping bag that traps the heat and can cause his temperature to go up again, unless sleeping bags are necessary for everyone else to keep warm.

CHILLS

An individual with a chill shivers uncontrollably and feels cold and miserable. These symptoms are produced by the entry of showers of microorganisms into the blood stream. In comparison with the usual chills resulting from exposure to cold, chills caused by infection are much more severe and produce violent, uncontrollable shaking of the entire body. Teeth chatter, the lips and nails turn purple, and the skin becomes pale and cold. (In years past, a chill could be diagnosed when a patient was shaking hard enough to make his bed rattle.) The cold feeling persists in spite of blankets and heating pads until the chill has run its course, usually five to fifteen minutes. Typically, a chill is followed by a fever that may reach high levels.

A chill is almost always the first sign of an infection, and treatment consists of caring for the underlying disorder. Pneumonia, meningitis, and "strep throat" are frequently introduced with a single shaking chill. Recurrent chills characterize malaria, infections of the kidneys or the liver and bile ducts, and generalized bacterial infections.

Occasionally individuals develop such chills fifteen to thirty minutes following prolonged severe exertion, particularly when they are not in good physical condition and food intake has been limited. Such chills appear to be related to a reduction in blood sugar (hypoglycemia) and are not a sign of infection.

SHOCK

Shock is a sign of severe disease and is most commonly caused by a sudden reduction in the blood volume, typically as a result of hemorrhage. Blood volume can also be reduced by disorders in which only fluid is lost. Large volumes of serum pour into the damaged tissues following a severe burn. Dehydration causes a reduction in blood volume and is lethal if severe and uncorrected.

When the blood volume is reduced, regardless of the cause, the arteries in the skin and muscles constrict, diverting blood to the vital organs. The heart pumps at an increased rate to circulate the remaining blood faster and enable a smaller volume of blood to carry more oxygen. When these mechanisms can no longer compensate for the reduction in blood volume, blood pressure falls. If untreated, severe shock eventually becomes irreversible in spite of therapy, and the person dies.

Shock also occurs in disorders not associated with an evident reduction in blood volume. Severe infections or heart attacks are often associated with shock. A period of shock of varying duration is characteristic of the terminal stages of any fatal disease. The mechanism by which shock is produced in those conditions is poorly understood, and efforts at treatment, other than therapy directed toward the underlying disease, are usually unrewarding.

Diagnosis

The severity of shock following hemorrhage depends upon the volume of blood lost and how fast it is lost. Signs of shock are usually more severe when blood loss is rapid than when loss is gradual, even though the amounts lost are identical. Estimating the volume of blood loss is not easy, and most individuals tend to overestimate. The area covered by a small amount of blood can be amazingly large.

Individuals of different sizes have roughly proportional blood volumes. A person 6 feet (180 cm) tall and weighing 175 pounds (80 kg) who is normally hydrated has a blood volume of about 6,000 cc. A person 5 feet 2 inches (155 cm) tall and weighing 110 pounds (50 kg) has a blood volume of about 4,000 cc.

Mild shock results from loss of ten to twenty percent of the blood volume. The person appears pale and his skin is cool, first over the extremities and later over the trunk. As shock becomes more severe, the subject often complains of feeling cold and is often thirsty. A rapid pulse and reduced blood pressure may be present. However, absence of these signs does not indicate that shock is not present because they may appear late, particularly in previously healthy young adults.

Moderate shock results from loss of twenty to forty percent of the blood volume. The signs of mild shock become more severe. The pulse is typically fast and weak or "thready." Blood flow to the kidneys is reduced as the available blood is shunted to the heart and brain, and the urinary output declines. A urinary volume of less than 30 cc per hour is a late indication of moderate shock. In contrast to the dark, concentrated urine observed with dehydration, the urine is usually a light color.

Severe shock results from loss of more than forty percent of the blood volume and is characterized by signs of reduced blood flow to the brain and heart. Reduced cerebral blood flow produces restlessness and agitation initially, but confusion, stupor, and eventually coma and death follow. Diminished blood flow to the heart can produce abnormalities of cardiac rhythm.

Treatment

Treatment for shock is much more effective if begun before the typical signs appear. The first measures instituted after controlling bleeding and ensuring adequate respiration should be for shock. Shock would obviously be expected after a severe hemorrhage, but some fractures of the spine, pelvis, and thigh, and many injuries to the internal organs, are associated with severe bleeding that produces no external evidence of hemorrhage. Shock should be anticipated with such injuries and with other disorders, particularly those that result in severe fluid loss, such as severe diarrhea.

Successful treatment of shock depends largely upon treating the cause. However, several measures should be taken regardless of the underlying disorder. The subject should be supine with his head at the same level as or lower than the rest of his body and his feet elevated ten to twelve inches (twenty-five to thirty centimeters). This position helps the venous blood in the legs to return to the body, making that blood available for more vital tissues. In severe shock, a lower position of the head may aid circulation to the brain.

The individual's body temperature must be maintained. Blankets or sleeping bags are not adequate in severe shock because the person can not produce enough heat to warm himself. An external heat source is needed, particularly in a cold environment. Warmth should be supplied before the body temperature has begun to fall.

Any impairment of respiration must be corrected; oxygen should be administered if it is available.

Pain, movement, or unpleasant emotional stimuli such as fear or the sight of blood often increase the severity of shock. If severe pain is present (someone in moderate or severe shock often does not feel much pain), the person does not have a head injury or other contraindication to such medication, and evacuation is going to be prolonged, a strong analgesic should be administered.

Circulation to the skin and muscles of the extremities is impaired in shock, and injected drugs may not be absorbed. When the patient recovers from shock and the circulation is restored, all of the injected medication could be absorbed at once, which would produce a severe overdose. Analgesics can be injected intravenously if a care provider is familiar with such therapy.

Morphine also helps to allay anxiety. With or without its use, the individual should be given all possible comfort and reassurance to minimize emotional turmoil. (See chapter 4, "Psychologic Responses to Accidents.")

The person may have to be moved from the path of falling rock or a potential avalanche or carried a short distance to a helicopter, but transport over greater distances, particularly evacuation by stretcher, should not be attempted until all injuries have been treated, shock has been controlled as well as possible, and he appears to be in a stable condition.

Low blood volume can be temporarily corrected to a considerable extent by the intravenous administration of a balanced salt solution. Blood plasma or plasma expanders are more effective but have potentially harmful side effects and should only be given by an individual knowledgeable about their use. These fluids do not replace the red blood cells needed to transport oxygen, and such therapy does have limited benefits. Blood is the optimum replacement for blood loss, but preservation, cross-matching, and transfusion are impossible without a blood bank.

Intravenous fluids should be given in anticipation of shock, particularly after injuries such as extensive burns or major fractures. (Accessing a vein suitable for inserting a needle for intravenous fluids is difficult once shock has appeared.) Fluids should be administered in amounts that approximate the volume of lost blood. (Blood loss is difficult to estimate accurately, particularly with injuries where most of the blood loss is hidden from view.)

A healthy adult with no heart disease is rarely harmed by under- or over-replacement of fluids by as much as one or two liters. For such individuals, as much as three to four liters of fluids may be administered fairly rapidly until the heart rate begins to slow and the patient appears to be responding to treatment. Thereafter, fluids should be given at a much slower rate, and no more than four liters should be given within the first eight-hour period. If blood loss is so great that more fluids are needed, the administration of a balanced salt solution alone probably would not be adequate treatment. (Individuals with extensive burns may need larger volumes of fluid and should receive them whenever they are available. See chapter 8, "Burns.")

If the subject does have heart disease, any error in fluid administration must be on the side of under-replacement. Excess fluids could lead to heart failure.

The adequacy of treatment can be determined by measuring the pulse rate, the blood pressure, and the urinary output. Pulse and blood pressure should return to levels close to normal within a few minutes to a few hours after replacement of the lost blood volume. A low urinary output and increasing pulse rate indicate the need for further therapy. Pulse rates, blood pressure, urinary output, and all therapy that has been administered must be carefully recorded so the individual's course can be accurately followed and his precise status known when care is assumed by a physician.

The treatment of shock associated with nontraumatic disorders is less clear cut, and the results are often less satisfactory. Individuals in shock from peritonitis or similar disorders may benefit from one or two liters of balanced salt solution per day, but more should not be given. Anyone who has suffered a heart attack but has sustained no blood loss must not be given fluids because they increase the work load on his already damaged heart.

UNCONSCIOUSNESS

An unconscious individual requires attention to four needs: protection from the environment, specific treatment for the cause of his unconscious state, replacement of fluids, and maintenance of an open airway. The first two requirements depend upon the circumstances in which the person is found and the cause of his condition. Fluid requirements are discussed under Fluid Balance in chapter 2, "Basic Medical Care and Evacuation."

The only specific care that can be given unconscious individuals in wilderness circumstances is the maintenance of an open airway to permit unimpeded respiration. Anyone with a disorder so severe that breathing ceases can rarely be kept alive by manual artificial respiration for more than a few hours.

If unconsciousness is the result of trauma, the subject must also be treated as if he had a broken neck. Fifteen percent of all head injuries that result in prolonged unconsciousness are associated with cervical fractures. Medications for sleep or pain are completely unnecessary, would further depress brain function, and must not be administered.

Maintaining an open airway is simple but vitally important. Skilled treatment of other injuries or heroic rescue efforts would be completely wasted by just a few minutes of airway neglect. No matter how precarious the situation, no rescue efforts can be justified until means for keeping the air passages clear during the entire evacuation have been established. An injured person must be left in an exposed and dangerous situation if rescue attempts would cause certain death by airway obstruction.

AIRWAY MAINTENANCE

The mouth and nose, throat, larynx, trachea, and bronchi form the passages through which air moves into the lungs and are known collectively as the airway. The mouth, throat, and tongue are constructed so that the base of the tongue moves backward and closes off the opening to the trachea during swallowing to prevent food or fluid entering the lungs. Partial obstruction of the larynx by the tongue during sleep results in snoring. However, the larynx is only partially blocked during natural sleep because the muscles that hold the tongue and structures of the throat are not totally relaxed (Fig. 3-1). In contrast, disorders resulting in unconsciousness produce such complete relaxation of these muscles that the tongue totally obstructs the passage of air (Fig. 3-2).

The easiest way to prevent such airway obstruction is to tilt the person's head back by placing one hand on the back of his neck and lifting while pushing down on his forehead or pulling up on his chin with the other hand. When the head is in this position, the tongue is pulled forward and can not fall back far enough to produce obstruction (Fig. 3-3). If the individual has no injuries that might be aggravated by turning him, particularly a broken neck or back, he may be placed on his side with his head facing downward. In this position his tongue tends to fall forward instead of backward and does not block the throat. However, his head should also be extended to help keep the airway open.

The adequacy of the airway is easily checked. If breathing is quiet, the airway is open. Snoring or noisy breathing, labored respirations, or the absence of respiratory movements indicates partial or complete airway obstruction.

If a broken neck is suspected, the airway can be opened by placing the fingers at the angles of the person's jaws and pulling forward. Alternatively, a finger or thumb can be hooked behind the teeth of his lower jaw and the jaw pulled forward. His neck should not be moved.

Disorders that produce unconsciousness are also frequently associated with vomiting. The vomit may be aspirated, completely obstructing the air passages or producing severe, often lethal pneumonia. To prevent such accidents, the unconscious person's head must be lower than his chest and turned to the side whenever he is vomiting or appears likely to vomit. If there is no reason not to do so, he can be placed on his side to help keep his airway open and prevent aspiration. (Unconscious persons must never be given food, liquids, or medications by mouth.)

If the individual does not recover consciousness within a few hours and evacuation requires a long stretcher carry over rough terrain, the maintenance of an open airway would be difficult. A plastic airway or tracheostomy is necessary. Many first aid kits contain plastic airways (oropharyngeal airways), which are flattened curved tubes that fit over the base of the tongue and allow air to enter the larynx (Fig. 3-4). (If the subject starts to regain consciousness and the tube causes him to gag and cough, he no longer needs it and it can safely be removed.)

Another way to keep the airway open is inserting a large safety pin through the meaty part of the tongue and holding the tongue forward by taping the pin to the chin or anchoring it in a similar manner. Although this technique sounds and appears brutal, it is simple, highly effective, and produces no permanent damage.

In rare circumstances a tracheostomy may be required.

Tracheostomy

A tracheostomy is an opening into the trachea through which a person can breathe if the upper air passages are obstructed. Although tracheostomies are commonly performed in hospitals, the occasions

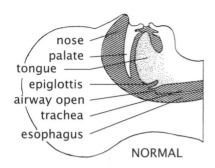

FIGURE 3-1. Structures of the mouth, throat, and airway in a normal, conscious subject

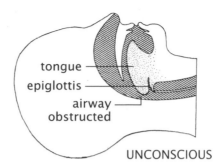

FIGURE 3-2. Position of the tongue and epiglottis in an unconscious subject

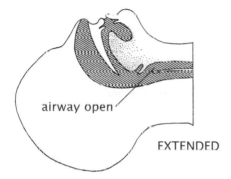

FIGURE 3-3. Position of the tongue and epiglottis in an unconscious subject with the head and neck extended to relieve airway obstruction

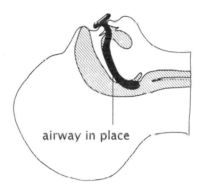

FIGURE 3-4. Oropharyngeal airway in place in an unconscious subject

when one would be needed in the wilderness are rare. Accidents that produce such severe facial fractures that the person is unable to breathe through the nose or mouth are probably the most common disorders for which such treatment is needed. A crushing blow to the larynx also can produce airway obstruction. Aspirated food can produce complete airway obstruction, but the food can usually be expelled by a Heimlich maneuver.

A tracheostomy is simply a hole in the trachea, and any reasonable technique for creating the hole and keeping it open is acceptable. The site for the tracheostomy must be selected carefully to minimize scarring and to avoid damage to other structures in the neck, particularly large blood vessels that could produce massive hemorrhage. (The location of the opening has little to do with how well the tracheostomy functions except that it obviously must be below any obstruction.) Most hospital tracheostomies are placed just above the sternum at the base of the neck. Inexperienced individuals must not use this site for tracheostomies because the thyroid and the common carotid arteries (two of the body's largest) may be encountered. Instead, an opening should be made in the cricothyroid membrane.

The thyroid cartilage forms the Adam's apple. The cricoid cartilage is the large cartilaginous ring just below the thyroid cartilage. The cricothyroid membrane connects these two structures (Fig. 3-5). (Help in identifying the cricothyroid membrane should be obtained from a program

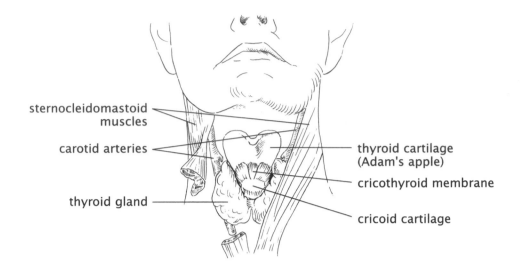

FIGURE 3-5. Location of cricothyroid membrane

provided by the Wilderness Medical Society or another such organization *before* such knowledge is needed to care for a patient.)

If possible, the person should be lying on a flat surface with his head extended backward to stretch the structures of his neck. The skin should be cleaned with soap and water and an antiseptic applied if time is available. The space between the thyroid and cricoid cartilages should be precisely identified. A one-quarter-inch skin incision can be made in the midline of the neck over the cricothyroid membrane with a scalpel or similar sharp blade, but one is not essential. The device being used should be inserted through the membrane into the trachea.

Several devices for crycothyroidostomy are commercially available, but the technique for using them must be learned before they are needed. An eight- to ten-gauge needle is suitable for this purpose and easy to use; a fifteen-gauge needle can provide an adequate airway for most individuals if nothing larger is available. Air can be heard moving in and out immediately.

The opening in the trachea collapses unless something is inserted to keep it open. Commercially available devices have a tube for this purpose. If a large needle is used to perform the tracheostomy, the needle can be left in place to provide an opening. The device must be anchored to keep it from falling out or from being jammed into the back wall of the trachea and obstructed.

The needle or tube should be left in place until the individual is under a physician's care. If, during a prolonged evacuation, an unconscious person should recover enough to not need the tracheostomy, the needle or tubing can be plugged so that it can be easily opened again. It can be removed if the individual clearly will not need it again. The wound almost always closes and heals with no further attention.

FOOD ASPIRATION ("CAFE CORONARY")

A common cause of respiratory obstruction is the aspiration of food, most commonly meat. Before the development of the Heimlich maneuver, a procedure that usually dislodges the food and that was named for its originator, an estimated 4,000 people died each year from this type of accident in the United States alone. Alcohol consumption is commonly associated with such events. Surprisingly large

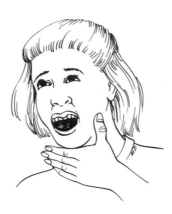

FIGURE 3-6. Signal that a person has choked on aspirated food, can not speak, and needs assistance, usually the Heimlich maneuver

food fragments can be impacted in the larynx. Whole radishes or chunks of poorly chewed food similar in size are typically found. The food plugs the larynx and obstructs the passage of air, usually completely. Because no air can move through the larynx, the individual can not speak, cough, or breathe.

While eating, the person suddenly indicates that he is choking, usually rises out of his chair, and after a brief struggle collapses. Because the food is jammed into his larynx, he can not speak. A signal has been devised for the individual to indicate that he is choking and consists of thrusting the V between the thumb and first finger of the hand against the throat (Fig. 3-6).

Attempts to dislodge the food by inserting a finger or a special device developed for that purpose through the mouth are rarely successful and may only force the food further down. Pounding on the back is usually fruitless. Such measures may be tried, but no more than a few seconds should be spent this way. Airway obstruction by aspirated food is a true emergency, and only three or four minutes are available to correct the problem.

The Heimlich maneuver consists of thrusting a hand or fist into the upper abdomen in such a way that the diaphragm is suddenly forced upward. The abrupt pressure on the diaphragm forces air out of the lungs and usually pops the obstructing food out of the larynx. The food is commonly ejected completely out of the person's mouth. The maneuver is so effective it can be used to evacuate aspirated objects that do not completely obstruct the airway.

The subject can be stood up if he is still conscious. Without delay, the rescuer's arms should be extended around him and one fist placed in the top of the V formed by the ribs just below the sternum. The second hand should be placed on top of the first, and both should be pulled inward and upward as sharply as possible (Fig. 3-7). Several attempts may be required to expel the food.

When performing the maneuver in this manner, little pressure should be placed on the subject's ribs. (Some is unavoidable.) Squeezing the ribs does not expel the food; thrusting against the diaphragm does. Squeezing the ribs has led to fractures and in a few cases multiple fractures.

If the individual is unconscious or obese, he should be placed on his back on the flattest surface that can be found. The rescuer should straddle the person (not kneel beside him) and place both hands, one on top of the other, on the upper abdomen just below the sternum. Pressing downward and toward the head briskly forces the diaphragm upward and dislodges the food (Fig. 3-8).

If the Heimlich maneuver is not successful after several tries, a tracheostomy must be performed. It should be done as quickly as possible. Artificial respiration through the tracheostomy may be necessary for a short time if the subject has stopped breathing. However, most poor outcomes have not resulted

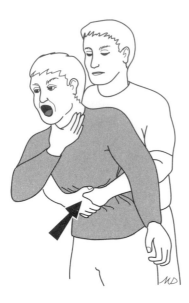 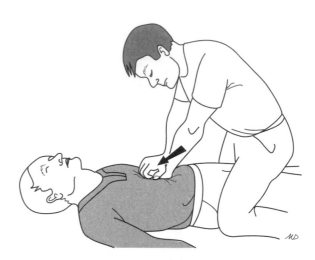

FIGURE 3-7. Position for Heimlich maneuver with the subject standing

FIGURE 3-8. Position for Heimlich maneuver with the subject lying down

from lack of success with the Heimlich maneuver but failure to use it in time to prevent permanent brain damage.

CARDIOPULMONARY RESUSCITATION

Occasions for effective cardiopulmonary resuscitation (CPR) in wilderness circumstances are rare. Resuscitative efforts for individuals with cardiac problems are futile unless advanced life support (ALS) can also be provided. However, individuals who have been struck by lightning can definitely be revived if efforts are begun promptly, and resuscitation should be attempted. Persons who have drowned can sometimes be revived, particularly if they have drowned in cold water and have been submerged for less than thirty minutes. A few individuals buried by avalanches can be successfully resuscitated. Even a person knocked unconscious in a relatively minor accident may temporarily stop breathing and require artificial respiration.

Resuscitation is usually not effective if the disorder that has caused breathing to stop or the heartbeat to cease is not corrected. Lung diseases such as pneumonia or high altitude pulmonary edema, severe infections, extensive trauma—particularly severe head, chest, or abdominal injuries—and severe shock of almost any origin are disorders for which cardiopulmonary resuscitation is not effective, particularly in wilderness situations.

Resuscitation takes time and energy; an unsuccessful attempt extracts a heavy emotional toll. Such expenditures may affect the survival of other members of the party in a threatening situation.

Attempts to resuscitate anyone who has a normal body temperature after fifteen minutes has elapsed without respiratory or cardiac action are futile. At a normal temperature, the brain can survive only about five minutes without oxygen before suffering permanent damage. After this period, deterioration is rapid, and by ten to twelve minutes death is inevitable. (Much longer periods without breathing—even an hour or more—are survivable if the body has been cooled.)

Individuals must be thoroughly familiar with resuscitative techniques, and must have perfected them with practice before they are needed, if efforts to apply them are to have a reasonable chance for success. Excellent CPR educational programs are widely available. Because those programs are so much more effective than the brief instructions provided in texts such as *Medicine for Mountaineering,* such instructions have not been included. (Instructions for other sophisticated procedures are included because they are not so readily available.)

Other Considerations

After a person has responded to resuscitation, he must be watched closely. A prolonged period of unconsciousness usually follows, even though he is breathing on his own. The airway must be kept open. Most individuals vomit and must be placed with their head lower than their chest and turned to the side to avoid aspiration. Shock must be anticipated and treated appropriately. The person should be evacuated as quickly as possible.

One of the most difficult questions concerning resuscitation is when to give up. The final decision in every case must be based on consideration of the circumstances in which the accident has occurred, the extent of injuries, the treatment required and administered, the people available for care of the victim, and the possibility of obtaining medical assistance within a short time. Artificial respiration must be continued for anyone whose heart is beating. On the other hand, anyone with a normal body temperature who requires cardiac massage has a much poorer prognosis. After thirty minutes, if spontaneous heart action has not resumed, and if the pupils are widely dilated and do not contract when exposed to light, the person is beyond further help. In contrast, resuscitative attempts for hypothermic individuals should be continued for a significantly longer time, preferably until the victim was been rewarmed to a body core temperature above 92°F (33°C).

In major medical institutions, less than five percent of the patients who receive CPR survive. Usually the injury or disease is too severe to begin with, or resuscitation is initiated too late. Resuscitative efforts for individuals with cardiac problems are futile unless advanced life support can also be provided. However, rescuers are often reluctant not to make the effort, even if the prospects for success appear remote. The rare individuals saved may make the efforts expended on others worthwhile, but the physical and emotional costs of unsuccessful attempts are high.

CHAPTER 4

PSYCHOLOGIC RESPONSES TO ACCIDENTS

PRINCIPAL CONTRIBUTOR:
Lawrence C. Salvesen, M.D.

Emotional reactions to traumatic accidents by accident victims and by their rescuers should be expected. Most responses are normal and tend to be consistent. Many are beneficial; only a few are harmful.

Anyone involved in an accident can benefit from attention to his psychologic responses. For some individuals, care for emotional needs is as essential as care for physical needs if they are to return to a functioning role in society.

PSYCHOLOGIC RESPONSES OF RESCUERS

Psychologic reactions by first responders have been well recognized by police, fire, and emergency medical services. Many have professional counselors on their staffs or on call to help with such reactions. In most situations, critical incident debriefing is provided for humanitarian reasons. However, financial considerations would justify counseling because individuals leave their jobs when the cumulative response to psychologic trauma becomes overwhelming and training replacements is expensive.

The potential magnitude of personnel losses was dramatically illustrated by the response to the crash of American Airlines Flight 191. This wide-bodied jet, a DC-10, lost the hydraulic system in one wing when the engine ripped away during takeoff. The flap on that side retracted, and the aircraft rolled inverted (rolled upside-down) and crashed. No one survived. The city of Chicago had staged a rescue drill only two weeks before this accident, and 351 rescuers were at the scene within twenty minutes. Experiencing hundreds of mutilated bodies was devastating for these responders, but no program to alleviate the emotional impact had been established. One year later, 275 of those individuals had left their positions for jobs that did not involve rescue!

Wilderness rescuers also respond psychologically to accidents, and their reactions require attention, but this need has not been as well recognized as the needs of police, fire, and ambulance service members. Such problems, labeled "rescue trauma," are well known to many rescuers, but few discuss them with their colleagues, possibly from fear of appearing unmanly or even unbalanced.

Dissociation

Performing well in rescue situations requires a high level of objectivity. The rescuer's emotional response to those involved in an accident and to their injuries must not interfere with caring for them. To maintain objectivity, most rescuers dissociate, or "split," their intellect from their feelings, and deny, or "block out," the emotional shock of the events surrounding them. Such defensive dissociation, "splitting," is effective but can not be kept up indefinitely. Eventually "mental circuits" become overloaded and rescuers develop symptoms of decompensation.

The symptoms are highly variable. Some rescuers become withdrawn and appear dazed, apathetic, forgetful, or tired. Others are open and expressive but become irritable, irrational, destructive, or violent. Some shut off their feelings and become less able to experience intimacy with their families and friends. Some rescuers become increasingly reliant on alcohol or other drugs.

Overload may come on suddenly, particularly after a major disaster that produces many casualties with mutilating injuries, or it may come on insidiously from the accumulated stress of a series of less distressing accidents. A rescuer's susceptibility to overload, his "rescue trauma threshold," may change from day to day as the result of events or circumstances entirely unrelated to the rescue, such as poor health, family problems, or insufficient sleep.

Sources of Stress

The many causes of rescue stress are interrelated, but they can be categorized as overt and covert. Overt sources of stress are immediately related to the accident. Sights or smells at the scene may assail the senses. The person to be rescued may be dead or may die during the rescue. Rescue equipment may be inadequate. The available personnel may be insufficient in number and lacking in knowledge and ability, resulting in great demands being placed on a few people. Wilderness accident casualties frequently must be evacuated over miles of difficult and dangerous terrain, often at night, which requires hours of exhausting labor. (Rescues require an average of twelve hours in the White Mountains of New England; they can require days in more remote areas when helicopters are not available.)

Covert sources of stress include fatigue or illness that may weaken the rescuer. He may be preoccupied with financial, legal, or family problems. The attitudes of other participants can be stressful. Rescuers with high expectations of success at the start of an operation may be frustrated by the death of the accident victim, by their or their co-workers' fallibility, and by lack of appreciation for their work, including inaccurate, critical, or even censorious reports in the media.

Another source of stress is the enforced inactivity a portion of the rescue team experiences after arriving at an accident scene. Dozens of stretcher-bearers are required to carry a loaded litter through difficult terrain, but only a few can administer medical treatment. While the rest wait, their energy and enthusiasm ebb. Some sink so low they need to be "psyched up" to evacuate the subject. The stress of this "middle period" is often overlooked and appears to result from feeling unneeded, from the "settling in" of fatigue, and sometimes from newness of the rescue experience.

Normal Reactions to Stress

Totally normal reactions to stress may be immediate or delayed. Immediate reactions that occur among rescuers at the accident site include anxiety and apprehension, doubts about their abilities, or hopelessness and despair, which are often mixed with denial or "splitting." All are normal. Some rescuers experience cognitive difficulties, forgetting where they put things and finding decisions hard to make. Rescuers in all types of incidents report nausea, a pounding sensation in their hearts, muscle tremors, cramps, profuse sweating, chills, headaches, and muffled hearing. These symptoms tend to dissipate within one to three days, but if the underlying emotions are not recognized and allowed to surface within a reasonably short period of time, they eventually work their way into the rescuer's daily life and can cripple him emotionally, cognitively, and physically.

Delayed stress reactions appear hours to weeks—sometimes months to years—after an accident and may be directed inward or outward. Inward reactions include depression, apathy, or feelings of guilt for not helping or for further injuring the subject. Nightmares, insomnia, or occasional visual flashbacks or physical symptoms such as headache, loss of appetite, or nausea may be experienced. Outward reactions typically include irritability, explosiveness, and in some cases anger with others who contributed to the stress of the incident, particularly with the press for inaccurate or distorted reporting. Like the immediate stress reactions, these delayed reactions are entirely normal.

Preventing Adverse Stress Reactions

Rescuers, whether amateurs or professionals, must be emotionally prepared for the worst casualties— the mutilated, dying, or dead—and for the worst situations. Watching helplessly while young, attractive accident victims die because they are inaccessible, equipment is inadequate, or they just do not respond to the best possible medical care is a devastating experience. In preparing for the worst, participants must be aware of their limitations and must balance their expectations with reality.

Rescuers must be prepared to serve under leaders who do not have time for explanations or who are not aware of the needs of their crewmembers. They must expect sparse recognition and abundant criticism, and they should not be surprised when rescue work turns out to be ninety percent drudgery and ten percent terror.

Despite training and experience, rescuers must withdraw from situations they find particularly stressful, such as accidents that involve family or friends, injuries to children similar to their own, and some specific injuries. The leader and his associates, as well as the rescuer, must respect such sensitivity.

Rescuers must realize that stress overload is virtually inevitable, regardless of training and experience, if sharing it with others does not relieve their accumulated emotional stress. To ensure the emotional health of rescuers, established preventive or therapeutic programs are essential.

Within twenty-four hours after a rescue, team members should engage in vigorous exercise to relieve tension and achieve greater muscular relaxation.

Within twenty-four to seventy-two hours after a stressful rescue, a mandatory "emotional debriefing" is held for the entire team. Effective sessions require an hour or more and promote expression and sharing of emotional reactions to the rescue—specifically the pain, sadness, terror, guilt, or feelings of helplessness experienced by each in different ways. These emotions must be expressed and accepted without shame or embarrassment. The participants must share their humanity and support each other.

The session must be entirely nonjudgmental. There can be no right or wrong, correct or incorrect, as long as emotions did not interfere with the rescue. To ensure absolute confidentiality, no records should be kept.

Although some groups can manage this process quite well by themselves, such exercises frequently are more effective when guided by someone experienced in stress management and not directly involved in the rescue. Completely resolving the stress may require more than one meeting, but all meetings should be conducted as close to the event as possible, preferably within three days. Delays of a week or more increase the risk of converting early, tenuous emotional reactions into entrenched, chronic disorders. The debriefing must be conducted without any alcohol or other drugs; to maximize the benefits, the minds of all must be fully functional.

After debriefing, rescuers must eat and rest well, rounding out the recovery of the entire organism. Only after physical and emotional recovery has been assured can the rescue team critique the rescue objectively, learning from successes as well as mistakes, and planning for the future.

Case Study One

A professional rescuer was on a Himalayan trek with a close friend who became seriously ill and clearly needed to be evacuated. The leader decided to split the party, most continuing to their objective, while the rescuer and two physicians stayed behind with the person who was ill. After the main party had moved on, that person's condition deteriorated catastrophically, and over a period of days the three rescuers worked virtually to the point of exhaustion to save him.

During this ordeal, the rescuer became aware of several strong feelings. He found that attending a close friend aggravated normal feelings of inadequacy and guilt, particularly guilt for not having more forcefully cautioned the person before he became so ill. He also felt guilt for not having resisted more vigorously the decision to split the party, which left the person who was ill with a support team barely able to provide for his care.

In retrospect, the rescuer realized that he had deferred to the leader because he was a physician, despite his own considerable judgement and experience. During and after the subsequent vigil, the subject began to question his confidence in the leader, in his associates, in himself, and even in the categories of people (doctors and nurses) who were members of the rescue group. His confidence was further eroded following reuniting of the party when "significant" people "acted like nothing had happened."

The rescuer kept these feelings hidden for some time, not realizing that others were experiencing the same emotions. Only months later, when he made an offhand comment that he was considering dropping out of the group, did he have an opportunity to share his pain and begin to reconstruct relationships. Since then he has made a variety of recommendations, particularly that the emotional residue of stressful situations be discharged through debriefings.

He also observed that even though support from associates is helpful, in the long run the benefits fade unless the rescuer recognizes the value of his efforts and learns from his mistakes, rather than wallowing in destructive self-criticism. To grow, everyone must accept responsibility for his actions, both good and bad.

Posttraumatic Stress Disorder

If rescuers do not work through their normal reactions, they risk developing a more severe abnormality, posttraumatic stress disorder. This condition has been repeatedly described and, depending on its origin, has been given widely varying names that include accident neurosis, shell shock, traumatic neurosis, combat fatigue, combat exhaustion, post-Vietnam syndrome, and neurasthenia. The term "posttraumatic stress disorder" unites these conditions under one label.

The features of posttraumatic stress disorder are as follows:

1. The individual has undergone a recognizable stressful experience that would evoke significant symptoms of distress in almost everyone.
2. The individual reexperiences the event in one or more ways:
   - Recurrent and intrusive recollections
   - Recurrent dreams of the event
   - Sudden acting or feeling as if the traumatic event were recurring due to the stimulus of an environment or thought associated with the event
3. The individual has numbed responsiveness to or reduced involvement with the external world that began some time after the event and is manifested by one or more of the following:
   - Markedly diminished interest in one or more significant activities
   - Feeling of detachment or estrangement from others
   - Constricted affect (emotionally flat or dull)
4. The individual usually has two or more of the following symptoms that were not present before the event:
   - Hyperalertness or exaggerated "startle" response
   - Sleep disturbances
   - Guilt about surviving when others have not, or about the behavior required for survival
   - Memory impairment or difficulty concentrating
   - Avoidance of activities that arouse recollections of the traumatic event
   - Intensification of symptoms by exposure to events that symbolize or resemble the traumatic event

Posttraumatic stress disorder has been subclassified as acute when symptoms appear within six months of the trauma and last less than six months; chronic when symptoms appear within six months and last longer than six months; and delayed when symptoms appear six months or more after the trauma.

Diagnostic studies suggest that with sufficient unrelieved stress, anyone would develop a posttraumatic stress disorder. Vietnam veterans who developed this disorder shared five characteristics that correlate with experiences of wilderness rescuers (Table 4-1).

Table 4-1	Stress Sources for Vietnam Veterans and Wilderness Rescuers
VIETNAM VETERANS	**WILDERNESS RESCUERS**
▼ A positive attitude toward the war before engaging in combat	▼ Unrealistic expectations
▼ A high level of combat exposure	▼ A high level of exposure to hazardous terrain or weather, and to massive trauma
▼ Immediate separation from the military service upon returning to the United States	▼ Infrequent opportunities to share emotional experiences; "suffering in silence"
▼ A negative perception of family helpfulness upon returning home	▼ Lack of support or appreciation
▼ A feeling that forces beyond their control were directing the course of their life	▼ Feeling that uncontrollable factors such as weather, timing, inadequate personnel or equipment, communication failures, or accidents involving members of the rescue group have determined the outcome of the rescue

Treating posttraumatic stress disorder is the province of professional therapists. However, the earlier the disorder is recognized, the faster and more successful is the recovery. Recognizing stressful events, taking measures to relieve the emotional pressures they engender, and recognizing the symptoms of emotional disorders are certainly within the abilities of rescuers and their friends and should be the responsibility of their leaders.

PSYCHOLOGIC RESPONSES OF ACCIDENT VICTIMS

The emotional responses of accident victims are similar to the bereavement or grief that follows loss of a loved one. Because many more individuals have experienced grief than have been involved in wilderness accidents, the emotional reactions to such events may be more understandable when compared with grief reactions. This comparison also demonstrates that most psychologic reactions to accidents are normal, even though they may seem abnormal to individuals who have not experienced such phenomena.

Grief Reactions

The period of mourning that follows the loss of a loved one can be lengthy and painful, but if grief is appropriately worked through, the survivor reconciles himself to the loss and resumes his life. Like other emotional states, bereavement is more easily resolved when shared with others.

Grief evolves through several stages, and the boundary between normal and abnormal is often blurred. Bereaved persons commonly display attitudes, beliefs, and behavior that smack of irrationality. Stunned shock and denial characterize the first stage of this emotional response, which has been labeled the protest phase: "He can't be dead!" Anger commonly follows and illogically may be directed at the person or circumstance that caused the loss, at the deceased, or at himself for not having prevented the loss, or even for surviving. The bereaved frequently manifest emotional pain by crying, weakness, loss of appetite, nausea, or sleep disturbances. Survivors may search for their loved ones or mementos of their loved ones (Fig. 4-1).

After days or weeks, bereaved individuals move into a stage dominated by despair. They experience anguish, grief, and depression, think slowly, display emotional pain, and continue to search for loved ones and remembrances of them.

After weeks or months, they move slowly into the detachment stage, during which they lose interest

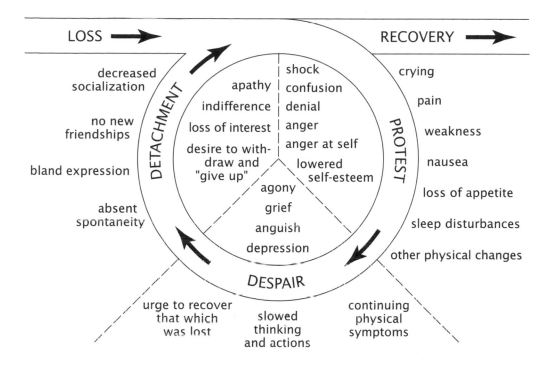

FIGURE 4-1. Diagram of reaction cycle associated with grief[1]

in life and want to withdraw and give up. They appear bland, lack spontaneity and social energy, and behave like robots or "zombies."

Normally the cycle of protest, despair, and detachment takes six to eighteen months. The bereaved finally work through their loss, say their final good-byes, and restructure their lives and personalities, reconciled with their loss. The success with which the bereaved can resolve his grief is proportional to his capacity to face the finality of death, whether the death of others or himself.

Sometimes grief can not be handled successfully. When the relationship has been an ambivalent mixture of love and hate, and hostile feelings have been denied, the bereaved may be tortured with guilt. His grief may go on indefinitely at great emotional cost.

Stress Imposed by an Accident

The normal emotional state of an individual involved in any sudden, unpredictable, and overwhelming crisis is similar to an acute grief state. If the incident is traumatic, the overwhelming emotion results from experiencing the possibility of death and fearing for his life. An accompanying sense of helplessness, of having lost control over his survival, adds to the impact. He is aware of seeking to escape and of being weak, vulnerable, and helpless. His self-esteem and sense of competence have been assaulted, and he sees himself as unable to keep out of harm's way or as having acted with poor judgement.

Hours to weeks after the incident, depending upon the individual and the nature of the incident, the accident victim is subjected to secondary stresses such as the prospect of being immobilized and isolated without food or shelter, the prospect of being totally dependent upon strangers for rescue, or the more distant prospect of not being able to go back to work or to continue other valued activities.

Responses by Accident Victims

During accidents, one-eighth to one-fourth of the people involved react effectively. They are often "too busy to worry." About three-fourths are stunned and bewildered. They show no emotion, are inactive or indecisive, and are usually docile. They may be totally unresponsive or behave in an automatic, robotlike manner. Manifestations of fear such as sweating, palpitations, tunnel vision, or a dry mouth may be present. This type of reaction is known as "psychologic shock" but should not be considered an abnormal reaction. A final one-eighth to one-fourth of people involved in accidents react inappropriately with incapacitating anxiety or hysteria.

Immediately after the accident, responses that are similar to the stages of the grief reaction occur. During the stage of protest or denial, the person may not be able to deny that a problem exists but refuses to admit the magnitude of the problem. The problem is understood intellectually but not emotionally, and the individual is blasé and unconcerned.

Some individuals are stunned and confused; others are vigilant and cool. Some are emotionally expressive, displaying anxiety, anger, sobbing, a sense of relief, or a tendency to blame others. Others are controlled, exhibit little distress, and appear composed. Both behaviors reflect denial and emotional exhaustion or "shock." Both reactions are normal, but the individuals need acceptance and assurance of the normality of their responses. They may be vulnerable to damaged self-esteem if they perceive their behavior as inadequate or abnormal.

A person may say, "This will hit me later." He should be reassured (or informed) that indeed it will hit him later and that his emotional responses may take time and talking out.

During the stage corresponding to the despair phase of the grief reaction, ninety percent of the individuals involved in accidents become aware of problems but regard them as overwhelming and unbearable. Tightening of muscles, sweating, restlessness, difficulty in speaking, sadness and weeping, irritability and anger, or passive dependency and childlike behavior are manifestations of strong emotions. Some persons develop a "zombielike" gaze—the "thousand-mile stare." Many need to tell and retell the experience.

During the stage corresponding to the detachment phase of the grief reaction, individuals begin to return to normal, accept their problems, and make efforts to solve them. They are more hopeful and confident, and emotions from the second stage are less intense.

The final phase of a disaster takes place six to twelve months after the incident and may last a lifetime. The source of stress is the personal and social aftereffects of the incident. The normal reaction after recovery from the accident is to return to normal activities. A sense of well-being returns, and individuals are able to make decisions and act on them. Grief that was encountered is successfully worked through. Many survivors develop altered attitudes toward life and death and display a definite philosophic mellowing and growth.

Abnormal reactions occasionally occur and have been labeled the "delayed stress syndrome." The characteristics of this disorder are posttraumatic stress disorder, psychosomatic or physical illness, depression, accident proneness, accidental death, or suicide. Professional counseling is often needed to work out the problems of this syndrome. However, proper emotional support during rescue can significantly reduce the severity of such disorders or prevent them altogether.

Abnormal Responses to Accidents

Abnormal psychologic reactions to trauma may affect four functional areas:

- ▾ Orientation to time, place, and person
- ▾ Observable motor and physical acts
- ▾ Verbal behavior
- ▾ Emotional or affective expression

Because typical abnormal behavior patterns are rather easily recognized, they are outlined without further discussion.

I. ORIENTATION

A. *Mild derangement (adequately aware of time, place, events, and person)*
1. Dazed, confused
2. Minor difficulty understanding what is being said
3. Minor difficulty thinking clearly or concentrating
4. Slow or delayed reactions

B. *Severe derangement (confused about time, place, events, and person but may gradually respond to information and reassurance [unlike individuals with brain trauma])*
1. Forgetful of own name and names of associates
2. Unclear about date—year or month
3. Unable to state clearly his location
4. Unable to recall clearly events of the previous twenty-four hours
5. Regresses to an earlier period of life
6. Complains about memory gaps of thirty minutes or more
7. Confused about who he is or what he does
8. Appears unaware of what is happening around him

II. MOTOR BEHAVIOR

A. *Mild derangement*
1. Wringing hands or clinching fists; stiff and rigid appearance; continuously sad expression
2. Some restlessness; mild agitation and excitement
3. Difficulty falling asleep or keeping down food
4. Rushing about trying to do many things at once but accomplishing little
5. Feelings of fatigue inconsistent with previous and concurrent activity
6. Halting or rapid speech that is out of character; difficulty getting words out

B. *Severe derangement*
1. Agitated movements; inability to sleep or rest quietly
2. Grimacing or posturing of recent onset
3. Markedly reduced activity; sits and stares; remains immobile for hours
4. Incontinence
5. Mutilation of self or objects for no reason
6. Repeated ritualistic acts of no functional significance; attempts to prevent the acts create resistance and excessive emotion
7. Excessive use of drugs or alcohol
8. Inability to carry out simple functions such as eating, dressing, organizing equipment

III. VERBAL BEHAVIOR

A. *Mild derangement*
1. Verbalizes hopelessness: "It's no use," "I can't go on"
2. States he can not make a decision; doubts his ability to recover
3. Overly concerned with small things and neglectful of more pressing, major problems
4. Denies any problems; overconfident; claims he can do everything without help
5. Blames the problems on others; has difficulty making plans or discussing future actions

B. *Severe derangement*
1. Hallucinations, auditory or visual, unverifiable by others
2. Verbalizes fear of losing his mind; claims the world seems unrecognizable and unreal; claims his body feels unreal and completely different
3. Preoccupied with an event or idea to the exclusion of anything else
4. Unrealistic claims that an agency, object, group, or spirit is out to harm him and others such as his family or friends
5. Expresses inability to make a decision to carry out familiar activities

6. Expresses a real fear of killing or harming himself or others; far exceeds simple statement of anger or hopelessness

IV. EMOTIONAL EXPRESSION

A. *Mild derangement (significantly different from most individuals but largely appropriate to situation)*

1. Frequent uncontrolled tearing and weeping; rehashing of traumatic events
2. Blunted expression of feelings; apathetic; seemingly withdrawn emotionally and unable to react with feeling to what is happening
3. Unusual laughter and gaiety
4. Overly irritable; quick to get angry over trivia

B. *Severe derangement (markedly unusual affect or emotion)*

1. Excessively flat emotionally; virtually no expression of feeling
2. Excessive emotional expression; inappropriate joy, anger, fear, or sadness for situation

Trauma or Disease Simulating Psychologic Abnormalities

A number of disorders, particularly those that reduce the availability of oxygen to the brain or cause metabolic derangements, produce abnormal behavior that simulates abnormal psychologic reactions. Hypoxia is common and results from altitude, but it is also produced by pneumonia, chest injuries, shock, and other disorders. Hypothermia typically produces changes ranging from forgetfulness and slow thought processes, through loss of coordination and greater mental dullness, to irrationality, and finally coma. Hyperthermia can cause headache, irritability, agitation, and mental dullness before progressing to stupor and coma. Hypoglycemia (low blood glucose or sugar) produces restlessness, irritability, lethargy, poor judgement, agitation, disorientation, and finally coma. Severe hypoglycemia is almost always a complication of diabetes, but milder glucose depletion occurs in normal individuals who are exhausted and have not maintained an adequate food intake. Dehydration can produce similar abnormalities.

Head injuries may result in immediate or delayed changes that include drowsiness, apathy, and irritability; disorientation; forgetfulness and wandering off; bizarre behavior, including homicidal or suicidal mania; or convulsions and finally unconsciousness. Signs such as unequal pupils or abnormal reflexes may be present. Severe infections of the nervous system can produce such signs, as can pneumonia or severe generalized infections. Intoxication by drugs (including alcohol) or drug withdrawal (particularly from alcohol, tranquilizers, and barbiturates) can have similar effects.

Generally, personality changes such as silliness, irritability, agitation, belligerence, and lethargy occur first. Loss of cognitive functions, which progresses from mild mental dullness through disorientation to time, place, and person (in spite of frequent reminders), loss of calculating ability and specialized knowledge, to loss of judgement and memory appear next. Eventually, obvious confusion with anxiety or hallucinations supervenes and may be associated with staggering and slurred speech, tremors, convulsions, and unconsciousness progressing to deep coma and eventual death.

If sedation is essential for evacuating a person whose behavior is uncontrollable, a tranquilizer is preferable. Barbiturates or narcotics complicate the neurologic abnormalities, depress respiration, and should be avoided.

Psychologic Aid for Accident Victims

Persons injured in an accident, uninjured members of the party, and rescuers must cope with the reactions at the scene of the accident or during evacuation. Assistance provided at that time can greatly diminish emotional aftereffects. Rescue leaders and their crew members must be prepared to provide as much psychologic help as possible with constructive, understanding listening.

The essence of psychologic care is listening effectively and creatively. The subject must be allowed to express his feelings openly and freely; the counselor must understand that such expression is the major purpose of the conversation. The counselor can not judge what the person should feel, and he certainly must not convey any such opinion to him. The counselor must look directly at the person who is speaking, giving his complete attention, and only asking questions or paraphrasing statements to emphasize his attentiveness or to make certain he fully understands what is being said.

Preferably, the counselor should be the same gender as the injured person. The counselor should remain in constant contact and should be the "head person" who remains by the subject's head throughout the evacuation.

Some goals rescue leaders and counselors should strive for are:

- ▼ To create acceptance of an injured person's feelings as normal reactions to stress
- ▼ To reduce feelings of guilt by not assessing blame for the accident
- ▼ To reduce panic and rage; to allow ventilation of feelings and to accept them
- ▼ To give realistic, honest answers balanced with judicious omissions
- ▼ To be aware of the special needs due to the person's sex when immobilized and dependent (as in a litter)
- ▼ To restore a feeling of well-being with food and water, warmth, attention to injuries, physical restraint when necessary, analgesia when indicated, and comfort and support through listening and touching
- ▼ To restore a sense of hope and of belonging through quiet, firm, and knowledgeable leadership with clearly understood goals and sensitivity to the need of injured or ill individuals and rescuers
- ▼ To maintain awareness that supposedly unconscious individuals often hear some of what is said around them

A person's self-esteem and sense of mastery are also based on his judgement of how well he responds to problem situations. Success heightens self-esteem; failure lowers it. The rescuer must constantly seek ways to help a person involved in an accident to preserve his dignity, particularly ways he can help in the rescue operation. Participation is essential for restoring and preserving self-esteem and a sense of mastery and control and for minimizing psychic trauma, guilt reactions, and delayed stress reactions. Rescue leaders must be aware of this need and do all they can to ensure it is met.

Some attitudes or actions rescue leaders and counselors must try to avoid are:

- ▼ Callousness or flippancy (the "M*A*S*H syndrome")
- ▼ Lying to provide unrealistic optimism and reassurance
- ▼ Talking around a subject without talking to him
- ▼ Authoritarian style; telling the subject how to feel or imposing ideas on him; not really listening
- ▼ Expecting a subject to function at top level too quickly
- ▼ Expecting too little of a subject, damaging his chances to salvage self-esteem
- ▼ "Chicken soup" style; oversolicitousness that interferes with a subject's recovery of self-esteem
- ▼ "Democratic" leader(less)ship; floundering by committee, with no definitive leader, goals, plans for achieving them, or communication within the party

Case Study Two

Some insights into the psychology of individuals involved in accidents and helpful recommendations for rescuers were made by Ray Smutek in his account of his own mountaineering accident and rescue. When describing his fall he recalls "accelerated mental activity, the detached overview of the situation, the recollection of past events. Most amazing was the absence of pain, coupled with a very acute awareness of the damage being done."[2]

He observes that potentially the most dangerous stage of an accident is immediately afterward, "not necessarily to the victim . . . I think the natural tendency in a situation like this is to rush to the victim, perhaps unbelayed. Action! Do something! Don't just stand there!" But Smutek continues, "this is not the time to rush; few situations require that immediate an action. There is only one thing that you should do immediately and that is to think."

He describes directing his immediate rescue and first aid to the extent that he was conscious and able to state what his injuries were and what he was capable of doing. Further in the article he says that the long wait for rescue "psychologically was the worst part of the entire episode. There was nothing to do but worry." He was very happy to have the company of a fellow climber and thinks everyone in a similar situation should have an "official comforter."

When rescue did come, some of the rescuers were "over their heads," and Smutek states, "nothing is more devastating to a person's morale than an obviously incompetent rescuer." Finally, he reports that administration of a painkiller muddled his mind and increased his anxiety because he could not understand the procedures to which he was being subjected. He feels that rescuers should use pain medication on a highly selective basis, particularly if that medication may interfere with a person's need to feel in control and be aware of what is going on.

These feelings clearly reflect Smutek's need to maintain a sense of self-efficacy. On the other hand, some people are not used to being in control and may be more comfortable being medicated or being told that everything is being cared for.

Case Study Three

In *The Breach,* Rob Taylor traces the various phases of his devastating accident on Kilimanjaro, his almost miraculous rescue, his prolonged recovery, and his reactions to them. Following a fall in which he suffered a severe compound fracture of his lower leg, he descended a perilously steep snow slope on his own and survived a solitary, exposed, life-threatening bivouac that lasted several days. During this ordeal his thoughts and behavior were strikingly organized. His self-control becomes more understandable when he says, "unrestrained emotions and unbridled feelings in the end, after the fact, are fine, but during the crisis they are illusory defenses."[3]

Nonetheless, while on the mountain Taylor experienced grief over the loss symbolized by the injury to his leg. He also felt anguish over the days of waiting for the unknown but was preparing for and accepting the worst. He writes of "the need to re-live the event" during his recovery and of becoming "daily more aware of the positive aspects of the pilgrimage . . . and (of a) renewal of a reverence and deep appreciation of the gift of life." Finally, he speaks of a heightened sense of self-definition, of altering his concept of death, and of coming to realize that he "must make the most of each encounter, each meeting" as a result of his experience.

Taylor recommends to rescuers the therapeutic use of concern, small talk, encouragement, and infectious optimism.

SELECTION OF RESCUERS

Enthusiasm alone is not an adequate qualification for wilderness rescuers. In addition to good physical condition, technical expertise, and support persons who are the same gender as the individuals involved in the accident, members of rescue teams should have the following characteristics:

- ▾ A reasonable personality that is not excitable, impulsive, or prone to harbor anger
- ▾ The ability to take the initiative
- ▾ The ability to cooperatively follow others
- ▾ Attentiveness to details of procedure and equipment
- ▾ A sense of humor
- ▾ Empathy and ability to feel for another's plight without being overwhelmed
- ▾ Optimism, although prepared for the worst
- ▾ The ability to minimize or shelve worry or fear and yet be able to accept those feelings as normal

PSYCHOLOGIC REACTIONS TO DEAD BODIES

When faced with the dead bodies of intimates or strangers, many people experience emotional difficulties. In *The Hour of Our Death,* Phillipe Aries states that people have long resisted believing that death deprives the body of all life.[4] He says, "belief in the sensibility of the cadaver has the support of the people, and what we would call folklore . . . though scientists consider such to be superstition." Reinforced by descriptions of "out of body" or "life after death" experiences, many people believe that the body still hears, feels, and remembers after death, and treat the dead gently for fear of hurting them or, in some cases, for fear of angering them.

Other reactions to dead bodies include anxious discomfort, horror and panic, fear of the unknown or of one's own death, and fear of contamination. A few people react with intellectual or morbid fascination and curiosity. Defensive behavior such as indifference, joking, hostility, or detachment is more commonly encountered.

In nursing and medical students, the fear of dying and the death of others decreases with increasing academic preparation and experience. However, the fear of their own death and dying remains the same or increases as they near the age at which their death is more likely.

Professional rescuers encounter death so commonly they lose any feeling of discomfort when near a body, at least when near the body of someone they do not know. For amateur rescuers who have fewer encounters with death, two methods for reducing the emotional shock of the experience have been suggested:

- ▼ Desensitization through gradual, nontraumatic exposure to death; or coming to terms with their own death by experiencing it in fantasy
- ▼ Discovering what is really essential for them to have accomplished during their lives, and taking steps to leave as little unfinished as possible

Anticipatory grief as a buffer for sudden and serious loss has demonstrated value. Many individuals have come to accept death as another stage of life, but that is the purview of religion.

ACKNOWLEDGMENTS

The author wishes to acknowledge his indebtedness to Grady P. Bray, Ph.D.; Jeffrey Mitchell, Ph.D.; George Everly, Ph.D.; Herbert Benson, M.D.; Roger Zimmerman, Ph.D.; and William Moss, EMT, for their professional expertise.

REFERENCES

1. Lamers W: *Death, Dying and Bereavement.* Symposium, Stockholm, Sweden, 20 June 1982. (Reproduced by permission.)
2. Smutek R: Good morning, I'm your guest victim for today. *Off Belay,* February 1978. (Quoted by permission of the author and publisher.)
3. Taylor R: *The Breach: Kilimanjaro and the Conquest of Self.* New York, Coward, McCann, and Geoghegan, 1981. (Quoted by permission of the author and publisher.)
4. Aries P: *The Hour of Our Death.* New York, Alfred Knopf, 1981.

CHAPTER 5

IMMUNIZATIONS, SANITATION, AND WATER DISINFECTION

In developing countries, infections, particularly gastrointestinal infections, are a constant threat. Preventing illnesses in wilderness areas, where disease is coupled with inaccessibility, has obvious advantages. Many infections can be prevented by immunizations and by sanitation measures, particularly water disinfection. (The prevention of malaria and some other infections for which immunization is not possible is considered in chapter 19, "Infections.")

IMMUNIZATIONS

Immunization is the easiest and most reliable method for preventing infections. Only a limited number of effective vaccines are available, but those that are only partially effective can significantly reduce the likelihood of infection and lessen the impact should the infection occur. (The immunologic principles upon which immunizations are based are discussed in chapter 20, "Allergies.")

History

The history of vaccine development is long. Well before Edward Jenner's discovery, which occurred more than 200 years ago, intentionally infecting a healthy person with the "matter" taken from a patient with mild smallpox was occasionally practiced. This procedure, which originated in the East, was based on the concept of "permanent immunity" (knowledge that an attack of smallpox effectively protected against any subsequent exposure), a concept that was well established at that time. Unfortunately, the infection did not always remain mild, and death sometimes occurred. Furthermore, the inoculated person could disseminate the disease to others.

Jenner had been impressed—even during his apprenticeship, which started at age thirteen—that a person who had suffered an attack of cowpox could not "take" the smallpox. His magnificent contribution was based on speculation that the protection provided by cowpox could be deliberately induced in another person. Jenner was not only a pupil of John Hunter, the great Scottish physician considered by many the father of surgery, but remained a close friend until Hunter's death, and was thoroughly familiar with Hunter's reliance on experimental investigation. Hunter typically would ask, "Why speculate—why not try the experiment?"

The story of the experiment is well known. In May 1796, Jenner found a young dairymaid, Sarah Nelmes, who had fresh cowpox lesions on her finger. On May 14, using "matter" from Sarah's lesions, he inoculated an eight-year-old boy, James Phipps, who promptly developed a slight fever and a small skin lesion. On July 1, Jenner inoculated the boy with smallpox "matter." No disease developed; protection was complete. (How many millions have lived because "informed consent" was not required at that time?)

In 1797, Jenner sent the Royal Society a short paper describing his results. His report of one of the greatest advances in medical history was refused! In 1798, having added additional individuals he had successfully vaccinated, Jenner published his results privately in a slender book entitled *An Inquiry into the Causes and Effects of the Variolae Vaccinae, a Disease Known by the Name of Cow Pox*. Subsequently, others tried to discredit Jenner or even claim credit for his findings.

Jenner's triumph became complete when smallpox was completely eradicated worldwide with basically the same vaccine he developed. The last case of naturally developing human smallpox occurred in Somalia in 1977. Ten years earlier, the annual number of deaths from smallpox worldwide had been estimated at two million. Currently, the vaccinia-based vaccine is considered more risky than the possibility of developing smallpox, and routine vaccination is not practiced in much of the world.

Jenner's vaccine was obviously a live virus vaccine, although it contained a closely related virus, not the smallpox virus. Louis Pasteur developed the first attenuated live virus vaccine. Through animal experimentation, he discovered that the spinal cords of rabid rabbits became noninfectious when dried for fifteen days. On July 6, 1885, he began his celebrated treatment of Joseph Meister—also an eight-year-old boy—who had been bitten by a rabid dog, with injections of spinal cord material that was fourteen days old. For subsequent injections he used progressively fresher material until he was injecting viruses that were hardly attenuated. Fortunately, far better vaccines for rabies have been developed, although the Pasteur vaccine was used as recently as 1953.

One of the safest and most efficacious attenuated live virus vaccines, that for yellow fever, was developed at the Institute Pasteur de Dakar, Senegal, in 1937. A single subcutaneous injection provides protection for at least ten years and possibly for life. Neutralizing antibodies have been detected in individuals immunized forty years earlier.

"Baby boomers" and older individuals can well remember the haunting fear of paralytic poliomyelitis that used to resurface every summer, and the monstrous iron lungs found in so many hospital wards. More than 20,000 paralytic infections occurred in the United States alone in 1952. Jonas Salk was beatified for developing the killed virus vaccine. (Viruses grown on monkey kidney cell tissue cultures were killed with formalin.) Albert Sabin became almost as well known a few years later for developing an oral attenuated live virus vaccine. Few recognize the names of John Franklin Enders, Thomas Huckle Weller, and Frederick Chapman Robbins, who were awarded the Nobel Prize for medicine for developing the techniques for growing the viruses, the real breakthrough.

The last indigenously acquired poliomyelitis (polio) infection in the United States occurred in 1979. The last naturally occurring infection anywhere in the Americas occurred in Peru in 1991, and in 1994 the entire Western Hemisphere was declared free of this scourge. By the end of the year 2000, poliomyelitis was expected to be eradicated worldwide by a vaccination campaign carried out by the World Health Organization with financial support from Rotarians International. That goal was not reached in 2000, but success is very near.

Contemporary vaccines are based on modern cell biology, including nucleotide analysis of gene sequences. A recombinant vaccinia-rabies oral vaccine eradicated terrestrial rabies throughout much of Europe in less than five years. A South Texas epizootic of rabies in coyotes and gray foxes that spread to dogs and resulted in two human deaths and thousands of human postexposure treatments was eliminated in less time with the same vaccine. This recombinant is composed of the genetic material that encodes the rabies G glycoprotein, the surface protein that promotes entry of the virus into a cell, inserted into vaccinia viruses. It is totally safe because the viral RNA is never encoded, and it is highly effective—as effective as vaccines that include the entire virion. The attenuated live virus vaccine that the recombinant replaced was capable of reverting to virulence, was lethal for rodents and skunks, and was ineffective for raccoons.

Perhaps closer to home is the hepatitis B vaccine, a recombinant in which the genetic material that encodes for the hepatitis B surface antigen (HBsAg) is inserted into the gene for *Saccharomyces cerevisiae*, common baker's yeast. HbsAg produced in this manner is the vaccine antigen.

The three currently licensed vaccines for *Haemophilus influenzae* type b immunization of children are recombinant vaccines in which the capsular polyribosylribitol phosphate (PRP) is combined with protein carriers that vary in polysaccharide size and method of chemical conjugation. PRP is a major virulence factor for the organism, and antibody to PRP is the primary contributor to serum bactericidal activity. However, PRP alone stimulates a T-cell–independent response characterized by:

▾ Induction of a poor antibody response in less than 18-month-old infants and children
▾ A variable and quantitatively smaller antibody response than that seen with T-cell–dependent antigens
▾ Production of a higher proportion of immunoglobulin M (IgM)
▾ Inability to induce a booster response

The conjugate vaccine stimulates a T-cell–dependent response and is effective in infants only six weeks old.

Sources of Up-to-Date Information

Recommendations for immunization change frequently. The Centers for Disease Control and Prevention (CDC) maintains complete information about all aspects of immunization at *www.cdc.gov.* This website is updated more frequently than the familiar "yellow book," *Health Information for International Travel,* which is issued annually.

The International Association for Medical Assistance to Travelers (IAMAT) is a volunteer organization of health care centers and physicians that provides travelers with access to physicians who speak English or French in addition to their native tongue and who meet IAMAT's standards, which are similar to U.S. standards. Membership in IAMAT and a directory of its affiliated institutions in more than 115 countries are free. The address of the U.S. affiliate is IAMAT, 736 Center Street, Lewiston, NY 14092. The organization has a website at *www.sentex.net/~iamat/index.html.* It offers a number of free publications, including informational pamphlets on malaria, schistosomiasis, and Chaga's disease, and its World Immunization Chart, which lists the potential risk for more than a dozen infections, country by country, in a quick reference format.

An International Certificate of Vaccination is the best way to record immunizations and is required for entrance into a number of countries.

Scheduling Immunizations

Months of planning and preparation usually precede foreign travel. Immunizations are a critical part of such preparations and must not be put off until the last minute.

Viral vaccines, including those for hepatitis A and B, and toxoid for tetanus and diphtheria can be given six months or more before departure because such immunizations persist for years. Bacterial immunizations for conditions such as typhoid fever are not as enduring and should be given closer to the date of departure. Immune globulin is not routinely given because effective vaccines for hepatitis A are now available.

Specific Vaccines
Bubonic Plague

Bubonic plague vaccine is prepared from bacteria killed with formalin. Its effectiveness has not been adequately tested, but vaccinated members of the U.S. military had a much lower incidence of plague (1 per 10^6 exposure-years) than unvaccinated civilians in Vietnam (333 per 10^6 exposure-years). A relatively high incidence of murine typhus indicated that the Americans were coming in contact with the *Xenopsylla cheopis* rat flea, which transmits both infections, so the vaccine appears to have been effective. Three vaccine injections are recommended: initially 1.0 cc, 0.2 cc one to three months later, and 0.2 cc five to six months after the second injection. All injections should be into the deltoid muscle. Currently, vaccination is recommended only for laboratory workers and for veterinarians and field workers such as mammalogists in areas where plague is enzootic or epizootic.

Cholera

Cholera immunization is not effective, is not recommended by the U.S. Public Health Service or the World Health Organization, and is not available in the United States. Cholera immunization is no longer required for entry into any country.

Vaccines produced from organisms genetically modified to eliminate virulence and administered orally to stimulate gastrointestinal mucosal immunity are being investigated. Two vaccines are being produced in Europe, but they have not been licensed in the United States.

Hepatitis A

A simple RNA virus that is most commonly transmitted by fecal contamination of water produces hepatitis A. Diligent water disinfection effectively prevents this infection, but although the mortality rate is only 0.3 percent, it causes approximately 100 deaths per year in the United States. It is far more common in developing countries, and vaccination for travelers is highly recommended. Two inactivated vaccines were licensed in the United States in 1995. Two injections six months apart provide excellent protection. The CDC provides no recommendations for boosters. High levels of immunity after six to eight years have been documented, and vaccination appears to be effective for twenty years or more.

Hepatitis B

Hepatitis B is caused by a large, complex DNA virus that is quite different from the hepatitis A virus and is primarily transmitted by body fluids, particularly blood and semen. However, contaminated water or food can transmit the infection. Two safe, effective vaccines are available. Three injections should be obtained, the second and third at intervals of one and six months after the first.

Everyone traveling into backcountry areas of developing countries should obtain hepatitis B vaccination, although individuals who have previously come into contact with this virus and developed natural immunity do not need to be vaccinated. Such subclinical infections are common in health professionals, individuals living with persons infected with hepatitis B, injecting drug users, and homosexual men. Testing for preexisting immunity is not cost effective for others.

Hepatitis D, or delta agent, is associated with hepatitis B infection and can be prevented by vaccination against hepatitis B.

Hepatitis C and E

Although hepatitis C and E infections are common, no vaccines are available.

Japanese Encephalitis

Japanese encephalitis is a major problem in much of Asia, but it is a very uncommon infection among travelers, among whom CDC investigators estimate the incidence to be less than one per million. Vaccination is recommended only for travelers who plan to spend one month or longer in endemic areas during the transmission season, which is different for each country. Precautions to avoid the mosquitoes that transmit the infection by using repellants, appropriate clothing, and mosquito nets must be exercised.

Immunization consists of three subcutaneous injections on days 0, 7, and 28. Boosters should probably be obtained after two years, but no adequate studies have been performed. Significant allergic reactions to the vaccine occur, which must be included in considerations of whether to obtain vaccination.

Lyme Disease

Lyme disease vaccine is made from lipidated outer surface protein A (OspA) of *Borrelia burgdorferi* expressed in *Escherichia coli*. Three injections are required; the second is given one month after the first, and the third eleven months later. Vaccination should be considered for persons age fifteen to seventy years who engage in activities such as recreation or property maintenance that result in frequent or prolonged exposure to tick-infested habitat. Vaccination may also be considered for persons age fifteen to seventy years who are exposed to tick-infested habitat but whose exposure is neither frequent nor prolonged. The vaccine has not been evaluated in younger or older individuals. Whether vaccination provides greater protection from infection than that afforded by measures to avoid ticks and by early diagnosis and treatment of infection is uncertain.

Lyme disease vaccination is not recommended for persons who have minimal or no exposure to tick-infested habitat, which is estimated to be ninety-nine percent of the U.S. population. Because the time of exposure is limited, travelers to Lyme disease–endemic areas within the United States are generally at lower risk for Lyme disease than those who permanently reside in endemic areas.

Measles

Measles can be a severe disease, particularly in adults. Many of the cases occurring in the United States are contracted in other countries. Whether or not they plan to travel, individuals born after 1956 who have not had a documented vaccination or a physician-diagnosed infection, or who do not have laboratory evidence of immunity, should receive the attenuated live virus measles vaccine. It produces lasting, probably lifelong, immunity, and has essentially eradicated the postmeasles complication of subacute sclerosing panencephalitis since its introduction.

Meningococcus

Outbreaks of meningococcal infection occur sporadically in developing areas. Major epidemics occur in the meningitis belt of sub-Saharan Africa (Fig. 5-1). Individuals traveling to countries in which such outbreaks are occurring should receive meningococcal vaccine before departure. Vaccination is required for entrance by Saudi Arabia and is recommended for India and Nepal.

The vaccine currently licensed in the United States, Menomune® A, C, Y, W-135, is composed of capsular polysaccharide antigens from those four serogroups. Much of the vaccine administered in other countries contains only the A and C antigens. Currently in Saudi Arabia an A, C vaccine is the only one available, even though the prevalent organism is the W-135 strain. In some areas, the prevalent organisms are of serogroup B, for which no effective vaccine exists.

Vaccination consists of a single subcutaneous injection of vaccine and is effective for three to five years. Vaccination can be administered at the same time as other vaccines but in a different deltoid or gluteal subcutaneous site.

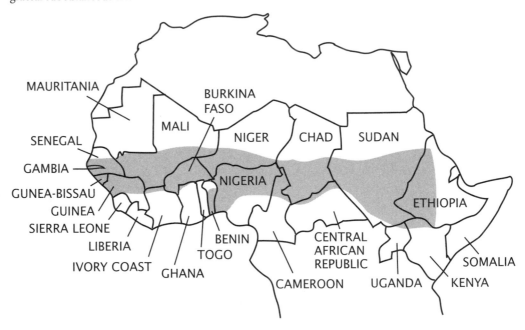

FIGURE 5-1. The sub-Saharan meningitis belt

Poliomyelitis

Until poliomyelitis (polio) eradication is completed, vaccination of children is essential to prevent epidemics from importation of viruses, which has been identified twice in Canada. Trivalent oral live virus (Sabin) vaccine provides more effective immunity for much longer than the inactivated virus (Salk) vaccine. However, a very small number of patients develop vaccine-associated paralytic polio following oral vaccination. In 1997, the Advisory Committee on Immunization Practices (ACIP) recommended that infants and young children receive two injections of inactivated virus before receiving the oral vaccine. (An improved injectable vaccine was licensed in 1987.) Recommendations will probably change after eradication is completed.

ACIP still recommends that fully vaccinated travelers obtain a single dose of oral or injectable vaccine before visiting developing countries for the first time.

Rabies

Preexposure vaccination for rabies has long been recommended by ACIP for anyone traveling to a rabies-endemic area (essentially all of South America, Central America, and Africa and most of Asia) for more than thirty days. One group of investigators in Kathmandu, Nepal, challenged this recommendation because the cost of vaccination is high and they determined the probability of exposure to be low. However, investigators from the World Health Organization rabies center in Bangkok questioned departing English-speaking travelers in the Bangkok air terminal, found a much higher incidence of exposure to dog saliva, and concluded that vaccination was advisable.

Furthermore, the World Health Organization investigators recommended intramuscular vaccination. Intradermal vaccination with human diploid cell vaccine (HDCV), which was approved by the Food and Drug Administration in 1987, does not produce antibody titers as high as those produced by intramuscular vaccination, and antibody titers do not persist as long. (The problem of intradermal versus intramuscular vaccination is moot in the United States as long as intradermal HDCV, the only product licensed for intradermal vaccination, is not available.)

A more compelling reason for rabies preexposure immunization is the worldwide shortage of rabies immune globulin. Postexposure rabies therapy consists of cleansing the wound to reduce the viral inoculum, administration of immune globulin to establish passive immunity, and administration of vaccine to provide active immunity. All three measures are considered equally essential, and rabies deaths have resulted from omission of any. Only approximately one-third of the human or equine immune globulin needed for postexposure therapy worldwide is currently being produced. In developing countries, most individuals exposed to rabies are not given immune globulin. Investigators at the travel clinic at the Pasteur Institute in Paris found that European travelers exposed to rabies were not given immune globulin unless they knew enough about postexposure rabies therapy to insist on its administration. (A recent study has clearly demonstrated that most travelers think rabies is no longer a problem and have no knowledge of postexposure therapy.)

Individuals who have been previously immunized do not need postexposure immune globulin. Vaccination on day 0 and day 3 after exposure is all that is required, but those vaccinations are essential. Rabies deaths have occurred in previously vaccinated individuals who did not receive postexposure vaccine. (Any dog or other bite or encounter with dog saliva in a rabies-endemic area must be considered a rabies exposure, and postexposure therapy must be instituted, regardless of the vaccination status of the animal.)

Rubella

Rubella (German measles) is one of the most widely documented causes of birth defects. The Centers for Disease Control and Prevention recommends that everyone, not just women, be vaccinated unless he has been previously vaccinated or has laboratory evidence of immunity. A single injection of attenuated live rubella virus vaccine provides lasting immunity.

Smallpox

Smallpox has been eliminated worldwide by a vigorous vaccination campaign carried out by the World Health Organization, an outstanding medical triumph. The last reported case of smallpox was in Somalia in 1977. Most countries have eliminated entry requirements for recent smallpox vaccination. The vaccine is considered more hazardous than the risk of contracting the infection and should not be administered.

Tetanus

The organisms producing tetanus are ubiquitous, and infections can result from trivial wounds. Because treatment for tetanus is not effective, the mortality rate is high. Immunization essentially completely prevents the devastating effects of such infections; therefore, inadequate protection against this disease is inexcusable. The initial series of tetanus toxoid immunizations is two injections four to eight weeks apart. A third inoculation should be obtained six to twelve months later. A booster should be obtained at least every ten years thereafter. However, if a booster has not been received within five years, one should be obtained before departing on a wilderness outing or following a contaminated wound.

Typhoid

Typhoid immunization is estimated to be only about seventy percent effective in preventing typhoid infection, but it does significantly reduce the severity of infections. Such immunization is recommended, sometimes strongly, for travelers outside of major cities in developing countries. Three vaccine preparations are available: an attenuated live oral vaccine (Vivotif Berna®), a recently developed injectable vaccine (Typhim Vi), and the older vaccine that has been available for many years (Typhoid Vaccine). The newer vaccines are preferable to the older preparation because they produce fewer side effects. The live vaccine is administered in four capsules that are taken every other day. The series should be repeated every five years. Typhim Vi is administered as a single intramuscular injection and should be repeated every two years.

Yellow Fever

Yellow fever is endemic in the equatorial regions of Africa and South and Central America. The possibility of resurgence in the Caribbean has appeared as the carrier mosquito Aedes aegypti has developed resistance to insecticides. Yellow fever has never been recognized in Asia, and its introduction could result in disastrous epidemics. For that reason, yellow fever immunization is required for travel in many Asian countries, particularly for persons arriving from countries where yellow fever is endemic. The attenuated live virus vaccine is one of the most effective available. A single inoculation provides immunization. Boosters are required every ten years, but prolonged persistence of immunity has been documented and is probably lifelong. Immunizations must be obtained from a World Health Organization Yellow Fever Vaccination Center, the locations of which can be obtained from local health departments.

The vaccine is prepared from viruses cultured in eggs. Persons allergic to eggs should not receive this vaccine.

TRAVELING WITH CHILDREN

For travel to developing countries, children should be up to date with all routine childhood vaccinations, particularly when they can be expected to have contact with local children and local caretakers. Travel-related time constraints may require infants and young children to have vaccinations at earlier than optimum ages (Table 5-1). The intervals between doses may have to be shortened, and only one or two doses of a three-part immunization schedule may be given. Such modifications usually decrease the immune response, and additional vaccinations must be given later, usually six to twelve months later (which causes no known untoward effects). Generally, immunizations given at an age earlier than that recommended should not be counted toward long-term immunity.

Table 5-1	Travel-Necessitated Schedule Changes for Routine Childhood Immunizations	
VACCINE	**AGE USUALLY GIVEN**	**REVISED SCHEDULE FOR TRAVEL**
MMR	12 to 18 months	6 months (followed by routine immunizations)
DPT	2, 4, and 6 months	Birth, 1 month, and 2 months
Hepatitis B	Birth to 2 months, 2 to 4 months, 6 to12 months	Birth, 1 month, 2 months, 18 months
Polio	2, 4, and 6 months	Birth, 1 month, and 2 months
Varicella	12 to 15 months	No change
Hib	2, 4, and 6 months	6, 10, and 12 weeks

Routine Immunizations

Measles, mumps, and rubella (MMR) vaccination is usually given between twelve and eighteen months of age in industrialized countries. Children traveling to developing countries should receive measles vaccine at six months. Mumps, rubella, and varicella are such benign infections in children that young that immunization for these disorders is not needed. Parents should check their own MMR immune states. Traveling with young children may increase their contact with other children who may not have been vaccinated, and these viruses produce severe infections in adults.

In industrialized countries, diphtheria, pertussis, and tetanus (DPT) immunization is given between two and six months of age. Infants can receive the first injection at birth, although waiting until one month of age is preferable.

Children usually receive hepatitis B vaccine at birth, one month, and between six and twelve months. For travel, the second and third vaccinations can be given at two and three months, and a fourth vaccination should be given between six and twelve months.

The new schedule for polio vaccination for children requires administration of injectable vaccine at ages two and four months and oral vaccine at fifteen months and four years. No data related to the effectiveness of vaccinating infants less than six weeks old are available, but polio is expected to have been essentially eliminated worldwide soon after this edition is published.

Close contact with children in developing countries may slightly increase the risk of acquiring *Haemophilus influenzae* type b (Hib) infection, but the vaccine is poorly immunogenic before two months of age.

Travel Immunizations

Children should receive preexposure rabies vaccine if they are to have prolonged stays in developing countries where rabies is endemic. One-half of all rabies deaths are in children fifteen years old or younger. Children are attracted to animals, are more likely to suffer bites, and may not report minor bites and scratches. (Preexposure rabies vaccination does not eliminate the need for proper wound care and additional vaccination after an animal bite. It does eliminate the need for administration of immune globulin, which is in severe short supply worldwide.)

Hepatitis A vaccine is not routinely given to children less than one year old (two years old in the United States). Younger infants who will be exposed to hepatitis A should be protected with immune globulin.

Meningococcal meningitis vaccine for serogroup A is not effective for children younger than three months. Vaccine for serogroup C is not effective for children younger than two years. Serogroup B is present in some countries, but no effective vaccine exists for those organisms.

Vaccines for typhoid fever have not been well studied in children younger than five to six years old. Younger children may not be able to swallow the capsules that contain the live, attenuated vaccine.

Yellow fever vaccinations in children less than nine months old have been associated with encephalitis and usually should not be administered. Infants from six to nine months may be vaccinated only when traveling to an area in which ongoing yellow fever is epidemic and they can not be protected from mosquitoes.

SANITATION

Sanitation plays a vital role in preventing infections. Many inhabitants of developing countries have never heard about the most rudimentary sanitation procedures, such as washing their hands after defecating. Even when they follow such practices, many do not understand their purpose and consider them idiosyncrasies of foreigners. When local inhabitants are employed as cooks or in similar roles, hand washing; disinfection of water for drinking, cooking, or even washing dishes; and sanitary food preparation must be vigorously enforced and closely supervised to prevent a lapse into old habits.

Locally obtained food must be regarded with the same distrust as the water supply. The only food that can be regarded as safe from contamination is that which has been thoroughly cooked under supervision. The plates on which it is served and the utensils provided are rarely washed in water hot enough to kill bacteria. Soap may not have been added to the water. The most common practice is simply to rinse these items with water that has not been disinfected. However, well-cooked food usually is safe—and often delicious—if the traveler provides his own plate, cup, and spoon.

Fruits that have been picked above ground level, cleaned, and peeled or sliced by the eater should be safe because bacteria can not enter the fruit as it is growing. However, fruits that have been previously sliced for display often have been cut with contaminated knives and sprinkled with undisinfected water to keep them attractive for potential buyers. Bacteria on the skin of oranges at the time they are squeezed can contaminate orange juice. Melons sold by the pound may be injected with undisinfected water to increase their weight. Leafy vegetables are often fertilized with human feces (night soil) and can not be adequately disinfected by washing. Even soaking in strong chlorine solutions is not effective.

All other foods must be assumed to be dangerous, particularly custards, cakes, bread, cold meats, cheeses, and other dairy products. Milk is a potential source of tuberculosis. Bottled carbonated drinks—water, sodas, and beer—are generally safe, but infections have resulted from drinking bottled noncarbonated water, which occasionally has not even been disinfected. Ice, even that served in airport lounges, is often made from undisinfected water.

Sites for garbage disposal and latrines should be downstream, downhill, downwind, and as far as possible from water sources. However, latrines that are too far away are not used, which can make campsites unpleasant and unsafe. Local inhabitants often must be instructed to use latrines. Developing Southeast Asian countries suffer epidemics of cholera at the beginning of each monsoon season because rain washes human feces from the streets into the streams that serve as the water supply.

WATER DISINFECTION

In recent years, widespread microbial contamination of backcountry water sources in the United States has been recognized. The single-cell parasite *Cryptosporidium* is essentially ubiquitous, and its universal presence has dictated changes in water disinfection techniques previously considered completely effective.

Developing countries do not build water systems that reliably supply uncontaminated water for drinking and cooking or sewage systems that prevent contamination of water sources. Many of their residents are resistant to the organisms in the water as the result of continuous contact since infancy, but deaths from diarrheal disease still number in the millions. Most water in developing countries is contaminated. Tap water is usually contaminated, even in the best hotels, although some establishments provide disinfected water for drinking. Tap water should not be used even for brushing teeth. Ice used to chill drinks is often unsafe. Even in remote areas, herdsmen and their cattle or sheep often contaminate small wilderness streams. Therefore, all water that is to be consumed or used in food preparation must be disinfected.

Desirable Characteristics of Water Disinfection Systems

A water disinfection system for use in the wilderness or developing countries must be:

▾ Simple and convenient
▾ Fast
▾ Small and lightweight
▾ Reliable

Wilderness users tend to be young and impatient; many will not use a system that is not simple and convenient or wait for a slow process. Water that is clear and appears uncontaminated will be consumed without disinfection. A system that is not small and lightweight will not be carried. A system that is not reliable should not be used by anyone.

Disinfection systems suitable for wilderness use are also suitable for urban use in countries with an unsafe water supply. However, long-term residents usually develop a more convenient system, optimally a system that combines a filter with chemical or ultraviolet treatment.

Goal of Water Disinfection

The goal of water disinfection is the elimination of waterborne microorganisms. Unlike urban systems, the techniques used to disinfect small quantities of water usually kill all organisms.

Three types of microorganisms must be eliminated: parasites, bacteria, and viruses. Some parasites are single-cell organisms such as amoebae and giardia; others are larger, multicellular organisms such as tapeworms or roundworms. When eliminated from the body, single-cell parasites often form thick, tough walls around themselves—cysts—that are much more resistant to chemical agents or heat than the unprotected organism. More complex parasites lay eggs that are excreted by the host.

Bacteria, which are intermediate in size between parasites and viruses, make up most of the bulk of feces and produce a wide range of infections, many of them potentially lethal.

Viruses are much smaller than bacteria and also produce a wide variety of infections. Many cases of "traveler's diarrhea" result from infection by waterborne viruses. Hepatitis A and polio have long been known to result from fecal contamination of water.

TECHNIQUES FOR WILDERNESS WATER DISINFECTION

Only two water disinfection methods suitable for wilderness use are available: heat and the combination of microfiltration and chemicals.

Heat

Heat is a reliable way to disinfect water. Simply bringing water to a boil destroys most organisms, although to eliminate cryptosporidia, the CDC and the Environmental Protection Agency (EPA) recommend boiling water for a full minute (three minutes above 6,500 feet [2,000 m] because water boils at a lower temperatures at higher altitude). Milk is pasteurized by heating it to 160°F (71°C).

Boiling is inconvenient and time consuming, particularly for small quantities of water. Fuel must be carried, particularly above tree line. If a fire is built, an unsightly residue is unavoidable without heavy, bulky firepans. Pressure cookers save time and fuel at all elevations (Table 5-2). No additional disinfection can be achieved by distillation.

Table 5-2	Boiling Temperature of Water at Various Altitudes
ALTITUDE	**TEMPERATURE**
Sea level	212°F (100°C)
10,000 ft (3,000 m)	194°F (90°C)
14,000 ft (4,300 m)	187°F (86°C)
19,000 ft (5,500 m)	178°F (82°C)
29,000 ft (8,800 m)	160°F (71°C)

Microfiltration

Cryptosporidia, and possibly some other parasites such as cyclospora, are resistant to halide disinfectants, which has made microfiltration an essential element of water disinfection. The CDC states that the labels for filters used to remove these parasites should carry one of the following statements:

▼ Tested and certified by NSF Standard 53 for cyst removal or reduction (applicable only to installed household filters)
▼ Reverse osmosis (no filters for backpackers use this process)
▼ Absolute (not nominal) pore size of one micron or smaller

The following do not "promise the filter removes cryptosporidium":
▼ Effective against giardia or against parasites
▼ Carbon filter
▼ Water purifier
▼ EPA approved
▼ Activated carbon
▼ Removes chlorine
▼ Ultraviolet light
▼ Pentiodide resins

As of August 1999, the websites for Katadyn Products, Northern Mountain Supply (SweetWater), Mountain Safety Research (MSR), and PUR Outdoor Products did not list any of the first three statements as qualifications for their products. General Ecology's (First Need®) website states its filter has a pore of "0.4 microns absolute." However, the others claim a pore size of 0.2 or 0.3 microns. All appear to be equally effective for removing cryptosporidia.

With pore sizes of 0.2 to 0.4 microns, these filter pores are much too large to remove viruses (Table 5-3). In fact, as the pores enlarge with use, they may allow passage of small bacteria, such as the vibrios that cause cholera. After filtration, the water must be chemically treated to destroy these organisms.

(First Need® claims that the "Structured Matrix™" of its filters removes viruses. Data about the removal of poliovirus type 1 and rotavirus SA-11 are presented, but the mechanism by which the viruses are removed is not stated.)

Some PUR, MSR, and SweetWater filters contain an iodine resin that destroys viruses. However, these products do not have any way of indicating when the iodine has been exhausted. The manufacturers claim that by the time the iodine has been used up, the filter is plugged and must be replaced.

Filters are relatively bulky (for backpacking) and expensive, and they can be rapidly obstructed by sediment in the water. The obstruction can be prevented with prefilters but in some systems can be relieved only by replacing the filter, which costs almost as much as the entire system. The Katadyne ceramic filter includes a brush for scrubbing away obstructing sediment.

Table 5-3	Size Comparison (Micrometers) of Organisms and Filter Pores
Filter pores	0.3 to 0.4 μm
Giardia cysts	6.0 μm
Cryptosporidium cysts	4.0 μm
Bacteria	1.5 to 3.0 μm
Viruses	0.004 to 0.06 μm

Chemical Disinfection Systems

Chemical disinfection systems combined with microfiltration provide the desired features of simplicity, speed, small size, and light weight, and they are reliable for all organisms. Although many chemicals are effective, only iodine or chlorine (halide) systems are readily available and have been proven by extensive use. Silver compounds are used in other countries but have not been approved by the Food and Drug Administration for use in the United States.

Iodine as a Water Disinfectant

During World War II, a search for a simple, reliable water disinfectant was initiated at Harvard University because chlorine-based systems were too undependable. The investigating team found that diatomic iodine (I_2) and the various ions resulting from the dissociation of molecular iodine in water consistently and reliably disinfects water containing as many as ten million bacteria per milliliter, a concentration approximately ten times greater than grossly polluted water. (The effectiveness of iodine was demonstrated on raw sewage from the Cambridge, Massachusetts, sewage system.) Unlike chlorine, iodine is fast, resists inactivation by organic compounds, is active over a wide pH range, and is available in stable preparations.

At 73°F (23°C), even in moderately turbid water with moderate amounts of organic color, an iodine concentration of 8 mg/l eradicates bacteria, viruses, parasites, and parasitic cysts other than cryptosporidia. A contact time of only ten minutes already includes a considerable margin of safety. (About ninety seconds is adequate for eliminating bacteria and viruses.)

However, an iodine concentration of 8 mg/l is needed only to destroy parasitic cysts. A concentration of 0.5 to 1.0 mg/l eliminates other microorganisms. If filters are used to eliminate cryptosporidia and other parasites, only such small concentrations are needed. The only currently available preparation that readily supplies such a limited quantity of iodine is a saturated iodine solution. Tablets could be broken up or dissolved in much larger quantities of water (two gallons).

Iodine Disinfection Precautions

In cold water (32° to 41°F [0° to 5°C]), the chemical activity of iodine is slower, just as all chemical reactions are slower at lower temperatures. An increase in contact time to twenty minutes has been recommended to ensure complete disinfection. However, in the original Harvard studies, ninety seconds of contact killed all nonparasitic organisms. Ten minutes was recommended to provide a margin of safety. Cloudy, heavily contaminated water requires more iodine to compensate for binding of the disinfectant by organic compounds; however, doubling the iodine concentration or doubling the contact time is sufficient.

If the water has been filtered, such precautions are probably unnecessary, but appropriate studies have not been published.

Masking Iodine's Taste

In water that has been filtered and disinfected with 0.5 to 1.0 mg/l of iodine, such a small concentration can not be tasted. If larger quantities of iodine are used and individuals find the taste objectionable, several methods for masking its taste are available. Because such procedures inactivate the iodine, they must not be used before enough time has elapsed for microorganisms to be destroyed.

Artificial flavorings added to hide the taste usually contain ascorbic acid, which reacts with iodine and impairs its antimicrobial activity. Potable-Aqua® is now supplied with ascorbic acid tablets—to be added after disinfection is complete—to eliminate the iodine taste. A less convenient technique is to convert the iodine to tasteless sodium iodide with an equal weight of sodium thiosulfate. The water can be filtered through activated charcoal, which, by adsorption, physically removes the iodine (and some odors, inorganic materials, and microorganisms, but not enough to make the water suitable for consumption).

In clear water, the rate at which microorganisms are destroyed by halogens is dependent on contact time and the iodine concentration. If time is available for more prolonged disinfection, lower concentrations of iodine can be used. One-half the standard concentration of iodine is equally effective as a disinfectant if allowed to act for twice the usual time; one-fourth the standard concentration is an effective disinfectant if allowed to act for four times the usual time. Even lower iodine concentrations could be used, but less than 2.0 mg/l usually can not be tasted. (Some individuals prefer a barely detectable trace of iodine as assurance the water has been disinfected.)

Persons with known thyroid dysfunction should determine how they react to water disinfected with iodine at home before relying on iodine water disinfection in the wilderness or while traveling. The uncommon individuals who are allergic to iodine, including iodine-containing compounds in radiographic contrast media, and those with thyroid dysfunction who react adversely, must not use iodine for water disinfection. For such individuals, a filtration system to physically remove bacteria, parasites, and parasitic cysts followed by chlorine to kill viruses offers a reliable alternative.

Acute Iodine Toxicity

Several publications have claimed that iodine used for water disinfection is dangerously toxic. The skull-and-crossbones symbol on bottles of tincture of iodine is familiar. However, iodine is only weakly poisonous. The third edition of Goodman and Gilman's *Textbook of Pharmacology* states "that iodine is highly toxic . . . is a popular fallacy." The lethal dose is 2 to 3 g, but survival after ingestion of 10 g has been reported. Iodine in such large quantities is a strong gastrointestinal irritant and causes immediate vomiting, which eliminates most of the iodine. Iodine remaining in the gastrointestinal tract is largely neutralized by the intestinal contents. (The immediate treatment for iodine poisoning is administration of starchy food.)

Accidental iodine poisoning is rare; almost all fatalities are suicidal, but successful suicide is uncommon if the victim receives medical care. Between 1915 and 1936, no deaths occurred among 327 patients who arrived alive at Boston City Hospital following attempted suicide with iodine.

Chronic Iodine Toxicity

Ingested iodine is absorbed as iodide, and an average adult requires 150 to 200 μg per day. Daily consumption of one to two liters of water disinfected with 8 mg/l of iodine would provide thirty to eighty times that amount, but individuals with normal thyroid function would not be affected by such quantities. (Even less effect would be produced by 0.5 to 1.0 mg/day.) The recommended daily dose of expectorant potassium iodide for asthmatics ranges from 1.2 to 8.0 g (0.9 to 6.0 g of iodine).

Iodine can cause fetal goiters that produce respiratory obstruction at birth, but the mothers of infants with iodide goiters are almost all asthmatics who have consumed one gram or more of iodine daily for many months or years.

Inmates of three Florida prisons drank water disinfected with 0.5 to 1.0 mg/l of iodine for fifteen years. No detrimental effects on the general condition or thyroid function of previously healthy persons were detected with careful medical and biochemical monitoring. Of 101 infants born to inmates who had been in prison for 122 to 270 days, none had detectable thyroid enlargement. However, all four individuals with hyperthyroidism became more symptomatic while consuming iodinated water.

These studies indicate that a system that incorporates a filter and adds only 0.5 to 1.0 mg/l of iodine would eliminate the risk of iodide goiter.

Iodine Preparations

Triiodide to Pentaiodide Resins

Many of the manufacturers of portable water filters have added secondary filters composed of iodine-containing resins. Water passing through the secondary filters is exposed to the iodine, which has been clearly demonstrated to kill bacteria and viruses. Because such devices should remove all microorganisms, they have been called water "purifiers" even though purification is not synonymous with disinfection.

However, these iodide resins are associated with several problems. The water is exposed to the resin for such a short time that some manufacturers have recommended that cold water be filtered twice.

A minute amount of iodine is released into the water as it passes through the filter, but the quantity is usually too small to taste and possibly too small to continue effectively disinfecting the water. However, with continued use, the iodine in the filter is totally removed. None of the filters currently available offer any means for determining when such exhaustion has occurred. Repeatedly replacing the filters after every 100 liters of water disinfected is expensive, and keeping the records needed to determine that the filter has been used for that quantity of water is tedious.

Tetraglycine Hydroperiodide

Tablets containing tetraglycine hydroperiodide are widely sold under trade names such as Globaline and Potable-Aqua®. One fresh tablet dissolved in one liter of water provides an iodine concentration of 8 mg/l, far more than needed if the water has been filtered. A major advantage of tetraglycine hydroperiodide tablets is their convenience. A small bottle of fifty tablets can be carried easily. Sealed bottles can be stored for months with little loss of iodine. (The manufacturer of Potable Aqua® claims four years.)

The principal disadvantage of tetraglycine hydroperiodide is its tendency to dissociate after exposure to air. In studies to document their stability, tetraglycine hydroperiodide tablets placed in a single layer in an open dish at 140°F (60°C) lost forty percent of their iodine in seven days. At room temperature and 100 percent humidity, the tablets lost thirty-three percent of their iodine in four days. Studies to determine the rate of dissociation of tablets in a small bottle opened several times a day for one or two weekends a month, the pattern of weekend outdoorsmen, have not been reported.

Tetraglycine hydroperiodide tablets (and other iodine preparations) add a definite brown color to the water if 8 mg/l are present. Tightly capping and refrigerating bottles of the tablets may help retard iodine loss, but they probably should be discarded a few months after opening. (The manufacturer of Potable-Aqua® recommends a year.)

Saturated Aqueous Iodine Solution

In 1975, F.H. Kahn and B.R. Visscher described a procedure for disinfecting water with a saturated aqueous solution of iodine. Iodine crystals (2 to 8 g, *United States Pharmacopeia* or USP grade, resublimed) are placed in a 30 cc (1 oz) clear glass bottle with a paper-lined Bakelite cap. (The details are important.) The bottle is filled with water, shaken vigorously, and allowed to stand for one hour to produce a saturated solution.

Originally, one-half of this saturated solution (15 cc) would be poured into one liter of water to be disinfected. If the temperature of the water in the 30 cc bottle is 68°F (20°C) or higher, which can be achieved easily by carrying the bottle in a shirt pocket, the iodine concentration in the disinfected water would be about 9 mg/l.

If the water has been filtered, a bottle cap of the solution (2 cc) provides an adequate amount of iodine.

Saturated aqueous iodine solutions have two distinct advantages:

▼ A bottle containing two grams of iodine can disinfect up to 2,000 liters of water.
▼ If crystals can be seen in the bottom of the bottle, enough iodine for disinfection is known to be present, so the system is totally reliable.

This technique for water disinfection has been denounced, even in terms such as "it can kill you," because in decanting the supernatant, iodine crystals could be poured into the water to be consumed. This hazard is insignificant. Iodine is so weakly toxic that three or four crystals do not produce any symptoms. Individuals who have used this technique extensively have found that small flakes of iodine are commonly caught by surface tension in the small bottle, poured into the large bottle, and ingested without producing any detectable ill effects. A jar with a sleeve in its neck to prevent decanting of the iodine crystals (Polar Pure®) is commercially available. On its surface, the jar also has a temperature indicator and data for calculating the volume of saturated iodine solution that would contain 8 mg of iodine. However, the jar is too large to comfortably fit into a shirt pocket.

A saturated aqueous solution of iodine has been singled out as being uniquely ineffective at low temperatures for eradicating giardia cysts. If microfiltration is used to remove cryptosporidia, this question is moot.

One real problem with saturated iodine solutions is the tendency for the water to freeze and break the bottle. (Such a small amount of iodine is dissolved in the water that the freezing temperature is not significantly lowered.) Leaving an air space in the bottle by not refilling it after its last use in the evening would allow the water to expand as it freezes and prevent breaking the bottle. Alternatively, the bottle must be kept inside a sleeping bag. (Glass is the only satisfactory container for aqueous iodine solutions.)

Saturated iodine solutions are widely used for water disinfection because they are convenient and reliable. For informed adults, extensive experience indicates that the method is safe, although children must not be entrusted with a potentially lethal quantity of iodine.

Tincture of Iodine

Tincture of iodine is useful for water disinfection primarily because it is so readily available. In industrialized nations such as the United States, tincture of iodine would be particularly valuable when a major disaster, such as an earthquake, has resulted in contamination of municipal water supplies, but water can not be boiled because electrical power has been interrupted and gas lines have been broken.

The major disadvantages of tincture of iodine are its taste and its iodide component. Many individuals find the iodine taste imparted by the tincture to be much stronger than that of other preparations containing similar quantities of iodine. The USP standard solution is two percent iodine and 2.4 percent sodium iodide in fifty percent ethanol. (Different concentrations are also sold as "tincture.") The iodide has no disinfectant activity and increases total iodine intake.

Tincture of iodine resists freezing. Also, it can be used to disinfect skin, but aqueous solutions are just as effective for that purpose and do not sting. Addition of 0.5 cc of a two percent solution to one liter of water provides an iodine concentration of 1.0 mg/l. The tincture must be stored in glass bottles.

Chlorine Disinfection

The effectiveness of chlorine for water disinfection is well documented. However, the disinfectant action of chlorine is pH sensitive, and if organic residues are present, chlorine combines with ammonia ions and amino acids to form chloramines, which release chlorine slowly and inconsistently.

Although most municipal water systems in North America use chlorine as a disinfectant, free chlorine levels in the water must be constantly monitored to ensure they are adequate for disinfection. Monitoring is not practical in the wilderness or in developing countries. Furthermore, chlorine compounds that have been advocated for wilderness water disinfection, such as Halazone® or chlorine bleaches, are unstable and of questionable reliability. Manufacture of Halazone® was discontinued in 1989.

Most bleaches for home laundry are five percent sodium hypochlorite solutions, which could disinfect water effectively, at least theoretically. Laboratory studies to evaluate the effectiveness of such agents have not been carried out. In addition, the solutions are very unstable, which renders them unsuitable for wilderness water disinfection because much of the chlorine is lost as the solution sloshes around while being transported. Solid or powder bleach preparations are not available in a form that allows an appropriate quantity for water disinfection to be easily determined.

If liquid bleach is used for water disinfection, the standard procedure is to add two drops to one liter of water with a temperature above 60°F (16°C) and allow it to stand for thirty minutes. If the water is colder, it should be allowed to stand for forty-five minutes. Chlorine is a much slower disinfectant than iodine.

Preparations such as SafeAqua and the Sierra Water Purifier use a granulated calcium hypochlorite–based system that follows a different approach. Initially, far more chlorine is added to the water than is needed for disinfection (superchlorination). In the presence of excessive chlorine, pH inactivation and binding by organic material are not significant. After the water has been disinfected, the chlorine is driven off.

These systems are much more suitable for disinfecting larger quantities of water—five to ten gallons or twenty to forty liters—than the one or two liters that would be carried in a backpack. The thirty percent hydrogen peroxide used to drive off the chlorine by the Sierra Water Purifier is caustic. (It is used in cosmetic dentistry to bleach teeth!) Some individuals have found that they get the solution on their fingers every time they use it and that it produces a burning sensation that lasts thirty to sixty minutes. The skin may be blanched, although no permanent injury is produced.

This procedure should be reliable; the presence of a "strong smell of chlorine" should be unmistakable. Additionally, the system is relatively small, lightweight, and reasonably simple, although two compounds must be added to the water instead of one. It is more expensive than the iodine-based systems but still is relatively cheap. Hydrogen peroxide, used to drive off the chlorine, imparts a "sparkle" to the water.

A zinc brush can be used to remove the chlorine instead of hydrogen peroxide or other agents. Because zinc catalyses the removal of chlorine instead of reacting with the halide, it is not used up and can last indefinitely. However, the brush is heavier and takes up more space.

TRAUMATIC AND NONTRAUMATIC DISORDERS

CHAPTER 6

SOFT-TISSUE INJURIES

Lacerations, abrasions, bruises, and blisters are the most common injuries occurring in the wilderness. They are called "soft-tissue" injuries to distinguish them from injuries to bones and ligaments.

The treatment of soft-tissue injuries has four objectives:
- ▾ Control of bleeding
- ▾ Control of infection
- ▾ Promotion of healing
- ▾ Preservation of function in the injured part

CONTROL OF BLEEDING

Direct pressure is the only effective means for controlling bleeding from a soft-tissue wound. The severed blood vessels must be collapsed to obstruct blood flow and permit clots to form. Pressure must be applied directly over the wound. Pressure points are not worth considering. Tourniquets are dangerous and are essentially never needed or even justifiable.

Bleeding from most skin wounds is from veins and capillaries. The pressure in these vessels is so low that simply holding a dressing on the wound for two to five minutes allows the blood to clot and plug the vessels. Deeper lacerations may cut larger veins that bleed more profusely, such as the veins visible beneath the skin of the arms and legs, but bleeding from these vessels can be easily controlled by compression because all veins have thin walls and the pressure within them is low.

Arteries have much thicker walls and are rarely cut. However, arterial blood is under much higher pressure, and blood loss is harder to control when these vessels are damaged. The only dependable way to identify arterial bleeding is to see blood spurting from the wound with each heartbeat. The color of the blood is not a reliable indicator of its source. Arterial bleeding also must be controlled by direct pressure.

If bleeding persists, even after direct pressure has been applied for fifteen to twenty minutes, particularly when an artery has been cut, the wound can be packed with sterile gauze and wrapped snugly with a continuous bandage.

Bandages that completely surround a limb may obstruct circulation to the rest of the limb. Absent pulses, bluish discoloration of the skin or nails, tingling sensations, and pain indicate that the blood supply to the tissues beyond the bandage is inadequate. Because swelling at the site of the wound can greatly increase the pressure beneath a circumferential bandage, the limb beyond the bandage must be frequently and carefully checked for circulatory impairment every few minutes. If the bandage initially is too tight, or becomes too tight, it must be loosened. After bleeding has been controlled, the circumferential bandage should be removed.

Movement may cause bleeding to recur after it has been controlled. To avoid further blood loss, severely injured limbs should be immobilized before the individual is evacuated. In expedition circumstances, delaying evacuation for two to three days to allow the clots within severed vessels to become more firmly anchored may be desirable.

CONTROL OF INFECTION

Wound infection results from contamination, and all open wounds are contaminated to some extent. Preventing infection by minimizing contamination and eliminating conditions that promote bacterial growth is far preferable to treating an established infection.

Wound Cleansing

After bleeding has been controlled, further contamination of soft-tissue injuries must be avoided. The person caring for the injured individual must wash his hands, preferably with an antibacterial agent such as pHisoHex® or a povidone-iodine preparation. Sterile gloves, if available, should be used, but only after the hands have been scrubbed. The skin around the wound should be vigorously cleaned, preferably by scrubbing with the same antibacterial agent. Washing dirt, dried blood, or other contaminants into the wound must be avoided.

Finally, the wound itself must be cleaned. A 20 or 50 cc syringe with a large-bore needle (eighteen gauge or larger), or even without a needle, is ideal for this purpose because a jet of water can be directed into the wound with sufficient force to rinse out any foreign material. (A plastic bag with a pinhole can be used as an improvised syringe.) Such rinsing produces little pain and does not damage the tissues. Obviously, only disinfected water is suitable for such cleansing. Foreign material, dead tissue, or even visible amounts of clotted blood left in the wound virtually ensure infection. Wound cleansing must be complete. The syringe must be repeatedly refilled and emptied into the wound. Sterile forceps should be used to remove any embedded debris that can not be rinsed away; small tags of dead tissue may be snipped off with sterile scissors.

For puncture wounds, bleeding should be encouraged to help remove bacteria and debris. The depths of such wounds are not reached by air, and anaerobic bacteria that thrive in such conditions, such as those that cause tetanus and gas gangrene, can produce devastating infections.

Antiseptics

Antiseptics have little value in the control of wound infections. They can not compensate for negligent wound cleansing, and, for wounds that are thoroughly cleaned, they provide little additional bacterial control. However, the informed use of the proper antiseptics is prudent, particularly for animal bites or other heavily contaminated wounds.

Antiseptics placed in a wound must be able to kill bacteria without injuring the tissues. Minimizing tissue damage is essential because no agent can kill all of the bacteria, and injured tissue provides an excellent medium for the growth of the remaining organisms. Only two readily available antiseptics meet these qualification: a 1:750 aqueous solution of benzalkonium chloride (Zephiran®) and a ten percent solution of a povidone-iodine preparation (Betadyne® and others). Povidone-iodine has two advantages over benzalkonium chloride: it is ideal for scrubbing hands or the skin around a wound (and is routinely used by surgeons), and it can be packaged in polyethylene bottles rather than glass. Benzalkonium chloride is not readily available in a form suitable for wilderness use.

Povidone-iodine can be used undiluted for cleansing skin before needle punctures, but for rinsing a wound it should be diluted ten to one or twenty to one with disinfected water. The wound should be flooded with the solution.

Antiseptics such as alcohol, tincture of iodine, or mercurial preparations damage tissues and should not be placed directly in an open wound.

Wound Closure

In the wilderness, soft-tissue wounds never need to be sutured. If a wound is left open, purulent material from infected areas drains to the outside. This purulent material can not escape from a sutured wound and is extruded into the surrounding tissues, spreading the infection. In hospitals, soft-tissue wounds are sutured under sterile conditions to promote healing and minimize scarring. However, such sterile conditions rarely can be duplicated in the wilderness, and the damage done by an infection in a sutured wound would greatly prolong healing and lead to far greater scarring and deformity. Furthermore, if an unsutured wound is not infected, the edges tend to fall together, healing is rapid, and scarring is minimal.

Minor wounds that appear to present little risk of infection can be held together with "butterflies" or tape that has been sterilized by flaming. Such devices can easily be removed and the wound opened and drained if infection develops. Wounds that are too large to close with tape should not be closed by anyone but a surgeon who knows how to obliterate the spaces beneath the skin surface and how to avoid producing further damage by the sutures.

The danger of introducing infection, and the far greater destruction of tissue that results from infection in a wound that has been sutured, far outweigh any benefits that might be obtained from early closure.

Diagnosing Wound Infections

If infection occurs in spite of preventive measures, early detection minimizes tissue damage and the threat to the person's health. The dressing over any wound except a burn should be changed daily until healing is clearly underway in order to look for signs of infection. The person's overall condition should also be monitored, particularly his temperature.

The signs of infection around the wound itself are primarily the signs of inflammation—pain, redness, swelling, heat, and limitation of motion. These signs can be found with every wound but are much more severe in the presence of infection. Pain from soft-tissue injuries usually begins to subside by the second or third day after injury. Persistence of severe pain beyond this period or an increase in pain suggests infection. Redness is usually limited to the margins of the wound. More extensive discoloration, particularly streaks extending upward along a limb, indicates infection. Severe swelling around a wound, particularly a simple cut with which swelling would not be expected, is a sign of infection, as is a detectable increase in the skin temperature. Swelling and pain combine to limit voluntary and involuntary motion, which is more obvious in the presence of infection.

An oral temperature of 100° to 101°F (37.8° to 38.3°C) can be expected for one or two days after any severe injury. A temperature elevation after a minor injury, a higher temperature, or an elevation persisting for a longer time is suggestive of infection.

Located throughout the body are collections of lymph nodes that trap bacteria and the debris from a localized infection and become enlarged and tender (Fig. 6-1). Tissue destruction occurs with any injury, and the regional lymph nodes often become enlarged, but in the presence of infection the nodes become more enlarged and painful. Lymph nodes in more than one area often are enlarged and tender with an infection.

The diagnosis of a wound infection is confirmed by the finding of purulent material—"pus"—in the wound or on the dressings. The discharge is usually creamy and light yellow, green, pink, or reddish in color depending upon the infecting organism. Occasionally the discharge may be clear and straw colored. A foul odor is often—but not always—present. Rarely, an infected wound produces a very scanty discharge. A diagnosis of infection is not necessarily wrong just because little purulent drainage is present.

The skin edges of an infected wound are sometimes sealed by coagulated serum, and exudate from the infection can not escape onto the dressings. If other signs of infection are present, the edges of the wound should be spread apart and the wound gently probed with a pair of sterile forceps. (This process is less painful if the wound is soaked in warm, disinfected water first to soften the coagulum.) If an infection is present, pus usually pours out when the wound is opened. If no infection is present, opening the wound usually does little harm except for the discomfort, which is of little consequence when compared with the damage that could result from an undiscovered infection.

Treating Wound Infections

Treatment for an infected wound consists of drainage and antibiotic therapy. The wound should be opened by prying apart its edges with a pair of sterile forceps. Because pus in infected wound tends to collect in pockets, the deeper parts of the wound must be probed to ensure that all such pockets are drained. If one is found, others should be expected. After drainage, gauze should be placed in the wound to keep it open. The gauze, preferably impregnated with petroleum jelly, should be changed whenever

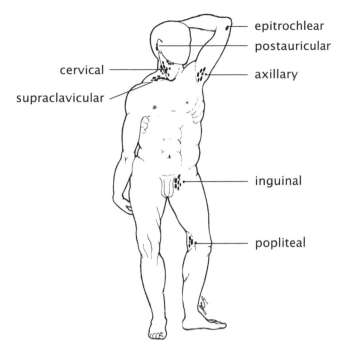

FIGURE 6-1. Locations of the major collections of lymph nodes

the wound is dressed. The edges of the wound should not be allowed to reseal as long as any evidence of infection is present.

Infected wounds covered by a crust of coagulated serum and pus, particularly those on the extremities, benefit from soaking in warm water. Moisture softens the crust and permits more thorough drainage. Heat causes the blood vessels to dilate, increasing the flow of blood to the tissues, which promotes healing and the eradication of infection. For infected small wounds on the extremities—or for large wounds if the subject can not be evacuated—the dressing should be removed and the wound immersed in warm, sterile water for periods of twenty to thirty minutes three to four times a day. An antiseptic such as povidone-iodine should be added to the water. Afterward, the skin should be carefully dried and a fresh dressing applied.

Antibiotics should not be given routinely to individuals with soft-tissue injuries because the probability of infection is low, antibiotics have only a limited ability to prevent soft-tissue infections, and the risk of allergic reactions and other adverse side effects is significant. However, for severe soft-tissue injuries or badly contaminated wounds, antibiotics should be administered prophylactically before signs of infection appear. In a remote situation, antibiotics should also be given to persons with major wound infections with the understanding that the major benefit would be to inhibit spread of the infection and not eradicate the infection within the wound.

If antibiotics are administered as a preventive measure, they should be given in large dosages for only two days; such a brief course of antibiotics does not allow the emergence of resistant bacterial strains. If a significant, established soft-tissue infection is being treated, however, high doses of antibiotics should be given for at least five days, or until all signs of infection are gone. If the subject is not allergic to penicillin, he should be given a penicillinase-resistant penicillin or a cephalosporin. Anyone with a history of an allergic reaction to penicillin should be treated with erythromycin, azithromycin, or trimethoprim-sulfamethoxazole.

BANDAGING

A bandage is usually composed of three layers, each with different functions.

Inner Layer

The inner layer of a bandage should be material, such as petroleum jelly–impregnated gauze, or a plastic such as Telfa®, that does not stick to the wound and allows the bandage to be changed relatively painlessly without aggravating the injury. Obviously, this material must be sterile.

Dressings

The middle portion of a bandage is referred to as a dressing and has five different functions:
- ▼ To prevent contamination in order to prevent infection or limit the infection to organisms already present
- ▼ To absorb wound drainage, which must not be allowed to contaminate clothing or other wounds
- ▼ To keep the skin adjacent to the wound dry to prevent maceration and infection
- ▼ To apply pressure on the underlying wound to aid in the control of bleeding or swelling
- ▼ To protect the wound from further trauma

In order to perform these functions, dressings must be sterile and bulky. Although special dressing materials are available, simple gauze pads that have been opened and crumpled to increase their bulk work almost as well and are easier to transport into wilderness areas.

Dressings that have been contaminated by purulent drainage should be handled with gloved fingers or with forceps or similar instruments that can be sterilized. Such dressings should never be touched with bare fingers and should be disposed of by burning. If more than one wound or more than one accident victim must be cared for, attention to the infected wounds should be put off until last, and the attendant must scrub his hands thoroughly after dressing each wound to prevent the spread of infection.

Outer Wrapping

The outer portion of the bandage also has more than one function:
- ▼ To hold the dressings securely in place
- ▼ To keep the dressings from being wet by water or perspiration, which inevitably carry bacteria
- ▼ To apply pressure to help control bleeding and swelling
- ▼ To splint and immobilize portions of the body, such as the hand

Materials that have some elasticity are easier to use and stay in place better. Such materials also compress the wound slightly, but an elastic bandage is more satisfactory if significant compression is needed. If the wound must be kept dry, it should be covered with waterproof tape, plastic, or some other waterproof material. However, moisture accumulates beneath waterproof tape and lifts it from the skin surface. If protection from outside moisture is not needed, porous tape should be used to hold the bandage in place. When the bandage is changed, the tape can be clipped off at the skin edges and new tape placed on top of the old to avoid the skin irritation that results from repeatedly stripping off the tape.

SPECIFIC INJURIES

Lacerations

Lacerations are slicing injuries that may be clean and straight or quite ragged. Such wounds commonly bleed. Infections are also a threat, particularly when small tags of dead tissue are present in ragged wounds. Blood vessels, nerves, or tendons may be damaged, but attempts to repair such structures outside of a hospital would cause further damage and increase the risk of infection. Individuals with such severe injuries should be evacuated.

Puncture Wounds

A puncture wound may extend deeply into underlying tissues. Hidden structures may be damaged, and infection is always a threat. Bleeding to wash out dirt and bacteria should be encouraged. Foreign bodies should be removed. A small wick of gauze can be inserted into the opening of the wound to prevent sealing and to allow the exudate from any infection to drain to the outside. In remote areas, antibiotic therapy is probably a justifiable precaution.

The greatest danger from such wounds is tetanus, which should be prevented with tetanus toxoid inoculations well before an outing is even contemplated.

Abrasions

Abrasions are scraping injuries produced by forceful contact with a rough surface. Severe bleeding is rare, and the objectives of treatment are to control infection and promote healing. Before bandaging, large fragments of foreign material should be removed from the wound with sterile forceps. Removing numerous small embedded particles usually aggravates the injury and does more harm than good. Many such particles are extruded during healing; the rest should be removed under more propitious circumstances.

The wound should be covered with a layer of nonadherent material such as gauze impregnated with petroleum jelly, over which should be placed a bulky dressing to absorb drainage and cushion against further trauma. During dressing changes, the inner layer should not be removed until it spontaneously separates from the wound surface. Similarly, crusts that form during healing should not be removed.

Infected abrasions usually produce purulent exudate, but the entire wound is open and drainage is not impaired. Dressings should be changed frequently and should be thick enough to absorb the exudate.

Skin Flaps and Avulsions

Forces roughly parallel to the skin surface tend to lift or tear out chunks of tissue. If the tissue is completely torn away, the injury is considered an avulsion. (A limb may be completely severed or avulsed, but few survive accidents in which such powerful forces are generated.) If the skin along one side remains intact, a skin flap is created. Small skin flaps are common, but occasionally larger flaps are produced.

If the full thickness of the skin is avulsed, the injury should be bandaged like an abrasion. As a general rule, wounds of this type that are more than one inch in diameter require skin grafting, so the subject eventually will have to be hospitalized. Large avulsions are incapacitating.

If a thick flap of tissue with fat or muscle attached to the undersurface has been produced, the subject must be evacuated. Such injuries heal poorly and tend to become infected. The wound should be thoroughly cleaned and the tissue flap replaced in its original position. If the tissue flap is large, a strip of gauze should be placed along the lip of the wound so that the edges do not seal and purulent exudate can escape if the wound becomes infected. The wound should be bandaged with a bulky compression dressing, and the entire limb should be immobilized. The flap, which must not be allowed to move or shift its position, is in essence a skin graft. If the wound is to heal, the flap must remain stationary while new blood vessels grow into the tissues.

The subject must be closely watched for signs of infection, and any wound infection that does occur must be promptly drained. Antibiotic therapy should be started at the time of the injury.

In expedition situations, evacuation may not be necessary if the wound appears to be healing satisfactorily without infection. The tissue flap is less likely to be moved inadvertently while the individual is lying in a tent than when he is walking or being carried over rough terrain. However, such wounds do not usually heal without infection, and evacuation may be much more difficult for a person with a severe injury that is infected. (When such wounds are treated in a hospital, the fat, muscle, or other tissue on the undersurface of the flap—the tissue that typically dies or becomes infected—is usually trimmed away, and only the skin is preserved.)

When the flap does not survive, it first acquires a dusky appearance and then becomes progressively darker until it is totally black. Uninfected flaps are dry and hard; infected flaps may be moist, foul smelling, and soft. Surgical excision and grafting are required for both, and the infection can be life-threatening.

Small skin flaps with little or no fat on the undersurface are an entirely different matter. The wounds must be cleaned and the flaps held securely in position by bulky bandages just as larger flaps are, but such wounds often heal with no complications or severe infection. The skin flaps commonly do not "take" or attach to the underlying tissue, but they protect the delicate new skin that grows in from the sides and allow it to cover the wound. By the time the wound is covered, the flap usually has dried up and fallen off. The new skin may need to be protected for a few days, but no further therapy is required. (A ruptured blister could even be considered a small skin flap in which the full thickness of the skin is not removed.)

Contusions

Contusions, or bruises, are crushing injuries that cause bleeding into the damaged tissues. Usually the subcutaneous tissue and muscle are injured without a break in the overlying skin. Most contusions are minor, almost insignificant injuries, but rarely the damage can be great enough to severely incapacitate the individual.

The ideal treatment for a severe contusion is immediate application of cold and rest until bleeding has ceased. However, such treatment may be impractical—even life-threatening—in some circumstances. Cessation of bleeding usually requires six to eight hours, but by that time the muscles may be so stiff and sore the person is unable to walk. Anyone with a severe contusion in a remote area may need to walk out, or at least back to his camp while he is still able to do so. After the muscles have stiffened, they often are too painful for vigorous exercise for three or four days, and weeks may be required for complete recovery.

If circumstances do not require immediate evacuation, the injured area should be elevated and cooled with wet towels or clothing, snow, or ice, which causes the blood vessels in the area to constrict, reduces bleeding into the tissues, and tends to reduce pain. (Cooling can hasten disabling muscle pain and stiffness and should not be used for lower extremity injuries if the subject must be able to walk.) If extensive swelling develops, the extremity may be wrapped with an elastic bandage that applies mild pressure. The wrapping should encompass the entire limb from the toes (or fingertips) to well above the area of injury, but it must not occlude the circulation.

After twelve to eighteen hours, movement of the injured area may be resumed, if tolerated, in order to speed resorption of the blood. After three days, heat may be applied to accelerate blood resorption and to relieve some of the muscle pain.

Stiffness persisting for more than two to three weeks in a muscle that has been severely bruised may herald the onset of calcium deposition in the injured tissue. Rarely, this process can continue until the entire clot has been transformed into bone—about twelve to eighteen months. The amount of muscle damage varies and is sometimes significant, so the condition should be recognized and treated to minimize disability. Diagnosis requires x-ray demonstration of the calcium deposits.

Wounds of the Hands and Feet

Wounds of the hands and feet are of special importance because these structures are anatomically complex. All wounds in these areas must be thoroughly cleaned, but no tissue should be trimmed away unless it is unmistakably dead. If these members are enclosed in a large bandage, the fingers or toes must be separated by gauze to prevent maceration of the skin from the dampness produced by perspiration. Such bandages should splint the hand in the "position of function," which is the position the

FIGURE 6-2. "Position of function" of the hand

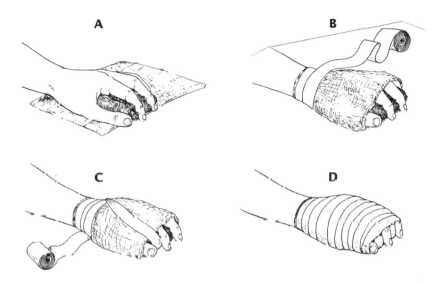

FIGURE 6-3. Technique for bandaging the hand in the "position of function"

hand takes when holding a pencil (Figs. 6-2 and 6-3). The color and sensation in the fingertips must be checked frequently to ensure that the bandage is not too tight. For severe injuries, antibiotic therapy should be instituted at the time of injury and evacuation begun immediately.

Blisters

Traumatic blisters are caused by friction that pulls the skin back and forth over underlying tissues. Eventually a cleft or tear develops in the midportion of the epidermis, the most superficial portion of the skin, and fluid collects in this cleft.

For a blister to develop, the epidermis must be thick and tough enough to resist destruction by the friction, which otherwise would produce an abrasion. Also, the skin and subcutaneous tissues must be bound to the underlying bone to some extent, or the friction would just move the skin and no shear stress would develop. Finally, the skin must be moist enough for the object producing the blister to adhere to the skin surface instead of sliding back and forth. Only the last condition can be modified to prevent blisters, but the first two conditions explain why blisters usually form at only a few specific sites such as the heels.

The most common cause of blisters is new or ill-fitting boots. Boots that are loose in the instep allow the foot to slide forward when going downhill, producing "downhill blisters," usually on the toes or front part of the foot. "Uphill blisters" are most common over the heel or the Achilles tendon at the back of the ankle.

Boots should fit properly and should be "broken in" slowly and thoroughly. Areas prone to blistering should be protected with adhesive tape or moleskin. Adherence between skin and boot should be minimized by keeping the feet dry with powder and by wearing a thick outer sock and a thin inner sock that allows slippage between the two socks. As soon as the pain or heat of an early blister—a "hot spot"—has been detected, the area should be covered with tape or moleskin. (Well-fitting boots do not provide enough space for thicker coverings, such as rings of padded material.)

Healing is faster, pain is diminished, and the risk of infection is greatly reduced when the blister roof is preserved. Blister fluid may have to be drained to allow the roof to become adherent to the base. To drain the fluid, the skin should be cleaned, preferably with an agent such as povidone-iodine, and a sterile needle inserted underneath the skin and into the blister from a point three to five millimeters beyond its edge.

If the roof of the blister has been torn away, the injury should be treated just like an abrasion—covered with a nonadherent inner layer and protected with a thicker outer layer. Second Skin® is a proprietary product developed to cover unroofed blisters that many people find to be effective. The feet should be kept as clean as possible to reduce the risk of infection.

7 FRACTURES AND RELATED INJURIES

CHAPTER

PRINCIPAL CONTRIBUTOR:
Joseph B. Serra, M.D.

Wilderness accidents often result in broken bones or joint and tendon injuries. The care for individuals with such injuries demands an understanding of them and their potential complications. The diagnosis of a fracture—or the absence of a fracture—without x-rays is particularly challenging.

Fractures vary widely in severity. Fractures of the small bones in the hands or feet may produce little pain or disability. The bone ends of a fractured hip may be driven into each other (impacted) in such a manner that the fracture is stable, produces little deformity, and causes little damage to the surrounding tissues. In contrast, bones can be so shattered that the limb feels as if no bone is present.

Fractures with a single, clean break are called "simple." If the bone ends are driven into each other with little or no displacement, the fracture is termed "impacted." If the bone is broken into one or more fragments, the fracture is "comminuted." Vertebral fractures in which the bone simply collapses as the result of trauma or osteoporosis are called "compression" fractures. When the surrounding skin is intact, the fractures are "closed." If the skin has been penetrated, the fracture is called "open" or "compound."

Many bone or joint injuries are of major significance, particularly in situations where immobilization without food or shelter is life-threatening. Disruption of major blood vessels can produce severe hemorrhage; vascular obstruction can cause gangrene of the extremity; breaks in the skin can lead to chronic infections; damage to nerves may result in paralysis.

DIAGNOSIS

The principal signs of a fracture are:
- Pain and tenderness
- Swelling and discoloration
- Deformity

Most fractures are painful. The pain is aggravated by movement or manipulation, and the fracture site is sensitive. Swelling and discoloration are usually present. However, these signs are not diagnostic and may occur with sprains or occasionally with simple contusions.

Obvious deformity is diagnostic of a fracture. Grating of the ends of the broken bones is also diagnostic but may be too painful to use as a diagnostic test. One or both ends of the bone can occasionally be seen in open fractures. A common sign of a fractured hip is shortening of the extremity by one to two inches and outward rotation of the foot.

Loss of function of the injured extremity is not a reliable sign of a fracture. Loss of function can be an emotional response to an injury. A few injuries are so painful that function is lost without fracture. Function may persist even though a fracture is present, particularly with compression fractures of vertebrae and fractures of small bones in the feet and hands.

In a wilderness situation, ascertaining that a fracture is present is not essential. If a fracture is suspected, its existence should be assumed until x-rays prove otherwise. Occasions commonly arise, particularly with ankle injuries, in which an extremity is severely injured but does not appear to be fractured. In a remote area, delaying evacuation until the character of the injury becomes evident may be desirable.

If a fracture is present but the extremity has been immobilized and elevated, the delay will rarely have an adverse effect on healing. If no fracture is present, the person may be able to walk out.

TREATMENT

Immobilization

The basic treatment for any fracture is immobilization, which minimizes further tissue damage by the bone ends, reduces pain, and decreases shock. Permanent immobilization by a cast or surgically implanted hardware allows the fracture to heal.

Immobilizing a fracture in a wilderness setting can be challenging if splints must be improvised. Any material that stabilizes the fracture can be used. A folded newspaper, magazine, or map is particularly effective for splinting fractures of the forearm and wrist. (Cardboard arm and leg splints have been used in downhill ski areas.) Ensolite pads can be used to splint forearms or lower legs; they make excellent cylindrical splints for knee injuries. Cross-country skis or ice axes can be used for lower leg splints. Pillows, heavy clothing, or sleeping bags can be used to splint ankles. Metal pack frames can be used for splints, and the pack straps can be used to hold the splint in place.

Bony prominences at the wrist, elbow, ankle, and knee must be padded to prevent discomfort and nerve damage from hard splint materials. The injured person must be given the responsibility for reporting any symptoms, or any change in existing symptoms, that may herald nerve or vascular compression.

A large and well-prepared outing should probably carry splints. Padded aluminum splints (Sam Splint®) are lightweight and relatively small and can easily be molded to form stable splints for fractures of the arms, wrists, lower legs, or ankles.

Inflatable splints are most suitable for immobilizing fractures of the lower leg and ankle (Fig. 7-1). These splints are lightweight, easy to apply, and help control hemorrhage by applying pressure over the leg when the splint is inflated. (The air pressure in the splint may need to be lowered briefly every one to two hours to ensure that the blood supply to the skin is not impaired.) Inflatable splints must be protected from puncture during evacuation. Changes in air pressure within the splint that occur with changes in altitude and environmental temperature must be anticipated. Heavier splints with zipper closures and screw-type air locks seem to work better than lighter, self-sealing splints, which are affected by large temperature changes.

To achieve immobilization, both the joint above and the joint below a fracture must be splinted. For a fracture of the forearm, the wrist and elbow should be immobilized. For a fracture of the lower leg, the knee and ankle must be stabilized.

Fractures of the thigh (femur) are often associated with severe bleeding and usually are very painful, particularly a few hours after injury when the surrounding muscles go into spasm. Immobilization of such fractures, particularly during evacuation, requires traction, which is described in more detail in the specific discussion of such injuries.

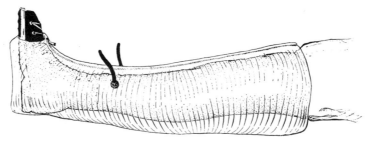

FIGURE 7-1. Inflatable splint for fractures of the lower leg and ankle

To apply a splint or to pack the injured person in a basket stretcher, a fractured extremity must be straightened, which can be accomplished most readily with traction immediately after the fracture has occurred. Later, muscle spasm and the individual's diminished tolerance for pain make manipulation more painful and more difficult.

A definite indication for manipulation of a fractured limb is loss of the blood supply to the limb beyond the fracture site. If the ends of fractured bones obstruct blood flow by pressing on an artery, or have lacerated the artery, the result is severe pain, numbness, and coldness in the affected limb, which typically is cyanotic or pale. If the bone ends are only pressing against the artery or vein, restoration to normal position may relieve the obstruction. If the vessel is actually torn, manipulation is usually not helpful. (Loss of sensation may also result from injury to a nerve.)

Bleeding

Some bleeding occurs with all fractures. Broken bones with sharp ends can cause extensive destruction of the surrounding soft tissues and profuse blood loss. Fractures of the pelvis or thighs are usually associated with severe bleeding. The hemorrhage often causes shock and can be lethal; however, it may produce little or no external evidence of bleeding. Anyone caring for a person involved in an accident who has either of these injuries—or multiple fractures of other bones—must be aware of the threat of shock and should institute treatment in anticipation of its appearance.

Open Fractures

The danger of infection makes open or compound fractures much more serious problems. Osteomyelitis, an infection of bone, can produce extensive bone destruction, may prevent healing of fractures, and occasionally leads to permanent deformities—even amputation. The infection may be difficult to eradicate with antibiotic therapy, and in rare individuals it can persist for years, producing general debilitation as well as local destruction.

Any fracture is considered open if the skin is broken, regardless of whether the skin was damaged by the bone ends or in some other way. A fracture produced by a penetrating injury, such as a gunshot wound, is considered open because the skin is no longer able to keep bacteria away from the injured bone.

If the bone ends protrude through a break in the skin, they should be rinsed with disinfected water until all visible foreign material has been removed before any attempt to straighten the extremity is made. Manipulation causes the bone ends to retract beneath the skin, and foreign material carried with them greatly increases the severity of the subsequent infection. The wound should be left open and covered with a bulky bandage. The individual should be evacuated as rapidly as possible. If evacuation can be completed in a few hours, antibiotics should not be administered unless they can be given intravenously. If evacuation must be delayed, high doses of oral or intravenous antibiotics should be given. The drug of choice is either a cephalosporin or amoxicillin/clavulanate.

Control of Pain

Pain from a fracture is greatly reduced by immobilization. Shortly after injury, pain medications are usually not needed during splinting. However, analgesics may be required for the inevitable jolts of a prolonged evacuation over rough ground.

If needed, morphine or meperidine should be injected intramuscularly every four hours. However, absorption of the drug from the injection site will be reduced if the individual is in shock, and repeated injections can lead to an overdose when normal circulation is restored. Pain medications usually are inadvisable for injured persons who are in shock. If such individuals do require analgesia, morphine should be injected intravenously in small amounts (two to four milligrams every fifteen to thirty minutes) until any necessary manipulation has been completed or the pain has been reduced to a tolerable level.

TRANSPORTATION

Immobilization of fractures and treatment for other injuries must be completed before the individual is moved unless his location is threatened by hazards such as falling rock, an avalanche, or an electrical storm. After obvious injuries have been treated, but before evacuation is begun, the person must be slowly and thoroughly examined to ensure that no additional injuries have been overlooked in the initial evaluation. Attention must be directed to the injured person's back, which is often neglected. If not treated, such injuries could be seriously aggravated during evacuation.

Individuals with fractures of the upper extremity, collar bone, or ribs and some persons with head injuries are able to walk. Such persons must be closely attended because weakness and instability can result from the injury or from drugs given for pain. Subjects with fractures of the lower extremities, pelvis, or vertebral column and subjects with severe head injuries usually must be carried. Considerable resourcefulness and sheer determination are required to successfully evacuate individuals with these injuries, particularly in bad weather.

SPECIFIC FRACTURES OF THE UPPER EXTREMITY

Hand and Fingers

Fractures of the fingers are usually obvious; fractures of the hand may be difficult to diagnose. If pain persists for several days, a fracture is probably present. The hand and fingers should be immobilized by bandaging the hand in the position of function with a wad of material in the palm. An elastic bandage or rolled-up pair of socks serves nicely for this purpose. If the fracture is adjacent to the wrist, a splint should be applied to the palm and the underside of the forearm. A forearm sling should be used to keep the hand elevated (Fig. 7-2).

Forearm

Forearm and wrist fractures are usually obvious. To stabilize wrist and forearm fractures, the hand and elbow must be included in the splint. After splinting, the injured arm should be suspended in two slings as with fractures of the upper arm.

Elbow, Upper Arm, and Shoulder

Fractures of the upper arm and shoulder can be distinguished from dislocations of the shoulder because the arm is held snugly against the chest. When the shoulder is dislocated, the forearm can not be brought into contact with the chest. The bone in the upper arm (humerus) is palpable throughout its entire length on the inner surface of the arm. Undisplaced fractures can be detected by gently running a finger along this bone.

Immobilization of fractures of the elbow, upper arm, and shoulder is best achieved with two slings. One supports the elbow, forearm, and hand. The second is tied around the body and holds the upper arm against the chest, which serves as the splint (Fig. 7-3). The elbow should not be flexed more than ninety degrees, to avoid impairment of circulation. If numbness of the little and ring fingers develops, the elbow should be padded to relieve pressure on the nerves located there. If only one triangular bandage is available, webbing or similar material can be substituted for one of the slings. A sling can be improvised by pinning the shirt sleeve to the front of the shirt with safety pins.

Collar Bone (Clavicle)

Fractures of the collar bone (clavicle) usually can be felt by running a finger along the bone. Such fractures are less uncomfortable if the shoulders are held back. The shoulders can be splinted in this position by webbing or rope that passes over the shoulder and under the armpit on opposite sides, forming a figure eight (Fig. 7-4). The strapping should be applied over the person's clothing, and the

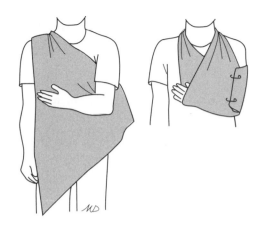

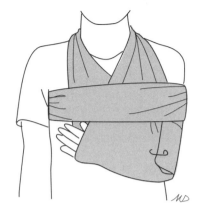

FIGURE 7-2. Application of a forearm sling

FIGURE 7-3. Forearm sling with an upper arm binder

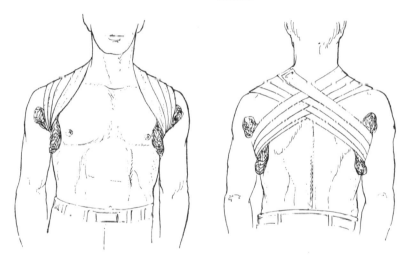

FIGURE 7-4. Figure-eight bandage for splinting a fractured collar bone

shoulders and armpits must be padded. The straps should be just tight enough for the individual to be able to relieve pressure on his armpit by holding his shoulders back.

SPECIFIC FRACTURES OF THE LOWER EXTREMITY

Foot and Toes

Fractures of the small bones in the foot may be difficult to diagnose. Some fractures result from accidents that seem insignificant, such as stepping off a curb, and are associated with relatively little pain. If pain persists for several weeks, the individual should consult a physician. Injuries of the toes and foot can be splinted by a well-fitting shoe or boot. Because they are usually wearing boots when injured, climbers and skiers rarely experience fractures below the ankle.

Fractures of the heel (calcaneus) result from a jump or fall when the individual lands flat-footed or on his heels on a hard surface. Pain usually prevents bearing weight on the injured foot during evacuation.

Ankle

Fractures of the ankle are often difficult to differentiate from sprains if the ankle is not dislocated. Swelling is often more severe with sprains. If pain in an injured ankle does not begin to subside in two or three days, the presence of a fracture should be assumed until x-rays can prove otherwise.

Ankle fractures can best be immobilized with a U-shaped splint that passes around the bottom of the foot and extends up along both sides of the leg. A flexible splint such as a Sam Splint® is ideal. Straightening may be necessary before a displaced or dislocated fractured ankle can be splinted and can best be achieved by applying gentle traction on both the heel and front part of the foot while rotating the foot and ankle into a more normal position.

A person with a minor injury, such as a fracture of the bony protuberance on the outside of the ankle (lateral malleolus) or a fracture of the bone in the foot just below the malleolus (fifth metatarsal), may be able to walk a considerable distance with a walking aid such as an ice axe after immobilization. An individual with more severe injuries may be able to hop short distances on the uninjured leg, but evacuation for distances greater than a few hundred yards usually requires a stretcher.

Lower Leg and Knee

Fractures of the lower leg are usually obvious if the tibia (the larger bone) or both bones are broken. Fractures of the fibula (the small bone on the outer side of the leg) may not be so apparent. Some individuals with a fibula fracture can walk gingerly on their injured leg.

Lower leg fractures should be immobilized in the same manner as fractures of the ankle, with a splint on either side of the leg or with an inflatable splint (see Fig. 7-1). Fractures that involve the knee require immobilization of the ankle and knee.

Kneecap

Fractures of the kneecap (patella) may be difficult to distinguish from a severe bruise. Occasionally, the fracture severs the tendons that pull the leg forward. To immobilize such fractures, a splint that extends from the ankle to the hip should be applied. A cylindrical splint is best, but if material to make one is not available, a straight splint should be applied to the back of the leg. With his knee well splinted, the person may be able to walk short distances.

Thigh

Fractures of the thigh (femur) are usually readily apparent because they are associated with pain and deformity. Adequate immobilization of a fracture of the thigh requires traction.

Such immobilization is needed to control bleeding. The strong thigh muscles cause the bone ends to override and damage the surrounding tissues, resulting in severe hemorrhage. Traction stretches the muscles to their normal length and compresses the blood vessels—particularly veins—within them, limiting the bleeding. Compression over the fracture site with a circumferential dressing such as an elastic bandage may also help control bleeding.

Traction is also required to control muscle spasms, which usually begin within an hour after the fracture, move the bone ends, and can be very painful. Spasms also increase damage to the surrounding muscle.

Traction splints consist of a padded ring or half-ring attached to a metal frame. The ring fits snugly against the buttock and is held in place by a strap that passes over the front of the leg at the groin. The frame is composed of metal rods that extend along both sides of the leg and are joined by a crosspiece beyond the foot (Fig. 7-5).

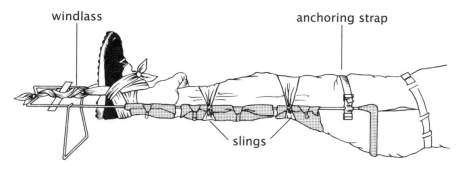

windlass   anchoring strap

slings

FIGURE 7-5. Fractured thigh immobilized by a traction splint

When a splint of this type is to be applied, the person's shoe or boot should be left in place. The ankle should be carefully padded to prevent obstruction of the blood supply to the foot, and a figure-eight bandage similar to that used for sprained ankles should be placed over the boot and padded ankle. The leg should be gently lifted by pulling on the foot, and the splint should be slipped into place and secured at the groin. A hitch slipped under the figure-eight bandage should be looped over the cross-piece of the metal frame and tied. A rod inserted through this hitch can be twisted to apply traction on the leg. The pull should only be strong enough to prevent the foot and leg from sagging when the splint is lifted, but the hitch has to be tightened periodically as the thigh muscles relax and lengthen.

Bandages should be used as hammocks to support the leg in the splint, and one bandage must completely surround the leg to prevent swinging from side to side. The lower end of the splint should be elevated so that no pressure is on the heel. The individual will be more comfortable, particularly during a long evacuation, if the knee is flexed five to ten degrees.

Pain in the foot after the splint has been applied indicates that the blood supply to the foot has been impaired. The figure-eight bandage must be disassembled at once and the ankle more carefully protected. Permanent injury, which may be more crippling than the fracture, can result if the circulation is not adequately protected. Such injury is more likely when traction splinting lasts overnight or longer. In a cold environment, careful attention to the circulation is required to prevent frostbite.

Rescue groups and wilderness expeditions should probably carry one or more Kendrick traction devices or Sager traction splints. If necessary, a makeshift traction splint can be made from two ski poles. The wrist straps can be hooked together and slipped up against the buttock like the half-ring of a manufactured splint. A handkerchief or strap can be used to tie the hand grips together across the front of the thigh like the belt on a standard splint. Bandages tied between the poles support the leg, and the hitch around the ankle is hooked to the baskets or ends of the ski poles. Other materials can be used similarly to improvise a traction splint, but improvised traction splints almost never work as well as a manufactured splint.

Ordinary splints that do not apply traction, such as those for fractures of the ankle and lower leg, should not be used for fractures of the thigh because they do not control bleeding or prevent muscle spasms. If materials to improvise a nontraction splint are available, they can be used for a traction splint.

An individual with a fractured thigh must be evacuated, preferably in a basket stretcher and by mechanical means, such as a helicopter. Because the basket stretcher must be carried to the injured person, a traction splint can be carried in at the same time. If avoidable, improvised splints should not be used during evacuation.

Hip

Fractures of the hip or its socket may be difficult to diagnose. Shortening of the leg and rotation to the outside, the typical signs of a fractured hip, may not be present if the fracture is not displaced. If a fracture is suspected, the person must not be permitted to walk on the injured leg.

Such fractures require no splinting other than binding the legs together.

SPECIFIC FRACTURES OF THE TRUNK

Pelvis

Fractures of the pelvis should be suspected following violent accidents, particularly if side-to-side or front-to-back pressure over the pelvis causes pain. Blood loss of major proportions is inevitable with pelvic fractures; it is rarely evident when the person is examined but commonly produces shock and may be lethal. Therapy for shock should be instituted if a pelvic fracture is suspected.

Splinters of bone from pelvic fractures frequently damage the organs in the pelvic area, particularly the urinary bladder. This complication should be suspected if the individual fails to void or passes only a few drops of bloody urine after the injury. (Injuries of the bladder are discussed in chapter 14, "Abdominal Injuries.")

No splinting is required for pelvic fractures because the muscles around the pelvis hold the bone fragments in place. The injured individual should be placed on a stretcher in a supine position and should be evacuated without being permitted to sit up or stand.

Vertebral Column Fractures

Fractures of the vertebral column (spine) in the back and neck are always accompanied by the possibility of injury to the enclosed spinal cord. The higher the level at which the fracture occurs, the greater is the risk of serious nervous system damage.

Pain or tenderness along the spine or anywhere in the neck following a fall should arouse concern about a vertebral fracture. Occasionally, such fractures present areas of swelling or discoloration similar to fractures elsewhere. Unusual prominence of one of the vertebral spines is sometimes found. However, pain alone demands that the existence of a fracture be assumed.

If an injured person is unconscious, the presence of a cervical fracture must be assumed. Approximately fifteen percent of individuals with a head injury severe enough to produce prolonged unconsciousness have fractures of the cervical vertebrae.

Spinal cord damage is often associated with pain that typically radiates to the front of the body or down the arms or legs. Numbness, tingling, and partial or complete paralysis may also be present. However, the vertebral column is commonly fractured without injuring the underlying cord, and the absence of symptoms of spinal cord damage is by no means evidence that a fracture has not occurred. Cord damage resulting from inadequate fracture precautions would turn an unfortunate accident into a genuine catastrophe. Paralysis resulting from a spinal cord injury is usually permanent.

The American Red Cross recommends that "amateurs" not try to evacuate a person thought to have a vertebral fracture. Transportation must be postponed until cervical collars, body boards, and basket stretchers, and emergency medical technicians experienced with their use, have been brought to the scene of the accident. In industrialized nations, such advice is excellent and should be followed if at all possible. However, in most of the rest of the world emergency medical technicians and the necessary equipment are not available.

During evacuation, a person with a confirmed or suspected vertebral fracture must be secured so that his body does not roll or twist as it is moved over rough terrain. A rigid support such as a metal basket or a broad wooden board is essential. A rolled-up jacket or a similar object should be placed under the small of the back to support the spine in that area. With injuries of the neck, a cervical collar must be installed or padding must be placed on both sides of the head and neck to prevent the head from rolling from side to side (Fig. 7-6).

An injured person with spinal cord damage and paralysis requires special attention during evacuation, particularly when evacuation takes more than twenty-four hours. Care must be given to the areas

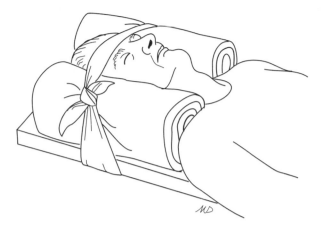

FIGURE 7-6. Technique for immobilizing the head of a subject with fractured cervical vertebrae

that support the body's weight—heels, buttocks, shoulders, and elbows. Pressure on these areas does not allow blood to circulate through the tissues. Normally such deprivation of the blood supply results in pain, and the person shifts his position. Individuals with spinal cord injuries may not be able to feel pain and may not be able to shift position. After a few hours of being deprived of blood, the tissues in these areas die, eventually resulting in ulcers known as "bed sores." To avoid this complication, the pressure points, particularly the heels and buttocks, must be carefully padded. Furthermore, this padding must be rearranged every two hours, day and night. The prevention of bed sores, which heal very poorly and are difficult to cure, requires diligent and truly devoted nursing care.

Most vertebral fractures that damage the spinal cord paralyze the urinary bladder and large intestine. Bladder care may require repeated catheterizations at least every eight hours or the insertion of an indwelling catheter.

OTHER FRACTURES

Rib fractures are discussed in chapter 11, "Chest Injuries." Skull fractures and fractures of the face and jaw are discussed in chapter 16, "Head and Neck Injuries."

DISLOCATIONS

A dislocation is an injury in which the normal relationships of a joint are disrupted. The bone may be forced out of a socket, as occurs in dislocations of the shoulder, elbow, or hip. But some joints, like those between the bones in the fingers, have no socket, and the joint surfaces are simply displaced. Bones may be fractured and adjacent nerves, blood vessels, and supportive structures may be injured.

The signs of dislocation are similar to those of a fracture: pain that is aggravated by motion, tenderness, swelling, discoloration, limitation of motion, and deformity of the joint. The findings are localized to the area around a joint, but comparison with the opposite, uninjured joint may be necessary to be certain that a definite abnormality is present. Frequently, the dislocated joint appears larger than normal due to overlapping of the bone ends. Pain and muscle spasm usually prevent use of the extremity for physical activities.

Dislocations should be reduced. The risk of causing additional damage is quite small, and any existing fractures of the joint surface will be better aligned after reduction. Furthermore, dislocations should be reduced as quickly as possible. The muscles surrounding a dislocated joint go into spasm quickly. The chances for successful correction of the dislocation decrease and the risk of further injury increases with the passage of time after injury.

Other advantages of early reduction of a dislocation are:

- ▾ Pain relief is often dramatic.
- ▾ The risk of circulatory or neural damage is reduced.
- ▾ Immobilization of the joint is easier.
- ▾ Transportation of the individual is easier.

Pain, pallor or cyanosis, swelling, numbness, or the absence of pulses beyond the dislocation are indicative of obstruction of the blood supply. Entrapment or compression of arteries is particularly likely to occur with dislocations of the elbow or knee. Prompt action may be required to save the limb from gangrene.

The individual performing the reduction should use other members of the party if they can help. He must ensure that the injured person understands and agrees with what he is attempting and the technique he plans to use. Strong analgesics (intramuscular or intravenous morphine or meperidine) are helpful; diazepam (Valium®) promotes relaxation of the muscles and the individual. Traction must be gentle and steady; forceful, jerking maneuvers must be avoided.

After any dislocation is reduced, the extremity should be splinted in the same manner it would be for a fracture. It may need to be immobilized for two to three weeks—sometimes longer.

Fingers

Dislocations of the fingers, which occur most commonly at the second joint, are usually obvious and may be corrected quite easily immediately after the injury. Reduction is best accomplished by holding the digit in a slightly flexed position and applying traction while pushing the end of the dislocated bone back into place (Fig. 7-7).

Dislocations at the base of the index finger and at the base of the thumb may not be reducible. With such injuries, surrounding ligaments and tendons often entrap the end of the bone, and surgery is required for reduction. An initial effort to reduce such dislocations should be made, but if unsuccessful, the hand should be splinted in the position of function and the individual evacuated.

After reduction, an injured finger can be splinted effectively by taping it to an adjacent uninjured finger.

Elbow

Dislocations of the elbow are usually obvious, particularly when compared with the opposite side. Most dislocations are posterior, and the tip of the dislocated ulna is very apparent. Movement of the joint is restricted.

FIGURE 7-7. Technique for reducing a finger dislocation

Elbow dislocations may be difficult to reduce. The slightly flexed forearm should be pulled downward while the upper arm is pulled upward by an assistant. A considerable amount of force is usually needed. As the joint separates, any sideways displacement of the bones should be corrected first. The forearm may need to be rocked back and forth very gently. If the joint is not fully reduced, gentle bending of the elbow may complete the correction. The ability to flex the elbow to ninety degrees or more is proof of reduction.

Immediately after the dislocation has been reduced, the pulse at the wrist should be checked. If the pulse is absent but the color of the hand is normal and pain is diminished, the absence is probably the result of arterial spasm, for which nothing needs to be done. If the pulse is absent, the hand is darkly colored or cyanotic, and pain is increasing, the artery to the forearm may have been entrapped when the bones of the elbow slipped back into position. The joint should be slightly separated again with traction (not dislocated again) and gently rocked back and forth to free the entrapped structures.

The arm and hand should be splinted with the elbow at a ninety-degree angle. Pulse and sensation should be checked again after the splint is applied. The elbow must not be wrapped circumferentially with tape or bandages because swelling does occur, and, if confined, it would compress blood vessels and nerves. Fracture of the bones of the elbow commonly occurs with the dislocation. A physician should be consulted as soon as possible, particularly if pain persists.

Shoulder

Shoulder dislocations result from strong jerks when the arm is rotated outward and held away from the body. A typical situation is a kayaker thrusting back and downward with a paddle (Fig. 7-8). Many individuals have recurrent dislocations, can readily identify the injury, and often are helpful with reduction.

Most shoulder dislocations are anterior (Fig. 7-9). Individuals with this injury are in pain and hold the upper arm and forearm away from the body in various positions, but the arm can not be brought into contact with the chest. (With a fractured humerus, the arm is usually held snugly against the chest.) The absence of the end of the humerus in the joint, which is located just lateral to the collar bone and below the shoulder, may be most easily recognized by loss of the normal roundness or fullness, particularly when compared with the opposite shoulder (Fig. 7-10).

Posterior shoulder dislocations are rare and are often difficult to diagnose. The forearm and upper arm are typically held across the chest in contact with the chest wall. The forearm can not be externally rotated away from the chest. A defect is usually present in the normal contour of the deltoid muscle,

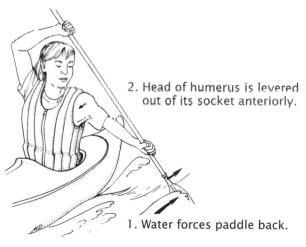

2. Head of humerus is levered out of its socket anteriorly.

1. Water forces paddle back.

FIGURE 7-8. Mechanism of shoulder dislocation by a kayaker

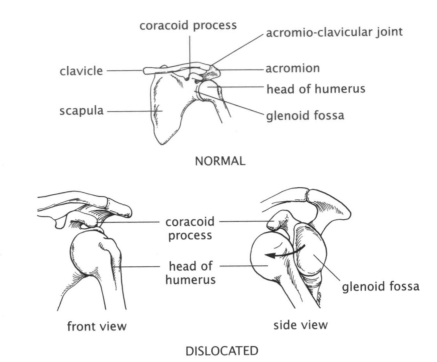

FIGURE 7-9. Normal and dislocated shoulder joints

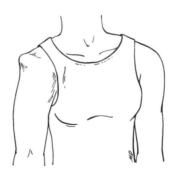

FIGURE 7-10. Appearance of a shoulder after anterior dislocation

which forms the outer point of the shoulder, and the head of the bone in the upper arm (humerus) sometimes can be palpated posteriorly.

Of the many methods for reducing a dislocated shoulder, two appear to combine the best chance for success with the least risk of additional injury.

The first uses traction by an attendant. The person should be lying flat with the injured arm held straight out from the side of the body. (A table for him to lie on would provide the best positioning, but a wilderness situation would require improvisation.) The arm should be flexed at the elbow and the forearm held in a vertical position. A loop of webbing, clothing, or similar material that has been tied loosely around the attendant's waist should be slipped over the arm and down to the elbow. After

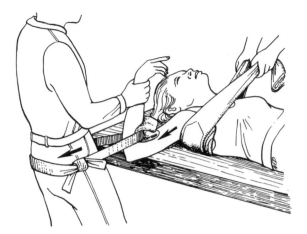

FIGURE 7-11. Technique for reducing a shoulder dislocation with active traction

padding the elbow, the attendant can apply traction by simply leaning backward. A second attendant must hold the injured person, preferably with a loop of clothing around the chest, to prevent traction moving his entire body (Fig. 7-11).

Communication with the injured subject helps achieve maximal relaxation. The humerus may be gently rotated by moving the forearm from side to side, and the head of the humerus may be gently pushed toward the socket with the fingers of the opposite hand. After a few minutes, reduction can be recognized by the palpable settling of the humeral head into its fossa, and is heralded by the relief of the individual, who is immediately more comfortable. If the forearm can be swung across the body and can lie in contact with the chest wall, reduction has been achieved.

A second method to restore the dislocated bone to its normal position is to attach a ten- to fifteen-pound weight to the person's wrist (Fig. 7-12). (A bucket of water is easy to attach.) The individual must be lying face downward on a flat surface with the injured arm dangling straight down. He should not grip the weight because that makes the arm muscles contract. They must be relaxed if reduction is to be achieved. After a somewhat longer time than that required by the first technique, the constant pull by the weight tires the muscles surrounding the shoulder, causing them to relax and permit the bone to slip back into its socket. If the dislocation is not corrected within an hour, traction should be discontinued, the arm splinted as well as possible, and the subject evacuated.

Following reduction of a shoulder dislocation, the arm should be immobilized for at least two weeks, preferably three, with two slings, one supporting the forearm and hand and the other holding the upper arm against the body. A recurrent dislocation of the shoulder may not require such long immobilization. The ultimate treatment of repeated shoulder dislocations is surgical repair of the lax ligaments that allow the dislocation, which may occur with disabling frequency after insignificant trauma until reparative surgery is performed.

Dislocated shoulders sometimes can not be reduced, and the discomfort makes rapid evacuation necessary. When the shoulder is dislocated, the arm is held in an awkward position that makes splinting difficult. Successful techniques use a strap or bandage to anchor the hand on top of the head. Sometimes the hand is held close to this position spontaneously, but the muscles would soon tire, producing increased pain in the muscles and in the shoulder. On ski slopes, effective splinting has been achieved with a rolled-up blanket secured in a figure-eight position like the splint for a fractured clavicle, with the bulk of the blanket in the armpit to support the upper arm (Fig. 7-13). In more remote wilderness settings, a similar splint would have to be devised.

FIGURE 7-12. Technique for reducing a shoulder dislocation with passive traction

FIGURE 7-13. Technique for splinting a dislocated shoulder that can not be reduced

Hip

Most hip dislocations are posterior and result from falls with the hip flexed. The force of impact transmitted longitudinally through the knee and femur drives the hip backward out of its socket. Strong forces are required to produce such injuries. Impact with the dashboard by the knees in an automobile accident is a common cause. Anterior hip dislocations are most commonly produced by falls in which the person lands directly on the outer aspect of his hip.

With a posterior dislocation, the hip is bent and the leg is rotated so that the knee is pulled upward and inward over the opposite leg. With an anterior dislocation, the hip may be bent backward or forward, but the leg is rotated so that the knee is turned outward, away from the body (Fig. 7-14). The key diagnostic clue with both types of dislocation is that returning the leg to a normal position for splinting or transportation in a stretcher is impossible. The position of the leg helps differentiate dislocations from fractures of the hip or thigh, with which the leg lies flat. Reducing a dislocated hip is difficult and painful, but it is worth attempting because reduction relieves pain, improves circulation to the femur, and greatly facilitates placement of the person in a basket stretcher and evacuation.

The technique for reduction is the same for anterior and poster dislocations. Two individuals are required. One holds the subject flat on the ground with his hands on both sides of the injured person's pelvis. The other straddles the injured leg and gently flexes the knee and hip to ninety degrees. After bending his knees and locking his hand behind the subject's knee, the second attendant can apply strong upward traction by simply straightening his legs (Fig. 7-15). The weight of the injured individual and the first attendant provide countertraction. Rotating the hip by moving the lower leg gently from side to side may help with reduction.

After reduction, the injured extremity must be splinted to the opposite leg. Gentle traction is beneficial if available; the person should be transported in a supine position.

Knee

Knee dislocations are major, sometimes disastrous injuries that result from forceful impact with the knee bent. In most instances, the ligaments and tendons around the knee are so extensively torn that dislocated knees pop back into position spontaneously. The nature of the injury can be recognized

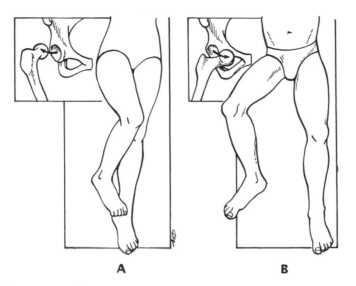

FIGURE 7-14. Posterior and anterior hip dislocations

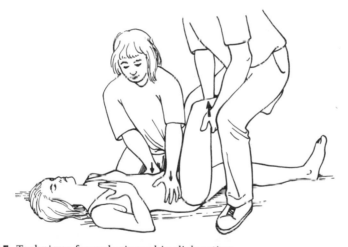

FIGURE 7-15. Technique for reducing a hip dislocation

by the pain and instability of the knee. If the knee remains dislocated, reduction can usually be achieved quite readily with traction on the lower leg. Pulses and sensation in the foot must be checked. Injury to the large vessels behind the knee occurs frequently. Such damage is suggested by painful swelling behind the knee developing immediately or hours after correction of the deformity and is confirmed by the absence of pulses. The leg should be splinted as securely as possible with precautions not to interfere with circulation. Dislocated knees are too unstable for walking over rough terrain.

Kneecap

Dislocations of the kneecap (patella) frequently are recurrent, much like shoulder dislocations. The kneecap is usually displaced to the outside, and the knee is held in a flexed position for comfort.

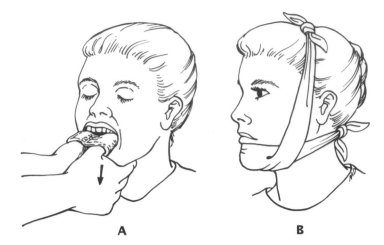

FIGURE 7-16. Technique for reducing a jaw dislocation and bandaging the jaw to prevent recurrence

Comparison with the opposite knee typically makes the abnormality obvious.

To reduce the dislocation, the leg should be gently straightened while the kneecap is pushed back into place. Straightening alone may be adequate.

The leg should be splinted as if the patella is fractured, but individuals are usually able to walk on the injured leg.

Ankle

Dislocated ankles are usually associated with fractures of the adjacent bones. They should be reduced and treated with the same techniques as fractures.

Jaw

An individual can become so completely relaxed while asleep that his jaw falls downward and slips out of its socket. When the person awakens, he finds that he can not close his mouth. In a remote situation, the resulting inability to swallow could lead to serious difficulties. Usually such complete relaxation follows the use of sleeping pills or overindulgence in alcohol.

Dislocations of the jaw can be safely reduced, usually rather easily. Both thumbs should be inserted over the molars of the lower jaw and pressed directly downward (Fig. 7-16). Considerable force is required to overcome the spasm in the jaw muscles, which are quite strong, but the jaw should slip back into place without too much difficulty. (The thumbs should be padded to prevent "bites" as the jaw pops back into its socket.) After reduction, persistent pain in the joint, which is located just in front of the ear, may be indicative of a fracture, and a physician should be consulted. If dislocations recur, the individual can wear a bandage to hold his mouth closed when he is asleep. The bandage should cover the tip of the chin and should be tied over the top of the head and around the back of the neck.

OTHER INJURIES OF BONE AND RELATED STRUCTURES

Contusions of Bone and Subperiosteal Hematomas

A blow that does not produce a fracture or dislocation may still cause sufficient damage to produce swelling in the fibrous bone sheath (periosteum) or bleeding between that tissue and the rigid portion of the bone (subperiosteal hematoma). The injured person complains of pain, the area is tender, and the bone may appear or feel larger than normal.

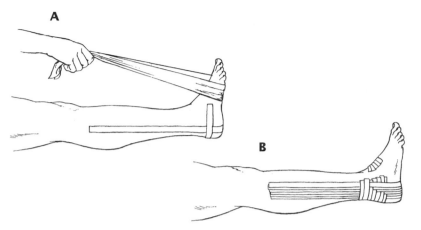

FIGURE 7-17. Technique for taping a sprained ankle after healing has begun. (The foot should be held perpendicular to the leg while the tape is being applied. The ankle should be taped only for the first three or four days of use after healing is under way.)

Treatment consists of applying cold and a pressure bandage for the first twenty-four hours following injury, and immobilization. After twenty-four hours, local heat should be applied, and activity can be allowed to the limits of pain tolerance. However, if a fracture or dislocation can not be ruled out, immobilization should be continued.

Sprains and Strains

Sprains and strains are stretching, tearing, or avulsing injuries of ligaments around a joint and often can not be differentiated from fractures without x-rays. They can be as disabling as a broken bone. The signs are similar to a fracture, although grating of broken bone ends and deformity are not present. Swelling is often quite marked, and discoloration may also be present. If an injury is obviously severe, the wisest course is to treat it as a fracture.

The treatment for sprains is summarized in the acronym "RICE," which stands for rest, ice, compression, and elevation. An elastic bandage can partially immobilize a small joint such as an ankle and applies compression that helps limit swelling. Applying cold immediately after an injury reduces hemorrhage and swelling. Absorption of blood and edema fluid can be promoted by elevating the injured area. Later, heat may be helpful, but it should not be applied until at least three days after the injury. Motion and use may speed recovery, but only when resumed after the initial swelling and hemorrhage have subsided.

Sprained ankles are the most common injuries of this type, and circumstances frequently require the subject to walk (or hobble) from the injury site. In most situations, a figure-eight bandage put on over the shoe or boot should support the ankle. Loops of the figure eight should pass around the back of the heel and under the sole of the foot, crossing on top of the foot. Support must be snug but must not obstruct the circulation. The injured person can no longer rely on the injured ankle, and the risk of further damage is significant.

If the ankle is to be taped, alternate interlacing layers of tape should be placed under the heel and straight up the leg, and around the back of the heel and straight out over the foot (Fig. 7-17). Tape must not completely surround the leg, or swelling (which could result just from immobilization) can impair blood circulation to the foot.

One of the most common downhill skiing injuries is a strain or tear of the ligaments of the knee. Occasionally, the cartilage that covers the joint surfaces is injured also. The knee should be splinted as if it were fractured, but the person may be able to walk after the knee has been immobilized. If standing or walking is painful, the individual should be evacuated by sled or stretcher. Such injuries frequently require a cast and four to six weeks or more to heal.

Muscle and Tendon Tears

A sudden, strong jerk with the bones and joints fixed in position, as occurs at the end of a fall, may rip a muscle from its insertion or may partially or completely tear the body of the muscle or tendon. Muscle tears or "pulls" can also result from vigorous activities, such as sprinting at top speed, and from sudden movements or changes in direction. A penetrating injury may sever a muscle or tendon. Complete separation of the muscle, or its tendon and attachments, results in loss of its function. Incomplete interruption seldom produces complete loss of function, but it is painful and predisposes the structures to subsequent injury.

Insertions are the points at which muscles or tendons are attached to bone. The most common sites at which insertion injuries occur are the fingertips behind the nails, the shoulder, the elbow, and the ankle. Rupture of muscles and tendons more commonly occurs in the calf, the front and back of the thigh, and the upper portion of the arm and shoulder. Pain, tenderness, swelling, and loss of motion are the usual findings. Sometimes a defect in the muscle or tendon can be felt.

Prehospital treatment should include applying cold, immobilization, and rapid evacuation. Definitive repair of such injuries is most successful if performed within twenty-four hours of the accident.

Muscle Compartment Syndromes

Some muscles are enveloped in a fibrous sheath or "compartment" that is only slightly distensible. Swelling of the muscle as the result of unaccustomed exercise or trauma can raise the compartment pressure to a level that impairs blood flow to the muscle. When deprived of its blood supply, the muscle dies, usually crippling the extremity.

Compartment syndromes are uncommon, but because they can produce permanent disability, they should be recognized and promptly treated. The anterior tibial muscle, which is located on the outside of the shin, is the muscle most commonly involved by compartmental compression. Most subjects have an obvious leg injury, typically a crushing injury. However, compartmental syndromes are insidious because they can develop following unaccustomed exercise. Occasionally, pressure on the leg during a period of unconsciousness, or injuries such as burns, can produce this disorder. A few individuals have experienced previous episodes of milder pain, particularly following vigorous exercise.

The initial symptom is pain in the involved muscles, which typically is much more severe than would be expected from the injury or exercise by which it is preceded. Passive movement or stretching of the muscle is also painful. Usually the muscle is obviously swollen and the overlying skin is tense and glossy. However, the most diagnostic feature is severe weakness or paralysis of the involved muscle. A person with an anterior tibial compartment syndrome can not flex his foot upward or resist pressure forcing it down. The foot may be cold and numb and the pulses may be weak, but such signs are inconsistent, and their absence is not an indication that a compartment syndrome is not present.

Outside of a hospital, two maneuvers may be beneficial: any constricting clothing or bandages should be removed, and the extremity should be positioned at or above the level of the heart. However, the only effective treatment is surgically opening the compartment to relieve the pressure. Because surgeons alone are familiar with the technique and the anatomy, subjects with this disorder must be evacuated to a hospital.

Evacuation is urgent. Treatment must be prompt to avoid permanent paralysis. Only thirty-one percent of one group of individuals treated within twelve hours had residual disability; ninety-one percent of those decompressed later had permanent functional deficits, and twenty percent required amputations. The usual functional deficit is an inability to flex the foot upward, called "foot drop," which usually requires a brace to support the foot when walking on a flat surface. On a wilderness trail, disability would be much greater.

Bursitis, Tendinitis, and Shin Splints

Bursitis, tendinitis, and shin splints are caused by inflammation of tendons or the flattened, cystlike spaces (bursae) that cushion the movement of tendons. These disorders are characterized by pain and stiffness that has a gradual onset, usually following unaccustomed use of a muscle for an extended length of time. The pain can be severe and frequently is first noticed the morning after such activities.

Splinting may relieve the immediate discomfort but often prolongs the problem. Moist heat and a mild analgesic may provide some relief; sometimes cold is more effective. The pain, which is rarely disabling, may persist for days, weeks, months, or years. Continued use of the joint through its full range of motion helps prevent stiffness.

Tenosynovitis

Inflammation and infection of the sheaths that surround tendons and lubricate their movements may result from unaccustomed overuse or a penetrating injury. In the field, such infections may develop several days after a small cut or puncture wound that did not appear significant at the time, particularly on the hands, fingers, or feet. Pain with motion of the involved tendon is the diagnostic finding. When infection is present, painful swelling, increased warmth, and redness are apparent. A crackling sensation in the affected tissue may be felt with pressure or movement of the tendon. Although sterile inflammatory episodes caused by overuse usually subside with rest, an infected tenosynovitis requires the attention of a physician, who sometimes must surgically drain the tendon sheath. If infection is suspected, a broad-spectrum antibiotic such as ceftriaxone (Rocephin®) should be started and the individual evacuated without delay. Failure to obtain surgical treatment can result in permanent loss of mobility of the tendon, or extension of the infection to adjacent tendons and body spaces and even greater loss of function.

Joint Effusion

Swelling, mild discomfort, increased warmth, and redness may appear in a joint after an injury—sometimes without any preceding trauma. The knee is most commonly involved, but other joints, particularly the elbow or wrist, can be involved. The cause may be outside the joint, as with "tennis elbow" or a similar condition involving the insertion of the tendons just below and to the side of the kneecap. Within the joint, effusions often result from deterioration of the cartilage following repeated injury. If inflammation but no infection is present, the discomfort and swelling may respond to rest, wrapping with an elastic bandage, moist heat, and a mild analgesic. An infected joint manifested by more obvious redness, greater pain and swelling, and fever that is sometimes high—requires immediate care by a physician, particularly when the person is febrile.

Ingrown Toenails

Ingrown toenails are best prevented by trimming the toenails straight across, without rounding the corners, and by wearing well-fitting boots and socks. If pain and redness occur during an outing, a wedge can be cut from the outer third of the nail. The offending sharp corner must be removed. Warm soaks hasten recovery; elevating the new corner of the nail with a pledget of gauze as it regrows may prevent recurrence.

Corns and Calluses

Corns and calluses should be prevented by wearing well-fitting shoes, but if they cause discomfort on an outing, they can be shaved flat with a razor blade after they have been softened by soaking in warm water.

BACK INJURIES

Strain and Spasm

Back pain is produced in many ways, such as by carrying heavy loads, by working in an unaccustomed stooped position, or by sleeping in an awkward position. However, treatment is frequently frustrating. The measures that provide the greatest relief are sleeping on a firm support, such as a mattress with a sheet of plywood underneath, and applying heat to the affected area. When sleeping outdoors, a mat that provides insulation but little padding is best. Heat may help relieve muscle spasm. Mild analgesics may mask the pain, but codeine may sometimes be necessary. A few individuals have severe, incapacitating pain from muscle spasms.

Ruptured Disc

Cushions of cartilaginous material separate the vertebrae of the spinal column. A ruptured disc is an extrusion of this semisolid material into the spinal canal so that it compresses the spinal cord or the nerves coming from the cord. The basic defect is degeneration and weakening of the ligaments that normally hold this cushion in place. Trauma is only the final incident. Unless the basic defect is present, trauma alone usually fractures the vertebrae instead of causing the disc to rupture.

Symptoms of a ruptured disc in the lumbo-sacral area are highly characteristic. Pain begins in the lower back, radiates to one side, and passes through the buttock and down the back of the leg. The pain may involve the outside of the leg but is rarely felt in the front or inner portion of the leg. The individual frequently walks with a decided limp. Pain when moving to and from a supine position is also characteristic.

As a result of the pain associated with movement, muscles in the lower back go into spasm. The vertebral column in the lower back is immobilized and does not bend when the individual leans to either side, which can be seen when he is examined from behind. An examiner's fingers can usually palpate this muscle spasm. Over the foot and lower leg on the affected side, loss of sensation to pin prick or the light touch of a wisp of cotton may be present.

The prehospital treatment for a ruptured disc is the same as for strain of the back muscles. However, the two conditions should be differentiated because each has a quite different outlook. Strain usually clears up in a few days, or perhaps a few weeks, with rest and proper treatment. Although the pain of a ruptured disc may disappear in a similar time with rest, it may be more prolonged and may be relieved only by surgery. Furthermore, a disc can produce permanent nerve injury and muscle weakness. Finally, even though symptoms disappear rather promptly, a recurrence is likely at any time.

In expedition circumstances these prognostic factors must be considered. Individuals with a previous history of a disc problem should consult an orthopedist or neurosurgeon before undertaking remote wilderness activities, particularly if evidence of sensory impairment is present.

SKI INJURIES

Ski injuries have decreased fifty percent in the last twenty-five years. Most of the reduction reflects fewer lower extremity injuries. However, anterior cruciate ligament (ACL) injuries make up twenty-five percent of all injuries, and the rate of ACL injuries has not declined.

Sprains of the ulnar collateral ligament of the thumb also remain high. Ski poles are implicated in this injury because they remain in the palm during falls on outstretched hands. This injury can largely be avoided by using ski pole straps only when skiing powder.

Many excellent articles on ski injuries have been written, and this discussion is limited mostly to the alarming rate of ACL injuries. The goal is to design equipment that will decrease the incidence of this injury. Until that is accomplished, education of skiers about the causes and avoidance of ACL injury appears to be the best way to reduce its incidence.

Carl Ettlinger and Robert Johnson have developed an ACL Awareness Program based on research conducted at a northern Vermont ski area. Giving their program to professional ski patrol members, ski instructors, and ski area employees has resulted in a fifty percent reduction in the incidence of ACL injuries.

Attempting to recover during a fall and forward thrusting of the tibia by the boot during a fall are two ways in which ACL injuries are produced. Ettlinger and Johnson have described the "phantom foot syndrome," which also can lead to ACL tears. This syndrome develops when the uphill arm is back and the skier is off balance to the rear, usually with his upper body facing downhill and his hips further downhill than his knees. The uphill ski is unweighted and all of the skier's weight is on the inside edge of the downhill ski, particularly the tail, which continues to carve into the hill. As a result, the skier's tibia is rotated inward, tearing the ACL.

To avoid ACL injury, skiers should keep their skis together or bring them back together if they have separated. Their arms should be forward with their hands over their skis. Skiers should not attempt to get up until they have stopped sliding, unless they are headed for an obstacle. If they fall, they should not land on their hands and should not straighten their legs.

More information about the program developed by Ettlinger and Johnson is available from Vermont Safety Research, P.O. Box 85, Sandhill Road, Underhill Center, VT 05490 (802-899-4738).

Ski injuries are preventable. The ultimate responsibility is with skiers, who should know their equipment, maintain it properly, have adjustments done by professionals, and develop an acceptable level of fitness.

SNOWBOARDING INJURIES

Snowboarding is the most rapidly growing winter sport and is gaining acceptance at most ski areas. Not many studies on injuries have been published, but an investigation of 415 injuries in the Lake Tahoe area has provided significant data.

Of those injured, seventy-five percent are males, with an average age of twenty years. At least sixty percent are in their first year of snowboarding. Many have never skied before taking up "boarding." Falls produce seventy-five percent of all injuries, mainly to wrists, shoulders, knees, and ankles. The fracture rate is much higher in snowboarders than in skiers. Wrist fractures are most common. Dislocations of shoulders and elbows also occur. Ankle sprains and fractures predominantly occur to wearers of soft boots. Those wearing hard-shell boots more commonly have knee injuries, similar to those experienced by skiers. However, snowboard injuries to the knees are mainly collateral ligament sprains, not anterior cruciate ligament tears.

The injury rate is slightly lower than that seen in skiers. Collisions account for five percent of the injuries, compared with seven percent in skiers. Significant research and development to improve bindings and types of release mechanisms is ongoing.

Prevention of injuries is directed at learning proper technique, including learning how to fall with less risk. Pads for elbows and knees and gloves with built-in wrist splints are available.

In addition, many snowboarders are new to the mountains and must learn to respect the mountains in winter, particularly the snow patterns and residuals of mountain storms. Three snowboarders died in 1998 within two weeks of a storm. All fell into tree wells filled with deep powder snow. Proper education and avoiding snowboarding alone in ungroomed or remote terrain could prevent such tragedies.

CHAPTER 8

BURNS

Minor burns, such as burns of the hands or fingers by hot pots or stoves, are common, and their care is straightforward—although they must not be neglected. Major burns are rare in the wilderness. Possibly the greatest risk is at high altitude when food is being cooked or snow is being melted for water inside a tent. In these situations, fuel spills or even explosions occur due both to the notoriously poor performance of stoves at high elevations and to hypoxic impairment of the individuals using them. Such accidents can be catastrophic if destruction of tents, sleeping bags, and clothing leaves people with severe burns exposed to an extreme environment.

Successful rescue of individuals with major burns from this kind of situation would require an incredible combination of medical knowledge, evacuation skills, dedication and determination, and sheer luck. The intravenous fluids and other supplies needed just to keep them alive for the first twenty-four hours would almost never be available in such circumstances. However, severe burns can occur in less remote circumstances, and few wilderness users would not try to provide the best care possible. Therefore, a discussion of the basic principles of care for major burns appears worthwhile, even though few opportunities for its successful application can be expected.

EVALUATING BURN SEVERITY

The depth, size, and location determine the severity of a burn. In the past, burns have been classified according to their depth as first, second, or third degree. First-degree burns were superficial, did not kill any of the tissues, and only produced redness of the skin. Second-degree burns damaged the upper portion of the skin, resulting in blisters. Third-degree burns destroyed the full thickness of the skin and could extend into the underlying tissues. This terminology has been modified, and first- and second-degree burns currently are lumped together as "partial thickness" because generally they are treated in the same manner. Third-degree burns are labeled "full thickness."

The area covered by the burn is of critical significance. Before the development of burn centers, few individuals survived full-thickness burns that covered more than fifty percent of their body surface. In contrast, few burns covering less than fifteen to twenty percent of the body are lethal when given proper care.

Location is also important. Burns of the face and neck, hands, or feet are more incapacitating due to the specialized organs and complex anatomy of these areas. Burns of the face may be associated with burns of the air passages or lungs, which often are lethal. Burns of the genitalia or buttocks are difficult to keep clean and usually become severely infected.

BURN SHOCK

The immediate life-threatening problem associated with major burns is shock—specifically "burn shock." When tissues are burned, the damaged capillaries allow blood serum to pour out into the burned tissues. This fluid loss reduces the blood volume and produces shock just like a major hemorrhage. A person with a major burn usually dies in shock within twelve to eighteen hours unless appropriate fluid therapy is instituted. Such fluids almost always must be administered intravenously. Individuals with severe burns are often unconscious or too stuporous to swallow fluids. If they can swallow, they often vomit anything taken by mouth. If they are not vomiting, the fluids often remain in the stomach and are not absorbed. Because appropriate fluids are rarely available in wilderness situations, a major burn in a remote area usually requires immediate evacuation by the fastest means available.

EVACUATION

As a general rule, all full-thickness burns larger than one inch in diameter eventually require surgical therapy—debridement and skin grafting. Therefore the only decision that must be made for individuals with burns of that size or larger is how urgently they should be evacuated. Help with this decision can be obtained from the following criteria for the classification of burn injuries established by the American Burn Association and the American College of Surgeons:

MAJOR
▼ Blistering partial-thickness burns of more than twenty-five percent of the body surface
▼ Full-thickness burns of more than ten percent of the body surface
▼ Significant burns of the face, eyes, ears, hands, feet, or perineum (genitals and buttocks)
▼ Significant associated trauma or coexisting disease

MODERATE
▼ Blistering partial-thickness burns of fifteen to twenty-five percent of the body surface, with less than ten percent full-thickness burns, and no involvement of critical areas

MILD
▼ Blistering partial-thickness burns of less than fifteen percent of the body surface, with less than two percent full-thickness burns, and no involvement of critical areas

Individuals with moderate or major burns require hospitalization and must be evacuated. If any question about the severity of the burn exists, the person should be evacuated. Experts have difficulty determining whether a burn is partial or full thickness immediately after it occurs, and inexperienced persons almost always underestimate both the depth and the area. Persons with major burns are often deceptively alert for several hours until fluid losses become severe.

Many individuals with less extensive burns must also be evacuated, particularly with burns of the hands or face, but speed is not as crucial. Fluid loss occurs with all burns, both partial and full thickness, but in previously healthy young adults does not achieve life-threatening proportions if the burns cover less than ten to fifteen percent of the body surface.

Care of a seriously burned individual demands a major commitment of time and personnel. Only a large group would have enough members for some to continue the expedition while others took care of even one burned individual.

TREATING THE BURN

Immediate Care

Immediately after the burn, all clothing and jewelry around the injury should be removed. If the burn is small and is not full thickness, immediate application of cold helps reduce the pain. Holding a towel soaked in ice water against the burned area or immersing the area in cold, soapy water usually is effective. More extensive partial-thickness burns and full-thickness burns should not be treated in this manner. Full-thickness burns are usually painless because the nerves in the skin have been destroyed.

The burn, like any other open wound, should be cleaned and covered with a dressing. In the field, cleaning can best be done with sterile cotton, liquid soap, and warm, disinfected water. If these materials are not available, the burn should be cleaned in the best way possible. All debris, dirt, and fragments of loose skin must be removed. These measures may be surprisingly painless if carried out gently.

The burn should be covered with a thin layer of an antibacterial ointment such as silver sulfadiazine in a petroleum jelly base (Silvadene®), over which should be layered gauze, a thick bulky dressing, and a snug bandage that applies pressure but does not interfere with blood circulation. The dressing or slings can be used to immobilize a burned extremity and reduce pain. Burned hands should be splinted in the "position of function," the position the hand assumes when holding a pencil (see Fig. 6-2).

Ointments or creams that do not contain appropriate antibacterial agents increase the risk of infection and should not be used.

Subsequent Care

The bandage should be left undisturbed for six to eight days. Changing the dressing increases the risk of introducing dirt and bacteria that could produce an infection. Furthermore, an accurate distinction between partial- and full-thickness burns can be made only about a week after the injury. If the burn is very superficial (first degree) and no blisters are found when the bandage is removed, no further treatment is required. Subsequent bandaging would be needed only to protect a sensitive area from trauma.

Unbroken blisters generally should be left intact. However, the blister fluid is an ideal medium for bacterial growth, and blisters larger than two to three inches (5 to 8 cm) in diameter probably should be opened (without contamination) to reduce the potential for infection. A protective dressing should be applied to prevent rupture of smaller blisters and infection and should be changed every three or four days until healing is complete.

Full-thickness burns six to eight days old are covered by a thick, leathery layer of parched, dead skin that may range in color from white to dark brown or black. The dead skin is usually insensitive to touch. If the depth of the burn—whether it is partial or full thickness—is uncertain, gentle probing with a sterile needle or pin is a good way of testing.

If the burn is full thickness, it should be rebandaged and the subject evacuated. Even under ideal conditions, these wounds essentially always become infected. They require operative care, including skin grafting, which can be provided only in a hospital.

Fluid Replacement

The most urgent aspect of treatment for a major burn is the administration of fluids to prevent or treat shock.

Calculating Fluid Volumes

A convenient formula for determining the volume of intravenous fluids to be administered during the first twenty-four hours following a major burn is:

$$\text{Weight (kg)} \times \text{Percent surface area} \times 3 = \text{Volume of fluid to be administered}$$

The body weight in kilograms (2.2 pounds = 1 kilogram) is multiplied by the percentage of the body surface covered by the burn, and that product multiplied by three equals the volume (in cubic centimeters) of fluids to be given. The percentage of the body area covered by the burn can be estimated from Fig. 8-1.

The fluid requirements for the first twenty-four hours after a burn for a 176-pound (80-kilogram) man with a thirty percent body surface area burn (approximately one arm and one leg) would be:

$$80 \text{ (kg)} \times 30 \text{ (\%)} \times 3 = 7{,}200 \text{ cc}$$

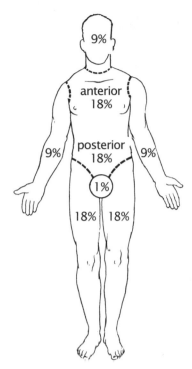

FIGURE 8-1. Percentage of total body surface area of various portions of the body

Approximately half of this fluid should be given in the first eight hours of treatment; the remainder should be given over the next sixteen hours. Although opinions differ about the ideal composition of the fluids, in a wilderness situation saline or Ringer's lactate are almost certain to be the only fluids available.

MONITORING

These calculations illustrate the tremendous volume of fluids required, but such exact volumes can not be given indiscriminately because the severity of the vascular injury produced by the burn and the functional capacity of the subject's heart and kidneys vary widely. (In some burn centers, the product of body weight times burn area is multiplied by four instead of by three.) Careful monitoring of the response to the fluids is just as essential as the calculations. Failure to give enough fluid can lead to shock. Administering too much can overload the cardiovascular system and lead to heart failure, particularly in older individuals who already have reduced cardiac reserve. A fine line separates inadequate fluid replacement and overload, and at high altitude the margin of safety is even narrower.

If the person remains confused or stuporous (in the absence of a head injury), his blood pressure is below normal, his pulse is weak and rapid, and his urinary output is below 50 cc per hour after several hours of treatment, fluids must be administered more rapidly and perhaps in larger quantities. Excessive fluid administration is indicated by a urinary output greater than 75 cc per hour; subcutaneous fluid accumulation causing swelling in unburned tissues, particularly in the legs or over the sacrum; or pooling of fluid in the lungs producing unusual shortness of breath. If these signs are present, the rate of fluid administration must be slowed, occasionally drastically. An indwelling urinary catheter is helpful for monitoring urinary output.

OTHER CONSIDERATIONS

Fluid requirements for individuals with burns covering more than fifty percent of the body surface should be calculated as if the burn were limited to that area. Larger fluid volumes overload the heart if given within twenty-four hours.

A severely burned person is usually thirsty, as are most individuals in shock, but thirst should be controlled with intravenous fluids, because fluids given orally usually cause vomiting and still greater fluid loss. (Fluids lost by vomiting must also be replaced with Ringer's lactate or saline.)

Subsequent Fluid Therapy

During the first twenty-four hours after a burn, Ringer's lactate or saline solutions should be used to replace the fluid and sodium lost into the burned tissues. Thereafter, five percent glucose should be used for fluid replacement. (Few expeditions would carry such fluids, but in some popular trekking areas, such as the southern approach to Everest, some fluids left behind by expeditions are available.)

Once shock has been prevented or corrected, fluid requirements are somewhat greater than normal, but not on the enormous scale of the first day after the burn. Also, the subject may be able to take fluids by mouth with only small (one- to two-liter) intravenous supplements. As always, urine volume is an excellent indicator of fluid status.

By the second or third day after the burn, the blood vessels in the burned tissues begin to recover and the fluids lost into those tissues are reabsorbed and excreted by the kidneys. Large volumes of urine may be passed, but in this recovery stage, fluid intake should not be restricted because the urinary output is high. Fruit juices that have a high potassium content may be particularly beneficial at this time.

Control of Pain

Inexperienced persons often are horrified by the appearance of a major burn and mistakenly administer unneeded pain medications, thinking the wound must be painful. However, the pain from a burn is quite variable. Superficial burns hurt at first but are usually relatively painless once they are covered and not exposed to air. Full-thickness burns are usually less painful because they destroy the nerves and produce anesthesia in the area of injury. In addition, shock tends to dull the pain. If the individual complains, pain should be controlled with as little medication as possible. Drugs stronger than a moderate analgesic are rarely needed. If strong analgesics are necessary, smaller doses (one-half to three-fourths the usual dose) should be tried before resorting to a full dose. Strong analgesics may aggravate the general effects of the burn and are almost never needed. Furthermore, if the individual is in shock when the drugs are administered, they are poorly absorbed. If absorbed later when the shock is corrected, an overdose can result.

Facial Burns

Burns around the face and neck are particularly dangerous because the flames and hot smoke may be inhaled, damaging the lungs. Persons with such injuries must be evacuated with extreme urgency. Burns of the face, nose, mouth, and upper respiratory tract cause swelling and obstruction of the airway. Treatment requires intubation with an endotracheal or nasotracheal tube or creation of an alternate airway by tracheostomy or cricothyroidostomy. If the flames and smoke reach the lower portion of the respiratory tract and the lungs are seared, no effective treatment is possible in the field. If the subject survives the initial injury, the burn and smoke cause fluid to collect in the lung in quantities that are often lethal. Subsequently, severe pneumonia is common. Fortunately such injuries are rare.

Burns of the upper airway should be anticipated after any facial burn, particularly if the skin around the nose and mouth is burned or the nasal hairs are singed. The subject typically becomes hoarse and begins to have difficulty breathing. Wheezes may be heard when listening to his chest. The most critical sign of an airway burn is coughing up black, sooty material, which should be considered diagnostic. Sometimes these signs do not become detectable until twenty-four to forty-eight hours after the injury, so individuals with facial burns must be closely watched.

Oxygen

Oxygen, if available, should probably be administered immediately to all individuals with severe burns occurring at high elevations. Burns can reduce respiratory effectiveness, and at high altitude such persons may not be able to breathe rapidly and deeply enough to compensate for environmental hypoxia. Fires in enclosed quarters such as a small tent, in which air circulation may be further reduced by a covering of snow, produce large amounts of carbon monoxide. An individual burned in such circumstances may have to cope with a reduced oxygen-carrying capacity of his blood due to carbon monoxide poisoning regardless of the altitude. Oxygen may be lifesaving until the subject can be evacuated to lower altitude, particularly for the first hour or two after the burn while the carbon monoxide is being eliminated.

Additional Measures

To prevent secondary streptococcal infection, penicillin G should be administered to individuals with major burns every six hours until they are in the care of a physician.

Individuals with burns covering more than twenty to twenty-five percent of their body surface usually develop paralysis of the stomach and intestine known as ileus. Because they continue to swallow air and saliva, the paralyzed stomach becomes distended and they vomit. To avoid these problems, a nasogastric tube should be inserted and gastric suction should be instituted. (See appendix B, "Therapeutic Procedures.") Fluids lost through the nasogastric tube should be replaced with Ringer's lactate or saline.

Dehydration following a burn, caused by the outpouring of fluids into the tissues, greatly increases the risk of thrombophlebitis. This complication should be anticipated and appropriately treated if it occurs. However, prevention by administering the required fluids and avoiding dehydration is far more desirable.

CHAPTER 9

HEART AND BLOOD VESSEL DISORDERS

PRINCIPAL CONTRIBUTORS:
Herbert N. Hultgren, M.D.
Blair D. Erb, M.D.

The heart and blood vessels circulate blood, which transports oxygen and nutrients to the body tissues and carries away carbon dioxide and "wastes." The heart consists of a four-chambered pump: right atrium, right ventricle, left atrium, and left ventricle. Blood travels from the left ventricle through the aorta and through repeatedly branching smaller and smaller arteries to capillaries barely large enough to permit passage of single red blood cells. In the capillaries, oxygen, carbon dioxide, and other substances are exchanged between blood and tissue. From the capillaries, blood continues its journey as it flows through larger and larger veins to return through the right atrium into the right ventricle. Blood is then pumped from the right ventricle through the lungs, where it replaces the oxygen it has lost and gives off carbon dioxide. It returns through the pulmonary veins and the left atrium to the left ventricle (Fig. 9-1). The result is a "figure-eight" circuit, one loop carrying blood through the lungs, where it is oxygenated, and the other carrying blood to the rest of the body.

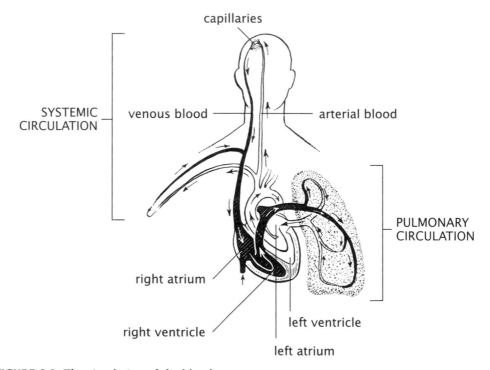

FIGURE 9-1. The circulation of the blood

Four valves permit the heart to function as an efficient pump. The tricuspid and mitral valves in the right and left ventricles close during cardiac contraction (systole), preventing reflux of blood into the atria. Simultaneously the pulmonic and aortic valves open, permitting blood to be pumped into the pulmonary artery and aorta. After systole has been completed and the heart muscle relaxes (diastole), the pulmonic and aortic valves close, preventing reflux of blood into the ventricles, and the tricuspid and mitral valves open, allowing the ventricles to fill.

Peripheral veins in the legs are compressed by the contracting muscles during exercise such as walking, squeezing blood toward the chest. Low pressure in the chest produced by the inspiratory phase of respiration results in a pressure gradient that moves blood from the extremities toward the heart. Consequently, an individual can be said to have "two hearts"—one in the chest that pumps blood through the arteries to the extremities, and a second in the legs, the muscles that pump blood through the veins back to the chest. Valves located in the veins prevent backflow during this process.

Delicate receptors sense blood volume, as well as oxygen and carbon dioxide concentrations, and adjust cardiac output by modifying heart rate and the volume of each heartbeat and hence the amount of blood supplied to different areas of the body. (See chapter 10, "Respiratory Disorders.")

PHYSICAL EXAMINATION OF THE CARDIOVASCULAR SYSTEM

Simple methods for examining the functions of the heart and circulatory system can provide highly significant information, even for inexperienced examiners. The examination should include:

▾ Determining heart rate and rhythm
▾ Judging arterial and venous pressure
▾ Evaluating the peripheral circulation
▾ Listening to the heart and lungs

Heart Rate and Rhythm

The heart rate can be measured most conveniently in the wrist at the base of the thumb, where pulsations in the radial artery can be felt. The pulsations are usually counted for fifteen or twenty seconds and multiplied by four or three to obtain the rate per minute. (Longer counts, sometimes as long as two or three minutes, may be needed for individuals with irregular rhythms.)

In some subjects, particularly those in shock, radial artery pulsations may be too weak to count, and the carotid or femoral pulse must be sought. The carotid pulse can be found on either side of the neck in the groove between the thyroid cartilage (Adam's apple) and the prominent muscle that extends from behind the ear to the top of the sternum (breastbone.) The femoral pulse can be found in the fold where the leg meets the abdomen about midway between the center of the pubic area and the lateral bony edge of the hip. Clothing must be removed before the femoral pulse can be palpated.

If shock is so severe that no pulses can be felt, the heart rate can be determined by listening with a stethoscope placed between the left nipple and the sternum. Each heartbeat is accompanied by two heart sounds of slightly different tone (lubb-dupp, lubb-dupp). Occasionally a faint third sound may be heard (lubb-dupp-dupp, lubb-dupp-dupp). Although heart sounds in normal subjects can be heard with the unaided ear pressed against the chest, the heart sounds are usually faint in shock and a stethoscope is often needed. A little prior practice by the examiner—even listening to his own heart—is useful.

The normal resting heart rate ranges from fifty (in a few well-conditioned individuals) to ninety beats per minute. The heart rate is slower during sleep. At high altitude, the resting heart rate may be as high as 100 beats per minute during the first few days of acclimatization.

Normally the heart rhythm is regular, but in young individuals it may change with respiration—speeding up during inspiration and slowing during expiration. Such variation is normal. When the person holds his breath, the rhythm becomes completely regular.

Arterial and Venous Pressure

When the pulse is barely palpable, the blood pressure is usually low. Strong, "bounding" pulses usually indicate a normal blood pressure and normal heart action. Arterial pulses are usually equal in both wrists, both sides of the neck, and both sides of the groin. Absence of a pulse on one side indicates arterial obstruction or injury.

When healthy persons are lying flat, the partially or fully filled neck veins can be seen extending from the middle of the clavicle (collar bone) to just below the lower jaw. When the subject is sitting upright or even partially upright (semirecumbent), filled neck veins should not be visible above the clavicle. Visible, distended neck veins in an upright position are abnormal and usually indicate heart failure or obstruction of venous blood flow to the heart.

Accurate measurement of blood pressure requires a blood pressure cuff (sphygmomanometer) and stethoscope. The cuff should be wrapped snugly around the arm above the elbow and inflated to a pressure of about 180 mm Hg or until the radial pulse disappears. The stethoscope bell should be placed over the inner aspect of the elbow crease with the arm extended. The pulsations of the brachial artery can often be felt here, and the best position for the stethoscope is over the artery. As the pressure in the inflated cuff is allowed to fall by slowly releasing air through the valve on or near the bulb, a thumping sound synchronous with the pulse appears. The pressure indicated when the sound is first heard is the systolic blood pressure. The pressure at which the sound completely disappears as the cuff pressure continues to fall is the diastolic blood pressure. If the radial pulse can be felt and a stethoscope is not available, the systolic blood pressure can be approximated by inflating the cuff and allowing the pressure to fall until the radial pulse first appears. This pressure is 10 to 20 mm Hg lower than the pressure determined by a stethoscope, but the method is reliable in an emergency. Normal blood pressure ranges from 105 to 140 mm Hg systolic and from 60 to 80 mm Hg diastolic.

Peripheral Circulation

The lips, tongue, and fingernails (nail beds) are normally pink, but when the oxygen concentration in the blood is low, they become blue or purple. This discoloration (cyanosis) is common at high altitudes and is usually severe in high altitude pulmonary edema. At lower elevations, cyanosis usually indicates inadequate oxygenation of the blood by the lungs and is caused by disorders such as airway obstruction, pneumonia, or chest injuries.

When the blood pressure is low and blood flow to the extremities is decreased, the nail beds and lips may be cyanotic even though oxygenation of the blood in the lungs is normal. This type of cyanosis is due to decreased blood flow and is commonly seen in shock.

Edema is an accumulation of excess water in the tissues and is not uncommon in women during the first few days at high altitude due to retention of salt and water. The face may be puffy in the morning, and the feet or ankles may be mildly swollen. More severe edema, particularly if progressive and lasting for more than one week, suggests heart failure or kidney disease and should be investigated.

Individuals who become short of breath with mild exertion, or who experience shortness of breath when lying flat that is relieved by sitting up, usually have fluid accumulations in the lungs (pulmonary edema). In young individuals at high elevations, high altitude pulmonary edema should be suspected. In older individuals at lower elevations, heart failure is a common cause. When listening to the chest of someone with pulmonary edema from any cause, crackling or bubbling sounds (rales) can be heard with each breath. (Asthma usually produces wheezes, or squeaking or groaning sounds, particularly during expiration. Auscultation of the lungs is discussed further in chapter 10, "Respiratory Disorders.")

Written records are vital in the care of anyone suspected to have heart disease. All observations, including the time of the observations, must be recorded. Examinations should be repeated at frequent, regular intervals, such as every two to four hours. Physicians need such records when the individual is evacuated, and they may make possible a prompt, accurate diagnosis by radio or cellular telephone.

HEART DISEASE IN THE WILDERNESS

Heart disease is common in individuals over age fifty, particularly men. However, many persons with heart disease live long and useful lives. Modern therapy, including surgery and medications, has extended life expectancy and reduced symptoms. Current management of heart disease encourages physical activity within specified limits, particularly among older people, and many of these individuals participate in wilderness activities.

In general, heart attacks, heart failure, or other cardiac emergencies are rare among individuals who maintain their physical fitness by regular exercise. Acute heart problems are much more common in individuals who only occasionally participate in vigorous activity, such as hunters or fishermen who are largely sedentary most of the year and participate in their sport only when it is in season. When such individuals engage in strenuous outdoor activities for which they are not physically conditioned, such as forcing their way through heavy underbrush or carrying a heavy pack or deer, heart attacks are much more likely to occur.

The Physician's Role

A person who partakes in wilderness activities without consulting his physician not only risks his own health but imposes upon his companions an unjustifiable responsibility for his care that they may not be prepared to provide. Individuals more than fifty years old who are likely to have coronary disease, or who have evidence of heart disease, should have an electrocardiogram, a chest x-ray, and an exercise test to evaluate their cardiac status and determine the risk of moderate to severe exertion at some distance from medical facilities. (See chapter 22, "Altitude and Common Medical Conditions.") The interview phase of the physician's examination is probably the most important part of the examination before an outing. Because a history of a successful previous similar venture is the best predictor of success in the new activity, the physician must have a clear understanding of the risks of the venture, the characteristics of the environment, and the health status of the individual. An informed decision to accept those risks can be made only with the assistance and recommendations of a concerned physician who understands the lure of wilderness recreation.

The individual must follow his physician's instructions and obtain prescribed medications. The outing leader should be familiar with the treatment the person is receiving and must be alert for complications that require additional care or evacuation. However, the person's physician is responsible for his medical management, not the trip leader. For longer trips or expeditions, the leader should be supplied by the physician with a detailed description of the individual's condition, restrictions on activity that should be observed, medications to be taken, and the anticipated signs or symptoms that could require additional therapy or evacuation.

THE HEART AND ALTITUDE

High altitude poses little threat to a normal heart. The level of exercise an individual can maintain is limited by the tissue oxygen supply. During severe exertion at sea level, oxygen supply is limited by cardiac output. To increase tissue oxygen to a maximum, the heart is pushed to work as hard as possible.

At high elevations, the oxygen supply to the tissues is limited by the smaller amount of oxygen in the atmosphere, not by cardiac output. As a result, the heart can not work at a maximal level. In fact, during maximal exercise at high altitude, the heart rate, which is a rough guide to the cardiac work being performed, is lower at maximal exercise than at sea level. If cardiac performance during exercise is normal at sea level, it will be normal at high altitude.

MAJOR HEART DISEASES

Coronary artery disease is the most common form of heart disease in men and women over age fifty. Progressive narrowing of the arteries that supply the heart results from deposits of cholesterol and other fats on the inner surface of the arteries (arteriosclerosis, or "hardening of the arteries") and can produce chest pain (angina pectoris), a heart attack (myocardial infarction), heart failure (cardiac dyspnea), or sudden death. Rupture of one of these fat deposits, or thrombosis where an artery is narrowed by such deposits, further impairs the cardiac blood supply and may cause angina, increase the severity of preexisting angina, or produce an acute myocardial infarction.

Angina Pectoris

Angina pectoris (or simply angina) is a sensation of pressure or deep-seated pain beneath the sternum that characteristically appears during exercise and disappears after a few minutes of rest. The discomfort may be described as crushing, a sensation of being squeezed, a feeling as if a weight were on the chest, a feeling as if a band were around the chest, or a deep burning sensation. It may be felt in the neck, jaws, or arms, as well as in the chest. If exercise is continued, the discomfort increases; pain is relieved by rest and nitroglycerin. The discomfort is predictable and rarely occurs at rest except during periods of emotional stress. Its duration is rarely longer than fifteen to thirty minutes. Angina is frequently accompanied by shortness of breath, which subsides as the discomfort eases.

Individuals who have suffered episodes of angina must bring nitroglycerin tablets with them into the wilderness. A person suffering angina should hold one of these tablets under his tongue until it has dissolved. Two or three tablets taken at three- to five-minute intervals may be necessary for relief. Nitroglycerin tablets should be kept in their original brown glass bottle with a metal screw cap and should not be kept longer than six months after purchase. Cotton wads should not be kept in the bottle, which should be tightly capped and kept away from heat and moisture to reduce or prevent loss of potency.

Individuals with only mild angina at sea level may experience increased symptoms during the first few days at higher altitudes. A decrease in physical activity, additional medications, and oxygen usually control the symptoms. If the person has medications such as beta blockers or calcium channel blockers, the dose may be cautiously increased. However, if symptoms persist, the individual should descend. (See chapter 22, "Altitude and Common Medical Conditions.")

Individuals with mild angina may safely take part in mildly strenuous outdoor activities if they follow their physician's instructions, do not overexert, and carry nitroglycerin tablets to relieve episodes of pain. Their low risk for catastrophic cardiac events must be established by appropriate studies, including an exercise test. They should be able to carry out moderately strenuous, continuous exercise, such as hill walking for several hours a day with minimal or no symptoms. Trips to remote areas far from medical facilities or prompt evacuation are not advisable.

Individuals who develop angina for the first time, or who experience unusually frequent or severe attacks of angina, should lie down, completely at rest, and should take nitroglycerin if it is available. Absolute rest, preferably with sedation, should be continued for at least six to eight hours—longer if the anginal episodes persist—after which the person should be evacuated with as little exertion as possible, preferably transported. Angina is an indication of severe heart disease and often is a prelude to a more serious event such as an infarct.

Myocardial Infarction

Myocardial infarction may occur in someone who has had angina, or it may occur in an individual who has never had chest pain. It is caused by obstruction of one of the arteries to the heart, usually by a blood clot, that results in death (necrosis or infarction) of part of the heart muscle.

Myocardial infarction is a common cause of sudden death and is a major medical emergency. Chest pain is the most common initial symptom and may appear at rest or during exercise. The pain resembles angina pectoris but is usually more severe, may last one to six hours, and usually is not relieved by nitroglycerin. Other frequent symptoms and signs are nausea, vomiting, difficulty in breathing, weakness, sweating, pallor, cyanosis, and cold extremities. The blood pressure may be low; the heart rate may be slow and irregular. (Elderly individuals may have an acute infarction with little or no chest pain.)

The person should lie down immediately and rest completely. Nitroglycerin should be tried, although it usually is ineffective. If the pain is not relieved in ten to fifteen minutes, a strong analgesic should be administered every two hours until the pain is relieved. If the individual is agitated, a tranquilizer should be given. If oxygen is available, it should be administered at a flow rate of four to six liters per minute with a face mask. If the person is short of breath, coughing, and can breathe more easily sitting up, he should be permitted to do so, preferably supported by a back rest. (Administration of oxygen should be continued.) Prompt evacuation, preferably by helicopter, is essential. A physician or advanced emergency medical technician should accompany the helicopter; cardiac resuscitation may be necessary at any moment.

Cardiac Dyspnea

Cardiac dyspnea is undue shortness of breath caused by heart disease and is indicative of heart failure. Dyspnea occurs with exercise but sometimes develops at night. The person awakens with a sense of suffocation and feels compelled to sit up or move out into fresh air to obtain relief. He is usually anxious, is breathing fast, and has a rapid heart rate. Rales or crackling sounds indicative of fluid in the lungs may be heard when listening to the chest.

Questioning usually discloses a history of high blood pressure, angina, a prior heart attack, or a heart murmur. In the few individuals who have no history of cardiac disease, the heart failure may be the result of an asymptomatic (silent) myocardial infarction or a marked rise in blood pressure. Nitroglycerin may be helpful, particularly if the blood pressure is high. Complete rest, sedation, oxygen, and a diuretic are the usual methods of treatment. The subject should be evacuated after twelve to twenty-four hours of rest with as little effort on his part as possible. If the dyspnea is severe, oxygen and a strong analgesic should be given even though no pain is present.

At high elevations, high altitude pulmonary edema should be considered, particularly if the subject has no history of heart disease and has recently ascended to that elevation. If high altitude pulmonary edema is suspected, rest, oxygen, and assisted descent to a lower altitude are necessary.

Sudden Death

Sudden death—instantaneous or within a few minutes of the onset of symptoms—is very rare in well-conditioned outdoorsmen who have never had symptoms of heart disease. The underlying cause in most cases is arteriosclerotic coronary artery disease, which may not have been suspected by the subject or the physician. Individuals who have a family history of sudden death, have high blood pressure, smoke, have high blood cholesterol concentrations, and have a sedentary lifestyle are predisposed to coronary disease. Investigation of sudden death during jogging or running has revealed that most of the individuals were known to have coronary artery disease or had experienced episodes of chest pain during exercise. Had they obtained a treadmill exercise test, the underlying coronary disease would probably have been detected.

Valvular Heart Disease

Many persons who have deformities of heart valves that cause heart murmurs are capable of strenuous physical effort without difficulty. However, with some types of valvular heart disease, such activities may produce complications such as cardiac failure, atrial fibrillation, or stroke. Any individual with a heart murmur or valvular heart disease should consult a physician to determine whether he should take part in wilderness activities. Leaders of an outing must be informed of that person's activity limits, medications to be taken, and complications that might be expected.

Noncardiac Chest Pain

Chest pain in most individuals is not a sign of heart disease, although an unfortunate number fear it is. Several common types of chest pain not related to heart disease are:

▼ Aching and soreness due to muscular effort. After unaccustomed physical work involving the arms and shoulders, such as climbing, cross-country skiing, carrying a heavy pack, or cutting wood, pain may be present in the upper chest muscles for two to three days. The ache is usually constant and may be aggravated by motion, and the muscles may be tender. Aspirin, ibuprofen, or acetaminophen, codeine, and rest are effective treatment. Reassurance should be provided.

▼ Chest discomfort due to anxiety. Nervous, anxious, or fearful individuals may notice a sensation of pressure in the chest that is associated with a sense of suffocation, trembling, dizziness, and occasionally numbness of the lips and fingers. The heart rate may be increased. Reassurance, rest, and mild sedation are usually the only measures needed. (See Hyperventilation Syndrome in chapter 10, "Respiratory Disorders.")

▼ Aching pain over the heart. After heavy exertion, some individuals note an aching pain over the area of the left nipple. The pain may be constant or intermittent and is often worse at night. Reassurance, rest, and a mild analgesic are all that is usually needed.

▼ Heartburn. A burning pain below the end of the breast bone, sometimes extending upward into the throat or jaw, may be noted after a meal, excessive consumption of spicy foods, coffee, tea, or alcohol, or the use of carbonated beverages. The discomfort is not related to effort and may last for one to three hours. Heartburn should not be mistaken for angina. Antacids or milk, smaller meals, rest, and reassurance are the most appropriate management. (See chapter 12, "Gastrointestinal Disorders.")

DISORDERS OF CARDIAC RHYTHM

Paroxysmal Tachycardia

Paroxysmal atrial tachycardia is characterized by a very rapid but entirely regular heart rate, sudden in onset, that is associated with a sensation of pounding in the chest, weakness, dizziness, and shortness of breath. True syncope (unconsciousness) is rare. The heart rate is very rapid (150 to 220 beats per minute or more) and completely regular. The pulses may be so weak that listening to the heart with a stethoscope is necessary to determine the rate. (When beating so rapidly, the heart does not have time to fill between contractions and the amount of blood pumped with each heartbeat decreases.) Individuals may have previously experienced similar attacks.

Preferably, the subject should rest and let the episode stop spontaneously. However, if the tachycardia does not stop within ten to fifteen minutes, a few simple maneuvers may be tried. The person can try forcefully blowing against pressure such as a paper bag or an air mattress. If that is unsuccessful, he can try holding his breath as long as possible. Inserting a tongue blade or a spoon handle in the back of the throat and making him gag may stop the attack. Immersing his face in water for as long as he can hold his breath sometimes works. If the individual has lost consciousness, a sharp blow over the heart with the edge of the hand (a "karate chop") may help. (The person obviously should be warned in advance, and the blow must not be heavy enough to fracture ribs!) In some instances, standing the person on his head has terminated episodes of tachycardia.

If these measures fail, the right carotid artery can be massaged, gently at first, but firmly if necessary. The subject usually is immediately aware that the attack has ended. Digitalis may prevent recurrent attacks. Because episodes of tachycardia tend to recur, the individual may require evacuation, particularly if the attack is his first and control has been difficult. However, paroxysmal tachycardia is almost never a sign of imminent cardiac disease.

Atrial Fibrillation

Atrial fibrillation is a rapid but irregular heartbeat (Fig. 9-2). The heart rate may be 100 to 180 beats per minute, and the onset may be sudden and resemble paroxysmal tachycardia. The important

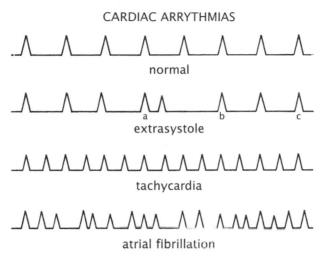

CARDIAC ARRYTHMIAS

normal

extrasystole

tachycardia

atrial fibrillation

FIGURE 9-2. Diagrammatic comparison of normal and abnormal cardiac rhythms. (Note: interval ab = interval bc.)

difference is the totally irregular rhythm of atrial fibrillation. Careful palpation of the pulse and listening to the heart may be necessary to be sure of the irregularity. At rates exceeding 160 beats per minute, irregularities are difficult to detect. Rest and sedation should be instituted. Normal heart action frequently returns spontaneously after a few hours. Maneuvers that stop paroxysmal tachycardia may not be of value for atrial fibrillation. If the attack does not respond to rest and sedation within twelve to twenty-four hours, the subject should be evacuated. Atrial fibrillation is a more significant disorder that may be a sign of serious heart disease.

Digitalis

Digitalis may be advisable if evacuation of a person with uncontrollable rhythm disturbances is difficult or unavoidably delayed. If the cardiac rhythm has not returned to normal within twelve to twenty-four hours, 0.25 mg of digoxin may be given every two hours until a total dose of 1.5 mg (six 0.25 mg tablets) has been administered. (The subject must not have taken digitalis during the previous week.) If irregularities persist and evacuation is impossible, an additional 0.25 mg of digoxin may be given once daily. The individual must rest; he should be sedated if necessary. Adequate fluids must be given to prevent the formation of clots that could cause embolism or a stroke in the irregularly beating heart. If nausea or vomiting occurs or the heart rate slows to less than sixty beats per minute, digoxin should be discontinued because these are signs of an overdose.

Syncope (Fainting)

Syncope is a transient loss of consciousness commonly referred to as fainting. Two general varieties are encountered.

- ▾ True syncope is complete loss of consciousness. The individual falls down, can not be aroused, and may display seizure activity. The duration may be seconds or minutes.
- ▾ Partial syncope is an incomplete loss of consciousness. The person feels "weak" or "faint" and slumps to a chair, a bed, or the floor, but consciousness and communication are maintained. After a few minutes the subject recovers but remains weak and unsteady for several minutes.

True syncope is present in only ten to twenty percent of the individuals referred to physicians with that diagnosis. Partial, or near, syncope makes up the rest. True syncope is a serious symptom, particularly if it has occurred more than once and without warning, and should be investigated in a hospital where sophisticated diagnostic studies can be performed. Many serious conditions, including brain tumors, heart tumors, and cardiac arrhythmias, may cause true syncope.

Most instances of partial syncope—and some cases of true syncope—are vascular or "vasovagal" in origin and also are situational. Common provocations are a crowded, overheated room, the sight of blood, recent arrival at high altitude, a large meal, or prolonged standing. In rare instances, partial syncope may occur during or immediately after heavy exertion, but in the absence of cardiac disease most such episodes are vasovagal also.

An individual with partial syncope typically becomes pale, sweaty, weak, and anxious. His pulse is usually slow and regular, but it may be weak. A history of similar episodes may be obtained.

Partial syncope can be avoided by having the person sit down with his head between his knees or lie down with his legs elevated. Fresh air and a cold, wet towel for his face usually aid recovery. If the individual has no history of cardiac disease or episodes of true syncope, hospitalization is not necessary. Precautions to prevent subsequent episodes should be observed.

Partial syncope may occur as a result of postural hypotension, a fall in blood pressure upon assuming an erect posture. The individual experiences faintness upon standing after a prolonged period of lying down or sitting, such as upon arising in the morning or after a large meal, particularly when alcoholic beverages have been consumed. The diagnosis is made by measuring the blood pressure in the supine position and in a standing position. A fall in systolic pressure of more than 20 mm Hg upon standing is abnormal. Postural hypotension is a common problem in persons who are receiving drug therapy for high blood pressure or coronary artery disease. Reassurance and a decrease in the medication dose are usually the only necessary measures.

Individuals who are more than sixty years old have a higher incidence of true syncope resulting from cardiac disease and are less likely to have benign, vasodepressor syncopal attacks. Such persons also are more susceptible to postural hypotension, particularly if medications for hypertension are being taken.

Cardiac Syncope

Cardiac syncope, usually a form of true syncope, is loss of consciousness caused by heart disease. Two forms are recognized: exertional and arrhythmic. Exertional syncope occurs during a burst of heavy effort such as walking fast uphill. Unconsciousness may occur suddenly or may be preceded by a "gray out" sensation, severe dizziness, or weakness. Convulsive movements may occur. Exertional syncope most frequently occurs in individuals with aortic stenosis (narrowing of the outlet valve from the left ventricle) but is occasionally seen in people with other forms of heart disease. Most affected individuals have a history of similar episodes.

Arrhythmic syncope occurs as the result of an abnormal cardiac rhythm, either a sudden increase in heart rate (tachycardia) or a marked slowing or temporary cessation of the heartbeat (heart block). The episode may occur suddenly, without warning, and the person may fall and be injured.

The blood pressure should be measured, the heart rate should be determined, and the rhythm should be evaluated. The individual should rest, with sedation if needed, for six to twelve hours and then be evacuated to a physician's care. Cardiac syncope may be an early warning of heart disease that can cause sudden death.

MINOR DISTURBANCES OF CARDIAC RHYTHM

Sinus Tachycardia

An anxious individual, after heavy exertion or at high altitude, may become aware of the pounding in his chest of a rapid, forceful heartbeat and fear he has heart disease. If the heart rate does not exceed 120 beats per minute and gradually slows with rest and sedation, a diagnosis of harmless sinus tachycardia may be made. No specific treatment except rest and reassurance is necessary.

Extrasystoles ("Skipped Beats")

Healthy individuals may notice occasional irregular thumping or "fluttering" sensations in their chest, particularly at rest or during the night. They may feel their pulse and notice occasional pauses between beats. Such irregular beats are called extrasystoles and are of no significance unless the person clearly has heart disease manifested by angina, myocardial infarction, or cardiac dyspnea. Rest and reassurance are usually the only measures needed. Avoiding stimulants such as coffee and tea or tobacco often entirely eliminates extrasystoles. Extrasystoles may be exacerbated at high altitude. (See chapter 22, "Altitude and Common Medical Conditions.")

If a bothersome irregularity of the heartbeat persists, if the skipped beats occur more than five times per minute, or if such irregularities have never been experienced before, evacuation to a physician's care may be desirable.

HIGH BLOOD PRESSURE (HYPERTENSION)

Ten to twenty percent of the over-forty population of the United States has an elevated blood pressure, and many individuals with high blood pressure pursue wilderness activities. For such individuals to be safe, the following guidelines should be observed:

- ▼ Persons with mild or drug-controlled hypertension should partake in wilderness activities only after consulting a sympathetic physician. On an outing, such individuals must supply their own medications and follow their physicians' recommendations carefully. Fluid intake should be adequate, and their diet should be low in salt and protein.
- ▼ Individuals with severe, uncontrolled hypertension, or complications of hypertension, should not venture into remote wilderness areas. The complications of uncontrolled hypertension—strokes, heart failure, coronary artery disease, decreased visual acuity, and kidney failure—could be disastrous in such situations.

Individuals with moderately high blood pressure may experience complications with which wilderness outing leaders should be familiar. These complications include cardiac dyspnea, angina pectoris, stroke, and severe headache, any of which is an indication for prompt evacuation.

Some persons with only moderate hypertension have periodic episodes of severe blood pressure elevation. Such episodes are typically associated with severe headache, confusion, forgetfulness, visual impairment, slurred speech, and other neurologic signs and symptoms. The blood pressure should be measured if such symptoms appear. If the systolic pressure exceeds 200 mm Hg, the individual should be forced to rest, with sedation if needed, and nitroglycerin should be given every hour to reduce the pressure. Evacuation should be arranged after six to twelve hours.

Some hypertensive persons experience an increase in pressure at high altitudes. The rise in pressure, which usually is not detectable unless the blood pressure is measured, is usually evident within one to two days at altitudes such as 6,000 feet (1,800 m). Individuals who have a significant rise in pressure at such moderate altitudes should consult their physicians, who may increase medication dosage when at high altitudes or may advise not going to high elevations at all. (See chapter 22, "Altitude and Common Medical Conditions.")

Individuals taking certain types of medication for high blood pressure (such as propranolol, a beta blocker) may not experience the usual increase in heart rate at high altitude. Some develop orthostatic hypotension. Individuals on a diuretic must continue to take potassium supplements if recommended by their physician. Diuretic-induced potassium depletion can result in muscular weakness but is relieved by potassium-rich foods such as dried fruits, nuts, soups, and fruit juices.

VASCULAR DISEASE

Claudication

Older individuals with arteriosclerosis of the arteries in their legs may experience pain in their calves, hips, buttocks, or thighs while walking uphill, particularly when carrying a heavy load. The pain occurs during effort, becomes more severe as effort is continued, and is relieved by rest. The medical term for this condition is claudication. When severe, it can appear while strolling on level terrain.

Claudication should be distinguished from common leg cramps, which occur at rest or during the night, are characterized by painful contraction of the muscles—not just pain—and usually involve the calf or foot.

If claudication is mild, a slower pace and a lighter load may permit the individual to continue. Smoking increases the severity of claudication and should be avoided. If claudication suddenly becomes severe or appears for the first time in the wilderness, the person should be evacuated with minimal effort on his part.

Varicose Veins

The veins of the extremities have numerous small valves within them to ensure that blood flows only in the direction of the heart. The blood pressure in veins is so low that the increase in intrathoracic or intra-abdominal pressure associated with straining or strenuous exercise would reverse the direction of the venous blood flow if these valves were not present.

In some individuals, the valves in the leg veins become incompetent, the direction of blood flow is no longer controlled, and the veins become dilated and tortuous (varicose). The return of venous blood from the limb to the heart may be impaired, causing persons with varicose veins to complain of aching in their legs, particularly after they have been on their feet for a prolonged period. The condition should be corrected surgically (by removing or ligating the affected veins) because it can lead to ulceration of the skin and other complications. The results are more satisfactory when surgical therapy is instituted early.

The greatest significance of varicose veins in the wilderness lies in the tendency for this disorder to increase fatigability of the legs and limit endurance. A second problem is the greater tendency for veins in the legs to thrombose as the result of stasis associated with the reduced venous blood flow typical of varicose veins. A less common problem is caused by the presence of greatly enlarged blood vessels just beneath the skin. Minor injuries that ordinarily would go unnoticed can penetrate one of these veins and produce relatively severe bleeding. Although the hemorrhage can be easily controlled, a person with varicose veins should be aware of this danger.

Individuals with varicose veins should consult a physician about proper management of their condition.

In the wilderness, persons with painful varicose veins should be encouraged to elevate their legs on pillows or a soft pad during rest stops to decrease the pressure within the veins. The pillow must not be placed immediately behind the knee, where it would compress the veins and reduce circulation. Relief may be obtained with a smooth elastic bandage or elastic stocking, which should be applied when the person is lying on his back and the veins are collapsed. (The bandages or stockings should be removed at night.) A hard knot or cord that is inflamed and tender indicates the blood in one or more of the enlarged veins has clotted. Thrombosis of such superficial veins is rarely a problem except for the discomfort. However, swelling of the foot or leg beyond the area where clotting has occurred is indicative of associated clotting of the deeper veins. Redness, swelling, and tenderness in the calf may be an indication of thrombophlebitis with its risk of clotting and embolism. To avoid pulmonary embolism, the individual should be treated as described in chapter 10, "Respiratory Disorders."

Table 9-1	Body Signals

PRIMARY

Cardiovascular
  Heart rate
  Pounding in the head (particularly in the temples)
  Chest pain, physiologic or pathologic
  Abnormal rhythms

Respiratory
  Mouth breathing begins at sixty percent of maximal physical capacity
  Can not hold a conversation above eighty-five percent of maximal capacity
  Air hunger
  Cough
  Periodic breathing associated with hypoxia and restless sleep
  Cyanosis

SECONDARY

Musculoskeletal
  Tremulousness in legs, knee pain, cramps
  Shivering
  Sweating

Gastrointestinal
  Abdominal distention
  Flatus associated with high altitude
  Loss of appetite associated with high altitude
  Dry mouth associated with high altitude

Genitourinary
  Urinary frequency (diuresis) associated with climbing

Sensory
  Visual changes: tunnel vision (associated with high altitude); loss of color discrimination (associated with high altitude); loss of night vision (associated with high altitude); central white spot (associated with high altitude)
  Diminished sense of touch
  Diminished sense of taste
  Diminished sense of smell (associated with high altitude)

Neurologic
  Headache
  Lack of analytical decisiveness
  Confusion or irrational behavior

PHYSICAL ACTIVITY IN THE WILDERNESS

The common denominator of outdoor ventures is physical activity, which increases the need for blood, oxygen, and nutrients in the muscles. The resulting demands placed on the heart and circulation may precipitate cardiovascular emergencies such as angina or myocardial infarction, rhythm disturbance, or heart failure, particularly in a hostile environment such as high altitude or cold weather.

Matching individual capacities with the characteristics of a proposed wilderness venture is useful.

One such classification divides ventures into four levels according to their physiologic demands:
- ▼ Extreme performance ventures such as high altitude Himalayan climbing
- ▼ High performance ventures such as hunting in the Rocky Mountains
- ▼ Recreational activities such as trail walking in national parks
- ▼ Therapeutic activities such as the highly individualized components of cardiac rehabilitation

The health status of participants can be matched with the nature of the venture. One such classification divides participants into five categories:
- ▼ Demonstrated high performance individuals
- ▼ Healthy vigorous individuals
- ▼ Healthy "deconditioned" individuals
- ▼ Persons at risk for the occurrence of disease
- ▼ Individuals who are manifestly ill

An experienced physician, in cooperation with the venture leader, may estimate the degree of risk for each individual. Safety can not be guaranteed, of course, but a scheme of this type may help match individuals with an appropriate venture and develop a smoothly functioning team.

Body Signals

An array of physiologic changes occurs during physical activity, and athletes learn to recognize them. They are useful for estimating the intensity of an activity and indicating the physiologic reserve remaining. These signs are referred to as "body signals" (Table 9-1).

Cardiovascular signals include heart rate, pounding in the chest or head, and chest pain and provide a useful marker for intensity of activity. Respiratory signals are also useful for this purpose or for pacing an activity. Mouth breathing, for example, occurs at about sixty percent of maximal capacity. Most activities of daily living are below thirty-five percent of maximal functional capacity.

Catecholamines such as adrenaline increase in linear fashion until approximately the sixty percent level is reached (the point at which mouth breathing begins). Above that level, the increase becomes much faster. Above eighty-five percent of maximal capacity (a level at which an individual can no longer hold a conversation), catecholamines increase almost exponentially, placing an individual with heart disease at risk of rhythm disturbances or a heart attack.

Other sensory symptoms may also be helpful in evaluating the intensity of physical activity. For example, tunnel vision—a narrowing of the visual fields—is noted during exertion at high altitude when an individual becomes hypoxic.

ADDITIONAL READING

Erb B: Predictors of Success in Wilderness Ventures: Physical Activity, the Environment and Fatigue. *Wild Med Lett* 1990; 7:8-9.

Erb B: Medical Selection of Participants in Wilderness Ventures. Syllabus, The Second World Congress on Wilderness Medicine, Wilderness Medical Society, 1995; pp 489-494.

Erb B: Human Performance in the Wilderness. Syllabus, The Second World Congress on Wilderness Medicine, Wilderness Medical Society, 1995; pp 343-349.

Hultgren H: Coronary Heart Disease and Trekking. *J Wild Med* 1990; 1:154-161.

Rennie D: Will Mountain Trekkers Have Heart Attacks? *JAMA* 1989; 261:1045-1046.

Sokolow M, McIlroy M, and Cheitlin M: *Clinical Cardiology.* Norwalk, Conn.: Lange, 1990.

CHAPTER 10

RESPIRATORY DISORDERS

PRINCIPAL CONTRIBUTOR:
Colin K. Grissom, M.D.

The respiratory system moves air in and out of the lungs to provide oxygen for the body and to eliminate carbon dioxide. The components of this system are the upper respiratory tract, the lower respiratory tract, the bellows, and the control system (Fig. 10-1):

▼ The upper respiratory tract includes the nose, mouth, and larynx (vocal cords and voice box). On inspiration, air moves through the upper respiratory tract and is filtered to remove foreign particles, saturated with water, and warmed to body temperature.

▼ The lower respiratory tract starts with the trachea just below the larynx and includes the divisions of the airways down to the alveoli, or microscopic air sacs, that make up the major

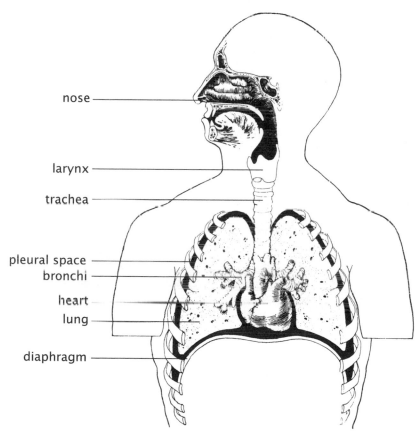

nose

larynx

trachea

pleural space
bronchi

heart
lung

diaphragm

FIGURE 10-1. Anatomy of the respiratory system

117

portion of the lung tissue, and in which oxygen and carbon dioxide are exchanged between blood and air. The trachea descends into the chest and divides into the right and left bronchi that supply air to each lung. The bronchi then repeatedly subdivide in each lung until, after some twenty-three divisions, the alveoli are reached. In the alveoli only a very thin membrane separates air in the sacs and blood in pulmonary capillaries.

▼ The bellows: during inspiration the diaphragm contracts and lowers, causing the chest wall to expand, which moves air into the lungs. During exercise, muscles of the neck and muscles between the ribs may also assist with expanding the chest. Expiration, or movement of air out of the lungs, occurs passively at rest as the diaphragm and chest wall relax. During heavy exercise, contraction of the abdominal muscles may assist with expiration by forcing air out of the lungs. A thin membrane, the pleura, covers the lungs, lines the inner surface of the chest wall, and eases the movement of the lungs within the chest.

▼ The control system consists of sensing cells that detect chemical changes in the circulating blood (chemoreceptors); sensing cells that detect movements of the chest wall, diaphragm, and lungs (neuroreceptors); and the network of nerves that carries information from these receptors to the brain, which controls the rate and depth of respiration.

Respiratory movements are controlled by a complex system of receptors, transmitters, and effectors throughout the body. Chemical receptors respond to lower oxygen, an increase or decrease of carbon dioxide, and a change in the acidity of the blood. These receptors signal the brain to increase or decrease the rate and depth of breathing (ventilation). One set of special receptor cells in the neck is called the carotid bodies. Other receptor cells are situated deep within a part of the brain called the respiratory center and respond to changes in the blood circulating through the brain and in the spinal fluid that bathes the brain.

Under ordinary resting conditions, approximately one-half liter of air is inspired with each breath. The normal respiratory rate is ten to twelve breaths per minute, and the corresponding normal breathing volume is five to six liters per minute. This volume is called the "tidal volume." After inhaling as deeply as possible, the total volume of air that can be forcefully exhaled is called the "vital capacity." The volume of air expired in the first second is called the "forced expiratory volume in one second." All three are commonly used measures of lung function. Even after a full forceful expiration, some air in the lungs can not be exhaled; this is called the "residual volume."

Sleep causes a decrease in the rate and depth of breathing—hypoventilation—that may result in a decreased blood oxygenation, particularly at high altitude. In contrast, exertion greatly increases ventilation because it increases the need for oxygen and the need for eliminating carbon dioxide. These demands stimulate the respiratory center in the brain to increase the respiratory volume to as much as 150 liters per minute during vigorous exercise. Even at rapid respiratory rates, the lungs supply oxygen to the blood and take up carbon dioxide with extraordinary efficiency and precision.

A variety of disorders can affect the function of the respiratory system. Head injuries or diseases of the brain may increase or decrease breathing. Airway obstruction can result from aspirated material or from injuries to the throat, usually sudden, and may halt effective breathing. Injury of the chest wall producing rib fractures can impair the bellows action of the chest wall and diaphragm. Even chest wall injuries without rib fractures can cause pain with inspiration that leads to splinting—not expanding the chest as much on the injured side. Air, blood, or fluid within the chest cavity may compress the lungs and prevent expansion during inspiration. An injury that damages the lung in such a way that inhaled air continuously leaks into the space between the lung and chest wall but can not be exhaled (tension pneumothorax) is life-threatening. Collections of fluid in the alveoli due to edema or infection can block the exchange of gases between inhaled air and blood.

Injury to the brain resulting in swelling or bleeding may depress the respiratory control system and cause hypoventilation. Sedative or analgesic drugs may also depress the respiratory control system, resulting in hypoventilation. In contrast, hyperventilation, an increase in the depth and rate of breathing, may occur in response to increased acid in the blood caused by kidney disease, uncontrolled diabetes, shock, or ingested toxic chemical agents or drugs.

SYMPTOMS

The principal symptoms produced by diseases of the lungs are shortness of breath (air hunger), cough, pain, and fever. All must be considered in order to diagnose the disorder that has caused them.

Shortness of Breath
- ▼ How and when did it begin?
- ▼ How is it affected by position?
- ▼ What makes it worse—or better?

Cough
- ▼ Is the cough dry or productive (sputum is coughed up)?
- ▼ What kind of material is coughed up?
- ▼ Does it contain blood, pus, or foreign material?

Pain
- ▼ Where is the pain?
- ▼ Did it begin suddenly or gradually?
- ▼ Is the pain mild or severe?
- ▼ What makes it worse?
- ▼ Is the pain stabbing, sharp, dull, or crushing?
- ▼ Is the pain constant or intermittent?
- ▼ How is the pain related to breathing?
- ▼ How is the pain related to other symptoms?

Fever
- ▼ How high is the temperature?
- ▼ Did it rise suddenly or gradually?
- ▼ Have chills or sweating occurred?

Many illnesses or injuries cause shortness of breath. At altitudes above 8,000 feet (2,400 m), shortness of breath with cough may indicate early high altitude pulmonary edema (HAPE). Because HAPE may progress rapidly to a life-threatening problem, early detection is important.

A persistent, dry, hacking cough is common at high altitude due to drying and irritation of the throat and is called altitude bronchitis. This form of bronchitis, or inflammation of the breathing tubes, is not due to infection but rather to breathing dry air. Cough at altitude, however, may also indicate lung disease or the presence of fluid in the lungs. Usually such fluid is reabsorbed, but it may develop into HAPE. The sputum is usually thin, watery, and pink or bloody with HAPE. (See chapter 21, "Disorders Caused by Altitude.") The cough due to infections of the lung is deeper and usually produces sputum that is green, yellow, or rust colored, and thick and stringy. With pulmonary embolism the sputum is usually bloody.

Pleuritic chest pain is pain caused by diseases of the lung with inflammation of the pleura, or injuries of the chest wall, and characteristically changes with respiratory movements. Deep inspiration typically causes sharp, stabbing pain. Pain that is dull or crushing and constant is more typical of heart disease. (See chapter 9, "Heart and Blood Vessel Disorders.")

PHYSICAL EXAMINATION

Even though the problem appears to be in the lungs, a complete physical examination should be performed. A rapid, hard pulse associated with fever is indicative of significant disease. Fever is usually a sign of infection, but it may occur with pulmonary embolism or high altitude pulmonary edema. Serious infection anywhere in the body causes fever, rapid pulse, and shortness of breath.

The first step in examining the chest is careful observation. Breathing difficulty, irregularities of respiratory rhythm, and differences in movement of the two sides of the chest are important. Obvious signs include rapid or labored breathing; shallow, irregular, or noisy breathing; and cyanosis (bluish discoloration) of the lips, nails, or skin. Flaring of the nostrils and tensing of the neck muscles are signs of severe respiratory difficulty. Efforts to breathe that do not move the chest indicate upper airway obstruction.

The respiratory rhythm should be observed while counting the rate. Minor changes of rhythm are of no significance; important irregularities are hard to overlook. In contrast, differences in the movements of the two sides of the chest may be subtle and should be sought during quiet respiration as well as during deep breathing.

Auscultation consists of listening to the sounds made by air passing in and out of the lung. A stethoscope makes the sounds easier to hear and is more convenient, but the sounds can be heard by pressing the unaided ear against the bare chest. Clothing must be removed or important sounds and signs may be missed.

Quiet breathing by normal lungs produces sounds so faint that they are barely audible except with a stethoscope. The person being examined must be instructed to breathe deeply through his mouth during the examination to amplify these sounds. All portions of the lungs should be examined to be sure no abnormalities are missed and the extent of any disease is recognized.

Many diseases of the lung cause fluid to collect in the small bronchi and alveoli, producing crackling sounds on inspiration known as rales. Fluid accumulation is typical of infection or edema of the lungs. A high-pitched sound heard on expiration, called wheezing, is more indicative of asthma or chronic lung disease due to cigarette smoking (chronic bronchitis or emphysema). With severe pneumonia or pulmonary embolism, a portion of the lung is often consolidated or airless due to fluid and inflammatory exudate in the alveolar sacs. Over these areas, the breath sounds are harsher and louder because consolidated lung transmits breath sounds from the bronchial tubes very effectively. They are called bronchial breath sounds because they are similar to the sounds heard directly over the trachea.

Infection or an embolus often produces inflammation of the pleura overlying the involved lung, which makes the pleural surface rough. Because the pleural surfaces no longer slide smoothly over each other, movement of the lung during respiration produces a squeaking sound similar to pieces of leather being rubbed together. This sound is called a "friction rub" or simply a "rub." Pain with a rub indicates pleurisy but does not define its cause.

If no sounds whatever are heard over a portion of the chest, fluid or air is usually in the space between the lung and the chest wall. Rarely, the absence of breath sounds may be due to obstruction of a large airway leading to that portion of the lung.

Auscultation of the lung, although it requires practice and experience, is not too difficult to learn and can be a valuable diagnostic aid, particularly in a remote wilderness situation.

CHRONIC LUNG DISEASE

The most common forms of chronic lung disease are asthma, chronic bronchitis, and emphysema. All of these are obstructive lung diseases characterized by increased resistance to airflow. Chronic bronchitis and emphysema are often associated with cigarette smoking. Chronic bronchitis is characterized by a chronic productive cough due to irritation of the airways. Emphysema, which is characterized by progressive destruction of lung tissue, results in loss of alveoli for exchange of oxygen and carbon dioxide. Asthma may occur in both younger and older persons and is characterized by intermittent episodes of increased airway obstruction clinically apparent as cough, wheezing, and decreased exercise capacity. Cold air, exercise, or allergens in the environment may trigger asthma. The first sign of chronic obstructive lung disease is a decreased forced expiratory volume in one second.

Another type of chronic lung disease is that caused by fibrosis or scarring. This form of lung disease is characterized by a decreased forced vital capacity.

Most individuals with severe chronic lung disease do not venture into the wilderness. Individuals with mild or moderate lung disease, however, may pursue such activities, and respiratory symptoms may occur during exertion or at altitudes above a few thousand feet (1,000 m) because chronic lung disease reduces the extra breathing capacity required in these situations. In addition, chronic lung disease reduces the extra breathing capacity required when infection, trauma, or shock stresses the body. Persons who know they have impaired respiratory reserve should seek the advice of a physician knowledgeable about the effects of altitude before ascent to any altitude, particularly altitudes above a few thousand feet, and particularly when they plan to exercise. (See chapter 22, "Altitude and Common Medical Conditions.")

DISORDERS OF BREATHING RHYTHM

Sleep Periodic Breathing at High Altitude

Sleep periodic breathing is almost universal at altitudes above 13,200 feet (4,000 m) and may occur at lower altitudes (above 6,600 feet or 2,000 m). The typical pattern begins with a few shallow breaths, increases in depth to very deep, sighing respirations, and then falls off rapidly. Respirations can cease entirely for five seconds or more before shallow breaths resume and the pattern is repeated. An observer may fear that the person is not breathing at all.

During the period when breathing has stopped, the person often becomes restless and sometimes awakens with a sense of suffocation. Acetazolamide eliminates sleep periodic breathing at altitude because it acts as a respiratory stimulant. Most sedatives worsen hypoventilation during sleep at altitude and should be avoided.

Sleep periodic breathing is so common at altitude that it should not be considered abnormal. Periodic breathing may be present on some occasions and not on others. However, it may be a sign of a serious disorder if it occurs for the first time during an illness or after an injury, particularly a head injury (Fig. 10-2).

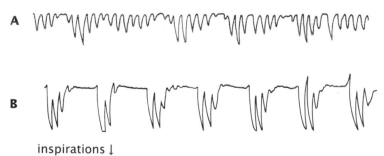

inspirations ↓

FIGURE 10-2. Actual tracings of periodic respirations: A, increasing and decreasing depth of respirations; B, two to three deep inspirations followed by total cessation of respiration for about twelve seconds

Some persons have intermittent upper airway obstruction during sleep that may cause snoring and an unpleasant morning headache and lethargy at altitude. This problem is called obstructive sleep apnea and is not relieved by acetazolamide. Another form of irregular breathing during sleep is central sleep apnea. Some defect in the respiratory control center in the brain causes alarming periods of absent breathing, followed by increasing respiration that rises to a peak and then decreases. This disorder resembles periodic breathing, but it occurs at any altitude and is not relieved by acetazolamide. (See chapter 22, "Altitude and Common Medical Conditions.")

Hyperventilation Syndrome

Hyperventilation (overbreathing) is common. The subject begins to breathe more rapidly and deeply than is appropriate and appears to be suffering from serious disease. However, this syndrome is almost entirely psychosomatic in origin. Individuals who hyperventilate tend to be nervous, tense, and apprehensive, although the disorder can occur in apparently stable persons. Among beginners, apprehension about hazards or fear of exposure might initiate this reaction. Knowledge of the person's emotional status, particularly unusual anxiety, helps establish the diagnosis.

When a person breathes too rapidly and deeply for more than a short time, an abnormally large amount of carbon dioxide is exhaled, altering the acid-base balance and increasing the alkalinity of the blood, which produces the characteristic symptoms of numbness or tingling around the mouth and in the fingers. Other associated signs and symptoms include a rapid pulse, dizziness, faintness, sweating, and apprehension. The person often complains "the air doesn't go down far enough" and breathes in gasps or takes frequent deep sighs. If hyperventilation persists, tingling in the fingers progresses to painful cramps or spasms of the fingers, hands, and forearms, which may be particularly frightening to the subject.

Even though the hyperventilation syndrome is suspected, the individual should be examined to ensure that no other problem is present. If none is found, reassurance and explanation are usually enough to reverse the disorder. The subject should be instructed to deliberately slow his breathing. If this is not effective, a tranquilizer may be necessary. Once recovered, the individual may feel weak and shaky and may have a headache. A treatment that has been recommended in the past is breathing into a paper bag. Currently this is not recommended, however, because it may cause dangerously low blood oxygen levels at high altitude or if an unrecognized lung problem is actually present at any altitude.

INFECTIOUS DISORDERS

Tracheitis

The trachea is the large airway leading from the throat to the middle of the chest where it divides into the two main bronchi. This structure sometimes becomes inflamed and occasionally infected. Usually the pain is in the throat below the tonsils or beneath the sternum and becomes worse with breathing. Coughing may cause pain in the same area and may produce thick sputum. The treatment of tracheitis is the same as that for bronchitis.

Bronchitis

Bronchitis, or more properly tracheobronchitis, is an infection of the major air passages to the lungs. Such infections are rarely disabling, but occasionally they progress to pneumonia. This disease frequently comes on during or after a cold, and may be called a "chest cold."

The predominant symptom of bronchitis is a persistent irritating cough that may be dry but frequently becomes productive after one or two days. The sputum may be green or yellow. Slight pain may be associated with the coughing and easy fatigability may be present, particularly at high altitudes. However, the person does not usually appear severely ill and has only a slight fever or none at all. If the infection involves the larynx (voice box), the individual may be hoarse (laryngitis). A few wheezes and rales may be heard throughout the chest, but these tend to disappear with coughing.

The treatment for tracheitis or bronchitis begins with adequate hydration. The subject should drink lots of warm fluids such as soups. If possible, he should inhale steam from a boiling kettle or pot to moisten the airways and "loosen" or liquefy the material in his bronchi so it can be coughed up more easily.

Rest, warmth, and nonsteroidal anti-inflammatory drugs are helpful. If the condition persists for more than two or three days, descent to a lower altitude may be necessary. Viruses cause bronchitis more often than bacteria, and antibiotics are not useful for treatment.

Increasing evidence suggests that even a mild upper respiratory infection increases the risk of HAPE.

Pleurisy

Pleurisy is pain localized to one side of the chest that is worsened by inspiration and is caused by inflammation of the thin membranes that cover the lungs and the inner surface of the chest wall. Pleurisy may occur with pneumonia, injury to the chest wall, collapse of the lung (pneumothorax), or pulmonary embolism. The principal symptom is pain with respiration. The pain usually is sharp and stabbing and usually is limited to an area on one side of the chest. Deep inspiration may elicit a particularly severe twinge. Pleurisy may be particularly uncomfortable and painful at altitude where respirations are more rapid and deeper than at sea level.

Physical signs are mild or absent. Motion of the affected side may be limited, and a few wheezes or rales may be heard over the involved area. Sometimes a leathery, rough, rubbing sound can be heard over the area where pain is worst. This "friction rub" is diagnostic of pleurisy but does not indicate its cause. The person may be more comfortable when lying on the affected side, limiting the motion of that part of the chest.

The treatment of pleurisy is dictated by the underlying cause. If the fever is high, the pulse is rapid, or the subject seems quite sick, pneumonia or embolism should be suspected. Pneumonia would require antibiotic treatment, and both pneumonia and pulmonary embolism dictate evacuation to a lower altitude. Recent trauma to the chest might suggest pneumothorax or blood in the space between the chest wall and lung (hemothorax) as a cause of pleurisy. Persistent pleuritic chest pain at altitudes above 14,000 feet (5,500 m) can be caused by rib cartilages torn by persistent coughing, and can be disabling. Pleurisy caused by moderate trauma to the chest wall, such as bruised or broken ribs without pneumothorax or hemothorax, may be treated with analgesics. Taping or splinting the chest increases the risk of pneumonia or collapse of part of the lung and is not recommended.

Pneumonia

Pneumonia is an infection of the lung tissue involving the alveoli and is most commonly caused by bacteria. Persons weakened by fatigue, exposure, or disease elsewhere in the body are particularly susceptible. Infected fluid accumulates in the alveoli, and the exchange of carbon dioxide and oxygen is impaired. If a large amount of lung is involved, low blood oxygen (hypoxia), combined with effects of toxic substances released from the bacteria, may cause death. Pneumonia should always be taken seriously.

Anyone with any type of pneumonia is oxygen deficient above 8,000 feet (2,400 m). Supplemental oxygen, if available, should be administered and individuals should be evacuated to lower altitude as soon as possible.

The symptoms of pneumonia vary with the causative organisms and the severity of the infection. Pneumonia usually causes a fever of more than 102°F (39°C) orally and rapid pulse and respiratory rates. Bacterial pneumonia often starts with one or more shaking chills followed by a high fever. The individual looks quite sick and may be very weak. Cough is a prominent symptom. The cough may be dry at first but usually becomes productive after one or two days. The sputum, which is usually green or yellow but sometimes has a rusty color, is thick and mucoid and frequently resembles pus.

Some bacteria tend to localize in a single segment of the lung that becomes consolidated. The physical signs are limited to that area of the lung and include rales or increased transmission of breath sounds on chest auscultation. Inflammation of the overlying pleura may occur and cause pleuritic chest pain that, when severe, feels like a stabbing pain with each breath. Pleuritic chest pain may be an early indication of underlying pneumonia. Pleuritic chest pain is more severe with deeper inspiration, which may cause reduced inspiration on the affected side that may be visible as asymmetric chest expansion, a condition called splinting.

Streptococcus pneumoniae is a common cause of "lobar pneumonia" limited to one or two lobes of the lung. Other bacteria that may cause pneumonia include *Haemophilus influenzae, Staphylococcus aureus,* and *Klebsiella pneumoniae.* "Atypical" organisms that may cause localized or widespread pneumonia include *Mycoplasma pneumoniae, Chlamydia pneumoniae,* and *Legionella.* Aspiration of gastric contents into the lung can result in pneumonia caused by a mixed bacterial population. All forms of pneumonia are treated with antibiotics. Diagnosis of the specific causative organism often is not possible, even in a hospital setting. Appropriate antibiotics that treat most or all of these common organisms include erythromycin, azithromycin, clarithromycin, or levofloxacin. Of these choices, erythromycin is less expensive but is not effective against as many organisms and is frequently associated with nausea.

Antibiotic administration should be continued for at least ten days. Stopping sooner can lead to a relapse with organisms that have become resistant to the drug. Because antibiotics may prevent identification of some less common infective organisms once the subject has reached a hospital, some physicians urge that no treatment be given until the organism has been identified. Despite these reservations, if hospitalization must be delayed for more than two or three days, or the individual is quite ill, treatment should be started at once.

Pneumonia caused by viruses or fungi does occur and is not effectively treated with antibiotics. Coccidioidomycosis is a fungal pneumonia common in the southwestern United States; histoplasmosis is a fungal pneumonia common in the Mississippi River Valley.

Recovery from pneumonia depends on the severity of the infection and the organism. Rarely can a person who has had pneumonia resume strenuous activity in less than two to three weeks.

OTHER PULMONARY DISORDERS

High Altitude Pulmonary Edema

Although HAPE was clearly described ninety years ago, only in the last forty years has it been recognized as a major problem. Before 1960, this disorder was usually mistaken for pneumonia, and acute pulmonary edema and pneumonia do have similarities. This serious problem can occur, and has been lethal, as low as 8,000 feet (2,400 m). It is more fully described in chapter 21, "Disorders Caused by Altitude."

Asthma

Asthma is a disease of the bronchi caused by allergy, exercise, or breathing cold air. Inhaling the substance to which the individual is allergic (the allergen), or inhaling dry or cold air that irritates the cells lining the airway, increases the secretion of mucus into the bronchi. Simultaneously, the muscles in the walls of the bronchi go into spasm, constricting these air passages. The narrowed bronchi filled with excess mucus obstruct the passage of air.

Asthma may be mild, severe, or—rarely—fatal. Although a first attack may occur at any time, most individuals are aware of their susceptibility long before engaging in wilderness activities.

Asthma is a recurring disease. Most people with this problem have suffered previous attacks and are under the care of a physician who can provide the medications that should be taken on a trip. Fortunately, individuals with mild asthma are not particularly limited in the wilderness activities in which they can participate; some may even breathe more easily at high altitude, where the air is thinner and freer of allergens and pollutants.

The most significant sign of asthma is difficulty in breathing, particularly during expiration. The expiratory phase of respiration is considerably prolonged, is associated with wheezing, and may require conscious effort.

An incessant, irritating cough is often present. Toward the end of an asthmatic attack, considerable quantities of very thick mucus may be coughed up. Fever is usually absent, but the pulse rate may be moderately increased. The respiratory rate is usually faster than normal in spite of the difficulty in breathing. When the person is examined, the chest may appear more expanded than normal at the end of expiration. Wheezing on expiration is usually audible throughout all parts of the lung.

The most important treatment for an acute asthma exacerbation is an albuterol inhaler. Albuterol occupies beta receptors in the smooth muscle of the bronchi and makes them relax. It also helps loosen mucus in the airways so that it can be coughed up. The dose is two puffs (inhalations) every four hours. Side effects of albuterol inhalation may include an increased heart rate and tremor. Most persons with asthma carry an inhaler with them. Steroid inhalers also are very effective in treating asthma on a continuing basis. For moderate or severe acute asthmatic exacerbations, steroids are given orally or intravenously in addition to inhaled albuterol.

At altitudes above 12,000 feet (3,600 m) asthma may further limit the amount of oxygen in the blood, and therefore supplemental oxygen is helpful. At sea level, supplemental oxygen is usually not necessary for mild or moderate asthma exacerbations.

On both short and extended trips, asthmatics should carry adequate medications for treatment of an exacerbation. Asthmatics ascending to altitude should be conservative in allowing adequate time for acclimatization. Although some asthmatics do better at altitude, others may suffer exacerbations due to the dry, cold air. In general, asthmatics are not known to have an increased risk for altitude illness, but they may be more susceptible to HAPE during an exacerbation.

Pneumothorax

Occasionally, lung tissue may rupture spontaneously, allowing air to leak into the chest cavity. Lacerations of the lung can also occur with penetrating or nonpenetrating injuries that fracture and displace ribs. The lung on the side of the air leak retracts due to its inherent elasticity and does not expand well during inspiration. As a result, pulmonary function is compromised. This condition is known as pneumothorax, meaning "air in the chest."

Rarely, the tear in the lung behaves like a valve, allowing air to enter the pleural space but not leave, which causes the pressure within the space to build rapidly. The pressure collapses the lung and can shift the heart and its surrounding structures (the mediastinum) toward the opposite side of the chest. If untreated, this disorder, called "tension pneumothorax" because the air is under increased pressure, may cause shock and result in death (Fig. 10-3).

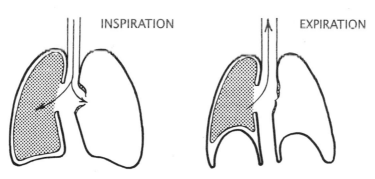

FIGURE 10-3. Pulmonary function with a tension pneumothorax[1]

Pneumothorax should be suspected when unexplained shortness of breath appears suddenly in an otherwise healthy, active person—particularly in combination with trauma to the chest. Sometimes the onset is associated with sudden pain. The diagnosis is confirmed when breath sounds can not be heard over the entire lung on the affected side. A tension pneumothorax should be suspected when shortness of breath is severe and the person is fighting for air. Lips and fingernails are usually purple (cyanotic). Sometimes the trachea just above the sternum is shifted to the side away from the pneumothorax; the point where the heart is felt may be shifted in the same direction.

No treatment is needed unless a tension pneumothorax develops. Then the pressure must be relieved by inserting a needle or tube into that side of the chest, a simple procedure that may be lifesaving but should be done only by a physician except in desperate circumstances. This procedure is discussed in greater detail in chapter 11, "Chest Injuries," and in appendix B, "Therapeutic Procedures."

Individuals with a spontaneous pneumothorax need to rest for a week or longer until the "leak" in the lung tissue has healed, as it usually does. In wilderness circumstances, the subject should be moved to a location where a physician's help can be obtained if tension pneumothorax develops. Persons who have had one episode of spontaneous pneumothorax are more vulnerable to others. They may consider surgery to try to eliminate the condition, and they certainly should learn, or have their colleagues learn, how to recognize and treat tension pneumothorax if it should develop.

VENOUS THROMBOSIS AND PULMONARY EMBOLISM

Blood clots in the veins of the legs (or rarely the arms)—venous thrombosis—are not uncommon and may result in serious complications. Blood clots in the large central veins of the thigh and pelvis—deep venous thrombosis—may break off and travel through the heart to the lungs, producing pulmonary embolism. The clots (emboli) obstruct the arteries in the lung (pulmonary arteries) and reduce blood flow through that organ, which interferes with the exchange of oxygen and carbon dioxide. Extensive embolism or obstruction of a major pulmonary artery, such as the artery to an entire lung, is rapidly fatal. Ascent to high altitude increases the risk of venous thrombosis and pulmonary embolism.

An increased tendency of the blood to clot (increased coagulability) and slowing or even cessation of blood flow in the veins (stasis) favor the development of venous thrombosis. Factors increasing the coagulability or stasis of blood are:

- ▼ Dehydration, which causes the blood to become thicker and more viscous
- ▼ An increase in the number of red blood cells due to high altitude, a normal mechanism of acclimatization that also increases the viscosity of blood
- ▼ Prolonged immobility, such as being stormbound for days in a small tent
- ▼ Resting in cramped, awkward positions
- ▼ Carrying heavy packs and standing immobile for long periods of time, which increase stasis in the legs
- ▼ Trauma to the pelvis or legs, which increases the tendency for clotting

Oral contraceptive drugs may promote the development of venous thrombosis and pulmonary embolism at altitude. Women taking such drugs should discontinue them three weeks before an outing if more than a few days will be spent above 10,000 feet (3,000 m).

Diagnosis of Venous Thrombosis

The most common symptom of venous thrombosis is deep, aching pain in the calf, inner side of the thigh, or back of the knee. The pain frequently comes on suddenly and is aggravated by walking. When the thrombosed vein is located in the calf, the overlying muscles are tender. Flexing the foot upward also causes pain in the calf. Usually the affected leg is swollen, which can be detected by measuring the circumference of both legs at identical five-inch intervals from the ankle to the upper thigh. A difference in circumferences of one-half inch is common and of no significance; greater differences are cause for concern. The limb may be pale, is sometimes cyanotic, and may have diminished arterial pulsation. A slight fever is sometimes present and lasts an average of seven to ten days. Blood clots in the veins of the thighs or pelvis may not cause obvious symptoms but may break off and travel to the lung, causing pulmonary embolism. Consequently, if a person is in pulmonary distress and other pulmonary disorders do not appear to be present, pulmonary embolism must be suspected even though signs of venous thrombosis are absent.

Diagnosis of Pulmonary Embolism

Pulmonary embolism is heralded by the sudden onset of pain in the chest. Cough, shortness of breath, and a rapid pulse usually accompany the pain. Later the pain becomes pleuritic and is aggravated by respiration, particularly deep breathing. The cough may produce bloody sputum. The respiratory and pulse rates are increased, and a slight fever is frequently present. Signs of consolidation (increased or absent breath sounds and dullness to percussion) may appear over the involved area a day or so after onset.

If the embolus obstructs a large pulmonary artery, the initial symptom may be the sudden onset of a sense of suffocation rather than pain. More severe shortness of breath, cyanosis, distention of neck veins, and signs of shock follow shortly. Pleuritic pain, cough, bloody sputum, and signs of consolidation usually develop a few hours later, although the pain of pleural involvement may be absent if the blood clot lodges in a central part of the lung.

A large pulmonary embolus will produce cardiovascular collapse and death within seconds. Smaller emboli cause respiratory difficulty, including shortness of breath, decreased exercise capacity, and sometimes hypoxia that may be more pronounced at altitude.

Prevention

Prevention is important but difficult. Anyone confined to a tent by a storm should change position and exercise his feet and legs for a few minutes every hour. Constricting clothing should be removed. Hospitalized postoperative subjects often wear snug elastic stockings that come up to the knee, but these are of doubtful benefit and would be impractical in the wilderness. Extra fluids are essential at altitudes above 12,000 feet (3,600 m), where dehydration promotes venous thrombosis, as well as hypothermia and other problems. An aspirin a day may help prevent venous thrombosis at high altitude because it inhibits platelet aggregation in the blood.

Treatment

Treatment of venous thrombosis and pulmonary embolism is the same. Both require anticoagulant drugs initially that are administered intravenously (heparin) or subcutaneously (enoxaparin), followed by several months of oral therapy with warfarin. These drugs must be closely monitored to prevent too much anticoagulation that might cause serious bleeding in the gastrointestinal tract or brain. Therefore, treatment of venous thrombosis or pulmonary embolism requires evacuation to a medical facility. Moderate analgesics are usually adequate for pain.

Once venous thrombosis develops, the individual should be immobilized. Walking or other movement may cause the clots to break off and embolize. The feet should be elevated slightly, and awkward positions should be avoided. A snug, but not tight, elastic bandage wrapped around the leg from toes to knees is thought by some to decrease the risk of embolism and is unlikely to worsen matters. Evacuation is essential, especially if pulmonary embolism has occurred. During evacuation, the individual should be carried as much as possible. If walking is unavoidable, the affected limb should be carefully bandaged. Not to evacuate such persons to hospital care is too risky, but every precaution must be taken to ensure that minimum activity and stress result (Table 10-1).

Table 10-1 Features of Various Pulmonary Disorders

	PNEUMONIA	HIGH ALTITUDE PULMONARY EMBOLISM	PULMONARY EDEMA
Onset	Gradual, 24 hours	Gradual, 12 to 36 hours after ascent	Sudden
Chills	Frequent at onset	Absent	Absent
Fever	Usual; often high	Mild or absent	Mild or absent
Sputum	Thick, stringy, green yellow, or rusty	Frothy; white or pink	May be bloody
Pain	Pleuritic; may be absent	None	Pleuritic
Fluid (edema)	Localized or diffuse; often mild	Usually diffuse	Localized if present
Physical Findings	Crackling rales; rub; loud, harsh breath sounds	Crackling rales; bubbling	Rub; harsh or absent breath sounds
Other	May follow a cold or bronchitis	No history of heart disease; recent ascent to 8,000 feet (2,400 m) or above	Signs of venous thrombosis

REFERENCES

1. Johnson J and Kirby C: *Surgery of the Chest*, 3rd ed. Year Book Medical Publishers, Inc., 1964. (Adapted and used by permission.)

CHAPTER 11

CHEST INJURIES

PRINCIPAL CONTRIBUTORS:
Ben Eiseman, M.D.
Bruce Paton, M.D.

Chest injuries are of particular significance because they interfere with the vital function of respiration. At high altitude, where the oxygen content of air is low, chest injuries that would be of minor consequence at low altitude can be life-threatening. In contrast to abdominal injuries, for which little can be done in a wilderness setting, a well-informed person can take steps to increase the chances for survival of individuals with chest injuries.

THE MECHANICS OF RESPIRATION

During inspiration, muscles in the chest wall pull the ribs upward. Simultaneously, the diaphragm contracts and flattens, expanding the chest and drawing air into the lungs. Expiration, in contrast, is passive and requires no muscular action. Elastic tissue in the lung, which is stretched as the lung expands during inspiration, retracts and reduces the volume of the lung during expiration, pushing air out of the chest (Fig. 11-1). (The anatomy of the respiratory system is described in chapter 10, "Respiratory Disorders.")

A thin membrane, the pleura, envelops each lung and the inner surface of the rib cage. The potential space between these two layers is called the pleural cavity. Normally the lungs fill the entire thorax, and, because negative pressure is present in the pleural cavity, the two layers of the pleura remain in intimate contact. There is, therefore, no real space in the pleural "cavity" under normal conditions. However, if the chest wall is perforated or a lung is punctured, air enters the pleural space through the defect and the elasticity of the lungs causes them to collapse. (See Pneumothorax, later in this chapter.)

Effect of Body Position

In the standing position the diaphragm lies low in the chest, permitting full expansion of the lungs.

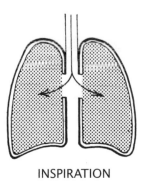
INSPIRATION

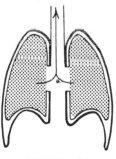
EXPIRATION

FIGURE 11-1. Normal pulmonary function[1]

When a person lies down, however, the abdominal organs push against the diaphragm, which is displaced toward the head, compressing the lungs and reducing ventilation. When an obese person is lying on his back, the abdominal organs may push the diaphragm up to the level of the nipples, seriously impeding gas exchange in the lungs.

Placing a person on his side permits the abdominal organs to shift away from the diaphragm and can improve ventilation, particularly in the upper portions of the lungs. In a sitting position, the abdominal organs tend to fall away from the diaphragm, improving respiration.

A person with a severe chest injury should be placed in the position that is most comfortable, but lying on his side or sitting may allow better respiration than lying flat. If blood loss has been significant, the individual may have to lie flat to maintain an adequate blood pressure.

CLOSED CHEST INJURIES

Broken Rib

A forceful blow to the chest may break one or more ribs, but the ribs are so surrounded by muscles that they rarely need to be splinted or realigned like other broken bones. Other than producing discomfort, most rib fractures are not serious injuries. However, the discomfort can be surprisingly disabling, and movement of almost any part of the body causes pain at the fracture site. Pain also interferes with motion of the chest wall and limits breathing. Rarely, one end of a broken rib is displaced inward, punctures the lung, and produces a pneumothorax.

A broken rib should be suspected when pain and tenderness at the point of impact follow a blow to the chest, particularly when deep breathing or movement aggravates the pain. Rarely can a defect be palpated at the point of fracture because the ends of the rib are held in position by surrounding muscles.

The pain of a broken rib may be severe enough to require analgesics for a few days. Almost any movement and sleep may be extremely uncomfortable for several weeks, particularly when lying on the injured side, but the pain gradually disappears as the bones heal. Sudden sharp pain at the site of injury for weeks after the injury should not arouse concern. Relief of pain so it does not interfere with breathing is the most important aspect of managing broken ribs (if there is no underlying lung injury), particularly at high altitude, in the elderly, and in individuals with reduced pulmonary function (such as smokers).

Adhesive strapping over the rib is not advisable, particularly at altitudes above 10,000 feet (3,000 m). Such immobilization reduces movement of the chest on that side even more, diminishes the capacity for exertion, and allows secretions to collect in the immobile lung. Pneumonia is a common complication of rib fractures. At lower elevations, if the pain can not be controlled with moderate analgesics, four or five strips of two- or three-inch adhesive tape can be applied along the fractured rib from the midline in front past the vertebral column in back. Taping provides some relief from pain, but the tape should be removed as soon as the individual has been evacuated—two to three days at the most. Wrapping the chest with an elastic bandage can provide similar immobilization, but because both sides of the chest are restrained, this technique reduces respiratory function more than taping only one side.

A blow to the chest may damage intra-abdominal organs—the liver if the blow has been low on the right side, the spleen by left-sided injuries, or the kidneys by a blow to the back.

Pneumothorax

Air in the pleural cavity, which is called "pneumothorax," allows the lung to partially or totally collapse (Fig. 11-2). When the air is introduced by rupture of a small bleb or air bubble on the surface of the lung, the pneumothorax is considered "spontaneous." If the air is introduced by an injury, the pneumothorax is "traumatic." Occasionally, a tear in the surface of the lung functions as a one-way valve, allowing air to enter the pleural space during inspiration but closing and not allowing air to escape during expiration. As a result the lung collapses, tension within the pleural space increases with

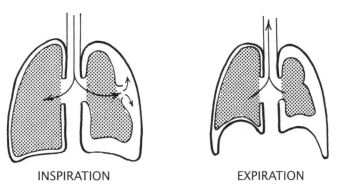

INSPIRATION   EXPIRATION

FIGURE 11-2. Pulmonary function with a punctured lung and intact chest wall[2]

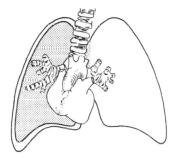

FIGURE 11-3. Collapse of the left lung and shift of heart and trachea to the right with left pneumothorax

every breath, and both respiratory and cardiac function can be severely impaired. This condition is called a "tension pneumothorax."

A spontaneous pneumothorax is heralded by the sudden onset of chest pain associated with shortness of breath. Such alarming symptoms in an older person and on the left side of the chest may suggest a heart attack. Although painful and frightening, spontaneous pneumothorax is rarely fatal. Some persons have repeated episodes and can recognize the disorder when it occurs. Individuals with spontaneous pneumothorax should be evacuated. If shortness of breath is not severe, they may even be able to walk out unassisted.

A key to the diagnosis of pneumothorax is the absence of audible breath sounds when listening to the chest, preferably with a stethoscope. With a tension pneumothorax, a shift of the trachea and the heart to the opposite side may be detectable (Fig. 11-3).

Although oxygen partially alleviates symptoms of pneumothorax, the only definitive treatment is removing the air trapped in the pleural cavity and allowing the lung to expand. To accomplish this, a needle or tube must be inserted into the pleural space. If the device is left in the pleura, a one-way valve or suction apparatus must be applied to maintain the negative pleural pressure and expand the lung. This procedure, called needle or tube thoracostomy, is usually performed in a hospital and should not be attempted in the wilderness except for individuals dying as the result of tension pneumothorax. Inexperienced individuals should not attempt the procedure at all. Only major expeditions or very well equipped rescue groups would be expected to carry the appropriate equipment and to include medical professionals who could perform this procedure.

Hemothorax

An accumulation of blood in the pleural cavity is known as a "hemothorax." Bleeding from vessels around a broken rib or from a punctured or bluntly injured lung may occur. Blood in the pleural space collapses the lung and interferes with its function, similar to air. If bleeding is severe, the person may go into shock and even die as the result of blood loss. If a hemothorax of lesser volume is left unattended, it can become infected. A large volume of blood left in the chest may form a constricting clot around the lung after several weeks. Although all of these possibilities are of concern, the immediate threat in a remote area is death from blood loss or impaired respiration. Such an event is unlikely unless a large vessel such as a pulmonary artery or vein has been torn, in which case the person usually dies before help arrives. Less severe bleeding usually stops spontaneously within a few hours.

The signs and symptoms of hemothorax are similar to those of pneumothorax: immediate pain, increasing difficulty in breathing, signs of decreased oxygenation (cyanosis, increased pulse rate, and decreased blood pressure), and the absence of breath sounds over the involved lung. Seldom can an observer in the wilderness differentiate pneumothorax from hemothorax. (Some individuals have both air and blood within the pleural cavity—hemopneumothorax.) Only a chest x-ray can determine accurately what has accumulated. The decision that must be made is whether the victim is stable or becoming worse.

Both pneumothorax and hemothorax are treated initially the same way. If air or blood is accumulating at a rate that seriously interferes with breathing, it has to be removed. (See tube thoracostomy in appendix B, "Therapeutic Procedures.") If the patient is stable, removing air or blood can be delayed until it can be accomplished in a hospital under sterile conditions. However, if a hemothorax or hemopneumothorax is suspected in a wilderness setting, medical help should be obtained as soon as possible, even if the victim is not in shock.

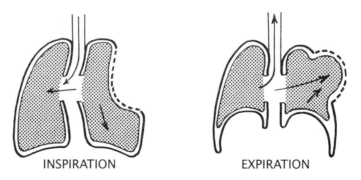

INSPIRATION   EXPIRATION

FIGURE 11-4. Pulmonary function with a flail chest[3]

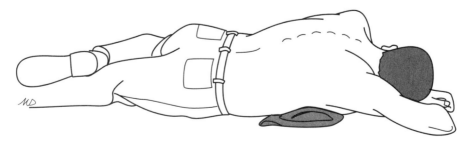

FIGURE 11-5. Subject lying on a rolled-up garment to support a flail chest

Flail Chest

Fracture of a number of adjacent ribs in two or more places can produce a mobile, freely floating plate of chest wall that moves back and forth during respiration, a condition called flail chest. When the chest expands, the loosened segment of chest wall moves inward; during expiration, the loosened plate is forced outward (paradoxical respiration) (Fig. 11-4). Because the chest wall moves without moving air into or out of the lungs, severe respiratory distress results, even if the damaged area is small. A large area of flail, particularly at altitudes above a few thousand feet (1,000 m), may be fatal and requires immediate attention.

The individual usually has received a severe blow to the chest and is fighting for air and breathing very rapidly. His lips, skin, and nails may be cyanotic. Examination of the bare chest discloses a mobile segment of chest wall that moves paradoxically with each respiration. A simple broken rib produces pain with breathing but does not interfere with the movement of air.

The loosened segment must be immobilized. In an emergency, the subject should be placed on his injured side (in spite of the pain) with a rolled-up piece of clothing beneath the loose segment of rib cage (Fig 11-5). The pressure effectively immobilizes the loosened portion of the chest wall and allows more adequate respiration. More permanent fixation of the rib cage can be achieved by taping or bandaging a large pad firmly over the mobile area. Oxygen should be administered, and the individual should be evacuated immediately.

PENETRATING CHEST INJURIES

A fall onto a pointed object such as an ice axe or ski pole may punch a hole in the chest wall and into the lung. Several injuries may result.

▼ If the opening in the chest is small and seals quickly but leaves a hole in the lung, air may leak into the pleural cavity, causing a pneumothorax (Fig. 11-6). The air leak may be large or small and could cause a tension pneumothorax.

▼ If the hole in the chest wall is large and air is sucked in and out of the chest cavity with every breath, the injury is obvious (Fig. 11-7). The opening should be sealed with a pad of sterile dressings, preferably with an inner layer of gauze impregnated with petroleum jelly (or clean cloth if that is all that is available). The pad should be taped securely over the open wound, but an edge that can lifted to allow air to escape should be available in case a tension pneumothorax develops.

Oxygen should be given immediately and should be stopped only when the subject's condition has definitely stabilized. Decompression of the chest with a chest tube may be necessary. Shock almost invariably accompanies a large penetrating wound of the chest and should be anticipated. In order to

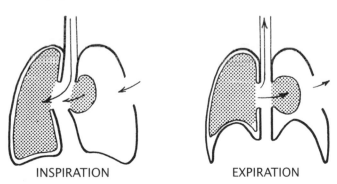

INSPIRATION   EXPIRATION

FIGURE 11-6. Pulmonary function with a punctured chest wall[4]

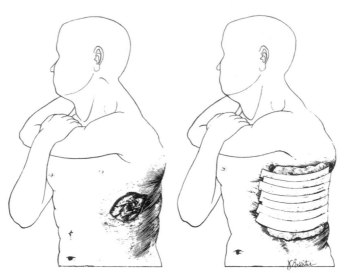

FIGURE 11-7. Open chest wound before and after bandaging

prevent secondary infection, a penicillinase-resistant penicillin or a cephalosporin should be given until evacuation is completed. If the person is allergic to penicillin, then erythromycin, clarithromycin, azithromycin, or levofloxacin can be administered.

All individuals with penetrating injuries of the chest must be evacuated at the earliest possible moment so that the hole in the chest wall can be permanently closed by surgery.

REFERENCES
1. Johnson J and Kirby C: *Surgery of the Chest,* 3rd ed. Year Book Medical Publishers, Inc., 1964. (Adapted and used by permission.)
2. Ibid.
3. Ibid.
4. Ibid.

12 GASTROINTESTINAL DISORDERS

PRINCIPAL CONTRIBUTOR:
Fred T. Darvill, M.D.

The gastrointestinal tract consists of the mouth and throat, esophagus, stomach, small and large intestines, liver, gallbladder, and pancreas. This system ingests food, converts it into forms that can be absorbed and used by the body, and excretes the waste.

The esophagus aids in swallowing and propels the food into the stomach, where it is digested for thirty to ninety minutes by enzymes and hydrochloric acid. The food next passes into the first part of the small intestine (duodenum), where enzymes from the intestinal mucosa and the pancreas further prepare the partially digested food for absorption. Bile, which is produced by the liver and stored in the gallbladder, helps emulsify fats so they can be absorbed. Absorption takes place in the middle and lower segments of the small intestine (jejunum and ileum). In the large intestine, water is extracted from the residual material. All of the blood from the small intestine first goes to the liver, where an array of complex biochemical reactions converts the absorbed nutrients to substances needed by other tissues and organs.

Diseases of many organs produce symptoms referable to the gastrointestinal tract, particularly nausea and vomiting. Illnesses originating in the gastrointestinal tract produce similar symptoms and often can not be distinguished without sophisticated diagnostic facilities. Furthermore, even when the nature of a disorder is known, specific therapy may not be available. Therefore, the treatment for most gastrointestinal disorders that appear for the first time in a wilderness situation or in a remote area of a developing country is limited to alleviating symptoms.

The signs of disease of the gastrointestinal system are nausea and vomiting, diarrhea, constipation, bleeding, jaundice, and pain. Pain that comes on suddenly is such an eminent problem that it is discussed separately in chapter 13, "Acute Abdominal Pain." Procedures for examining the abdomen are also described in that chapter.

NAUSEA AND VOMITING

The causes of vomiting are innumerable and include such widely differing disorders as motion sickness, head injuries, metabolic disorders, infections, pregnancy, ulcers, environmental heat, and appendicitis.

If the patient is stuporous or unconscious, a single bout of vomiting can be disastrous because the vomited material may be aspirated into the trachea and bronchi. Lethal respiratory obstruction can be produced if the volume of aspirated material is large. If a smaller amount of vomit is aspirated into the lungs, the resulting severe pneumonia is difficult to treat. At the first sign of vomiting, an unconscious patient must be rolled onto his side with his head lowered. His waist may be lifted twelve to eighteen inches if he has not been involved in an accident that could have produced a fractured spine. (If a blow to the head is responsible for the unconsciousness, the individual should be assumed to have a broken neck.) The head-down position must be maintained until vomiting has ceased and the vomit has been cleared from his mouth. **The patient must not be allowed to aspirate the vomited material.**

Protracted vomiting sometimes ruptures small blood vessels in the lining of the stomach, and small amounts of blood appear in the vomited material. Chronic use of aspirin or other nonsteroidal anti-inflammatory drugs (NSAIDs) or excessive alcohol consumption can irritate the stomach and cause vomit to be bloody. When ulcers of the stomach or duodenum cause vomiting, the vomit may contain large quantities of blood.

Vomiting caused by minor disorders often stops without any treatment. After the first bout, the individual usually feels better and is able to resume limited activity. If vomiting does not stop within a few hours, a serious underlying disease must be considered. Vomiting may be an important sign of brain injury, an acute abdominal disorder such as intestinal obstruction or appendicitis, drug overdose, and many other diseases. If a patient has one of these disorders, controlling vomiting with medications could delay diagnosis and definitive treatment.

When no underlying disease can be identified, vomiting can be treated symptomatically. If medications can be taken orally, prochlorperazine (Compazine®) can be given. Therapy should continue until the patient has been asymptomatic for at least four hours. If oral drugs can not be retained, prochlorperazine or promethazine (Phenergan®) rectal suppositories can be inserted every four to six hours until oral medications can be kept down. Treatment for more than twenty-four hours should be avoided. Drowsiness is a common side effect of all drugs used to treat vomiting. While taking prochlorperazine orally or using either of the suppositories, the patient must not take part in activities in which drowsiness or inattentiveness could result in injury.

If vomiting is prolonged, the body becomes depleted of fluid and salt. On rare occasions, vomiting can not be stopped until the fluid and salt have been replaced. Treating such intractable vomiting requires intravenous fluids. If fluids for intravenous therapy are not available, the patient must be evacuated.

Following recovery, fluids should be replaced as quickly as possible to correct dehydration. The patient should eat bland foods, preferably liquids, for about twenty-four hours.

Motion Sickness

Susceptible individuals may develop nausea and vomiting when traveling by car on a winding road, by airplane when turbulence is substantial, or by boat when the water is rough. Symptoms may be improved by limiting the motion: moving to the front seat of a car, the center of a ship, or over the wing of an airplane. Lying still with the eyes open can sometimes reduce symptoms of motion sickness.

Several medications can prevent or decrease motion sickness if taken one hour or more before the motion is encountered. Three can be purchased over the counter. Dimenhydrinate (Dramamine®) is an old standby. Either meclizine (Bonine® and Antivert®) or cyclizine (Marezine®) is more effective for some individuals. Transdermal scopolamine (Transderm Scop®), another option that requires a prescription, consists of a patch placed behind the ear from which scopolamine is absorbed through the skin. All may cause sedation (drowsiness) as a side effect. Scopolamine may also cause dry mouth and blurred vision, but it is usually the most effective of these agents.

Dimenhydrinate, meclizine, and cyclizine should be taken every four to six hours as long as a risk of motion sickness exists. The scopolamine patch lasts three days but can be removed earlier.

Travelers taking other medications or with existing medical conditions should contact their physician before taking any of these medications to ensure that no drug interaction or adverse effect on their illness is likely.

DIARRHEA

Diarrhea is the most common and the most notorious of traveler's illnesses. However, the most common cause is simply a change in food or water. Many other causes are equally benign, although some diseases characterized by diarrhea can be life-threatening.

Mild Diarrhea

Mild diarrhea consisting only of soft, unformed stools and one to four bowel movements a day has many different causes. A change in food, water, or surroundings is the most common. Excitement or anxiety frequently produces such symptoms. Diseases of other organs may be accompanied by mild diarrhea.

These disorders may last for days or even weeks. However, the diarrhea is only bothersome—not incapacitating—and usually clears up without any therapy. Antimicrobial agents do not help and should be avoided. One capsule of loperamide (Imodium®) each morning may be helpful.

Individuals with persistent chronic diarrhea after returning from a developing country should consult a physician. The cause of such disorders may be a parasitic infestation such as amebiasis that can become a major illness if untreated.

Invasive and Noninvasive Diarrhea

In situations where microbiologic laboratories that can identify the causative organisms are not available, distinguishing between "noninvasive" and "invasive" diarrhea allows appropriate therapy to be administered. Noninvasive diarrhea is caused by organisms that do not invade the lining of the intestinal tract (the mucosa) but remain in the intestinal lumen and release toxins that are absorbed and produce diarrhea. (Viruses invade the cells lining the intestinal tract but produce a noninvasive type of diarrhea.) Most traveler's diarrhea is noninvasive. The diarrhea produced by these organisms most commonly is less severe than that caused by invasive organisms, but cholera, which usually is severe and can be lethal, is a noninvasive infection.

In contrast, invasive organisms actually penetrate the intestinal mucosa and can spread throughout the body. Typhoid fever, a form of invasive diarrhea, typically involves all of the body tissues. Invasive bacterial infections often are associated with chills and fever, and with pus, mucus, or blood in the stool, and should be treated with antimicrobial agents. Antidiarrheal agents are not recommended because they may aggravate and prolong the illness.

With the exception of cholera, antimicrobial agents should not be administered for noninvasive diarrhea. They usually are ineffective, but even when they are helpful they can lead to the emergence of antibiotic-resistant strains of organisms. Antidiarrheal agents may be helpful for these disorders.

Traveler's Diarrhea

Most acute gastroenteritis occurring in visitors to other countries, particularly developing areas, is noninvasive diarrhea known as "traveler's diarrhea." About one-third of visitors from the United States, Canada, and Europe will develop diarrhea during travel in such countries. Residents of developing countries coming to the United States or Europe sometimes develop the same disorder, which has many colorful names: the Aztec two-step, Delhi belly, Montezuma's revenge, or simply *turista*. Such infections are not limited to travelers and involve the native population as well.

Enteropathogenic *Escherichia coli* (*E. coli*) organisms secrete a toxin that causes noninvasive diarrhea and are the most common cause of traveler's diarrhea. These bacteria are normally found in everyone's large bowel, and individuals develop resistance to toxins from the strains found in their environment. However, exposure to strains to which the individual has not developed resistance often produces illness.

Other noninvasive bacteria also cause traveler's diarrhea. A high percentage of the severe diarrheal disorders acquired in the wilderness and in developing countries are of viral origin. The high incidence of parasitic infestations such as cryptosporidiosis was not appreciated until the 1980s. Giardia have occasionally been associated with traveler's diarrhea.

Infection is usually spread by fecal contamination of water or food and is more common in countries with inadequate sewage disposal and water disinfection. However, the illness may be contracted anywhere.

Traveler's diarrhea can be prevented in several ways. Avoiding infection is clearly best but is not always easy. Water is the major source of infection. Even in modern hotels, tap water is usually contaminated and must be disinfected before being used just for brushing teeth. (Many of the better—and more expensive—hotels provide bottled water for drinking and brushing teeth.) However, some of these hotels may still serve drinks containing ice prepared from undisinfected water. Beer, bottled soft drinks, and bottled carbonated water are safe. Bottled noncarbonated water usually is safe, but some unscrupulous street vendors refill bottles with undisinfected water.

Bringing water to a boil, regardless of altitude, kills all organisms that cause diarrheal diseases. Most are destroyed by appropriate exposure to iodine. Unfortunately, cryptosporidia and possibly cyclospora, two diarrhea-producing parasitic infestations recognized in the last twenty-five years, are resistant to chlorine and iodine and must be removed by filtration. Infectious bacteria may survive well in food stored in a refrigerator, at room temperature, and even at temperatures too hot to touch comfortably. Food and beverages are safe only if they have been brought to boiling or near-boiling temperatures before consumption.

Previously peeled fruits and salads containing leafy vegetables are well-recognized sources of infection. Fruits with a protective rind that is not eaten are generally safe, but such fruits split open for display in markets are often splashed with undisinfected water so they will remain attractive. Melons sold by the pound are often injected with undisinfected water to increase their weight. All fruits and vegetables should be thoroughly washed in disinfected water and peeled by the consumer.

Contamination of food during preparation must be avoided. Modern concepts of sanitation, even such simple measures as hand washing after defecation, are totally alien to many inhabitants of developing countries. They must be monitored to ensure they wash before preparing food. Stool cultures to detect carriers of infectious diseases are desirable for the indigenous personnel in large parties, particularly those engaged in preparing meals, but they are essentially impossible to obtain. Disinfection of water used for food preparation as well as for drinking may be necessary. Unfortunately, such precautions are not universally effective and are difficult to sustain for a prolonged time.

The incubation period for traveler's diarrhea is usually twelve to forty-eight hours, and the disorder usually lasts two to five days. The onset is characterized by rapidly developing generalized abdominal distress culminating in waves of cramps and diarrhea. During spasms of pain, a patient may draw his knees up against his abdomen for relief. However, the periods between spasms are relatively free of pain. Nausea is common and may be accompanied by vomiting. Occasionally, nausea and vomiting are the dominant features of the illness.

Mild generalized abdominal tenderness may be present, particularly in the lower abdomen, and the bowel sounds are usually much louder than normal. Chills and fever are mild or absent.

The diarrhea is frequently explosive in onset and is characterized by copious, watery, foul-smelling stools. The number of stools varies from three or four to as many as twenty or more in twenty-four hours. Mucus is occasionally present in the stool, particularly when stools are numerous, but pus and blood are absent.

Antimicrobial agents can prevent traveler's diarrhea, but physicians are justifiably reluctant to recommend their routine use. All antibiotics have potentially significant side effects. They predispose individuals to the development of invasive bacterial infections and can induce drug resistance in bacteria, increasing the risk of infection by organisms that are antibiotic resistant and more dangerous.

An over-the-counter drug, bismuth subsalicylate (Pepto-Bismol®), prevents traveler's diarrhea in approximately sixty-five percent of the individuals taking it. The liquid form is so bulky that its use is impractical, but the tablets are effective (two tablets four times a day). This drug has no major toxicity and is considerably safer for prophylactic use than antimicrobial agents. Aspirin, which also is a salicylate, should not be taken concomitantly with Pepto-Bismol®.

The essential element of treatment for vomiting and diarrhea is fluid and salt replacement. (The relief of other symptoms, although desirable, is of secondary importance.) These disorders often produce significant dehydration, although lethal dehydration is uncommon in healthy adults. Worldwide, 3.3 million deaths per year are caused by diarrhea, eighty percent of them in children less than two years old. Vomiting or diarrhea would definitely aggravate the dehydration almost invariably encountered at high altitudes.

Table 12-1 Oral Fluid Replacement Solutions

Sodium chloride	3.5 g/l	*or*	1/2 level teaspoon/l
Sodium bicarbonate	2.5 g/l	*or*	1/2 level teaspoon/l
Potassium chloride	1.5 g/l	*or*	1/4 level teaspoon/l
Glucose	20 g/l	*or*	6 level teaspoons/l
	or		
Sucrose (table sugar)	40 g/l	*or*	12 level teaspoons/l

U.S. PUBLIC HEALTH SERVICE FORMULA (CENTERS FOR DISEASE CONTROL AND PREVENTION)

Glass no. 1
    8 ounces fruit juice
    1/2 teaspoon honey or corn syrup
    1 pinch table salt

Glass no. 2
    1/2 teaspoon baking soda (bicarbonate)
    8 ounces water (disinfected)
    Drink equal amounts from each glass, alternating between the two.

Urine volume and color are reliable indicators of dehydration; small volumes (less than 500 cc daily) of dark yellow or orange urine indicate substantial fluid depletion.

To replace fluids and salts, fruit juices, broths, and soups can be consumed. Rehydration with a sugar and salt solution may be more effective. (The sugar is a key ingredient because it promotes absorption of the salts.) Two formulas for replacement solutions are provided in Table 12-1. Others can be found in standard references.

The components of oral replacement solutions can be packed in small units at home, can be purchased in prepackaged form, or can be made up in the field. The rather crude measurements listed (teaspoons) are sufficiently accurate for anyone with normally functioning heart and kidneys, which will retain what is needed and excrete the rest. Furthermore, diarrheal salt losses vary more than such measures. Disinfected water must be used to dissolve the salts and glucose. Patients with moderate diarrhea (five to ten watery stools per day) should drink one to three liters of solution in addition to their usual water intake every twenty-four hours. Patients with more severe diarrhea (ten or more watery stools per day) should drink enough solution to equal the volume of the estimated losses and an additional one and one-half to two liters per day. No salt-free water should be consumed until rehydration is achieved and the diarrhea is substantially improved.

Treatment of nausea and vomiting with oral prochlorperazine (Compazine®) or prochlorperazine or promethazine (Phenergan®) suppositories may be required for adequate amounts of oral fluids to be consumed. Bismuth subsalicylate (Pepto-Bismol®), two tablets every six hours, may also be helpful.

Whether drugs that specifically control diarrhea should be used is controversial. Some evidence suggests these agents may prolong the illness even though the frequency of bowel movements is decreased. A compromise that appears reasonable is to administer medications only to control severe cramps or in circumstances where frequent bowel movements would be hazardous or substantially inconvenient and uncomfortable. For example, the need to leave a tent in an ice and snow environment five to ten times a night would justify the use of a medication to lessen the frequency of bowel movements.

Paregoric (tincture of opium), codeine, and diphenoxylate (Lomotil®) are effective agents, but they are potentially habituating and are available only by prescription. Loperamide (Imodium®) has similar actions, and tablets are available without a prescription. These drugs vary in their effectiveness for different individuals. The drug most effective for each specific patient should be administered. If the initial drug is not effective, one of the others may be tried.

Patients with severe diarrhea (more than ten stools a day) that has persisted for more that a few days, particularly if chills and fever are present and the stools contain blood, mucus, or pus, should seek a physician for diagnostic studies and treatment. If such care is unavailable, many authorities recommend treating such prolonged or severe traveler's diarrhea with an antidiarrheal agent such as loperamide for two days and an antibiotic such as ciprofloxacin (Cipro®) or trimethoprim-sulfamethoxazole (Bactrim DS® and Septra DS®) every twelve hours for five to seven days.

The amount of rest required varies widely. Few are able to continue vigorous activities. Most must restrict physical activity until symptoms improve or resolve.

Persons taking antibiotics for infections not involving the gastrointestinal tract should be aware that diarrhea often is a side effect of such therapy. It should resolve a day or two after the medication is stopped, but if diarrhea persists or worsens, and abdominal cramps, fever, weakness, and malaise develop, colonic infection with *Clostridium difficile* may be the cause. Testing for the toxin is the optimum guide for therapy, but facilities are not available in the wilderness or outside of major cities in developing countries. The antibiotic should be stopped if the condition for which it is being taken is not considered life-threatening—a judgement call. Metronidazole (Flagyl® and others) may be administered four times a day until a sophisticated medical facility can be reached. Alcoholic beverages can cause severe vomiting for patients receiving metronidazole and should be avoided while taking the drug and for three days afterward.

SPECIFIC CAUSES OF DIARRHEA

Staphylococcal Enteritis

Staphylococcal enteritis is a type of acute gastroenteritis caused by a toxin produced by staphylococci. These bacteria are present on the hands of about half of the population, and contamination of food during preparation is common. Any food may harbor the organisms, but salads made with mayonnaise, sweets such as custards and cream pies, meat, and milk are the most common. The staphylococcal toxin is produced when contaminated food is allowed to stand unrefrigerated for several hours, which allows the organisms to multiply and produce toxin. Subsequent reheating—even boiling—does not destroy the toxin or prevent illness. To prevent contamination and growth of the organism, food must be consumed or refrigerated immediately after it is prepared. (Food contamination with other organisms that have a very short incubation period can produce an identical disorder.)

The onset of cramps and diarrhea, with or without nausea and vomiting, occurs one to six hours—an average of three hours—after contaminated food is ingested, and is frequently abrupt. The diarrhea lasts until the gastrointestinal tract is emptied, rarely more than five to six hours. Most of the individuals who have eaten the contaminated food develop the disease, which establishes the diagnosis. Antibiotics are not effective; they do not neutralize the toxin. Antidiarrheal agents may help.

Giardiasis

For years, frantic alarms about the perils of giardiasis have aroused exaggerated concern about this infestation. Governmental agencies, particularly the National Park Service and the U.S. Forest Service, have filtered hundreds of gallons of water from wilderness streams, found one or two organisms (far less than enough to be infective), and erected garish signs proclaiming the water "hazardous."

Giardiasis is not a new problem. These organisms have always been present in wilderness streams and in the water supplies for most cities. They often have not been detected because they are not isolated by routine bacterial cultures. This protozoal parasite is found all over the world. Many animals harbor and excrete the organisms, resulting in contamination of wilderness streams, but the organism has been found in the municipal water supplies of a number of large U.S. cities, as well as in cities as diverse as St. Petersburg and Kathmandu.

In humans, the noninvasive parasites live in the upper intestinal tract, where they form numerous cysts that are passed in the stool. The cysts do not produce active disease, but they are resistant to disinfectants and other agents in their environment and do transmit the infestation. Fecal contamination of water is the most common route of transmittal. Less common, but significant, is direct passage of cysts or organisms from stool to the hands of a food preparer and to the food itself. Filtration removes the organisms. Iodine in a concentration of eight parts per million effectively kills parasites and cysts within ten minutes (twenty minutes if the water is cold—32° to 40°F or 0° to 5°C). Bringing water to a boil also kills the cysts.

Symptoms of giardiasis vary widely. Most infested individuals have no symptoms at all. In one incident carefully studied by the Centers for Disease Control and Prevention (CDC), disruption in a city's water disinfection system allowed the entire population to consume water heavily contaminated with giardia. Only eleven percent of the exposed population developed symptomatic disease, although forty-six percent had organisms in their stools. In the same study, 8.5 percent of the population of a neighboring city was found to have totally asymptomatic giardia infestations.

Characteristic symptoms, when they occur, are mild to moderate abdominal discomfort, abdominal distention due to increased intestinal gas ("rotten egg burps"—belches that smell like hydrogen sulfide—are typical), and mild to moderate diarrhea. Stools are soft, may be liquid, and are bulky and foul smelling. They do not contain blood, mucus, or pus. Two to four bowel movements a day are typical, but a few individuals have more severe symptoms. Cramps may occur. Mild to moderate generalized symptoms of illness—weakness, loss of appetite or even nausea, and chilly sensations—may appear. Without treatment, infestation lasts seven to ten days. Apparently most people develop some type of immunity after that time, because symptoms and the organisms disappear and recurrent symptomatic infestations are rare.

Rare individuals, less than one percent of those with infestations, fail to rid themselves of the organisms and develop chronic infestations that can cause malabsorption, loss of weight, ulcerlike stomach pain, and other chronic disturbances. Such prolonged infestations may result from mild immunologic deficiencies.

Occasionally, giardiasis has been associated with the explosive onset of voluminous diarrhea characteristic of traveler's diarrhea. Travelers, including physicians, often overdiagnose giardiasis. However, if a laboratory is not available and typical symptoms persisting for six to seven days have not been relieved by measures effective for traveler's diarrhea, a therapeutic trial of one of the drugs effective against this parasite may be justified.

Several drugs are effective. Metronidazole (Flagyl®) for five to ten days is the usual therapy in the United States. Cures have been obtained with a single large dose of this drug. When alcohol is consumed while taking metronidazole, severe vomiting results. Therefore, alcohol must be avoided during and for three days after taking this drug.

Quinacrine (Atabrine®) for one week is probably more effective, but this drug has a bitter taste, commonly causes nausea and vomiting, and is not tolerated as well. Yellowing of the skin is a nonsignificant side effect of quinacrine. The benign discoloration should not be confused with jaundice.

Furazolidone (Furozone®) is effective against giardia (and most gastrointestinal infectious organisms, including cholera). It may cure giardiasis unresponsive to metronidazole and quinacrine. The adult dose is 1,000 mg four times a day for seven to ten days.

Tinidazole is an agent similar to metronidazole that is sold under the trade name Tinebah® and can be purchased over the counter in many developing nations. Visitors to those countries have often taken it for disorders presumed to be giardiasis. The advantages of Tinebah® are its ease of administration—four tablets taken at the same time—and avoiding abstinence from alcohol. However, in view of the similarity of this agent to metronidazole, both advantages should be regarded with skepticism.

Cryptosporidiosis

Cryptosporidia were discovered in laboratory mice in 1907 and have been known to produce diarrheal disease in a variety of animals, including domestic animals. These organisms were not thought to infect humans until 1976, when the first human infection was diagnosed. In the subsequent decade, infections by the parasite were recognized mostly in immunocompromised individuals, primarily persons with acquired immunodeficiency syndrome (AIDS) or malnutrition. Only since the early 1980s has cryptosporidiosis been recognized as a major worldwide cause of diarrhea in otherwise healthy individuals.

Cryptosporidia are ubiquitous. The organisms have been found in up to ninety-seven percent of the large streams, lakes, and reservoirs in the United States. Infections occur on every continent but Antarctica and cause up to twenty percent of the cases of diarrhea severe enough for individuals to seek medical attention.

Cryptosporidia present a particular problem in wilderness situations because the organisms resist iodine and chlorine disinfectants. These parasites must be eliminated from water by filtration. Most filters sold for wilderness water disinfection have pores small enough to remove them.

After ingestion, the organisms implant in the cells lining the small intestine. Mature organisms are released into the intestinal lumen as thick-walled (eighty percent) or thin-walled (twenty percent) cysts. The thick-walled cysts are excreted, but the thin-walled cysts can reimplant and maintain the infestation.

In immunocompetent hosts, the incubation period is two to fourteen days. Typical symptoms are watery diarrhea, crampy pain, anorexia, malaise, and "gas." Approximately ten to fifteen percent of infected individuals are asymptomatic. Others may have more than seventy stools a day. The volume of diarrheal fluid may exceed twenty-five liters a day, mostly in immunocompromised individuals. Obviously, dehydration is common. Eating aggravates the diarrhea and pain, so many patients do not eat, resulting in weight loss.

More than eighty therapeutic agents have been tried; none has produced any benefit. Eradication of the infection depends entirely on the development of immunity by the host. As a result, immunocompromised individuals rid themselves of the organisms slowly—or not at all. For patients with human immunodeficiency virus (HIV) infection or receiving chemotherapy that suppresses their immune system, infestation may prove fatal. Malnourished children have impaired cellular immunity and are prone to severe cryptosporidiosis.

Therapy consists entirely of fluid replacement. Gatorade®, bouillon, and oral rehydration fluids have been recommended. The disorder lasts from two days to a month, typically about two weeks. It may recrudesce. Infective cysts may be shed for a longer time.

Cyclosporiasis

Cyclospora cayetanensis is a parasite first reported in New Guinea in 1977 and found in New York and Peru in 1985. Among the names it was given were "blue-green algae." Cyclosporiasis has now been reported from all over the world. This organism gained notoriety in the United States in 1996 when 1,465 infections were reported to the CDC. Investigation clearly indicated that most of the infections were related to consumption of raspberries shipped from Guatemala. However, most of the infections occurred east of the Rocky Mountains, which suggests that contamination of the raspberries may not have occurred in Guatemala.

Waterborne outbreaks have also occurred. In Nepal in 1992, twelve of fourteen British soldiers were infected by cyclospora in their drinking water. The water had been chlorinated, which suggests that cyclospora, like cryptosporidia, may be halide resistant.

Cyclospora involve the small intestine and are capable of completing their entire life cycle within a single host. However, infected individuals excrete cysts that require days to weeks to become infectious. As a result, direct human-to-human transmission of infection is unlikely. Humans are the only identified host for this parasite.

Infection typically causes watery diarrhea with frequent, sometimes explosive, stools. Other symptoms can include loss of appetite and substantial weight loss; bloating and increased flatus; cramps, nausea, and vomiting; and muscle aches, low-grade fever, and fatigue. Untreated illness may last for a few days to a month or longer and may follow a remitting-relapsing course. As would be expected, some infected individuals are asymptomatic. Diagnosis is dependent upon identifying the organism in stool.

Trimethoprim-sulfamethoxazole (TMP-SMX), one double-strength tablet twice a day for seven days, is effective treatment. No alternative drugs for individuals who are intolerant of this agent have been identified.

Irritable Bowel Syndrome

Irritable bowel syndrome, also known as "mucous colitis" or "spastic colon," is a common disturbance of large intestinal function that may result in either diarrhea or constipation. The syndrome is at least partially emotional in origin and is often related to stress. Most individuals with this disorder have had a history of similar symptoms. Onset during a wilderness outing would be unusual.

Abdominal pain relieved by defecation, looser stools at pain onset, more frequent stools at pain onset, abdominal distention, and the passage of mucus are commonly associated with this condition. Stools may be thin and tapered (pencil shaped).

Recognizing the nature of the disorder and reassuring the patient are important aspects of treatment. For patients with constipation, a high-fiber diet, possibly supplemented with psyllium husk fiber (Metamucil®), may be helpful. For diarrhea, loperamide up to four times a day may be helpful.

Other types of drug therapy, which must be administered by a physician, include cholestyramine, Bentyl®, and Librax®, which includes a tranquilizer. Other psychoactive drugs such as Elavil® and Prozac® have been used. Treatment is directed at the control of symptoms because no cure for this condition is known. All interventions may be ineffectual. Fortunately, the condition is not life-threatening.

SEVERE DIARRHEAS

Severe acute and subacute diarrhea is mostly of bacterial origin and, like less severe diarrhea, is most frequently transmitted by fecal contamination of drinking water. In areas where these diseases exist, all water must be carefully disinfected. Other precautions are described in the discussion of traveler's diarrhea.

Experienced physicians have difficulty distinguishing different invasive bacterial diarrheas in the wilderness. Nonphysicians in this situation can not expect to be able to make correct diagnoses. Individuals in any of the following categories who are considered to have an invasive gastrointestinal bacterial infection should contact a medical center with a bacteriologic laboratory as soon as possible:

- ▾ Children under three years of age and adults over sixty-five, particularly those with other significant illnesses
- ▾ Women who are pregnant
- ▾ Anyone with severe diarrhea lasting more than forty-eight to seventy-two hours that is associated with any of the following:
  - ▾ Stools that contain blood or easily detected pus
  - ▾ Pronounced abdominal tenderness
  - ▾ Fever—morning temperature over 99°F (37.2°C); evening temperature over 100°F (37.8°C)
  - ▾ Dehydration (loss of more than five percent of usual body weight)

If timely evacuation is impossible, appropriate antimicrobial drugs should be administered. Under these circumstances, pregnant patients present a special problem, because some of the drugs normally used may harm the developing child. Loperamide (Imodium®) is safe. TMP-SMX is relatively safe for the first eight months but should be avoided at term. The safety of ciprofloxacin (Cipro®) during pregnancy and the first eighteen years of life has not been established.

Precautions are necessary to avoid spread of the infection. A patient with one of these diseases should be isolated as much as possible. Attendants should be limited to one or two individuals who are scrupulous about cleanliness.

The attendants should wear protective rubber or plastic gloves and must scrub their hands vigorously, preferably with an antibacterial soap such as pHisoHex® or soap containing Betadine®, after any contact with the patient. All feces and vomit should be buried where contamination of water will not occur, preferably after being mixed with an antiseptic such as one percent Cresol®. All utensils and other instruments should be immersed in boiling water. Indispensable items, such as clothing or sleeping bags that can not be boiled, should be aired in bright sunlight for at least one or two days after the patient is recovering.

Invasive Bacterial Infections (Dysentery)

Invasive bacterial infections, or bacillary dysentery, are caused by a wide variety of bacteria, including *Salmonella, Shigella, Campylobacter, Yersinia, Aeromonas, Clostridium,* noncholera vibrios, and occasionally by other organisms. These organisms are found in temperate as well as tropical areas, but severe cases of bacillary dysentery occur most frequently in tropical or semitropical climates.

Salmonellae are particularly widespread. Virtually all domestic animals, including household pets—dogs, cats, birds, and turtles—and many wild animals harbor these bacteria. The number of asymptomatic human carriers has been estimated at two persons per thousand.

Contaminated water and food spread infections. Any item of food or drink can be contaminated. For salmonella, the greatest single source of human disease is poultry products (both meat and eggs) and raw meat of other types. Lack of hydrochloric acid in the stomach—as the result of disease or therapy for peptic ulcer—and alteration of the normal microbial flora in the intestinal tract by antibiotics increase susceptibility to infection by these organisms.

The incubation period varies from one to six days with an average of forty-eight hours (somewhat shorter for salmonella). The onset is often rather abrupt and is characterized by severe, intermittent abdominal cramps followed by diarrhea that may be copious and soon progresses to watery, foul-smelling stools. The stools contain large amounts of mucus and pus and occasionally moderate amounts of blood, particularly four to five hours after the onset. Nausea is common, but vomiting may not occur. Infection usually is associated with a fever of 100.5° to 102°F (38° to 39°C) or higher and chilly feelings or frank, shaking chills. Abdominal tenderness may be pronounced, is most marked in the lower portion of the abdomen, and is frequently accompanied by spasm of the abdominal muscles. Abdominal pain may be sufficiently intense, localized, and associated with enough rebound tenderness to suggest an acute abdominal disorder requiring surgery. The patient is obviously ill and may be prostrate.

After six to eight hours the symptoms abate somewhat, but the disease may take seven to ten days to run its course. Considerable variation in the severity of symptoms is observed, even among persons infected at the same meal.

The most important aspect of treatment for invasive bacterial gastroenteritis is prompt correction of dehydration. Large amounts of fluids should be administered (see Table 12-1). Intravenous fluids may be necessary for more severe cases. A bland diet may be given if it can be tolerated.

A hot water bottle or other source of warmth placed on the abdomen may reduce some of the pain and tenderness. Drugs to stop the diarrhea are not recommended because they tend to produce intestinal paralysis, which prevents the patient from taking fluids orally. These agents also may make the fever and overall disability worse. However, many individuals take such medications.

These infections should be treated with antibacterial agents. Ciprofloxacin (Cipro®) every twelve hours is the drug of choice; TMP-SMX every twelve hours is the second choice. (In Latin America, twenty-five percent of *Shigella* organisms are resistant to TMP-SMX.) The usual duration of therapy is one week.

Although antimicrobial therapy frequently produces marked improvement in twenty-four hours or less, it must be continued for at least five days or longer if symptoms persist.

Patients with these infections require rest; most should be in bed. Victims of bacillary dysentery frequently require seven to ten days to recover their strength after symptoms have disappeared.

Enterohemorrhagic *E. coli*

Enterohemorrhagic *E. coli,* serotype 0157:H7, produces an infection of the colon that is often manifested by bloody diarrhea. Undercooked meat, particularly beef, is often the source of infection, which is sometimes complicated by anemia, kidney failure, and impaired brain function. No specific treatment is available. Seriously ill patients require hospitalization in an institution that can provide supportive therapy. Antimotility drugs should be avoided because they aggravate the illness.

Cholera

Cholera, once a scourge throughout the world, is almost nonexistent where modern sanitation and water purification methods are practiced. However, infections that claim many lives are common in some areas. A major outbreak recently killed thousands in Peru, Ecuador, and Colombia. In Southeast Asia, monsoon rains wash feces that has collected on the ground and in the streets into streams and rivers and regularly—almost annually—precipitate epidemics. Effective treatment is unavailable for the poor in many developing countries.

Although cholera is transmitted primarily by contaminated water, the infection may also be contracted from food, particularly items that are not cooked. Injected vaccines are ineffective. Oral vaccines are being developed and tested. Vaccination is not recommended by the CDC and other authorities, is not available in the United States, and is not required for entry by any country.

Fortunately, the cholera vibrio can not survive very long outside the human body. As a result, most infections occur near areas of significant population and thus in areas where hospitals are available. However, undiagnosed patients with mild symptoms and carriers, although much rarer than carriers for the salmonella that cause typhoid fever, may spread the organisms a considerable distance from hospitals. The rapidity with which prostration appears in severe infections usually prevents evacuation and mandates treatment in the field.

Cholera can become overwhelming with amazing speed, leaving the patient severely dehydrated and in shock from fluid loss within one to three hours. An uncooked seafood dish contaminated with cholera organisms served after takeoff on a jetliner flight from Lima, Peru, to Los Angeles, California, produced fifty-three infections, one of which was fatal before the flight could be completed. However, the usual incubation period for cholera is one to three days, during which the victim may notice mild diarrhea, depression, and lassitude. The end of the incubation period is signaled by the explosive onset of voluminous watery diarrhea.

The gastrointestinal tract is quickly emptied, and the stools lose their fecal character and foul odor. The patient is constantly dribbling stools consisting almost entirely of water. Flecks of mucus that look like grains of rice floating in water have resulted in the name "rice water stools" for this material. The stools rarely contain blood.

Frequently, no warning of the need to defecate is felt, resulting in repeated, often uncontrollable bowel evacuations. Similarly, vomiting may occur without antecedent nausea, although vomiting is uncommon after the onset. As the patient becomes dehydrated, fever and a rapid pulse appear. The blood pressure frequently drops below normal, and the weak pulse becomes difficult to feel. The features become gaunt, the eyes shrunken, and the skin shriveled and dry. Urinary output falls to less than 500 ml per day.

The treatment for cholera is fluid replacement. The entire volume of stool and vomit must be replaced with oral or intravenous salt solutions. Stool volumes should be measured for replacement to be accurate. Intravenous administration of fluids is often necessary during the early stages of the disease, particularly if vomiting is substantial, and may be lifesaving if the patient is severely dehydrated and in shock. Two to four liters of saline or Ringer's lactate may be required in the first hour, and as much as eight or more liters during the first day. After dehydration has been corrected and the patient is no longer in shock, he usually is able to take fluids orally (see Table 12-1).

Victims of cholera are severely ill and obviously require bed rest. A canvas cot with a hole in the center through which the patient can defecate without having to move helps make him more comfortable and facilitates the collection and measuring of the stools during the first few days of the illness. Feces must be disposed of carefully to avoid contamination of water supplies and infecting others.

A single dose of tetracycline (2 g) or doxycycline (300 mg) is the preferred antibiotic therapy for adults. In areas where tetracycline resistance is prevalent, ciprofloxacin (1 g) should be substituted. For children, TMP-SMX or erythromycin should be administered. **Antibiotics are only an adjunct to therapy and can not substitute for fluid and electrolyte replacement.** Sedatives make care of the patient more difficult and are not useful.

Cholera is not very contagious and is spread principally by feces. Sanitary disposal of feces and vomit must be strictly enforced, and all contaminated articles, including clothing, bedding, and utensils, must be cleaned.

The acute phase of the infection rarely lasts more than three to five days. The patient usually is able to eat a bland diet by the third day. However, several weeks are required for full recovery.

Typhoid Fever

Typhoid fever is a generalized as well as a gastrointestinal infection caused by *Salmonella typhi*. The organisms invade the wall of the small bowel and enter the blood stream. Occasionally, people (called "carriers") who have recovered from typhoid fever continue to harbor the organisms in the gastrointestinal tract and excrete them in their stools. The bacteria can survive for months under natural conditions. Uncooked foods, salads, raw milk, and contaminated water are the most important sources of infection.

The incubation period is seven to fourteen days. Symptoms during the first week consist of fever, headache, and abdominal pain. The onset is usually insidious. Often there is no change in bowel habits during the initial ten days of illness. Near the end of the first week, enlargement of the spleen may be detectable. A brief, somewhat diagnostic rash can be seen in seventy percent of light-skinned individuals about seven to ten days after the onset of symptoms. The rash consists of "rose spots" that are deeply red, usually few in number, two to four millimeters in diameter, often present in clusters, blanch on pressure, and occur most often on the lower chest and upper abdominal wall. During the second week of illness, fever becomes more continuous and many patients are severely ill. The pulse rate is often slow in comparison to the severity of the fever, an important diagnostic feature. Cough and nosebleeds may occur. In the third week, extreme toxicity, irrationality or confusion, and greenish "pea soup" diarrhea may occur. The latter may presage the dire complications of perforation of the intestine or intestinal hemorrhage. For survivors, the fourth week often brings improvement in their status. However, typhoid fever is a long-lasting and debilitating infection.

For typhoid fever, supportive care and maintenance of fluid intake are important. Antipyretic agents such as aspirin, ibuprofen, or acetaminophen may cause severe sweating and may lower blood pressure. Cautious use is acceptable only if sponging with tepid water does not control the high fever.

The antibiotic treatment of choice is either ciprofloxacin for ten days or ceftriaxone 2 grams daily intravenously for five days. Chloramphenicol is no longer commonly used because typhoid bacteria from Mexico and Vietnam are often resistant to chloramphenicol, and this drug may rarely cause a potentially lethal anemia after prolonged therapy. The usual duration of therapy is two weeks.

Before travel to an area where typhoid may be encountered, immunization for typhoid and paratyphoid fever should be obtained. Although immunization does not completely prevent infection, it does reduce the severity of the disease and reduces the incidence of complications. An oral typhoid vaccine is now available.

Amebiasis

Amebiasis is caused by the invasive parasite *Entamoeba histolytica*. Although generally thought of as a tropical disease, amebiasis is by no means limited to such areas.

These organisms invade the wall of the large intestine. The adults form cysts that are passed in feces and spread the infection. The cysts are most commonly ingested in contaminated water. Food that has been fertilized with human excreta, carelessness in food preparation, and insects—particularly flies—are other sources of infestation. Iodine in appropriate concentrations and boiling destroy the cysts effectively; filtration removes them.

Amebiasis is usually a very mild disorder in its early stages, and symptoms may be entirely absent. Mild diarrhea with soft stools and a moderately increased number of bowel movements is more common. Occasional individuals develop constipation rather than diarrhea. A few patients have more severe symptoms, including numerous watery stools that contain mucus or even blood, and abdominal cramps. However, a period of mild gastrointestinal dysfunction usually precedes the onset of the more severe stage.

Easy fatigability, a low fever, and vague pains in the muscles, back, or joints are frequently present. Nervousness, irritability, and dizziness occasionally develop. Typically, no abnormality can be found by physical examination, although slight tenderness in the right lower quadrant of the abdomen is sometimes present. The chronicity and mildness of the diarrhea and a history of exposure to conditions in which infection is likely suggest the diagnosis. Laboratory facilities are required to make a definitive diagnosis.

If amebiasis is suspected, metronidazole should be given three times a day for five to ten days. Occasionally, metronidazole may not completely eradicate the infection.

Persons visiting an area in which amebiasis is prevalent should consider examination for infestation upon their return. The organisms may lie quietly within the large intestine for years and then spread to the liver, where they form abscesses from which they occasionally even invade the lung. This form of the disease has a high mortality rate.

CONSTIPATION AND RECTAL PROBLEMS

Healthy adults rarely need to be concerned about constipation. The concept that normal individuals should have a bowel movement every day is a myth perpetrated on bowel-conscious people by herb peddlers and overprotective mothers. Bowel rhythm can vary widely. For some individuals three stools a day is normal; others have one stool every three days. A change in bowel habits for which no cause can be identified may be significant, but new foods or alteration in daily schedule can produce such changes.

The type of food consumed plays a large part in determining the character and frequency of stools. Foods that are almost completely absorbed, such as liquids or carbohydrates, can not be expected to produce a copious stool. The converse is true for foods with a large unabsorbed residue such as bran or leafy vegetables. Reduced food intake due to illness or dieting leads to smaller stool volume.

Constipation is more accurately defined as the passage of hard, dry stools rather than a specified frequency of bowel movements. Reduced intake of fluids and disruption of normal schedules with infrequent rest stops (travel by air) all tend to cause constipation. An adequate fluid intake (one and one-half to two quarts a day) and consumption of fruits and other foods that loosen the stools and of bran or high-fiber cereals that provide bulk help maintain normal bowel function.

In general, laxatives have very little prophylactic or therapeutic value. If, in an unusual situation, laxatives become necessary, the best and safest is Milk of Magnesia®, either one or two tablespoons or two to four tablets at bedtime.

Fecal Impaction

Under conditions in which the urge to defecate is resisted, such as weather or illness that confines individuals to their tents, the normal bowel reflexes may become insensitive and permit stool to accumulate in the rectum. Dehydration may cause the water in the stool to be reabsorbed with such avidity that a bulky, hard residue that can not be evacuated in a normal manner results.

The best way to determine whether impaction has occurred is to insert a lubricated and (if available) gloved index finger into the rectum. If a mass of hard stool is found, it must be extracted. The mass of stool should be broken up with the index finger and the fragments removed as gently as possible (Fig. 12-1). Injury of the rectal and anal tissues should be avoided. Following manual removal of the impaction, the causes of the impaction should be corrected.

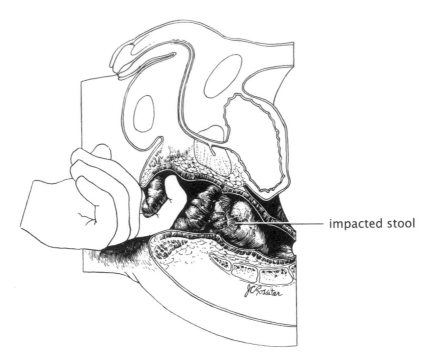

impacted stool

FIGURE 12-1. Digital removal of a fecal impaction

Although breaking up and extracting a fecal impaction is aesthetically unpleasant, no alternative exists. Enema fluids will not enter the solidified fecal mass; laxatives have no effect on the dilated, flaccid rectal wall. Paradoxically, fecal impaction may be accompanied by the passage of a number of small, watery stools—the only material that can get past the impacted mass.

Anal Fissure

With constipation, the stool may become so hard and bulky that its passage causes a small tear (fissure) in the skin of the anus. Subsequent bowel movements are painful and may be associated with a small amount of bleeding.

Avoiding bulky, hard stools by consuming adequate fluids often allows the fissure to heal. A low-residue diet that is low in fiber and consists of foods that are almost totally absorbed, such as milk, soups, and carbohydrates, may avert bowel movements for several days and allow healing, but this diet is constipating. Straining at stool should be avoided indefinitely. Supporting the body so its full weight is not on the toilet seat during defecation avoids aggravating the injury. The anal area should be cleaned gently after each bowel movement. Aggressive wiping (particularly with coarse paper), scratching, and rubbing should be avoided.

Mineral oil, one tablespoon (15 cc) twice a day, lubricates the stool and reduces the pain with bowel movements. (Mineral oil is not a laxative—only a lubricant.) If pain persists between bowel movements, a bland anesthetic ointment such as dibucaine may be applied. The ointment or a rectal suppository containing dibucaine may have to be inserted into the anal canal. Healing is also aided by the application of one percent hydrocortisone ointment.

Persistent pain or bleeding should be brought to the attention of a physician as soon as possible.

Hemorrhoids

Hemorrhoids ("piles") are abnormally dilated veins that protrude from the anus. They are usually present before a journey begins but can be aggravated by the constipation that commonly develops with new foods and irregular schedules. Hemorrhoids usually are more annoying than disabling, but they can be a source of considerable itching and discomfort and can cause severe pain if they become prolapsed and thrombosed. Hemorrhoids bleed modestly following a hard or bulky bowel movement, but serious bleeding is rare. The blood is usually noted on the toilet paper or on the outside of the stool; blood mixed with stool suggests bleeding from within the colon, a much more serious problem.

Individuals with substantial hemorrhoids should have them assessed by a colorectal surgeon before a major wilderness outing. If hemorrhoids become bothersome in the field, measures to soften and lubricate the stool—most important, a generous fluid intake—and one tablespoon of mineral oil twice a day may provide relief. Bearing down during bowel movements should be avoided. Sitting in warm water for fifteen to thirty minutes several times a day helps relieve symptoms but interferes with outdoor activities. Bulk formers such as Metamucil® may be helpful during an acute episode. Hemorrhoidal suppositories may relieve symptoms. Application of an anesthetic cream to the painful area four times a day also should provide relief.

Thrombosed Hemorrhoid

The blood within a hemorrhoid occasionally clots, resulting in significant anal pain that may come on gradually or suddenly. A purple nodule that is firm and tender can be seen protruding from the anal opening or can be felt just inside. Clots smaller than one-half inch (1.25 cm) in diameter are best allowed to resolve spontaneously. Clots larger than one inch (2.5 cm) may require surgical therapy. The severity of the pain should determine how clots between these two sizes should be treated.

An incision in the top of the thrombosed hemorrhoid and evacuation of the clot can provide relief of pain that frequently is dramatic. Days of distress can be avoided if the thrombosed hemorrhoid is large. Before incision, the anus should be washed with soap and water. A moderate analgesic can be given before incision. Ice or snow pressed against the nodule provides surprisingly effective anesthesia. The incision should be left open and pads should be left in the intergluteal cleft to reduce soiling by blood. Warm baths help relieve pain and anal muscle spasm.

Rectal Abscess

Abscesses in the tissues surrounding the rectum and anus usually follow long-standing anal problems such as fissures or hemorrhoids, which should be corrected before a prolonged wilderness outing. Abscesses in this location are not basically different from abscesses elsewhere in the body.

The cardinal symptom of a rectal abscess is throbbing pain in the region of the anus. Malaise, fever, and chills are common, and the patient may appear acutely ill. Examination usually reveals the characteristic signs of an abscess—a mass that is red, tender, and warm. The abscess may come to a point ("head") in the skin adjacent to the anus. A few rectal abscesses are located deeper beneath the skin and can only be felt during digital examination of the rectum.

Rectal abscesses should be treated just like abscesses anywhere else—incision and drainage. If the abscess comes to a point in the skin beside the anus, an incision can be made in the center of the fluctuant area. If a deeper abscess is felt or the surrounding inflammation is extensive, the patient should be evacuated. Only a surgeon should drain such abscesses. Serious complications can follow an abscess in this location that is not properly treated. If the patient has a fever, amoxicillin/clavulanate or levofloxacin and metronidazole should be administered during evacuation.

PEPTIC ULCER AND RELATED PROBLEMS

A peptic ulcer is a crater in the lining of the stomach or intestine produced by the digestive action of the enzymes and acids from the stomach (Fig. 12-2). The cause of peptic ulcers is not well understood, but stress may play a role. Most ulcers, particularly duodenal ulcers, are associated with infection by *Helicobacter pylori*. Infection with this organism is also associated with two gastric malignancies: adenocarcinoma and lymphoma. However, the manner in which this organism produces these disorders is as yet unknown. Drugs such as steroids and NSAIDs, particularly aspirin, are also associated with ulceration. Celebrex® and Vioxx® are less likely to cause ulcers or bleeding than other NSAIDs currently available.

An uncomplicated ulcer is not usually disabling, although the pain can be substantial. An ulcer is dangerous because it may hemorrhage or perforate. These disabling, life-endangering complications require immediate evacuation to a medical center. Perforation is discussed in chapter 13, "Acute Abdominal Pain."

The characteristic symptom of an ulcer is gnawing pain, usually located in the upper portion of the abdomen near the midline. The pain is quite localized and the patient usually can pinpoint it with his fingertip. Typically, the pain comes on one to four hours after eating or between midnight and two o'clock in the morning. Bland food, milk, or antacids usually relieve the pain.

The pain is thought to be caused by the effects of stomach acid on the ulcer. Acid is a factor in all peptic ulcers. Food and antacids tend to neutralize the acid and thus relieve the pain. The characteristic times at which the pain occurs are the periods when there is no food in the stomach to counteract the acid. (No explanation for the absence of pain in the early morning, when the stomach is totally empty, has been found.)

Treatment

The basic therapy for ulcers associated with *H. pylori* is eradication of the infection, but diagnosis and treatment of such infections is complex and can only be carried out by a physician. Supplemental ulcer therapy is primarily directed toward reducing the acidity of the stomach contents. Antacids have been used

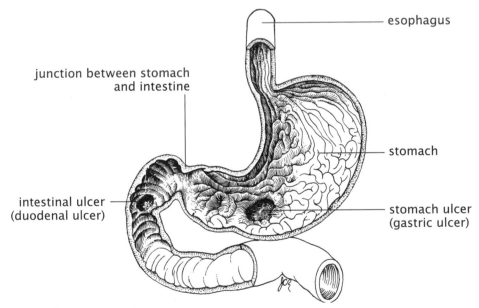

FIGURE 12-2. Gastric and duodenal ulcers

in the past and are still valuable. However, newer, more effective approaches include drugs that block the secretion of acid and other agents that create a barrier between the acid and the ulcerated area.

Antacids are best taken between meals. Consumption within an hour of other anti-ulcer drugs should be avoided. Because overdosage with antacids is rarely a problem, more frequent doses may be administered if pain persists. Liquid antacids are more effective than tablets but are less portable. Many liquid preparations are available. Some tablets are ineffective. The most effective tablet is Alkets®. Titralac® and Robalate® are also effective but sometimes are not as readily available. Rolaids®, Tums®, or other agents may be taken if none of the three preferred tablets is obtainable.

Antacid therapy became less important after histamine H_2 receptor antagonists (H_2 blockers) became available. Famotidine (Pepcid®), ranitidine (Zantac®), cimetidine (Tagamet®), and nizatidine (Axid®) are H_2 blockers currently being used; all are equally effective in appropriate dosage. The first three are now available over the counter. Famotidine and nizatidine are best taken once a day at bedtime and are simpler to administer. The other two drugs must be taken more frequently.

Sucralfate (Carafate®) forms a complex that adheres to the surface of the ulcer and protects it from the action of acid, digestive enzymes, and bile salts.

The most potent medications now available are the proton pump inhibitors. Omeprazole (Prilosec®) was the first drug of this class to become available, but it is available only with a physician's prescription.

Any NSAID being administered should be discontinued. Aspirin in any form must be strictly avoided; it increases the risk of bleeding fifteenfold. Smokers with ulcers should cease smoking entirely; less desirably, they should substantially decrease their nicotine usage. Alcohol and caffeine should be avoided. A mild tranquilizer may help highly stressed individuals.

Symptoms normally improve within a few days, but full healing takes six to eight weeks. Physical activity may continue during treatment, but strenuous exertion, particularly if stressful, is best avoided for at least a week after the institution of appropriate therapy. Persistent symptoms in spite of the institution of treatment merit the care of a physician.

Indigestion

Indigestion is a nonscientific term for nonspecific abdominal symptoms that usually are transient or periodic and are rarely indicative of a serious disorder. The symptoms of indigestion may be confused with those of an ulcer. Because an ulcer poses a threat of severe complications but indigestion does not, the conditions should be correctly diagnosed.

The symptoms of an ulcer and indigestion usually differ in several respects. Instead of pain, indigestion more commonly produces a sense of fullness, excessive belching, or regurgitating small amounts of food or sour stomach contents, although a burning sensation may be present beneath the breastbone (heartburn). Sour stomach contents may reach the back of the throat. Ulcer pain usually occurs in the central upper abdomen; indigestion may be felt in any portion of the abdomen. Indigestion symptoms usually get worse with eating; ulcer symptoms are usually improved during and for an hour or so after food consumption. The symptoms of indigestion become less noticeable with time and the passage of food from the stomach, also the opposite of ulcer symptoms. Indigestion symptoms are intermittent; ulcer symptoms are more persistent.

No drug therapy for this condition is mandatory. Medications that may provide symptomatic relief include antacids, H_2 blockers, chlordiazepoxide and clidinium (Librax®), and propantheline (Pro-Banthine®). (Librax® and Pro-Banthine® should not be taken within eight hours of each other.) Acetaminophen (Tylenol®) can help control discomfort. In addition, eating small meals six times a day may be helpful.

Heartburn responds promptly to the administration of a liquid antacid. H_2 blockers also provide relief, but it is usually less prompt and longer lasting. Combining both drugs often produces better symptom control than either alone. Therapy with proton pump inhibitors may be needed for severe symptoms associated with reflux of gastric contents into the esophagus. Patients with this condition should not eat for several hours before going to bed so that their stomachs will be empty, and should try to sleep with their head and shoulders elevated so that gravity can help prevent reflux.

GASTROINTESTINAL HEMORRHAGE

One of the most serious problems that can occur in the wilderness is massive hemorrhage from the stomach or intestines. Even with expert treatment, about ten percent of elderly patients hospitalized with this condition die. (Death rates in young, otherwise healthy adults are lower.) Because blood transfusions and other forms of intensive medical and surgical care are required to treat this life-threatening disorder, every effort must be made to get the individual to a hospital as quickly as possible.

If, in a remote area, helicopter transport can not be achieved promptly, the condition must be managed in the field. Attempting litter evacuation or walking out with assistance while active bleeding is occurring is unwise. Fortunately, a young person usually stops bleeding within twelve to twenty-four hours. Six to twelve hours after bleeding appears to have stopped, a choice between remaining in camp at rest for one to three days and attempting to reach a hospital must be made. A slow pulse, cessation of vomiting, and a normal brown color of the stools are indications that relatively little blood has been lost and that bleeding has stopped. However, rebleeding can occur at any time. Careful consideration must be given to the unique circumstances found in every situation.

The patient is usually very weak after a significant bleeding episode and requires assistance during evacuation. He should by no means attempt to continue vigorous activities, even though he feels well at rest.

Except for the occasional individuals who bleed slightly after prolonged retching, essentially all gastrointestinal bleeding in otherwise healthy young adults is due to peptic ulcer. However, even though the ulcer is almost always present before the hemorrhage, it may be totally asymptomatic.

The signs and symptoms of serious gastrointestinal bleeding include:
- ▼ Faintness or weakness, which is more prominent when erect than when lying down
- ▼ Vomiting obvious blood
- ▼ Vomiting "coffee ground" material (blood that has been partially digested in the stomach)
- ▼ Rectal passage of obvious blood
- ▼ Passage of liquid or solid "tarry black" stools (blood that has been digested in the intestines) (Iron, which is contained in vitamin and mineral preparations, and Pepto-Bismol can cause the stools to have a dark color.)
- ▼ Shock

No medications currently available stop heavy bleeding from peptic ulcers. However, high-dosage omeprazole (twice the usual dosage two times a day) often significantly reduces the rate of bleeding. The H$_2$ blockers may be helpful if omeprazole is not available.

When the bleeding ceases, drugs lessen the likelihood of rebleeding. In addition, smoking must cease! Aspirin and other NSAIDs, alcohol, and caffeine must be avoided. The individual should rest as much as possible. If a substantial amount of blood has been lost and the individual becomes light-headed when erect, he should be kept supine. If signs of shock, particularly low blood pressure, appear, appropriate treatment should be instituted.

DISEASES OF THE LIVER

Jaundice

Jaundice is produced by diseases of the liver. One of the numerous functions of the liver is to remove from the blood the pigment resulting from the normal destruction of old red blood cells. When disease severely damages the liver, the bilirubin not removed from the blood accumulates in the body and imparts a yellow or bronze color to the whites of the eyes and later the skin.

Bilirubin is excreted into the intestine through the bile ducts and, following further changes in the intestinal tract, imparts the normal brown color to the stool. If the pigment is excreted into the intestine in small amounts or not at all, the stools become pale or "clay colored." Excess bilirubin is partially excreted by the kidneys, imparting a brown color to the urine and causing the foam produced by shaking to have a yellow color instead of the normal white appearance.

When jaundice is suspected, the patient should be examined in daylight. Flashlights and other artificial lights usually produce a yellowish color that can simulate jaundice.

Hepatitis

Hepatitis, an inflammatory disorder of the liver caused by infection with viruses that selectively involve that organ, is the most important cause of painless jaundice likely to occur for the first time in wilderness conditions. (Jaundice associated with pain is discussed in chapter 13, "Acute Abdominal Pain.") Patients with previous attacks of jaundice should be evaluated by a physician and instructed in the treatment for their condition before undertaking an outing. Untreated malaria and other conditions cause jaundice on rare occasions by the excessive destruction of red blood cells. However, such disorders can usually be recognized from other findings.

A number of distinct hepatitis viruses are now recognized: hepatitis A, B, and C; the delta agent (hepatitis D); and hepatitis E, F, and G. Hepatitis A is an RNA virus that is spread principally by fecal contamination of water and food, particularly shellfish. Infections are common but almost never fatal; well over ninety percent of infected individuals have such minor symptoms they do not realize they are ill. If jaundice does develop, it rarely lasts more than a month. However, such individuals are usually unable to continue a wilderness outing. Chronic liver disease does not follow hepatitis A infections. Effective vaccines are available. Individuals not known to have been previously infected should be vaccinated before traveling to developing nations, particularly if they visit such areas frequently. Gamma globulin may be advisable for unvaccinated individuals who can not defer travel for the four weeks needed for vaccination to be effective.

Hepatitis B is caused by a DNA virus that is spread principally by body fluids through personal contact, particularly sexual contact. As with hepatitis A, most individuals do not realize they have an infection, but up to ten percent may be quite ill, a few die, and approximately five percent develop chronic liver disease. Approximately half of the individuals with chronic liver disease develop cirrhosis (scarring of the liver), an eventually lethal disorder. Hepatitis B is directly responsible for many cases of hepatocellular carcinoma (a malignancy arising in the liver), the most common malignant tumor on a worldwide basis, although it is uncommon in the United States. A safe and effective vaccine for hepatitis B is available. Everyone probably should be vaccinated, but it is essential for medical workers, others who come in contact with blood, and travelers to developing countries.

The delta agent (hepatitis D) is an incomplete DNA virus that can produce infections only in association with hepatitis B. Therefore, immunization for hepatitis B prevents hepatitis D. Hepatitis D may be acquired simultaneously with hepatitis B or subsequently. Patients with both infections simultaneously have a higher risk of more severe disease. Acute hepatitis B infection may become rapidly fatal, and chronic hepatitis B is more likely to progress to cirrhosis when associated with hepatitis D infection.

Many of the infections previously termed non-A, non-B hepatitis are now known to be caused by hepatitis C, a viral agent identified in 1989 that accounts for roughly twenty percent of the cases of acute hepatitis and a much higher percentage of chronic, long-standing infections in the United States. Acute infections are often asymptomatic and undiagnosed. About fifty percent of hepatitis C infections result in chronic liver disease, which is often asymptomatic but may cause persistent fatigue. Approximately twenty-five percent of the patients with chronic hepatitis C develop cirrhosis, an ultimately lethal disorder, within twenty-five years of acquiring the infection. After twenty years, one to four percent of patients with hepatitis C develop hepatocellular carcinoma. After cirrhosis is established, one to five percent of patients develop this tumor. Significant alcohol consumption increases the risk of such severe complications.

Ninety to ninety-five percent of hepatitis following blood transfusion has been caused by hepatitis C, although procedures for screening for this infection introduced in 1990 have almost eliminated this problem in the United States. In developing nations screening procedures often are not available or not affordable, and the risk of acquiring hepatitis C infection is much higher.

Hepatitis C is an RNA virus that is transmitted through broken skin or mucous membranes. Intravenous drug use accounts for fifty percent of the infections, sexual contact for ten percent, blood transfusion for five to ten percent, and exposure to blood by nurses, ambulance attendants, and similar medical professionals for five percent. The routes of inoculation for the remaining one-quarter of the infections are unidentified. Blood tests for this recently recognized virus are available, but development of a vaccine has not yet been accomplished. Gamma globulin probably is of no value for preventing infection.

Another form of non-A, non-B hepatitis—an important form worldwide—is hepatitis E, which is rarely encountered in the United States. The virus was first identified in 1989 and has been linked to epidemics in Africa and Asia and to two outbreaks in Mexico. Infection usually results from ingestion of water contaminated with sewage, and can be prevented by routine disinfection. Infection can also be spread by close personal contact. Like hepatitis A, hepatitis E usually produces an acute infection that is rarely fatal and heals without producing chronic liver disease. However, in some outbreaks the mortality rate in pregnant women has been as high as twenty percent. No diagnostic blood test is available, but the virus can be identified in stool samples. No vaccine is available. The effectiveness of gamma globulin for preventing or ameliorating the infection is unknown.

Hepatitis F and G are recently discovered blood-borne infections about which little is known.

The onset of hepatitis may be abrupt or insidious and follows an incubation period ranging from three weeks to six months. The earliest symptoms are loss of appetite, general malaise, and easy fatigability. Later a low fever and nausea and vomiting appear. Many smokers have a peculiar loss of taste for cigarettes. In individuals with more severe infections, the symptoms increase in severity. Light-colored stools and dark urine may precede the appearance of jaundice by several days. Vague upper abdominal discomfort and tenderness may be present, particularly in the right upper quadrant, but severe pain is absent. After the appearance of jaundice, some patients experience ill-defined joint or muscular pains. A highly variable skin rash may be present, and some patients have generalized itching. When jaundice does develop, it often lasts three to six weeks. Malaise, easy fatigability, and loss of appetite may persist for several more months.

No effective treatment for the acute episodes of any type of hepatitis infection is available. A study of previously healthy young adults in the U.S. Army indicated that restriction of exercise had no effect on the course of the disease for that rather select group of individuals. Most wilderness explorers would fall into the same group of previously healthy, relatively young adults. However, most subjects do not feel capable of more than very mild exercise. A nourishing diet, high in proteins and carbohydrates and supplemented with vitamins, should be provided.

All drug therapy should be avoided if possible, including alcohol and drugs to promote sleep. The liver metabolizes most drugs. When that organ's function is impaired by hepatitis, such metabolism may be much slower than normal. If the drugs are not completely metabolized between doses, they can accumulate in the blood and may reach toxic concentrations.

Most individuals with hepatitis should be evacuated. Recovery usually takes so long that delaying evacuation until the person is well is impossible. In addition, complications that require a physician's care may develop.

Treatment of chronic hepatitis B with lamivudine for one year has produced favorable results and is well tolerated. Improvement is usually sustained after therapy is terminated. Hepatitis C can be treated with interferon and ribavirin, but these drugs must be injected, and therapy is prolonged, expensive, and only partially successful. Prevention is essential!

Cirrhosis

Hepatic cirrhosis is a progressive scarring or fibrosing process that results from chronic hepatitis B and C infection, prolonged alcohol abuse, and many other disorders and is ultimately lethal. Jaundice and ascites, an accumulation of fluid in the abdomen, are common complications. The scarring in the liver blocks the flow of blood returning from the intestines. In order to return to the circulation, the blood must find other channels, which results in the enlargement of veins in several areas, most prominently the lower esophagus. Death often results from massive bleeding from these enlarged esophageal veins (known as varices), which can not be controlled by the measures that limit bleeding from peptic ulcers. Liver failure is also a common cause of death for patients with cirrhosis. Such problems are rare in wilderness situations because individuals with these conditions rarely feel well enough to visit the backcountry.

Acute Hepatic Necrosis

Acute hepatic necrosis is a disorder that is usually fatal within a week. Toxic fungi (*Amanita* mushrooms); large quantities of some drugs such as acetaminophen (Tylenol®), particularly when associated with excessive alcohol consumption; and certain chemicals such as carbon tetrachloride can produce this disorder. However, knowledge of these hazards has become more widespread, and the most common cause of acute hepatic necrosis now is probably acute hepatitis.

Patients rapidly deteriorate, become jaundiced, and sink into a coma from which they can not be roused. The only effective treatment is liver transplantation, which rarely can be performed rapidly enough, even in major medical centers.

13

ACUTE ABDOMINAL PAIN

PRINCIPAL CONTRIBUTOR:
Ben Eiseman, M.D.

Travelers to remote areas who consume food and water from questionable sources are familiar with the abdominal pain associated with acute diarrhea. They know that these symptoms, although painful for a few days, are self-limited and gradually subside. Distinguishing such relatively trivial conditions from serious diseases that are life-threatening if left surgically untreated can be difficult. Inappropriate delay in evacuating an individual to a medical facility where surgical intervention is available may seriously compromise the outcome, but unnecessary evacuation can disrupt a carefully planned expedition. Three options are available in such circumstances:

▼ Observing the individual to determine whether the character of the pain changes
▼ Administering antibiotics
▼ Evacuation

A few questions are helpful in making a preliminary decision:

▼ Do others in the party share identical complaints? The most common cause of abdominal pain in wilderness conditions is infectious gastroenteritis (traveler's diarrhea), which is discussed in chapter 12, "Gastrointestinal Disorders."
▼ Has the individual had similar attacks of abdominal pain? If so, his symptoms probably have the same cause, and previously effective treatment should be repeated.
▼ Does the person have a known medical disorder? What medications is he taking? Patients often fail to mention medications that they use routinely in their urban or suburban environment, such as aspirin, anticoagulants, medications for hypertension, bronchodilators, antihistamines, diuretics, mood elevators or depressants, and even insulin. Such drugs may produce unexpected symptoms and alter the course of a disease when taken in a harsh wilderness environment.
▼ Is the pain or tenderness localized to a single point in the abdomen? Such localization often suggests an inflammatory process that requires operation.
▼ Is the abdomen diffusely tender and rigid? A "boardlike" abdomen commonly signals generalized peritonitis that requires immediate evacuation and operation.
▼ Is the person seriously ill? Is he delirious, febrile, jaundiced, or dehydrated? Is he thirsty? (Thirst is sometimes a sign of shock.) Does he feel warm?
▼ Does the person seem likely to overreact to discomfort? Being in a wilderness environment can be highly stressful for some inexperienced persons.

DIAGNOSIS

A definitive diagnosis may be impossible during the early phases of a disease, but a tentative or working diagnosis, with the understanding that it may be altered as signs and symptoms change, is appropriate because it provides guidance for the next step. Once the abdominal pain and other indications of disease are well developed, an astute examiner can usually match the signs and symptoms with the pattern of a well-defined disorder (see Fig. 13-3).

HISTORY

Important information to be obtained in the history includes:
- ▼ Time and nature of pain at its onset. Was it sharp, dull, sudden, or gradual?
- ▼ Location of pain. Is it right or left of the midline, above or below the umbilicus?
- ▼ Progression of pain and tenderness since onset. Is the pain increasing or decreasing? Has it shifted from one part of the abdomen to another? Has the nature of the pain changed? For example, has generalized discomfort become localized sharp pain?
- ▼ Is nausea, vomiting, or diarrhea present?
- ▼ Are chills, fever, or other signs of disease present?
- ▼ Does the urine contain blood?
- ▼ Does the individual have a history of similar episodes, pain relieved by food or milk, indigestion caused by fried or fatty food, previous abdominal surgery, or a missed menstrual period?

PHYSICAL EXAMINATION

The unhurried examination should be performed in the quietest place available, with the patient as comfortable and as secure as possible. However, in the wilderness, medical emergencies frequently arise

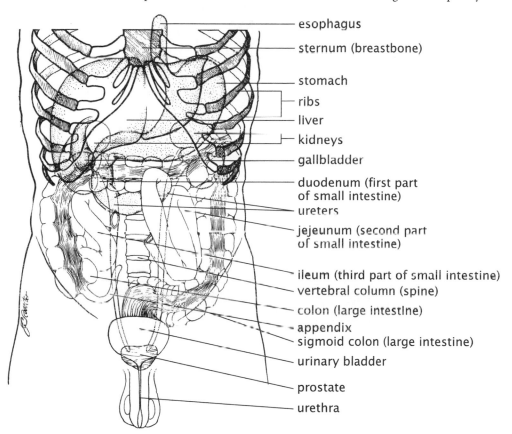

esophagus
sternum (breastbone)
stomach
ribs
liver
kidneys
gallbladder
duodenum (first part of small intestine)
ureters
jejeunum (second part of small intestine)
ileum (third part of small intestine)
vertebral column (spine)
colon (large intestine)
appendix
sigmoid colon (large intestine)
urinary bladder
prostate
urethra

FIGURE 13-1. Organs of the abdominal cavity

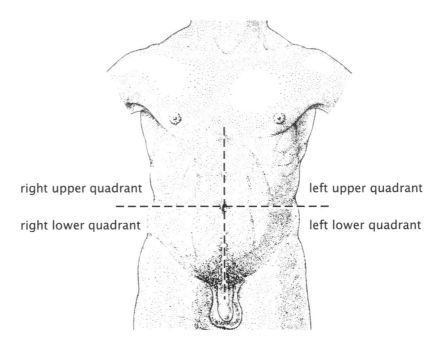

FIGURE 13-2. The four quadrants of the abdomen

at night, and a frightened individual may have to be examined inside a cramped tent with a headlamp the only light source.

The entire abdomen from crotch to nipple line should be bared and examined visually first (Fig. 13-1). Abdominal surgical scars suggest intestinal obstruction caused by postoperative adhesions. Abdominal distention is indicative of intestinal obstruction, either mechanical obstruction or paralysis of the intestinal muscles (ileus) by inflammation. A mass or hernia should be specifically sought. The abdomen should be watched to determine whether attacks of cramping pain are accompanied by abdominal muscular spasm.

Trying to detect abnormal bowel sounds by listening to the abdomen, preferably with a stethoscope, may be an exercise in futility for an inexperienced examiner, but the absence of bowel sounds over a period of several minutes is an indication of ileus, usually resulting from peritonitis.

Palpation of the abdomen is essential for localizing the disorder and making a diagnosis, but it must be performed gently, patiently, and carefully. The examiner's hands should be as warm as possible to avoid inducing muscle spasm with cold fingers.

The individual should be asked to tell where the pain is greatest and point with one finger to that site. The examiner should stay away from that point during the initial examination. Jabbing at the tender spot usually results in tensing the abdominal muscles, which can block subsequent attempts to detect subtle tenderness and muscle guarding. Gentle pressure at a site distant from the suspected disorder may elicit pain referred to the site of inflammation and clarify the diagnosis. A typical example is pressure in the left lower abdominal quadrant referred to the right lower quadrant in cases of acute appendicitis (Fig. 13-2).

Frequently, the individual experiences pain when pressure by the examining hand is released. This is called rebound tenderness and is a sign of peritoneal inflammation, which may be caused by blood or infection.

CONSULTATION

Progress in telecommunication technology, particularly cellular telephones, has made obtaining medical consultation in a wilderness environment easier. Those providing medical care in such a situation should never hesitate to seek advice. Before a consultation, the care provider should prepare answers—preferably written—to the questions listed above and record the findings of the history and physical examination, including the person's name, address, age, and gender.

If the individual is being observed overnight, calls can be scheduled at three- to four-hour intervals so that any changes in his condition can be reported and evacuation plans can be ready at first light.

CONDITIONS THAT DO *NOT* REQUIRE EVACUATION

Gastroenteritis

With acute gastroenteritis, others who have shared the same food or drink often have similar signs and symptoms. The typical onset is gradually increasing diffuse abdominal distress that soon changes to waves of cramping pain that may be severe. The pain is often associated with an overwhelming urge to defecate. The stools soon become watery and in severe cases may contain flecks of blood. The acute pain characteristically subsides following each diarrheal stool, and the individual may be relatively free of discomfort until another episode of cramps begins.

A feeling of weakness or malaise and a low-grade fever often appear with the diarrhea, and the person may become dehydrated. Vomiting occurs only rarely.

Differentiating gastroenteritis from appendicitis may be difficult in the early hours of the disease. Diarrhea is seldom associated with appendicitis but is typical of gastroenteritis. The pain of appendicitis is steady and unrelenting, whereas discomfort caused by gastroenteritis is usually intermittent and cramping in nature. The pain or discomfort from appendicitis may start near the midline but characteristically shifts to the right lower quadrant of the abdomen. In contrast, the pain or discomfort of gastroenteritis is typically generalized.

Differentiating the two conditions is important because appendicitis must be treated by early operation, whereas gastroenteritis is usually self-limited and rarely requires evacuation. As detailed in chapter 12, hydration is necessary for gastroenteritis, but oral intake of any kind is difficult for a nauseated individual with appendicitis and should be avoided, unless evacuation is expected to require more than twenty-four hours.

Mittelschmerz

Midway between menstrual periods, some women experience discomfort from the slight amount of bleeding associated with normal ovulation. Mature women recognize the cause of such discomfort and have become accustomed to it. Younger women unfamiliar with this symptom may, under the stress of a wilderness environment, confuse this process with appendicitis, particularly when ovulation is from the right ovary.

The diagnosis is based on the timing of the discomfort (halfway between menstrual periods). Physical signs of inflammation are minimal, and the disorder usually disappears without treatment in twenty-four hours.

Salpingitis

This gynecologic infection, also known as pelvic inflammatory disease, occurs in sexually active women of any age. Most infections are of the fallopian tube, through which eggs move from the ovary to the uterus. The organism is usually either *Chlamydia* or *Gonococcus*. Women with salpingitis are sexually active, typically with multiple partners, and have suprapubic tenderness, a mild fever, and occasionally some vaginal discharge. The characteristic symptom is the gradual onset of pelvic and suprapubic discomfort. Women with this condition seldom appear acutely ill or toxic, and some have had previous

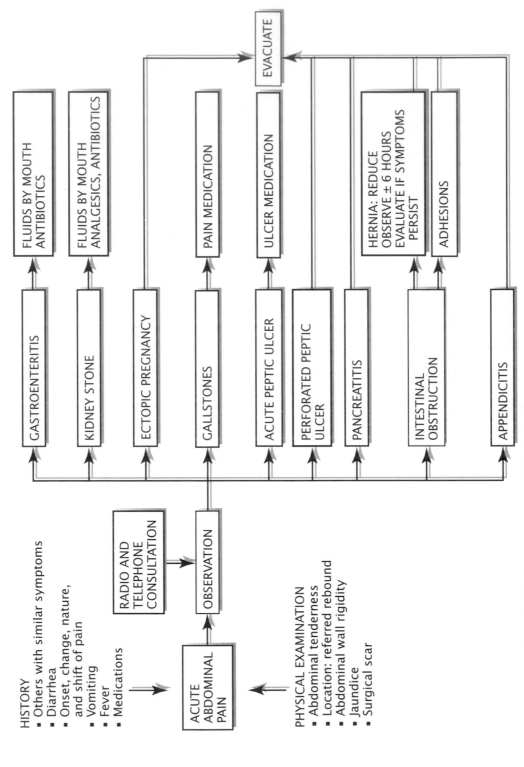

FIGURE 13-3. Algorithm for diagnosing acute abdominal pain

attacks. However, occasionally the condition results in an abscess that can rupture and produce generalized peritonitis. When on the right side, salpingitis may be confused with acute appendicitis.

The treatment consists of antibiotics. (See chapter 19, "Infections.") Evacuation is rarely necessary.

Kidney Stone

When minerals in the urine precipitate to form a stone, it may remain in the kidney or may pass through the narrow tube (the ureter) that connects each kidney to the bladder. The resulting pain typically is quite severe and usually is sudden in onset and cramping in nature. It may be localized to the flank but usually radiates down to the groin and into the scrotum or labia. If the stone passes through the ureter into the bladder, the pain decreases in severity and soon disappears.

The diagnosis can be confirmed by identifying blood in urine collected in a clear glass container or passed into snow. However, the pain of a kidney stone can be confused with that of an incarcerated (irreducible) inguinal hernia or appendicitis.

If the stone does not pass through the ureter into the bladder, pain persists, although it may gradually diminish to a dull ache in the side. Fever, chills, generalized malaise, and red blood cells in the urine typically accompany the pain. The urine may contain pus if a kidney infection supervenes. (See chapter 18, "Genitourinary Disorders.")

If the stone passes into the bladder, the pain quickly subsides and there is no longer an emergency. Once the stone has passed, an early recurrence of another stone is rare, but the individual should consult a urologist upon completion of the trip. Treatment consists of antibiotics and drinking large volumes of water to increase urine volume and help wash the stone into the bladder.

Peptic Ulcer

Peptic ulcer is described in greater detail in chapter 12, "Gastrointestinal Disorders." It characteristically produces discomfort in the upper part of the abdomen, begins some hours following a meal, and is relieved by eating bland food or milk. Duodenal or gastric ulcer usually is a chronic disease. The individual may have previously been told he has a peptic ulcer, and may even have been taking such medications as antacids, H_2 blockers, or proton pump inhibitors.

If the discomfort is localized and not significantly different from previous ulcer pain, treatment with medications is usually all that is necessary. If the pain comes on suddenly, is unusually severe, or is associated with signs of peritonitis, all of which indicate perforation, evacuation is mandatory.

Acute Cholecystitis

The gallbladder is a thin-walled sac that lies beneath the liver in the right upper quadrant of the abdomen and stores bile secreted by the liver. When food containing fat empties from the stomach into the intestine, the gallbladder contracts, forcing bile through the common bile duct into the intestine, where it mixes with the food.

Bile salts in the bile occasionally precipitate and form stones, which may remain in the gallbladder or pass through the bile duct into the intestine. Most individuals with gallstones are middle-aged, often overweight, and usually have a history of intolerance for fried or fatty foods. Stones passing through the bile duct produce greater pain but are not associated with other signs and symptoms of acute cholecystitis.

Individuals with acute cholecystitis usually have had uncomplicated gallstones (cholelithiasis) for a number of years. Why acute cholecystitis develops in a few of these individuals is not known. The manifestations include:

▼ Sudden onset of acute, stabbing pain in the right upper quadrant, associated with nausea and vomiting
▼ A faint yellow color of the white part of the eye (sclera) or the skin (jaundice)
▼ Occasionally, a history of similar attacks of pain diagnosed as being associated with gallstones
▼ Tenderness that is maximal in the right upper quadrant

If left untreated, the individual often continues to vomit and to have right upper quadrant pain and a mild fever for a few days before his condition improves. A subsequent attack is highly probable, but whether to have the gallbladder removed to prevent such attacks is a matter for the patient to consider with his physician after returning from the wilderness.

Analgesics should be administered to relieve pain; severe pain may require a narcotic such as meperidine. (Morphine and other opiates should not be administered.) Antibiotics are needed only if symptoms are prolonged or the attack does not resolve spontaneously. As soon as vomiting stops, the individual can start drinking small amounts of water and eating a gradually increasing, fat-free diet. He may not feel like moving for a few days but seldom needs evacuation unless complications develop.

Acute Pancreatitis

Acute pancreatitis is an uncommon but dramatic cause of acute abdominal pain. As the name implies, it is inflammation (not an infection) of the pancreas, which lies across the upper part of the abdomen. The condition characteristically involves young or middle-aged persons who have a history of alcohol abuse. This disorder typically is heralded by the sudden appearance of severe upper abdominal pain that is associated with nausea and vomiting. It frequently follows an episode of alcohol overindulgence. The individual is usually immobilized by the severity of the pain. The entire abdomen is tense and tender.

Individuals with acute pancreatitis are frighteningly ill and in severe pain. Unless an attendant is acquainted with the condition, he may experience pressure to "do something—anything." Fortunately, the disorder usually runs its course after a few hours or days and the person gradually improves and is able to take liquids by mouth. He should abstain from alcohol.

Treatment consists of analgesics (not morphine or other opiates) to minimize pain, and symptomatic care. For the rare individual whose condition continues to deteriorate, evacuation may be necessary to provide intravenous fluids for hydration.

CONDITIONS THAT *DO* REQUIRE EVACUATION

Appendicitis

Appendicitis is the most common acute abdominal condition requiring immediate evacuation from a remote region. Early operation is needed to avoid rupture of the inflamed appendix and contamination of the entire peritoneal cavity, which can cause generalized peritonitis and even death. Acute appendicitis can occur at any age and in either sex. Only a previous appendectomy excludes the diagnosis.

In the early stages, this condition may confuse expert clinicians and may resemble flu or similar infections. The first symptoms are vague generalized abdominal distress, nausea, and vomiting. Rarely is persistent diarrhea present, which often is helpful in differentiating appendicitis from gastroenteritis. In the early stages, the abdomen may be soft with some generalized lower abdominal tenderness not greater on one side or another. As the disease progresses, slightly greater tenderness is found on the right side.

At this stage, the individual should be kept under careful and frequent observation to determine whether the pain and tenderness change location. In four to six hours, the abdominal pain and tenderness usually shift from the midline to the right lower quadrant. Maximal pain and tenderness usually is midway between the umbilicus and the bony protuberance of the pelvic iliac crest (McBurney's point). Pressure applied anywhere over the abdomen is referred to this site, which overlies the appendix. Pain is felt in that location when the individual coughs or when pressure on the abdomen is suddenly released (rebound tenderness).

If treatment is delayed and the appendix ruptures, generalized peritonitis usually develops. This complication is manifested by high fever, toxicity, vomiting of any fluid or food taken by mouth, and rigidity of the abdominal muscles.

Before such advanced signs and symptoms develop, the astute examiner should have tried to obtain consultation by radio or cellular telephone and should have decided that evacuation is necessary. Delay invites rupture with its severe consequences.

As soon as the diagnosis of appendicitis is made, a broad-spectrum antibiotic such as amoxicillin/clavulanate should be administered to minimize the spread of the infection elsewhere in the body, although it will not stop progression of the appendicitis. The individual should be allowed only sips of water by mouth to relieve feelings of dryness. Any additional fluid taken by mouth would not be absorbed and would usually induce more vomiting.

Ruptured Ectopic Pregnancy

A ruptured ectopic pregnancy should be suspected in any sexually active woman experiencing the sudden onset of severe lower abdominal pain who also has a history of missing one or more menstrual periods, and who has evidence of blood loss (weakness, dizziness on standing, increased pulse rate, low blood pressure). Without definitive treatment, the signs of bleeding such as continued low blood pressure and increased heart rate progress—even to the point of shock.

The only definitive way to stop the bleeding is to surgically remove the fallopian tube, which obviously requires evacuation to a hospital. When possible, consultation with a gynecologist should be obtained.

Intestinal Obstruction

Obstruction of the intestinal tract produces pain and ultimately causes nausea and vomiting. If the obstruction is in the upper part of the small intestine near the stomach, vomiting usually begins soon after obstruction occurs. An obstruction lower in the bowel first produces an accumulation of gas and fluid in the obstructed segment of intestine. The onset of vomiting is later, and the abdomen is noticeably distended by dilated loops of intestine.

The onset of acute small bowel obstruction is usually sudden and unexpected and is characterized by waves of severe, sharp colicky pain that seem to involved the entire abdomen. Each rush of gas and fluid propelled against the obstruction by peristalsis is accompanied by a spasm of acute pain felt throughout the entire abdomen. Because the flow of intestinal contents is blocked, diarrhea is absent. Not even gas is passed.

Regardless of the cause of the obstruction, the treatment needed is based upon two considerations:

▼ Is the obstruction complete, or is it incomplete and can be relieved?

▼ Is the intestine proximal to (upstream or behind) the obstruction still alive and capable of recovering (viable) and is it intact (unperforated)?

If the obstruction is complete, if it does not quickly resolve and permit intestinal contents to pass beyond the site of obstruction, or if the viability of the intestine is suspect, immediate evacuation is needed. A decision must be made as quickly as possible to avoid perforation and catastrophic peritonitis. A few hours of close observation are required, during which efforts should be made to identify the cause of the obstruction.

The two most common causes of small bowel obstruction are postoperative adhesions and an irreducible (incarcerated) hernia, which is usually inguinal.

Adhesions

Some tissue reaction follows any operation on the organs within the abdominal cavity. Clean, uninfected wounds produce little inflammation and leave little observable change. After some operations, particularly those associated with infection, adhesions—essentially scar tissue that binds the loops of intestine together—may form. Some individuals are much more prone to develop adhesions than others. Adhesions can constrict the intestines and produce kinking, both of which can obstruct the flow of intestinal contents. These lesions, which usually occur together, are the most common cause of small bowel obstruction. A surgical scar on the abdominal wall strongly suggests adhesions as the cause in a patient thought to have intestinal obstruction. Although such obstructions are most frequent in the days and weeks following operation, they may not occur for weeks, months, or even longer following operation.

Almost nothing can be done in a wilderness setting to relieve obstruction due to adhesions. The only decision to be made is whether obstruction is complete and the individual should be evacuated immediately, or whether the obstruction is incomplete and may soon be relieved spontaneously. Only a few hours are available for this decision. If the obstruction is unrelieved, perforation results and could be catastrophic. A venerated surgical maxim states, "The sun must not rise or set on a patient with an obstructed small intestine" (without operation). In a wilderness environment, this translates into deciding within about six hours whether the obstruction is being relieved—whether the individual is passing gas, has had a bowel movement, is experiencing less pain, and has diminished abdominal distention. Consultation is advisable because no treatment except intravenous fluid administration is possible. Antibiotics may be advisable if perforation is suspected.

Incarcerated Hernia

Most hernias ("ruptures") are protrusions of the intestines through an abnormal weakness or opening in the abdominal wall (Fig. 13-4). Most occur in the groin or inguinal region. Occasionally (particularly in women), the hernia may be relatively unobtrusive, appearing as a slight bulge below the inguinal crease—a femoral hernia. Some hernias develop in surgical incisions. Hernias are detectable by routine physical examination and should be repaired before major wilderness excursions, certainly before a major expedition.

Hernias become important when the intestine can not be "reduced" (returned to its proper location within the peritoneal cavity). Obstruction of the bowel can result and is evidenced by pain and tenderness at the site. If the blood supply to the intestine is obstructed, the pain and tenderness become intense and the bowel can perforate, resulting in peritonitis.

In contrast to adhesions, if an incarcerated hernia causes intestinal obstruction, reducing the hernia can relieve the obstruction, which in some circumstances could be life-saving. When an unreduced hernia is identified, every effort should be made to reduce it. The individual should be flat on his back and as relaxed and as comfortable as possible. If much pain is being experienced, an analgesic, even a

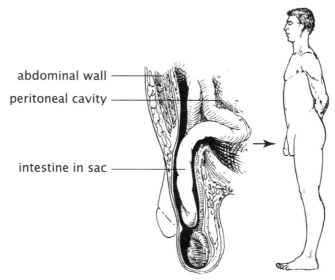

abdominal wall

peritoneal cavity

intestine in sac

FIGURE 13-4. Anatomy of an inguinal hernia

narcotic, can be given to maximize muscular relaxation. The intestine should be pushed back into the peritoneal cavity with gentle but continuous pressure. A quarter of an hour or more may be required, and the process can not be hurried. Usually the hernia contents slip back into the peritoneal cavity and the obstruction is relieved. The longer reduction is delayed, the more difficult it is, and the greater the likelihood that the blood supply to the entrapped bowel will be compromised.

The patient should be advised to obtain subsequent surgical repair of the hernia, but once reduced, recurrence is unlikely in the early postreduction period. Most such patients can resume normal activity, although actions producing increased intra-abdominal pressure that might push the intestine back into the hernia should be avoided.

If, despite all efforts, the hernia can not be reduced and it remains tender, or the patient continues to vomit and show signs of obstruction, evacuation is mandatory in order to achieve operative reduction, relief of obstruction, and resection of any irretrievably damaged small intestine.

14

ABDOMINAL INJURIES

PRINCIPAL CONTRIBUTORS:
Ben Eiseman, M.D.
Eugene E. Moore, M.D.

The definitive treatment for a severe abdominal injury consists of surgery, which is out of the question in a wilderness setting. Therefore, management of severe abdominal trauma in such situations consists of recognizing the severity (or triviality) of an injury and deciding whether immediate evacuation is required. As with all injuries, a conservative approach should be adopted. If any question exists about the diagnosis, the worst should be assumed.

Under no circumstances should pseudoheroic attempts at surgical intervention be made. The results would be uniformly fatal without proper anesthesia, sterile operating conditions, or the proper instruments. Operative intervention under primitive conditions by untrained hands would be more deadly than most injuries. Even the most severe trauma can occasionally be successfully managed without surgery.

DIAGNOSIS

Before any decision can be made concerning the care for someone involved in an accident, an accurate diagnosis must be made (see Fig. 14-3). The first step is obtaining an account of the accident. Exact details of the mishap, including the site and direction of a blow to the abdomen, are helpful in

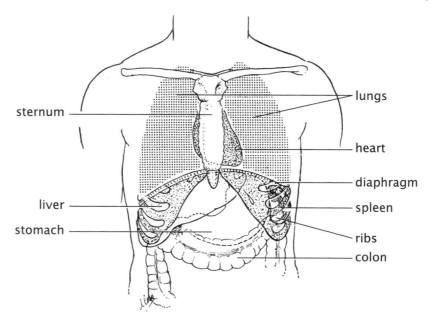

FIGURE 14-1. Location of the liver and spleen in relation to the lower ribs anteriorly

diagnosing the abdominal injury. A blow to the left upper quadrant of the abdomen or lower part of the chest may rupture the spleen. A blow to the corresponding area on the right side would injure the liver. Trauma to either flank or the back may damage a kidney (Figs. 14-1 and 14-2).

The abdomen must be carefully examined as described in chapter 13, "Acute Abdominal Pain." Close attention should also be given to blood pressure, pulse rate, respiratory rate, color of the skin and fingernails, and other signs of shock. The vital signs must be recorded hourly for at least the first twelve hours after injury. The urine should be examined for blood.

Attention must not be focused on the abdomen to the extent that other injuries are overlooked or neglected. At some time in the subject's care, preferably early, a complete examination—including an examination of the back—must be performed.

If the individual is to be evacuated to a physician, a written account of the accident and all diagnostic findings, along with a detailed record of subsequent events, should accompany him. The exact time of the accident, all medications and the time they are administered, hourly measurements of pulse and respiratory rates, and observations about his general condition must be written down.

TREATMENT

Because the individual may require immediate evacuation to a surgical facility, he should be carried with all reasonable haste to a point from which he can be evacuated. The sooner this can be accomplished, the better such persons withstand the subsequent rigors of bleeding or peritonitis. Individuals with severe abdominal injuries usually require litter evacuation of some kind.

Abdominal trauma frequently produces rather severe pain, but the pain may not be proportional to the severity of the injury. Even minor abdominal trauma may be quite painful at first, although the discomfort usually subsides in the hours that follow. In general, the person should be kept comfortable with moderate or strong analgesics. Intravenous administration may be necessary if shock is present. If injected intramuscularly, these drugs may not be well absorbed, and an overdose could occur after the circulation is restored. The subject should be made comfortable but not "snowed under." If he can be

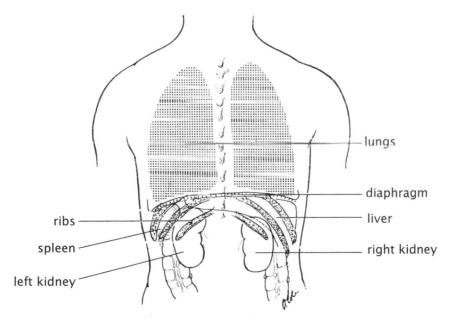

FIGURE 14-2. Location of the liver, spleen, and kidneys in relation to the lower ribs posteriorly

evacuated promptly, analgesics should not be given, because such medications tend to mask some vital diagnostic signs. If evacuation is not necessary or must be delayed, more liberal use of analgesics, particularly strong analgesics, can be made.

Severe abdominal trauma may produce bleeding into the peritoneal cavity, rupture of abdominal organs, or both. Peritonitis inevitably results, although the inflammation following hemorrhage is due to irritation by blood rather than infection. Gastric distention, absence of bowel sounds, nausea and vomiting, and other signs of peritonitis are usually present. (The diagnosis and treatment of peritonitis are described in greater detail in chapter 13, "Acute Abdominal Pain.")

Shock usually follows abdominal trauma, particularly trauma that causes intra-abdominal hemorrhage, and should be anticipated and treated.

NONPENETRATING INJURIES

Blunt or nonpenetrating injuries to the abdomen may produce:
- ▼ Contusion of the abdominal wall
- ▼ Internal bleeding due to a ruptured spleen, liver, or kidney
- ▼ Rupture of other internal organs such as the urinary bladder or, rarely, the intestines
- ▼ Combinations of the above

Contusion of the Abdominal Wall

Any blow to the abdomen causes a bruise that may be very painful. Although the area of impact may be quite tender, the abdomen around it is not so sensitive. If the internal organs have been injured, tenderness is usually diffuse. In the first hour after injury, deciding whether a severe blow has produced merely a bruise or serious intra-abdominal damage may be quite difficult. Therefore, a delay of several hours may be necessary before the severity of the injury can be determined. A large black-and-blue area may blossom forth twenty-four to thirty-six hours later as blood lost at the time of injury works its way out under the skin. This discoloration is of no significance, does not require treatment, and subsides spontaneously in time regardless of its extent.

After a tumbling fall, as may occur on boulders or on a steep ice slope, bruises often appear in areas that the person had not realized were injured. Frequently the individual feels far more sore and stiff a day or two after a fall than immediately after the injury. If no associated injuries are present, the person usually recovers after a few days of rest and mild to moderate analgesia every four to six hours.

Internal Bleeding

A blow to the abdomen may rupture the liver, spleen, kidney, or a combination of the three. Rupture is more likely if the blow falls immediately over the organ. The liver lies in the right upper quadrant; the spleen lies in the left upper quadrant. Both are tucked under the rib cage but can be injured by blows to either the upper abdomen or to the lower part of the chest. A blow from the back may damage the kidneys, which lie on either side of the backbone. These organs are solid and may shatter when hit directly. Blood from an injured liver or spleen flows unimpeded into the abdominal cavity. The hemorrhage usually does not stop without surgical intervention. In contrast, the kidney is enveloped in a tough, fibrous sheath that contains the bleeding. Blood from a ruptured kidney appears in the urine.

Ruptured Kidney

A ruptured kidney is usually manifested by:
- ▼ History of a blow to the flank
- ▼ Pain, tenderness, and discoloration at the point of injury
- ▼ Blood in the urine

History
- Details of injury
- Symptoms
- Preexisting factors

Physical examination
- Mental status
- Heart rate, blood pressure
- Temperature
- Abdominal signs
- Associated injuries

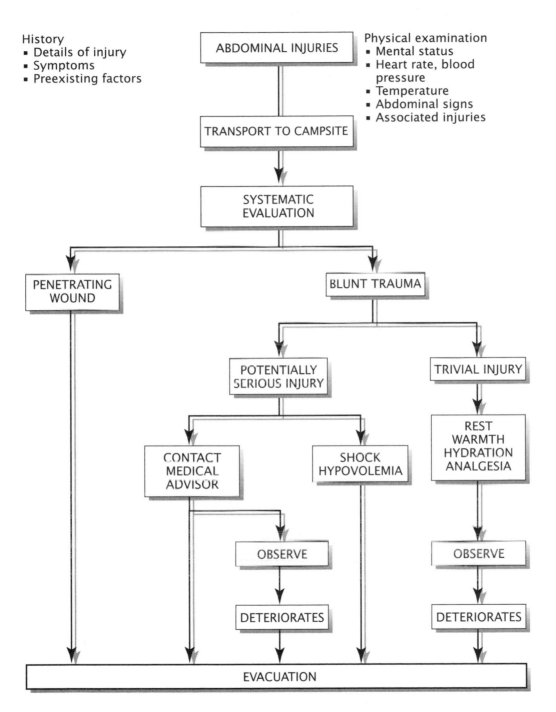

FIGURE 14-3. Algorithm for managing abdominal injuries in the wilderness

Bleeding from kidney injuries usually stops spontaneously; rarely is an immediate operation necessary. The presence of large amounts of blood in the urine for more than six hours, a drop in blood pressure, or a consistently elevated pulse rate are indications that bleeding has assumed dangerous proportions. The individual should be treated for shock and evacuated as rapidly as possible. If bleeding from a damaged kidney stops, the subject must still wait ten to fourteen days before resuming vigorous activity because delayed bleeding sometimes occurs.

Ruptured Liver or Spleen

The individual characteristically has a history of a blow to the upper abdomen or lower chest. Pain, tenderness, and evidence of contusion are usually found in the area of impact, and one or more ribs may be broken. Shortly after the injury, intra-abdominal pain appears, first in the region of the injury and later more diffusely throughout the abdomen. The pain is usually aggravated by breathing deeply and may be associated with pain in the shoulder.

An individual with either of these injuries usually appears to be in reasonably good condition at first, but as hours go by his condition deteriorates. His pulse becomes weak and rapid, and pallor, restlessness, and other signs of shock appear. With the spread of pain, the abdomen becomes tender, and rebound tenderness, distention, absence of bowel sounds, and other signs of peritonitis develop.

A person with an injury of the spleen may recover from the initial accident only to bleed massively when a clot breaks loose from the splenic surface several days or even a week later. Signs of intra-abdominal hemorrhage appear rapidly after such events.

Subjects with such injuries must be evacuated to the care of a surgeon as rapidly as possible. Hemorrhage rarely stops spontaneously; most individuals bleed to death if not surgically treated. The sooner an operation can be performed, the better are the chances of survival.

During evacuation, shock must be anticipated—if it is not already present—and treatment should be started. Pulse, respiratory rate, and blood pressure should be recorded at least every hour to assist the surgeon who is to assume care of the subject.

Ruptured Intra-abdominal Organ

Severe blunt abdominal trauma may rupture one of the hollow intra-abdominal organs such as the intestines or the urinary bladder. The contents of the damaged organ are spilled into the abdominal cavity, producing peritonitis. The urinary bladder is rarely ruptured unless it is full at the time of the injury. Urinary bladder rupture usually is associated with a fractured pelvis.

Following injury, the pain gradually becomes worse and spreads over the entire abdomen as peritonitis becomes generalized. Diffuse tenderness, abdominal distention, vomiting, and fever soon appear. If the bladder is ruptured, no more urine is voided except for a few drops that are mostly blood.

Treatment is the same as that for peritonitis of any cause. (See chapter 13, "Acute Abdominal Pain.")

PENETRATING ABDOMINAL INJURIES

Perforating injuries of the abdomen are rare in the wilderness, but occasionally they are caused by a fall onto a sharp object or even by a gunshot wound. These injuries are extremely serious and require operative treatment. Not only are the abdominal organs injured, but the abdominal cavity is contaminated from external sources, resulting in severe peritonitis.

The diagnosis is usually obvious, but a perforating abdominal wound may be overlooked following a shotgun injury in which the pellets have scattered widely. Attention must not be limited to the area of most obvious injury. The person should be stripped of all clothes and the entire abdomen and back carefully checked for pellet holes.

Evacuation should be carried out as quickly and rapidly as possible. During evacuation, the individual should be treated for peritonitis. Shock should be anticipated and treated.

A sterile dressing should be placed over the wound. In contrast to the usual care given soft-tissue injuries, the wound should not be washed or cleaned, because such efforts only introduce more infection. Any loops of bowel protruding through the wound should be pushed back into the abdomen with the cleanest technique possible, and the wound should be covered with a dressing that is sufficiently snug to prevent the bowel from popping back out again. This dressing should not be changed once it is in place because further contamination of the wound would result and no benefit can be expected.

CHAPTER 15

NEURAL DISORDERS

The nervous system has two major components: the central nervous system (CNS), which consists of the brain and spinal cord, and the peripheral nervous system, which is made up of the numerous nerves that transmit impulses from and to the CNS. Almost everything that happens in the body—voluntary and involuntary movement, respiration, blood circulation, even endocrine function—is controlled or regulated by the nervous system. The diseases of this complex system are numerous and often disabling. However, most of these diseases come on too slowly to create problems on a wilderness outing, even on trips lasting several months.

SIGNS AND SYMPTOMS

The signs and symptoms produced by diseases of the nervous system consist of:
- ▼ Altered intellectual function
- ▼ Impaired control of movement (motor disturbances)
- ▼ Sensory disorders
- ▼ Loss of function of specific nerves
- ▼ A group of unrelated, less specific signs that includes headache, nausea and vomiting, and changes in pulse rate and blood pressure

Altered Intellectual Function

Alterations of intellectual function usually produce personality changes first, most commonly increased irritability or silliness. Impairment of the individual's contact with his surroundings shows up later and is manifested initially by forgetfulness and confusion, but it can progress to hallucinations, delirium, or complete loss of consciousness (coma).

Motor Disturbances

Motor disturbances, when early or mild, result in loss of coordination that causes stumbling or falling or the inability to perform delicate or repetitive movements with the hands. More severe dysfunction causes weakness, convulsions, or total paralysis.

Sensory Disturbances

Sensory disturbances most commonly consist of paresthesias, tingling or prickly sensations similar to those felt when a limb "goes to sleep." Such sensations may not be indicative of nervous system disease. Acetazolamide, which is frequently administered to treat or prevent acute mountain sickness, commonly produces similar symptoms. Total anesthesia is rare. Anesthesia of an entire limb or portion of a limb in a "stocking" pattern is due to "hysteria" rather than organic disease. The distribution of nerves does not allow this pattern of anesthesia to be produced by disorders that are not of emotional origin.

Individual Nerve Loss

Dysfunction of nerves that originate in the brain causes highly varied symptoms. Disturbed function of nerves to the eyes may cause blindness (occasionally limited to only a portion of the field of vision), paralysis of eye movements, or double vision. The pupils may fail to contract when exposed to light or may differ greatly in size. Vision may be blurred.

Disorders of nerves to the muscles of the face, a common complication of Lyme disease, cause weakness or paralysis of facial movements and drooling on the affected side. Swallowing is impaired when the nerves to the muscles of the throat are affected, and fluids may be regurgitated through the nose or aspirated into the lungs. Disturbances of the nerves to the ear cause ringing or buzzing, vertigo, or hearing loss. Damage to other nerves may cause loss of smell, loss of taste, severe facial pain, weakness of the muscles of the neck, or impairment of respiration.

Damage to the nerves originating in the spinal cord causes paralysis or sensory disturbances, commonly anesthesia, in the portion of the body supplied by the injured nerves. Reflexes such as the knee jerk may be lost.

Other Signs and Symptoms

Blood clots, tumors, infections, or any disorder that increases the pressure within the skull can cause nausea and vomiting, the latter typically occurring without warning. A slow pulse and a wider than normal separation of diastolic and systolic blood pressures are also typical of increased intracranial pressure. Headache associated with nervous system disease is often severe. Fever with CNS infections is often high. In other nervous system disorders, the temperature is normal or only slightly elevated.

COMMON NERVOUS SYSTEM DISORDERS

The common nervous system disorders are usually not very serious and are frequently brief in duration.

Headache

Headache is a very common ailment suffered occasionally by all but a few fortunate individuals. Often a specific cause for a headache can not be identified, and the disorder is thought of as a disease in itself, although it is often a symptom of another illness. Headache after a rapid ascent to altitude is common and is usually a symptom of acute mountain sickness.

The pain of a headache may be located in the back of the neck, behind the eyes, or all areas in between. Little significance can be attached to the location of the pain except when it is limited to one side of the head, which is typically a sign of vascular headaches (migraine).

A severe, persistent headache in an individual who usually does not suffer from headaches may be a sign of serious disease. Headache associated with confusion, forgetfulness, dizziness, nausea and vomiting, and rarely convulsions or loss of consciousness may be the result of an acute increase in blood pressure (hypertensive encephalopathy). This disorder usually occurs in persons with preexisting hypertension and requires prompt treatment. (See chapter 9, "Heart and Blood Vessel Disorders.") Headache associated with fever and a stiff neck are characteristic of meningitis. Following a head injury, increasing severity of a headache may be indicative of the development of a blood clot within the skull. (See chapter 16, "Head and Neck Injuries.")

Acetaminophen, ibuprofen, or aspirin every three to four hours relieves the pain of most headaches; acetaminophen or aspirin and codeine taken with the same frequency is adequate for most of the remainder. Individuals with frequent headaches should consult a physician. Some causes of recurrent headaches, such as brain tumors or high blood pressure, are quite serious, but they usually come on so slowly that they would cause problems in the wilderness only on a protracted expedition. However, a few individuals with brain tumors have first noticed symptoms when they developed high altitude cerebral edema. (See chapter 21, "Disorders Caused by Altitude.")

Fainting (Syncope)

Fainting is a common disorder that usually is not a sign of organic disease. It typically follows emotional stress and sometimes occurs without an identifiable cause. When fainting is the result of disease, the disorder most often involves the heart and not the nervous system. Therefore this condition is discussed in chapter 9, "Heart and Blood Vessel Disorders."

Convulsions

Convulsions may be a sign of disease of the nervous system, but they also occur with diseases that only affect the brain indirectly. Convulsions associated with renal failure are not uncommon. Many convulsions, particularly in young people, are solitary events that never recur and for which no cause can be established.

Epilepsy, a condition in which a person suffers repeated convulsions, can be controlled with medications. Convulsions rarely recur as long as the prescribed treatment is diligently followed. A person with epilepsy need not refrain from wilderness activities if his disorder is controlled and he is conscientious about taking his medications. His outing partners should be informed of his condition so they can learn the measures to take should a convulsion occur. However, the stigma once attached to epilepsy is completely unwarranted.

The onset of a convulsion is usually sudden and may be marked by a sound of some kind. The person characteristically loses consciousness and falls to the ground, his body twisting and writhing, his limbs twitching, jerking, or flailing about. The jaw may be involved and he may bite his tongue. He may salivate profusely and may defecate or void uncontrollably.

In any single convulsive episode, all or none of these features may be present. Sometimes only slight twitching of the extremities is present. A person who is unconscious from a head injury may exhibit only a series of jerking movements that gradually increase in intensity and then subside. Limbs paralyzed by injury do not move.

Nothing can shorten or terminate the convulsive episode. The only helpful measure is to keep the subject from injuring himself. His arms and legs should be restrained only enough to prevent striking nearby objects as he flails about. Attempts to hold the extremities absolutely still may produce muscular or tendinous injuries. Clothing around his neck should be loosened to prevent strangulation.

The convulsion usually lasts only one or two minutes but can persist for five minutes or even longer. A period of unconsciousness almost always follows and can last from a few minutes to several hours. The coma may be so deep that the individual is completely unresponsive, even to painful stimuli, and requires the same care as any comatose person, particularly maintenance of an open airway. He should be permitted to awaken without stimulation and allowed to rest until strength has returned and he feels that he has fully recovered. He must not be left alone for at least twelve hours, the time in which recurrences are most likely.

A physician should examine anyone suffering an unexplained convulsion without delay so that any underlying disease can be diagnosed and treated.

MENINGITIS AND ENCEPHALITIS

Meningitis is an infection of the membranes surrounding the brain and spinal cord usually caused by bacteria. Encephalitis is an infection of the brain itself, most commonly by a virus. These diseases produce similar signs and symptoms, in the wilderness would be treated the same, and are discussed as a single category. (Rabies, a form of encephalitis, is discussed in chapter 25, "Animal Bites and Stings.")

These diseases are spread by human contact or by insects, particularly mosquitoes. Meningitis can result from the direct spread by bacteria from a chronic infection of areas such as the sinuses, ears, or mastoids, or from an open fracture of the skull. A number of organisms can cause meningitis or encephalitis, and each organism varies in the effects it produces. The signs, symptoms, and severity of this group of infections cover a wide spectrum.

Headache, usually severe, is the most common initial symptom. Fever is usually present and may be high. Nausea and vomiting sometimes occur. Paralysis is rare and usually affects only one or two nerves, those originating in the brain more commonly than those from the spinal chord. Confusion, delirium, or coma may ensue and are fairly common with encephalitis.

The most specific diagnostic signs of CNS infections result from involvement of the fibrous membranes that cover the brain, which are severely inflamed with meningitis and to some extent with encephalitis. Movement of these membranes by bending the neck or back causes pain. In order to prevent such movement, the muscles surrounding the vertebral column go into spasm. A subject with one of these disorders is unable to touch his chin to his chest, although normally that maneuver is very easy. If he is placed on his back and his leg is lifted with the knees bent, straightening the leg causes pain in the back. This maneuver pulls on nerves in the leg, which produces movement of the spinal cord and its coverings, resulting in pain.

The treatment for bacterial meningitis and encephalitis consists primarily of control of the infection. Large amounts of antibiotics are needed and should be given intravenously, if possible. High blood concentrations of the antibiotic are required for therapeutic quantities to get into the brain and cerebrospinal fluid, where the infection is located. Ceftriaxone (Rocephin®), 2 grams intravenously twice daily, is the drug of choice for individuals who are not allergic to penicillin. Penicillin (3 million units) or ampicillin (3 grams) given every four hours can be used if ceftriaxone is not available. If the individual has anaphylactic reactions to penicillin, chloramphenicol should be substituted. Four to six grams per day of this drug should be administered in four equal doses, given either orally or intravenously.

Fever accompanying these infections can be high and should be lowered orally if it goes above 104°F (40°C). Acetaminophen, ibuprofen, or aspirin can be given every four hours. Cooling by covering the arms and legs with wet cloths or clothing and fanning may be required.

The headache that accompanies these disorders is frequently severe but can usually be controlled with acetaminophen, ibuprofen, or aspirin—possibly combined with codeine—every four hours. Medications for sleep or medications for pain stronger than codeine should not be given because they depress brain function.

Fluid balance must be maintained; intravenous fluids may be necessary. Coma requires the same care as unconsciousness from any cause. Evacuation to low altitudes or oxygen administration is desirable. The subject should be isolated with only one or two attendants to prevent spread of the disease. Evacuation to a hospital is always desirable and often essential.

STROKE

"Stroke" is a term for a group of disorders that are also called "cerebrovascular accidents" because rupture or obstruction of arteries in the brain destroys the tissue they supply. The most common of these disorders are hemorrhage, which can obliterate significant portions of the brain, and clotting within an artery, which causes the death (necrosis or infarction) of tissue supplied by that blood vessel.

Most strokes result from arteriosclerosis (hardening of the arteries), are associated with high blood pressure, and occur in older people. However, strokes can occur in young adults with severe, untreated hypertension. The dehydration and increased numbers of red blood cells typical of high altitudes increase the risk of stroke.

The individuals most likely to have strokes in the wilderness are members of support teams such as porters. Many of these individuals have never had any professional medical care, not even a routine physical examination, and high blood pressure could not have been detected. They should be screened for hypertension, as well as other diseases, particularly infectious diseases such as tuberculosis, and affected individuals should be excluded from the expedition, although the political situation in many areas does not permit such discrimination. (A physician should examine participants in such expeditions beforehand so that hypertension or other disorders predisposing to strokes can be detected and treated.)

Although many persons survive strokes, frequently with surprisingly little or no disability, the prognosis is still serious, particularly at high altitudes where cold and reduced atmospheric oxygen add to the stress.

The onset is quite variable. With milder strokes, headache is commonly present. Other symptoms, which may be transient, include:

▼ Weakness of an arm or leg or one-half of the body
▼ Vague, unusual sensations such as tingling, "pins and needles" sensations, or numbness
▼ Visual disturbances such as blurred vision or partial blindness (which may not be noticed by the subject)
▼ Difficulty with speech, both speaking and understanding the speech of others
▼ Personality changes such as combativeness, indecisiveness, or irritability

More severe strokes may be preceded by a headache, but unconsciousness follows fairly quickly and rapidly progresses to a deep coma in which no response to any stimuli can be elicited. (These events may take place almost instantaneously.) Breathing is noisy and may be very irregular (Cheyne-Stokes respirations). Paralysis is usually present, most commonly affects one side of the body, and may include the face as well as the extremities. However, the paralysis may be difficult to evaluate if the individual is comatose.

Regardless of the severity of symptoms, anyone with a stroke should be evacuated to lower altitude without delay. Oxygen should be administered at altitudes above 8,000 feet (2,400 m). An open airway must be maintained if the individual is unconscious. Elevated blood pressure should be treated if medications are available. After a lower elevation is reached, a conscious individual with hypertension should rest for several days. A physician's care is essential. If the subject has only transient symptoms, more disabling damage can often be prevented. For individuals with more severe disease, such recovery as will occur requires months.

16 HEAD AND NECK INJURIES

Brain injuries are clearly life-threatening, but other head injuries, particularly fractures of the jaw or facial bones that obstruct the airways, also can be lethal. Eye injuries can be almost as devastating. Care for all such injuries must be based on knowledge of the measures that should be taken and of potential complications that must be avoided.

BRAIN INJURIES

Brain injuries are among the most common causes of death in wilderness accidents. Usually the only care possible for persons with such injuries outside of a hospital is maintenance of an open airway, although injuries to other areas of the body also must be treated.

Unconsciousness following a blow to the head indicates the brain has been injured. The severity of the injury correlates roughly with the duration and depth of coma. A person who responds in some fashion when called by name, or responds to pinching or similar painful stimuli, usually has not suffered serious brain damage and often regains consciousness in a short period of time. Someone who is completely flaccid and has dilated pupils, a slow pulse, and irregular respirations has a more severe injury. Widely dilated pupils that do not contract when exposed to light usually indicate brain damage that few survive. Bleeding from within the ears is a sign of fracture of the base of the skull, which is often associated with lethal injury to the brain.

Occasionally a person who has received a blow to the head may regain consciousness only to lapse into coma later as the result of continued bleeding within the skull (see Subdural Hematoma, later in this chapter). Considerable perspicacity is required to recognize the subtle changes of this disorder at a time when effective treatment can be instituted.

Treatment

No specific treatment can be given for a brain injury in the field. The person must be evacuated to the care of a neurosurgeon. An open airway must be maintained during evacuation if the subject is unconscious. Burial is the only reason for evacuating an unconscious individual in a manner in which the airway is not kept open!

Evacuating a comatose subject is so difficult that waiting until he has regained consciousness is highly desirable. In a particularly exposed and hazardous situation, such as on a sheer rock wall, a delay of several hours is fully justified. However, if the subject is not awake at the end of this time or shows signs of deepening coma, he can not be expected to regain consciousness without medical treatment. Even if he does regain consciousness later, recovery is usually so slow that he can not assist in his rescue, although he would be able to keep his airway open. The absolute necessity for maintaining an airway during evacuation, and the difficulty in doing so during descent from such a position, may require that a climber be left on a wall with one or more of the party to care for him while the rest go for help.

Approximately fifteen percent of all severe head injuries are associated with a broken neck. All individuals who are unconscious as the result of a traumatic head injury must be immobilized as if they were known to have a cervical fracture.

Injuries to other areas of the body must be found and treated. Diligence is required when the person is unconscious and not able to point out painful areas. Many serious injuries are neglected for long periods because the individual is lying on his back and no one examines that area. Any lucid interval must be utilized to ensure that no injuries have been missed. Shock rarely results from brain injury alone, and the presence of shock should prompt a search for other injuries, particularly damage to the abdominal organs and fractures of the legs or pelvis.

Oxygen should be administered to everyone with a brain injury, regardless of altitude, if it is available. Such injuries depress respiratory function at a time when an adequate supply of oxygen for the brain is essential.

During evacuation, the person should be transported in the supine position, ideally with his head slightly elevated to promote drainage of blood from the brain and help reduce swelling and congestion. However, if he is vomiting, his head must be lower than the rest of his body to prevent aspiration. The presence of severe facial fractures greatly magnifies the difficulty of maintaining an open airway. If a tracheostomy can not be performed, considerable ingenuity may be needed to keep the person breathing. (See chapter 3, "Special Problems.")

Pulse, respiration, and blood pressure should be recorded at hourly intervals for the first twelve hours after injury, and every four hours afterward, until evacuation is complete. Such records are of vital importance for an individual with a brain injury because they often reflect his status more accurately than any other data, even sophisticated electronic monitoring or laboratory results.

If the subject is not hospitalized, either because he regains consciousness promptly or the injury does not appear to be of sufficient severity, or because circumstances prevent hospitalization, he should be monitored for at least a week after his injury. A blood clot within the skull may produce no signs or symptoms at the time of the accident, but it can enlarge and prove lethal a few days or weeks later if not promptly recognized and treated.

SUBDURAL HEMATOMA

Among the brain's unique features is its snugly fitting envelope of bone, the skull. Although the skull is essential for protecting the very soft brain from injury, its presence occasionally is a disadvantage. Bleeding or swelling, which accompany injuries to any tissue, compress the brain within this rigid covering and frequently produce damage and dysfunction far out of proportion to the original injury. A hemorrhage that would be of no significance at another site often causes death when confined within the skull.

Occasionally, a blow to the head, although not severely injuring the brain at the time, tears some of the blood vessels around the brain. Blood from the torn vessels pours into the narrow space between the brain and the skull and produces a clot that compresses the brain. This condition is called "subdural hematoma" (Fig. 16-1). Death is usually the final outcome if the clot is not evacuated or is evacuated too late.

The speed with which this clot develops depends on the number and size of the blood vessels that have been damaged. Following severe injuries, bleeding may become apparent within a few hours. In other individuals, signs of injury do not appear for two or three weeks, occasionally even longer. Even though the bleeding stops, the clot can continue to enlarge because the osmotic pressure created by proteins released from destroyed red blood cells pulls in water. The prognosis correlates fairly well with the speed with which the hematoma becomes evident. A person with a subdural hematoma that develops within twenty-four to forty-eight hours has a poor prognosis. One that develops two to three weeks after injury is associated with a much more favorable prognosis—if detected and removed promptly.

An epidural hematoma is a similar disorder that usually follows a fracture of the skull. The clot is located between the bone and its covering fibrous membrane, the dura, but the effect on the brain is the same. The damaged blood vessels producing an epidural hematoma are usually medium-sized arteries, rather than the veins that produce a subdural hematoma. As a result, signs of an epidural hematoma usually come on faster and are more severe.

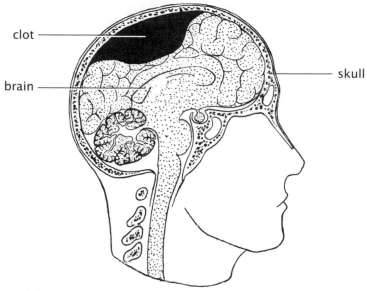

FIGURE 16-1. Subdural hematoma

Diagnosis

Typically, an individual who develops a subdural hematoma has suffered a blow to the head that left him unconscious for thirty to sixty minutes, but then he has regained consciousness and appears normal. Some time later he begins to exhibit signs and symptoms of brain dysfunction and, after a variable period of time, lapses into unconsciousness again.

The subject is in critical condition when coma occurs the second time and must be evacuated immediately if he is to have any chance for survival. A much more favorable outcome is usually possible, and evacuation is certainly much easier, if signs of the developing clot can be recognized before unconsciousness ensues.

Although few subdural hematomas follow injuries that produce unconsciousness of less than twenty minutes' duration, hematomas occasionally follow less severe injuries and may rarely develop after a blow that does not produce unconsciousness at all. The recipient of any significant blow on the head must be closely watched. However, the period of twenty minutes is a valuable reference point for evaluating the seriousness of a head injury. Anyone unconscious for a longer time must be considered to have a significant risk of developing a subdural hematoma.

The intellect is the highest function of the brain and is frequently the first to be impaired in central nervous system disorders. Changes in personality, such as silliness or irritability, are often the first to appear; confusion and irrational speech or behavior show up later. Anyone rendered unconscious by trauma may be mildly confused or irrational for a few hours after regaining consciousness, but such signs are suggestive of a more serious disorder if they persist for more than twenty-four hours or begin to get worse instead of improving.

Headaches may follow almost insignificant injuries. However, headache associated with nausea, with or without vomiting, usually indicates significant, although not necessarily severe, brain injury. Stumbling, loss of coordination, loss of ability to stand with the eyes closed, and weakness are signs of more severe cerebral damage. Inequality of the pupils (that did not previously exist) is a definite and important sign of brain injury and should be specifically sought.

None of these signs is diagnostic of a subdural hematoma. Diseases of other organs can produce most of them. However, deterioration in a person's condition, an increase in the severity of signs and symptoms of brain injury, or the concurrence of several such signs following a head injury should prompt immediate evacuation. Paralysis, loss of sensation, disturbances of vision or hearing, and loss of consciousness are signs that develop later in the course of the disorder. Evacuation should not be delayed until these late signs have appeared.

Treatment

Treatment for a subdural hematoma consists of its surgical removal, which can not be performed safely outside of a hospital. The only recourse is evacuation to the care of a neurosurgeon. The more quickly evacuation is accomplished, the better are the person's chances for complete recovery.

A rapidly developing subdural hematoma in a remote area is of such grave significance, and the difficulty evacuating an unconscious subject so great, that the occurrence of a head injury on a weekend outing or similar short trip should prompt immediate termination of the outing while the individual is still able to walk to a location where medical care is available. On a more extended expedition, the person should at least be returned to a point from which he can be evacuated if he becomes incapacitated.

SKULL FRACTURE

Skull fractures are often surprisingly difficult to diagnose. Nonfatal fractures may occur with relatively little brain injury and no detectable deformity. (In contrast, fatal brain injuries can occur without an associated skull fracture.) A few fractures result in a small portion of the skull being depressed into the brain. Larger depressed fractures, or fractures accompanied by any obvious deformity, are usually lethal.

With a skull fracture, the typical signs of a fracture in any other bone—pain, tenderness, swelling, and discoloration—are often masked (or mimicked) by contusions or lacerations of the scalp that produce swelling and bleeding. Occasionally, signs typical of a fracture are present on the opposite side of the head from the point of impact. In this location, pain, tenderness, swelling, and discoloration are indicative of a fracture. This injury, the so-called *contre-coup* fracture, is produced by the coincidence of the forces created by the impact at a point on the opposite side of the skull. Paradoxically, the skull may not be fractured at the point where the blow actually landed.

Fractures of the base of the skull frequently produce bleeding from the ears or nose. (The blood comes from within the ears or nose, not from lacerations of the surrounding skin.) Similarly, the clear, straw-colored fluid that surrounds the brain, cerebrospinal fluid, may leak from defects in the bones of the ear or nose after a basilar skull fracture. However, such a great impact is required to produce a fracture of the base of the skull that the associated brain injury is lethal, either immediately or within two or three days, for all but a few persons.

Fractures of the skull may also involve the bony orbit of the eye. When this type of fracture is present, the eye on the injured side typically drops back into its socket and appears sunken when compared with the opposite eye.

Until x-ray examination can determine whether a fracture is present, the safest course is to assume that any head injury that has resulted in more than transient unconsciousness has also fractured the skull. Under expedition circumstances, a headache persisting for more than two or three days, the appearance of other signs of fracture or brain injury, or blood or cerebrospinal fluid leaking from the nose or ears should prompt immediate evacuation to an area where definitive diagnostic studies can be carried out and appropriate treatment can be instituted.

No specific treatment for skull fractures can be given outside of a hospital. The subject should be evacuated promptly. Special precautions to prevent further injuries to the head may be needed. Injuries to other areas of the body must receive attention. Prophylactic antibiotics do not prevent meningitis following a traumatic skull fracture and should not be administered.

SCALP INJURIES

Scalp injuries differ from other skin injuries in two important respects: the scalp contains numerous blood vessels that bleed profusely from minor injuries, and infected scalp wounds are more threatening because the infection can spread to the brain. Fortunately, the scalp is more resistant to infection than most other soft tissues.

The treatment of scalp injuries is similar to the care for skin or soft-tissue injuries anywhere else. Special care must be taken to flush all foreign material out of the wound. Pressing down firmly with the fingertips or with a gauze pad on both sides of the injury can control bleeding.

A foreign body embedded in the skull or brain should not be disturbed. The wound should be bandaged with the object in place. Thick dressings must be applied to prevent dislocation of the object during transport, and the individual must be evacuated immediately. If evacuation requires more than a day, he should be given ceftriaxone 2 grams intravenously, if possible, every twelve hours.

If the underlying bone is visible while a scalp wound is being cleaned, it should be examined (but not probed) for a fracture.

FACIAL INJURIES

Soft-Tissue Injuries

The tissues of the face have a greater blood supply than most other areas, tend to heal faster, and have greater resistance to infection. Tags of skin around facial wounds should not be trimmed away unless they are so badly damaged that survival is obviously impossible. Many such skin fragments can be saved and may reduce the need for skin grafting at a later date. Preserving these fragments may also reduce scarring.

Fractures

Facial fractures are uncomfortable, but, except for lower jaw fractures, they do not require splinting and seldom interfere with locomotion. Delayed treatment is often the preferred method of caring for hospitalized individuals with such injuries. Therefore, treating facial fractures is rarely an urgent problem. However, such fractures can make the maintenance of an open airway quite difficult, particularly for unconscious individuals. A fractured jaw may permit the tongue to drop back into the throat, completely obstructing the passage of air. Extensive fractures of the nose and adjacent bones can allow the nasal air passages to collapse.

Brain injuries, skull fractures, and fractures of the neck frequently accompany facial fractures and must be recognized and treated.

Fractures should be suspected after any forceful blow to the face that produces pain, tenderness, swelling, and discoloration. Survivable fractures rarely cause any obvious deformity, except for some fractures of the nose or jaw. Some discontinuity of the bones can occasionally be felt. A broken nose bleeds rather profusely. Double vision is a sign of fractures of the bones about the eye.

Except for fractures of the lower jaw, facial fractures do not require splinting. A broken jaw can be splinted with a bandage that passes under the chin and over the top of the head, binding the lower jaw to the upper. However, individuals splinted in this manner may have difficulty breathing, particularly if they are stuporous or comatose. Fractures of the jaw should not be splinted if the person needs to breathe through his mouth.

The maintenance of an open airway in a person with facial fractures may require diligence and perseverance. A finger must be swept through the mouth of an unconscious individual with a broken upper or lower jaw to remove tooth or bone fragments and prevent them from entering the airway. If a tracheostomy can not be performed and an oral airway is not available or not tolerated, the subject may have to be transported in a face-down position, particularly if severe bleeding or swelling is present. Obviously, his face must be kept free of pillows, sleeping bags, and the stretcher while he is in this position.

Nosebleeds

Nosebleeds are common following minor injuries to the nose. Fractures of the nasal bones are usually accompanied by rather severe bleeding. Nosebleeds without any antecedent trauma are even more common and may be severe. Anyone with repeated or severe nosebleeds should consult a physician because such incidents may be signs of a serious disorder.

An individual with a nosebleed should be in an upright position, seated or standing, and leaning forward. Leaning backward or lying down permits blood to drain back into the throat, where it is swallowed, which usually produces nausea and vomiting.

Many different maneuvers for stopping nosebleeds have been devised. Almost all are equally ineffective. However, most nosebleeds stop spontaneously, and no specific treatment is needed. Pinching the nostrils together along their full length is probably as effective as any other maneuver.

If bleeding persists, a cotton pledget can be moistened with decongestant nose drops or spray and formed into an elongated roll. After both nostrils have been blown clear of clots or mucus, the cotton roll should be inserted in the side that is bleeding. The nose should be held closed with gentle pressure for three to five minutes. After the pressure has been released, another two or three minutes should be allowed to pass, and then the cotton roll can be gently removed. If bleeding persists, this procedure can be repeated as often as necessary until the bleeding is controlled. This technique is usually effective eventually, even with nasal fractures.

EYE INJURIES

Eye injuries must always receive immediate and careful attention. Apparently trivial injuries can cause total loss of vision if neglected. Eyelid injuries can be almost as devastating as injuries of the globe.

Globe Injuries

Eye injuries are usually obvious, particularly for the person who has one, but they may be overlooked if he is unconscious. Such injuries must always be sought in the presence of head or facial injuries, particularly injuries of the opposite eye.

Penetrating or lacerating injuries of the eye produce visible damage. Contusions can cause hemorrhage within the eye and loss of vision with no externally visible sign of injury. Injuries of the nerves and muscles of the eye, or of the surrounding bone, can produce double vision or loss of vision. Because the eye is located within a protective socket of bone, injuries are often associated with damage to the adjacent bone and soft tissues.

The treatment outside of a hospital for all visible or suspected eye injuries (including sudden, unexplained loss of vision) consists of bandaging the eye and evacuating the individual to an ophthalmologist. Removal or any other manipulation of foreign bodies almost inevitably produces greater damage and should not be attempted. Delays of ten to fourteen days in treating such injuries usually make no difference in the final results.

All dirt and debris should be washed away as gently as possible with lukewarm, disinfected water or saline. No attempts should be made to remove blood clots attached to the eye. Distinguishing between blood clots and retina that has been extruded through a wound is usually impossible. Eyelid injuries must also receive careful attention.

During evacuation, the eye must be covered. An opaque shield containing a small hole in the center should cover the uninjured eye. This type of shield permits the wearer to see only straight ahead and minimizes eye movements, thereby splinting the injured eye.

Penicillin or amoxicillin/clavulanate should be given orally every six hours to persons with penetrating injuries if evacuation requires more than one day. Moderate or strong analgesics may be given every four hours for pain. Medications for sleep or tranquilizers may be required, because such injuries arouse much anxiety. The subject should be kept quiet during evacuation. He must not be permitted to touch his injured eye or finger its bandage.

Eyelid Injuries

Vision can be destroyed by injuries of the eyelids as well as by injuries to the eye itself. If the eye is not continuously moistened by the tears that the lid spreads over its surface, it rapidly dries, which kills the cells lining the cornea and usually leads to scarring and blindness.

The torn or lacerated eyelid, after being washed free of all dirt and foreign material, should be returned as closely as possible to its original position. The eye must be completely covered. A snugly fitting bandage should be applied to hold the fragments in place. The opposite eye should also be snugly bandaged to prevent blinking or other movements that would disturb the alignment of the injured lid.

Rarely, the entire lid may be ripped away. If the lower lid is lost, the upper lid can be pulled down with adhesive tape to cover the entire eye. If the upper lid or both eyelids are lost, the exposed eye should be covered with a thick layer of ophthalmic ointment. A sterile dressing of soft material should be placed over the eye and held in place with a snug bandage.

Individuals with such severe eyelid injuries should be evacuated as fast as possible. Antibiotics are not necessary and should not be given unless the injury is unusually contaminated. Tears contain antibacterial substances that eliminate most bacteria.

Minor lacerations, scratches, or abrasions that do not perforate the eyelid are not serious injuries and should be treated in the same manner as similar skin injuries elsewhere.

Foreign Bodies

Foreign bodies in the eye are very common, are usually easily removed, and are rarely followed by significant complications. Such objects most commonly adhere to the inner surface of an eyelid and can be removed by pulling one eyelid over the lashes of the other. If necessary, the eyelid can be folded outward over a match stem or similar object, and the foreign material can be brushed away with the edge of a clean handkerchief or a wisp of sterile cotton (Fig. 16-2). Occasionally, the foreign material produces mild conjunctivitis; this should be treated as described in chapter 17, "Eye, Ear, Nose, and Throat Disorders."

A foreign body may become embedded in the superficial layer of the eye itself. An ophthalmologist should remove the offending object, but in circumstances where a physician is not available, attempts can be made to brush it away with a sterile cotton swab or the corner of a folded handkerchief. If the object can not be brushed away, it can occasionally be removed with the tip of a needle. Obviously, great care must be exercised. If these measures are not successful, the eye should be bandaged and

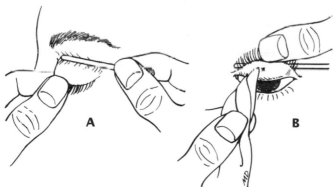

FIGURE 16-2. Technique for everting an eyelid and removing a foreign body

medical assistance obtained. The subject should be treated for conjunctivitis even though evidence of infection is not present.

Foreign objects that appear to actually penetrate the eye should never be removed or manipulated by anyone other than an ophthalmologist.

EAR INJURIES

Ear injuries are uncommon. Most are simple skin injuries and should be treated like similar injuries located anywhere else. More severe injuries are often associated with severe head or brain injuries.

One important cause of ear injuries is cleaning the external canal with long, narrow objects such as match stems. The admonition "never put anything in your ear smaller than your elbow" is wise, particularly in a remote area. If an accumulation of wax, a foreign body, or a small insect causes problems, it should be removed by irrigating the ear with lukewarm water, preferably with a soft rubber bulb designed specifically for this purpose.

Occasionally, a traumatic injury causes a blood clot beneath the skin of the external portion of the ear. If the clot is large enough to cover one-third or more of the ear, it can cause a permanent "cauli-flower ear" if allowed to persist. Such clots should be drained to avoid this type of scarring. The skin should be cleaned and swabbed with an antiseptic. Then one or more one-eighth inch (3 mm) incisions should be made and the blood expressed with gentle pressure. Removal of all of the blood is not necessary and would probably aggravate the underlying injury.

Barotrauma

The middle ear and the paranasal sinuses are lined by thin mucous membranes and filled with air. These chambers have narrow openings to the nose or throat through which air moves to equalize the pressure within the chamber with atmospheric pressure. The opening into the middle ear, the eustachian tube, is much longer than the openings into the sinuses and is more easily obstructed. As a result, barotrauma is more common in the ear (Fig. 16-3).

As atmospheric pressure decreases during an ascent to altitude, air usually leaves these chambers without difficulty. However, increasing atmospheric pressure during a descent to lower elevations tends to close the chamber openings. Active measures such as swallowing or yawning may be required to open the eustachian tube. A light "pop" is often heard as the pressure is suddenly equalized. However, when the difference in pressure between the middle ear and the atmosphere is 90 mm Hg or more, the eustachian tube can no longer be opened by swallowing. In air, this pressure differential requires a change in altitude of about 3,750 feet (1,150 m) near sea level and can develop only when descent is rapid, as occurs in aircraft or rarely in automobiles on steep mountain roads. However, under water, such pressure differences can develop with a descent of only a few feet, particularly near the surface. Colds or nasal allergies cause swelling of the mucosa around the eustachian tube or the ducts into the nasal sinuses, which can partially obstruct the openings and hinder pressure equalization.

If the pressure within the chambers is not equalized with the atmosphere, a sense of fullness or pain develops. Hearing is diminished if the middle ear is involved. As the pressure differential increases, the ears and sinuses become more and more painful. Involvement of the middle ear also can cause sensations of noise, light-headedness, and hearing loss.

As soon as an individual becomes aware of symptoms in his nose or ears, he should begin trying to equalize the pressure. Scuba divers, for whom barotrauma is a constant threat, commonly pinch their nose shut and forcibly exhale against the obstruction to open their eustachian tubes. Subjects with colds or hay fever should be aware of their increased risk of barotrauma and should not dive, or at least should use decongestants to reduce mucosal swelling before a dive. A decongestant spray is usually adequate; oxymetazoline sprays are longer lasting. The spray must be applied a second time after an interval of several minutes so it can enter the deeper recesses of the nose. A systemic decongestant can also be taken

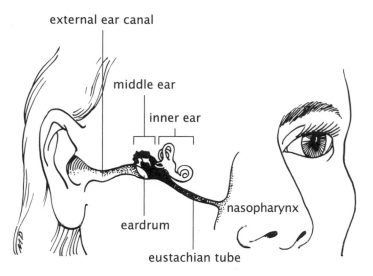

FIGURE 16-3. Anatomy of the ear and eustachian tube[1]

in advance of the descent. (Decongestants are often combined with antihistamines, which often cause drowsiness. Such combinations should not be taken if drowsiness is likely to create problems.)

If precautions are not successful or are neglected, or the individual is unconscious, an aerotitis media or aerosinusitis may develop. The reduced pressure (negative pressure) within the chamber causes hemorrhage into the mucosa, which usually is quite painful. However, it rarely causes any other problems, and the pain usually disappears within twenty-four hours. The person should be given a systemic decongestant to promote drainage. Acetaminophen, ibuprofen, or aspirin, with codeine if needed, may be given to help relieve the pain.

NECK INJURIES

Injuries to the neck can damage vital structures. Massive hemorrhage usually follows injury of the large blood vessels. Hoarseness, coughing up blood, or extensive swelling that feels spongy or "crackles"—a condition known as crepitance, produced by the introduction of air beneath the skin—indicates injury to the air passages. Persons with such injuries must be evacuated without delay. Swelling associated with the injury may lead to airway obstruction, so preparations should be made for a tracheostomy. If the bandage over the wound encircles the neck (which is undesirable but is often the only way to keep the bandage in place), it must be loose enough to accommodate subsequent swelling that could result in obstruction of blood flow.

REFERENCES
1. Adapted from *Dorland's Illustrated Medical Dictionary,* 26th ed. Philadelphia, W.B. Saunders, 1981.

CHAPTER 17 EYE, EAR, NOSE, AND THROAT DISORDERS

Diseases of the eyes, ears, nose, and throat, the most common of all disorders if the common cold is included, are inconvenient rather than disabling, and except for allergies are of relatively short duration. However, all diseases of these organs, even colds, carry some threat of severe complications and must be respected and treated carefully, particularly in the wilderness. Because loss of vision is so devastating, the eyes must be protected and disorders must be treated with particular care.

DISORDERS OF THE EYE

Conjunctivitis

Conjunctivitis is an inflammatory disorder of the delicate membrane that covers the visible white portion of the eye surface (the sclera) and the inner surface of the eyelids. Inflammation is most frequently caused by irritation from a foreign body, smog, or smoke, but it is sometimes the result of a bacterial or viral infection. "Pink eye," a common type of conjunctivitis that can reach epidemic proportions, is produced by the bacteria that were the most common cause of pneumonia in preantibiotic days. Trachoma, a form of chlamydial conjunctivitis, is the most common cause of blindness in those areas of the world where it occurs frequently, particularly Southeast Asia.

A person with conjunctivitis feels as if he has something in his eye, even after the foreign body has been removed. Movement of the eye aggravates the irritation. The eye appears red and the blood vessels on its surface are engorged. The flow of tears is increased. Exudate may be crusted on the margins of the eyelids and the eyelashes and may seal the lids together during sleep.

If the conjunctivitis results from smoke or a similar irritant, steroid-free eye drops that contain an antihistamine and a decongestant (such as Vasocon-A®, Optihist®, or Vernacel®) can provide symptomatic relief and reduce swelling of the eyelids and excessive tearing.

If exudate indicates that an infection is present, an antibiotic ophthalmic ointment or solution (eye drops) should be placed beneath the lower lid every four hours until symptoms have disappeared. Antibiotic preparations should not be used except when clearly indicated. Allergy is fairly common, and the allergic reaction can be worse than the original condition.

If symptoms persist for more than three days and the conjunctivitis appears to be severe, tetracycline should be administered orally every six hours. Dark glasses or blinders with only a pinhole to see through help reduce the discomfort. If the conjunctivitis is clearly infective, contact between the subject and other members of the party should be limited.

Subconjunctival Hemorrhage

Occasionally, exertion or coughing (sometimes no identifiable event) causes hemorrhages that range in size from a few millimeters to almost the entire visible part of the sclera. Although alarming, these hemorrhages are of no real significance, are not related to high altitude retinal hemorrhages, and require no treatment. They disappear in ten to fifteen days, depending upon the size of the hemorrhage. Hot compresses applied to the eye may speed resolution a little but are not at all necessary.

Eyeglasses and Contact Lens

All eyeglasses worn in the wilderness, whether needed to correct visual defects or for protection from sunlight, should be made of shatter-resistant (tempered) glass. A second pair should be carried in a secure place where they can not be broken or lost. In an emergency, cardboard with a central pinhole provides effective sunlight protection and also affords surprisingly good correction for individuals with refractive errors.

Wearers of contact lenses frequently have greater problems with the lenses at higher altitudes, particularly at the elevations encountered in Himalayan mountaineering. A variety of problems occur, including slipping and loss of the lenses, but hypoxia of the cornea appears to be the principal problem. The minimum surface oxygen tension for normal corneal function is about 15 mm Hg. At altitudes above 25,000 feet (7,600 m), where the oxygen level is low, contact lenses decrease the surface oxygen tension to levels that are uncomfortable, which appears to be the reason they are not as well tolerated at such elevations.

Radial Keratotomy

Radial keratotomy is a form of surgical therapy for refractive errors. Climbers ascending to altitudes above 20,000 feet (6,000 m) have found that hypoxia induces swelling that changes the curvature of the eye and eliminates some or all of the surgically produced correction. Such individuals must be prepared with ordinary glasses and goggles that cover them. (See chapter 22, "Altitude and Common Medical Conditions.") Photorefractive keratectomy is a different type of procedure and is not associated with this problem.

DISORDERS OF THE NOSE

The Common Cold

A number of viruses cause upper respiratory infections (colds). (Some generalized viral infections, particularly measles, often mimic a cold during their initial stages.) The viruses are spread by personal contact. Chilling may play a role in contracting the disease by increasing susceptibility to infection, but in the absence of the causative viruses, cold exposure alone can not produce infection. Secondary bacterial infections and allergy to the virus or bacteria cause many of the symptoms of a cold.

A sense of dryness, scratchiness, or tickling in the throat or back of the nose usually appears first and is followed in a few hours by nasal stuffiness, sneezing, and a thin, watery nasal discharge. After forty-eight hours, when the disease is fully developed, the eyes are often red and watery, the voice husky, and the nose obstructed. An abundant nasal discharge is present, and taste and smell are diminished. A cough is commonly present and typically is dry at first; later, a moderate amount of mucoid material may be coughed up. The individual characteristically is uncomfortable but not seriously ill. Fever is usually absent but may be as high as 102°F (39°C). The throat may be sore, but exudates are not present (see Streptococcal Pharyngitis, later in this chapter), and the lymph nodes around the neck and jaw usually are not enlarged.

No effective treatment for a cold has been developed, although some measures to alleviate the symptoms are available. The disease usually lasts seven to ten days. Strenuous activity during the first few days when symptoms are most severe should probably be avoided, particularly at higher altitudes, in order to reduce the probability of complications such as sinusitis or bronchopneumonia. Moderate exercise at low altitudes and limited work at higher altitudes for the additional three to six days required for complete recovery are usually well tolerated.

A decongestant nasal spray may be used to reduce nasal congestion and obstruction. However, symptoms may be worse after the decongestant wears off, particularly after short-acting decongestants. Decongestant sprays should probably be reserved for the times when they are needed most, such as at night to permit restful sleep. When first administered, a decongestant usually relieves obstruction by reducing the swelling of the mucous membrane over the more prominent portions of the nasal passages. A second spray five to ten minutes later may be necessary to reach the recesses of the nasal cavity. Swelling in these areas should be relieved to promote drainage and reduce the risk of bacterial sinusitis. A systemic decongestant or a combined decongestant and antihistamine taken orally may be beneficial.

Antibiotics have no significant effect on the viruses that cause colds and for most individuals should not be administered. The rare serious complications of colds may require antibiotic therapy, but such therapy should not be given until the conditions actually develop. Prophylactic antibiotic therapy should be avoided, even at high altitudes, because the bacteria producing any subsequent infection could become resistant to the antibiotics. However, the uncommon individuals who almost invariably develop a bacterial bronchitis or bronchopneumonia following a cold should be considered exceptions to this rule.

Sinusitis

Sinusitis is an infection of one of the paranasal sinuses, air-filled spaces within the bones of the face that are lined by a thin mucous membrane similar to that of the nose and are connected with the nose by narrow canals (Fig. 17-1). The sinuses serve to make the skull lighter in weight than it would be if these areas were occupied by solid bone.

Sinusitis most commonly results from obstruction of the canals that drain the sinuses, usually produced by swelling of the mucous membrane around the opening due to a cold or allergy. Mucous collects within the sinus, becomes infected, and the infection spreads to the surrounding tissues.

Sinusitis, although accompanied by a headache, is rarely disabling by itself. Complications do occur, and spread of the infection to the bones of the skull or to the brain itself can result in chronic osteomyelitis, meningitis, or a brain abscess. However, these potentially lethal complications usually follow prolonged chronic sinusitis, which should be eradicated before an extended wilderness outing.

Acute sinusitis usually accompanies or follows a cold or hay fever. The most prominent symptom is headache, which may be located in the front of the head, "behind the eyes," or occasionally in the back of the head. A purulent discharge frequently drains into the nose and back into the throat, where it may be swallowed ("postnasal drip").

Fever rarely gets higher than 102°F (39°C) and may be entirely absent. Tenderness may be present over the involved sinus. Infection in the maxillary sinuses may produce pain or tenderness in the teeth of the upper jaw. If a small flashlight or penlight is placed in the subject's mouth with his lips closed over it, fluid in the maxillary sinuses can be detected by the failure of the sinus to be illuminated. (This examination must be carried out in darkness, and a normal individual should be examined at the same time for comparison. If both sinuses are involved, as often happens, an inexperienced examiner would be unable to recognize any abnormality.) The frontal sinuses can be illuminated by pressing the flashlight into the upper inner corners of the eye sockets, just below the eyebrows.

The treatment of sinusitis consists of drainage and antibiotic therapy. A decongestant nasal spray should be administered at regular intervals to reduce the swelling of the nasal mucosa and permit

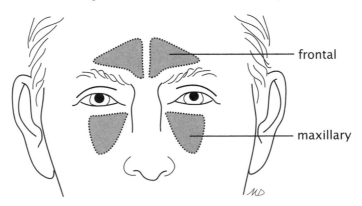

frontal

maxillary

FIGURE 17-1. Location of the frontal and maxillary sinuses

drainage through the canals that enter the sinuses. Spraying should be repeated ten minutes after the first application to make sure the spray reaches the recesses where the openings of these canals are located. A systemic decongestant should also be administered. In a remote area, amoxicillin/clavulanate, a cephalosporin, or a tetracycline should be given orally every six hours. Treatment should be continued until all signs of sinusitis have been absent for two days.

Acute sinusitis usually clears up within a few days. Symptoms persisting for more than seven to ten days may be indicative of a complication and should prompt serious consideration of evacuation. Swelling around the eyes or nose is a definite sign of spread of the infection, and an indication that immediate evacuation is needed.

Nosebleed

Nosebleed is commonly a result of trauma, but many nosebleeds do not follow an injury. Regardless of the cause, the treatment is similar. Care for this problem is discussed in chapter 16, "Head and Neck Injuries."

SORE THROAT (PHARYNGITIS)

Sore throat is a common symptom that is produced by a number of different conditions.

Drying

Prolonged mouth breathing, particularly in hot, dry climates, or in cold climates at high altitudes where air has a very low relative humidity when warmed to body temperature, causes drying of the mouth and throat, resulting in a sore throat. An irritating, dry, hacking cough is usually present. Recognizing the existence of conditions that cause drying of the throat and excluding the presence of other diseases characterized by a sore throat can identify this condition. Drying of the throat is not accompanied by chills or fever, or by enlargement of the lymph nodes of the neck or under the jaw. The throat may be mildly inflamed, but exudates are not present.

Treatment of any kind is usually disappointing. Lozenges containing anesthetics or antibiotics are available. However, hard candy or rock sugar melted in the mouth (not chewed) is probably just as effective, is much less expensive and easier to obtain, and does not carry the dangers associated with indiscriminate antibiotic use. Lozenges should be taken only about every four hours, but candy can be consumed freely. Additionally, the candy has nutritional value, which is important at high altitudes, where loss of appetite makes the ingestion of any food a problem.

Viral Pharyngitis

In conditions that do not produce drying, viral infections are the most common cause of sore throats. Viral pharyngitis (viral sore throat) commonly accompanies a cold but may not be associated with infection elsewhere. The person usually does not feel or appear seriously ill, although a few individuals feel much worse than most others. Fever may be present but is rarely higher than 101°F (38.5°C). The throat is inflamed, but exudates are not present and enlargement of lymph nodes is rare.

Before accepting a diagnosis of viral pharyngitis, streptococcal pharyngitis must be ruled out.

Viral sore throat usually clears up in three to six days without therapy. Lozenges may provide some relief, but hard candies melted in the mouth are equally effective. Antibiotics are of no benefit and should be avoided unless streptococcal infection is seriously suspected. However, distinguishing between these two infections without laboratory facilities may be impossible.

Streptococcal Pharyngitis

Streptococcal pharyngitis, or "strep throat," is encountered less frequently than other causes of sore throat but can be treated much more satisfactorily. This infection is caused by bacteria known as streptococci and is potentially dangerous because it can lead to rheumatic fever, which may damage the heart valves, or glomerulonephritis, a kidney disease.

Individuals with streptococcal pharyngitis typically feel and appear ill. Fever is usually present and may reach 103°F (39.5°C) or higher. Chills often occur. The throat appears beefy red, and exudates, which are similar to the pus found in boils or infected wounds, can be seen as white or pale yellow points or patches scattered over the throat, particularly on the tonsils. The lymph nodes in the neck and under the jaw usually are enlarged and tender.

Fever, exudates, enlarged lymph nodes, and general malaise serve to differentiate strep throat from other forms of pharyngitis. However, malaise may not be marked, lymph node enlargement may not be prominent, and fever may not be very high. Therefore, any sore throat should be regarded with suspicion. In a remote area, if the possibility of streptococcal infection appears significant, antibiotic therapy should be instituted.

Treatment for streptococcal pharyngitis consists of the oral administration of penicillin every six hours for ten days. Symptoms and signs of the disease usually disappear completely within twenty-four to forty-eight hours. Nonetheless, therapy must be continued for ten days to ensure complete eradication of the infection and the prevention of complications, particularly rheumatic fever. Individuals allergic to penicillin should be treated with erythromycin.

DISORDERS OF THE MOUTH

Toothache

Toothache is most often due to an infection. The infection initially produces a cavity in a tooth, but later it can spread to the surrounding bone and soft tissue to produce an abscess. Adequate dental care should almost completely prevent abscesses, but such infections are fairly common among inhabitants of developing countries for whom dental care is not available.

Usually a cavity is obvious. The tooth may have broken off so that only a jagged stump remains. Swelling in the gum and jaw indicates that the tooth has become abscessed. One whole side of the face may be swollen. Fever and occasionally chills often accompany an abscess.

A small wad of cotton soaked in oil of cloves and inserted in the cavity usually reduces the pain, if no abscess is present. Mild or moderate analgesics every four hours also help relieve discomfort.

The presence of an abscess is an indication that the tooth should be pulled. However, extraction by anyone other than a dentist should be attempted only in remote situations, and only when dental forceps are available. An antibiotic such as penicillin, ampicillin, or ceftriaxone should be administered intramuscularly or intravenously thirty minutes before the extraction to help destroy the bacteria invariably released into the blood stream during such procedures. Chills and fever are common in the twenty-four hours after the tooth is pulled. If the person is to be evacuated to a dentist for the extraction, he should be given penicillin or amoxicillin/clavulanate every six hours until evacuation is completed.

An analgesic may or may not be needed. Sometimes extraction of an abscessed tooth is surprisingly painless.

Canker Sores

Canker sores are small, painful ulcers that appear in the mouth without apparent cause. They first appear as small blisters that soon rupture, leaving small, white ulcers surrounded by an area of inflammation. Such sores may be caused by herpes simplex infection.

No therapy is effective for these ulcers, but they disappear in a few days without treatment. A mouthwash consisting of one teaspoon (4 cc) of sodium bicarbonate (baking soda) in a glass of water is soothing. A mouthwash of half water and half three percent hydrogen peroxide solution helps prevent secondary infection.

Herpes

Herpes (also known as "cold sores" or "fever blisters") is a viral infection (herpes simplex) that produces small, painful blisters, most commonly on the lips and skin around the mouth. The viruses persist in the tissues, so blisters recur in the same location. Herpes sores commonly result from sunburn of the lips or face, may accompany severe infections such as pneumonia or meningitis, but most commonly they can not be associated with any disorder.

An initial small, painful swelling rapidly develops into one or more small blisters containing clear fluid and surrounded by a thin margin of inflamed skin. The blisters may rupture, particularly if they are traumatized, resulting in bleeding and crusting. Fever or other symptoms are rarely experienced.

The application of a local anesthetic ointment (Nupercainal®) may provide some symptomatic relief, but no specific treatment is available. The blisters usually heal in five to ten days, and although uncomfortable and perhaps unsightly, they usually cause no significant disability. Avoiding sunburn helps prevent herpes sores.

EAR INFECTIONS

Ear infections frequently occur in infants and young children but are uncommon in older persons. Swelling of the mucous membrane or enlargement of the adenoids in young people easily blocks the eustachian tube that drains the middle ear. However, this tube is larger in adults and these disorders rarely produce obstruction. In the absence of eustachian obstruction, ear infections are uncommon.

A cold, sinusitis, or hay fever usually precedes the ear infection. The principal symptom is pain in the ear. Fever or malaise may be present. Infrequently, a purulent discharge from the ear can be found.

Therapy consists of the oral administration of amoxicillin/clavulanate or trimethoprim-sulfamethoxazole every six hours until all signs of infection have been absent for two days. A systemic decongestant should also be given to help reduce swelling around the opening of the eustachian tube. A hot water bottle and mild to moderate analgesics every three to four hours help reduce the pain. Warm (not hot), bland oil such as olive oil inserted into the ear also helps relieve the pain.

18 GENITOURINARY DISORDERS

The urinary tract is made up of the kidneys, ureters, urinary bladder, and urethra (Fig. 18-1). The genital system includes the ovaries, fallopian tubes, uterus, vagina, and external genitalia in females; the testes, epididymides, vasa deferentia, seminal vesicles, prostate gland, and external genitalia in males. The kidneys filter blood and excrete unneeded substances and water. Urine is transported by the ureters from the kidneys to the urinary bladder, where it is held until voided through the urethra.

Normally hydrated adult males of average size with normal renal function form approximately 1 cc of urine per minute. About 60 cc is formed per hour; 1,500 cc is excreted per day. Persons with smaller or larger bodies produce somewhat smaller or larger urine volumes, although urinary output does not vary directly with size. Dehydration reduces urine volume; overhydration increases urinary output.

ACUTE URINARY TRACT DISORDERS

The most common symptoms or signs of acute urinary tract disease are:
- ▾ Pain in the back or flank
- ▾ Burning with urination
- ▾ Blood in the urine
- ▾ Changes in urine volume
- ▾ Chills and fever (sometimes high)

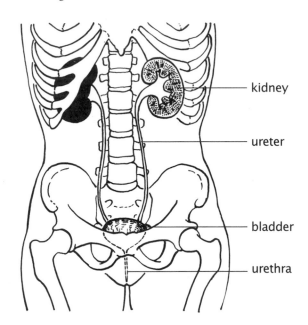

FIGURE 18-1. Anatomy of the urinary tract

Back pain is often indicative of kidney disease, particularly when located to one side of the vertebral column at the point where the lowest ribs join it. However, the pain frequently radiates to the sides just above the pelvis and around to the groin.

A burning sensation with voiding is unmistakable, is often described as the sensation of passing gravel, and usually results from inflammatory diseases of the urinary bladder, prostate, or urethra.

Bleeding can be obvious or may produce only cloudy or "smoky" urine. If the urine is allowed to stand so the cells can settle out, a red sludge often can be seen at the bottom of the container, confirming the presence of blood. Surprisingly small amounts of blood can be detected in this way.

Changes in urinary volume, except for very large deviations, usually go unnoticed unless the urinary output is measured. In the wilderness, dehydration is by far the most common cause for a change in urinary output. However, some renal diseases can result in total or near-total cessation of kidney function. In rare cases, a larger volume of very dilute urine is excreted.

Cystitis

Cystitis is inflammation of the urinary bladder that occurs with or without infection. This disorder is rare in young males but is common in females. When cystitis is associated with acute pyelonephritis, symptoms of the latter usually predominate.

The principal symptom of cystitis is burning or pain during voiding. The pain may increase somewhat as the bladder is emptied but disappears gradually after flow has stopped. The frequency of voiding may be increased because the irritated bladder feels full with a smaller urine volume. Fever or other symptoms are rare. Slight bleeding sometimes occurs; rarely, bleeding may be severe enough to make the urine obviously bloody.

Usually no treatment is needed for cystitis, and the symptoms disappear in two or three days. If symptoms are severe, persist for a longer time, or are associated with fever, then ampicillin, a cephalosporin, trimethoprim-sulfamethoxazole, or ciprofloxacin may be administered. These drugs are excreted by the kidneys and reach high concentrations in the urine. Ampicillin or a cephalosporin should be given orally four times a day; trimethoprim-sulfamethoxazole or ciprofloxacin should be given orally twice a day. Therapy should be continued for at least a week, or until the person has been completely free of symptoms for two days, if that takes longer. Large quantities of fluids must be consumed also.

Pyelonephritis

Pyelonephritis, an infection of one or sometimes both kidneys, is characterized by the rather sudden onset of high fever, often with chills, and pain over the kidney. The subject often feels and appears ill. Pain of moderate severity is usually present. Pressing or gentle pounding with the fist just below the lower rib on either side of the vertebral column reveals tenderness. Symptoms of cystitis are often present, and slight to moderate bleeding may occur.

The individual should drink large quantities of fluids, at least twice the usual daily requirement. Fluid intake and urinary output should be recorded. Evacuation from altitudes above 14,000 feet (4,300 m) is desirable.

Antibacterial therapy is important. Trimethoprim-sulfamethoxazole, ampicillin, a cephalosporin, or ciprofloxacin should be given as described above and should be continued for five days after all signs of disease have disappeared or for a minimum of ten days. Individuals with repeated episodes of pyelonephritis should consult a physician because irreversible kidney disease can result. Additionally, an underlying disorder such as renal stones may be present.

Acute Renal Failure

Renal failure, a drastic reduction or total cessation of kidney function, occasionally follows a severe injury, particularly if the person is in shock for several hours or longer. (Certain poisons, drug reactions, and other disorders can also cause acute renal failure.) If the person can be kept alive through the period of reduced renal function, which may last from a few days to several months, complete recovery is usually possible.

The principal manifestation of renal failure is reduced urinary output. Dehydration may also cause a low urinary output, but when a dehydrated subject is given fluid, the urinary volume increases. An individual with acute renal failure can not increase his urinary output, no matter how much fluid he is given. With dehydration, the urine is concentrated and has a deep yellow or orange color; with acute renal failure, the small amount of urine produced is typically dilute. Any adequately hydrated subject with a urinary output of less than 400 cc per day of dilute urine following a severe injury should be considered to be in renal failure.

Weakness, loss of appetite, nausea, vomiting, diarrhea, muscle twitching, confusion, convulsions, and eventually coma appear sometime after the onset of renal failure, usually three to ten days after injury. In most cases, few symptoms related to diminished renal function are present for the first two or three days. However, weakness becomes apparent on about the third day, and the other symptoms soon follow.

Urinary retention due to spasm of the bladder muscles, and rupture of the urinary bladder, simulate renal failure because urinary output ceases. However, urinary retention is usually accompanied by a strong urge to urinate, as well as by pain in the bladder or lower abdomen. (If urethral catheterization discloses the bladder to be empty, urinary retention can be ruled out.) Following bladder rupture, evidence of an abdominal or pelvic injury, including abdominal pain and tenderness, is usually obvious. (See chapter 14, "Abdominal Injuries.") However, acute renal failure can also be associated with an injury in which the bladder is ruptured.

Evacuation is urgent. Only well-equipped medical centers would have the dialysis (artificial kidney) facility required to keep someone with acute renal failure alive for more than a few days.

During evacuation, fluid intake must be carefully controlled to prevent overloading with water. To establish the diagnosis of acute renal failure, the person's previous state of hydration must be determined. If he appears to have been dehydrated, enough fluids must be given to correct that situation. If renal output does not return, subsequent fluids must be administered very carefully. Each day's fluid intake should be limited to one quart plus a quantity roughly equal to the urine volume. Unusual fluid losses caused by vomiting, sweating, or high elevation must also be replaced. (See Dehydration at Altitude in chapter 2, "Basic Medical Care and Evacuation.")

If nausea and vomiting, which are usually present after the third day, prevent taking fluids orally, intravenous fluids must be administered. The quart of water, the previous day's urinary output, and any unusual losses through the lungs should be replaced with a five or ten percent glucose solution. Fluids lost through vomiting and excessive sweating should be replaced with a balanced salt solution. To ensure that the volume replaced matches the amounts that have been lost, urine volume, losses from other sources, and oral or intravenous intake must be measured and recorded.

While he can, the subject should be encouraged to eat sweets such as hard candy or glucose tablets. However, citrus fruits and fruit juices must be avoided because they contain potassium, which can be toxic for a subject with reduced renal function.

Medications should be avoided because the kidneys excrete most drugs. In the absence of renal excretion, their concentration can rapidly build to toxic levels.

Acute Glomerulonephritis

Glomerulonephritis is a common disease of the renal glomeruli, the portion of the kidneys in which the blood is filtered. Chronic dialysis or kidney transplantation is required for chronic glomerulonephritis more often than any other disorder. However, chronic glomerulonephritis would rarely have such a rapid onset that it could cause problems on even an extended wilderness outing. Acute glomerulonephritis can appear much more rapidly.

Acute glomerulonephritis usually follows a strep throat or some other streptococcal infection by a few days or a few weeks and can be largely prevented by treating the initial streptococcal infection with penicillin. (A few individuals do not have identifiable preceding infections.)

Swelling or puffiness of the face, which is most striking upon arising in the morning, blood in the urine, and headache are the most common signs. A low fever and loss of appetite, nausea, and vomiting may be present. More severe disease is characterized by edema, particularly of the feet and ankles, and acute renal failure. The blood pressure commonly is elevated.

The urine may appear bloody, but more frequently blood can only be detected after the red blood cells have been permitted to settle to the bottom of a container. Protein is almost always present in the urine (proteinuria), and boiling causes the protein to precipitate as a thick, flocculent coagulum that resembles egg albumen. Proteinuria is the key feature for the diagnosis of glomerulonephritis. If present, the individual probably has this disorder; if absent, he does not.

The person should rest, and salt, which tends to promote edema and high blood pressure, should be restricted. Penicillin, four times a day, should be given for ten days in case a lingering streptococcal infection is present. Evacuation is desirable, but in a truly remote area it may not be mandatory if a urinary output of more than 500 cc per day can be maintained. If the subject's urine volume falls below 400 cc, he should be considered to have acute renal failure (which can result from glomerulonephritis), his fluid intake and output must be monitored, and he should be evacuated to a hospital.

OTHER URINARY TRACT DISORDERS

Renal Stones

Because the characteristic symptom of renal stones is severe pain, this disorder is discussed in chapter 13, "Acute Abdominal Pain." Bloody urine and burning with voiding can also accompany the passage of a stone.

Hematuria

Hematuria, which means bloody urine, may be associated with traumatic injuries, tuberculosis, or tumors of the urinary tract, as well as the disorders discussed above. Traumatic urinary disorders are discussed in chapter 14, "Abdominal Injuries." Adequate treatment for tuberculosis or tumors is impossible in the wilderness.

Visibly bloody urine may be produced by cystitis, usually disappears in about twenty-four hours, and is accompanied by symptoms of cystitis. In the absence of signs of a specific disorder, hematuria should prompt immediate medical consultation to determine the cause and institute appropriate therapy. Hematuria can be an indication of a serious disorder. (The loss of blood itself is almost never of sufficient volume to be disabling.)

Hemoglobinuria

Severe injuries, burns, severe infections, and other disorders can destroy red blood cells and release hemoglobin into the blood. This pigment is excreted by the kidneys and imparts to the urine a faint pink to deep red color that resembles bloody urine.

Hemoglobinuria must be distinguished from hematuria, which is caused by entirely different conditions. If urine that contains hemoglobin is permitted to stand, no blood settles to the bottom of the container. Acute renal failure sometimes follows disorders producing hemoglobinuria if the individual becomes dehydrated or goes into shock. Immediate administration of enough fluids to significantly increase urinary output helps prevent this complication.

Occasionally, strenuous exercise alone results in hemoglobinuria or myoglobinuria. (Myoglobin is a protein similar to hemoglobin that originates in muscle and can also be released by crushing injuries.) Such disorders can also cause acute renal failure, but they usually disappear with rest. The subjects must maintain a generous fluid intake to reduce the chances of renal failure.

The pigment from some foods or dyes, particularly beets, occasionally imparts a reddish color to the urine. However, the individual can usually remember the ingestion of these substances, and the pigment disappears from the urine within a few hours or days. Hemoglobinuria that is not associated with renal failure requires no therapy other than a high fluid intake.

FEMALE GENITAL PROBLEMS

Although gynecologic problems are common and widely variable, few appear so rapidly that they create problems on a wilderness outing. An examination by a physician beforehand should disclose any potential disorders and permit their correction before the outing is underway.

Two problems that could occur are dysmenorrhea and abnormal bleeding.

Dysmenorrhea

Dysmenorrhea means painful menstruation. Pain is caused by many different abnormalities, including a wrongly positioned uterus and the passage of blood clots. Most women with dysmenorrhea have had it most of their postpubertal lives, and encountering it for the first time on a wilderness outing would be most unusual. Exercise often relieves dysmenorrhea.

The pain typically is cramping, may be disabling (although it usually is less severe), and usually is worse the first day or two of menstrual periods. Mild or moderate analgesics usually mask the pain. Prostaglandin antagonists such as ibuprofen are most effective.

Diminished physical activity may be of some benefit. Women bothered with this problem—and they are numerous—have usually learned to deal with it long before it could create problems in a wilderness situation.

Abnormal Bleeding

Abnormal uterine bleeding can take the form of excessive bleeding with menstrual periods, bleeding between periods, or both. Although numerous disorders can produce such bleeding, commonly no cause can be identified, particularly in perimenopausal women. No specific treatment can be given in a wilderness situation. The bleeding is rarely severe enough to create blood loss problems. If a hemorrhage of massive proportions does occur, packing the vagina with tampons, gauze, or anything available may help slow the bleeding during evacuation, although complete control of bleeding by such means probably can not be obtained. Such problems must be exceedingly rare; exercise helps control abnormal bleeding for many women.

Pregnancy

Pregnancy, at least in its early stages, does not necessarily require curtailment of a woman's customary activities, but some precautions should be observed during wilderness activities. Fifteen to twenty percent of all pregnancies terminate in spontaneous abortions; most occur during the first three months of pregnancy. Occasionally, such abortions are associated with severe bleeding that can not be stopped without hospital facilities. A woman in this stage of pregnancy should probably not enter an area so remote that evacuation within twelve to twenty-four hours could not be readily accomplished.

During the last three months of pregnancy, the enlarged uterus and the baby it contains often cause problems with balance. Activities that require balance are usually difficult. A fall could injure the mother, baby, or both, even though such falls would not injure a woman who was not pregnant. Premature labor, whether caused by a fall or occurring spontaneously, could result in the birth—in less than optimal circumstances—of a small, immature baby who could not survive without the facilities available in a hospital.

The specific problem of altitude and pregnancy is discussed in chapter 22, "Altitude and Common Medical Conditions."

Occasionally, pregnancy creates or aggravates other medical problems, such as diabetes, hypertension, or cardiac disease. The mother should consult her physician for any special care that such problems would require on a wilderness outing.

Contraceptives

One aspect of pregnancy, its prevention, does have direct implications for high altitude activities. Oral contraceptives appear to cause an increased incidence of venous thromboses and pulmonary embolism. High altitudes also predispose to the development of these disorders. (See chapter 10, "Respiratory Disorders.") Women taking part in outings requiring a prolonged stay at altitudes above 10,000 feet (3,000 m) should discontinue oral contraceptives several weeks in advance. If some other form of contraception is needed and an intrauterine contraceptive device (IUD) is selected, it should be inserted several months in advance to be sure it is well tolerated. These devices occasionally cause problems such as perforation, bleeding, or infection that could be difficult or impossible to control in the wilderness, but most of these complications show up during the first few months the devices are used.

MALE GENITAL PROBLEMS

Few male genital problems appear with sufficient speed or at a young enough age to cause problems in mountaineering situations. Two exceptions are acute epididymitis and torsion of the testes (Fig. 18-2), two entirely different disorders that have similar features and may be difficult to distinguish, even for a physician.

Epididymitis and Testicular Torsion

Epididymitis is an inflammatory disorder of the epididymis, an organ adjacent to the testis in which sperm collect before passing through the vas deferens to the seminal vesicle. Epididymitis sometimes is the result of gonorrheal infection, but cultures are rarely taken from the inflamed tissues. Most epididymitis probably has no relation to venereal infection; many cases may not result from infection.

Torsion refers to twisting of the testis within the scrotum. The spermatic cord, which contains the vas deferens and the arteries and veins supplying the testis, also is twisted, and the blood vessels, particularly the veins, are occluded. If the occlusion is not relieved, which usually requires surgery, the testis is deprived of its blood supply and "dies" within a few hours.

Both of these disorders are quite painful. The scrotum is often distended and may be inflamed,

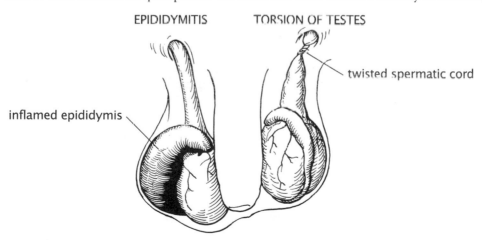

FIGURE 18-2. Testicular disorders

particularly with epididymitis. The testis is usually swollen and quite tender. The pain of testicular torsion may appear rapidly; epididymitis usually develops more slowly. An enlarged, firm, nodular epididymis may be felt with epididymitis. Elevation of the scrotum and the application of cold packs are frequently helpful with epididymitis; elevation of the scrotum usually does not help relieve the pain of testicular torsion. With testicular torsion, the affected testis may be higher in the scrotum than the opposite testis because twisting shortens the cord.

The individual should rest as much as possible. (Many physicians keep patients with epididymitis confined to bed.) Both disorders are too painful for vigorous activity. A cephalosporin, trimethoprim-sulfamethoxazole, or ciprofloxacin should be administered with either disorder. If the individual has a history of gonorrhea or exposure to gonorrhea within the previous two months, he should be treated as if he had gonorrhea. Subjects with testicular torsion who can not be evacuated right away need antibiotics to prevent the establishment of an infection in the dead tissue of the testis.

Almost everyone with either of these disorders must be evacuated. Individuals with testicular torsion require surgery, even if it can not be carried out quickly enough to save the testis. Individuals with epididymitis require rest and antibiotics. Two to three weeks may be required for complete healing. Resumption of activity before all symptoms have completely cleared frequently reactivates the disease. However, epididymitis has little tendency to spread to other tissues and probably could be adequately treated in base camp in truly remote circumstances.

SEXUALLY TRANSMITTED INFECTIONS

Of sexually transmitted infections (STIs), syphilis, gonorrhea, and herpes are the most common. Hepatitis B is spread largely by sexual contact in developed nations, but it is not considered a venereal disease and is discussed in chapter 12, "Gastrointestinal Disorders." Human immunodeficiency virus (HIV) also is spread by sexual contact. That infection and the acquired immunodeficiency syndrome (AIDS) it produces are discussed in chapter 19, "Infections."

All STIs are spread by intimate personal contact. Infection from toilet seats or similar sources essentially does not occur because the organisms can not survive outside of the body.

At the present time, the only dependable way to completely prevent such infections is to avoid sexual contact with infected individuals. Condoms are helpful but do not completely prevent infection. Prophylactic antibiotic therapy has many disadvantages in addition to the significant risk of allergic reactions to the drugs.

Syphilis

Syphilis is produced by the spirochete *Treponema pallidum.* This infection has an interesting history. It apparently originated in the western hemisphere, was transported to Europe by members of Columbus's crew, and in an amazingly short time spread all over the world. The great variation in its clinical features, its long duration, and its ability to involve any of the body's organs and mimic many other diseases have been particularly fascinating. The discovery of penicillin therapy was a dramatic triumph.

Syphilitic infections have three stages. The primary stage is that of the chancre, a one-quarter to one-half inch (6 to 13 mm), painless ulcer that appears at the site of inoculation. Most chancres appear on the genitalia, but they are occasionally found on the mouth or lips, or the skin of other parts of the body. In women, chancres may be located within the vagina or on the uterine cervix, where they are not easily seen. Sometimes primary chancres never appear, or they go unnoticed, particularly when hidden in a location such as the vagina.

The secondary stage of syphilis is characterized by the appearance of a skin rash about six weeks after the primary lesion. However, many individuals do not manifest this stage of the disease. The appearance of this rash is highly variable, although it does not produce blisters, and it usually has a wide distribution, including the palms and soles and the mucous membranes of the mouth. The rash does not itch, and infected individuals usually have no other significant symptoms. It usually lasts from a few days to a few weeks.

In its third, or tertiary, stage, syphilis can produce fatal cardiac disease or disabling brain disease. However, tertiary syphilis takes years to develop and can be prevented by appropriate antibiotic therapy.

A precise diagnosis of syphilis requires laboratory facilities not widely available in developing countries. Treatment in the wilderness should be based on a history of sexual contact and the presence of a primary chancre or the secondary skin rash. The infection is most contagious during the primary and secondary stages.

The preferred treatment for all stages of syphilis is penicillin. Benzathine penicillin G, a single intramuscular injection of 2.4 million units in each buttock, should be administered for primary or secondary disease. Alternatively, single daily intramuscular injections of 600,000 units of procaine penicillin G may be given for eight days. Individuals allergic to penicillin can be treated with erythromycin or tetracycline, 500 mg four times a day for fifteen days, but follow-up care should be obtained from a physician after a wilderness outing to ensure that the infection has been totally eradicated.

Gonorrhea

Gonorrhea is a common, widespread infection that in males is usually limited to the lower genital tract, principally the urethra. Infection at this site is associated with a purulent discharge, but the diagnostic feature is pain (often severe) with voiding. Residual infection may persist, particularly in the prostate, or the infection may spread to other parts of the body.

In females, gonorrhea is a much more insidious infection. Seventy-five percent of infected women have no initial symptoms at all. The infection must be diagnosed by bacterial cultures from the vagina or uterine cervix. Treatment must be based on a history of sexual contact with an infected individual when laboratory facilities for a definitive diagnosis are not available.

Gonorrhea is also a much more threatening disorder in females. Spread of the infection to other organs is much more common. Extension to the fallopian tubes produces painful infections with symptoms similar to those of appendicitis. (See Salpingitis in chapter 13, "Acute Abdominal Pain.") Permanent sterility often results. Spread of the infection to one or more joints can produce a destructive arthritis; involvement of the heart can cause disabling cardiac disease. Infections also occur in other tissues.

Unfortunately, strains of gonorrhea resistant to penicillin have emerged in recent years and are now worldwide. In wilderness situations, all gonorrhea should be assumed to be penicillin resistant and treated with a single oral dose of ciprofloxacin or ofloxacin or with a single intramuscular injection of ceftriaxone. In addition, tetracycline or doxycycline should be given orally for seven days.

Genital Herpes

In spite of the attention it has attracted, genital herpes infection is little different from herpes occurring on the lips and known as "fever blisters." Although the genital infection is transmitted by sexual contact, it has the same tendency to recur in the same location that oral herpes does. Because the tissues are somewhat more sensitive, infections on the genitalia may be more uncomfortable than those around the mouth. No curative treatment has yet been developed; acyclovir (Zovirax®) does shorten the symptomatic period and the duration of virus shedding.

Other Considerations

Everyone with a suspected or known venereal infection should consult a physician for treatment. An untreated infection can be disastrous. The ease with which syphilis and gonorrhea can be treated has created a lack of concern for all such infections. To encourage individuals to obtain the therapy they need, many states have laws that permit physicians to treat minors without reporting the infection to parents or guardians.

19

INFECTIONS

PRINCIPAL CONTRIBUTOR:
C. Kirk Avent, M.D.

Infections occur whenever microorganisms invade body tissues and multiply or develop within them. Humans normally have harmless organisms in such sites as the skin, throat, and intestines that rarely cause disease. However, when the body's defenses against infection are deficient, when organisms that are not harmless are present, or when an injury allows organisms to enter tissues in which they are not normally present, infection may result.

Infections transmitted directly or indirectly from one person to another, such as influenza and streptococcal sore throat, are termed "contagious." Others, such as urinary tract infections or appendicitis, though infectious, are not contagious. Many of the infections of concern to wilderness enthusiasts are transmitted by vectors such as mosquitoes (malaria and yellow fever) and ticks (Rocky Mountain spotted fever and Lyme disease). Few infections likely to occur in the wilderness are so contagious that they require isolation precautions.

A boil or abscess in the skin typifies the pain, swelling, redness, and heat produced by the inflammation accompanying localized infections. An infection localized to a small area such as the superficial layers of skin usually does not cause fever and other systemic symptoms. If a localized infection extends deeply, however, organisms may enter the blood stream and disseminate throughout the body. Patients with such widespread infections usually have chills, fever, and malaise. Additional symptoms may include headache, nausea, vomiting, and back pain.

When localized signs of disease accompany fever, identification of its cause is not difficult. For example, burning pain on urination, frequent passage of small amounts of urine, and discomfort over the bladder or kidneys indicate that a urinary infection is probably the cause of associated chills and fever. Similarly, if pleuritic chest pain is accompanied by a cough productive of thick, yellow sputum, the diagnosis is pneumonia. The infections discussed in this chapter are those that involve the skin and selected other generalized infections. Infections of specific organs are discussed in the chapters dealing with those organs or systems.

ANTIBIOTICS

Although a large number of antibiotics have been developed for the treatment of infectious diseases, organisms vary greatly in their sensitivity to individual drugs. An antibiotic that is effective against the specific causative organism must be used for each infection. For example, streptococci commonly cause sore throats and skin infections and may be sensitive to the penicillin family of antibiotics. Bacteria that may not be sensitive to penicillin but are susceptible to the quinolone family of antibiotics cause typhoid fever and bacillary dysentery. Identifying the organism causing an infection so that the most appropriate antibiotic can be administered is highly desirable, but this usually is not possible in the wilderness or even in remote towns and villages.

In order to eradicate an infection, antibiotics must be given in quantities large enough to produce blood and tissue concentrations that kill or inhibit the growth of the causative organisms. Dose recommendations should be followed carefully. If nausea or vomiting prevents oral administration, or the antibiotic is not effective when given orally, it must be administered by intramuscular or intravenous

Table 19-1 Significant Febrile Illnesses Likely to be Encountered by Mountaineers and Adventure Travelers

FEVER WITH MACULES[1] AND PAPULES[2]	FEVER WITH PETECHIAE[3]	FEVER WITHOUT RASH
Rocky Mountain spotted fever	Rocky Mountain spotted fever	Typhoid fever
Dengue fever	Dengue fever	Malaria
Typhoid fever	Malaria	Infectious mononucleosis
Lyme disease	Meningococcal disease	Plague
Infectious mononucleosis	Relapsing fever	
Hepatitis B	Yellow fever	
Measles	Viral hemorrhagic fevers	
Rubella	Epidemic typhus	
Tularemia		
Relapsing fever		
Colorado tick fever		
Toxic shock		

[1]A macule is a flat patch of discolored skin.
[2]A papule is a small, raised area of skin.
[3]Petechiae are small, dark red or purple spots containing blood.

injection. Intravenous administration of drugs and fluids outside of a hospital has become more feasible with the development of disposable plastic administration sets and may be necessary when high blood concentrations of antibiotics are required, as in meningitis.

Once therapy with an antibiotic has been started, it should be continued until all organisms have been killed and until all signs and symptoms of the infection have been absent for several days. Treatment usually lasts from five to twenty days, depending on the infection. Ending therapy after shorter periods may result in relapse by organisms resistant to the drug.

Antibiotics should not be given prophylactically to prevent infections, except under special circumstances. For example, most individuals with colds or minor wounds should not be given an antibiotic to prevent pneumonia or a wound infection. Administration of antibiotics in this manner not only does not prevent subsequent infection, it may allow resistant organisms to multiply and produce an infection that is difficult to treat.

The most frequently used antibiotics are the two beta-lactam families, the cephalosporins and the penicillins. Penicillin V (Pen Vee K® and others) and cephalexin (Keflex®) are well absorbed from the intestines and are the usual form given orally. If an intramuscular injection is necessary, procaine penicillin G is used. The intravenous preparation of penicillin G is aqueous or crystalline penicillin G, and a frequently used intravenous cephalosporin is ceftriaxone (Rocephin®). Dicloxacillin or cephalexin is given for less severe staphylococcal infections. Ampicillin and cephalexin are usually effective against organisms that produce urinary tract infections. Trimethoprim-sulfamethoxazole (TMP-SMX) (Bactrim®, Septra®, and others), a combination of two agents, one of which is a sulfonamide, is useful for treating a wide variety of infections, particularly typhoid fever and bacillary dysentery, but also urinary tract infections, skin infections, and pneumonia. Ciprofloxacin and levofloxacin are quinolones that are usually used to treat bacillary dysentery, urinary tract infections, and traveler's diarrhea. Because it affects growing bones, ciprofloxacin should not be given to children.

Some individuals are allergic to the penicillins and may have severe, even fatal, reactions to either oral or intramuscular administration. (See Anaphylactic Shock in chapter 20, "Allergies.") Anyone about to receive a penicillin (or any other drug, for that matter) must be carefully questioned about

INFECTIONS

previous allergic reactions. If a patient has a history suggestive of a serious penicillin allergy, a chemically different antibiotic effective against the infecting organism should be substituted. Allergies to other antibiotics and to sulfa drugs also occur.

BACTERIAL INFECTIONS

Infections of the respiratory tract, urinary tract, and skin are the most common bacterial infections. These disorders are usually innocuous if treated properly. If mistreated, however, disastrous, widespread infection can result.

Abscesses

Abscesses, boils, carbuncles, and pimples are localized skin infections that differ only in size. They are usually caused by staphylococci, which frequently are resistant to penicillin. Staphylococci release enzymes that cause clotting and obstruction of blood vessels and lymphatics surrounding the site of the infection. Because the vascular obstruction blocks the spread of bacteria, the infection usually remains localized, but the vascular obstruction also hinders access by white blood cells and antibiotics. Other enzymes released by these bacteria destroy tissues around the infection, producing a cavity filled with the mixture of bacteria, white blood cells, and liquefied tissue known as "pus."

The treatment for such disorders consists primarily of drainage and is similar to the treatment for infected wounds. Pimples and small abscesses do not need to be surgically opened. They should be covered until they rupture spontaneously. Squeezing pimples forces the bacteria into the surrounding tissues and tends to spread the infection. A particularly dangerous area for such infections is the "danger space" around the nose and below the eyes. Squeezing a pimple in this region may force bacteria into veins and lymphatics that carry them directly to the brain.

Larger abscesses may have to be incised in order to drain. After the surrounding and overlying skin has been cleaned with a preparation such as povidone-iodine (Betadine®), alcohol, or clean water and soap, a small incision into the abscess should be made with a sterile scalpel or razor blade. A local anesthetic may be necessary. When the abscess has drained, it should be gently probed with sterile forceps to make certain no pockets of infection remain. The skin should be cleansed again, and a small piece of sterile gauze should be inserted into the opening so it can not seal off. Finally, the entire area should be covered with sterile dressings.

Antibiotics are unnecessary for a small, uncomplicated abscess. If the abscess is larger than one inch (2.5 cm) in diameter or if fever, chills, or other symptoms are present, dicloxacillin or cephalexin (Keflex®) should be given orally every six hours until all evidence of infection has been absent for two days.

Similar antibiotic therapy should be instituted, even without signs of blood stream or secondary infection, if the patient has multiple abscesses or is a diabetic, because diabetes predisposes one to severe infections.

Cellulitis

Cellulitis is a bacterial infection of the skin and underlying tissues produced by organisms that do not cause obstruction of blood vessels, typically streptococci. Such infections do not tend to remain localized, and the bacteria can spread to other areas more easily. The site of the infection is usually red, swollen, hot, and tender. Fever is usually present.

Because the blood vessels remain open, these infections can be successfully treated without drainage. Dicloxacillin, a cephalosporin, or TMP-SMX should be administered orally every six hours until all signs of infection have been absent for two days. The patient should rest quietly until the infection has cleared. Due to its propensity to spread, cellulitis is a more dangerous infection than an abscess, and its potential for complications must be respected.

Bacteremia

Bacteremia is defined as the presence of bacteria in the blood stream. The organisms may multiply in the blood and produce infections throughout the body. Bacteremia is usually preceded by a localized infection such as an infected wound, a urinary tract infection, or an abscess, but it may also accompany intestinal infections, such as typhoid fever.

Bacterial blood stream invasion produces chills, high fever, sweating, and prostration. Specific signs may indicate spread of the infection to other parts of the body. Severe headache, a stiff neck, and nausea and vomiting typify involvement of the brain or its covering (meningitis). Cough, shortness of breath, and pain with breathing suggest pneumonia.

Prompt administration of antibiotics may be lifesaving. Ceftriaxone (Rocephin®), 2 grams intravenously once daily, and gentamicin, 1 mg/kg of body weight every eight hours, is a generally effective regimen in the absence of meningitis. If only aqueous penicillin G is available, 20 million units a day should be given intravenously. Patients who do not respond to treatment within seventy-two hours should be evacuated.

Patients with bacteremia should be provided with rest, warmth, a soft or liquid diet, and adequate fluids. Medications for pain and sleep are often helpful; aspirin, ibuprofen, or acetaminophen may be given to reduce fever. A record must be kept and should include the patient's temperature and the times any drugs are administered.

Rocky Mountain Spotted Fever

The triad of fever, severe headache, and rash occurring in the spring, summer, or fall should suggest the possibility of a rickettsial infection. Rickettsial organisms are smaller than bacteria but larger than viruses. They have a worldwide distribution and are transmitted to humans by the bites of arthropod vectors, such as ticks, lice, and fleas. Rocky Mountain spotted fever is not only the most severe of the rickettsial infections, it is the most prevalent rickettsial disease in the United States. Other spotted fevers are among the emerging infectious diseases occurring with increasing frequency in the United States and around the world. Rocky Mountain spotted fever is caused by *Rickettsia rickettsii*, which is transmitted to humans by the bite of a wood or dog tick.

Two to fourteen days after the bite, mild chilliness, loss of appetite, and a general run-down feeling appear. These mild symptoms are followed by chills, fever, pain in the bones and muscles, severe headache, and confusion. Between two and six days after the onset of symptoms, small red spots appear on the skin around the wrists and ankles and spread over the entire body, frequently including the palms of the hands and the soles of the feet. These spots are actually hemorrhages into the skin; in severe cases, large, blotchy, red areas may appear all over the body. The patient appears seriously ill without an obvious cause. Untreated infections last about two weeks and have a mortality rate of twenty to thirty percent; treatment reduces the rate to three to ten percent.

Diagnosis is aided by a history of a tick bite in an endemic area. The most important endemic area is the middle Atlantic coastal states; fewer cases of Rocky Mountain spotted fever are seen west of the Mississippi (including the Rocky Mountains, despite the name), but the disease can occur in any of the forty-eight contiguous states (Fig. 19-1).

For normal-sized adults, tetracycline, 500 mg to 1 g four times a day, doxycycline, 100 mg every twelve hours, or chloramphenicol, 1 g four times a day, should be given orally until the temperature has been normal for two to three days; the medication must be taken for a total of at least seven days. Tetracycline and doxycycline are the preferred agents, but, in spite of its potential for rare cases of fatal bone marrow damage (see appendix A, "Medications"), chloramphenicol should be used during pregnancy. General measures such as bed rest, fluid replacement, anti-fever medications every four hours if needed, and medications for sleep are also important.

Rocky Mountain spotted fever can be prevented by careful daily inspection for ticks when in an endemic area. The ticks should be carefully extracted with tweezers, and the wound should be

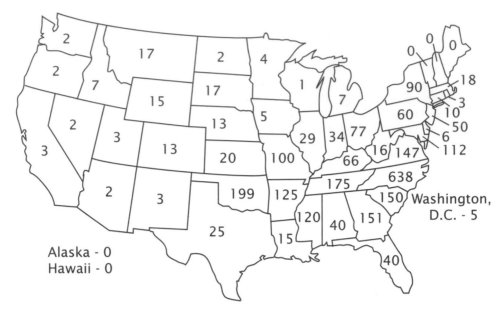

FIGURE 19-1. Rocky Mountain spotted fever cases in the United States, 1994–1998

thoroughly cleansed. Individuals moving about in brush in an endemic area should keep their shirtsleeves rolled down with the cuffs buttoned. Shirt collars should be buttoned, heads should be covered, and long trousers should be closed by gaiters or tucked into boot tops. No reliable vaccine is available.

Ehrlichiosis

Though generally a milder illness, ehrlichiosis has many of the same symptoms as Rocky Mountain spotted fever and is also transmitted to humans by ticks. Two varieties of ehrlichiosis exist in the United States. One has roughly the same distribution as Lyme disease; the other is concentrated in the South and the mid-Atlantic states. Fever, headache, nausea, and muscle aches begin a week to ten days after a tick bite. One-third of patients have a rash. The clue to diagnosis is the development of typical symptoms following a tick bite in one of the high-risk geographic areas of the United States. Low white blood cell and platelet counts are frequently found on laboratory testing. Doxycycline, 100 mg by mouth twice daily for seven days or until the patient has been afebrile for three days, is the treatment of choice.

Relapsing Fever (Tick Fever)

Tick fever occurs in mountainous areas of the western and west central states. It is a blood stream infection by a spiral bacterium *(Borrelia recurrentis)* transmitted to humans by a tick bite or, in some areas, by lice. The ticks live on rodents, including chipmunks and squirrels, and small animals such as rabbits. About two to fifteen days after the bite, chills, fever, severe headache, muscle aches and pains, joint pains, a cough, and often nausea and vomiting appear. A rash may appear on the body and limbs. Bleeding from the nose, lungs, or gastrointestinal tract may occur but usually is not severe. The initial attack lasts two to ten days and may be followed by an asymptomatic remission lasting three to ten days. During the remission, fever is absent and the patient feels well. A relapse, during which the previous symptoms recur in milder form, usually occurs seven to ten days later in untreated patients. In untreated patients, three to ten relapses may occur before complete recovery. Identification of the organism in the blood is desirable. Tetracycline or erythromycin should be given in doses of 500 mg every six hours for five to ten days to shorten the symptomatic period and prevent relapses.

Plague

Plague is a serious infection caused by *Yersinia pestis,* an organism transmitted to humans by contact with infected rodents, rabbits, and cats, or by flea bites. Not particularly widespread, the organism is found chiefly in the southwestern United States and in rural areas of South America, Africa, and Asia, particularly Vietnam. After multiplying in the skin following a bite, the organisms spread to regional lymph nodes and produce large swellings called buboes, which are responsible for the name "bubonic plague." Fortunately, involvement of the lungs is rare; when pneumonia does occur, the infection is termed "pneumonic" rather than "bubonic," and it becomes transmissible by droplets in the air. The illness is characterized by high fever, chills, prostration, and shock. It may be rapidly fatal, particularly in the pneumonic form. Treatment with streptomycin and tetracycline should be started whenever the infection is even suspected and should be administered by a physician.

Tularemia

Another infection transmitted to humans from wild rodents such as rabbits and muskrats is tularemia. Humans acquire infection by skinning infected animals or by being bitten by ticks. A red swelling develops at the site of inoculation, then enlarges and ulcerates. The fever, chills, headache, and nausea that accompany spread of the organism to the blood stream begin suddenly two to ten days after inoculation. An enlarged spleen, rashes, and prostration may complicate severe cases. Treatment with streptomycin and tetracycline should be given by a physician.

Lyme Disease

Lyme disease results from infection by *Borrelia burgdorferi,* an organism transmitted to humans from deer and mice by *Ixodes* ticks. Although concentrated in the Northeast, upper Midwest, and Pacific coast (Fig. 19-2), Lyme disease occurs throughout the United States and in parts of Europe, Asia, and Australia. More than 10,000 cases are diagnosed in the United States yearly, making it the most common vector-borne illness in the country.

The *Ixodes scapularis* ticks that transmit Lyme disease are much smaller than common dog ticks, and bites frequently go unnoticed. The nymphs, which are responsible for most human bites, are smaller than the adults—about the size of a poppy seed. As a rule of thumb, arthropods easily identified as ticks by individuals who are not familiar with the appearance of *Ixodes scapularis* are not of that species.

The risk of developing Lyme disease from a tick bite in New England, where one quarter to one-half of all *Ixodes scapularis* ticks harbor the organism, is only in the range of one to five percent and is greatest in late spring and early summer. Infection is rare unless ticks remain attached for more than twenty-four hours. Transmission sometimes requires as long as four days.

The first and most characteristic symptom, usually occurring three to ten days after exposure, is a single red skin eruption that spreads from the site of the tick bite, sometimes clearing in its center as it grows larger. The disc is flat and does not contain small blisters. Because the lesion erupts at the site of the bite, it is frequently located at underwear lines, which is as far as the tick could progress. This eruption spontaneously fades in two to four weeks. Fever, malaise, and muscle aches resembling the flu may accompany the rash. In this stage, treatment for fourteen to twenty-one days with oral doxycycline, amoxicillin, or cefuroxime axetil (Ceftin®, Zinacef®) is effective.

During later stages, which may be days to months after the original illness, headaches, fatigue, a stiff neck, and pain and swelling in joints and muscles may appear. Even later, in the third stage, serious nervous system, joint, and skin complications may develop in untreated patients. The diagnosis of

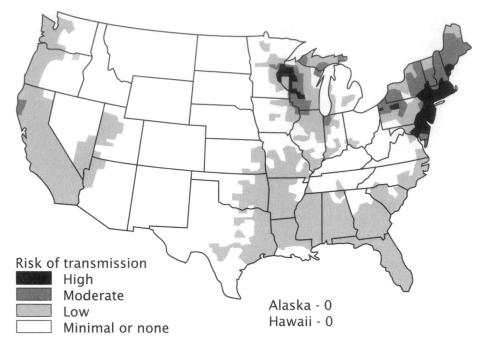

Risk of transmission

■ High
▓ Moderate
▒ Low
□ Minimal or none

Alaska - 0
Hawaii - 0

FIGURE 19-2. Categories of risk for Lyme disease in the United States

Lyme disease in later stages is based on blood tests for antibodies to the organism. Treatment in the later stages is with different drugs or for longer times and is best undertaken by a physician.

A Lyme disease vaccine, LYMErix®, is approved for administration to individuals fifteen to seventy years old. It is given in three injections, the second and third being administered one month and twelve months after the first. The vaccine is recommended only for those who live for extended periods in areas of high risk or who have frequent or prolonged occupational or recreational exposure to tick-infested habitats. Temporary visitors to areas of high or moderate risk do not need vaccination.

VIRAL INFECTIONS

Influenza

Influenza, or "flu," a viral infection caused by influenza viruses A or B, is an acute, self-limited disease that lasts five to six days and is spread by sneezing, coughing, or close contact with an infected person. Epidemics are common, particularly in winter months. The incubation period is one or two days. The onset is heralded by chilliness, fever, weakness, lassitude, headache, loss of appetite, and characteristic aching muscle pains. A dry, hacking cough is prominent and may be severe. The runny nose and sinus congestion of the common cold are absent. Fever usually lasts two to three days and occasionally reaches 104°F (40°C).

Signs and symptoms of respiratory tract involvement usually differentiate influenza from other systemic infections. Fever, muscle aches, and cough distinguish it from a common cold. A history of contact with other persons with influenza is helpful in making a diagnosis. Gastrointestinal symptoms are usually absent, but diarrhea may occur.

Symptoms are partially relieved by rest, warmth, a light diet with abundant liquids, and medications such as aspirin, acetaminophen, or ibuprofen every four hours. Medication to promote sleep and reduce cough may be helpful. Specific antiviral treatment with oral oseltamivir (Tamiflu®) or inhaled zanamivir (Relenza®) is expensive, is effective only if started within forty-eight hours of the onset of symptoms, and shortens illness by only a day.

Antibacterial drugs have no value for the routine treatment of influenza. If fever returns after several days or a cough productive of purulent sputum indicates a secondary bacterial pneumonia has developed, it should be treated with an antibiotic having a broad spectrum of activity, such as a cephalosporin or quinolone.

Infectious Mononucleosis

Infectious mononucleosis is a common viral infection of young adults spread through close personal contact. Although sometimes incapacitating, it is usually a mild illness. Fatal complications such as splenic rupture, secondary bacterial infections, severe anemia, and low platelet counts are rare.

The most characteristic symptom of infectious mononucleosis is a persistent, severe sore throat. Other complaints are not specific: fever, fatigue, and loss of energy. Lymph nodes in various portions of the body are usually enlarged, especially those in the neck.

The triad of sore throat, lymph node enlargement, and fever is classic, but infectious mononucleosis is notorious for its great variability. A skin rash, headache, weakness, loss of appetite, and generalized aching may be present. Mild liver involvement is frequent; more severe involvement with jaundice occasionally occurs.

No specific treatment is available. Antiviral and antibacterial drugs are of no benefit. Serious complications, such as hepatitis or an obstructed airway due to enlarged lymph nodes, can be treated by a tapering, five-day course of corticosteroids (Medrol® Dosepack). Acetaminophen or other anti-inflammatory drugs reduce symptoms. Saltwater gargles may help the sore throat. An adequate fluid intake should be stressed, because the sore throat may discourage oral intake. Rest is important, and the patient's activity should be limited until fever resolves. Because minor abdominal trauma could easily rupture the enlarged and fragile spleen, climbing with a waist loop and other activities in which such injury is likely should be avoided. Recovery in most cases takes two to four weeks. If jaundice or skin hemorrhage is present, the patient should be evacuated.

Dengue Fever

Dengue is a febrile illness associated with a rash that is transmitted to humans by *Aedes* mosquitoes, the same vector that transmits malaria. A virus of the same family as the yellow fever virus causes the disease. In recent years, dengue has emerged as a major public health problem, particularly in the Americas, where the disease has the same geographic distribution in the tropics as malaria. It is the most important mosquito-borne viral infection affecting humans in that area. Because *Aedes* mosquitoes live in urban environments, the disease is more common there than in rural environments, making it less of a risk to wilderness travelers. After an incubation period of four to seven days, individuals experience the sudden onset of high fever, headache, joint pain, nausea, vomiting, and a blotchy, red rash. Severe muscle pain is so typical that one of the names for the infection is "break-bone fever." After a brief period of improvement, fever and symptoms may recur. Almost everyone recovers, but bleeding, hepatitis, and neurologic complications may occur. A vaccine is under development but is not yet available.

Colorado Tick Fever

Colorado tick fever is a viral disease transmitted by the wood tick. It occurs in all western states and is far more common there than Rocky Mountain spotted fever. Infections usually occur in spring and early summer when ticks are active. Four to six days after exposure, chills and fever appear, along with headache and generalized aching. The eyes may be unusually sensitive to light. The initial attack lasts about two days, at which time the fever and other symptoms disappear, only to recur two to five days later. The outlook for complete recovery is good, even though no specific treatment is available.

Bed rest, fluids, and aspirin are helpful. A physician should evaluate the patient to be sure that Rocky Mountain spotted fever, a more serious disorder that requires antibiotic treatment, is not present.

Yellow Fever

Yellow fever is an infection of humans and monkeys caused by a virus transmitted by the *Aedes* mosquito. The disease occurs chiefly in South America and in sub-Saharan Africa. Following an incubation period of three to six days, chills, fever, headache, and backache begin. The heart rate may be slow in relation to the severity of the fever. Most patients recover completely after a few days without progressing to the severe form of the disease. In a few patients, however, fever returns; the patient becomes flushed, feels nauseated, starts vomiting, and is seriously ill. The eyes may be bloodshot and the tongue appears red. Bleeding from the gums and into the skin may occur. Vomiting "coffee ground" material or black stools indicates that bleeding is occurring in the stomach or intestines. Jaundice is typical and gave the disease its name.

The treatment of yellow fever consists of bed rest and a liquid or soft diet high in carbohydrates. Fluid and salt replacement may be necessary because dehydration accompanies vomiting, diarrhea, and high fever. Nonsteroidal anti-inflammatory drugs for discomfort and bedtime medications for sleep are helpful. No specific treatment is available. If travel into a yellow fever area is planned, vaccination should be obtained. (See chapter 5, "Immunizations, Sanitation, and Water Disinfection.")

California Encephalitis Virus

California encephalitis is the most common childhood central nervous system infection in the United States and occurs throughout the eastern and midwestern states. Most infections occur in males under age fifteen and are usually manifested by mild meningitis or encephalitis. Recovery is almost always complete. The virus is transmitted to humans by mosquitoes.

Hantavirus Pulmonary Syndrome

The hantavirus pulmonary syndrome was first recognized in New Mexico in 1993. It was given its somewhat awkward name to distinguish it from hantavirus infections in other parts of the world that disrupt kidney function and are associated with a pronounced bleeding tendency. The first signs of the pulmonary syndrome are fever and unexplained respiratory distress. At the onset, the illness is generally flulike: fever, muscle aches, headache, and cough. Bilateral infiltrates are seen in chest radiographs. Progression to respiratory failure and death frequently is quite rapid—twenty-four to forty-eight hours. Currently about one-third of the people who have a recognizable infection die. (Some people get infected but do not get sick. They can be recognized because they have antibodies to the virus. How often such subclinical infections occur is unknown.) Individuals with this condition often are healthy and in good physical condition. The first individual in whom this infection was recognized (after his death) was a marathon runner.

Hantaviruses are excreted in the urine of infected white-footed deer mice, the same rodent that serves as a reservoir for Lyme disease. In the Four Corners area where the infection was first recognized, hantavirus infection was found in thirty percent of the deer mice, which do not become ill but shed the organisms in saliva, urine, and feces. Human infection occurs when infected saliva or excreta are inhaled as aerosols. (Persons visiting laboratories where infected rats were housed have been infected after only a few minutes of exposure.) Dried rodent excreta that are introduced directly into broken skin or the eyes may also infect humans.

No effective therapy for hantavirus infection is available. The disease is best controlled by environmental hygiene that excludes rodents from the home and work environment. For campers, the Centers for Disease Control and Prevention (CDC) recommends the following commonsense precautions:

▼ Tents or sleeping bags should not be placed near areas attractive to rodents, such as garbage dumps or woodpiles.

- ▾ Rodent-infested cabins should be avoided.
- ▾ Tents with floors or cots should be used for sleeping—bare ground should be avoided.
- ▾ Food should be kept in rodent-proof containers.
- ▾ Garbage should be disposed of properly.
- ▾ Water should be disinfected.
- ▾ Dead mice should be handled with gloves.

Hemorrhagic Fever Syndromes

Hemorrhagic fevers are dramatic, frequently fatal illnesses. Coma, bleeding from the intestines and skin, and liver and kidney failure are the usual causes of death. Ebola is the most notorious of these fevers, probably because the fatality rate ranges from fifty to eighty percent, but is far from the most common. (Many Ebola and other hemorrhagic fever deaths occur in areas with rather primitive hospital facilities. Whether the death rate would be so high with sophisticated medical care of the type available in industrialized countries is unknown.)

Yellow fever is a form of hemorrhagic fever that is lethal for approximately five percent of infected individuals. A few patients with dengue develop hemorrhagic fever. Rift-Valley fever, Crimean-Congo hemorrhagic fever, and Seoul hemorrhagic fever occur in Africa, Asia, and parts of Europe. Lassa fever occurs in Africa and its incidence is second only to yellow fever. Infections by similar viruses occur in South America, and three individuals infected by a similar virus, the whitewater virus, have recently been identified in the United States. Fortunately, these viruses are limited in their geographic distribution and are unlikely to involve wilderness and adventure travelers who avoid centers of infection. No effective treatment is available, but Ebola virus can be transmitted simply by touching the skin of an infected individual, so contacts must be made only when protected by rubber gloves.

PARASITIC DISEASES

Malaria

Malaria is caused by protozoa of the genus *Plasmodium* and is transmitted by the bite of infected mosquitoes. It is by far the most common infection worldwide, with 300 to 500 million infected individuals. More than one million deaths occur each year as the result of malaria, ninety percent of them in Africa, and most of them in children.

Malarial parasites are ingested along with the blood of an infected person or animal at the time a female *Anopheles* mosquito bites. The parasites undergo fertilization and reproduce in the mosquito's gut. They are transmitted to humans when the mosquito injects saliva into the skin during a subsequent bite. In the human, parasites invade red blood cells, multiply, and release daughter parasites, destroying the red blood cells in the process. The daughter parasites invade other red blood cells and the process is repeated. The periodic release of parasites produces recurrent episodes of fever; the destruction of red blood cells can eventually result in anemia.

The initial symptoms of malaria are muscular soreness and a low fever, which appear about six to ten days after a bite by an infected mosquito. Four to eight days later, the typical chills and fever appear. Shivering, chattering teeth, cold and clammy skin, and a feeling of chilliness that is not relieved by heating pads or blankets characterize the chills. An hour later, the febrile stage begins with a flushed face, a feeling of intense heat, headache, often delirium, and temperature as high as 107°F (41.5°C). This stage lasts about two hours and is followed by drenching sweats and a fall in temperature. Headache, backache, and muscular aches may be very severe.

The repeated occurrence of febrile episodes at regular intervals such as every day, every other day, every three days—occasionally at irregular intervals—is characteristic of malaria. In severe cases, vomiting, diarrhea, severe anemia, dark urine containing elements of destroyed red blood cells, shock, and coma may occur. Enlargement of the liver or spleen may be present.

Treatment consists of general supportive measures and specific drug therapy. Rest in bed and maintenance of body warmth during the chill is highly desirable. Because water losses by sweating may be severe, a large fluid intake should be encouraged. Fluids and salt lost by vomiting or diarrhea also must be replaced. A careful record of temperature and pulse should be kept. If possible, blood smears should be made during the chill for later identification of the parasites. During an acute episode of malaria, the subsequent period of therapy, and for two weeks following recovery, strenuous exercise should be avoided to prevent rupture of the spleen.

Specific treatment for malaria should be given by a physician familiar with its various types and manifestations. The most effective general regimen for chloroquine-sensitive malaria consists of chloroquine and primaquine. For a normal-sized adult, 1.0 g of chloroquine phosphate should be given initially and should be followed by 0.5 g in six hours and 0.5 g on the second and third days. Fifteen milligrams of primaquine should be given every day for fourteen days.

Plasmodium falciparum malaria is the most dangerous form of malaria for two reasons: it produces the most severe disease, and strains resistant to chloroquine have been found throughout the world except for isolated pockets in Central and South America. Expeditions into areas where malaria is present should carry mefloquine, quinine, pyrimethamine, and doxycycline to treat chloroquine-resistant falciparum malaria. Instruction by a physician should be obtained before using these drugs.

Before leaving for a region in which malaria is present, a traveler's clinic or the CDC should be consulted to determine whether chloroquine-resistant falciparum malaria has been found in that area. Chloroquine prophylaxis effectively prevents malaria caused by strains that are not resistant. One-half gram of chloroquine phosphate should be taken on the same day of each week, beginning two weeks before entering an endemic area and continuing for five weeks after leaving. Any illness occurring within five weeks after leaving a malarial area should be reported to a physician.

If travel is anticipated into areas where chloroquine-resistant malaria is present, mefloquine (Lariam®) should be taken—a single 250 mg tablet once weekly beginning one week before travel and continuing for four weeks after return. Contraindications include pregnancy, psychiatric illness, and seizures. Consultation with a physician knowledgeable about travel medicine should be arranged well before the anticipated date of departure.

In cities and towns frequently visited by tourists, malaria is uncommon, and malaria-carrying mosquitoes are rarely found at elevations above 6,000 feet (1,800 m). In malarial areas, contact with mosquitoes should be minimized with screens or mosquito netting, protective clothing, and insect repellents. The best available repellent is N,N-diethyl-*m*-toluamide (DEET). It remains effective for up to eighteen hours, a considerable advantage over odor repellents, which are effective for only two to four hours. Avoiding malarial areas may be easier than taking chloroquine for five weeks, because this drug occasionally causes itching, gastrointestinal complaints, and a variety of other side effects.

Babesiosis

Babesiosis is a malarialike parasitic disease occurring primarily along the northeast coast of the United States and in Mexico, Yugoslavia, and Ireland. The organism is transmitted from mice and voles to humans by the bites of *Ixodes* ticks, the same arthropod that transmits Lyme disease and ehrlichiosis. The illness is characterized by fever, chills, sweats, headache, and muscle aches. Because red blood cells are destroyed by the parasite, anemia may result. The disease is usually self-limited, and most patients recover uneventfully. In a few patients, particularly those who have had their spleens removed, the disease may be severe, even fatal. Treatment with quinine and clindamycin is usually effective.

Schistosomiasis (Bilharziasis)

Schistosomiasis is a parasitic infection caused by three different species of the genus *Schistosoma*. Schistosomiasis affects more than 200 million people worldwide, but most infested people have no symptoms or clinical evidence of disease. Depending upon the particular species, infestation can cause complications in the liver, bowel, or urinary tract. The life cycles of all species are similar. After the eggs leave the human host in stool or urine, they hatch into tiny miracidia that penetrate any of several species of freshwater snails. (The absence of an appropriate snail host in the waters of the United States probably accounts for the absence of disease in this country.) Within the snail, the miracidia mature into free-living cercariae. When released from the snail into water, the cercariae are able to infest humans by penetrating intact skin, a step that requires about thirty minutes. After two days, the organisms spread through the blood stream to the lungs and liver. A month later, the worms mature and migrate through veins to their final dwelling place in the intestines or urinary bladder. Adult worms live five to ten years.

The clinical manifestations of schistosomiasis occur in stages and are produced by the effects of the organism. Skin penetration by the cercariae usually is not associated with any reaction, but repeated exposure may lead to a red rash called swimmer's itch or schistosome dermatitis.

Sometimes, with particularly heavy infestations, fever, chills, headache, and a cough occur when adult worms form and eggs are first produced. Such episodes are known as Katayama fever or acute schistosomiasis. The liver, spleen, and lymph nodes are enlarged, and eosinophilia is present.

The chronic effects of infestation are produced when the body responds to the eggs. Adult *S. mansoni* and *japonicum* live in the intestines and release their eggs into blood that goes to the liver. Scarring occurs around the eggs, producing obstruction to liver blood flow. First the liver and then the spleen become enlarged. In late stages, catastrophic gastrointestinal bleeding and liver failure may occur.

Different complications are associated with infestation by *S. haematobium* because the adults live in the veins around the urinary bladder instead of in the intestines. Scarring from the eggs of these organisms produces obstruction of the bladder and ureters. Blood in the urine and painful urination are the usual symptoms. Eventually, the chronic irritation associated with the infestation can lead to malignant changes. Squamous cell cancer of the urinary bladder is uncommon in most of the world but is one of the most common malignancies in areas where schistosomiasis is endemic.

The three main *Schistosoma* species are found in freshwater lakes and rivers worldwide. Infections caused by *S. mansoni* are found throughout tropical and subtropical Africa, Arabia, South America (Brazil, Venezuela, and Suriname) and the Caribbean. *S. japonicum* occurs in Southeast Asia and the Philippines, and *S. haematobium* occurs in Africa and the Middle East.

The diagnosis of schistosomiasis is made by finding the characteristic eggs in the stool or urine of individuals with any of the clinical manifestations of infection, such as dermatitis, Katayama fever, or liver disease. A blood test is available through the CDC.

Safe and effective oral drugs have recently been introduced for the treatment of schistosomiasis. The most broadly effective is praziquantel (Biltricide®), which is given as a single dose of 40 mg/kg for *S. mansoni* or *S. haematobium* and as 20 mg/kg three times in one day for *S. japonicum*. Only a physician should undertake treatment. The drugs kill the organisms but do not eliminate them from the body, and they produce inflammatory reactions similar to those produced by living eggs, although the reactions are considerably less severe.

Avoiding infestation is far more satisfactory and can be achieved by staying completely out of stagnant water (lakes or ponds) or slowly moving water (slowly flowing streams or rivers) in areas where the parasites are found. No swimming, bathing, or even wading should be allowed in infested water. No other effective preventive measure exists. The snails that form an essential part of the schistosome life cycle do not live in rapidly moving water, so the schistosomes are not found there. However, the water does not have to be completely still, and significant infestations have occurred among rafters on slowly moving streams—infestations that did not occur during flood season on the same rivers when the water was flowing much faster.

Onchocerciasis

Onchocerciasis, "river blindness," is one of the most common causes of vision loss in developing countries. It is caused by a filarial parasite transmitted to humans by the bite of black flies found near rivers in higher elevations of tropical Africa, Central America, and South America. Adult worms live in hard, painless nodules under the skin. The adults release microfilaria that cause intense itching in the skin and irritation of the eye. The diagnosis is made by examining skin biopsies or examining the eye for the organism. Effective treatment is now available with ivermectin (Stromectol®).

Chagas' Disease

Chagas' disease, or American trypanosomiasis, is found from southern South America to northern Mexico. The causative organism, *Trypanosoma cruzi,* is transmitted from infected animals to humans by the bite of several kinds of reduviid bugs that inhabit the walls and ceilings of poorly constructed houses. After a bite, usually at night, redness and swelling occur locally, followed by fever, headache, generalized lymph node swelling, and enlargement of the liver and spleen. Ten to thirty years later, signs of irreversible damage to the heart, esophagus, or colon appear. No clearly effective form of treatment in the late stages of disease is available. Nifurtimox may be useful early. Infestation should be avoided by not sleeping in such houses. Tents are far safer.

Trichinosis

Trichinosis is a parasitic disease caused by eating improperly cooked pork containing larvae of the roundworm *Trichinella spiralis.* After the larvae are ingested, they attach themselves to the wall of the small bowel, mature, and produce eggs. The larvae that are released when the eggs hatch spread throughout the body through the circulation and localize in muscles.

If infestation is heavy, penetration of the intestinal wall by the larvae one to four days after ingestion produces nausea, vomiting, abdominal cramps, and diarrhea that resemble food poisoning. The migration of the larvae to the muscles seven days after ingestion produces fever, chills, muscular weakness, a skin rash, and swelling of the face and tissues around the eyes. Headache may be severe.

The diagnosis is based upon the onset of characteristic symptoms following the ingestion of uncooked pork or improperly prepared pork products such as salami. A skin test is also available. No specific treatment for trichinosis has been of proven value except thiabendazole, which should be given by a physician. Symptomatic treatment consists of rest, aspirin and codeine, and sedatives to promote restful sleep. Prednisone may be beneficial in the early stages of the disease. All pork must be thoroughly cooked. In addition, freezing at 0°F (-18°C) for twenty-four hours or 5°F (-15°C) for twenty days usually kills all trichinae.

Acquired Immunodeficiency Syndrome

Acquired immunodeficiency syndrome (AIDS) is characterized by susceptibility to unusual infections and malignant tumors caused by a defect in the immune system. The disease results from the destruction of normal lymphocytes by the human immunodeficiency virus (HIV). Since its identification in 1981, the disease has spread worldwide. In sub-Saharan Africa, more than two million persons die from AIDS annually.

The period of time between infection by HIV and the development of AIDS can be many years. During this latent phase, the infected person has no symptoms but is capable of transmitting the infection by sexual contact, by blood, and by mothers to infants. Transfusions of blood or blood products, injections with needles or syringes contaminated with blood, infected mothers giving birth, and splashing contaminated blood into open wounds are some of the ways blood can transmit the virus.

Kissing, sharing utensils, using the same toilets, drinking from the same containers, touching, and other nonintimate contacts do not transmit the virus and are safe. Persons who are infected with HIV but otherwise in good health should not be excluded from wilderness outings. Before traveling to a foreign country, however, such individuals should determine whether a negative test for HIV is required for entry or a visa.

Blood transfusions are extremely risky in any country that does not effectively screen blood for HIV. A traveler's clinic or the CDC can supply up-to-date information (see *www.cdc.gov/travel/*). Similarly, injections from reused syringes or needles are dangerous. The safest ways to avoid sexual transmission of infection are abstinence or monogamous sexual relations with a person known to be uninfected. Condoms reduce but do not eliminate the risk of infection.

20

ALLERGIES

When foreign substances enter the body, the immune system responds by forming "antibodies" that combine with the foreign materials to facilitate their elimination. When the foreign substances (antigens) are bacteria or viruses, antibodies play a large role in preventing or eradicating infection. Other foreign antigens also elicit an antibody response.

Once a person has contacted an antigen, antibodies persist in his blood for years or even his lifetime. These persistent antibodies provide permanent immunity following infections such as measles or mumps. Vaccines are composed of dead or weakened organisms that induce immunity by eliciting an antibody response without producing a full-blown infection. Many vaccines do not elicit an antibody response as effective as that following an actual infection and must be repeated every few years.

Antibodies are proteins known as immunoglobulins. Various types of immunoglobulins are classified as G, M, A, E, and D and are usually abbreviated IgG, IgM, and so on. Occasionally, a person reacts to an antigen by forming an excessive amount of antibody, particularly IgE, the principal antibody responsible for allergic reactions. Contact with that antigen—or allergen, as antigens that produce allergic reactions are called—results in a strong IgE response that releases histamine and related substances to produce the allergic reaction.

The periodic injection of gradually increasing amounts of an allergen can sometimes overwhelm the antibody response. This process, known as desensitization, eliminates or greatly reduces the allergic reaction. If desensitization is stopped, the original allergic condition usually returns. Nonetheless, desensitization can be useful in helping to control allergic reactions such as hay fever.

The substances to which an individual may become allergic are unlimited. Foods, pollens, animal dander, and dust are the most frequent offenders. Reactions to therapeutic agents are also common. Insect stings and penicillin are notorious for causing anaphylactic reactions, an uncommon type of allergic reaction that is explosive in onset and is often lethal if not effectively treated.

HAY FEVER

Pollens, dust, and other allergens in the air are the most common causes of hay fever—acute nasal allergy. Hay fever is rare in a world of ice and snow, whether at high altitude or extreme latitude, but it is a common and occasionally severe problem in warmer climates. The nasal membranes are red and swollen, causing nasal stuffiness and nasal discharge. Frequent sneezing is common. The eyes are often red; excessive tearing is common.

An individual with recurrent hay fever that is so severe it hinders his routine activities should consider desensitization. He should consult his physician or allergist to determine the medications that are most effective for him personally. Effective treatment for hay fever usually combines an antihistamine with a decongestant. However, some drugs and drug combinations are more effective for certain individuals than others. Antihistamines that produce little or no drowsiness have recently become available. The combination of triprolidine, an antihistamine, with pseudoephedrine, a decongestant (Actifed®, Histafed®, and others), is widely used to help control nasal allergies and the stuffiness of colds. A four percent solution of cromalyn sodium sprayed into the nose is effective for preventing the nasal symptoms of hay fever but has little effect on eye symptoms.

HIVES

Hives are often caused by food allergies—chocolate, seafood, and fresh fruit are the most common offenders—but can occur as an allergic reaction to almost any substance, including dusts and pollen, insect bites and stings, or drugs, occasionally even to drugs as commonly used as aspirin. Hives appear quickly following contact with the allergen, are often widely scattered, and consist of red or white raised wheals (bumps) that itch intensely. Hives may rapidly appear and disappear several times from a single allergen exposure. Repeated exposures to the same allergen usually reproduce the attacks indefinitely. However, the condition is more miserable than serious.

The treatment for recurrent episodes of hives consists of antihistamines. Those used for motion sickness are usually effective. Cornstarch packs or baths, or bland lotions, may help reduce itching. Spontaneous recovery occurs without treatment if further exposure to the allergen is avoided.

CONTACT DERMATITIS

A rash occasionally develops following contact with jewelry, the case of a wristwatch, or a similar material. Often the cause can not be determined, and the rash may not be located at the point of contact. The rash is usually more annoying than disabling, typically is composed of multiple small blisters on a red background, and may itch or burn. Severe cases should be treated in the same manner as poison ivy dermatitis.

Poison Ivy, Poison Oak, and Poison Sumac

Poison ivy, poison oak, and poison sumac produce an acute contact dermatitis due to the urushiols that are components of their sap. Poison ivy and poison oak are closely related plants found throughout the United States and grow as shrubs or vines. Their leaves grow in clusters of three, a distinctive pattern that allows them to be easily recognized (Fig. 20-1). Poison ivy leaves tend to have smooth edges, and poison oak leaves tend to be more lobulated or serrated; but the patterns overlap, and distinguishing between the two is not important. Poison sumac does not have this identifying feature, but it grows

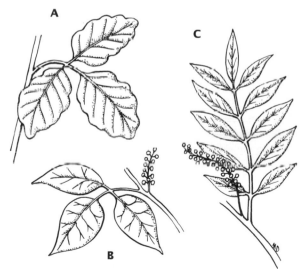

FIGURE 20-1. Typical appearance of the leaves of poison oak (A), poison ivy (B), and poison sumac (C)

only in marshy areas east of the Mississippi and is encountered much less frequently.

The rash typically develops at the point of contact but may appear at sites that are far removed. It usually appears on the hands and face only a few days after contact, but as long as a week may pass before it appears at other locations. The rash usually disappears in the same order it appeared after four to seven days.

Red streaks or patches that itch appear first, followed in twelve to twenty-four hours by blisters that typically are arranged in lines. The blisters often break, resulting in oozing and crusting of the surface. Usually, swelling of the underlying tissues, burning, and itching are present. Scratching should be avoided because it can introduce infection or cause scarring, but scratching does not spread the rash. The blisters are filled with serum, not the urushiol that causes the dermatitis.

Treatment depends upon the extent of the rash. If the area covered is small, no therapy at all may be needed. Calamine lotion may relieve itching. For more extensive eruptions, itching may be relieved by cool saltwater compresses (two teaspoons [8 cc or 8 g] of salt per quart of water) applied for ten minutes four times a day. A steroid ointment such as 0.25 percent hydrocortisone can be applied in limited amounts after the compresses.

Patients with extensive, disabling poison ivy dermatitis require systemic steroid therapy. In urban surroundings, such patients have been defined as those sick enough to seek a physician's care. The physician should prescribe the medication.

Desensitization for poison ivy has been tried, but the side effects are as bad as the rash. No desensitizing agent has been approved by the Food and Drug Administration (FDA). Many over-the-counter preparations for poison ivy contain antihistamines, analgesics, or even antibiotics that can produce a secondary allergic reaction that may be worse than the original problem.

ANAPHYLACTIC SHOCK

Anaphylactic shock is an acute, massive allergic reaction that involves essentially the entire body. Fortunately, such reactions are uncommon, for death can occur within five to ten minutes if treatment is not administered immediately. (Deaths due to anaphylactic reactions undoubtedly still go unrecognized, are attributed to heart attacks or some similar disorder, and may be significantly more common than appreciated.)

Insect stings are one of the more common causes of anaphylactic shock. In the United States, deaths due to allergic reactions to insect stings far outnumber those caused by all other venomous animals, including poisonous snakes, spiders, and scorpions. (See chapter 25, "Animal Bites and Stings.")

Drugs are another prominent cause of anaphylactic shock. The most common offenders are penicillin and foreign serum such as horse serum. Because the danger of anaphylactic shock is so great, these agents must be administered to patients who are or may be allergic to them only when absolutely essential (such as after a severe snake bite envenomation). Even then, they should be given only in a hospital, where the allergic reaction can be monitored and controlled. Anaphylactic reactions to drugs are most common following injection, but they have been caused by oral medications. Very rarely, anaphylactic reactions have been caused by food.

Diagnosis

The symptoms of anaphylactic shock usually appear five to fifteen minutes after exposure to the allergen. Occasionally, an hour may pass before symptoms appear, and very rarely twenty-four hours can elapse, particularly after oral ingestion of the offending substance.

The dominant feature of anaphylactic shock is severe respiratory distress that appears and progresses rapidly. Swelling of the tissues of the upper air passages, particularly in the larynx, where the airway is already narrowed by the vocal chords (laryngeal edema), narrows the air passages and can produce lethal respiratory obstruction. Narrowing of the bronchi within the lungs—bronchospasm—produces respiratory difficulty that is similar to asthma but is much more severe. The cause, a spasm of the muscle in the walls of small bronchi that results in severe constriction, is also similar. With anaphylaxis, the onset is more abrupt and usually develops within minutes. Sometimes a sense of pressure beneath the sternum is noted.

The skin is the next most common organ affected by anaphylaxis. Hives may be present and are widely distributed. Angioedema or localized swelling may occur on an extremity or around the eyes or mouth.

Nausea, vomiting, abdominal pain, and diarrhea may reflect involvement of the gastrointestinal system. Involvement of the eyes and nose causes changes that resemble a sudden, severe attack of hay fever. The eyes are swollen and red and the flow of tears is greatly increased. A red, swollen mucosa and mucoid discharge plug the nose. Rarely, involvement of the cardiovascular system can result in shock or a cardiac arrhythmia that can be fatal.

Treatment

Anaphylactic shock is a true medical emergency for which minutes may make a difference between therapeutic success and failure. Treatment must be instituted without delay and consists of the injection of 0.3 cc of a 1:1,000 aqueous solution of epinephrine (adrenaline). The route of administration is determined by the patient's condition. If the reaction is caught early, when only moderate respiratory distress is present, the adrenaline should be injected subcutaneously. If the patient is in severe respiratory difficulty, the epinephrine should be injected intramuscularly so that it can be absorbed more rapidly.

Epinephrine in 1:1,000 dilution is available in several forms in the United States. EpiPen® is a preloaded syringe that can be injected almost instantaneously with only one hand. After the cover is stripped away, the needle can be jabbed into the thigh or any other convenient location, through clothing if necessary. Although the ability to make an injection with one hand would be useful for a few individuals such as rock climbers, such speed is rarely needed, particularly after the first injection. Although the syringe contains 2.0 cc of solution, only a single 0.3 cc dose can be delivered. Ana-Kit® contains a syringe loaded with 1.0 cc of epinephrine that can deliver two 0.3 cc injections, but not as rapidly as the EpiPen®. Epinephrine is made by several pharmaceutical manufacturers; it is available from Wyeth-Ayerst in Tubex®, a preloaded syringe that contains 1.0 cc of solution, essentially all of which can be used. Detailed directions accompany all of these devices, but an allergic individual should develop a strategy specifically for himself with the physician who writes the prescription for the device.

Some inhalers for asthmatics contain epinephrine. Such preparations are not recommended for anaphylactic shock because the response to them is inconsistent. Although they are cheaper than the injectable preparations and undoubtedly better than nothing, they are not totally reliable for the treatment of severe anaphylactic reactions—the type that most needs reliable therapy.

Injections of epinephrine should be repeated every twelve to fifteen minutes if needed. In fact, patients must be closely watched because many individuals relapse in fifteen to twenty minutes as the epinephrine wears off.

Respiratory obstruction due to laryngeal edema usually responds to epinephrine but may require tracheostomy.

Other steps can help a patient with anaphylaxis, but none can substitute for epinephrine. Following insect stings on an extremity, placing a tourniquet above the site can provide more time for the individual to be transported to a medical facility where epinephrine is available. Oxygen should be administered during the period of respiratory difficulty regardless of altitude. Other forms of treatment for shock should be instituted. Appropriate care should be given if the patient is unconscious. Antihistamines may help control the itching of hives and other symptoms, but they should be administered only after anaphylaxis has been controlled.

Prevention of anaphylactic shock by avoiding the allergen or by desensitization is far safer than treatment. Desensitization for insect sting allergy with purified venoms is effective for some individuals. However, even after desensitization, individuals subject to anaphylactic shock from insect stings or similar uncontrollable allergens should always carry epinephrine. Effective desensitization for allergies to drugs such as penicillin is not practical.

ENVIRONMENTAL INJURIES

21 DISORDERS CAUSED BY ALTITUDE

PRINCIPAL CONTRIBUTOR:
Charles S. Houston, M.D.

For centuries, travelers returning from high mountains have reported unpleasant symptoms, even fatalities, and have ascribed them to poisonous shrubs, emanations from ores—even the breath of dragons. Only 100 years ago was the real cause shown to be lack of oxygen, which had been isolated a century earlier.

Although approximately twenty percent of air is oxygen, no matter what pressure it is under, the weight of the overlying atmosphere—atmospheric or barometric pressure—decreases as altitude above the earth's surface increases. When a person ascends to a higher altitude, fewer molecules of oxygen—or any of the other gases that make up air—are available in the atmosphere. At 18,000 feet (5,500 m), the atmospheric pressure, and the pressure of oxygen in the air, is approximately half that at sea level. On top of Mount Everest (29,002 feet [8,824 m]), atmospheric pressure and the amount of oxygen available is one-third that at sea level. (Because the air at the poles is colder and more dense, the atmosphere is vertically compressed. Ascending individuals pass more quickly through the atmospheric mass, and any significant elevation is physiologically higher than it would be nearer the equator.)

Both decreased pressure and lack of oxygen cause problems at altitude, but the conditions called mountain or altitude sickness are due only to lack of oxygen—hypoxia. (In contrast, if inhaled oxygen pressure is too high—breathing 100 percent oxygen, for instance—inflammation of the lungs often develops within a few hours.) The manner in which the body takes in oxygen, circulates it throughout the body, and gets rid of carbon dioxide is described in chapter 10, "Respiratory Disorders."

The rate of ascent is the most important determinant of whether an individual develops mountain sickness. The faster the ascent, the more likely is illness to develop. (Going up very fast in an unpressurized aircraft, a balloon, or a decompression chamber produces acute hypoxia, which causes problems quite different from the mountain sickness discussed in this chapter.)

Significant differences between individuals exist, and a schedule of ascent that suits most members of a group may be too fast for some. Only some of these differences are known, but among them are recently recognized genetic variations. These differences are inherent and have nothing to do with an individual's physical condition, determination, or courage. The effects of hypoxia are aggravated by cold (hypothermia), low blood sugar (hypoglycemia), exhaustion, and dehydration. Furthermore, these and other conditions—including carbon monoxide poisoning—often mimic mountain sickness. Nevertheless, on a high mountain, hypoxia should be assumed to be the cause of any symptoms. "Waiting to see what happens" when symptoms are severe all too often makes the situation worse and can lead to death that could have been prevented.

MOUNTAIN ALTITUDES

Mountain altitudes can be divided into three levels that are physiologically significant. (Table 21-1 lists conversions between feet and meters.)

Table 21-1 Conversions Between Feet and Meters

FEET TO METERS

FEET	METERS	FEET	METERS
1	0.30	14,000	4,267
10	3.05	15,000	4,572
100	30.48	16,000	4,877
1,000	301	17,000	5,182
2,000	608	18,000	5,486
3,000	914	19,000	5,791
4,000	1,219	20,000	6,096
5,000	1,524	21,000	6,401
6,000	1,829	22,000	6,705
7,000	2,134	23,000	7,010
8,000	2,438	24,000	7,315
9,000	2,743	25,000	7,620
10,000	3,048	26,000	7,925
11,000	3,353	27,000	8,230
12,000	3,658	28,000	8,534
13,000	3,962	29,000	8,839

METERS TO FEET

METERS	FEET
1	3.281
10	33
100	330
1,000	3,281
2,000	6,562
3,000	9,843
4,000	13,123
5,000	16,404
6,000	19,685
7,000	22,966
8,000	26,247
9,000	29,528

8,000 to 12,000 Feet (2,400 to 3,600 Meters)

In the United States, hundreds of thousands of tourists—skiers, climbers, and others—ascend to these altitudes, at which most altitude illnesses occur. Although newcomers ascending above 5,000 feet (1,500 m) may notice a decrease in athletic performance, not many have any other symptoms. A few unusually susceptible individuals may have mild mountain sickness as low as 8,000 feet (2,400 m), but serious altitude illnesses such as pulmonary or cerebral edema are rare at that altitude. The incidence of mountain sicknesses in new arrivals increases from twenty-five to forty percent as altitude increases from 9,000 to 12,000 feet (2,700 to 3,600 m). (In this text, these elevations are referred to as "altitude" or "moderate altitude.")

Table 21-2	Gas Pressures at Various Altitudes (mm Hg)					
Meters	Feet	BarP	Pio_2	Pao_2	$Paco_2$	Sao_2(%)
0	0	760	149	94	41	97
1,500	5,000	630	122	75–81	39	92
2,286	7,500	570		69–74	31–33	92–93
4,600	15,000	425	76	48–53	25	86
5,500	18,000	379	69	40	29	71
6,100	20,000	352	63	37–45	20	76
7,620	25,000	291		32–39	13	68
8,848	29,029	253	42	26–33	9.5–13.8	58

Abbreviations: BarP = barometric pressure; Pio_2 = pressure of inspired oxygen; Pao_2 = arterial oxygen pressure; $Paco_2$ = arterial carbon dioxide pressure; Sao_2(%) = arterial oxygen saturation

12,000 to 18,000 Feet (3,600 to 5,500 Meters)

Several hundred mountains in North America reach these altitudes and are visited by hundreds of climbers, many of whom get sick. Most high altitude base camps in the Andes, Himalayas, and other Asian ranges are above 14,000 feet (4,200 m), but the experienced climbers who attempt these peaks usually know how to avoid mountain sickness. This is not true of trekkers, and a great many fall ill; a few die. Rapid ascent to such altitudes without prior acclimatization is dangerous and can cause all of the different types of altitude illness. (In this text, these elevations are referred to as "high altitude.")

18,000 to 29,000 Feet (5,500 to 8,800 Meters)

The great mountains of Asia, Africa, and South America attract experienced mountaineers who know to avoid illness by careful acclimatization. Those susceptible to mountain sickness infrequently go so high. These individuals do occasionally fall victim to severe altitude-related illness, but most of their difficulty comes from prolonged stays above 20,000 feet (6,100 m) that cause loss of physical and mental fitness rather than acclimatization problems. Humans live permanently at altitudes up to 17,500 feet (5,400 m), where the pressure of oxygen in the atmosphere is about 80 mm Hg (Table 21-2), but above this do not thrive. Above 20,000 feet (6,100 m), humans deteriorate rapidly. (In this text, such elevations are referred to as "extreme altitude.")

RESPONSES TO INCREASING ALTITUDE

As individuals ascend to higher elevations, the body makes adjustments to sustain its supply of oxygen. These alterations begin almost immediately, and over days evolve into changes that are called acclimatization.

Short-Term Changes
Increased Rate and Depth of Breathing

An early and important response to lack of oxygen is an increase in both the rate and depth of breathing. This natural and logical response brings air deeper into the lungs, flushes out the carbon dioxide and the oxygen-depleted air in the alveoli, and brings the alveolar oxygen pressure closer to that of the outside atmosphere. Persons whose response—termed the "hypoxic ventilatory response"—is brisk appear to be less susceptible to mountain sicknesses. Those with a "blunted" response may be slightly more susceptible or may simply take longer to adjust. However, increased depth and rate of breathing is the first and most important effect of oxygen deficiency.

At sea level, the work of breathing requires only about five percent of the oxygen used by the body. At higher altitude, the respiratory muscles must work harder and require a larger share of the inhaled oxygen. Near the summit of Mount Everest, climbers who are not using supplemental oxygen are estimated to be consuming approximately two-thirds of their inhaled oxygen just in the work of respiration.

At high altitudes, the lungs rather than the heart fail to keep up with demand and limit the amount of work that can be done. The decreased ability to perform physical work is proportional to the altitude. The rate is approximately three percent per thousand feet, but the decline is even faster at extreme altitude. Acclimatization improves the ability to work somewhat, but even the best-acclimatized person can not reach sea level work capacity.

Decreased Oxygen Saturation

At sea level, the hemoglobin in arterial blood leaving the lungs carries almost its full capacity of oxygen and is ninety-five percent or more saturated. As altitude increases, the saturation decreases proportionally. Resting arterial oxygen saturation at 15,000 feet (4,500 m) is approximately eighty-five percent. During exercise at sea level, arterial saturation remains normal, although it may fall slightly with very strenuous effort such as running a 440-yard (400-meter) race. During exercise at high altitude, the lower alveolar oxygen pressure results in incomplete loading of red blood cells with oxygen, and saturation falls dramatically. The decrease is proportional to the exercise level and the altitude. Because the working muscles do not get as much oxygen as they need, climbers take more frequent rests, allowing the saturation to rise again. At extreme altitudes, the muscles of respiration may tire more rapidly than those of the legs and arms (Figs. 21-1 and 21-2).

Changes in pH

Increased breathing "washes out" carbon dioxide from blood, making it more alkaline. (The pH is higher.) The increased alkalinity is responsible for some of the symptoms that occur at higher elevations. It also plays a role in producing altitude illness, particularly acute mountain sickness (discussed below), because the higher pH of blood and cerebrospinal fluid limits the increased ventilatory response.

Increased alkalinity stimulates the excretion of bicarbonate in the urine, which tends to restore the pH of the blood toward normal. The drug acetazolamide (Diamox®), discussed below, increases bicarbonate excretion and has been called an "artificial acclimatizer."

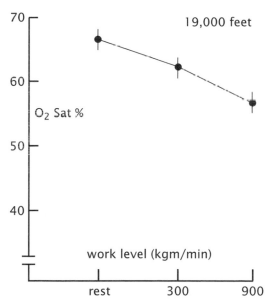

FIGURE 21-1. Blood oxygen content (saturation) under varying working conditions at an altitude of 19,000 feet

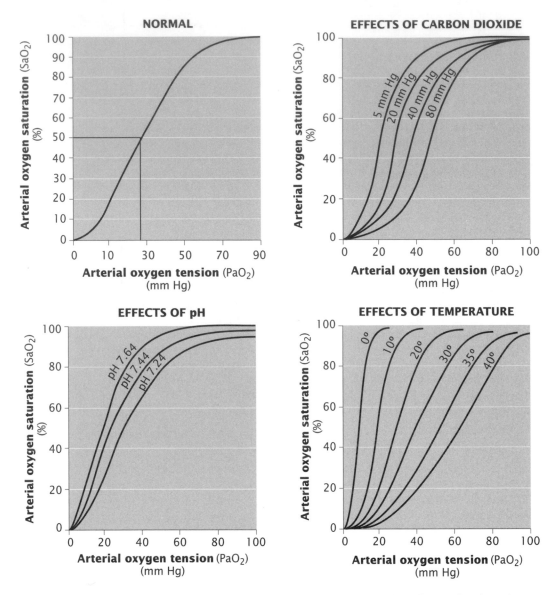

FIGURE 21-2. Oxygen-hemoglobin dissociation curves: normal and the effects of carbon dioxide, pH, and temperature

Pulse Rate and Cardiac Output

During a climb, the pulse rate rises with the workload but subsides during rest. The extent of increase and the speed with which it returns to normal are a function of altitude and, to a certain degree, are indicators of acclimatization. A slow resting pulse that increases little during work and rapidly returns to resting level is a sign of physical fitness at sea level and also indicates that an individual is adjusting well to higher elevations.

For a short while after reaching altitude, the volume of blood pumped by the heart (the cardiac output) at any level of exercise is greater than normal. However, it soon decreases to normal, and after a

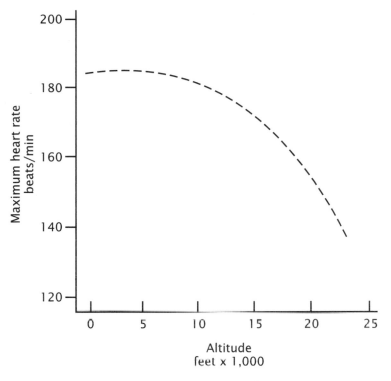

FIGURE 21-3. Decline of maximum heart rate with altitude

few days falls below sea level quantities during rest or comparable exercise. Cardiac output remains at this lower level for a week or two and then rises to or above the sea level value. This sequence depends on the altitude and, obviously, on the health of the heart.

The maximum heart rate that can be attained during heavy exercise is lower at altitude (Fig. 21-3). The maximum achievable heart rate at sea level decreases with age and is roughly 200 minus one-half of one's age. Heavier exertion does not raise this level much but can put a significant strain on the laboring heart.

A crude but useful indication of the load on the heart is the "double product"—the systolic (higher) blood pressure multiplied by the pulse rate. Obviously, these increase with work and with altitude. The double product can estimate the combined effect and can be helpful in deciding whether a person with heart disease can safely go to altitude.

Blood Volume

Rapid ascent to altitude is accompanied by a prompt decrease in blood volume because fluid moves out of the blood vessels into the tissues and cells. The decrease is five to ten percent of the sea level blood volume, which is equivalent to removing about a pint of blood plasma. The fluid may remain as edema in the tissues for some days.

This loss of fluid causes an apparent increase in red blood cells, although the actual number of circulating red cells does not increase for many days. If the individual consumes additional fluids, the blood volume may be slowly restored by a shift of fluid back into the blood from the tissues.

An increased urine output and inadequate fluid intake at higher elevations may further decrease blood volume. Maximal work capacity is significantly impaired by a blood volume reduction of this magnitude. If the missing fluid is not restored, the thicker blood has a greater tendency to clot. In veins, such clotting is called thrombophlebitis and is a real hazard of high altitude, particularly if the individual is inactive. (See chapter 9, "Heart and Blood Vessel Disorders.")

Sleep Hypoxia

During sleep at altitude, ventilation is often decreased, and wide fluctuations in the respiratory rate—periodic breathing—may occur. Sometimes alarming periods (ten to twelve seconds) of not breathing (apnea) are followed by a period in which the depth and rate of breathing increase. Often the depth and rate rapidly increase to a level greatly above normal but then subside until apnea intervenes again.

The generally accepted explanation for periodic breathing is that the brain's respiratory control centers become less sensitive during sleep so that respiration decreases or stops. Very soon, blood carbon dioxide has risen so high—and oxygen has fallen so low—that breathing starts up again with ever-increasing depth until the blood gases have become more normal. At that point, respirations tail off again. Periodic breathing often begins as a person reaches a moderate elevation, persists or even becomes more marked with acclimatization, and may be an important cause of deterioration during prolonged stays at extreme altitude.

At 14,000 feet (4,200 m), where resting oxygen saturation is about eighty-six percent in people who are awake, periodic breathing, which is almost universal, may cause saturation to fall as low sixty percent.

Acetazolamide may not change waking hemoglobin saturation but almost completely eliminates the wide swings caused by periodic breathing. At 14,000 feet (4,200 m), for example, acetazolamide limits the lower level of saturation during sleep to about eighty-two percent. Sedatives and tranquilizers make sleep hypoxia worse and should be avoided at altitude. On the other hand, a small dose of acetazolamide taken at bedtime is a simple and safe way to improve sleep, despite the slight diuresis it may cause.

Sleep hypoxia may account, in part, for the inability of many individuals to sleep well at altitude. It may also explain why headache and other symptoms of acute mountain sickness are more severe in the morning hours, and why both high altitude pulmonary edema (HAPE) and high altitude cerebral edema (HACE) often become worse during the night. Part of the beneficial effect acetazolamide has for acute mountain sickness probably results from decreased sleep hypoxia.

Sleep hypoxia decreases physical working capacity during the day, which provides one physiologic explanation for the wisdom behind the mountaineer's dictum "sleep low and climb high." Climbers have noted better physical performance when low-flow oxygen has been used during sleep because this decreases the fall in arterial oxygen saturation. Chronic lack of sleep on a mountain, like hypoxia, interferes with intellectual function, particularly at extreme altitude, and increases the likelihood of mistakes.

Acclimatization

The evolution of the short-term changes described above to long-term adjustments constitutes acclimatization. Survival and effective functioning at 18,000 feet (5,500 m), and the ability of some persons to work without supplemental oxygen as high as 29,000 feet (8,800 m), is dependent upon the ability to adjust, or acclimatize, to lack of oxygen. Taken abruptly from sea level to the summit of Mount Everest, an unacclimatized person would have only five to ten minutes of decreasing consciousness before lapsing into coma and dying in about thirty minutes. Birds can fly higher for much longer periods, but no mammals, including humans, live permanently above 17,500 feet (5,300 m), suggesting that this is the upper limit to which they can acclimatize.

Acclimatization can best be described as a series of integrated changes by which the oxygen reaching the tissues is brought closer to that in the ambient air. It is a gradual process taking days and weeks to mature, but a well-acclimatized person can tolerate altitudes that would incapacitate a person newly arrived from sea level. It is a remarkable process, one that also enables many persons who are hypoxic at sea level as the result of illness to lead nearly normal lives.

The most important changes in acclimatization are those that occur upon first arrival at altitude:
▼ Increased respiratory volume
▼ Increased cardiac output
▼ Elevation of pulmonary artery pressure
▼ Apparent increase in red blood cells due to a shift of fluid from blood to tissues

In addition, complex changes in the way cells use oxygen, hormonal changes that control electrolyte migration, changes in urine output, and redistribution of blood flow to more critical parts of the body all promote normal function at low oxygen pressures.

Increased Respiratory Volume (Ventilation)

An increase in the depth and to a lesser extent the rate of respiration—increased ventilation—brings more outside air into the alveoli, increasing the oxygen available to diffuse into blood. The increase is most obvious during exercise. Those who have just arrived at even moderate altitude may experience unusual shortness of breath during only moderate exertion. Ventilation is the function that limits exercise at extreme altitude.

Increased Pulmonary Artery Pressure

Many conditions that reduce the oxygen pressure in the lungs, whether at altitude or at sea level, increase the blood pressure in the pulmonary arteries. The elevated pressure tends to open more capillaries in all parts of the lung (many of which are closed during quiet respiration at sea level) to maximize the capacity of the pulmonary circulation to absorb oxygen. One explanation offered for high altitude pulmonary edema (HAPE) is that increased arterial pressure, transmitted directly to the capillaries, forces fluid through their thin walls into the alveoli.

Interestingly, lack of tissue oxygen due to anemia or carbon monoxide poisoning does not increase pulmonary arterial pressure because the alveolar oxygen is normal. On the other hand, sleep apnea, which can lower alveolar oxygen several times each minute, can increase pulmonary arterial pressure permanently and is thought to increase systemic blood pressure.

Increased Cardiac Output

As stated, during the first few days at altitude the volume of blood pumped by the heart at rest or at any exercise level is higher than at sea level, which increases the amount of oxygen delivered to the tissues. However, after seven to ten days the cardiac output becomes less than at sea level, and more time is required for any specific amount of work, whether brisk exercise such as running or more prolonged activities such as carrying a load. With a longer stay at altitude, cardiac output rises again; at extreme altitude, it is above sea level values. The ability of the heart to pump blood does not limit work at extreme altitude, even during heavy exercise. The ability—or inability—to move air restricts work at great heights.

Increased Number of Red Blood Cells

Shortly after arrival at altitude, an apparent increase in the concentration of red cells in the blood results from movement of water out of the blood into the tissues. However, hypoxia stimulates release of a hormone called erythropoietin, which is formed in the lungs and kidneys. This hormone is a powerful bone marrow stimulant, and within the first few days after ascent, red blood cell production actually increases. The blood eventually may contain many more cells than at sea level. This increase in red cells, measured as the percentage of whole blood volume occupied by cells (hematocrit), is the best known and historically was the earliest described change in acclimatization, although it is not the most important.

The increased number of red cells enables blood to carry more oxygen, but this increased capacity may be offset by the increase in blood viscosity. A serious danger of clot formation in the veins (thrombophlebitis) appears when the hematocrit rises above sixty percent. (At sea level, normal hematocrit in males is forty-two to fifty-two percent; in females it is thirty-seven to forty-seven percent.)

Changes in Oxygen-Carrying Capacity

Red blood cells contain the enzyme 2,3-diphosphoglycerate (DPG), which facilitates the release of oxygen from hemoglobin to the tissues. The concentration of DPG in the blood increases at higher altitudes and produces a "leftward shift" of the hemoglobin saturation curve that allows release of a larger volume of transported oxygen for a smaller drop in oxygen pressure, at least below 20,000 feet (6,100 m). At higher elevations, the increased alkalinity caused by loss of carbon dioxide helps blood take on oxygen in the lungs.

Changes in Body Tissues

Acclimatization by long residence at altitude causes more subtle changes that enable near-normal function by the oxygen-consuming tissues, particularly muscle, despite low oxygen pressures. These changes include:
- ▼ An increase in the number of capillaries within the muscle
- ▼ An increase in myoglobin, the intramuscular oxygen-carrying protein
- ▼ An increase in the concentration of intracellular oxidative enzymes
- ▼ An increase in the size of mitochondria, the tiny structures in the cells that contain oxidative enzymes

These changes allow more than fifteen million people throughout the world to live at 17,000 to 17,500 feet (5,150 to 5,300 m).

Some populations that have lived at high altitude for many generations (for example, in the high Andes, Caucasus, or Ethiopia) develop physical changes characteristic of their specific race. These generational changes are better called adaptation than acclimatization, and they convey a few special abilities, such as prolonged endurance, at high and extreme altitudes and some superiority in endurance sports, such as marathon running, at sea level.

Other Considerations

Acclimatization is an ongoing process that takes many weeks to mature. The time required for different processes varies greatly, and also varies between individuals. The respiratory and biochemical changes level off in a few weeks, but the number of red blood cells requires longer to reach a maximum. At that time, secretion of erythropoietin switches off, but the bone marrow continues to produce the same number of red cells.

Above 20,000 feet (6,100 m), deterioration outstrips acclimatization, and after ten to fifteen days at such altitudes, climbers can not continue without great risk.

ACHIEVING ACCLIMATIZATION

Individuals vary so widely in their ability to acclimatize—not only in the degree of acclimatization they can achieve but also in the time required—that no program fits everyone. Generally speaking, the slower the climb, the better will be the acclimatization.

Using "siege tactics," climbers attempting a very high mountain climb to a higher camp, return to rest at base camp, carry supplies to a higher camp, and repeat the process, stocking successively higher camps. After a few weeks, a summit attempt can be made from the highest camp. Most climbers accept the adage "climb high, sleep low," and after carrying a load to a higher camp, they prefer to return to a lower elevation for the night.

Other experienced mountaineers prefer "alpine style." The individuals live at base camp, each day climbing a little higher but returning to base. A high degree of acclimatization can be achieved this way. After four to six weeks, when the weather looks promising, the party can move up rapidly, sometimes straight through to the summit (unless the climb is technically very difficult). This approach has the obvious advantage of minimizing the carrying of loads and consumption of supplies, and it allows an attempt to be made whenever the weather is promising. No altitude deterioration occurs.

A modification of these two approaches is currently popular: a small party stocks camps as it climbs, acclimatizing by occasional rest days, and then goes to the summit at an auspicious time.

All of these protocols keep climbers high on a mountain for relatively short periods, so they are less likely to suffer from altitude deterioration and are less likely to be caught by bad weather. However, if one or more members of the party become ill or injured, no stocked camps to which the group can retreat are available.

On modest mountains, acclimatization is not necessary, but to avoid mountain illnesses, tourists, climbers, skiers, and other visitors going to 8,000 to 10,000 feet (2,400 to 3,000 m) should not exercise vigorously for a day or two after arrival. Highly susceptible individuals would be wise to spend two or more days and nights at an intermediate altitude, perhaps 5,000 feet (1,500 m). Shorter stays at such altitudes seem to offer little benefit.

The customary advice to take one day to climb each 1,000 feet (300 m) above 10,000 feet (3,000 m) is conservative and does not apply to everyone. Above 12,000 feet (3,600 m), people should find their own pace. The expedition leader should pace the party to take care of the slowest—or perhaps send that person down.

Persons who have only a short time to vacation at a mountain resort are reluctant to "waste" time acclimatizing. Some have mountain sickness, sometimes quite severe; others do not. Acetazolamide is a safe and effective way to gain some artificial acclimatization for those who can not or will not take time to acclimatize naturally, and perhaps is wiser than spoiling a short vacation.

Those going to higher mountains usually need a number of days to walk to base camp, gaining altitude en route. This is a good way to acclimatize if heat, exertion, or the diarrheal and other illness so common in developing countries do not lead to dehydration and wasting. Such illnesses commonly have a greater impact on an expedition than weather or terrain.

Acclimatization is thought to be lost at about the same rate at which it is gained. Once acclimatized, not descending for at least a week to ten days appears prudent. Furthermore, a fully acclimatized individual who descends to a lower altitude for longer than a week to ten days is at some risk of developing HAPE upon returning (discussed below).

In recent years, many persons planning a trip to moderate altitude have tried to acclimatize by spending an hour once or twice a day in a low oxygen room or breathing a low oxygen gas mixture. A number of sports clubs and hotels in several countries offer such facilities, and the process has been studied in a few research laboratories. Although some results of the research are persuasive, no convincing data fully prove that repeated short exposures to hypoxia can stimulate acclimatization or decrease the likelihood of acute mountain sickness.

Some climbers who have made many trips to high mountains believe that the body acclimatizes more rapidly and completely on later climbs. Only anecdotal evidence supports this conviction, although it seems reasonable. Others think that increased familiarity with living and climbing at high altitudes is responsible for the apparently greater acclimatization.

Apart from acetazolamide, no artificial aids to acclimatization are known. Susceptibility to mountain sicknesses decreases with increasing age (one of the few benefits of aging), but the ability to acclimatize also seems to decline slightly as people get older. Good physical fitness is helpful but only insofar as it increases muscular efficiency, thus decreasing the need for oxygen.

A fascinating and almost unexplored problem is the nearly normal life that can be led at high altitudes by some individuals who have heart or lung disorders that make them moderately hypoxic at sea level. Is this the result of acclimatization, adaptation, or simply tolerance?

Climbers who have reached the summit of a very high mountain such as Mount Everest without supplementary oxygen have some inherent physiologic advantages that can not be entirely predicted by sea level studies. They are able to sustain very heavy exercise much longer than others. They are experienced mountaineers with highly developed skills that enable them to climb efficiently and fast, with minimal energy expenditure. Their lungs have a higher than normal diffusing capacity, and they usually have a normal or increased ventilatory response to hypoxia. Experience has given them confidence, reducing the anxiety felt by novices. These characteristics give them an increased tolerance for hypoxia. Even when made acutely hypoxic at sea level, they seem to fare better. However, some of those who have gone the highest without illness actually have a lower than normal hypoxic ventilatory response and must take longer to acclimatize.

SUMMIT OF MOUNT EVEREST

The barometric pressure on the summit of Mount Everest, as measured directly in 1981, is 253 mm Hg, or one-third sea level atmospheric pressure. That pressure is 17 mm Hg higher than had been predicted, apparently due to the greater thickness of the atmosphere at the equator. The pressure may vary by the equivalent of 100 to 300 feet (30 to 90 m) due to weather-related changes in atmospheric pressure, which means that on "high barometer" days, the summit is physiologically a few hundred feet lower. On the summit of Mount Everest, the arterial oxygen pressure is about 28 to 32 mm Hg, or approximately one-third that of sea level. The carbon dioxide pressure is approximately 10 to 13 mm Hg (normal at sea level is 35 to 48 mm Hg for adult males), depending on when and how, relative to overbreathing, the sample is taken.

THE SPECTRUM OF MOUNTAIN ILLNESSES

Almost no one should get altitude sickness. A few simple measures prevent altitude illnesses in most healthy individuals, and individuals who experience more than minor, temporary discomfort have only themselves to blame. Only persons with a few specific conditions are prone to altitude illness.

Acute Mountain Sickness

Acute mountain sickness (AMS), the most common disorder that afflicts those who go too high too fast, results from the effects of lowered oxygen pressure on the brain. Brain cells are probably damaged only by extreme hypoxia; changes in the circulation of the brain and the accumulation of fluid (edema) are thought to be responsible for the symptoms of AMS. Low oxygen pressure dilates cerebral blood vessels, which occurs despite the constricting effect of low carbon dioxide levels resulting from increased ventilation.

The symptoms of mild or moderate AMS are quite realistically described as those of a bad hangover: headache, nausea, and sometimes vomiting. The severity of symptoms depends upon the rate of ascent, the altitude reached, and—quite often—individual susceptibility. Symptoms usually start twelve to twenty-four hours after arrival and begin to subside by the third day. The headache is throbbing, tends to be at the back of the head, and is worse on awakening in the morning. Dizziness, fatigue, dry cough, loss of appetite, disturbed sleep, and general malaise are common. The individual feels miserable.

One normal response to ascent is a temporary increase in urine volume, but with AMS the volume is usually decreased and the victim retains fluid. Broadly speaking, those people who have the least increase in ventilation and the lowest oxygen levels retain water and are the sickest. One attractive but oversimplified explanation for the symptoms of AMS is that rapid ascent causes generalized water retention, but in susceptible people more fluid collects in the brain.

A few individuals develop an unsteady gait (ataxia), an important sign of brain involvement. If a person begins to stumble and fall and becomes drowsy and apathetic, he or she should be considered to have cerebral edema. (Pulmonary edema is often present too, increasing the hypoxia.) Such individuals are in great danger, and rapid descent—with supplemental oxygen, if possible—is essential.

AMS can be prevented by gradual acclimatization at intermediate altitudes or by medication. The incidence, or frequency, of AMS increases with altitude (Table 21-3). Only a few persons have AMS at 8,000 feet (2,400 m), but after going rapidly from near sea level to over 14,000 feet (4,200 m), more than half have symptoms.

Children are more susceptible than adults. Recognizing symptoms of AMS in infants or young children who can not verbalize their symptoms requires awareness of the problem. The incidence decreases with advancing age, possibly because the normal cerebral atrophy of aging leaves more space for a swollen, edematous brain.

None of the symptoms of AMS is diagnostic of the condition. Similar symptoms may occur in people who are exhausted, dehydrated, hypoglycemic, hypothermic, suffering from carbon monoxide poisoning, taking prescription or recreational drugs, or developing an infection. Usually, the individual's history of rapid ascent, together with absence of other obvious causes, makes the diagnosis clear. A high fever suggests infection; AMS seldom causes fever unless complicated by another condition.

Anyone who has recently come to high altitude and has the symptoms listed above should be assumed to have AMS. If the individual's condition gets worse in spite of rest, he should be taken to a lower altitude. Supplemental oxygen is helpful for providing restful sleep but is not a substitute for descent if a person is ill.

AMS, like all altitude illnesses, often leads to disordered thinking. Decisions may have to be made for the individual, who may have to be forced to accept them. Problems have developed when persons—particularly trip leaders—have refused to accept the decision of a doctor. When the affected individual is a physician, problems may become even worse.

Carbon monoxide combines preferentially with hemoglobin and displaces oxygen. Using a stove in a small, sealed tent can lead to carbon monoxide poisoning, which not only adds to altitude hypoxia but has caused a number of deaths. This possibility must always be considered, even though the treatment—rapid descent and oxygen—is the same as that for altitude illnesses.

Individuals with AMS should avoid heavy exertion, although light activity is better than complete rest. Sleep is not helpful because respirations are slower during sleep, which may make symptoms worse.

Table 21-3 Incidence of Acute Mountain Sickness (AMS)

ACTIVITY	LOCATION, YEAR	ALTITUDE	INCIDENCE (%)
Skiing	Rocky Mountains, 1993	6 to 7,000 ft (1.8 to 2,100 m)	18
		7 to 9,000 ft (2.1 to 2,750 m)	22
		9 to 10,000 ft (2.7 to 3,050 m)	27
Skiing	Rocky Mountains, 1989	6,765 ft (2,060 m)	20
		6,900 ft (2,100 m)	26
		8,900 ft (2,700 m)	40
Skiing	Rocky Mountains, 1985	8,600 ft (2,000 m)	12
		9,500 ft (2,900 m)	17
Skiing	Rocky Mountains	9,000 ft (2,750 m)	12
Climbing	European Alps, 1989	6,700 ft (2,050 m)	9
		10,000 ft (3,050 m)	13
		12,000 ft (3,650 m)	34
		15,999 ft (4,900 m)	54
Trekking	Nepal, 1976	14,000 ft (4,250 m)	42

The groups studied were large enough to be statistically significant, although they were not sorted by age, sex, or activity except in the last study.

At night, sedatives should be avoided because they also decrease respiration. Low-flow oxygen at night is very helpful.

Affected persons should drink extra fluids and eat a light, high-carbohydrate diet. Aspirin, acetaminophen, or ibuprofen is helpful for headache. Tobacco and alcohol should be avoided.

Acetazolamide is a good preventive for most people and seems to speed acclimatization. A prescription is required, because this drug is contraindicated for individuals with certain kidney, eye, or liver diseases. The dose recommended by most authorities is 125 mg twice daily, beginning one day before ascent and continuing for two to five days after arrival. (Some individuals have been unable to obtain 125 mg tablets; the correct dosage must be achieved by breaking 250 mg tablets in two. Extended-release tablets deliver the drug somewhat erratically.)

Tingling sensations in the lips, fingers, or toes is a common side effect that indicates that an adequate dose has been taken. Carbonated beverages (particularly beer) have a less pleasant taste, caused by the effect of the drug on taste buds, and some people notice an increase in urine volume, but these symptoms subside when the drug is stopped. Because this drug is chemically related to sulfa drugs, persons sensitive to them may not be able to take acetazolamide. It makes a few individuals more sensitive to sunlight, but otherwise it is remarkably free from adverse effects.

The best treatment for AMS after it has developed is descent or oxygen; both are essential for severe illnesses. Acetazolamide is less helpful for treatment than it is for prevention, but it may help some. Ibuprofen seems to be better than aspirin for headaches, and cyclizine (Marezine®) or prochlorperazine (Compazine®) may relieve the nausea. Dexamethasone is less helpful for prevention but is quite good for treatment of AMS. Gingko biloba and clonidine have been found to be helpful in a few limited studies.

Some temporary relief from the symptoms of AMS can be achieved by voluntarily taking ten to twelve deep breaths every four to six minutes. If overdone, this maneuver can cause dizziness and tingling of the lips and hands due to "blowing off" too much carbon dioxide. So-called grunt breathing is no more effective than the overbreathing it requires.

AMS is common and is usually self-limited, but it deserves attention because it can easily evolve into more serious illnesses, such as HAPE or HACE. Vigilance must be maintained so more serious types of mountain sickness can be detected early.

High Altitude Cerebral Edema

High altitude cerebral edema (HACE) is now considered part of the spectrum of acute mountain sicknesses. In a few people with AMS, usually at altitudes above 12,000 feet (3,600 m), symptoms of brain edema become worse, sometimes with alarming speed. Ataxia or staggering gait, which can be demonstrated early by having the individual touch his nose with his finger or walk a straight line heel-to-toe, can become so bad that the person can not stand or get into his tent or sleeping bag. He may not be able to get dressed, tie his shoelaces, or handle a knife and spoon.

The individual becomes confused, often begins to have hallucinations, loses memory, and develops impaired judgement. These disabilities may rapidly worsen to psychotic behavior, coma, and death.

In an extreme case, a person with a worsening headache, vomiting, and lassitude for several days may retire to his tent to sleep and lapse into a coma. His companions may become aware of his condition only when they can not wake him. Indeed, he may not even respond to painful stimuli. The individual may have weakness or paralysis of a limb; rarely, he may have a seizure. He looks pale and blue (cyanotic), and often rales can be heard in the lungs, indicating the presence of pulmonary edema. Autopsies on individuals who have died of HACE have disclosed swelling of the brain and the presence of small and large hemorrhages ranging in number from few to many.

Because HACE can cause death or—rarely—lasting brain damage, early diagnosis and treatment are essential. Recent arrivals at high altitude—and, occasionally, someone who has been there for several days—who develop confusion or ataxia combined with a persistent bad headache should be considered to have HACE. They should be given oxygen and taken to a lower altitude immediately. (Volunteer physicians in the Himalayan Rescue Association do not allow trekkers to take time to pack up their gear.) They should be accompanied during descent because ataxia may progress rapidly and individuals may fall and be injured. Usually, descent of a few thousand feet brings relief if accomplished promptly, but leaving a person with HACE alone is unwise—and possibly risky—even at a lower altitude.

Some individuals appear to be unusually susceptible to HACE and other altitude-related disorders and have suffered more than one episode. Once HACE has occurred, even if recovery is rapid at a lower altitude, it may recur. Several HACE recurrences have proven fatal. Individuals are best advised to end their trip once severe HACE has occurred.

After descent, the person must be hospitalized as soon as possible so that other causes of his condition can be carefully ruled out. Dexamethasone is the preferred treatment and does not decrease blood flow to the brain. It should be administered promptly, orally, if the victim is still conscious, or intravenously. Intravenous mannitol and diuretics, which are often given to patients with cerebral edema from other causes at sea level, usually are not effective and may reduce the circulation of blood to the brain and impede recovery.

HACE may occur without any signs of AMS or HAPE, but some people with severe HAPE lose consciousness and develop signs and symptoms of cerebral edema, occasionally with little cough or shortness of breath. Apparently, the additional hypoxia caused by pulmonary edema leads to cerebral edema. For this reason, the lungs should be examined carefully in all persons with central nervous system signs at high altitude. A chest x-ray obtained as soon as possible often contains evidence of pulmonary edema in persons with HACE.

Other neurologic disorders may occur at high altitude and can confuse the diagnosis of cerebral edema. (See chapter 22, "Altitude and Common Medical Conditions.") Not uncommonly, changes in vision, such as the flashing lights (scotomata) that often occur during or before a migraine attack, are noticed. Gradual or sudden blindness, usually lasting a few minutes to an hour, has been described. These episodes are probably migraine equivalents, even without headache or a history of migraine, but they are not well understood. Brief spells of dizziness, double vision, and weakness in a hand, arm, or leg have also been described at high altitude; they may be caused by migraine or a transient ischemic attack (TIA), a brief decrease in blood flow to the brain that sometimes occurs at sea level in persons with arteriosclerotic vascular disease. Strokes do occur in the mountains but are not common.

When descent is difficult or impossible due to nightfall or weather, a party can buy time by placing the individual in an inflatable bag in which the pressure can be increased to simulate descent of two or three thousand feet. The original device of this type was the Gamow Bag, but several hyperbaric bags are now available. Treatment in a bag does not replace descent or continuous oxygen; it only buys a little time. Once removed from the bag, the person may relapse. Hyperbaric bags weigh eight to ten pounds and are costly. Whether to include one in the medical equipment requires careful thought, particularly since litigation related to inadequate preparation is becoming more frequent.

High Altitude Pulmonary Edema

High altitude pulmonary edema (HAPE) is the second most common type of severe altitude illness. It usually occurs in the same context as AMS—a healthy person ascends too rapidly from low altitude. It frequently complicates AMS and sometimes is associated with HACE. HAPE is a condition in which the alveoli of the lungs are filled with fluid that has oozed through the walls of the pulmonary capillaries. As more alveoli fill with fluid, oxygen exchange is progressively decreased and the blood oxygen pressure falls, decreasing the oxygen supply to all cells, most dangerously to the brain. The individual is literally drowning in his own fluids. Unless effectively and promptly treated, the individual may lapse into coma and suffocate.

Symptoms of HAPE usually begin two to four days after arrival at altitude and consist of excessive shortness of breath on moderate exertion; a sense of "tightness in the chest," especially at night;

weakness; and often—but not always—an irritative cough that soon produces frothy, blood-streaked sputum. A person with HAPE is typically much more tired than other members of the party, an important early symptom. Because the hypoxia of altitude is made more severe by the fluid in the alveoli, the symptoms of AMS are often worsened. Coughing is also an important early sign, although this may also be due to irritation from overbreathing dry air.

The pulse rate is usually rapid (110 to 160 beats per minute), even after several hours of rest, and the respirations are fast and labored (twenty to forty per minute). The lips and nails are bluish (cyanotic), and the skin is pale and cold. Bubbling or crackling sounds (rales) may be heard when listening to the lungs with the unaided ear or with a stethoscope. Sometimes rales are heard on one side only, usually in the middle of the right lung. Occasionally they are almost inaudible. Symptoms and signs usually become worse during the night.

Due to the further decrease in oxygen reaching the brain, a person with HAPE does not think clearly. He may become confused or even delirious, which suggests that some degree of HACE is also present. When this occurs, the outlook is poor. Unless treated quickly and effectively, the person is likely to die.

HAPE is not due to heart failure or pneumonia, although years ago it used to be mistaken for those disorders. The cause lies in alterations in the pulmonary circulation. High altitude, sleep apnea, or hypoxia from any cause, including heavy exercise, causes a rise in pulmonary artery blood pressure. Normally, the smallest pulmonary arteries (arterioles) constrict, protecting capillaries from excessive pressure and flow rates. In individuals who develop HAPE, arteriolar constriction may not be uniform throughout the lungs. Arterioles constrict in some areas but not in others. Consequently, in those parts of the lung where no constriction occurs, high pressure and flow are transmitted directly to the capillaries, and they leak fluid into the alveoli.

Probably no one is completely immune; HAPE occurs even in experienced and acclimatized mountaineers, if they go too high too fast and work too hard. Individuals who are HAPE susceptible and have repeated episodes of HAPE have been recognized. These unfortunate persons respond to high altitude—or to the hypoxia of sleep apnea—with an abnormally large increase in pulmonary artery pressure, particularly during exercise. This susceptibility may be genetic, perhaps due to failure of certain tissues to generate nitrous oxide (NO), one of the most important compounds controlling the tone of small blood vessels. The defect may be either an absent or abnormal gene sequence, or some other defect in nitrous oxide formation.

Most persons ascending to moderate altitude accumulate a small amount of fluid between the thin layers of the membrane lining the alveoli—interstitial edema—that hinders the diffusion of oxygen. Such edema may also develop during strenuous exertion. Usually this fluid is absorbed as fast as it forms, but if not, HAPE or the exercise equivalent begins. The evolution of interstitial to alveolar edema is caused by rapid ascent, particularly when associated with strenuous exercise.

If altitude gain is fast enough or strenuous enough, HAPE may strike even well-acclimatized individuals. For reasons that are not understood, some well-acclimatized high altitude residents, even though not unusually susceptible, develop HAPE when they return to high altitude after a week or ten days near sea level. Such "reentry HAPE" is more frequent in children.

The incidence of HAPE and HACE varies with the terrain. A climber living in Seattle can ascend and descend Mount Rainier (14,410 feet [4,400 m]) in a weekend. Because that climber will be climbing fast, AMS is likely (the incidence is greater than fifty percent), but a fast descent is possible if symptoms become bad. On Denali (Mount McKinley), which is much larger and higher (20,300 feet [6,200 m]), deep snow, heavier packs, severe weather, and longer distances not only demand greater work but also increase the likelihood of HAPE and HACE and make rapid descent to safety much harder.

The risk of developing HAPE after a rapid ascent to 12,000 feet (3,600 m) is about one in two hundred (0.5 percent) in adults and is higher in children.

The diagnosis of HAPE is based on a history of rapid ascent, strenuous exertion, a past history of mountain sickness, and the signs and symptoms described above. When a chest x-ray can be obtained, the abnormalities are usually diagnostic, but the x-ray may be normal. Sometimes radiographic changes are misdiagnosed as pneumonia.

High altitude pulmonary edema may progress very rapidly, particularly during the night. Any worsening of the condition demands prompt descent.

The most important treatment is descending to a lower altitude. If the individual can not walk, he must be carried. Descent of as little as 2,000 to 3,000 feet (600 to 900 m) often results in prompt relief. The speed with which individuals can recover from HAPE is remarkable. If oxygen is available, it should be given without delay. Rescue parties should bring oxygen if the victim can not be moved (for example, because he has a major injury). Deaths have occurred when the seriously ill person has worked too hard during his evacuation.

Studies have shown that nifedipine, which relaxes the pulmonary arterioles and reduces pulmonary artery pressure, is effective for treating HAPE. It may lower the systemic, as well as the pulmonary artery, blood pressure and cause faintness—even collapse—and should be given only by a medical professional familiar with its effects. Nitroglycerin is also effective for a short time, but it has other effects that make it undesirable if an alternative exists.

In the past, furosemide was used to remove fluid from the lungs, but this strong diuretic can cause a large urine output, resulting in a drop in blood volume and collapse. Persons who could walk with a little help have been converted to litter cases. With pulmonary edema due to heart failure, fluid can be removed from the lungs by a diuretic because the drug lowers the pressure in the left ventricle and encourages absorption of the edema fluid. Because HAPE is not caused by heart failure, a diuretic should not be expected to be helpful. Morphine may be helpful, particularly for persons who are very apprehensive and have marked shortness of breath, but it should only be given by a physician.

If descent is impossible or must be delayed, one of the portable hyperbaric bags can be used to buy time, but this is not a substitute for descent.

As soon as the victim reaches a medical facility, a chest x-ray should be obtained. Diagnostic pulmonary densities may persist for several days after apparent recovery. Residual weakness and fatigue may persist for one to two weeks, although recovery usually is surprisingly rapid.

Prevention of HAPE is the same as that for AMS: gradual ascent with time for acclimatization. Heavy physical exertion should be avoided for the first few days after a rapid ascent to high altitude. Nifedipine is not recommended for prevention except for the rare individuals unusually susceptible to HAPE. They may be helped by acetazolamide, started on the day before ascent and continued for three to five days after arriving at a high elevation.

The rare individuals who have congenital absence of one of the pulmonary arteries are very susceptible to HAPE and may develop this disorder after ascending to as low an elevation as 6,000 feet. If such persons must go higher, great care is necessary. Nifedipine may be helpful but has not yet been tested in such individuals.

Table 21-4 lists the common high altitude illnesses.

OTHER HIGH ALTITUDE CONDITIONS

High Altitude Retinal Hemorrhage

Hemorrhage into the retina, the layer of sensitive light receptors in the eye, is common above 14,000 feet (4,300 m). The incidence increases with altitude but is rare below 12,000 feet (3,600 m). Usually the hemorrhages are small and cause no symptoms, but rarely the bleeding involves the macula, the area of most acute central vision, and can cause blurred vision or even a tiny area of blindness.

The hemorrhages are painless and usually can be detected only by looking at the retina with an ophthalmoscope. Occasionally, the hemorrhages are larger, involve more of the retina, and cause blurring or loss of vision in portions of the visual field for that eye.

Table 21-4	Common High Altitude Illnesses

ACUTE MOUNTAIN SICKNESS (AMS)
  Headache or nausea with or without vomiting
  Sleep disturbance
  Undue fatigue or shortness of breath

HIGH ALTITUDE CEREBRAL EDEMA (HACE)
  Increasing headache
  Confusion
  Ataxia (clumsiness when walking or using hands)
  Progressively worsening disorientation
  Coma and death

HIGH ALTITUDE PULMONARY EDEMA (HAPE)
  Increasing shortness of breath, particularly on exertion
  Irritative cough later producing pink sputum
  Extreme fatigue progressing to unconsciousness

HIGH ALTITUDE RETINAL HEMORRHAGES
  Rarely cause symptoms except when in macula
  Macular hemorrhage causes central blind spot
  Visible only with an ophthalmoscope
  Most resolve in ten to twenty days

HIGH ALTITUDE SYSTEMIC EDEMA
  Painless swelling of face, ankles, and hands
  Scanty, dark yellow urine
  Also caused by exercise at low altitude
  Subsides with passage of more urine

Several investigators have not found a significant relationship between hemorrhages and other forms of altitude illness, but other observers consider the bleeding predictive of poor acclimatization. The hemorrhages do not appear to be identical to retinal hemorrhages associated with conditions such as diabetes or hypertension at sea level. The exudates that often occur in these conditions are extremely rare with high altitude hemorrhages.

Most hemorrhages disappear in a week or two, even at high altitude, but bleeding into the macula can leave small, central blind spots that persist for many years. Persons who have hemorrhages on one climb are neither more nor less likely to have them again. Because a blind spot can persist after a macular hemorrhage, a few specialists advise individuals with such defects not to return to high altitude.

A small minority believes that retinal hemorrhages are evidence of tiny pinpoint hemorrhages in the brain and are a contraindication to going higher—or even to going to any altitude in the future—but hemorrhages are so common that this seems to be an extreme position.

There is no treatment—or need to treat—high altitude retinal hemorrhages because most absorb in a week or two. Nevertheless, persons with very large hemorrhages or macular bleeding should descend to a lower elevation because further exposure may worsen the condition.

The hemorrhages are related to dilatation and increased blood flow in the small blood vessels of the retina due to lack of oxygen. They also occur with severe carbon monoxide poisoning and severe hypoxia from other causes at sea level. Possibly the increased pressure resulting from hypoxia causes small tears in these thin-walled vessels.

High Altitude Systemic Edema

Swelling of the feet and hands may occur during or after ascent to high altitude. Considerable swelling of the face and eyelids is often present in the morning. This edema is usually accompanied by a decrease in urine output, but it may not be associated with symptoms of AMS. Although this condition sometimes is a nuisance, it is harmless and clears up within a few days.

Almost identical edema and fluid retention can develop following strenuous exertion near sea level, which makes it difficult to assign it to altitude alone. Salty foods and salt tablets should be avoided because an increased sodium intake aggravates the condition. Nevertheless, a high fluid intake is necessary to avoid dehydration. It is ironic that the blood may be concentrated due to edema and the body dehydrated despite the fluid in the tissues. Acetazolamide given for AMS may diminish the edema through its mild diuretic action.

NUTRITION AT ALTITUDE

Some—but not all—extreme altitude climbers lose weight during a climb. Losses of as much as forty pounds occur in a few individuals. Because these individuals usually are physically fit with little excess body fat, most of the weight loss is from muscle. The cause of such weight loss is not well understood.

The maintenance of adequate food and water intake is difficult at extreme altitudes. Appetites are poor, and high altitude climbers usually eat and drink much less than they need. At least some of the fatigue and weakness experienced at such altitudes is due to inadequate nutrition, dehydration, and possibly potassium loss accompanying high energy expenditure.

Impairment of food absorption in the gastrointestinal tract has been suggested but not confirmed as a cause for the weight loss, which reportedly can not be prevented by forced feeding. The tastelessness of the freeze-dried foods carried by most expeditions may be more significant. Climbers often go hungry at high and extreme altitudes rather than eat food that they do not crave.

Menus should consist largely of foods enjoyed by all party members, but foods to satisfy individual tastes must also be carried. Diets should contain large amounts of sweets, which are usually consumed in large quantities at high altitude. Fatty foods or highly condensed rations may not be well tolerated. During days of heavy exertion, many climbers find that frequent, small, high-carbohydrate snacks are consumed better than less frequent, larger meals.

On prolonged expeditions where fresh vegetables and fruits are not available, possible vitamin C deficiency can be prevented with ascorbic acid. Most packaged drinks such as lemonade or orange juice contain vitamin C. Approximately six months is required for signs of vitamin deficiency to appear in individuals previously in good nutritional condition.

If vitamin intake appears to be inadequate, one or two multivitamin tablets per day can be taken. A higher vitamin intake or special vitamins such as E or B complex are of no benefit at high elevations. Vitamin requirements are only minimally increased by the rigors of an expedition, and a standard diet contains much more vitamins than are needed. Any excess is simply excreted in the urine. Excess vitamins A and D—and possibly others—are definitely harmful.

EXTREME ALTITUDE DETERIORATION

Acclimatized persons can live a normal life span at elevations as high as 17,500 feet (5,300 m) and can live and work for several weeks at up to 20,000 feet (6,100 m). At higher elevations, deterioration rather than further acclimatization occurs. The cause is a combination of continuing hypoxia, dehydration because of the difficulty of melting snow for water, hypoglycemia due to loss of appetite, and exhaustion stemming from severe exertion and inadequate rest resulting from frequently broken sleep. Those who persist in going higher after a long stay at such high elevation are at risk of not returning.

The number of red cells in the blood may increase far above usual sea level values, and the concentrated, viscous blood flows more slowly, causing poor perfusion of vital organs. This blood also has a greater tendency to clot within blood vessels, producing serious, possibly even lethal, damage.

Spending as little time as possible at extreme altitude and periodically descending for recovery at lower altitude for several days can minimize high altitude deterioration. An adequate fluid intake is essential. The urine volume must be greater than 500 cc every day, preferably two to three times greater, and urine color should be clear or light yellow, not deep yellow or orange. Efforts must be made to eat an adequate amount of food despite a poor appetite. An adequate caloric intake is needed more than specific nutrients. Nutritional deficiencies do not develop in healthy individuals during the short periods that expeditions are at high altitude.

Oxygen during sleep—two liters per minute through a face mask—is beneficial. No drugs are known to minimize deterioration, but sleeping with low-flow oxygen does make a difference.

Removing blood and replacing it with fluid to reduce viscosity may extend stays at high altitude, but such extreme measures are not justified when simple descent can solve the problem safely.

THROMBOSIS, STROKES, AND PULMONARY EMBOLISM

After a period of immobility, such as being confined in a tent by a storm, associated with dehydration and exhaustion, blood clots may form in the leg or pelvic veins (and, more rarely, in arm veins). Occasionally, such clots break free and are carried to the lungs, where they lodge in a pulmonary artery, a condition known as thrombotic pulmonary embolism. Warning signs are a swollen, painful leg or arm, followed by the sudden onset of chest pain, cough, and worsening shortness of breath. Sudden death is not uncommon in pulmonary embolism, which is discussed at greater length in chapter 10, "Respiratory Disorders."

Rarely, blood may clot in the blood vessels of the brain. A stroke that produces temporary or permanent paralysis, commonly limited to one side of the body, is the usual result. (Strokes are discussed more thoroughly in chapter 15, "Neural Disorders," and chapter 22, "Altitude and Common Medical

Table 21-5 Less Common High Altitude Disorders
ALTITUDE DETERIORATION
Slowly develops after ten to fifteen days above 20,000 ft
Loss of appetite; weight loss
Exhaustion
Impairment of memory and judgement
CHRONIC MOUNTAIN SICKNESS
Develops only in long-term residents above 15,000 ft
Bluish, ruddy coloration
Excessive red blood cells
Various aches and pains
Gradual heart failure
THROMBOPHLEBITIS AND PULMONARY EMBOLISM
Caused by dehydration and inactivity
Painful swelling of leg or arm
Sharp pain in chest and bloody sputum
TRANSIENT ISCHEMIC ATTACK (TIA)
Brief weakness, paralysis, numbness, or vision change
Clears within an hour or less
May be migraine equivalent
CEREBROVASCULAR ACCIDENT (STROKE)
Brief numbness or paralysis
May progress to severe paralysis or unconsciousness
Slow, if any, improvement

Conditions.") All such disorders of blood clotting may cause death or disability and require prompt descent, oxygen, and hospitalization.

CHRONIC MOUNTAIN SICKNESS

Rare long-time residents at 15,000 to 17,000 feet (4,500 to 5,200 m) form red blood cells far in excess of what is normal at that altitude. This greatly thickened blood places such a heavy load on the heart that eventually that organ fails. Symptoms are a dusky reddish purple complexion, easy fatigue, generalized aches and pains, and, later, swelling of the legs and abdomen.

Victims recover after a few weeks at sea level, but the condition recurs if they return to high altitude. Drawing off 500 to 1,000 ml of blood every two weeks only slows, and may eventually worsen, the condition. Descent is the only effective treatment.

A similar condition known as chronic alveolar hypoventilation can develop at sea level. Chronic mountain sickness is an uncommon disorder observed only in persons who have lived at a high altitude for many years. It apparently never occurs in climbers, even after weeks at high elevations.

Table 21-5 lists the less common disorders that can occur at high altitudes.

PREEXISTING MEDICAL PROBLEMS AND ALTITUDE

Many people considering a trip to a large, high mountain—and sometimes those considering a trip to a lower mountain—ask about medical conditions that may become worse at high altitude, and whether the risk is unacceptable. Generally, any condition that causes hypoxia at sea level is aggravated by going above 5,000 feet (1,500 m), but several specific conditions may cause problems:

- ▼ Chronic lung disease with low arterial oxygen saturation
- ▼ Pulmonary hypertension
- ▼ Congenital absence of a pulmonary artery
- ▼ Cyanotic congenital heart disease
- ▼ Previous stroke or pulmonary embolus
- ▼ Heart failure
- ▼ Severe angina
- ▼ Sickle cell disease

These conditions are discussed in chapter 22, "Altitude and Common Medical Conditions." However, individuals searching for adventure and trying to "get away from it all" must remember that they are also getting away from prompt, sophisticated medical care and must assume responsibility for themselves.

CHAPTER 22

ALTITUDE AND COMMON MEDICAL CONDITIONS

PRINCIPAL CONTRIBUTOR:
Peter H. Hackett, M.D.

More and more people with a variety of medical conditions are traveling to higher elevations for recreation or work. Many, particularly retirees, are choosing to live there. The increased need for knowledge about the mix of illness and altitude has stimulated investigation, but for many conditions, not enough information is available for conclusions about the risks to be drawn. This chapter considers the effect of altitude on preexisting illnesses, pregnancy, children, and the elderly, as well as the converse effect of illnesses on acclimatization to altitude.

(Huge differences exist between the effects of moderate, high, and extreme altitudes. To emphasize those differences, to achieve a uniform usage, and to avoid misunderstanding, the practice used in chapter 21, "Disorders Caused by Altitude," has been followed in this chapter. That is, "altitude" and "moderate altitude" are used for elevations of 8,000 to 12,000 feet (2,400 to 3,600 m), "high altitude" is used for elevations of 12,000 to 18,000 feet (3,600 to 5,500 m), and "extreme altitude" is used for elevations of 18,000 to 29,000 feet (5,500 to 8,800 m).—Ed.)

ALTITUDE STRESS

Ascent to altitude affects people in various ways. Expansion of air from the reduced pressure can cause problems in any space that contains air or gas, such as sinuses, middle ears, lungs, the intestines, or even a pneumothorax. Dysbarism, as such problems are called, is more common with rapid ascent in airplanes, but even gradual ascent to terrestrial elevations can be associated with problems such as dental pain produced by expansion of gas trapped beneath a filling.

On the other hand, less dense air may flow through airways more easily and improve lung function. Decreased air resistance improves performance in athletic events such as jumping, vaulting, and sprinting, and it allows balls to travel farther.

The major physiologic stress of altitude is, of course, hypoxia. As barometric pressure falls with increasing altitude, the partial pressure of oxygen declines. Compared to sea level, Denver, Colorado, has seventeen percent less atmospheric oxygen pressure; Aspen has twenty-five percent less oxygen pressure; and only half the sea level pressure of oxygen is present at approximately 18,000 feet (5,500 m). In addition, weather, season, and latitude affect barometric pressure. Low atmospheric pressure produces bad weather. Pressure at high altitude is lower in winter, and lower farther from the equator for any given altitude. Environmental hypoxia is directly related to barometric pressure, not altitude.

Many individuals experience hypoxemia—lower blood oxygen—in everyday life, such as during sleep, during airline travel, or as the result of lung disease. Commercial aircraft have cabin pressures equivalent to altitudes as high as 8,500 feet (2,600 m), and airline crew members experience hypoxemia. Oxygen saturations of eighty to ninety-three percent (normal at sea level is ninety-five percent or higher) and an average low point of 88.6 percent were found in a recent study. The effects of such hypoxemia are inconsequential in healthy individuals, but persons with illnesses affecting oxygen transport could suffer adverse effects.

Temperature decreases at a rate of approximately 3.5°F per 1,000 feet (6.5°C per 1,000 m) gain in altitude. Cold and hypoxia combine to produce hypothermia and frostbite, and cold may contribute to high altitude pulmonary edema (HAPE).

Because particulate matter, water vapor, and cloud cover diminish with increasing altitude, solar ultraviolet radiation increases by approximately four percent per 1,000 feet (300 m) gain in altitude, increasing the risk of sunburn, photosensitive reactions, snow blindness, and, with lifetime exposures, skin cancer and cataracts. On windless days, reflection of sunlight from snow can produce intense heat, and heat-related illnesses are more common than generally appreciated.

Because smaller amounts of airborne particulate matter are present, altitude can be beneficial for those with allergic asthma or other allergic conditions and for individuals whose reactive airway disease is aggravated by pollutants. However, air pollution at higher elevations is now increasing throughout the world.

Humidity is decreased at higher elevations, particularly at high and extreme altitudes, because the air is cold. (The vapor pressure of water at 5°F [-15°C] is only 1.24 mm Hg.) Furthermore, in wilderness situations, water can only be obtained above snowline by melting snow or ice. Such difficulty obtaining water, combined with increased water loss from the skin and lungs, often leads to dehydration in healthy climbers. Compromised cardiovascular systems, diuretics taken for heart failure or hypertension, and pregnancy (perhaps) aggravate this problem. Drying of the airways increases the risk of tracheal and bronchial plugging, particularly in those with chronic lung disease.

EFFECT OF ALTITUDE ON RESPIRATORY DISORDERS

Movement of oxygen from air to blood, the first stage of oxygen transport, is the function of the respiratory system. Components of this system include the controls of ventilation (the movement of air into and out of the lung), the mechanics of respiration, matching of ventilation and perfusion by blood in the lung, and gas exchange across the alveolar-capillary membrane.

Disorders of Ventilatory Control

Any disorder that diminishes ventilation or the ventilatory response to lowered oxygen or increased carbon dioxide, such as a stroke, trauma that injures the brain, neuromuscular diseases, obesity resulting in diminished respiration (hypoventilation), chronic obstructive pulmonary disease (COPD) (including asthma), and sleep apnea, poses a greater risk at altitude. Medications may have the same effect. Long-acting benzodiazepines such as diazepam (Valium®) reduce nocturnal arterial oxygen saturation at altitude.

Carotid Surgery

Carotid body responsiveness to hypoxia is necessary for optimal acclimatization to altitude, and a lessened response to hypoxia has been linked to susceptibility to altitude illness. The carotid body is commonly damaged or ablated during carotid artery surgery (usually for arteriosclerotic narrowing or occlusion). Investigative studies found that the ventilatory response to the hypoxia of 5,000 feet (1,600 m) observed before surgery was abolished by the procedure. Similarly, individuals with bilateral carotid body resection for treatment of asthma or emphysema lack adequate ventilatory responses to acute altitude hypoxia. However, although altitude acclimatization might be impaired in such persons, whether the relative hypoventilation leads to altitude illness remains to be determined. Nonetheless, these individuals can be easily identified and should be cautioned about altitude exposure.

Sleep Disordered Breathing and Apnea

Persons with abnormal breathing rhythms during sleep at sea level, such as snoring, obstructive apnea, or sleep disordered breathing (SDB), particularly the elderly, may have greater nocturnal hypoxemia at altitude and a consequent increase in abnormal cardiac rhythms, an increased pulmonary artery pressure, and a greater susceptibility to altitude illness. A period of apnea at altitude would produce greater hypoxemia than at sea level. However, altitude-induced changes in ventilatory control and breathing conceivably could improve certain apnea syndromes. Unfortunately, virtually nothing is known about the interaction of SDB with altitude, even though SDB has been invoked in the pathogenesis of acute altitude illnesses, including HAPE. (In contrast, normal periodic breathing at altitude has not been related to development of acute mountain sickness (AMS) and, in fact, is associated with a brisk hypoxic ventilatory response, which is generally considered beneficial at altitude.)

At altitude, individuals using a continuous positive airway pressure (CPAP) machine without pressure-compensating features as treatment for SDB need to make adjustments, because altitude decreases the delivered pressure. The error is greater with higher altitudes and higher initial pressure settings.

Lung Disorders

Impairment of gas exchange by hypoventilation leaves afflicted individuals with a lower arterial oxygen pressure than their healthy counterparts. Physiologically, individuals with lung disease are already at a higher altitude and may suffer even greater effects with ascent. In addition, greater hypoxemia may exacerbate their underlying lung disease—for example, increasing pulmonary artery pressure by exaggerating hypoxic pulmonary vasoconstriction.

High Altitude Residents

Lung disease is the most common cause of impaired oxygen transport and would be expected to affect those living at altitude. Studies of high altitude residents have found an increased morbidity from COPD, as well as a propensity to migrate to lower altitude.

In South America and Asia, the problem of acquired lung disease is greater. A high incidence of pneumoconiosis—lung disease resulting from inhalation of particulate foreign material—is found at high altitude in central Ladakh, located at the base of the Korakorum range in Pakistan and Kashmir. This disorder is attributed to dust storms that stir up silica and to the absence of chimneys in residents' homes.

Cigarette smoking is also a major cause of lung disease. Altitude and smoking are independently associated with mortality from COPD in the United States. In an analysis by states, COPD mortality rose by 1 per 100,000 people for every additional 5.4 packs of cigarettes smoked per person per year, and for each 300 feet (95 m) increase in altitude.

Stable Hypoxemic Disease in Lowlanders

Sea level and low altitude residents (lowlanders) with lung disease would be expected to tolerate altitude less well. In addition, altitude might unmask lung disease that has gone undetected. Acute hypoxia associated with air travel has received considerable attention, but much less is known about more prolonged hypoxia, such as a stay at a ski resort.

In one study of eight hypoxemic patients with moderate, uncomplicated COPD who ascended to 6,300 feet (1,920 m) for four days, the subjects had only mild symptoms on ascent, primarily mild fatigue and insomnia. However, arterial oxygen pressure declined from 66 mm Hg at sea level to 51 mm Hg while at rest and from 63 to 47 mm Hg with exercise. (Normal resting arterial oxygen pressure at sea level for healthy young adults is 85 to 100 mm Hg.) The patients did acclimatize. Their arterial carbon dioxide pressures dropped abruptly and declined further over four days, and their arterial oxygen pressures increased, the responses seen in healthy persons. The researchers concluded that travel to this moderate altitude is safe for such patients and speculated that their preexisting hypoxemia may have produced the equivalent of altitude acclimatization, decreasing the likelihood of AMS. Despite the researchers' plea for further investigations with sicker patients at higher altitudes, subsequent studies have not been done.

In studies of acute hypoxia and air travel, the ability to blow out a match, which assures adequate expiratory flow, and the ability to walk up a flight of stairs without distress have been recommended as simple screening tests. Supplemental oxygen during flight has been suggested for those who "fail" these tests. These and other, more sophisticated tests may predict oxygenation during transient (lasting up to four hours) modest hypoxia, but their usefulness is limited because sea level arterial oxygen levels do not correlate well with how people fare at altitude. These studies also did not address how individuals might do with longer stays at altitude and with associated stresses such as sleeping, physical activity, smoking, angina, hypertension, or other problems. Despite these limitations, a physician attempting to evaluate the risk of altitude for a subject with COPD may want to use the predicted initial resting arterial oxygen pressure at altitude as a way to determine the need for supplemental oxygen (Fig. 22-1).

Efforts to predict oxygenation at altitude in children with hypoxemic lung disease have found that hypoxic challenge with fifteen percent oxygen is a better way to identify individuals who might require supplemental oxygen during flight or in the mountains than measuring breathing capacity and oxygen saturation. The main value of provocative testing is to determine the need for oxygen while at rest at altitude, but further assessment of oxygen saturation during activity and sleep is needed to ensure a correct oxygen prescription.

Oxygen therapy may be required for persons who are symptomatic at altitude or for those predicted

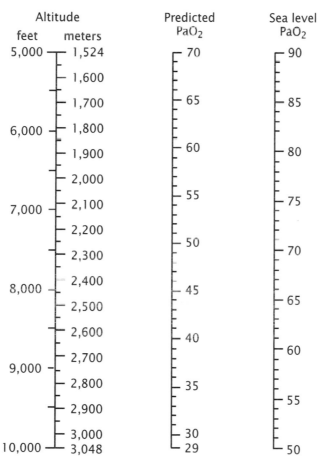

FIGURE 22-1. Nomogram for predicting PaO_2 at altitude based on sea level PaO_2

to become severely hypoxemic. For those already on supplemental oxygen, the amount of inspired oxygen should be increased by the ratio of higher to lower barometric pressures. Whether acetazolamide and medroxyprogesterone acetate, both of which aid acclimatization by stimulating ventilation, might be useful (or harmful) in individuals with COPD, especially with elevated blood carbon dioxide concentrations, is unknown. Individuals should have pulmonary function optimized before ascent to altitude and should receive instructions on medication use (including oxygen) if problems develop.

In summary, information regarding the effect of altitude on chronic lung disease is extremely limited. Predicting who will tolerate and who may be harmed by the additional hypoxia of altitude often is a difficult, possibly futile, undertaking, leaving old-fashioned clinical judgement based upon the overall health and capacity to function of each individual as the best guidance available.

Asthma

Data on mortality and morbidity from asthma in high altitude residents are scant. The available information suggests that asthma may be less of a problem at high altitude than at sea level, both for residents and sojourners, because allergens and pollution are decreased. Studies worldwide have reported improvement in childhood asthma at altitude, which has been a popular treatment for asthma in Europe for many decades.

Surprisingly, in view of the possibility of greater hypoxemia during asthmatic bronchoconstriction at altitude, no association between asthma and HAPE or AMS has been reported. Nor has unexpected asthma exacerbation in lowlanders at altitude been described. Likewise, no information documents the value of a variety of logical clinical aids for prevention, including increased hydration or the use of an airway warming mask.

Whether a severe asthma attack at altitude puts a person at greater risk than such an attack at low altitude—an important question—is unanswered.

EFFECT OF ALTITUDE ON CARDIOVASCULAR PROBLEMS

During ascent and the first few days of residence at altitude, the cardiovascular systems of healthy individuals make important adjustments. These physiologic changes may be limited in those with underlying disease, or these adjustments may stress the compromised cardiovascular system and aggravate illness. The principal initial adjustments are increases in resting and exercise heart rate, increases in blood pressure and systemic vascular resistance, increases in cardiac output and velocity of contraction, and contraction of the veins in the skin, muscle, and intestines resulting in increased central blood volume. Largely mediated by increased sympathetic nerve activity, the net effect is an increase in cardiac work, cardiac muscle oxygen consumption, and coronary blood flow. After four to eight days at altitude, most of these changes diminish, and with prolonged exposure, cardiac output, coronary blood flow, and eventually blood pressure may fall to below sea level values. An elevated pulmonary blood pressure, however, persists.

Hypertension

The effect of altitude on blood pressure depends on many variables: length of exposure, degree of hypoxemia, genetic and dietary variables, and cold exposure. Long-term high altitude residence has been associated with lower systemic arterial pressures than sea level residence in South and North America, Africa, and Asia. Prolonged high altitude exposure has also been found to inhibit progression of hypertension. A preliminary survey in Tibet found an incidence of hypertension higher (9.4 percent) than that in South American high altitude natives (4.5 percent), but that difference is attributed to ingestion of large amounts of salted tea by Tibetans.

The effect of acute exposure to altitude on blood pressure is not entirely clear, in part due to differences in study methodologies. Many studies indicate that blood pressure increases during the first week or two at altitude, more so with greater altitude. However, a few investigations have reported no significant change in blood pressure, or even a slight decrease.

Whether individuals who have high blood pressure at sea level have an exaggerated hypertensive response on initial ascent to altitude has not been systematically evaluated. Anecdotally, some individuals have developed severe hypertension. Such occurrences, whatever their frequency, are not trivial problems in view of the large number of hypertensive patients visiting ski resorts and trekking at high altitude.

The magnitude of the blood pressure change in hypertensive individuals may depend upon the hypoxic stress. At lower elevations, the average increase appears to be minimal, although individual variability is great. Heart rates also increase. The authors of one study concluded that the blood pressure increase in individuals with normal and elevated pressures was not important at 4,000 feet (1,200 m), but it could become so at 10,000 feet (3,000 m).

With acute exposure to higher elevations, hypertensive individuals have a greater blood pressure response than normotensive persons (individuals with normal blood pressure). Importantly, individual variation is considerable, and a few hypertensive persons have an exaggerated pressure increase. Unfortunately, the studies that have been done have not been continued after the first hours at altitude, so whether blood pressure continues to increase over a period of days, as it does in normotensive persons, is an important unanswered question. Also unknown is whether more prolonged stay at altitude might reliably reduce arterial pressure to below sea level values, as has been reported in normotensive persons after five to ten years.

Clearly, the scientific basis for advising individuals with hypertension about ascent to altitude is limited. Because some patients may become markedly hypertensive, and because there is no way at present to predict an individual's response, careful blood pressure monitoring appears to be prudent.

Which medication is best for altitude-aggravated or altitude-induced hypertension and whether antihypertensive medication regimens effective at low altitude may be insufficient upon ascent to altitude are significant questions not yet answered.

Individuals with hypertension may experience other untoward effects of altitude in addition to increased blood pressure. They have a greater increase in pulmonary blood pressure in response to hypoxia, which could predispose to high altitude pulmonary edema, a relationship yet to be explored. Additionally, the central nervous systems (CNS) of hypertensive persons respond in an exaggerated manner to hypoxia. The prevalence of periodic breathing at altitude could cause hypertensives to experience very high levels of sympathetic stimulation during sleep, increasing their risk of exaggerated systemic hypertension, pulmonary hypertension, and abnormal cardiac rhythms. Normotensive persons were recently found to have elevated nocturnal blood pressure at altitude. Although these concerns about hypertensive individuals are hypothetical, the issues of untoward events during sleep and susceptibility to HAPE warrant further attention.

Coronary Artery Disease
High Altitude Residents

Various studies suggest that the incidence of coronary artery disease and consequent death rates is lower in lifelong high altitude residents. Firm conclusions are difficult because such variables as age, genetics, smoking, exercise, diet, and migration to lower altitude due to illness have not been controlled, but the evidence is not to be discounted. No study has ever suggested an increased incidence of ischemic heart disease in high altitude residents.

Lowlanders Ascending to Altitude

With acclimatization, a normal heart can tolerate even extreme hypoxemia without ischemic changes or impaired function. A theoretical basis for exacerbation of coronary artery disease at altitude exists, however. Cardiac work is slightly increased, and the usual compensatory increase in coronary blood flow may not be attained in those with arteriosclerotic coronary artery disease. In fact, arteriosclerotic coronary vessels that can not dilate may actually constrict, resulting in ischemia (an inadequate blood supply).

To assess whether these concerns are significant, four questions must be considered: (1) Can altitude unmask previously unknown coronary artery disease? (2) Can altitude exacerbate stable ischemia? (3) Does altitude increase the risk of myocardial infarction or sudden death? and (4) Does altitude provoke abnormal rhythms? (See chapter 9, "Heart and Blood Vessel Disorders.") Anecdotal reports make it clear that these events may all occur at altitude, as they do at sea level, but whether altitude is a contributor is unclear. Additional considerations are the possible influence of cold and the risk of ischemia in those who have no signs or symptoms of coronary artery disease, particularly the elderly. Finally, what recommendations make ascent to altitude safer for those with known or unknown coronary artery disease?

Does Altitude Unmask Coronary Artery Disease?

Investigation decades ago found that severe hypoxia is stressful for a heart with coronary artery disease, but it is less stressful than exercise. In a direct comparison, sea level exercise produced more ischemia-related electrocardiographic (ECG) changes in individuals with known coronary artery disease than did inhalation of ten percent oxygen while at rest. (Normal air contains twenty percent oxygen.) As a result, exercise testing has become the preferred way to screen. Of several thousand patients with suspected coronary disease who were tested for twenty minutes with ten percent oxygen, none developed serious cardiac events or died. When hypoxia and exercise were combined, however, the results were different. When seventy asymptomatic soldiers (ages thirty to fifty years) who already had nonspecific ECG changes were evaluated, hypoxia at rest resulted in further ECG changes in four. However, ten subjects developed changes with exercise at sea level, and twenty developed changes with the combination of hypoxia and exercise. Although these studies are interesting, they assessed only ECG changes, and only in persons with pretesting ECG abnormalities. Nonetheless, hypoxic exercise appears to be better able to unmask coronary artery disease (by ECG) than hypoxia at rest or exercise while breathing air containing a normal amount of oxygen. If acute hypoxic exercise can unmask ECG evidence of coronary artery disease, altitude exposure may do so as well.

Because the blood concentrations of catecholamines such as adrenaline are increased during the first few days at altitude, exertion varies, sleep may exaggerate hypoxemia, temperatures are lower, and other stresses are present, a stay at altitude may stress the coronary circulation as much as or more than acute hypoxic exercise.

Does Altitude Exacerbate Stable Cardiac Ischemia?

Small increases in heart rate and blood pressure on initial ascent to altitude may cause angina or induce angina in those with coronary artery disease. (See chapter 9, "Heart and Blood Vessel Disorders.") Altitude alone may aggravate angina, at least immediately after ascent. Several investigators have concluded that individuals with coronary artery disease who are well compensated at sea level do well at a moderate altitude after a few days of acclimatization, but during that period their threshold for angina may be lower and activity should be limited. However, two subjects had untoward events—one an increase in angina and a second a myocardial infarct—a relatively high incidence of complications. Further study to better define those who are at risk is needed.

A reunion of the U.S. Army 10th Mountain Division in Vail, Colorado, at an elevation of 8,250 feet (2,500 m) provided an opportunity to observe a number of elderly individuals (mean age 69.8 ± 4.4 years) over a period of four days after ascent from near sea level. Of seventy-seven men and twenty women, twenty were known to have significant coronary artery disease. Thirty-eight had abnormal ECGs on arrival at high altitude. Over the four days at high altitude, no clinically significant ECG changes occurred, nor did any clinical events suggestive of ischemia. These elderly subjects with both symptomatic and presumed asymptomatic coronary artery disease (and frequently hypertension) tolerated moderate altitude well and had no exacerbation of their stable ischemia.

Does Altitude Increase the Risk of Myocardial Infarction and Sudden Death?

Data are inadequate to draw firm conclusions about the risk of myocardial infarction and sudden death at altitude in those with coronary artery disease. The limited available evidence does not identify an increased risk, particularly in individuals who have been exercising regularly at low altitude.

COLD, ALTITUDE, AND ISCHEMIA

Whether cold provokes myocardial ischemia at altitude has not been studied but seems likely. At sea level, breathing cold air or exercising in a cold environment by individuals who already had exercise-induced angina limited their exercise tolerance even more. The cold-induced increase in heart rate and blood pressure was similar to that reported at moderate altitude in temperate conditions. Therefore, cold and altitude might interact to incite effort-induced angina. Because locations at altitude are commonly cold, this question of interaction deserves pursuit.

RISK OF ACUTE ISCHEMIC EVENTS IN THOSE WITHOUT CORONARY ARTERY DISEASE

In addition to arteriosclerosis, coronary artery spasm has also been invoked as a possible mechanism for cardiac ischemia at altitude. Spasm would not be surprising at altitude because the sympathetic stimulation and respiratory alkalosis that typically occur are known coronary vasoconstrictors. However, only one individual with altitude-induced coronary artery spasm has been identified.

ADVICE FOR PERSONS WITH CORONARY ARTERY DISEASE REGARDING ALTITUDE

The stress of altitude on the coronary circulation appears to be minimal at rest but significant in conjunction with exercise. Patients exercising at altitude are more at risk than those merely sitting in a car or an airplane. European studies imply that an exercise program at sea level before exercising at altitude is essential for reducing the risk of sudden death.

Ideally, no one with any of the following risk factors for coronary artery disease should undertake unaccustomed exercise at altitude without a physician's supervision—certainly not those with known coronary artery disease:

- ▾ Family history of coronary artery disease before age fifty-five
- ▾ History or presence of hypertension
- ▾ Resting ECG changes indicative of ischemia (ST depression of any magnitude)
- ▾ Prior episode of chest pain

Asymptomatic men over age fifty with any risk factors should have an exercise treadmill test before altitude exposure (Table 22-1). Individuals with low risk of coronary artery disease as determined by the exercise test can be reassured and given such medical management as they may need. (Individuals who have had myocardial infarcts or coronary artery surgery are considered high risk only if they have abnormal results from the exercise test.) High-risk patients may require radiographic examination of the coronary arteries (coronary angiography) to determine appropriate management.

An increasingly frequent question is whether patients who have had coronary artery surgery are at increased (or perhaps decreased) risk at altitude. The complete lack of data makes advising a patient difficult. Conservative physicians may follow the adage "better safe than sorry," but others argue that forbidding such adventure is unwarranted and without scientific basis. Advice for such patients requires individual evaluation; a trial at an intermediate altitude at the expected workload may be useful. As always, nothing substitutes for sound clinical judgement.

POSSIBLE BENEFICIAL EFFECTS OF ALTITUDE FOR CORONARY ARTERY DISEASE

Some studies have suggested potential benefits from altitude exposure for those with coronary artery disease. In experimental animals, and in studies of cardiac rehabilitation programs at 12,375 feet (3,750 m) for sea level dwellers with heart disease carried out in Russia and Kyrgyzstan and in Peru, definite benefits have been found and no adverse effects have been encountered. A French group has suggested skiing at moderate altitude as part of a program to lower cardiovascular risk. Given the

Table 22-1	Evaluation of Coronary Artery Disease in Individuals over Age 50 Who Wish to Ascend to Altitude				
SYMPTOM	**EVIDENCE OF CORONARY ARTERY DISEASE**	**RISK FACTORS[1]**	**TESTING**	**RISK CATEGORY[2]**
None	None	None	ETT[3] optional	Low
None	None	One or more	ETT normal	Low
None	None	One or more	ETT abnormal, T scan[4] normal	Low
None	None	One or more	ETT abnormal, T scan abnormal	High, needs angiogram
None or stable angina		Healed MI[5], healed MI found by ECG, or history of coronary artery surgery	ETT normal or questionable	Low
None or stable angina		Healed MI, healed MI found by ECG, or history of coronary artery surgery	ETT strongly positive	High
Age less than 50 years	None	None	ETT not indicated	Low
Age less than 50 years	None	One or more	ETT optional	Low

[1]Risk factors: family history of coronary artery disease before age 55, history or presence of hypertension, ST depression of any magnitude in the resting ECG, and prior episode of chest pain.
[2]Risk categories: low risk = minimal risk for a coronary event (angina, infarct, sudden death) over five years (two to four percent); high risk = risk for a coronary event in five years of ten to twenty percent; requires coronary arteriography.
[3]ETT = exercise tolerance test. Negative or minimally positive: patient can walk nine minutes or more (through stage 3 of Bruce protocol) without chest pain and with 1 mm or less ST segment depression on ECG. Strongly positive: patient walks six minutes or less (Bruce protocol) and has either chest pain or 2 mm or more ST depression on ECG.
[4]T scan = thallium nucleotide scan of myocardium.
[5]MI = myocardial infarct.

physiologic and biochemical similarities of altitude acclimatization and aerobic conditioning, these proposals merit attention.

Does Altitude Provoke Abnormal Cardiac Rhythms?

In older individuals who ascend to altitude, a number of investigators have noted an increased number of extrasystoles (skipped beats). (See chapter 9, "Heart and Blood Vessel Disorders.")

However, the extrasystoles appeared benign and did not suggest a propensity to life-threatening abnormal rhythms. Biochemical studies indicated that increased secretion of adrenaline and related compounds was the most likely cause. Most persons returned to normal after a few days, and no dire events have been reported.

Persons with troublesome or severe rhythm disorders have not been evaluated systematically at altitude. No anecdotal reports of exacerbations of supraventricular tachycardia or other common rhythm abnormalities have been published, and no information about whether or to what extent ascent to altitude increases risk for those with specific rhythm disorders at sea level is available.

Heart Failure

A tendency toward acute decompensation in individuals with a history of heart failure upon arrival at altitude has been observed, but systematic studies have not been made. Although the hypoxemia of moderate altitude does not depress myocardial contractility, the tendency toward fluid retention in some individuals at altitude—sometimes manifested as AMS—could aggravate heart failure. Because such fluid balance changes may occur, persons with heart failure need to be cautious about altitude exposure. However, no data on the magnitude of the risk or who would be most at risk are available.

Presumably, prevention and treatment at altitude would be the same as at sea level, although low-flow oxygen would probably have greater benefit by reducing hypoxic stress. Persons who know they have heart failure should consult their physicians about increasing their diuretic medication at altitude and should monitor their blood pressure, as well as their weight, peripheral edema, and chest congestion.

Congenital Heart Disease

The hypoxia of high altitude elevates pulmonary arterial pressure and resistance. As a result, individuals with congenital disorders such as atrial and ventricular septal defects (abnormal openings between the right and left atria or ventricles), patent ductus arteriosus (an opening between the aorta and pulmonary artery), and partially corrected tetralogy of Fallot (a complex combination of congenital defects) might have increased pulmonary hypertension and shunting from the pulmonary to the systemic circulation at altitude. Children born at altitude with atrial and ventricular septal defects have greater pulmonary hypertension than those born at lower elevations. Whether such individuals develop greater arterial oxygen desaturation at altitude because the pulmonary hypertension of altitude increases shunting depends on the severity of preexisting pulmonary hypertension and that induced by altitude hypoxia. Shunting would be expected to contribute to altitude illness, including HAPE, as well as to dyspnea, although these individuals tend to have a lower hypoxic ventilatory response as a result of their chronic hypoxia. An interesting, and related, question is whether defects resulting in reduced pulmonary blood flow, such as tetralogy of Fallot, might protect individuals from HAPE.

Whether patients with persistent pulmonary hypertension after corrective surgery for septal defects may have problems at altitude is unknown. When patent foramen ovale (a type of atrial septal defect) was found in persons with HAPE, it raised the suspicion that shunting and hypoxemia may have contributed to the illness, but further investigation disclosed others with patent foramen ovale who did not develop high altitude pulmonary edema.

Pulmonary Vascular Disorders

In addition to congenital cardiac defects, any illness resulting in pulmonary hypertension (increased blood pressure in the lungs, which normally is much lower than the pressure in the rest of the body) may be a relative contraindication to altitude exposure. Hypoxic pulmonary vasoconstriction would probably exaggerate pulmonary hypertension. Given the prominent role of pulmonary hypertension in the pathophysiology of high altitude pulmonary edema, any such illness may predispose to that disorder. Conditions for which this caution would apply include unilateral absent pulmonary artery and restrictive lung diseases, both of which have been associated with HAPE.

Persons with primary pulmonary hypertension (PPH) would be expected to be more symptomatic—to be more short of breath, to have more frequent fainting episodes, and to be weaker on exertion. However, some individuals with this disorder are able to tolerate altitude. Hypoxic gas breathing can be used to identify an individual's response to hypoxia.

Persons with PPH who must travel to altitude may benefit from calcium channel blockers, isoproterenol, or low-flow oxygen. These individuals must also be aware of a probable increased susceptibility to HAPE. A lowland woman with pulmonary hypertension secondary to fenfluramine developed two episodes of HAPE: the first at 7,600 feet (2,300 m), the second at only 6,100 feet (1,850 m) although she was skiing as high as 7,750 feet (2,350 m).

Other conditions that may produce pulmonary hypertension include bronchopulmonary dysplasia, recurrent pulmonary emboli, and mitral stenosis. Whether pulmonary hypertension is primary or secondary to some other disorder, individuals with this condition should be aware of the hazards of altitude, including right-sided heart failure and HAPE. Pulmonary hypertension is at least a moderate contraindication to ascent to altitude.

EFFECT OF ALTITUDE ON HEMATOLOGIC PROBLEMS

Abnormal Hemoglobin

The hypoxia of altitude is a well-recognized problem for those with sickle cell disease. Even pressurized aircraft cabin altitudes (up to 8,250 feet [2,500 m]) will cause twenty percent of those with hemoglobin SS–thalassemia disease, hemoglobin SC–thalassemia disease, and sickle cell–thalassemia disease to have thrombotic vaso-occlusive crises. Indeed, for some, ascent to altitude has triggered their first awareness of their condition. People with sickle cell disease living at an altitude of 10,000 feet (3,000 m) in Saudi Arabia have twice the incidence of crises, hospitalizations, and complications as their counterparts at low altitude.

Splenic infarction at altitude may be more common in those with sickle cell trait (hemoglobin AS) than those with homozygous disease (hemoglobin SS), who totally infarct their spleens early in life. The differential diagnosis of left upper quadrant pain at altitude (even as low as 5,000 feet [1,500 m]) should include splenic infarction—in Caucasians as well as those of African ancestry. The incidence of problems in individuals with sickle cell trait, however, is quite low, and ascent to altitude, even with vigorous exercise, is not contraindicated, in contrast to those with sickle cell disease. The U.S. Army, for example, does not consider soldiers with the trait unfit for duty at high altitude.

Oxygen Affinity

Hemoglobin with altered oxygen affinity may affect acclimatization to high altitude. When individuals with genetically left-shifted oxygen dissociation curves were taken to 10,200 feet (3,100 m), they surprisingly did not develop a fast pulse or rapid respirations and were superior in their exercise performance. At least at this altitude, increased loading of the hemoglobin in the lung presumably resulted in improved oxygen transport. Whether a decreased oxygen affinity would be detrimental has not been addressed.

Anemia

Given the central role of hemoglobin in oxygen transport, a low hemoglobin level might be expected to affect tolerance to altitude. However, neither the extent of ventilatory acclimatization nor the incidence or severity of AMS has been found to correlate with hemoglobin concentration.

Persons with iron deficiency, even without frank anemia, have reduced exercise performance at altitude (as at sea level), as well as reduced erythropoietic (bone marrow stimulation) response. Iron deficiency is particularly common in women who are not careful about replacing iron lost in menstrual blood. No data are available on the role of anemia in susceptibility to altitude illness.

EFFECT OF ALTITUDE ON NEUROLOGIC CONDITIONS

Migraine

The important question of whether altitude aggravates migraine has not received sufficient attention. That the headache of AMS and that of common migraine may be nearly indistinguishable presents obvious problems in diagnosis and determination of incidence. The mechanisms for migraine and the headache of AMS could be similar. To test this hypothesis, sumatriptan, an effective drug ($5HT_1$-receptor agonist) for treating migraine, was evaluated as therapy for the headache of AMS. The results were mixed, and further study is required.

One group in which migraine is easier to identify at altitude is high altitude natives, a population that does not suffer from AMS. At 14,200 feet (4,300 m) 12.4 percent of a population of Peruvian natives suffered migraine headaches, but only 3.6 percent of a similar population at sea level had that problem.

In a group of 379 adult men subsequently studied at 14,200 feet (4,300 m) by the same investigators, the incidence of migraine headaches was 32.2 percent and correlated with increasing age, hemoglobin values, and chronic mountain sickness. For all types of headaches, the incidence was 54.6 percent, far higher than reported in Peruvian and other populations living at low altitude. The authors postulated that the incidence of migraine in this population might be higher due to the combined effects of hypoxia, polycythemia, and reduced cerebral blood flow. Because migraine in this population may be related to chronic mountain sickness, a disorder that develops over a period of years, the implications for high altitude sojourners are unclear.

Whether ascent to altitude increases the frequency or severity of headaches in lowlanders with migraine is not yet determined, but it is clear that ascent can trigger migraine in both those with and those without a prior history of migraine at sea level. In one study, migraine developed repeatedly in susceptible subjects during simulated exposure to altitudes between 9,000 and 11,000 feet (2,750 and 3,400 m). For others, while frequency may remain stable, the severity may change. Migraine must be included in the differential diagnosis of a severe headache at altitude, even with apparent AMS, particularly when associated with visual or other focal neurologic deficits. Whether hypoxic gas breathing at sea level can identify individuals in whom altitude may trigger an attack has not been investigated.

STROKES, TRANSIENT ISCHEMIC ATTACKS, AND OTHER CEREBROVASCULAR DISORDERS

Whether the incidence or severity of cerebrovascular disease (CVD) and stroke is different in high altitude natives than in sea level populations is unclear. Surveys conducted in rural areas of South America and Asia over a range of 5,100 to 14,200 feet (1,550 to 4,300 m) have suggested a lower incidence of CVD. However, a recent epidemiological study reported that the prevalence ratio for CVD at 11,200 feet (3,400 m) in Peru was close to the worldwide average. Discerning the true relationship between altitude and cerebrovascular disease requires careful control for racial characteristics and lifestyle while comparing low and high altitude populations.

Rarely, stroke has been reported in previously healthy sojourners at altitude and typically has been ascribed to dehydration, forced inactivity, and polycythemia. Stroke may also be a complication of high altitude cerebral edema (HACE); clotting in cerebral blood vessels is a common finding at autopsy.

Clinically, cerebral venous thrombosis (most strokes are arterial occlusions) is easily confused with HACE. A number of reports emphasize the need for physicians to consider this diagnosis in individuals with persistent neurologic symptoms after descent from altitude. In a recent series of patients eventually diagnosed with cerebral venous thrombosis, all had recently been on long air flights, and one had been mountaineering. An accompanying editorial suggested that hypercoagulability or increased viscosity might be responsible and emphasized that this condition is relatively easy to treat and must not be missed.

Whether acute altitude exposure contributes to a hypercoagulable state that predisposes individuals to strokes is a subject of debate. The interesting question of whether altitude might unmask cerebral arteriosclerosis and vascular insufficiency in asymptomatic individuals has not been addressed.

Transient, focal neurologic abnormalities in the absence of HACE have been attributed to transient ischemic attacks (TIAs). However, other possible etiologies include cerebrovascular spasm (migraine equivalent), focal edema, and hypoxia in zones of minimal cerebral blood flow. Most of these individuals have been young, healthy mountaineers, not older individuals who would be expected to have arteriosclerotic vascular disease, the usual cause of TIAs. One report described six cases of transient blindness that appeared to result from a cerebral rather than an ocular process. Supplemental oxygen or carbon dioxide breathing promptly reversed the condition, which suggested vascular spasm rather than occlusion. Descent provided slower relief. Others have described similar incidents, as well as other problems suggestive of TIAs. In all cases, recovery was complete, and the few individuals subsequently evaluated by magnetic resonance imaging had no detectable abnormalities. The exact etiology of these focal neurologic events remains a mystery and warrants further study.

Because cerebral blood vessels dilate during ascent to altitude, persons with cerebrovascular structural abnormalities, such as arteriovenous malformations or aneurysms, may be at risk. Individuals with such abnormalities that have hemorrhaged have been encountered. Persons with known cerebrovascular malformations should perhaps be advised to avoid significant altitude exposure.

Brain Tumors

Brain tumors can be unmasked upon ascent to altitude, presumably because the intracranial blood flow changes and the brain volume increases. Four such individuals have now been recognized. In none of the persons had the tumors been previously diagnosed.

Seizures

Acute, severe hypoxia may cause seizures, a fact more relevant and better known to aviation medicine and of questionable relevance for sojourners who take time to acclimatize and go to more moderate altitudes. In fact, seizures appearing for the first time in sojourners at altitude without an underlying seizure focus—with or without high altitude cerebral edema—appear to be rare.

In persons with seizure disorders, exacerbation due to altitude has been anecdotally observed when they were not taking their medication. The mechanism of exacerbation might be related to either the respiratory alkalosis of altitude, similar to the hyperventilation used in electroencephalograph laboratories to trigger seizure events, or to the hypoxia. Persons with seizure disorders have had no increase in frequency or severity of seizures when medications were continued at altitude.

In contrast to these apparently unusual events, syncope, or fainting, is common at altitude. Since syncope of any cause may be associated with seizure activity (convulsive syncope), confusion of convulsive syncope with a true seizure is inevitable. Systematic studies of patients with seizure disorders are sorely needed to determine whether altitude is a risk for these individuals.

Whether an individual with a grand mal seizure at very high altitude might be at greater risk for residual brain injury is another unanswered question.

DIABETES MELLITUS

Do diabetics have more problems at altitude? The onset of severe diabetic ketoacidosis in five trekkers at altitude, three of whom died, raises suspicion of a problem, but whether incidence or severity is increased at altitude is unknown. Some reports have questioned the reliability of self-monitoring blood glucose devices at altitude, but a recent study demonstrated reliability of one system at 8,800 and 12,100 feet (2,668 and 3,665 m) in Colorado.

OPHTHALMOLOGIC CONDITIONS

The parts of the eye most affected by altitude are the cornea and the retina. The most common corneal problem is snow blindness caused by the increased ultraviolet light and increased reflection from snow of such light at altitude. (See chapter 24, "Heat and Solar Injuries.")

Hypoxia also affects the cornea. Because the cornea obtains almost all of its oxygen by diffusion from the atmosphere, the decline in partial pressure of oxygen at high altitude causes a decline in corneal oxygen tension. This disturbs corneal fluid balance, and the hypoxic cornea swells, particularly when the eyelids are closed during sleep, which produces additional hypoxia. Because the swelling is uniform, no change in corneal curvature and no visual abnormalities occur.

Persons who have had radial keratotomy (RK) for refraction correction, however, no longer have structurally normal corneas. Deep radial incisions have been made to allow the central cornea to flatten, improving farsighted vision. On ascent to high altitude, however, swelling of the hypoxic cornea is not uniform and significant visual changes may result (Fig. 22-2). The degree of refractive change is progressive with higher altitude. A variety of studies have demonstrated that the swelling is the result of hypoxia and is not caused simply by lower barometric pressure.

The implications are significant, as was dramatically documented on a recent expedition to Mount Everest by a climber who had undergone RK. Over several hours at 27,400 feet (8,300 m), his visual difficulty progressed to the point of near-blindness. He suffered severe frostbite, nearly died, and required an enormous rescue effort. Similar visual changes have been reported in other climbers to high altitude and may occur below 10,000 feet (3,000 m). The problem is likely to become worse with the decreasing accommodation typical of aging.

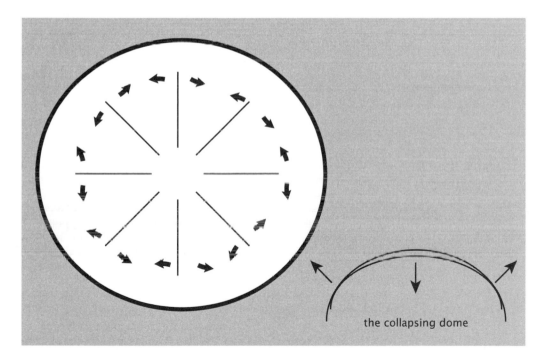

the collapsing dome

FIGURE 22-2. Effect of altitude on cornea after radial keratotomy (RK): Circumferencial expansion from edema causes peripheral steepening with corresponding cental flattening.[1]

ALTITUDE AND COMMON
MEDICAL CONDITIONS

In contrast, with photorefractive keratectomy (PRK), a laser technique for shaving the anterior cornea uniformly in which no incisions are made, no changes in vision occur at high altitude. In studies done at 13,800 feet (4,200 m), corneal swelling was observed in individuals with both RK and PRK, but only the RK subjects developed refractive changes.

Individuals contemplating surgical correction of myopia who may travel to high altitude should choose PRK over RK. Those who have had RK performed can correct their vision only with appropriate spectacles.

High altitude retinal hemorrhages are discussed in chapter 21, "Disorders Caused by Altitude." Whether altitude may contribute to or aggravate the retinal microangiopathy of hypertension, diabetes, or other diseases is not known, and no research has addressed the effect of ascent to altitude by such patients. Even if these populations exhibited a "normal" incidence of retinal hemorrhage at high altitude, such an event could increase the probability of visual impairment. Although retinal hemorrhages are rare below 15,000 feet (4,500 m), except in persons with AMS or HAPE, whether the threshold altitude is the same in the diseased retina is unknown, and caution is warranted.

EFFECT OF ALTITUDE ON PREGNANCY

A normal mother breathing room air at sea level has an arterial oxygen pressure (PO_2) of 85 to 100 mm Hg. The PO_2 in the uterine veins is approximately 40 mm Hg. The PO_2 in the umbilical vein going to the fetus (analogous to a systemic artery in the adult) is 30 to 35 mm Hg. The PO_2 in the umbilical artery coming from the fetus (similar to the pulmonary artery) is 10 to 15 mm Hg. Such low oxygen pressures are normal for a fetus, and this "low oxygen" environment is remarkably stable. The shape of the fetus's oxygen dissociation curve and the high affinity of its hemoglobin for oxygen minimize changes in maternal arterial oxygenation.

The placenta acts as a buffer in several ways: it maintains a constant carbon dioxide gradient (10 mm Hg), is relatively impermeable to bicarbonate ions (to protect the fetus from maternal changes in acid-base balance), and maintains the fetal oxygen environment. Additional changes that maintain fetal stability include increased ventilation by the mother (even in high altitude residents, who normally are insensitive to chronic hypoxia) and increased oxygen extraction by the fetus. As a result, oxygen consumption remains stable even when stressed with a fifty percent reduction in either placental blood flow or blood oxygen content. (The fetus must avoid a high PO_2 because that triggers the drop in pulmonary vascular resistance and closure of the ductus arteriosus that normally occurs following birth.)

Given a stable fetal environment, what degree of maternal hypoxia can be detrimental, and what evidence is there for compromise of the lowland fetus or mother upon ascent to high altitude?

Studies of High Altitude Residents: Implications for Pregnant Lowlanders

In native residents at an altitude of 6,000 feet (1,830 m), umbilical cord arterial and venous oxygen tensions are the same as at sea level. A slightly lower carbon dioxide pressure reflects mild maternal hyperventilation. At altitudes over 10,000 feet (3,000 m), fetal response to hypoxia is evidenced by an increased hematocrit (two to three percent higher), increased fraction of fetal hemoglobin, and increased erythropoietin in the umbilical cord blood.

Studies from all of the world's high altitude regions have identified various effects of high altitude residence on pregnancy. The best documented is intrauterine growth retardation, which leads to healthy, full-term infants who are small for gestational age. Where sophisticated medical care is accessible, intrauterine growth retardation is not associated with increased rates of morbidity or mortality unless the infants are also premature. Intrauterine growth retardation, however, does indicate an apparent effect of hypoxia on the developing fetus.

Similar reductions in birth weight are seen with mothers who smoke, but unlike the high altitude infants, the infants of mothers who smoke have higher perinatal mortality rates at every birth weight. This important difference indicates that effects on fetal growth can occur independently of effects on mortality, and also that smoking produces more abnormalities that affect fetal growth and well-being than just reduced oxygen transport. Reduced size for gestational age at sea level is also associated with preeclampsia, maternal hypoxic lung disease, maternal cyanotic congenital heart disease, and various anemias, all of which have diminished fetal oxygen/nutrient delivery as a common pathway. Unlike some of these other conditions, particularly preeclampsia, low birth weight due to high altitude does not appear to be associated with increased morbidity and mortality for full-term infants.

Various investigations suggest that the mechanism of intrauterine growth retardation at high altitude is, in large part, lower uteroplacental blood flow and "relative ischemia" of the placenta. Three factors are thought to explain this decreased placental blood flow: a smaller maternal blood volume increase, less uterine artery dilatation, and lack of appropriate redistribution of blood flow to the uteroplacental circulation. How hypoxia could produce these changes is unknown, but impaired placentation, the process by which the placenta "invades" the uterus to establish its blood supply, has been suggested. Recent studies have indicated that hypoxia causes shallower placentation and higher vascular resistance, similar to that seen in preeclampsia. Although this finding must be confirmed in normal high altitude placentas, this work does question whether hypoxic exposure could be detrimental during placentation (the first nine to twelve weeks of pregnancy). A corollary question is whether high altitude exposure is advisable for lowland women with any suggestion of impaired placentation or fetal compromise, such as hypertension or preeclampsia, at any time during pregnancy.

In high altitude residents, intrauterine growth retardation is not linear throughout pregnancy. Only after thirty-two weeks of gestation does fetal growth at high altitude become appreciably slower than at sea level. Does this observation mean that the otherwise healthy pregnant lowlander need not worry about impaired fetal growth at high altitude until after thirty-two weeks of gestation? Or is the stage set for intrauterine growth retardation earlier in the pregnancy, such as during placentation, so that altitude exposure after this time has no effect on growth? Is the intrauterine growth retardation of altitude residents even relevant to lowlanders? Without answers to these questions, admonishing all women to avoid altitude exposure throughout pregnancy, as some have done because they are concerned about intrauterine growth retardation, seems premature.

At the present time, no evidence indicates that altitude exposure, at least to moderate altitudes, increases risk to the healthy pregnant lowlander or her fetus.

Acute Ascent—The Altitude Sojourner

Clinical and physiologic investigations of pregnant lowlanders ascending to altitude are conspicuously missing, particularly to altitudes over 8,250 feet (2,500 m). Thousands of pregnant women travel to the moderate altitude of ski resorts for recreation. The absence of any reported adverse effects is reassuring, but the safety of altitude exposure during pregnancy has not been systematically evaluated. Is adding the stress of exercise (skiing) to that of hypoxia a cause for concern?

The few studies available are encouraging. A study of submaximal and maximal aerobic work at sea level and 6,000 feet (1,830 m) after two to four days of acclimatization found that fetal heart rate responses were not changed from sea level. A study of pregnant subjects who exercised after ascent to 7,350 feet (2,225 m) produced similar results. The experience of the airline industry is also reassuring. Exposures are brief, but cumulative time at cabin altitudes up to 8,000 feet (2,400 m) is high. Pregnant cabin crew are generally permitted to fly until seven months of gestation. Untoward effects have not yet been demonstrated in this large population, though studies are continuing.

In summary, the only available data, though rather inadequate, suggest that short-term exposure to altitudes up to 8,250 feet (2,500 m) with exercise is safe for lowland women with normal pregnancies.

Effect of Acute Hypoxia on Fetuses

The only observed effect of acute hypoxia on the fetus is an increase in heart rate. Results have been variable, but only a slight increase (tachycardia) is the usual response to moderate maternal hypoxia (twelve percent or fifteen percent inhaled oxygen). A slower heart rate (bradycardia) is the response to more severe hypoxia (ten percent oxygen). In experimental animals, severe acute hypoxia (ten percent oxygen), with an average maternal arterial PO_2 of 40 mm Hg, resulted in no change in uterine or umbilical blood flow, but substantial increases in fetal heart rate.

Investigators have suggested that hypoxic gas breathing could detect placental insufficiency and potential labor and delivery problems because fetuses with abnormal responses, such as prolonged recovery from tachycardia, would be more likely to have fetal distress during labor. Another way to assess relative hypoxia or ischemia of the uteroplacental unit is to determine the fetal response to breathing oxygen. An improved physiologic function with oxygen would imply correction of a deficit. Although no reports of this intervention at altitude can be found, maternal hyperoxia at sea level had no effect in normal pregnancy or mild preeclampsia. However, it does cause observable changes (increased heart rate and increased fetal breathing movements) in severe preeclampsia, in fetal growth retardation, and in small-for-gestational-age infants.

These studies suggest that a compromised placental-fetal circulation could be unmasked at altitude. In the absence of such complications, the fetus seems to tolerate a level of acute hypoxia far exceeding moderate altitude exposure.

Recommending that women with any complication of pregnancy avoid unnecessary altitude exposure seems prudent. An ultrasound or other assessment may help reassure the clinician and mother about the absence of the more common complications. For women with no known abnormalities, there appears to be little risk to the fetus or the mother undertaking a sojourn to an altitude at which oxygen saturation remains above eighty-five percent most of the time (up to 10,000 feet [3,000 m]), but the data are very limited. Altitude alone does not determine whether the fetus becomes stressed. The maternal (and fetal) arterial oxygen pressure and arterial oxygen saturation are critical. A woman with HAPE at 8,250 feet (2,500 m), for example, is much more hypoxic than a healthy woman at 16,500 feet (5,000 m). Altitude illness, especially pulmonary edema, must be carefully avoided. Similarly, smoking, lung disease, and other disorders of oxygen transport render the pregnant patient at altitude more hypoxemic and at a higher physiologic altitude.

Clinicians concerned about unmasking placental insufficiency at altitude may find hypoxic gas breathing challenge a useful but uncalibrated tool. The safety of modest hypoxia on the fetus and mother at different stages of pregnancy and at different altitudes (different levels of hypoxia), whether persons at risk for untoward effects can be identified before exposure, and the interaction of hypoxia with other stresses such as exercise clearly require more investigation. Studies comparing large populations of women with and without altitude exposure during pregnancy would be particularly useful for pregnant lowlanders trying to make informed decisions about the potential risks of altitude.

CHILDREN AT ALTITUDE

In general, children tolerate moderate altitude well. Children who have been born and grow up at high altitudes seem to have no more problems than adults. Whether the incidence of AMS and other altitude disorders in infants and young children is the same as adults or somewhat higher is controversial. In one study, fourteen children, ages three to thirty-six months, ascended from 5,275 feet (1,609 m) to 11,440 feet (3,488 m). Three children developed AMS, an incidence similar to that in adults. As in adults, the higher the altitude and the faster the ascent, the greater the incidence of AMS. A few observers have thought that children acclimatize somewhat more slowly.

Identifying children with AMS can be a problem. Children frequently become ill with vague viral illnesses that create symptoms similar to those of AMS—headaches, irritability, loss of appetite, inability to sleep, and fatigue. Infants and young children can not verbalize what is bothering them. Parents are advised to avoid high altitudes with children so young. If they go to such altitudes and their children become ill, parents should assume the children have altitude sickness and descend immediately.

Air travel appears to be safe for children with upper respiratory infections, nasal allergies, and ear infections. Children may experience pain in flight, but permanent damage from barotrauma appears to be extremely rare. Nasal sprays and decongestants may decrease the risk of discomfort, but some studies suggest that these agents have limited effectiveness in children. Middle ear infections seem to protect children from pain because fluid fills the middle ear space and pressure differences can not develop. Flying is safe for children with tympanic membrane tubes.

Conventional wisdom recommends nursing infants or giving them bottles during ascent and descent and when they cry during flight. The rationale is that the infants are crying because they are experiencing barotrauma or they are dehydrated. No data support these recommendations, and feeding may make the infants more uncomfortable. Air in the intestine expands twenty percent during flight. Sucking and eating introduce more air. Infants probably should be fed no more often when flying than when at home.

One study has suggested that the lower oxygen pressure in airliner cabins at cruising altitudes may be hazardous to infants. When forty infants were subject to the oxygen levels found in aircraft, approximately 6,000 feet (1,800 m), four developed irregular breathing and such decreased blood oxygen levels that the study was interrupted. However, these studies were carried out in a laboratory. Millions of infants travel on airliners without apparent adverse effects.

ALCOHOL AT ALTITUDE

Alcohol ingestion at altitude is widespread. A recent epidemiologic study indicated that sixty-four percent of tourists ingest alcohol during the first few days at 9,240 feet (2800 m). Two questions regarding alcohol are frequently asked: (1) Does alcohol affect acclimatization? and (2) Does altitude potentiate the effects of alcohol? In regard to acclimatization, determination of blood gases one hour after ingestion of 50 g of alcohol (equivalent to one liter of beer) at 550 feet (171 m) and again after four hours at 10,000 feet (3,000 m) in ten subjects disclosed that alcohol had no effect on ventilation at the low altitude. However, at higher altitude, alcohol depressed ventilation as gauged by a decreased arterial oxygen pressure (from 69 to 64 mm Hg) and increased carbon dioxide pressure (from 32.5 to 34 mm Hg).

Whether this amount of ventilatory depression would contribute to AMS, and whether repeated doses would have greater effect, was not tested. Nonetheless, alcohol might impede ventilatory acclimatization and should be used with caution at altitude (as elsewhere).

Conventional wisdom proffers an additive effect of altitude and alcohol on brain function. However, in a variety of studies mostly related to aviation, no influence by altitude was detectable.

The possibility of interactions between alcohol and altitude deserves more study. The limited data on blood gases at altitude after alcohol ingestion support the popular notion that alcohol may slow ventilatory acclimatization. Considerable data, however, refute the belief that at least up to 12,000 feet (3,660 m), altitude increases the effect of alcohol. How altitude and alcohol might interact at higher elevations is unknown.

FUTURE DIRECTIONS

Assessing the effect of altitude on myriad medical conditions is a difficult task requiring multiple approaches. The most fruitful avenue of research would be a large, ongoing epidemiologic data system, similar to the surveillance systems used for detecting adverse drug reactions or environmental toxicity. Many of the questions regarding the interaction of altitude with age, disease, and pregnancy require such a large-scale approach. Physicians and other health professionals at high elevations in North America and other continents that attract tourists are ideally situated for this type of investigation.

In addition to recognizing the effects of altitude on preexisting conditions, focused surveys of hotel and resort guests can yield data on prevalence of medical conditions in a general population. Occupational health personnel, as well as local health care providers, could make valuable contributions to

ALTITUDE AND COMMON
MEDICAL CONDITIONS

an epidemiologic survey assessing the health of individuals who live at high altitude locations, particularly in the high altitude locations of South America and Asia. Focused, detailed studies of selected medical conditions or populations, such as the elderly and those with coronary artery disease investigated in the U.S. Army 10th Mountain Division study, play an important role in understanding how specific conditions are affected by altitude hypoxia. This model can be applied to neonatal and pediatric age groups, pregnancy, and migraine sufferers, to name but a few of the more pressing problems that merit investigation. Such groups are also well suited for outcome studies.

Acute hypoxic stress tests need to be correlated with the effects of intermediate and long-term acclimatization. Study of high altitude natives will continue to provide information of importance for sojourners. For example, intrauterine growth retardation in high altitude natives alerts us to the possible effects of hypoxia on the fetus of the sojourner as well. Understanding its mechanism would help assess its relevance for altitude visitors and help determine whether such effects can be prevented or minimized. Finally, as the molecular bases of adaptation to hypoxia and to disease unfold, new breakthroughs might minimize hypoxic stress and maximize wellness in those persons with medical conditions who choose to visit altitude because it adds to their enjoyment or quality of life.

REFERENCES

1. Adapted from an illustration by Tom Mader. (Reproduced with permission.)

CHAPTER 23

COLD INJURIES

The common disorders produced by cold are hypothermia and frostbite. Hypothermia is a decrease in the core temperature of the body that impairs intellectual, muscular, and cardiac function. Frostbite is a localized injury characterized by freezing of the tissues. Preventing and treating these disorders requires knowledge of the way heat is lost or gained and the body's responses to cold.

MECHANISMS OF HEAT EXCHANGE

Heat is lost or gained from the environment by four routes:
- Radiation
- Evaporation
- Convection
- Conduction

Radiation

Radiation, the largest source of heat loss in sedentary individuals in temperate climates, is a form of direct energy emission, much of it as infrared radiation. Heat is exchanged directly with the environment and can be quantitated by the formula

$$J_Q = EK(T_S^4 - T_A^4)$$

where J_Q = heat gain or loss; E = emissivity, which varies with skin color; K = Stefan-Boltzmann constant (5.67051×10^{-8}); T_S = skin surface temperature; and T_A = air temperature. As this formula indicates, heat loss is determined by the difference in temperature between the skin and the atmosphere or surrounding objects such as rocks, trees, snow, or ice. Radiant heat loss increases as the environment grows colder.

In an environment that is warmer than the skin surface temperature (about 95°F [35°C]), radiant heat is absorbed by the body. The inability to lose heat by radiation in such environments can contribute to heat illness.

Clothing has little effect on heat loss by radiation. The heat radiates from the body to the clothing and from there to the atmosphere (Fig. 23-1). Efforts to develop clothing materials that reflect heat back to the body have met with little success. However, radiant heat loss becomes a major problem only in extremely cold situations (below -20° to -30°F [-29° to -35°C]). If clothing adequately limits heat loss by other routes, particularly convection, the body can compensate for the increased radiant heat loss encountered in most cold wilderness environments.

Evaporation

Perspiration is continuously being produced in small amounts, even in cold climates. This "insensible" perspiration evaporates from the skin, extracting approximately 580 calories of heat for each cubic centimeter lost. Additional heat is lost from the respiratory passages as inspired air is warmed to body temperature and moistened to 100 percent relative humidity. In temperate conditions, twenty to thirty percent of all heat loss results from evaporation, about two-thirds of which takes place on the skin.

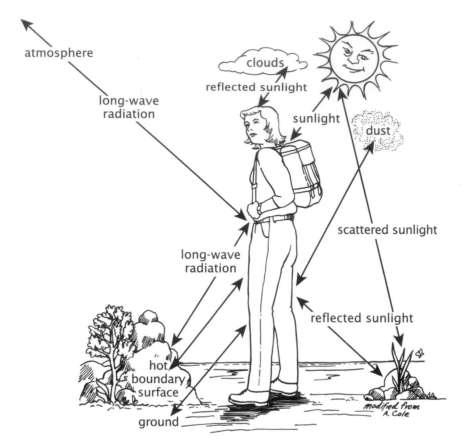

FIGURE 23-1. Heat loss by radiation

Heat and water losses from the lungs become much larger at high elevations, where breathing is deeper and more rapid to compensate for the lower quantity of oxygen in the atmosphere. As much as four liters of water and 2,300 kilocalories (Kcal) of heat can be lost daily through the lungs at high altitudes (1,000 calories = 1 kilocalorie).

Heat loss from the respiratory tract can not be reduced in any practical manner. Mouth breathing increases fluid and heat loss somewhat, but the amount is insignificant in comparison with the quantity of heat lost through other sources. Outdoorsmen must be aware that this heat and water loss is occurring, must eat enough food to regenerate the heat, and must drink enough liquids to replace the water.

Heat loss from insensible perspiration also can not be effectively limited. Vapor barrier systems, which consist of a layer of material impermeable to water vapor (usually plastic) between layers of insulation, have been tried. Since the barrier prevents water vapor loss, the air beneath the barrier quickly becomes saturated, perspiration can not evaporate, and heat loss by that route should be eliminated. However, perspiration does not cease, and the clothing underneath the barrier becomes saturated with water. Wet clothing is hazardous because it no longer limits convective heat loss.

No vapor barrier system works well at temperatures above freezing because too much water accumulates. Even at lower temperatures, the only vapor barrier system widely used was in footwear (Korean, or "Mickey Mouse," boots). Although such boots did keep feet warm, application of antiperspirants to the feet and frequent sock changes were needed to avoid injury by perpetual wetness. (These boots are no longer manufactured.)

Convection

Air in contact with skin is warmed to the skin's temperature. When the warmed air is displaced, cool air that replaces it is also warmed. Because the heat that warms the air comes from the skin, body heat is lost as the warmed air moves away.

Convective heat loss is an almost continuous process, but the amount of heat required to warm air (the specific heat of air) is so small that little heat is lost by this route in temperate climates. In a cold atmosphere, convective heat loss is greater because more heat is required to warm the colder air. However, the greatest convective heat losses occur when the air is moving. Even a mild breeze greatly increases heat loss because the layer of warmed air next to the skin is constantly being replaced with cooler air.

The amount of heat extracted by moving air increases as the square of the velocity, not in direct proportion to its speed. A wind of eight miles an hour removes four times as much heat, not twice as much, as a wind of four miles an hour. A strong wind can remove tremendous amounts of heat.

The increased heat loss that occurs with moving air is called "wind chill." Table 23-1 illustrates the additional cooling produced by wind in a cold environment. For instance, a temperature that poses little threat in still air, such as 15°F (-9.5°C), can be life-threatening in a wind of twenty to twenty-five miles per hour (mph), or thirty-two to forty kilometers per hour (kph).

Because convective heat loss can increase so enormously, it is the major cause of terrestrial hypothermia in the wilderness. Fortunately, clothing can greatly reduce this type of heat loss. Insulating clothing such as down or wool forms a myriad of small pockets in which air is trapped—the essence of thermal insulation. Windproof outer garments prevent displacement of the air within and between layers of clothing.

Convection also is a major route of heat loss in cold water. The water next to the skin extracts heat and is warmed, but any movement, such as swimming, displaces the warmed water, which is replaced by more cold water. Because the specific heat of water is so high, tremendous amounts of heat can be lost through convection, much more than can be generated by physical activity, even by strong, excellently conditioned swimmers. Individuals accidentally immersed in cold water can stay warmer by holding still to reduce water movement and limit heat loss than they can by swimming to generate heat. (Unless the shore or a boat is a very short distance away, active swimming should be avoided.) Positions that limit the area of the body surface exposed to water also help reduce heat loss (Fig. 23-2). Two or more persons should huddle together to limit their contact with water.

Conduction

Heat is conducted from the body when it is in contact with water, snow, rocks, or any cold object that is a good conductor. Air is not a good conductor. Water, an excellent conductor, has about twenty-five times the conductivity of air. More importantly, water has approximately 3,500 times the volumetric heat capacity of air. (To raise the temperature of a specific volume of water, a specific amount requires 3,500 times as much heat as could be required to raise an identical volume of air the same amount.) Conductive heat losses are high for anyone immersed in cold water without protective clothing.

Conductive heat losses can become significant in the wilderness when a person is seated or lying on ice, snow, or a cold rock. One cause of conductive heat loss is lying or sleeping on the ground without adequate insulation. Foam pads eliminate most of the conductive heat loss by this route. (Air mattresses, which allow air to circulate freely, provide less insulation than foam pads.) Thin, poorly insulated boots allow heat to be conducted from the body through soles in contact with snow. Although conductive heat loss alone is rarely a major cause of hypothermia, except during cold water immersion, heat loss by this route can aggravate convective heat losses and should be avoided.

Conductive heat losses become greater when clothing is wet.

Table 23-1 Wind Chill Chart

WIND (MPH)	EQUIVALENT TEMPERATURE (DEGREES FAHRENHEIT)													
WIND (KPH)	EQUIVALENT TEMPERATURE (DEGREES CELSIUS [CENTIGRADE])													
Calm	35	30	25	20	15	10	5	0	-5	-10	-15	-20	-25	-30
	2	-1	-4	-7	-9	-12	-15	-18	-21	-23	-26	-29	-32	-34
5 mph	33	27	21	16	12	7	1	-6	-11	-15	-20	-26	-31	-35
8 kph	1	-3	-6	-9	-11	-14	-17	-21	-24	-26	-29	-32	-35	-37
10 mph	21	16	9	2	-2	-9	-15	-22	-27	-31	-38	-45	-52	-58
16 kph	-6	-9	-13	-17	-19	-23	-26	-30	-33	-35	-39	-43	-47	-50
15 mph	16	11	1	-6	-11	-18	-25	-33	-40	-45	-51	-60	-65	-70
23 kph	-9	-12	-17	-21	-24	-28	-32	-36	-40	-43	-46	-51	-54	-57
20 mph	12	3	-4	-9	-17	-24	-32	-40	-46	-52	-60	-68	-76	-81
32 kph	-11	-16	-20	-23	-27	-31	-36	-40	-43	-47	-51	-56	-60	-63
25 mph	7	0	-7	-15	-22	-29	-37	-45	-52	-58	-67	-75	-83	-89
40 kph	-14	-18	-22	-26	-30	-34	-38	-43	-47	-50	-55	-59	-64	-67
30 mph	5	-2	-11	-18	-26	-33	-41	-49	-56	-63	-70	-78	-87	-94
48 kph	-15	-19	-24	-28	-32	-36	-41	-45	-51	-53	-57	-61	-66	-70
35 mph	3	-4	-13	-20	-27	-35	-43	-52	-60	-67	-72	-83	-90	-98
56 kph	-16	-20	-25	-31	-33	-37	-42	-47	-51	-55	-58	-64	-68	-72
40 mph	1	-4	-15	-22	-29	-36	-45	-54	-62	-69	-76	-87	-94	-101
64 kph	-17	-16	-26	-30	-34	-38	-43	-48	-52	-56	-60	-66	-70	-74

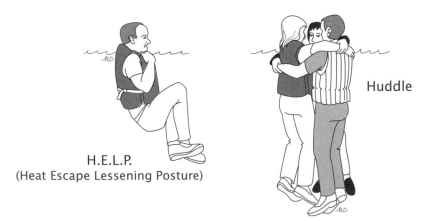

H.E.L.P.
(Heat Escape Lessening Posture)

Huddle

FIGURE 23-2. Methods for reducing the body surface area exposed to cold water

PHYSIOLOGIC LIMITATION OF HEAT LOSS

Physiologic mechanisms for limiting heat loss are largely limited to constriction of blood vessels in the skin and in the arms and legs. (Humans evolved in a tropical climate, and the body's mechanisms for increasing heat loss are much better developed than those for reducing heat loss.) Vasoconstriction reduces cutaneous blood flow, which allows the tissues to cool. Because the skin temperature is lower, less heat is lost by radiation and by convection.

As a result of their long, narrow shape, the arms and legs have a greater relative surface area than the body and tend to lose heat more readily. Narrowing of blood vessels in the extremities reduces blood flow and heat loss, and also tends to keep the heart and brain supplied with warm blood so they can function after the rest of the body has become significantly chilled.

PREVENTING HYPOTHERMIA

A human's greatest protection against the cold is his intellect. At ambient temperatures below about 82°F (28°C), an unclothed human body loses more heat to the environment than its heat-generating processes can produce and its heat-preserving mechanisms can retain. Almost everywhere they live, humans are dependent upon intellectually devised clothing and shelter to insulate them from the environment and reduce heat loss to levels for which metabolism and physiology can compensate.

Informed, intelligent behavior is even more necessary in the severe cold of high altitude and extreme latitude. Threatening situations must be recognized in time for effective countermeasures. Preparation is essential because clothing adequate for such climates can rarely be improvised. Even when available, such clothing must be worn properly. Shelter often can be improvised, but a skier with a snow shovel is far more capable of improvising a satisfactory shelter than a skier without one.

Water and Food

Avoiding hypothermia in a cold climate requires water, food, and clothing. Failure to replace normal water losses through the kidneys, skin, and lungs, or abnormal losses by other routes, results in dehydration, which decreases the blood volume and, in a cold environment, impairs heat production by exercise. Dehydration can be accompanied by weakness, fatigue, dizziness, and even a tendency to faint when standing, which impede efforts to deal with a threatening environment.

Dehydration also contributes to other problems. Constriction of peripheral blood vessels, which takes place so the smaller volume of blood goes to vital organs, increases the risk of frostbite. Severe shock may develop following minor injuries. Clots tend to form in the legs and can result in pulmonary embolism. (See chapter 10, "Respiratory Disorders.")

In a dehydrated state, the sensation of thirst is diminished or absent, and a conscious effort to consume adequate fluids must be made. With mild exertion, water intake should be at least two quarts per day. With heavier exertion or at high altitude, three to five quarts are needed. In a world of snow and ice, fuel is required to melt snow for drinking water. Eating snow does not provide an adequate volume of water, and body heat is lost in warming ingested snow to body temperature.

An adequate fluid intake is indicated by urine that has a light yellow color and a volume of at least one liter every twenty-four hours. Few outdoorsmen would measure urine volume, but they should be able to appreciate a reduced frequency for voiding, particularly the absence of a need to void after a night's sleep. They certainly can recognize the deep yellow or orange color of concentrated urine indicative of dehydration. When voiding into snow, orange "snow flowers" are an ominous sign.

Food is needed for physical activity and heat production. Eating small amounts of food at frequent intervals helps prevent depletion of energy stores during the day. Some experienced outdoorsmen seem to be munching almost continuously, and often have developed personal mixtures of nuts, dried fruits, candies, and other high-calorie food. Such mixtures are sold as "gorp" or "trail mix."

In a survival situation, experience has demonstrated that food is one of the most important ingredients of success. Any source of food, even wild animals such as birds or rodents, which may have to be eaten uncooked, is preferable to the fatigue and depression that result from not eating and that can contribute significantly to hypothermia.

Clothing

Clothing for cold climates must not only protect from the cold, it must be able to compensate for changes in environmental temperature and for heat production by exercise. The most flexible cold-weather clothing systems are composed of three layers: an inner layer (underwear); one or more middle, insulating layers; and an outer, windproof (and perhaps water-repellant) shell. The middle and outer layers can be opened or removed when environmental temperature or heat production increases. Additional insulating layers can be added as the temperature falls or the person becomes inactive.

In a multilayered clothing system, each succeeding layer must be slightly larger than the one beneath. If the layers are the same size, the outer layers compress the deeper layers and reduce their insulation value. Each layer must provide a one-quarter inch air space between it and the layer beneath.

However, the outer layer must not be too large. It must be snug enough to be warmed by the wearer's body so that its inner surface temperature does not fall to the dew point. If that occurs, moisture collects on the inner surface and wets the insulating layers, greatly reducing their effectiveness.

In a cold climate, sweating must be avoided. Sweat moistens the clothing, greatly reducing its insulation value, and more heat is lost as the perspiration evaporates. Outer layers must be opened or taken off as soon as activity begins, not after the individual has become hot and begun to perspire. These layers must be put back on or closed as soon as activity ceases, not after the individual has become cold and requires more heat to warm him again.

Clothing Materials

No third-party testing facility, such as the Underwriters' Laboratory, exists for clothing. Buyers are at the mercy of advertising agents serving the manufacturers and sellers. The most reliable indicator of a fabric's or garment's performance is its persistence in the marketplace for two or three years or more.

Effective cold-weather clothing must have two properties: insulation and permeability. Insulation is the ability of the clothing to entrap air and prevent convective heat loss. The insulating properties of a material are dependent upon its thickness and how well it inhibits the movement of air. Permeability refers to the ability of water vapor to move through the fabric. Water vapor resulting from the evaporation of sensible or insensible perspiration on the skin must be able to move through clothing to the atmosphere. If the clothing is impermeable, the vapor condenses and the clothing becomes wet.

A variety of natural materials are used in clothing for outdoor wear. Wool, cotton, silk, and goose down are the most popular. All but down are usually combined with synthetic materials such as nylon, polypropylene, polyester, and acrylics to impart specific desirable characteristics to the fabric.

Underwear

Polypropylene became popular for underwear in the 1970s. Because it is hydrophobic and allows moisture to wick from the skin surface to the surface of the fabric, where it evaporates without cooling the skin, it provides a greater sensation of warmth. Furthermore, polypropylene retains most of its insulating properties when wet. The disadvantages of polypropylene include its retention of body odors (it can become quite foul after repeated use), its tendencies to become brittle when heated and to pill when dried in a clothes dryer, and its tendency to become baggy. The last problem has been corrected to some extent by adding nylon to the fabric.

Polyester fabrics have to a large extent replaced polypropylene because, in spite of being slightly more expensive, they do not have the same disadvantages. Capilene®, Coolmax®, Thermax®, and Thermostat® are the trademarks of polyester fabrics. These fabrics keep the skin cool and dry through a wide range of activities, but to achieve this effect, these fabrics must be worn next to the skin, not over cotton underwear or as a jacket.

Wool remains an excellent fabric for underwear, but it has fallen from popularity and is difficult to find. Adding one tablespoon of olive oil to the wash water can eliminate the scratchiness that wool tends to develop after repeated washings. Some people like the feel of dry silk, but when silk becomes wet, it feels unpleasant. The fabric holds twenty-five percent of its weight in water.

Insulation

Wool is the oldest and one of the best insulating materials for cold-weather clothing. Its major disadvantage is its greater weight than pile or fleece, but it is still popular for caps and gloves. Wool is one of the few materials that maintains its insulating properties when wet. However, with prolonged wetness the inner core of wool fibers can absorb water, which makes the fabric considerably heavier. Totally drying this core requires a large amount of heat—generally extracted from the wearer's body.

Synthetic fabrics have largely replaced wool. Pile fabrics, introduced in the 1970s, are lighter and are hydrophobic. However, they tend to lose their pile and to pill badly with wear and laundering, and they have largely been replaced by fleece.

Fleece is a similar polyester fabric but with stiffer fibers than pile, and superior qualities. It is produced in different thicknesses: microfleece for underwear and 100, 200, and 300 weights for outer garments. This material breathes well, and is lightweight, durable, and fast drying. It is easy to cut and sew and has largely replaced pile as a fabric for outdoor clothing.

Goose down is the best available insulating material for its weight—when it is dry. True down is the philoplume of geese or ducks and historically was handpicked from those animals, but that material is no longer available. Down now comes from killed animals and is composed of less mature plumes that do not loft as well. However, down garments drape well, do not constrict movement, loft after compression, and are comfortable. When wet, down mats together and loses most of its insulating properties. However, when precipitation is in the form of dry snow, which is typical of high altitudes, down is the insulating material of choice.

Synthetic fibers can provide insulation similar to down and retain their insulating properties when wet. Although various materials have been tried, manufacturers currently are using a blend of three different deniers (thicknesses) to gain high loft. The disadvantages of such materials are their greater weight (about fifty percent heavier than down) and their bulk or lack of compressibility.

Mat materials are extruded, densely packed fine fibers. Because the fibers are so thin, they slightly limit radiant heat loss, but they lose this advantage when laundered. These materials resist compression and do not drape well. Thinsulate® is the dominant brand of this type of fabric, the use of which is limited largely to ski clothing.

Outer Shell

The outer shell must be windproof in order to protect the insulating qualities of the underlying clothing. Tightly woven fabrics made of synthetic fibers are most commonly used. The shell usually must be water repellant also. The ideal fabric that would allow all water vapor to pass through freely but keep out all liquid water has yet to be developed. The best available fabrics are laminates such as Gore-Tex® and urethane-coated materials, which have small pores close enough together to resist penetration by liquid water but large enough for most water vapor to pass through. Soiling limits the functionality of these fabrics.

Protecting Hands and Feet

When the body is cool, the blood vessels in the hands and feet constrict, reducing heat loss through those tissues, but also reducing their temperature and commonly causing severe discomfort. The most effective way to prevent cold extremities is to keep the body warm, a lesson some outdoor enthusiasts seem to have difficulty learning.

For the hands, mittens are much warmer than gloves. Radiant heat is lost from the surface of protective garments; the larger the surface area, the more heat that is lost. Because the fingers are such narrow cylinders, increasing the thickness of gloves by more than one-quarter inch increases the surface area to such an extent that the increased heat loss eliminates any benefit from the increased insulation. Because mittens do not have such a large relative surface area, their thickness can be increased to a much greater extent without a concomitant increase in heat loss.

The basic components of mittens are an outer shell and an insulating layer. An inner layer of a thin fabric such as nylon or silk—usually a glove—is useful if the mittens have to be removed to manipulate clothing or equipment. The outer shell should be an abrasion-resistant material, typically nylon. Wool works well for insulation, but down and synthetic materials are also used. Many different types of one-piece mittens have been developed, particularly for skiing. Many are quite expensive but are not more effective than a simple, inexpensive wool mitten with an outer nylon shell.

One of the warmest types of footgear yet devised was the U.S. Army double vapor barrier boot known as the white Korean boot. However, this type of footwear was too soft for kicking steps in hard snow and was difficult to fit with crampons. It is no longer being manufactured. For the severely cold climates typical of high altitudes, double or triple boots are best for climbers. The outer boot is usually constructed of hard, protective plastic, and the inner boots are made of softer insulating material. Older double boots were made of leather, which is entirely adequate but is heavier than plastic. Leather "breathes," which allows moisture to escape, and leather can expand to accommodate swelling of feet and ankles due to an upright position or altitude. It remains the best material for single boots in moderately cold climates.

Head Protection

The voluminous blood flow to the head is a potential source of major heat loss. In cold weather, effective headgear, such as wool caps, is essential. Balaclavas that cover the neck and lower face are desirable for severe conditions. Hoods do not fit closely enough to be as effective, but they do provide additional protection when worn over caps, at least if the hood is insulated.

An insulating scarf (usually wool) or neck gaiter reduces heat loss from the large blood vessels that are close to the skin surface in the neck.

CAUSES OF HYPOTHERMIA

Hypothermia results from inadequacies. In a wilderness environment, hypothermia results from:
- ▾ Inadequate protection from the cold
- ▾ Inadequate clothing
- ▾ Inadequate food for metabolic fuel to be burned during exercise
- ▾ Inadequate fluid intake resulting in dehydration

In an urban environment, where hypothermia is significantly more common, the causes are:
- ▾ Inadequate youth (old age)
- ▾ Inadequate money for housing, heat, clothing, and food
- ▾ Inadequate sobriety

In both situations, inadequate "smarts" is an almost universal component of the cascade of events that leads to hypothermia!

RECOGNIZING HYPOTHERMIA

Hypothermia can usefully be divided into two forms: mild and severe. A person with mild hypothermia has a body temperature that is lower than normal but is not so incapacitated that he can not stand or walk with assistance. Usually his temperature is above 90° to 92°F (32° to 33°C).

A person with severe hypothermia is intellectually impaired, usually can not walk, and may be unconscious. His body temperature is typically below 90°F (32°C), although the temperature at which such severe impairment appears varies significantly (Table 23-2).

Table 23-2	Stages of Hypothermia
MILD HYPOTHERMIA	
98°–95°F *(37°–35°C)*	Sensation of chilliness, skin numbness; minor impairment in muscular performance, particularly in fine movements with the hands; shivering begins
95°–93°F *(35°–34°C)*	More obvious incoordination and weakness; stumbling; slow pace; mild confusion and apathy
93°–90°F *(34°–32°C)*	Gross incoordination with frequent stumbling, falling, and inability to use hands; mental sluggishness with slow thought and speech; retrograde amnesia
SEVERE HYPOTHERMIA	
90°–86°F *(32°–30°C)*	Cessation of shivering; severe incoordination with stiffness and inability to walk or stand; incoherence, confusion, irrationality
86°–82°F *(30°–28°C)*	Severe muscular rigidity; semiconsciousness; dilatation of pupils; inapparent heartbeat or respirations
Below 82°F *(below 28°C)*	Unconsciousness; eventually death due to cessation of heart action at temperatures approximating 68°F (20°C) or below

Temperature is not a practical basis for recognizing severe hypothermia in the wilderness because obtaining a temperature is so difficult. Profoundly hypothermic individuals often have their jaws clamped so tightly that oral measurements are impossible. Rescue personnel uniformly refuse to try rectal measurements, particularly in a threatening environment. Such reluctance is probably fortunate, because moving a subject to take such measurements would precipitate ventricular fibrillation much of the time.

Mild Hypothermia

The key to early recognition of mild hypothermia is awareness of the risk of hypothermia and the speed with which it can develop. Even in the summer, cold, wet conditions can be dangerous, particularly when a wind is blowing. Anyone who is physically active and generating heat, but who still feels cold, must realize that he is going to become even colder when that activity ceases. If he can not produce enough heat to warm himself while exercising, he certainly can not do so when resting and must have more clothing or shelter (or an external heat source) to provide protection from the environment.

Close observation of each other by members of the group is a vital element of hypothermia prevention. Every member of a party must be responsible for observing everyone else.

Feeling cold is the most typical early symptom of hypothermia. Painfully cold hands or feet are common. As body temperature continues to fall, muscular coordination is lost. Fine movements can not be performed with the hands, but if the individual is walking and not using his hands, such loss may not be detectable. The first sign of incoordination may be slowing of pace or stumbling, particularly on rough ground or loose rocks. As hypothermia becomes more severe, stumbling becomes worse and the individual may fall. Characteristically, he lags behind, which should be an unmistakable warning for the rest of his group. If he is left unattended, subsequent deterioration in his condition will go unobserved. Shivering may further impair his ability to walk over rough terrain.

The intellect is also impaired as hypothermia develops. Personality changes, particularly irritability, are typical. A common early sign is refusal to admit that anything is wrong. Some individuals are apathetic and unconcerned about their deteriorating condition. Slow thought and speech may manifest mental sluggishness. Confusion and retrograde amnesia subsequently indicate a greater decline in body temperature.

A mnemonic for remembering the signs of mild hypothermia is "umbles." The hypothermic subject mumbles and grumbles (personality changes) and fumbles, stumbles, and tumbles (loss of coordination).

At this point, the presence of hypothermia should be obvious—unless the other members of the group are hypothermic also. Failure to institute corrective measures can result in progression to severe hypothermia.

Severe Hypothermia

Severe hypothermia should be defined by the person's condition, not by a specific body temperature. However, the signs typical of severe hypothermia usually appear when body temperature has fallen to about 90° to 92°F (32° to 33°C) or below.

Shivering usually becomes uncontrollable when body temperature has dropped to between 93° and 94°F (34°C). As the temperature drops lower, usually about 2°F (1°C) lower, shivering gradually disappears. The disappearance of shivering is considered by many to be the first sign of severe hypothermia. It should be easily recognizable.

As body temperature drops further, muscular incoordination becomes so severe that the individual can not walk without assistance. Eventually he becomes unable to stand without support.

Intellectual impairment is greater, but the impairment may be subtle. A common and important sign of severe hypothermia is neglect or carelessness about protection from the cold. Coats and pants are left unzipped; hoods are not pulled up; caps or mittens are not worn. Sleeping bags or blankets are not snug around the head; fires are neglected. Sometimes severely hypothermic individuals urinate in their pants.

Individuals who seemed to be acting quite sensibly have made gross errors in judgement that have caused problems for an entire group. A typical individual with severe hypothermia may appear to be capable of cooperating with other members of the group but does not.

Eventually, confusion and irrationality progress to incoherence, semiconsciousness, and finally total unconsciousness and a failure to respond to any stimuli. (Some writers divide severe hypothermia into moderate and severe stages, with severe hypothermia being identified by loss of consciousness. Because that division has no practical value for wilderness situations, it is not used in this discussion.)

As an individual begins to lose consciousness, he may develop a sensation of extreme warmth and, if unattended, actually remove his clothing or climb out of a sleeping bag. Such bizarre behavior is not uncommon, and its occurrence in urban surroundings may arouse suspicion that the person has been assaulted, particularly if the person is female. Sometimes the individual's clothing has been neatly folded, an unlikely occurrence during an assault. Although the reason for such behavior is not really known, one proposed cause is dilatation of the blood vessels in the skin, which produces a sensation of warmth that prompts the semicomatose person to disrobe or climb out of his sleeping bag. The diversion of blood flow from the brain to the skin by the cutaneous vasodilatation is probably the last straw that drops the person into complete unconsciousness

As a severely hypothermic individual's condition deteriorates, his body functions slow drastically. A comatose subject's breathing may be so slow and shallow that it appears absent. His heart rate also slows dramatically and can become so weak that it can not be palpated.

Unquestionably, a number of individuals with severe hypothermia who were actually still alive have been pronounced dead and denied medical assistance. In the wilderness, few hypothermic individuals should be declared dead unless their measured body temperature has fallen to environmental levels. Only after unsuccessful rewarming can death be certain.

No one should be considered cold and dead until he has been warm and dead!

TREATING MILD HYPOTHERMIA

Recognizing mild hypothermia is critical. Its treatment is simple—all those things your mother told you to do when you went outside in the cold. Effective measures decrease heat loss and increase heat production.

Decreasing heat loss by convection can be achieved by putting on more clothing: sweaters, caps, mittens, jackets, parkas, windpants, or whatever is available. Protection from the wind by parkas or windpants, rocks or trees, natural shelters such as caves or even crevasses, or manmade shelters such as cabins or snow caves reduces convective heat loss, or "wind chill." Replacing wet clothing with dry clothing restores insulation and reduces evaporative heat loss. The warmer environment provided by a fire—or just body heat within a windproof shelter—reduces radiant heat loss.

Heat production can be increased significantly. Shivering is an involuntary muscle activity that generates heat at a rate equivalent to walking fast. Much more heat can be generated by vigorously exercising the large muscles in the legs and back. Such exercise is even more useful if it helps a hypothermic person get out of a hostile environment. However, if escape from the predicament is not possible, "purposeless" exercise, such as repeatedly stepping up onto a stone or log, can generate heat. A metabolic energy source—food—is needed if increased heat production is to be maintained.

Heat-producing exercise can not be continued indefinitely. Nor can enough heat be produced by exercise to compensate for the large quantity of heat lost in cold water or in a snowstorm if the individual is inadequately protected.

Once hypothermia has been corrected, measures to prevent its recurrence are essential. Obviously, a rewarmed person must not be returned to the environment in which he became hypothermic with no additional protection. Hypothermia would probably recur faster because his energy stores would be depleted.

TREATING SEVERE HYPOTHERMIA

Severe hypothermia is a complex disorder for which the simple measures that effectively treat mild hypothermia are inadequate because severely hypothermic subjects can not generate enough heat to rewarm themselves. An external heat source must be provided. In addition, ventricular fibrillation must be avoided while the individual is being rewarmed.

Ventricular Fibrillation

Ventricular fibrillation is a life-threatening condition in which the thousands of muscle fibers that make up the heart contract independently. Because all of the muscle fibers must contract together for the cardiac chambers to squeeze out blood, no blood is pumped when the fibers are not synchronized. The effect would be the same if the heart were not beating at all.

The hypothermic heart is extremely prone to ventricular fibrillation. It has appropriately been compared to a mousetrap, ready to snap with the slightest bump or jolt—often without a recognizable precipitating event. Individuals have begun fibrillating in hospital emergency rooms even though the possibility of that event was well recognized and every effort to avoid it was being made.

Severely hypothermic individuals can not be placed in a basket stretcher and carried out of the wilderness. The unavoidable jarring and bouncing associated with evacuation over rough terrain almost inevitably provokes fibrillation. Although profound hypothermia prolongs the time an individual can survive the absence of effective blood circulation without sustaining significant neurologic damage, that time is limited to one hour or slightly longer.

Rescuers must realize that a severely hypothermic individual in ventricular fibrillation who can not be evacuated by helicopter, or in less than an hour by stretcher, is usually in a hopeless situation. He must receive cardiopulmonary resuscitation (CPR) to avoid neurologic damage, but CPR can not be administered while he is being carried on a stretcher. Cardioversion (defibrillation with electrical shocks) is almost never effective until the heart has been warmed to about 90°F (32°C). In a situation threatened by hazardous weather, avalanche, or other danger, rescue leaders may be achieving the greatest benefit by extracting their team and—although difficult—abandoning the unfortunate hypothermia victim.

Individuals with severe hypothermia in the wilderness must either be evacuated by helicopter or rewarmed on the spot. Leaders of major rescue organizations have realized that essentially none of the severely hypothermic individuals carried out of the wilderness by hand without rewarming have survived. They now try to rewarm such individuals where they are found.

Rewarming

Severely hypothermic persons require external heat sources for rewarming because their metabolism is so slow they can not generate enough heat to rewarm themselves, even if completely protected from the environment.

Theoretically, the most effective rewarming methods would rewarm the core of the body first—"central rewarming." Because the heart would be among the first tissues rewarmed, it would be protected from fibrillation. In hospitals, central rewarming can be achieved with heated peritoneal or pleural dialysis fluids, heated gastric lavage, or heart-lung machines for individuals without effective cardiac function.

However, experience has demonstrated that central rewarming is not essential for most individuals who have functioning hearts. Many hospitals in which hypothermia is a common problem, which includes those in most northern and high altitude U.S. cities, rely primarily on external rewarming with forced heated air (the Bair Hugger device). Heated, humidified aerosols may provide some central rewarming, but the amount of heat transported by such systems is miniscule.

The development of wilderness rewarming techniques has met with only limited success. Three general procedures are currently followed:

▼ Protection from the environment
▼ External rewarming
▼ Central rewarming

When an individual who is severely hypothermic, particularly one who is stuporous, is first found, he should not be allowed to move. To minimize the risk of ventricular fibrillation, he should not be allowed to sit up or even roll over unassisted. If the individual is in water, he should be passively removed as gently as possible. If he is covered with snow, the snow should be brushed away with as little movement of the person as possible.

The person should be examined briefly to establish a diagnosis of hypothermia and to ensure injuries that need treatment are identified.

If shelter is available, the person should be moved into it—carried in a flat or prone position if possible to avoid pooling of blood in the lower portion of the body as the result of cardiovascular instability. If the shelter is a tent, it should be pitched at a site that minimizes the distance the individual must be transported. Snow caves are warmer. The shelter can be warmed with heated stones or similar objects. A gasoline stove should not be lighted inside the shelter unless it is well ventilated. Carbon monoxide accumulates in poorly ventilated structures when gasoline stoves are burning.

An ideal way to heat a well-ventilated structure is to boil water. The increased humidity reduces heat loss by evaporation from the respiratory tract.

Wet clothing should be removed, cut off if necessary to avoid moving the subject. If no dry clothing is available, the wet clothing should be wrung out and replaced. Some fabrics, particularly wool, pile, or fleece, and garments filled with man-made fibers such as polyesters, retain much of their insulating capabilities when wet. Saturated down-filled garments are almost worthless.

The hypothermic individual should be insulated from the ground, snow, or whatever surface he is lying on. Insulating pads are ideal, but clothing, leaves, grass, boughs from evergreen trees, newspaper, whatever is available can be used.

The person must be protected from the environment—low temperature, wind, and wetness—as well as possible. Sleeping bags and insulating clothing are ideal. Anything available can be used. Constricting clothing, particularly boots, should be loosened (but not removed) to reduce the risk of frostbite.

A fire can be built if materials are available (the person is below the tree line). A reflector placed behind the fire directs more heat to the individual being treated.

No effective methods for field rewarming are available in most remote areas. Putting a severely hypothermic individual in a sleeping bag is not adequate because sleeping bags only insulate; they do not generate heat. Heated stones, hot water bottles, even another individual in the sleeping bag add only a minimal amount of heat, not nearly enough to rewarm a person who is cold enough to be unconscious.

External rewarming transfers so little heat that all available techniques must be employed. Folded sheets or blankets soaked in hot water and placed in plastic bags, hot water bottles, or similar warming devices placed along the sides of the neck, chest, and abdomen and in the inguinal areas, where the body wall is thin, is one of the more effective methods. (Obviously, if enough warming instruments are available, they can be placed anywhere.)

Placing a normothermic individual in the sleeping bag with a hypothermic person transfers only a minimal amount of heat through body-to-body contact.

Central rewarming can also be achieved in a wilderness situation, but it requires specific equipment and individuals familiar with the techniques. The methods are simple, and cold-weather rescue teams should include individuals proficient with them.

The most widely used method employs heated air saturated with water vapor. The quantity of heat carried by the air is minimal, because so little heat is required to raise the temperature of air (Fig. 23-3). Furthermore, the depth and rate of respirations are greatly reduced with severe hypothermia, and the volume of inhaled air is less than half of normal. However, physicians who have used this system consider the benefits greater than can be explained by the small amount of heat the system is capable of transferring.

The air must be saturated with water, or the evaporation of water from the respiratory tract would extract more heat from the body than the heated air could supply. Most of the heat transferred to the body results from condensation of the water vapor. In a cold wilderness environment, a heated aerosol also eliminates the small heat loss from the respiratory tract.

Emergency technicians may be able to insert an endotracheal tube and ventilate the individual at a normal volume of five to six liters per minute, which would increase the heat gain. However, the tubing must be modified to increase "dead space" and carbon dioxide retention in order to avoid severe respiratory alkalosis, which also predisposes to ventricular fibrillation. At altitudes above 10,000 feet (3,000 m), heated, humidified oxygen may be more useful.

Severely hypothermic individuals are inevitably dehydrated, and all benefit from correction of the dehydration. Because most are unable to ingest fluids orally, rehydration fluids must be given intravenously. However, the peripheral veins of a dehydrated, severely hypothermic person are collapsed, and accessing a vein is quite difficult, even for experienced individuals.

Administration of heated intravenous fluids has been suggested as a means of rewarming. However, four liters of fluids heated to 104°F (40°C) and administered over a period of two hours to an individual with a temperature of 77°F (25°C) could not transfer more than 60 Kcal of heat per hour to the subject. That would raise the body temperature of a 176 lb (80 kg) individual less than 1°C per hour. More fluids would result in fluid overload and must not be given. At subfreezing temperatures, more heat would be lost by radiation to the environment. The subject would benefit more from evacuation to a warm shelter.

Gastric lavage, introducing heated fluids through a tube inserted into the stomach and replacing the fluids as they cool, is a technique for central rewarming that has been employed in hospitals. Because this technique is simple and is associated with little risk of significant complications, it could be adapted for use outside of the hospital.

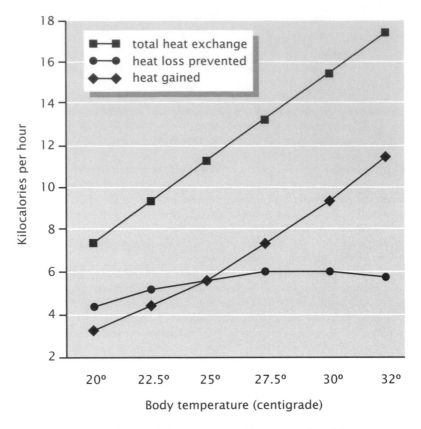

FIGURE 23-3. Maximum calculated heat exchange (heat gained and heat loss prevented) from inhaling a humidified aerosol heated to 104°F (40°C) at an environmental temperature of 5°F (-15°C). Actual heat exchange would be lower. (Respiratory tidal volume assumed to be 2.0 l/min at core temperatures of 20°C, 22.5°C, 25°C, 27.5°C, 30°C, and 32.5°C.)

In a hospital, severely hypothermic individuals being rewarmed with noninvasive techniques increase their temperature at a rate of 0.9° to 2.7°F (0.5° to 1.5°C) per hour. In the wilderness, rewarming would be slower. Rescuers must be prepared to spend many hours—perhaps one or more days—rewarming a person before moving him. Stoves and abundant fuel for heating water must be available so heating devices can be renewed as they cool.

Cardiopulmonary Resuscitation

CPR is essential for profoundly hypothermic subjects who have no effective blood circulation, and who can survive for only about an hour without sustaining significant neurologic damage, particularly when evacuation is prolonged. However, the probability of success is so limited that risks to rescuers or other members of the party can not be justified. CPR should be initiated in the wilderness only by a team of experienced individuals in a safe, relatively protected environment. If a hostile environment poses a major threat to the team, CPR should be postponed or abandoned entirely.

Individuals with a detectable heartbeat, no matter how slow, should not receive CPR or assisted ventilation because ventricular fibrillation would almost certainly result. Three minutes or longer should be spent trying to detect a carotid pulse before assuming that a severely hypothermic person has no effective cardiac activity.

A portable electrocardiograph (ECG) monitor to detect cardiac activity in subjects with severe hypothermia may be necessary, and rescue groups should probably carry such units. (In a wilderness environment, portable ECG monitors can not be relied upon for distinguishing between abnormalities such as asystole, ventricular fibrillation, or baseline artifacts, but they do reliably indicate the presence of a heartbeat by portraying QRS complexes.) Hypothermic subjects with a functioning heart commonly have a reduced blood pressure, and blood pressure determination may be further hindered by the absence of the Korotkoff sounds used to measure pressure.

CPR should be given at one-half the usual rate to severely hypothermic persons. Such individuals have such a slow metabolism that they need limited amounts of oxygen and are producing little carbon dioxide. A slower rate of ventilation avoids excessive carbon dioxide loss and respiratory alkalosis. A slower rate of cardiac compression also provides a longer interval for the heart to be filled with blood by the slow circulation.

CPR should be instituted immediately following a witnessed cardiac arrest or fibrillation, particularly when transportation to a hospital is expected to require more than a few minutes. CPR probably should be administered for individuals with unwitnessed cardiac arrest who appear to be resuscitatable, but each situation is unique, and more definitive recommendations are not possible. CPR should not be initiated if the subject can be transported to a hospital in minutes.

CPR should not be initiated for fibrillating hypothermic subjects considered unsuitable for resuscitation due to their situation, or for individuals with extremely low body temperature, associated severe illness or injuries, a noncompressible chest, prolonged cardiac inactivity, or drowning with more than one hour of witnessed submersion.

The role of drugs in preventing fibrillation is unclear; perhaps no role exists. Anecdotal evidence indicates that lidocaine is not effective at body temperatures below 90°F (32°C). Other agents have not been evaluated.

FROSTBITE

Frostbite is a cold injury produced by freezing of the tissues. The hands and feet, the ears, and the face, particularly the tip of the nose, are most commonly injured. The hands and feet are farthest from the heart, and their blood supply is further reduced by vascular constriction when the body is cold. The ears are thin and have a meager blood supply; the rims are often frozen. Portions of the face, particularly the tip of the nose, are often exposed.

Constriction of blood vessels in the extremities to conserve heat for the central portion of the body can be so rigorous that circulation to those areas almost ceases. Cold also damages the endothelial cells that line blood vessels, causing plasma to leak through their walls. Loss of plasma causes the blood to sludge inside the vessels, further impairing circulation.

As the circulation is diminished, the tissues begin to freeze. Ice crystals form within and between the cells and grow by extracting water from the cells. However, freezing does not necessarily kill cells. In laboratories, cells frozen for long periods of time can be thawed and grown in cultures.

The ultimate damage from frostbite results from the damage to vascular endothelial cells. When the tissues are warmed, blood exposed to these damaged cells clots and completely obstructs the circulation. The result is identical to the effects of thrombosis in arteriosclerotic arteries—the tissue supplied by that artery dies (is infarcted).

Prevention

Frostbite can occur in any environment in which the temperature is below freezing, but it is commonly associated with hypothermia. When a contributing condition can be identified, it is usually impaired circulation. Immobility contributes to impairment of the circulation, particularly in soldiers under fire in wartime or in substance abusers, but boots that are too tight or encircling, tightly fitting garments are common offenders.

On rare occasions, frostbite can result from unprotected contact with cold metal or liquids, most commonly gasoline or ethyl alcohol, that remain liquid at temperatures far below the freezing temperature of water.

Avoiding the conditions by which it is produced, particularly hypothermia, is the best way to prevent frostbite. Clothing that keeps the trunk warm also keeps the extremities warm by eliminating the need for blood vessel constriction to preserve heat. "If your feet are cold, put on a sweater" is a time-proven adage. Also essential is footgear that does not constrict the circulation, such as white Korean ("Mickey Mouse") boots.

Cigarette smoking constricts the blood vessels in the skin and aggravates local cold injuries such as frostbite.

Diagnosis and Prognosis

The early signs of frostbite are cold, pain, and pallor of the affected tissues. Some individuals suffer little pain. Pain disappears as the tissues begin to freeze, a highly significant warning sign. As freezing progresses, the tissues become even whiter, all sensation is lost, and the tissues become quite hard. With extensive frostbite, such as that affecting an entire hand or foot, the tissues often have a dull purple color.

Frostbite of the face, tip of the nose, or ears can be recognized by pain and pallor of the affected tissues.

The extent and severity of frostbite are notoriously difficult to judge accurately while the tissues are still frozen or immediately after thawing. However, a few hours after thawing, prognostic signs begin to appear. Minor frostbite ("frostnip") that involves only the tips of the fingers or toes, the tip of the nose, or small areas of the face or ears produces redness and swelling that lasts for a few days but leaves no permanent damage.

With more severe injuries, blisters develop after rewarming and may cover entire digits (Figs. 23-4 and 23-5). If the blisters contain clear fluid and extend to the tips of the digits, the underlying tissues can be expected to recover. If the blisters do not extend to the tips of the digits, the unblistered tissues are usually lost. When the blisters are filled with bloody fluid, much of the underlying tissues can not recover. The most severe frostbite injuries are not followed by blisters and retain a deep purple color.

After a week to ten days, the dead, frostbitten tissues develop a thick black covering called an "eschar." Eventually, usually after four to six weeks, the dead tissue, including entire fingers or toes, separates spontaneously.

Treatment

The preferred treatment for frostbite is rapid rewarming in a water bath. However, opportunities for such therapy are rare because most frostbite injuries have thawed before the individual arrives at a site where rewarming can be performed. Climbers or cross-country skiers usually have to be evacuated before they can be rewarmed, and thawing of the frostbitten tissues during evacuation often is unavoidable. Individuals with urban frostbite, who greatly outnumber those with wilderness frostbite, delay an average of twelve hours before seeking medical care.

Rewarming can best be carried out in a hospital, where the person can be kept warm and supplies for rewarming and later care are available. Treatment in a wilderness environment should be attempted only when the following conditions can be met:

▼ The person does not need to use the frostbitten extremity until healing is complete. Specifically, he does not need to walk on a foot that has been frostbitten and thawed. The greatest damage from frostbite occurs when frozen tissues are thawed and refrozen. Walking on a frozen foot produces far less damage.

▼ The person can be kept warm during rewarming and afterward for as long as recovery requires. If the person's body is cold, the blood vessels in his extremities will be constricted. Rewarming

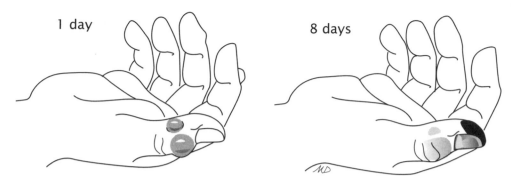

FIGURE 23-4. Frostbite of the thumb and fingertips one and eight days after injury

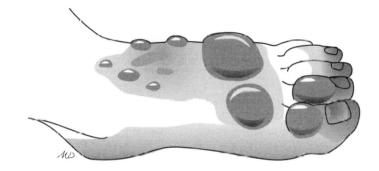

FIGURE 23-5. Frostbite of the feet manifested by blisters that do not reach the tips of the toes

in such circumstances leaves badly injured tissues without an adequate blood supply at the time it is most needed.

▾ Adequate facilities for prompt rewarming, including abundant supplies of warm water and accurate methods for maintaining the temperature of the rewarming bath, are available.

Even though the frostbitten extremity has thawed, rewarming probably still has beneficial effects if administered within twenty-four hours of injury. After longer intervals, rapid rewarming is of little value.

During rewarming, the water temperature should be maintained between 100° and 108°F (38° and 42°C). Higher temperatures damage the tissues. The water must not feel uncomfortable to an uninjured person's hand. A large water bath permits more accurate temperature control and warms the frozen extremity more rapidly, often resulting in less tissue loss, particularly when freezing has been deep and extensive.

The extremity should be stripped of all clothing and any constricting bands, straps, or other objects that might impair the circulation. The injured member should be suspended in the center of the water bath and not permitted to rest against the side or bottom.

During rewarming, hot water must be added to the bath periodically to keep the temperature at the desired level. (A frozen hand or foot is essentially a block of ice and cools the water.) The injured extremity should be removed from the bath and not returned until the water has been thoroughly mixed and the temperature measured.

An open flame should not be used to keep the water bath warm. The frostbitten extremity may come in contact with the heated area and be seriously burned because sensation in the tissues has been lost.

Warming usually requires thirty to sixty minutes; it should be continued until the tissues are soft and pliable, or until no further changes in color are seen.

During rewarming, the frostbitten tissues usually are quite painful. Strong analgesics may be needed during or after rewarming.

Following rewarming, the individual must be kept warm and the injured tissues must be elevated and protected from any kind of trauma or irritation. A framework should support bedclothes to avoid pressure or rubbing on the injured area. To avoid infection, blisters should not be ruptured.

The subject should be evacuated immediately. Healing requires weeks to months, depending upon the severity of the injury. Subsequent care in the field should be directed primarily toward preventing infection. Cleanliness of the frostbitten area is extremely important. Soaking the extremity in disinfected, lukewarm water to which a germicidal soap has been added may be helpful. A small amount of dry, sterile cotton or gauze should be placed between fingers or toes to avoid maceration. Antibiotics should not be given routinely, but if infection appears to be present, amoxicillin/clavulanate, a cephalosporin, or cloxacillin should be administered every six hours until a physician's care is obtained.

Smoking should be strictly avoided because it reduces the already deficient blood supply to the damaged area. Movement of the extremities should be encouraged but should be limited to movements that can be carried out without manipulation or assistance from others. Most individuals with frostbite need continuing reassurance and emotional support.

Surgery has little or no role in the immediate therapy of frostbite. Unfortunately, some surgeons with no experience with this injury are so alarmed by the appearance of frostbitten extremities that they insist upon immediate amputation. Tragic mutilations have occurred. Many individuals have refused amputation and recovered with minimal or no tissue loss.

With essentially no exceptions, surgery must be delayed until demarcation of the dead tissues is complete and unmistakable. At that time, surgical debridement of infected eschars or incision of constricting eschars that completely surround a digit and are obstructing circulation may be needed. However, surgery is usually not required until six to eight weeks after the initial injury, and then only to complete amputation of frostbitten tissues or to reconstruct hands or feet.

Individuals who have suffered frostbite have increased sensitivity to cold and are more susceptible to cold injury because the blood vessels in the injured tissues have been permanently damaged.

TRENCH FOOT

Trench foot is a nonfreezing cold injury that is almost always a military problem. In the 1982 Falkland Islands fighting, approximately fourteen percent (70 of 516) of the hospitalized British battle casualties had trench foot. Only soldiers with the most severe injuries were hospitalized; estimates of the number with lesser injuries ranged as high as 2,000.

Trench foot results from wetness and cold that is uninterrupted for days or weeks. The feet do not have to be immersed in water; simply being wet produces the condition. Symptoms rarely appear in less than four or five days, and even then only in severely cold, windy weather—as was encountered in the Falklands.

The disorder was first clearly described during the Napoleonic campaigns, particularly during the retreat from Moscow, but it received its name during World War I from the men who spent weeks with their feet in the cold water that flooded the trenches. The British had more than 115,000 casualties from trench foot and frostbite in that conflict. Similar injuries in individuals who spent weeks with their feet in cold water in rafts or lifeboats after their ships had been sunk or their aircraft had crashed led to the name "immersion foot." Other names exist, but trench foot is the most clearly and widely recognized.

The cold induces intense vasoconstriction, which deprives the feet of an adequate blood supply. (The separate roles of cold and poor circulation in producing injury have not been distinguished.)

After five to seven days (or longer), the feet become red, swollen, and quite painful. British soldiers with trench foot in the Falklands screamed in pain when putting their boots on in the morning (but stormed into battle anyway!).

Treatment is simple. It consists of keeping the subject warm with his feet dry, elevated, and protected from bedclothes. Nothing more. Nerve damage can cause persistent pain so severe that amputation is required, but such injuries are rare. The British had no immediate amputations in the Falklands. Sensitivity to cold is usually lifelong and can disqualify troops for continued military service.

Prevention of trench foot is also simple. World War I commanders ordered their troops to dry their feet and put on dry socks every day, which reduced their trench foot casualties to very low numbers, even though the men were returned immediately to flooded trenches.

Outdoorsmen, particularly participants in water-based activities, must be aware of the potential for injury in wet, nonfreezing weather. They must carry dry socks and must take time to dry their feet, change their socks, and dry their boots. They should encounter many fewer distractions while attending to such precautions than do soldiers in combat.

CHAPTER 24 HEAT AND SOLAR INJURIES

Heat injuries are more common in urban situations than in the wilderness. Many are related to poverty that prevents access to cool (air-conditioned) environments. The outcome of severe heat illness, particularly heat stroke, often is death or permanent disability. Avoidance of heat illness requires recognition of the circumstances in which it occurs and familiarity with the measures that can prevent it.

Solar injuries are all too common, particularly in societies that consider suntan an essential element of physical attractiveness.

HEAT ILLNESS

Normal Heat Loss

Normal human body temperature is maintained within a narrow range by sensitive temperature control centers in the hypothalamus. Heat produced within the body is dissipated to the environment so that a temperature between 97° and 100°F (36° and 38°C) is maintained.

Largely through muscular activity, most individuals generate 2,000 to 5,000 kilocalories (Kcal) of heat per day, depending upon their size, physical activity, and state of nutrition. The body must get rid of this heat to prevent a devastating increase in temperature. If no heat were lost, the body temperature of a sedentary individual weighing 154 lb (70 kg) producing only 2,000 Kcal per day would climb approximately 62°F (34°C) to 160°F (71.4°C) in twenty-four hours. (The temperature would climb at that rate as long as he was alive!)

Humans lose heat largely through their skin. The lungs are the principal route of heat loss (panting) for hairy animals, and at high altitudes deeper, more rapid breathing of cold, relatively dry air causes significant heat loss in humans, but in temperate or hot climates much less heat is lost through the lungs. The skin acts much like the radiator of a liquid-cooled engine. Blood is warmed as it passes through exercising muscles and cooled as it circulates through the skin. The thermostat on an engine increases the flow of coolant through the radiator when the engine is hot; comparable mechanisms increase blood flow to the skin by dilating cutaneous blood vessels when exercise heats the body.

The radiator for an engine is cooled only by air passing over it. Heat is lost from the skin in this way also (convection), but in a hot climate by far the largest heat loss is through evaporation of perspiration. Evaporative cooling is highly effective because a large amount of heat is required to change water from a liquid to a vapor. The evaporation of one cubic centimeter (1 cc) of water at a skin temperature of 95°F (35°C) requires 577 calories, enough to reduce the temperature of one liter (1,000 cc) of water approximately by 1°F (or 577 cc of water by 1°C). Most of this heat is extracted from the body.

Evaporative cooling is limited because the maximal sweating rate for individuals not acclimatized to heat is about 1,500 cc per hour. Evaporation of that much perspiration would eliminate the heat produced by running six miles at a pace of ten minutes per mile, which is not a particularly fast pace. Acclimatization takes about one week, results in an increased tolerance for exercise in a hot environment, and is produced by mechanisms that increase the maximum sweating rate but reduce salt loss. Water deprivation does not accelerate or otherwise contribute to the acclimatization process.

Exertional and Nonexertional Heat Illness

Heat illness results from the inability of the body to get rid of heat it has produced. Two distinct disorders have been identified. Exertional heat illness results from an increase in heat production so great that all of the heat can not be dissipated even though the heat-losing mechanisms are functioning well. Nonexertional heat illness results from impairment of heat-losing processes by disease and can occur even though heat production is low or normal. Heat illnesses occurring in healthy individuals participating in vigorous wilderness activities are essentially all the result of exertion, and nonexertional heat illness is not considered in this discussion.

A fever raises body temperature by resetting the "thermostat" at a higher level. Fever can be controlled with drugs such as aspirin, ibuprofen, or acetaminophen. Such drugs have no effect upon the elevated temperature associated with heat illness because the thermostat has not been changed. Only heat production has changed.

Preventing Exertional Heat Illness

The only way exertional heat injuries can be prevented is by recognizing climatic conditions in which heat can not be dissipated and sharply curtailing physical activity. Those conditions are easily defined: an environmental temperature of 95°F (35°C) or higher and a high relative humidity.

The average skin temperature is 95°F (35°C), slightly lower than core temperature. At environmental temperatures above this level, heat can not be lost by convection because the air temperature is higher than skin temperature. Heat can not be lost by radiation because the environment is hotter than the skin surface. (Heat would be gained by radiation.) The only way heat can be lost in such circumstances is by evaporation. (Mechanisms of heat loss are described in chapter 23, "Cold Injuries.")

At a high relative humidity evaporation is greatly diminished, and heat can not be lost by that route. **In humid conditions at temperatures greater than 95°F (35°C), heat can not be lost effectively by any route!** In the southeastern United States, where hot, humid conditions are common in the summer, experienced residents know that a man dripping with perspiration is in danger of heat illness. If perspiration were evaporating and cooling him, it would not accumulate on his skin.

To avoid heat illness in such circumstances, heat production must be reduced to the lowest possible level. Vigorous exercise must cease. In tropical areas, where temperatures and humidity are usually high, the midday siesta is a sensible way to minimize the risk of heat illness during the time when the threat is greatest.

In past years, the most frequent causes of exertional hyperthermia in the United States have been distance running (including jogging) and football practice in late summer, which combines vigorous physical activity, a uniform that inhibits evaporation of sweat, and a hot, often humid environment. Recognition of the hazard associated with these activities has led to scheduling such events in early morning, when temperatures are lower. Wearing plastic or rubberized suits while exercising in order to lose weight is another dangerous practice. Such suits increase body temperature, sometimes to high levels, because they do not allow perspiration to evaporate. Fortunately, this practice also has been largely abandoned in recent years, probably more from the realization that only water—not fat—was being lost than recognition of the danger of heat illness.

Individuals taking certain therapeutic drugs also have an increased risk of heat illness. Anticholinergic drugs taken for peptic ulcer, irritable bowel syndrome, and other disorders impair sweating. Any of the many diuretics used to treat hypertension and heart failure can lead to dehydration. The phenothiazine tranquilizers such as prochlorperazine (Compazine®) and chlorpromazine (Thorazine®) interfere with central nervous system temperature control. Individuals taking these and other medications must be particularly cautious in hot environments.

Water Replacement

Staggering quantities of water must be consumed to replace perspiration losses in desert conditions. During 1964 U.S. Army maneuvers in the deserts of southern California, for which daytime temperatures of 100° to 110°F (38° to 43°C) were expected, participants were required to drink eight quarts of water every day. Not a single case of heat illness occurred, which was considered almost miraculous at the time. Israeli soldiers operating in the Sinai Desert during the 1967 war with Egypt were allotted ten liters of water a day and had no heat illnesses, which were punishable by court martial in that army. The Egyptians, who received only three liters a day, suffered numerous fatalities due to heat illness.

Thirst alone does not ensure an adequate fluid intake. Individuals must make a conscious effort to consume the quantities needed. During desert operations, military commanders are held responsible for ensuring that their men meet the daily intake requirements. An augmented salt intake has been considered essential for preventing heat illness in the past. Soldiers in the California desert were required to take three to five grams of salt—six to ten tablets—every day. That recommendation was abandoned because the diet of residents of most industrialized nations was thought to contain enough salt for stressful heat conditions. However, the pendulum appears to be swinging in the other direction, and a generous salt intake appears to be advisable.

Heat Syncope and Heat Exhaustion

Heat illnesses range in severity from very mild to lethal. Typical patterns of illness have been given specific names, but the types of heat injury must be recognized as different manifestations of the same basic disorder. Mild heat illnesses have the potential for becoming severe and must be treated with care.

Heat syncope and heat exhaustion are similar, relatively mild forms of heat illness to which dehydration contributes significantly. In an effort to increase heat loss, the blood vessels in the skin dilate to such an extent that the blood supply to the brain is diminished. Reduction in blood volume by dehydration contributes to the lower cerebral blood flow. The result is a disorder essentially identical to ordinary fainting (syncope) except for its cause. Initially, the victim feels faint and is usually aware of a rapid heart rate. Nausea, vomiting, headache, dizziness, restlessness, and even brief loss of consciousness are not uncommon. The presence of sweating and the skin color are variable.

Some investigators have separated these two disorders on the basis of body temperature, which is normal with syncope but elevated to 102° to 104°F (39° to 40°C) with heat exhaustion. No sharp division between heat exhaustion and heat stroke is possible. Some physicians consider anyone with an elevated temperature and evidence of brain dysfunction, such as dizziness or brief unconsciousness, to have heat stroke, which may be wise in view of the dire consequences of that disorder.

Heat syncope should be treated in the same manner as fainting. If the individual recognizes preliminary symptoms, he should lie down, or at least sit down, to avoid injury. If lying down, his feet should be elevated. A cooler environment is desirable; the subject should at least be protected from direct sunlight. He should be given fluids, particularly fluids containing salt, and should not engage in vigorous activity for at least the rest of that day. Only after he has completely restored his body fluids and has a normal urine output should he cautiously resume exercise in a hot environment.

An individual with heat exhaustion should be treated in the same way, but his body temperature must be closely monitored. If his temperature is above 104°F (40°C), or continues to climb after he has been taken out of the sun and is at rest, he should be actively cooled. Victims of heat exhaustion have an even greater fluid deficit that must be corrected. Such persons must be very careful about resuming physical activity and probably should be examined by a physician beforehand.

Heat Stroke

Heat stroke (also called "sunstroke") is the most severe form of heat illness. Fatalities are common, as are permanent residual disabilities. The onset typically is very rapid and is characterized by changes in mental function. Confusion and irrational behavior are most frequent, but incoordination, delirium, and unconsciousness often follow. Convulsions occur commonly. The pupils may be dilated and unresponsive to light.

The rectal temperature is almost always above 104°F (40°C) and is commonly above 107°F (42°C), which is the upper limit for most clinical thermometers. A rectal thermometer reading to 113°F (45°C) is usually needed to measure the temperature of heat stroke victims. It would not be carried unless severe heat stress had been anticipated, in which case effective preventive measures should have been instituted. If the temperature is not measured for some time after the onset of the illness, it may have fallen.

The skin feels hot. If the victim has been actively exercising, he is usually covered with perspiration at the time he collapses. Later he may have dried, particularly if cooling has been instituted. The hot, dry skin long associated with heat stroke is typical of individuals with the abnormal heat loss that accompanies nonexertional heat illness, not those with exertional heat illness. However, sweating does decrease during exercise and can fall to quite small volumes, particularly when exercise has been prolonged and the individual has become dehydrated.

Both pulse and respiratory rates are increased. Shock is usually present.

Cooling should be instituted as rapidly as possible. Heat stroke is one of the few true medical emergencies in which a delay of only a few minutes may significantly alter the outcome. If the patient is unconscious, an open airway must be maintained. Shock should be treated by elevating the feet and by any other methods that are feasible.

The individual should be moved to the coolest spot possible; he must be shaded from sunlight. To cool persons with heat stroke in hospital emergency rooms, their clothing is removed, they are covered with wet sheets, and large fans are placed to blow directly across their body from two directions. In the wilderness, similar methods should be devised. Clothing should be soaked with water. If the clothing is removed or is scanty, the extremities and trunk should be covered with wet towels or similar fabric and the body should be fanned to increase air circulation and evaporation. Immersion in water would be useful. Any reasonable method for cooling the victim should be employed.

In a wilderness environment that produced heat stroke, ice or snow would not be available. In an urban environment, they probably should not be used. A heat stroke victim should be cooled by evaporation. Alcohol sponging should not be used. Isopropyl alcohol may be absorbed through the skin, particularly by children, and is toxic.

During cooling, the extremities should be massaged to help propel cooled blood back into the organs of the body and head. Oxygen should be administered if available.

After the temperature has been reduced to 102°F (39°C), active cooling should be slowed to avoid hypothermia, but the patient must be closely monitored to ensure that his temperature does not climb back to higher levels. Rebound is particularly common three to four hours after cooling. Drugs do not effectively reduce body temperature, may aggravate complications, and should not be administered.

As soon as possible, the victim should be evacuated to a hospital, particularly if he has been unconscious for more than a few minutes. The complications of heat stroke include failure of essentially every organ system—particularly the heart, liver, and kidneys. Blood clotting abnormalities, gastrointestinal ulceration with bleeding, biochemical alterations, and extensive brain damage also occur. Unconsciousness of more than two hours' duration is an indicator of a poor prognosis that is usually followed by permanent disability or death.

Heat Cramps

Heat cramps are severe, spasmodic contractions of one or more muscles, most commonly the leg muscles. Cramps may last up to fifteen minutes or even longer, and the muscles are usually painful for several days afterward.

Stretching the muscle usually can stop cramps almost immediately. For example, extending the leg and pulling the foot upward can stretch the calf muscle. Kneading or pounding the muscle is less effective and probably contributes to the residual soreness.

Cramps usually appear in the most heavily worked muscles and may be produced, in part, by an excessive water intake without accompanying salt, resulting in dilution of the salt in the extracellular fluid. Cramps are more common in circumstances that tend to cause salt depletion; they can be prevented to a large extent by consuming large quantities of salt and water.

INJURY BY SOLAR RADIATION

Sunlight has been considered beneficial because it plays a significant role in vitamin D synthesis. However, questions about that assumption are being raised. Some investigators argue that all sun exposure is harmful, not just excessive exposure, because DNA can be damaged by any amount of ultraviolet radiation. Everyone is familiar with sunburn, but many individuals are not as well aware of—or choose to ignore—the degenerative changes associated with repeated exposure that eventually lead to cancer. Three hundred thousand new skin cancers are diagnosed every year in the United States, and the incidence is increasing.

Melanoma is the most aggressive form of skin cancer, and the incidence of this malignancy has almost tripled in the last four decades, a faster increase than any other malignant tumor. Approximately 32,000 new cases and 7,000 deaths from melanoma occur annually in the United States. This tumor has become the most common cancer in Caucasians between ages twenty-five and twenty-nine. Sunlight is the most significant environmental element causing this tumor. Intermittent exposure, particularly early in life, appears to increase risk more than cumulative exposure. Three or more episodes of blistering sunburn during childhood or adolescence predispose individuals to melanoma.

Much of the energy in solar radiation has shorter (ultraviolet) or longer (infrared) wavelengths than visible light. Most biologic damage is caused by ultraviolet radiation, which has wavelengths less than 400 nanometers (nm) (1 centimeter = 10^7 nanometers = 10^8 angstroms). Ultraviolet (UV) radiation is divided into UVA, which has a wavelength of 315 to 400 nm, and UVB, which has a wavelength of 280 to 315 nm (Fig. 24-1). For many years, only UVB was considered to be harmful, but that is now known to be incorrect.

Even when a person is shielded from the direct rays of the sun, much ultraviolet radiation can still reach him due to atmospheric scattering. This "sky radiation" may contribute half of the total ultraviolet radiation and tends to be greater when high, thin cirrus clouds are present. Indeed, total ultraviolet radiation can be greater on an overcast day than on a cloudless day. Such radiation is particularly insidious because it is so inapparent.

Ultraviolet exposure at high altitudes is greater than at sea level because the atmosphere is thinner and filters out less sunlight, particularly in the harmful wavelengths. The rate of increase is four percent per 1,000 feet (300 m). Snowfields and glaciers reflect about seventy-five percent of the incident ultraviolet radiation; in a cirque or bowl, reflection can increase the radiation even more. Individuals participating in water sports are exposed to direct radiation and large quantities (up to 100 percent) of reflected radiation. High altitude sail boarding can result in great ultraviolet exposures.

Sensitivity to Sunlight

Individuals vary widely in their sensitivity to sunlight. Redheads are particularly sensitive. Blue-eyed blondes are more susceptible to sunburn than brunettes. Individuals of northern European ancestry are more sensitive than Mediterranean, Indian, African, and other peoples whose skin contains more protective pigment (melanin). Children are more susceptible than adults.

Sensitivity to sunlight may be increased by wide a variety of drugs, such as sulfonamides and their derivatives (trimethoprim-sulfamethoxazole); oral antidiabetic agents; the phenothiazine tranquilizers (Thorazine®, Compazine®, Phenergan®, and Sparine®); thiazide diuretics (Diuril®); most tetracyclines, particularly doxycycline (Vibramycin®), which may been used to prevent traveler's diarrhea; and the barbiturates. Many other substances such as biothionol, which is used in soaps; many first aid creams and cosmetics; green soap; many plants and grasses such as fig leaf, certain meadow grasses, wild parsnip, celery, and others; dyes used in lipstick; and coal tar or coal tar derivatives increase sensitivity to sunlight.

Ultraviolet A and Ultraviolet B

UVA makes up ninety-five percent of all solar ultraviolet radiation and varies less with altitude and time of day than UVB. UVA increases pigmentation and increases the thickness of the outer layer

SPECTRAL DISTRIBUTION OF SUNLIGHT

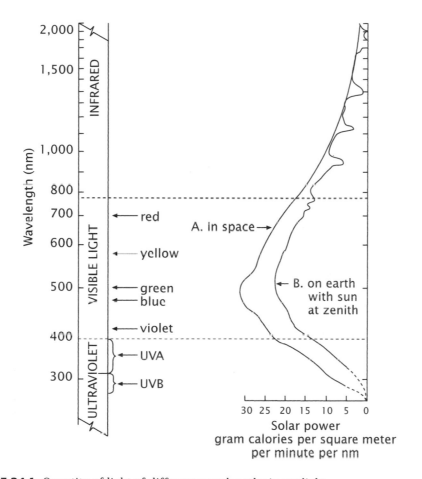

FIGURE 24-1. Quantity of light of different wavelengths in sunlight

of the skin, producing a suntan that is protective because the pigment and the thickened skin reduce the penetration of ultraviolet radiation. UVA penetrates the skin more deeply than UVB and potentiates the changes produced by UVB. UVA damages the elastic fibers in the skin and is primarily responsible for such aging changes as wrinkling.

UVB, although it makes up only five percent of all solar ultraviolet radiation and penetrates less deeply than UVA, is the major cause of sunburn and of skin cancer. This type of ultraviolet radiation damages the DNA in skin cells, which ultimately leads to malignancy.

Sunburn

Mildly excessive exposure to UVB produces redness (due to dilatation of cutaneous blood vessels) and slight swelling and induration. Greater exposure causes pain and blistering. Severe burns may be associated with chills, fever, or headache. Sunburn of the lips is often followed by painful herpes simplex infections ("fever blisters" or "cold sores").

Gradually increasing exposure to sunlight permits natural tanning and thickening of the skin and helps avoid sunburn, although sunscreens should still be applied. For many redheads, and some other light-skinned individuals, adequate tanning is impossible. Such persons may benefit from the use of trioxsalen (Trisoralen®), but this is a potent drug that must be taken only under the close supervision of a physician, preferably a dermatologist.

The sun protection factor (SPF) is a value that indicates how much longer an individual can tolerate direct sunlight when protected by a sunscreen than with no protection. When protected by a sunscreen with an SPF of 12, a person whose skin would begin to turn red after five minutes of unprotected sun exposure could stay in the sun for twelve times longer, or sixty minutes, before his skin would begin to redden.

Clothing is protective against UVB, but the level of protection is dependent upon how tightly the fabric is woven. If the fabric is held up to a light bulb and images can be seen through it, the SPF is less than 15. If light gets through but no images, the SPF is 15 to 50. If no light comes through, the SPF is greater than 50. If the fabric is wet, it does not provide as much protection. Clothing made from sun-protective fabric can be purchased from Sun Precautions, 2815 Wetmore Avenue, Everett, WA 98201, 800-882-7860, *www.sunprecautions.com.* Hats with wide brims (three inches or wider) provide protection of the face and neck. Baseball-style caps protect only the forehead, or only the back of the neck if worn backward.

Protective creams or lotions that contain sunscreens are the typical methods for protecting exposed skin from sunlight. They should be applied liberally and frequently. Most individuals do not use enough—about one ounce a day—nor do they apply screens as often as needed—every one to two hours. The face and neck should be carefully protected because they are essentially always exposed. The nose, cheeks, neck, and ears are most frequently sunburned. The lower surfaces of the nose and chin are commonly burned by reflected radiation.

Larger and more frequent applications are needed when sweating and after immersion in water, and wiping the neck and face tends to remove the preparation. Sunscreens labeled "water-resistant" are effective after forty minutes or less of immersion. Products labeled "waterproof" are effective after eighty minutes of immersion. No products resist immersion indefinitely.

The earliest chemical sunscreen, para-aminobenzoic acid (PABA), was introduced in the 1970s. It caused contact dermatitis (see chapter 20, "Allergies"), particularly in young children; was water soluble and short lasting; and stained clothing. It is rarely used now. Cinnamates or salicylates, which are highly water insoluble, are used in most currently available preparations, even though they cause sensitivity reactions.

Price has little relation to the effectiveness of sunscreens. Investigators for Consumers Union, publisher of *Consumer Reports,* found equally effective adult sunscreens to range in price from $0.66 to $4.28 per ounce.

Most of the day's UVB radiation is received during the four hours in the middle of the day, and protection from solar injury is particularly needed during this interval—the time when a person's shadow is shorter than his height. Protection from UVA is needed during essentially all hours of sunlight.

Protective agents that block out all ultraviolet radiation contain opaque pigments such as titanium dioxide (A-Fil®) or zinc oxide (Zincofax Cream®). Red Veterinary Petrolatum® is also effective. Such agents should be used on the nose, lips, and ears, which are easily sunburned and are not covered by clothing. (Products containing benzophenones, such as Uval® and Solbar®, also screen out all ultraviolet radiation but were developed primarily for individuals with skin diseases that require complete protection. These agents are easily removed by sweating and are not suitable for protection during recreational sun exposure.)

Treating Sunburn

If prevention has been neglected or has been inadequate, application of cold, wet dressings soaked in a boric acid solution (one teaspoon per quart of water) or a one to fifty solution of aluminum acetate may relieve discomfort. Soothing creams may be helpful if swelling is not severe. Anesthetic sprays or ointments are effective but can produce significant allergic reactions. Steroid preparations, such as 0.25 percent hydrocortisone ointment or an aerosol containing prednisolone, help reduce inflammation and may reduce pain if applied early. However, steroid preparations probably slow healing and repair, may increase susceptibility to infection, and must be used sparingly. Extensive or unusually severe sunburn must be treated as a second-degree burn.

Skin Cancer

Repeated sun exposure over a period of many years, even for individuals who are darkly pigmented, produces degenerative skin changes that are cosmetically unattractive and commonly lead to cancer. Degenerative skin changes are particularly likely in persons who spend much time in intense sunlight, such as ski patrol, lifeguards, and white-water rafting guides. Tanning clearly provides incomplete protection.

Individuals who spend much of their time in sunlight must reduce the severity of such changes by conscientiously applying sunscreens whenever they are exposed, regardless of the risk of sunburn. However, the best protection is clothing, particularly long-sleeved shirts and wide-brimmed hats that shade the face.

Snow Blindness

The surface of the eye (cornea and conjunctiva) absorbs ultraviolet radiation just like the skin. Excessive exposure can result in sunburn of these tissues, producing snow blindness (photophthalmia). Any source of ultraviolet radiation—the sun, ultraviolet lamps, and electric welding equipment—may produce photophthalmia. During the period of exposure, no sensation other than the intensity of the light serves to warn the victim.

Symptoms may not develop until eight to twelve hours later. The eyes feel irritated or dry at first, but as symptoms progress, they feel as though they are full of sand. Moving or blinking the eyes becomes extremely painful. Even exposure to light may cause pain. Swelling of the eyelids, redness of the eyes, and excessive tearing occur. A severe case of snow blindness may be disabling for several days and may even lead to ulceration of the cornea, permanently damaging the eye.

Preventing Snow Blindness

Snow blindness can and should be prevented by consistently wearing protective goggles or sunglasses. Any lens transmitting less than ten percent of the erythemal band of sunlight (below 320 nm) is satisfactory. Glasses should be large and curved or have side covers to block the reflected light coming from below and from the sides. When ultraviolet radiation exposure is high, as it would be on a concave high altitude snowfield, goggles are safer, even though they may be less comfortable and tend to fog. If only glasses are available, a sunscreen should be applied to the eyelids to prevent burning. Spare goggles or glasses should be carried, but emergency lenses can be made of cardboard with a thin slit or pinhole to see through. The eyes may be alternately covered so that only one eye at a time is exposed to the sunlight.

Eye protection is just as necessary on a cloudy or overcast day as it is in full sunlight. Snow blindness can occur during a snowstorm if the cloud cover is thin.

Treating Snow Blindness

Snow blindness heals spontaneously in a few days. The pain, which may be quite severe, may be relieved temporarily by cold compresses and a dark environment. Early and frequent (hourly) applications of an ophthalmic preparation containing an anti-inflammatory steroid help relieve the pain, lessen the inflammatory reaction, and shorten the course of the illness. The person must not rub his eyes. Local anesthetics should not be employed because they rapidly lose their effectiveness and may lead to damage of the delicate corneal surface.

CHAPTER 25

ANIMAL BITES AND STINGS

All animal bites are associated with a high risk of serious infection. The mouths of all animals—including humans—contain innumerable bacteria, many of which are introduced into the wound when a bite is inflicted. Human bites tend to produce particularly virulent infections.

All bite wounds should be treated as contaminated soft-tissue injuries. They must be washed copiously with soap and water, and an antimicrobial agent such as benzalkonium chloride or povidone-iodine should be applied. Under no circumstances should the wound be sutured. It must be left open, covered with a sterile dressing, and watched closely for signs of infection.

Because the mouths of animals contain so many bacteria, treatment for tetanus (toxoid injection) should be administered if the individual has not had a recent booster.

RABIES

Rabies is a catastrophic viral infection that has been known and justifiably feared since antiquity. In all of history, only four humans who have developed clinical rabies are known to have survived. All four were vaccination failures, and two had severe residual neurologic damage. (One was blind and quadriplegic.) Although rare in industrialized nations, rabies remains a scourge in developing countries that can not afford the canine vaccination programs required to keep the infection under control. In India, twenty-five thousand to fifty thousand people die every year from rabies. The incidence is probably similar in Africa (Ethiopia, for example, has a high incidence of rabies), but surveillance and reporting is so inadequate that the true rate is unknown. At the beginning of the twenty-first century, rabies ranks eleventh among infectious causes of death worldwide.

Rabies within the United States

In the United States, human rabies has been controlled by vaccinating domestic animals, mostly dogs and cats, and eliminating stray animals. Dog rabies diminished from 5,688 cases in 1953 to 95 cases in 1986. Human rabies has concomitantly declined from approximately 350 cases in the 1940s to ten cases in the1980s, seven of which were acquired outside the United States. Two of the other three were of bat origin, and the third was from a skunk. From 1990 through 2000, twenty-six rabies infections were acquired in the United States. All but two were caused by rabies virus strains associated with bats (Fig. 25-1).

Essentially all mammals are susceptible to rabies and capable of transmitting the infection, but transmission by rodents has not been documented. The United States and Canada are unique in that rabies epizootics are recognized in a number of wild animals: raccoons, skunks, foxes, and bats. Bat rabies is endemic in all areas of the continental United States, both urban and rural, including Alaska (Fig. 25-2).

An epizootic in raccoons that began in the late 1970s has spread to involve the entire East Coast (Fig. 25-3). No human rabies infections have resulted from this epizootic, although extensive vaccination programs have been required after humans contacted animals infected with the raccoon virus. A coyote and gray fox epizootic in southern Texas was originated by unvaccinated dogs from Mexico. It spread to Texas dogs and resulted in two human rabies deaths (one in 1991 and one in 1994). Thousands of humans had to be vaccinated. This epizootic has been controlled by dropping bait containing vaccine from aircraft, the largest program of this type ever carried out.

FIGURE 25-1. Human rabies acquired from bats, 1980–2000 (26 cases total)

FIGURE 25-2. Rabies in bats, 1998 (989 cases total)

Transmission of Rabies

In an infected animal, the rabies virus travels through nerves from the central nervous system to the salivary glands and is present in the saliva. Transmission of the infection occurs when a wound is contaminated with the saliva of a rabid animal. The virus can not penetrate intact skin but can pass through an intact mucous membrane such as the lining of the mouth, nose, or eyelids. Licking alone can transmit the infection. The average incubation period between the time of the bite

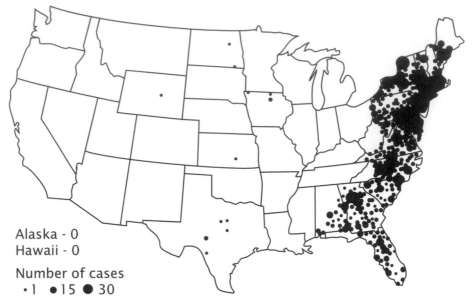

FIGURE 25-3. Rabies in raccoons, 1998 (2,872 cases total)

and the appearance of a clinically evident infection is thirty-five days. (Approximately one percent of human rabies infections have an incubation period of one year or more.) The virus travels along nerves at a relatively constant speed to reach the brain. As a result, bites on the extremities allow more time for treatment than bites about the face, which are particularly dangerous and must be treated urgently.

The manner in which bat rabies is transmitted to humans is unknown. Only two of the twenty-six individuals infected by rabies viruses originating in bats had a clear history of a bite by a bat, but many of the infections were diagnosed after death or so late in the course of the illness that the individuals could not be questioned. Infection has been transmitted by breathing aerosolized rabies virus in a medical laboratory and in Frio Cave near Uvalde, Texas, which is inhabited by huge numbers of bats, many of which are rabid.

Treating a Bite by a Rabid Animal

The treatment for rabies, known as immunoprophylaxis, is a race to develop protective immunity before clinical infection appears. Treatment must be initiated as soon as possible after the bite is inflicted. Therapy begun after the subject begins to show signs of rabies is ineffective.

The treatment of any animal bite has three components:

▾ Diagnosis of rabies in the attacking animal
▾ Treatment of the bite wound
▾ Immunotherapy

In the United States, if the attacking animal is a domestic dog, cat, or ferret that has been vaccinated for rabies within the past year and can be captured, it should be confined under observation for ten days following the bite. If the animal is healthy at the end of that time, it is safe to assume the animal did not have transmissible rabies at the time the bite was inflicted, and immunotherapy is not required.

All other animals, including wolf hybrids, should be killed and their heads shipped under refrigeration to a laboratory where the brain can be examined to determine whether rabies virus is present. Public health services are responsible for maintaining reliable laboratories and for transporting the heads.

If the animal can not be killed or captured, or if the encounter occurs in a developing country, the animal must be assumed to be rabid regardless of the manner in which it was behaving or whether it has been vaccinated. Rabies in animals follows a highly variable course. The notorious "mad dog" foaming at the mouth is almost never seen. Unprovoked attacks are the most common indication of rabies.

The behavior associated with rabies by animals other than dogs, cats, and ferrets is not well known. Occasionally the only sign of rabies is the absence of fear of humans, which may even appear to be a show of friendliness. Animals such as skunks, which usually scurry away from any threatening situation, may actually pursue humans. Because rabid behavior is not known, quarantining such animals for ten days is not a reliable way to determine whether they are infected.

The only exceptions to this caveat would be those few areas where rabies does not occur. Hawaii, for example, is free of all forms of wildlife rabies. (All animals brought into the islands are quarantined, regardless of their vaccination history, to prevent the introduction of this infection.)

Cleansing of the bite wound is just as vital as administration of immune globulin and vaccine in the care for persons exposed to rabies. The severity and speed of onset of any infection is dependent upon the number of viruses or bacteria introduced. Rinsing saliva out of a bite wound reduces the number of rabies viruses that can enter the tissues, slows the onset of infection, and provides time for vaccination to be effective.

Washing should be done with large quantities of soap and water, and the wound subsequently should be flushed with benzalkonium chloride or povidone-iodine. Washing is of such urgency that it should be instituted without delay. Someone else should catch or kill the attacking animal. If soap and water are not available, anything on hand—even a favorite whiskey—should be used.

Immunotherapy for rabies consists of administering serum from an individual or animal already immune to rabies—rabies immune globulin—followed by vaccine to build up immunity to the rabies virus. The immune globulin provides passive immunization while the body is building active immunity in response to the vaccine. In the United States, only immune globulin of human origin is licensed. In developing nations, usually only equine (horse) globulin is available.

Twenty international units per kilogram of body weight (20 IU/kg; 2.2 lb = 1 kg) of rabies immune globulin of human origin (or 40 IU/kg for equine globulin) should be injected around the wound. If a single bite is on a finger or toe, as much globulin as possible should be infiltrated immediately around the wound and the rest as closely as possible in the tissues of the hand or foot. (Infiltration of large volumes of globulin into a finger is painful.) If multiple wounds are present, the globulin can be diluted with saline and injected around all of the wounds. (Additional globulin should not be given because it interferes with active immunization by vaccine.) Epinephrine to treat an anaphylactic reaction should be available, but such reactions are rare.

Following an exposure, one milliliter (1 cc) of rabies vaccine should be injected into the deltoid muscle on the day of the bite (day zero) and on days three, seven, fourteen, and twenty-eight. The injections must be made into the deltoid (shoulder) muscle (or the anterior thigh for small children). Rabies has developed following gluteal (buttock) injections because the vaccine is not absorbed well from this site.

The rabies vaccine most widely used in the United States is human diploid cell vaccine (HDCV), which is prepared from viruses grown on human diploid fibroblast cell cultures and is largely free of the serious side effects that were common with older vaccines. Rabies vaccine absorbed (RVA), which is prepared on fetal rhesus monkey lung cell diploid cultures, is just as effective but has not been as widely available. In 1997, the Food and Drug Administration (FDA) licensed another vaccine, purified chick embryo vaccine (PCEV), for use in the United States. This vaccine has been used in other countries for many years and is equally safe and effective. PCEV does not contain albumen, as HDCV does, and may cause fewer allergic reactions.

Because a few cases of human rabies develop following prolonged incubation periods (at least two cases developed after six years), postexposure therapy should be administered regardless of how much time has elapsed.

Bat Exposures

Because the manner in which rabies is transmitted by bats is essentially unknown, the following four measures are recommended:

▼ Dwellings should be "bat-proofed" by carefully covering all possible entrances, particularly roof ventilation openings, with wire screens. Protection from bats in unscreened dwellings or when sleeping outdoors can be achieved with mosquito netting.

▼ Contact with bats should be assiduously avoided, particularly bats that are behaving unusually. Bats are nocturnal, and any activity during daylight hours should be considered abnormal. Diseased bats often are unable to fly. Bats should be caught with nets; disabled bats should be scooped into a container. These animals must never be picked up or handled with unprotected hands.

▼ Anyone who has contact with a bat, regardless of whether a bite is thought to have been inflicted, should receive postexposure prophylactic therapy unless the bat can be caught and tested for rabies.

▼ Anyone, particularly a child, who awakens from sleep and finds a bat in his room should receive postexposure prophylaxis, unless the bat can be caught and tested for rabies. (Tennis rackets are useful for capturing bats. Injuring the animal is not a consideration because they must be killed to examine their brains for rabies.)

The problem of rabies transmission by bats is best addressed through education. Reducing the bat population is not an acceptable approach, is probably impossible, and would almost certainly be an ecological disaster because bats play such a major role in insect control.

Rabies in Developing Countries

Any bite or contact with saliva from any animal in a developing country should be considered an exposure to rabies, regardless of the animal's vaccination history. The vast majority of such exposures are to dogs, although in a study from Nepal ten of fifty-one bites were inflicted by monkeys leaping for food held by tourists visiting the Swayambunath Temple.

Individuals exposed to rabies while visiting developing countries can not depend upon local physicians or institutions for reliable treatment. In many areas, vaccine prepared from infected animal brains is used to immunize individuals exposed to rabid animals because it is inexpensive. This vaccine has been described as the "crudest" biological preparation administered to humans. It varies considerably in its potency and effectiveness and probably is not effective for severe exposures with multiple bites about the head and neck. Twenty-four injections are required and are quite painful, and the vaccine is associated with a high incidence of side effects, a number of which are disastrous. Vaccination should be refused unless the recipient is certain the preparation is a cell-culture vaccine. (Essentially all such vaccines are reliable.)

The amount of rabies immune globulin being produced worldwide is estimated to be about one-third the quantity needed for treating all individuals exposed to rabies. In developing countries, immune globulin is rarely administered. Travelers to those countries treated in local facilities are not given immune globulin unless they know enough about rabies postexposure therapy to insist upon its administration.

If a reliable source of therapy, such as the CIWEC Clinic in Kathmandu, Nepal, or the Queen Saovabha Memorial Institute in Bangkok, Thailand, is not available, U.S. citizens exposed to rabies should go immediately to the nearest American embassy. These embassies have physicians on their staffs or available to them and are required to be able to obtain reliable vaccine within twenty-four hours or less. (Citizens should not allow themselves to be turned away by uninformed personnel.) In addition, the embassies of Canada and Great Britain have usually welcomed the opportunity to assist citizens of the United States in an emergency.

Human Preexposure Rabies Vaccination

Human preexposure rabies vaccination consists of three intramuscular injections of 1 cc of vaccine on days zero, seven, and twenty-one or twenty-eight. In 1987 the FDA approved vaccinations with only 0.1 cc of vaccine intradermally on the same schedule. (The volume injected is one-tenth that administered intramuscularly.) However, the antibody level produced by intradermal injections is not as high, and does not last as long, as that produced by intramuscular injections. Some authorities recommend that only intramuscular injections be administered.

If a vaccinated individual subsequently has contact with a rabid animal, he still must be treated with vaccine. However, rabies immune globulin is not needed, and only two vaccine injections (1 cc injected into the deltoid muscle) on day zero and day three after exposure are required. The duration of therapy is much shorter, but at a time when rabies immune globulin may be difficult or impossible to find in many areas, eliminating the need for immune globulin may be a more significant consideration.

The Centers for Disease Control and Prevention (CDC) divides individuals at risk of developing rabies into three groups. Group I has the highest risk and consists of rabies laboratory workers. Group II has a lower but significant risk and includes spelunkers, as well as veterinarians, animal control workers, and fish and game wardens in areas of high rabies incidence. For these individuals, the CDC recommends vaccination and serologic testing or boosters every two years.

Group III, which has a definite but still lower risk, includes travelers to areas with a high incidence of rabies, veterinarians and animal control workers in areas of low rabies incidence, and veterinary students. For these individuals, the CDC recommends vaccination without subsequent serologic testing or boosters.

Reliability of Rabies Postexposure Therapy

In its 1992 report, the World Health Organization Expert Committee on Rabies made this remarkable statement: "Prompt and thorough cleansing of the wound, and administration of purified equine or human rabies immunoglobulins and cell-culture rabies vaccine immediately after exposure virtually guarantee complete protection." The report also stated that "pregnancy and infancy are never contraindications to post-exposure rabies vaccination."[1] Recent investigations indicate that immunosuppression, including human immunodeficiency virus (HIV) infection and acquired immunodeficiency syndrome (AIDS), is also not a contraindication.

POISONOUS SNAKE BITES

Poisonous snake bites are unquestionably serious, potentially deadly accidents. Nonetheless, the danger from a single bite has been greatly exaggerated, particularly in the United States, where an average of less than fifteen people die each year as the result of bites by poisonous snakes and half of those have refused therapy. Less than one percent of poisonous snake bites in this country are lethal. In other parts of the world, where many snakes have much more toxic venom and sophisticated medical care is not available, poisonous snake bites are a more serious problem.

Worldwide, the treatment of poisonous snake bites remains a subject of controversy and confusion. (Even the material used to treat snake bites is referred to in the English literature as antivenom, antivenin, or antivenene.) No venom is injected in approximately twenty-five percent of poisonous snake bites (reportedly eighty percent of king cobra bites). In another twenty-five percent, envenomation is mild. Individuals with such bites recover regardless of how they are treated (unless they are killed by the therapy). In addition, many nonpoisonous snakes are incorrectly identified as venomous. Recovery by these individuals following many types of therapy, some of which—such as electric shock—seem bizarre, has led to acceptance of such treatment as beneficial. A sensationalist press has aided the wide dissemination of misinformation.

Families of Poisonous Snakes

The world's poisonous snakes have been divided into three groups. Within the family *Elapidae* are the North American coral snakes (eastern, western, and Sonoran), the Indian krait found in India and Pakistan, the tiger snake of Australia, the death adder of Australia and New Guinea, the Indian king cobra (which occurs in most of Southeast Asia, including Indonesia and Formosa, and reportedly is responsible for more deaths than any other species), the mamba of East Africa, and the ringhals of South Africa.

The subfamily *Viperinae* of the family *Viperidae* includes the puff adder, found in most of Africa and southern Arabia; the saw-scaled viper, which ranges from northern and western Africa to northern India; the Palestine viper of the Middle East; and the Russell's viper, found from West Pakistan to Formosa. No members of this family are found in North or South America.

The subfamily *Crotalinae* of the family *Viperidae* are of major importance in North and South America. They include all of the North American rattlesnakes, as well as the copperheads and cottonmouth moccasins, the fer-de-lance and neotropical rattlesnakes found from Mexico to Argentina, and the bushmaster found from Costa Rica to the Amazon River basin. Also in this family are the habu, which occurs in the Ryukyu Islands of Japan, and closely related species in Formosa and the southeastern part of the People's Republic of China.

Identification of Poisonous Snakes of the United States

The poisonous snakes of the United States are the rattlesnakes, the copperheads and cottonmouth or water moccasin, and the coral snakes. In the United States, poisonous snakes, except the coral snakes, are pit vipers and have a characteristic triangular head and heavy body. The body markings are rarely sufficiently unique for species identification by inexperienced individuals.

These snakes are called "pit vipers" because they have a small pit located between the eye and the nostril—a feature found only in these poisonous species—that is an infrared sensing organ instrumental in detecting the small, warm-blooded animals that these snakes eat (Fig. 25-4). The pit vipers are also characterized by single scales reaching across the undersurface of the body posterior to the anus. Most other snakes have double scales (Fig. 25-5).

If fangs are present, a snake is undoubtedly poisonous, but searching for fangs is hazardous. The fangs may be folded back against the roof of the mouth, which makes them difficult to identify. One or both fangs may be broken off; three or four are occasionally found. Rattles are of obvious significance, but the absence of rattles is not, because the rattle may be broken off. The Catalina Island rattlesnake sheds its rattle with its skin and never has more than one.

Coral snakes are small, thin, brightly colored snakes with small heads and are quite different from the pit vipers. Adjacent red and yellow bands identify them. The nonpoisonous king snakes and other harmless species with similar coloration have adjacent red and black bands. A helpful mnemonic is: **"Red and yellow—kill a fellow. Red and black—venom lack."**

Vipers have large heads and heavy bodies and tend to resemble pit vipers, but they lack pits. Elapids from other parts of the world do not at all resemble their American counterparts. Elapids have small heads and thin bodies like the coral snakes, but few have such brilliant coloring. Except for a few species with distinctive hoods (mostly cobras), they have an appearance similar to many nonpoisonous snakes. The poisonous snakes of Australia, including the innocent-sounding brown snake and the more appropriately named death adder and tiger snake, are elapids. Many of the poisonous snakes of Africa, including the notorious black mamba, are elapids. To individuals accustomed to the heavy-bodied American crotalids or pit vipers, these snakes appear harmless, but their venoms are vicious. Travelers who are not knowledgeable should avoid all snakes in areas inhabited by these reptiles.

Snake Venoms

The venoms of all poisonous snakes contain similar toxins. To classify snakes according to a single target for their toxin is misleading and can result in inadequate medical therapy.

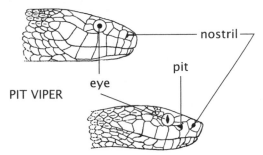

NONPOISONOUS

nostril

pit

eye

PIT VIPER

FIGURE 25-4. Comparison of the heads of pit vipers and nonpoisonous snakes

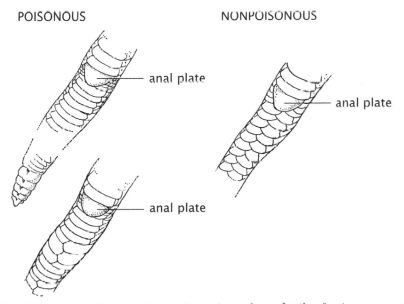

POISONOUS

NONPOISONOUS

anal plate

anal plate

anal plate

FIGURE 25-5. Comparison of the scales on the undersurface of tails of poisonous and nonpoisonous snakes

Vascular toxins damage the walls of blood vessels and inhibit blood clotting. The combination of the two results in bleeding into the tissues at the site of the bite, as well as spontaneous bleeding from the gums, nose, or gastrointestinal tract. The damaged blood vessels allow proteins and fluid to leak into the tissues, which produces swelling at the point where the bite occurs. Such fluid loss in combination with the destruction of red blood cells and blood proteins reduces the circulating blood volume and leads to shock, a consistent feature of severe envenomation by snakes of all species.

The ultimate effect of the neurotoxins is paralysis, most importantly respiratory paralysis. However, abnormal sensations such as tingling or prickly feelings and partial paralysis of the eyelids are more common. Although pit vipers have been described as having predominantly hemolytic toxins, characteristic early symptoms following the bites of some rattlesnakes are numbness and tingling of the lips and a metallic taste, both of which result from the effects of the toxin on neural tissues.

Crotalid venoms do tend to have higher concentrations of hemolytic toxins; elapid and viperine toxins tend to have higher concentrations of neurotoxins. However, more than a dozen different venom components have been identified. Different species within the same family have venoms of different composition.

Venom concentrations also vary. Some, like that of the copperhead, are rather weak, while others, like that of the Mojave rattlesnake, are concentrated and quite potent. Additionally, larger snakes are able to inject a larger volume of venom than smaller snakes. The concentration of the venom, the concentrations of its individual components, and its total volume are different in the same snake at different times of the year.

Because the venom of a copperhead is so mild, persons bitten by these snakes require little more than supportive therapy. Antivenom is almost never needed for adults bitten by a single snake. In a compilation of more than 400 copperhead bites in eastern North Carolina, only two deaths could be found. In both instances, the unfortunate individuals had been bitten simultaneously about the head by three or more snakes.

In contrast, the eastern diamondback rattlesnake, a large species, produces a venom that is only moderately toxic, but the volume is so great that bites by this snake require vigorous treatment. In the United States, this species is responsible for more poisonous snake bite deaths than any other. Most of the bites occur in Florida.

The Mojave rattlesnake is small but has very potent venom with a high concentration of neurotoxins. The effects of envenomation by this species tend to be delayed, may not become fully apparent until twelve hours after the bite, and may be much more severe than indicated by the initial reaction.

Diagnosis of Envenomation

Although identifying the species of snake inflicting a bite is desirable, it is not essential. In the United States, catching or killing the snake is not advisable because the risks are greater than the benefits. In some areas of the world, broad-spectrum antiserum is not available (for some species it is not effective), and specific antiserum must be administered. If the snake can not be precisely identified, specific therapy may be impossible.

Inspecting the bite occasionally helps in determining that the snake is poisonous. Typically, the fangs of a pit viper produce two small puncture marks, which are a reliable indication that the snake was a member of this family. However, characteristic fang marks are distinctly uncommon. The target is usually moving, and the snake's strike is rarely accurate. Only one fang may strike, or the fangs may only graze or scratch the skin. The snake may have had one fang broken off. Some snakes have three or even four fangs. The fang marks may be hidden among the marks from the other teeth if the snake has embedded its fangs so deeply that the other teeth have also penetrated the skin. Although only the fangs have entered the skin, a U-shaped row of teeth marks from the bottom jaw may be present.

Even though an attacking snake can be positively identified as poisonous, the individual it has bitten does not require specific treatment unless envenomation has occurred (venom has been injected). Poisonous snakes attack humans in sheer terror, not for food. Sometimes snakes strike without opening their mouths or extending their fangs. Occasionally venom is only sprayed on the surface of the skin. Even when the fangs pierce the skin, no venom or only a very small quantity is injected in approximately twenty-five percent of the bites by poisonous snakes occurring in the United States. Reportedly, for king cobra and sea snake bites, the incidence of nonenvenomation is about eighty percent, but reliable data are probably not available.

If the subject has been bitten but not envenomated, the bite should be treated like any other animal bite. It must be thoroughly cleaned. Because the wound is a puncture wound, bleeding should be encouraged and tetanus prophylaxis should be administered.

Crotalid Envenomation

The reaction following the bite of a crotalid (pit viper) is one of the best indications that the snake was poisonous, and is the only indication that envenomation has occurred and treatment may be needed. This reaction begins within minutes after the bite. It is usually severe following an eastern diamondback rattlesnake bite but may be less marked after other pit viper bites. The reaction may be deceptively mild following the bite of a Mojave rattlesnake and almost nonexistent after a massagua or pygmy rattlesnake bite.

The earliest symptom is pain or burning at the site of the bite, although some people experience relatively little pain. Shortly afterward, the area begins to swell as fluid pours out into the tissues. Bleeding usually produces a purple or green discoloration, but this change may take several hours to appear.

If no further symptoms develop, the envenomation is mild and antiserum therapy is rarely needed. However, the individual should be taken to a hospital, even though he has only a mild reaction. Evidence of more severe envenomation may take several hours to develop.

Following moderate envenomation, the swelling and discoloration extend further from the site of the bite, large blisters that contain clear or bloody fluid appear, and the regional lymph nodes, particularly in the armpit or the inguinal crease, become enlarged and tender. Numbness or a tingling sensation about the mouth or tongue, sometimes extending into the scalp or involving the fingers and toes, and often associated with a metallic or rubbery taste, commonly follows the bite of eastern diamondback and some western rattlesnakes and is an indication of moderate envenomation.

Severe envenomation is heralded by systemic reactions. The subject becomes weak and dizzy and develops signs of shock, particularly cold and clammy skin and a weak pulse.

Prehospital Care for Crotalid Bites

Most of the poisonous snake bites within the United States occur in situations where hospitalization is less than two hours away. The average interval between bite and hospitalization has been reported to be thirty-five minutes. When a subject can be hospitalized in such a short time, the only treatment needed is limiting the spread of the venom and immobilizing the extremity.

Tourniquets have been recommended to help reduce spread of the venom, but if applied incorrectly they can do more harm than good. Tourniquets that obstruct the flow of arterial blood are too painful to be tolerated by a conscious person for more than a few minutes. If left on for an hour or more they can cause gangrene.

A properly applied tourniquet should only obstruct lymphatic flow. The tourniquet should be made from a band at least one inch wide and should not be so tight that a finger can not be inserted beneath it without difficulty. Thin rubber straps, such as those used to obstruct the venous circulation while drawing blood, are considered ideal and should be applied in the same manner.

Wrapping the bitten extremity snugly and immobilizing it with a splint is a technique devised for inhibiting the spread of venom from Australian elapids. This procedure is not recommended for crotalid bites. Most bites by crotalids are not life-threatening, and the primary goal of therapy is to limit local tissue damage. Immobilizing the venom allows it to continue to digest the tissues in that area and significantly increases the resulting destruction. Travelers to Asia and Africa should learn the technique so that it can be used for treating snake bites inflicted in those areas.

Controversy about snake bite therapy still exists regarding incision and suction. Everyone agrees that the Sawyer extractor is the only effective device and the only one that should be used. Oral suction is useless. However, some investigators feel that suction is of no value and should not be used. Others think it might provide some benefit. Incisions are not recommended, but application of the extractor over the snake bite immediately after it has been inflicted may remove a limited amount of venom.

The immobilized extremity should be kept at the same level as the heart, and the person should be transported to a hospital with as little effort on his part as possible. Movement, even just walking, increases the circulation of blood and speeds the spread of venom through the rest of the body. Furthermore, the effects of activity are frequently worse than would be expected from this consideration alone. The person should be lying still if possible. No drugs, including alcohol, should be administered. No other treatment should be attempted.

An individual bitten by a poisonous snake who is by himself in a remote area has no choice but to walk out. If a companion is present, the companion should make sure the person is warm and comfortable and then try to obtain help, preferably a helicopter. If the party is large enough, the subject can be carried out. Even jostling on a makeshift stretcher probably stimulates blood flow and venom absorption less than attempting to walk out. However, stretcher evacuation would be slower than walking out. Every situation is different.

Antivenom Therapy

Antivenom is the only specific treatment for poisonous snake bite. The administration of antivenom can be hazardous and should not be attempted by anyone other than a physician, and even then only in situations (such as in hospital emergency rooms or intensive care units) where potentially lethal allergic reactions can be monitored. Allergic reactions of the type known as serum sickness occur in almost all antivenom recipients, including those not previously allergic to horse serum.

A few individuals carry single vials of antivenom when traveling in snake-infested areas so they can be prepared to treat themselves should they be bitten. This practice is not only useless but dangerous for the following reasons:

  ▾ A snake bite victim who needs crotalid antivenom needs at least five to fifteen vials (and sometimes as many as forty)—not one.
  ▾ If the antivenom were administered and a major allergic reaction occurred, the individual or others in his party would not be able to provide effective therapy.
  ▾ Carrying antivenom could impart a false sense of security that could lead to inadequate precautions to avoid poisonous snakes.

The antivenom that has been most widely available in the United States is a polyvalent, or general-purpose, crotalid antivenom made by Wyeth Laboratories and effective against all North American pit vipers. A new antivenom, CroFab™, was licensed by the FDA in October 2000. This antivenom is produced by injecting venom into sheep, harvesting the IgG, and chemically fractionating and digesting that immune globulin to produce purified Fab fragments. Clinical trials have demonstrated that CroFab™ is safe and effective, and that it is associated with a lower incidence of immediate and delayed hypersensitivity reactions.

Coral Snake Bites

The coral snakes are the only elapids native to the United States. These snakes are found in the coastal states from southern North Carolina to Texas. The eastern coral snake inhabits this area from Mississippi eastward; the western coral snake is found in Louisiana and Texas. The Sonoran coral snake is found in a limited portion of southern Arizona.

These North American elapids are shy and rarely seen; bites are even less common. Reportedly, children may play with these snakes for hours without being bitten. Envenomation appears to occur in less than forty percent of the bites that are inflicted. Coral snake bites make up less than two percent of all snake bites in the United States.

Fatalities from coral snake bites apparently have not occurred since the development of specific *Micrurus fulvius* antivenom. This antivenom is effective for bites of the eastern coral snake, *Micrurus fulvius fulvius,* and the western coral snake, *Micrurus fulvius tenere.* It is of little value for bites by the Sonoran coral snake, *Micruroides euryxanthus,* but envenomation by this species is not severe. No deaths following its bite have been reported.

Coral snakes tend to bite and hang on, sometimes chewing for as long as a minute, which contrasts strikingly with the lightning strike of pit vipers. The bites are rarely associated with the local reaction—severe pain and swelling—typical of crotalid bites. Puncture marks from the fangs usually can not be identified, particularly if the person is intoxicated and can not provide a reliable account of the bite, which is a common occurrence. Some pain may be present and may radiate up the limb. Often the first sign of elapid envenomation is painful enlargement of the regional lymph nodes. With severe envenomation, numbness and weakness of the limb appear within one to two hours, sometimes less.

Later signs and symptoms include drowsiness, apprehension, weakness, tremors of the tongue or other muscles, difficulty swallowing, nausea, and vomiting. Pronounced weakness of the eye or eyelid muscles may occur; pupils may be pinpoint in size. Breathing may be labored. Convulsions may occur. Eventually, in inadequately treated, severely envenomated individuals, unconsciousness and paralysis are followed by death in shock from respiratory and cardiac failure.

Antivenom is the only effective therapy for coral snake bites and should be administered as quickly as possible without waiting for signs and symptoms of envenomation. The limb can be wrapped to immobilize the venom, and it should be splinted. The individual should be rapidly transported to a hospital with as little effort on his part as possible. Incision and suction or other forms of nonhospital treatment are of no value.

Bites by Exotic Poisonous Snakes

Bites by snakes that are not native to the United States occasionally occur among collectors, amateur and professional herpetologists, and exhibitors. The treatment for such bites is essentially identical to that for coral snake bites: immobilization of the venom by wrapping the limb, splinting, and transportation to a medical center. Incision and suction or cooling have no value in treating such bites.

Antivenoms for bites by exotic species of snakes, and physicians experienced in treating such bites, may be available through zoos. Poison control centers and university-associated herpetologists also can be valuable sources of information and assistance. The Antivenin Index in Oklahoma City (405-271-5454) maintains a twenty-four-hour service to assist in locating antivenoms and provide advice about the treatment for snake bites. Another source of information is the Poisondex central office in Denver (800-332-3073).

In other countries, such information and antivenoms may not be so easy to obtain. The nearest hospital would probably be the most reliable source of information and assistance, particularly in areas where snake bites are common.

Other Considerations

If a person who has been bitten by a poisonous snake in a wilderness area can not be evacuated for several days (after which evacuation may not be needed), antibiotics may be needed to combat wound infection. A tranquilizer every four to six hours may help keep the individual quiet and allay anxiety, but it must not be given to a stuporous or unconscious person. Pain should be controlled with moderate analgesics. Strong analgesics may have harmful effects and should not be administered. Alcohol, which increases absorption of the venom and physical activity by the subject, must be avoided.

Most snake bite fatalities result from shock, regardless of the species of snake or whether the venom is primarily hemolytic or neurotoxic. This complication should be anticipated and treated.

Every person with a poisonous snake bite is different, and the treatment for each must be individualized. Children and elderly persons tolerate poisonous snake bites poorly and require more vigorous treatment. Children can require huge quantities of antivenom. Bites occurring in the spring, when the snake has just emerged from hibernation and its venom is more concentrated, are more severe than bites occurring at other times of the year. Bites about the head or trunk are more dangerous than bites on the extremities and require more aggressive treatment.

Avoiding Poisonous Snakes

Poisonous snakes and their bites are best avoided, not treated. Several simple measures could prevent almost half of all envenomations:

- ▼ Poisonous snakes should not be teased or handled, even after they are dead. Reflex strikes with envenomation can occur for several hours after death.
- ▼ Unprotected hands should not be inserted under logs or stones or into cracks or crevices that have not first been visually inspected.

▼ Snakes are nocturnal animals. After dark, special care must be taken to avoid them. Walking barefoot and collecting firewood after dark are two activities that contribute to poisonous snake bites.

▼ Snakes rarely strike higher than the ankle. Loosely fitting long pants and hiking boots that cover the ankles prevent many bites.

SPIDER BITES

Almost all spiders produce toxic venoms, but their fangs are too small and weak to penetrate the skin, the venom is too weak, or the volume of venom is too small to pose a significant threat for humans. The black widow, *Latrodectus mactans,* is the only spider found in the United States that is capable of routinely producing serious illness by its bite. The tarantula native to the U.S. Southwest bites only after extreme provocation. Its weak and ineffective fangs can only penetrate thin skin, such as that on the sides of the fingers, and the effects of the bite are no worse than an insect sting.

In other parts of the world are spiders that can cause severe, even fatal poisoning in humans. Other species of *Latrodectus* produce effects similar to the black widow, as do the bites of large, hairy tarantulas found in areas such as Brazil or Peru. The Sydney funnel web spider, a *Latrodectus* species limited in distribution to the area within 100 miles of Sydney, Australia, is capable of inflicting a bite that can be lethal for healthy young adults.

Some spiders, most notoriously the brown or violin spider, *Loxosceles reclusa,* inflict bites that occasionally cause extensive damage at the site but usually have less severe generalized effects. The jumping spider, *Phidippus,* is the most common biting spider in the United States. Bites by this spider, trapdoor spiders, orbweavers, spiders of the *Chiracanthium* species such as the garden spider, and more than one hundred other species produce local reactions that ulcerate, and less often produce systemic symptoms. However, individuals with these bites almost never require hospitalization. Spiders usually cling to the site of the bite. (If the spider can not be found, some other arachnid such as a bedbug should be suspected.) Anyone that has been bitten should bring the spider to be identified.

Rarely, an individual may be bitten repeatedly by a relatively harmless spider or insect and develop an allergy to the toxin produced by that species. Subsequent bites can produce severe, even fatal allergic reactions. Fortunately, such events are rare. The treatment for such reactions is identical to the treatment for allergic reactions to insect stings.

Black Widow Spider Bites

The female black widow typically is coal black and has a prominent, spherical abdomen that may be as large as one-half inch (1.25 cm) in diameter. This appearance is so distinctive that finding the characteristic markings on the undersurface of the abdomen is rarely necessary. The typical markings consist of red or orange figures that usually resemble an hourglass, but they may be round, broken into two figures, or have some other configuration. Markings of the same color but in varying patterns are sometimes present on the back, although only the undersurface markings are considered characteristic. In some southwestern states, black widow spiders have irregular white patches on their abdomens. Different species of *Latrodectus* in other countries have a similar appearance. (The male is smaller, has a brown color, and is harmless.)

Black widows weave coarse, crudely constructed webs in dark corners, both indoors and out. Almost half the black widow bites reported in the medical literature in the first four decades of the twentieth century were inflicted on the male genitalia by spiders on the underside of outdoor toilet seats. However, this spider is timid and would rather run than attack an intruder.

Forty to fifty years ago, five to ten deaths a year resulted from black widow spider bites, although they were limited almost entirely to small children or elderly individuals in poor health. Recognition and treatment of such bites has improved so much that deaths are rare within the United States. (Bites in children weighing thirty pounds or less would still have a mortality rate of about fifty percent if untreated.) In healthy adults, black widow spider bites cause painful muscle spasms and prostration for two to four days, but complete recovery essentially always follows. Antivenom treatment usually is not recommended for adults.

The bite may feel like a pinprick, may produce a mild burning sensation, or may not be noticed at all. Small puncture wounds, slight redness, or no visible marks may be found at the site of the bite. Within about fifteen minutes, painful muscle cramps develop at the point of the bite and rapidly spread to involve the entire body. The characteristic pattern of spread is by continuity. From a bite on the forearm, the cramps spread to the upper arm, to the shoulder, and over the chest to involve the rest of the body, including the legs. The abdominal muscles are characteristically rigid and hard, although the abdomen is not tender. Weakness and tremors are also present.

A typical subject is anxious and restless. A feeble pulse and cold, clammy skin suggest shock. Labored breathing, slurred speech, impaired coordination, mild stupor, and rare convulsions (in children) suggest a disease involving the brain. Bitten individuals are often covered with perspiration. Dizziness, nausea, and vomiting are common. If the spider or its bite have not been observed, the signs and symptoms may lead to an erroneous diagnosis of an acute abdominal emergency.

Symptoms typically increase in severity for several hours, occasionally as long as twenty-four hours, and then gradually subside. After two to three days essentially all symptoms have disappeared, although a few minor residua may persist for weeks or months.

Treatment consists of efforts to relieve the painful muscle spasms and antivenom for small children. No treatment at all should be directed to the site of the bite, with the possible exception of applying an ice cube to relieve pain. Incision and suction is damaging and useless and should not be performed.

Essentially nothing can be done outside of a hospital; small children must be hospitalized. Antivenom or the drugs to control spasms would rarely be available anywhere else. Antivenom is usually administered to children under twelve. It is usually not administered to healthy adults between ages sixteen and sixty, and only to individuals of small body size with severe symptoms who are twelve to fifteen years old. Instructions with the vial of antiserum should be followed.

Periodic injections of 10 cc of a ten percent calcium gluconate solution or 10 cc of methocarbamol have been used to treat muscle spasms but now are considered to be of no value. A tranquilizer (diazepam) may provide some relief. Hot baths are occasionally helpful. Strong analgesics are helpful but rarely provide complete pain relief.

Brown Spider Bites

The brown or violin spider, *Loxosceles reclusa*, incorrectly labeled the "brown recluse spider," has received attention as the cause of "necrotic arachnidism." Following the bite of this spider, a blister surrounded by an area of intense inflammation about one-half inch (1.25 cm) in diameter appears. Pain is mild at first but may become quite severe within about eight hours. Over the next ten to fourteen days, the blister ruptures and the involved skin turns dark brown or black. Eventually the black, dead tissue drops away, leaving a crater that heals with scarring.

A few individuals have large skin losses that require grafts to cover the defect. Some children have lost considerable portions of their faces. Such events have attracted great notoriety for this spider, even though much smaller wounds are far more typical. Bites by *Loxosceles reclusa* are commonly reported incorrectly well outside of its habitat, which is limited to the southeastern and south central portion of the United States and ends at the Texas–New Mexico border.

Generalized symptoms that may appear within thirty-six hours of the bite include chills and fever, nausea and vomiting, joint pain, and a skin rash or hives. With severe reactions, red blood cells are broken down (hemolysis) and platelets are destroyed (thrombocytopenia), which can result in a significant anemia and bleeding tendency. Fatalities have occurred, mostly in children, but are rare.

Essentially nothing can be done for such bites in a wilderness situation unless appropriate injectable medications are carried along. If the person can be hospitalized within less than eight hours, the site of the bite can be surgically excised. Such therapy is rarely necessary and should be reserved for bites from spiders clearly identifiable as *L. reclusa,* so the spider must be captured (intact, if possible) and brought to the hospital to be identified. After eight hours, the area involved may be too large to be excised. Corticosteroids may also be administered. Dexamethasone, 4 mg administered intramuscularly every six hours until the reaction starts to subside, and then in tapered doses, is one recommended program. Others include injection of hydrocortisone or dapsone beneath the bite. Nothing is very satisfactory.

SCORPION STINGS

Scorpions are found throughout most of the United States, but those species lethal to humans, *Centruroides,* are limited to Arizona, New Mexico, Texas, southern California, and northern Mexico. In this area, scorpions are a significant problem. Sixty-nine deaths resulted from scorpion stings in Arizona between 1929 and 1954. During the same period, only twenty deaths resulted from poisonous snake bites. With improved medical management of the complications of scorpion stings, no deaths resulting from such stings have occurred in Arizona for more than twenty years.

Scorpions are eight-legged arachnids that range in length from three to eight inches (7.5 to 20 cm) and have a rather plump body, thin tail, and large pinchers. They are found in dry climates under rocks and logs; buried in the sand; in collections of lumber, bricks, or brush; and in the attics, walls, or understructures of houses or deserted buildings. The problems with scorpions in Arizona are clearly related to their tendency to live in the vicinity of human habitation where children are frequently playing.

Stings can be avoided by exercising care when picking up stones, logs, or similar objects under which scorpions hide during the day. Because scorpions are nocturnal, walking barefoot after dark is inadvisable. Shoes and clothing should be shaken vigorously before dressing in the morning, particularly when camping outdoors.

The lethal species of scorpions are often found under loose bark or around old tree stumps. They have a yellow to greenish yellow color and can be distinguished from other species by a small knoblike projection at the base of their stinger (Fig. 25-6). Adults measure three inches (7.5 cm) in length and three-eighths inch (1 cm) in width. One subspecies has two irregular dark stripes down its back.

The sting of a nonlethal scorpion is similar to that of a wasp or hornet, although usually somewhat more severe, and should be treated in an identical manner. (Scorpion venom is not identical to insect venom, and individuals allergic to insect stings usually are not allergic to scorpion stings.)

Initially the sting of a *Centruroides* species produces only a pricking sensation and may not be noticed. Nothing can be seen at the site of the sting. (Swelling and red or purple discoloration are indications that the sting has been inflicted by a nonlethal species.) Pain follows in five to sixty minutes and may be quite severe. The sting site is quite sensitive to touch and is the last part of the body to recover. Tapping the site produces a painful, tingling or burning sensation that travels up the extremity toward

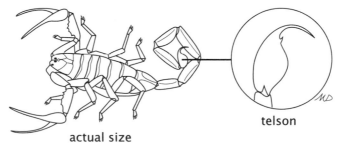

actual size

FIGURE 25-6. *Centruroides* scorpion. *Enlargement:* typical bulb and stinger

the body. (Stings by other species of scorpions can occasionally produce a similar sensation.) Sensitivity may persist for as long as ten days, although other symptoms usually disappear within ten hours.

Individuals who have been stung typically are extremely restless and jittery. Young children writhe, jerk, or flail about in a bizarre manner that suggests a convulsion. Their movements are completely involuntary. However, in spite of their constantly moving bodies, the children can talk. Although they appear to be writhing in pain, they usually state that they do not hurt. Convulsions have been described, but the true nature of these events is questionable. Visual disturbances such as roving eye movements and a fluttering type of movement known as nystagmus are common. Occasionally a child complains that he can not see, but nothing abnormal can be found when examining his eyes, and sight returns spontaneously in a few minutes. Children under six years of age may develop respiratory problems such as wheezing and stridor, and a few may need assisted respiration.

Persons who have been stung typically have an elevated blood pressure, which may be an important diagnostic sign because hypertension is rare in children. The blood pressure usually returns to normal within four to six hours and becomes life-threatening only in infants.

Elderly individuals with preexisting health problems and small children stung by *Centruroides* species should be taken to a medical facility that has the equipment and supplies necessary to monitor these individuals and deal with any complications that may arise. An ice cube applied to the site of the sting may help reduce pain, but no other therapy is possible outside of a hospital. In locations such as the Grand Canyon, where prompt evacuation is not possible, diazepam can be given to children to control the purposeless movements.

Other countries have species of lethal scorpions much more deadly than those in the southwestern United States. Mexico reportedly has had as many as 76,000 scorpion stings resulting in 1,500 deaths in a single year. The stings of such scorpions must be treated with antivenom, which is rarely available outside of a hospital, particularly for someone who is not fluent in the local language. Death from the stings of such scorpions is usually the result of sudden, very severe high blood pressure. Adrenergic blocking agents such as propranolol may be effective for treating such stings and could be carried by visitors to the countries where such lethal species of scorpions exist.

ALLERGIC REACTIONS TO INSECT STINGS

Between fifty and one hundred deaths result annually from allergic reactions to Hymenoptera stings (bees, wasps, hornets, and fire ants) in the United States, more than the deaths from rabies, large animal attacks, poisonous snakes, spiders, and scorpions combined. Approximately one of every two hundred people in the United States has experienced a severe reaction to such stings. Fatal reactions can be prevented or successfully treated in individuals known to have such allergies, but many deaths still occur in persons whose allergic status has not been previously recognized. The problem of allergies and the severe, lethal allergic reactions known as "anaphylactic shock" are discussed in chapter 20, "Allergies."

An individual allergic to insect stings usually experiences milder allergic reactions before having a potentially fatal reaction. Two types of nonlethal reactions occur: local reactions and systemic reactions.

Local reactions are characterized by severe swelling limited to the limb or portion of the limb that is the site of the insect sting. Almost all insect stings are associated with some swelling, but the area of swelling is usually 3 inches (7.5 cm) or less in diameter. With severe local reactions, a major portion of an extremity, such as the entire forearm, is swollen, and may be painful, associated with itching, or mildly discolored.

Systemic reactions occur in areas of the body some distance from the site of the sting. Most typical are hives, which may be scattered over much of the body. Generalized itching or reddening of the skin also occurs. Persons with more severe reactions may have hypotension (low blood pressure) and difficulty breathing. (Clearly, the last two reactions could be fatal if severe.)

Investigators of insect hypersensitivity reactions have recommended that individuals who have had a systemic reaction to an insect sting undergo skin testing with Hymenoptera venoms. (If the results of skin tests are inconclusive, more sophisticated measurement of venom-specific IgE antibodies can be carried out.) About half of the people who have had a systemic reaction and who also have a positive skin test would be expected to have a severe, possibly fatal reaction if stung again. Desensitization with purified insect venoms—not whole-body extracts—is recommended for these individuals. (In one study of children who had experienced an anaphylactic reaction following a sting, only nine percent of subsequent accidental stings led to severe reactions. None of the reactions was more severe than the original reaction, which led to the conclusion that immunotherapy was unnecessary for such individuals.)

Desensitization can be a drawn-out, uncomfortable procedure but also can be life-saving. Starting with very small quantities, increasingly larger amounts of the insect venoms are injected subcutaneously until the allergic reaction is "neutralized." The individual is still allergic to the Hymenoptera venoms, but the antibodies responsible for producing the allergic reactions are "used up" by the repeated injections of the material with which they react. Generally, even after successful desensitization, injections must be continued at approximately monthly intervals for years or indefinitely. If the desensitization injections are stopped, the former allergic condition often reappears.

Desensitization must be carried out under the close supervision of a physician experienced with the procedure. Severe, life-threatening allergic reactions to the desensitization injections can occur, and a physician must be on hand to deal with them. However, a physician watching for a reaction can treat it effectively. Allergic reactions to insect stings in a wilderness environment without a physician in attendance are a far greater threat.

Desensitization, or even skin testing, is not recommended for individuals who have large local reactions because these are rarely followed by systemic reactions. However, carrying epinephrine (adrenaline) is recommended for individuals who have had either type of reaction.

For individuals experiencing an anaphylactic reaction, 0.3 cc of a 1:1,000 solution of epinephrine should be injected subcutaneously as soon as symptoms are detected. Second (and sometimes third) injections are often needed at intervals of twelve to fifteen minutes.

Rock climbers and some other wilderness users who have systemic allergic reactions to insect stings have a unique risk of fatal reactions because they are subject to stings in locations such as rock walls where others can not treat them immediately and they can treat themselves only with difficulty. Such persons should seriously consider desensitization. They also must be prepared to treat an anaphylactic reaction at any time.

FIRE ANT STINGS

Both the black fire ant, *Solenopsis richteri,* and the red fire ant, *Solenopsis invicta,* appear to have entered the United States in the early twentieth century through the port of Mobile, Alabama. These insects were originally expected to occupy most areas where the average minimum annual temperature was higher than 10°F (-12°C), but identification of hybrids that are more tolerant of cold indicates that these insects will ultimately infest one-quarter of the U.S. land area. As recently as 1950, fire ants were limited to the western half of southern Alabama and the adjacent eastern part of southern Mississippi. In 1989 they were found in most of South Carolina, Georgia, Alabama, Florida, Mississippi, and Louisiana; the southeastern two-thirds of Texas; and parts of Missouri and North Carolina. They are expected eventually to occupy the rest of Texas, most of California (sparing only the northern and central Sierra Nevada), and the coastal areas of Oregon and Washington.

In infested urban areas, thirty to sixty percent of the inhabitants are stung by fire ants every year. Stings are more common among children, on the legs, and during the summer. The ant grabs the skin with powerful mandibles and, if undisturbed, stings repeatedly, rotating its body so it can reach different sites. Almost everyone stung by an ant develops a wheal-and-flare reaction—a pale bump that itches and is surrounded by a thin rim of skin that has turned red. This reaction resolves in about thirty to sixty minutes, but within twenty-four hours it evolves into a sterile pustule (a pimple or small boil). The skin over the pustule sloughs in two to three days. No therapy is effective for the pustule, but scratching can lead to infection that may require antibiotic therapy.

Between one-fourth and one-half of the individuals who have been stung develop large local reactions that are red, swollen, firm, and "itch like crazy!" In extreme cases, compression of nerves or blood vessels develops, and a few individuals have required amputation. Elevation of the extremity, steroid therapy, and antihistamines can largely prevent such extreme reactions. Topical steroid ointments such as 0.25 percent hydrocortisone, local anesthetic creams, and oral antihistamines reduce the itching associated with more common, less severe reactions.

About one-half to one percent of stings are followed by anaphylactic reactions, and at least thirty-two deaths have resulted. Most of the individuals had been stung fewer than five times. Anaphylactic reactions can occur hours after a sting. Such reactions should be treated in the same manner as any other anaphylactic reaction. (See chapter 20, "Allergies.")

No method for controlling the population of fire ants over a large area is currently available. Avoiding contact with the insects is virtually impossible for individuals who live in infested areas. Those who develop anaphylaxis following a sting should be desensitized. Whole-body extracts of fire ants, unlike whole-body extracts of other hymenoptera, contain substantial (although variable) quantities of venom and are effective for desensitization. Thousands of residents of infested areas are receiving such therapy. Anyone who has had an anaphylactic reaction to the sting of one of these insects should at least consult a physician about desensitization.

LARGE ANIMAL ATTACKS

Attacks by large animals are uncommon in North America in comparison with Africa or India. However, a significant number of injuries and a few deaths are caused by such assaults each year. The North American animals included in this discussion are:
- ▾ Bears (black bears, brown bears, and polar bears)
- ▾ Bison
- ▾ Cougars
- ▾ Alligators
- ▾ Ungulates (moose, elk, and deer)
- ▾ Coyotes and wolves

In addition, the following large animals found in Asia and Africa are briefly considered:
- ▾ Elephants
- ▾ Tigers
- ▾ Lions
- ▾ Leopards
- ▾ Crocodiles
- ▾ Black rhinoceroses
- ▾ Hippopotamuses
- ▾ Cape buffalos
- ▾ Hyenas

Bears

Approximately ten bear attacks on humans and one fatality are reported in all of North America (including Canada) each year, but the incidence is increasing, probably because more humans are encroaching on bear habitat. Brown bears are responsible for most of the attacks and fatalities, but polar bears and black bears also attack and occasionally kill humans.

Black Bears

Black bears, which have many color variations, including brown and honey colors, are numerous in the forested areas of the United States. They have no natural enemies and have become a nuisance for campers in some national parks. Because these animals have always lived in forested areas, they have learned to hide or climb trees when threatened. Therefore, truly wild bears infrequently attack humans. Sows with cubs usually do not behave aggressively. Bears that have become habituated to humans do occasionally assault people, particularly individuals who approach too closely.

Black bears rarely make predatory attacks on humans, although a few such attacks have been reported, and two individuals (one in North Carolina and one in Montana) reportedly have been killed by black bears recently.

Aggressive behavior—shouting, waving arms, walking toward the bear and making threatening gestures—almost always frightens away black bears.

Brown Bears

Brown bears, both grizzlies and Kodiaks, are larger and more aggressive than black bears. Attacks on humans, a number of which are fatal, are periodically reported from Glacier National Park in Montana and from Alaska and Canada. Unlike black bears, brown bears do behave aggressively. Sows with cubs are particularly aggressive and are responsible for eighty percent of brown bear attacks.

These bears usually try to avoid interacting with humans. Hikers in the wilderness are advised to make noise by shouting, talking loudly, or singing as they hike to avoid surprising brown bears. (The effectiveness of "bear bells" is unproven.) Particular vigilance must be exercised when traveling into the wind because bears can not smell approaching humans. Signs of a bear's presence, such as tracks or scat, must be sought. Partially eaten carcasses should be given a wide berth because bears usually return to finish their meal. Vultures circling over such a carcass indicate its presence and also warn that a bear may be near.

One of the best ways to avoid injury by brown bears is to travel in a group. No attacks on groups of four or more people have been reported, and attacks on two or three individuals are far less common than attacks on persons traveling alone.

Brown bears have lived in open environments, not in forests, and have not learned to be frightened by aggression. The best behavior when a brown bear is encountered is to be as unthreatening as possible. Eye-to-eye contact should be avoided. Walking slowly backward is the best way to get away. Running is not advisable because it attracts the bear's attention, and bears can run much faster than humans.

"Playing dead" if the bear approaches is often—although not always—successful. Individuals should curl up on the ground with their arms over their head for protection. Brown bears often make only one bite or one swipe with a paw, and injuries to an arm are far more survivable than injuries to the head. A hiker wearing a pack can try to shoulder it over his head for protection. One common mistake made by individuals playing dead is getting up too quickly. People using this protective maneuver must be absolutely certain the bear has left. The rule is: "Wait until you're sure he's gone, and then wait some more." When bears return to someone who has played dead, they often are more aggressive than during the first curious examination.

Bear sprays (pepper sprays) for deterring an attacking bear have been devised, but their effectiveness has not been proven. Guns are not allowed in national parks, and anyone considering carrying a gun for protection must remember that only a large-caliber round precisely aimed in minimal time would be effective against a charging bear. Wounding the bear simply makes him angry.

Occasionally brown bears make predatory attacks on humans, commonly individuals in tents. When faced with such an attack, the only recourse is to fight back. Fighting back is effective with surprising frequency, probably because the bear is looking for an easy meal, not one he has to fight for. Brown bears habituated to humans more commonly make predatory attacks and consume the bodies of those they have killed.

Polar Bears

Human encounters with polar bears are uncommon because few humans live in the areas where these bears are found. The number of attacks by polar bears is too small for effective preventive behavior to have been devised. Anecdotal reports of polar bear behavior range from portraying animals that attack without provocation to portraying animals that totally ignore humans.

Injuries Produced by Bears

Bears often attack the face or head first. Injuries are produce by biting and by clawing and batting with the forelegs. Claws and teeth produce lacerations that sometimes are extensive. Fractures, including skull fractures, are common.

Bison

Most attacks by bison occur in Yellowstone National Park, the home of the largest herd of free-ranging animals. An average of three attacks occurs annually. Four fatalities have resulted from these attacks since 1975.

Most bison attacks are considered to be provoked, often by tourists who approach the animals too closely for photographs. However, totally unprovoked attacks sometimes occur. Bison can weigh as much as 2,000 lb (900 kg) and can run as fast as 35 mph (57 kph). Their potential for inflicting injury must be respected.

Injuries from bison attacks include gorings and blunt trauma. The bison's horns may appear inconspicuous but can produce deeply penetrating injuries. Gorings typically involve the buttocks, posterior thighs, and back because the individual is running away from the bison. Stomping, butting, and tossing by the bison produce blunt injuries that include fractures of essentially any bone.

Cougars

More than sixty cougar attacks have been reported in North America since 1970, mostly in Colorado and California, and the incidence and fatality rate appear to be increasing, in part because humans are encroaching on cougar habitat. However, cougars no longer have any natural enemies and to a large extent are protected from hunting, so the population is growing. Furthermore, cougars are territorial. Older, more mature animals drive young animals out of their territory (or kill them) as soon as the young are ready to leave their mothers. Some of the attacks on humans may have occurred because young cougars have been driven into areas closer to human habitation.

Attacks are usually unprovoked and predatory. Cougars consume humans they have killed. More than twenty-five percent of the victims have been children.

When faced by a cougar, threatening behavior is best for warding off attacks. Individuals should make noise and open their coats so they look as large as possible. Running only invites attack. If actually assaulted, humans should fight back. Cougars are looking for a meal, not a fight.

Individuals who live near cougar habitat should avoid making their homes attractive for cougars. Not only are pets such as dogs and cats an enticement for hungry cougars, residents must not plant vegetation that is attractive for rabbits or other small animals on which these large cats prey.

Injuries are produced by biting and by clawing and are mostly lacerations. Fractures result less commonly than they do from attacks by larger animals.

Alligators

In a recent period of seventeen years, 127 attacks by alligators, resulting in five fatalities (a rate of approximately four percent), were reported. Alligator attacks are predatory. Typically, the alligator grabs its victim with its jaws and rolls under water. Individuals who are attacked should fight back.

To avoid alligator attacks, individuals should not swim at dusk, when alligators are active; should not swim with a dog, which might attract alligators; and should not swim alone. Avoiding swimming in bodies of water or streams known to be inhabited by alligators seems reasonable. However, these beasts can move with surprising speed on land, and individuals standing on the shore and not in the water have been attacked.

Alligator teeth produce large lacerations, commonly located on the body as well as the limbs. The alligator's efforts to roll its victim under water can produce fractures, many of which are open. Many of the wounds become infected.

Moose, Elk, and Deer

Attacks by these ungulates are usually provoked, typically by someone inadvertently walking up on them in a forested area. These animals are herbivores, and the attacks are not predatory. If the encounters are in a forest, individuals under attack can climb a tree, or get behind a tree and use it as a shield from the attacking animal. To avoid attacks by these animals, people should not invade their space, particularly during the fall, when they are in rut. Females with calves should be avoided.

Injuries produced by these animals include goring with their antlers and injuries produced by trampling or kicking with their hooves, which can be vicious weapons. Butting and even biting injuries also occur.

Wolves and Coyotes

Healthy wolves almost never attack humans. Wolves are one of the few animals that will desert their young when approached by humans. No wolf assaults in the wild have been reported in North America. In contrast, no other animal becomes as ferociously aggressive when infected by rabies. It seems likely that this species' reputation for savagery is based entirely on the behavior of rabid animals. (Wolf attacks producing 112 deaths a year have been reported from Siberia. The number that was rabid is unknown.)

Coyote attacks are uncommon, and because these animals are small, attacks are usually directed at children. A number of the attacks have occurred in urban surroundings, indicating that the animals were either ill (possibly rabid) or desperately hungry.

Individuals under attack should fight back. They should not appear docile or try to pet any dog acting aggressively. Children should not be left unattended in areas accessible to coyotes. The injuries produced by wolves and coyotes are essentially the same as those produced by other dog bites—lacerations and punctures.

Care for Individuals Attacked by Animals

The wounds inflicted by attacking animals are not significantly different from the soft-tissue injuries and fractures produced by other traumatic incidents, except for the greater risk of infection. However, prehospital care for these individuals is complicated by one major problem: scene safety. Will the attacking animal return? Each situation is different, and therefore no specific rules can be made, but this problem must not be forgotten or ignored.

Otherwise, care for the victims of animal attacks is similar to the care for other accident victims. Rescuers first on the scene should check the ABCs: airway, breathing, and circulation. (See chapter 2, "Basic Medical Care and Evacuation.") The severity of the individual's injuries must be ascertained, and at some point all clothing should be removed to ensure that no wounds go undetected and untreated.

Bacteria almost always heavily contaminate animal wounds. Lacerations and puncture wounds must be carefully explored and debrided and must be vigorously irrigated with disinfected water. Foreign material is often introduced by animal wounds and must be carefully sought. Only after thorough cleaning can the wounds be dressed and splinted. Animal wounds should not be sutured; the risk of infection is too great.

Hand wounds are common because the hands are used to defend against the attacking animal. Such wounds deserve special consideration because the structures are anatomically complex and hand function is an integral part of most day-to-day activities. Individuals with severe wounds should probably be evacuated as soon as possible. Puncture wounds are common, particularly following bites, and must be appropriately treated.

Everyone bitten by a wild animal should receive postexposure rabies therapy. Tetanus immunization should be administered if the individual has not had a recent booster.

Antibiotic therapy is particularly significant following an animal bite because the wounds are so contaminated. The organisms typically found in bite wounds from some animals are:

- ▾ Cats—*Pasteurella* and *Pseudomonas*
- ▾ Bears—*Micrococcus* and *Streptococcus*
- ▾ Ungulates—*Pasteurella* and *Acinetobacter*
- ▾ Crocodiles—*Aeromonas*

Antibiotic therapy should be directed toward the specific pathogens associated with the attacking animal species, if possible. Otherwise, broad-spectrum antibiotics should be administered. Amoxicillin/clavulanate is probably the drug of choice. A cephalosporin or a quinolone should be administered if amoxicillin/clavulanate is not available.

African and Asian Large Animal Attacks

Elephants

Attacks by elephants, the largest of the "large animals," produce 200 to 500 fatalities a year. Most attacks are provoked, although "rogue" elephants occasionally appear. Trampling, goring, tossing the individual with the trunk, or crushing him with the knees produces the injuries.

Big Cats

Tigers kill 600 to 800 humans a year in India. This animal is the number one "man-killer" worldwide. Lions are responsible for 300 to 500 deaths a year in Africa. Leopards kill about 400 individuals a year in Africa. A number of the victims are killed by the attack, but many die from infection.

Crocodiles

In Australia, sixteen attacks and four deaths from attacks by crocodiles were recorded over a ten-year period. In contrast, crocodiles kill more than one thousand individuals a year in Africa. Crocodiles have been witnessed "scavenging" for babies and young children in the Nile.

Black Rhinoceroses

These beasts kill many people in Africa. They have such poor eyesight that they may charge anything that moves, even trains.

Hippopotamuses

This ungainly appearing animal can move at speeds as fast as 45 mph (74 kph). It is responsible for 200 to 300 human deaths a year. It is known to swim underwater and attack boats, biting canoes in half. However, most attacks occur on land and are inflicted on individuals who refuse to believe how rapidly hippos can run.

Cape Buffalos

These animals are notorious for unprovoked attacks, but they kill only 20 to 100 persons a year.

Hyenas

These animals attack sleeping people (including campers), commonly decapitating them or producing massive facial trauma. They are more consistent "man-eaters" than lions or tigers.

REFERENCES

1. *WHO Expert Committee on Rabies, Eighth Report.* Geneva, World Health Organization, 1992 (WHO Technical Report Series, No. 824).

APPENDIXES

A

MEDICATIONS

Usual dosages for medications recommended in this text are provided only in this appendix. The precautions that must be observed with the administration of these agents are included with the dosages. By this means, anyone using the drug will be warned of risks without that warning having to be repeated each time the drug is recommended. (Rare individuals may have unpredictable adverse reactions to any drug, even aspirin. Warnings about such idiosyncratic reactions are not included.)

The doses that are listed are those that can be safely administered to a young or middle-aged adult in good health. The doses of some drugs for children or elderly individuals are significantly different. The doses for individuals with liver or kidney disease are also different. Administration of the stated doses of these drugs to such persons could have deleterious, possibly lethal, results.

For some medications a range of doses has been given, indicating that the dose should be adjusted for the patient's weight or for the severity of his disease.

Essentially all drugs have two types of names: a generic name and one or more trade names. (Drugs also have names based on the chemical structure and official names listed in the *United States Pharmacopeia* or *National Formulary,* but these are rarely used.) Generic names, assigned by the American Medical Association–United States Pharmacopeia Nomenclature Committee, are widely used. Some generic names are similar to chemical or official names; many are not.

In the United States, a drug has only a single generic name regardless of the number of companies that manufacture it. In contrast, if the drug is produced and sold by more than one manufacturer, each gives it a different trade name. (A few pharmaceutical manufacturers sell their products only under generic names.) Trade names are registered trademarks that can be used only by the manufacturer that has developed them. Trade names are devised to be more easily remembered than the generic name so that physicians will prescribe that manufacturer's product. Some are similar to generic names; many are not.

In this text, medications have been listed by their generic names with some of the better-known trade names in parentheses to help with identification. (For some agents—aspirin or penicillin, for instance—generic names are more familiar and are the only ones listed.) Many generic names are unfamiliar to people who are not medical professionals but are known by pharmacists and by most physicians through whom these drugs must be obtained. Generic names used in countries other than the United States may be totally different, even in other English-speaking nations. (A U.S. committee assigns U.S. generic names.)

MEDICATIONS FOR THE RELIEF OF PAIN

Drugs that relive pain are known as analgesics or local anesthetics. Analgesics can be classified as mild, moderate, and strong. The best-known mild analgesics are aspirin, acetaminophen, ibuprofen, and codeine. These and a number of more recently developed mild analgesics are called nonsteroidal anti-inflammatory drugs (NSAIDs). Moderate analgesia is provided by codeine combined with acetaminophen or aspirin and by a combination of acetaminophen and hydrocodone (Vicodin®). The commonly used strong analgesics are morphine and other opiates, so called because they were originally derived from opium, and meperidine (Demerol®).

The strong analgesics are called narcotics, a vague term that has no basis in chemical or pharmacologic properties. ("Narcotic" is defined as any drug that numbs, soothes, or induces a dreamlike state.)

The major hazard associated with strong pain-relieving drugs is cerebral depression that

impairs respiration. No one with a known or suspected head injury or neurologic illness should be given strong pain medications.

Addiction is not a major hazard of these agents—possibly not even a significant hazard—for individuals receiving analgesics for legitimate reasons. Almost everyone who undergoes major surgery—thousands of people every day—receives strong analgesics postoperatively to control pain. Subsequent addiction is vanishingly rare. Many of the drugs that relieve severe pain also produce euphoria, which is clearly beneficial for the victim of a major accident or illness. Addiction results when these drugs are taken for their euphoric effects alone.

Codeine and the strong analgesics (and many other agents) are classified as "controlled substances" in the United States, and the Drug Enforcement Agency, an arm of the U.S. Treasury Department, not the Public Health Service, regulates their distribution. They are difficult to obtain for anyone who is not a licensed physician (or a habitual drug user). Problems with regulatory agencies, particularly for individuals who are not physicians, can be lessened by precise records that detail the total amount of such agents on hand, where they are stored, the security of that location, persons authorized to remove the agents from storage, the names of individuals treated, and the time, place, quantity, and reason for administering the drugs.

To minimize the risk of addiction, the following precautions should be observed:

▼ Strong analgesics should not be administered except when clearly needed for the relief of pain (or the few other conditions for which some are effective, such as the treatment of the pulmonary edema of heart failure with morphine).

▼ A less potent analgesic should be substituted for a stronger agent as soon as pain has diminished to a level at which the milder drugs can provide relief.

▼ If therapy with a strong analgesic must be continued for more than seven days, a switch from one of the opiates (morphine and others) to meperidine or vice versa helps prevent addiction.

▼ Strong analgesic administration should not be continued for more than twelve to fourteen days except in extraordinary circumstances, but such circumstances could occur in the wilderness. Evacuation of a person with a painful fracture from a remote area such as Antarctica or the Himalayas could well take more than two weeks. Failure to provide analgesia, even if addiction resulted, could be devastating.

If a potent analgesic is needed, one should be used, and it should be given in adequate quantities to relieve pain. A person with severe pain desperately needs the rest and relief that these drugs alone can provide. Halfway measures, such as inadequate doses or inadequate drugs, are of almost no value at all.

Aspirin

Aspirin is a mild analgesic that is as effective for the relief of minor pain as any available single drug except the strong analgesics. The other mild analgesics that are as effective are acetaminophen, ibuprofen, and codeine. Aspirin is often not highly regarded because it is so familiar.

All aspirin is the same; all brands sold in the United States are identical in quality and effectiveness even though the prices differ as much as 1,000 percent. Combination with other compounds (except codeine and related drugs) offers no significant analgesic benefits.

An apparently unrelated action of aspirin and other mild analgesics are their ability to reduce fever, which is a major reason it provides symptomatic relief for colds. More significantly, aspirin is valuable for the reduction of high fevers that threaten brain damage.

Precautions

Aspirin is poisonous when taken in large quantities. In the United States it is one of the two most common causes of poisoning in children. (The other is acetaminophen.) Like all medications, aspirin, particularly flavored "children's" aspirin, must be inaccessible to children.

Aspirin is a strong gastric irritant. A study at a major university medical center found that more than ninety percent of the individuals hospitalized for gastrointestinal bleeding had been taking aspirin. Persons with peptic ulcers or related disorders, including severe indigestion, should not use this drug. The addition of buffering agents or antacids does not increase analgesic potency, but it can reduce the gastric irritation that aspirin commonly produces. However, for this purpose enteric coating is more effective.

Aspirin should not be used in circumstances in which it might mask a fever that could be the first indication of an infection. (Codeine is probably the best substitute in this situation.)

Dose

650 mg (10 grains) orally every four hours.

Acetaminophen

Acetaminophen (Tylenol® and others) is a minor analgesic that is just as effective as aspirin for relieving minor pain and for reducing fever. However, acetaminophen has much less tendency to cause stomach irritation. The increased dose in "extra strength" preparations has no benefit for individuals who are not unusually large.

Precautions

Acetaminophen in large quantities (10 to 15 g) produces severe liver damage. (At one time it was the drug most commonly used for suicide in Great Britain.) Treatment for an overdose must be initiated within a few hours after the drug has been ingested or it will be totally ineffective. This medication should be used with caution for individuals known to have liver disease. Many over-the-counter preparations for colds or sinus problems include acetaminophen, but this information is provided only in the list of contents in very small print. Such preparations should not be combined with acetaminophen alone.

Dose

325 to 650 mg orally every three to four hours.

Ibuprofen

Ibuprofen (Motrin®, Nuprin®, and others) is a prostaglandin antagonist that is sold primarily as a minor analgesic. Its analgesic properties are essentially the same as aspirin or acetaminophen. Its greatest value has been for dysmenorrhea (painful menstrual cramps) because its antagonism to prostaglandins tends to make the uterine muscle relax. (The anti-inflammatory effects make this drug useful for arthritis, but that is not an acute disorder that requires care in wilderness circumstances.) Ibuprofen also is an effective fever-reducing (antipyretic) agent.

Precautions

Ibuprofen is a gastric irritant, like aspirin, although some patients who can not tolerate aspirin have no problems with ibuprofen. Persons with a history of peptic ulcer or severe indigestion should not take it. All individuals receiving this drug must be aware of its potential to produce gastrointestinal ulceration and bleeding and must be alert for signs or symptoms of those disorders.

Ibuprofen also has a tendency to cause fluid retention. Whether it would aggravate symptoms of acute mountain sickness (AMS) or high altitude pulmonary edema (HAPE) has not been studied, but it should be used with caution in circumstances in which those disorders could appear.

Dose

For dysmenorrhea—400 to 600 mg orally every four hours. (Tablets may contain 200, 300, 400, 600, or 800 mg; most tablets sold over the counter are 200 mg.)

Codeine

Codeine is an opium derivative that can augment the analgesia provided by other minor analgesics. The analgesic effect of codeine alone is no stronger than aspirin or acetaminophen, but the analgesia produced by combining codeine with one of these two agents is approximately twice that of either alone. Most codeine sold in the United States is in combination with one of these two drugs.

Codeine is legally classified as a "controlled substance" in the United States because it is an opium derivative, not because it is an addicting drug of abuse. In almost all other countries, including developed countries with sophisticated drug regulations such as Great Britain, codeine is sold over the counter. Codeine has almost none of the euphoric effect of other narcotics, and addiction is essentially nonexistent.

Codeine is a valuable substitute for other minor analgesics when masking a fever might delay recognition of an infection.

Precautions

Symptoms of indigestion or heartburn occur frequently in individuals who have such symptoms with other drugs, alcohol, or spicy foods. Some individuals experience nausea and a small number may vomit. Constipation is common following codeine administration.

Codeine, like all of the opium derivatives, causes spasm of the muscles controlling outflow from the biliary system (sphincter of Oddi) and should be used sparingly for persons with liver disease, gallstones, acute cholecystitis, or acute or chronic pancreatitis.

Dose

32 to 64 mg (1/2 to 1 grain) orally, usually in combination with 625 mg of aspirin or acetaminophen.

Hydrocodone and Acetaminophen

Hydrocodone and acetaminophen, a combination sold as Vicodin®, is an analgesic approximately as strong as the combination of codeine and acetaminophen or aspirin.

Precautions

Like other moderate to strong analgesics, Vicodin® should not be given to persons with head injuries or other disorders affecting the brain. It is habit forming when used excessively or inappropriately.

Dose

One or two tablets (containing 5 mg of hydrocodone and 500 mg of acetaminophen) every four to six hours. More than eight tablets should not be taken in a twenty-four-hour period.

Morphine

Morphine is a potent analgesic that has been so widely used for so long, and so effectively relieves severe pain, that it has been called "God's own medicine." It is one of the oldest and most valuable agents in a physician's armamentarium.

In addition to its analgesic properties, morphine has a strong sedative effect that helps calm injured persons and limit thrashing about, which could aggravate wounds or hinder evacuation. This sedation and morphine's euphoric effect also help relieve the anxiety that follows an accident.

Precautions

Morphine, like all sedatives, depresses brain function. Therefore, **morphine must never be given to a patient with a central nervous system injury or disease,** even a mild disorder, because morphine would usually further impair cerebral function. After the administration of morphine or a related drug, determining whether subsequent changes in the patient's condition were the result of progression of his disorder or the effects of the drug would be impossible. A person who is unconscious does not require analgesia.

Since the brain controls respiration, morphine also depresses respiratory function. It must be used cautiously for patients with chest injuries or pulmonary diseases, particularly at higher altitudes. However, relieving the pain of a severe chest injury may allow a patient to cough and breathe more deeply (in the absence of an accompanying brain disorder).

Morphine causes nausea and vomiting in some individuals; it is constipating for almost everyone and can contribute to the development of fecal impaction. This drug may cause spasm of the muscles controlling outflow from the urinary bladder, resulting in urinary retention requiring urethral catheterization, particularly following abdominal injuries. Like codeine, morphine causes spasm of the muscle controlling biliary outflow and should be used with caution for patients with liver, gallbladder, or pancreatic diseases. Meperidine produces such spasm much less frequently and should be used when these patients need a potent analgesic.

Morphine is addicting, should be used only when specifically needed for the relief of severe pain, and should be discontinued when less potent drugs can provide adequate analgesia.

Oral administration can produce satisfactory analgesia if enough of the drug is given (orally administered morphine is only one-third to one-sixth as effective as the injected drugs), but absorption is slower and thirty to sixty minutes are required for the drug to take effect. More rapid onset can be obtained with sublingual tablets held under the tongue until dissolved. Rectal suppositories also are effective, particularly for individuals who are nauseated. Following intramuscular injection, analgesia can be expected after ten to fifteen minutes; the onset following intravenous injection is immediate. Individuals with previous experience with intravenous drug administration should use the intravenous route of administration for persons in shock. The drug must be injected slowly over a period of several minutes, and the injection should be stopped if pain relief is achieved before the full dose is administered.

Dose

For individuals weighing 150 lb (70 kg) or more, 16 mg intramuscularly, 12 to 16 mg intravenously, or 20 to 30 mg orally every four hours. For individuals weighing less than 150 lb (70 kg), 12 mg intramuscularly, 9 to 12 mg intravenously, or 15 to 20 mg orally every four hours.

Meperidine

Meperidine (Demerol®) is a synthetic analgesic first introduced in 1938. It is not an opium derivative, as are codeine and morphine. The analgesia provided by meperidine is equal to that of morphine, but meperidine does not have as much sedative and euphoric effect and the overall relief from severe pain may not be as satisfactory as that obtainable with morphine. However, meperidine does have some euphoric effect, which some authorities consider to be the reason it is so frequently used to treat severe migraines.

Precautions

Meperidine was developed as a potent analgesic because it was thought to have fewer side effects than morphine. However, meperidine definitely depresses cerebral function, must not be given to patients with central nervous system injuries or diseases, and must be used very carefully for patients with respiratory disorders.

Meperidine does cause fewer problems with biliary outflow than morphine. It appears to cause nausea and vomiting, constipation, or urinary retention less commonly, but such problems do occur.

Meperidine is definitely addictive, but addiction may take longer to develop and may occur less frequently because meperidine produces less euphoria. Precautions to avoid addiction must be observed. For patients who require a potent analgesic for longer than seven to ten days, switching from morphine to meperidine at that time may help avoid addiction.

Dose

100 mg orally or intramuscularly, or 75 to 100 mg intramuscularly or intravenously, every three to four hours.

Dibucaine Ointment

Dibucaine (Nupercainal®) is a local anesthetic that is neither a narcotic nor related to procaine or cocaine, and can be used by individuals allergic to those agents. Although the ointment can provide temporary relief from the pain and discomfort of many minor disorders, it is used most commonly for hemorrhoids and related anal problems.

Precautions

Few precautions are necessary, although no more than one ounce of the one percent ointment should be used in a single twenty-four-hour period. Allergy to this agent may develop, usually produces a rash covering the area to which the ointment has been applied, and commonly causes more discomfort than the condition for which this medication was being used.

Lidocaine

Lidocaine (Xylocaine®) is an injectable local anesthetic that is widely used for dental procedures and for minor surgery, including suturing lacerations. (The same agent is also used to prevent some cardiac rhythm abnormalities, but that use is not considered here.) Epinephrine may be added to lidocaine solutions to constrict blood vessels at the site of injection, reduce the speed of absorption, and prolong local anesthesia. Lidocaine ointment is available and should be used in the same manner as dibucaine ointment.

The concentrations of solutions for injection range from 0.5 to 2 percent; a 1 percent solution appears most useful for wilderness circumstances, although the higher concentrations provide more of the agent in a smaller volume.

Precautions

For the uncommon individuals who are allergic to lidocaine this drug must not be used. Adverse reactions include anaphylaxis (see chapter 20, "Allergies") and convulsions.

During injections of lidocaine, repeated aspirations should be made with the syringe to ensure the drug is not being injected into a blood vessel.

Dose and Administration

The usual injection consists of 5 to 10 cc of a one percent solution, although more is occasionally needed. The solution should be injected into and just beneath the skin first and into deeper tissues after the skin has been anesthetized. Before each injection, the plunger of the syringe should be pulled back to ensure the needle is not in a blood vessel. Anesthesia is almost immediate, usually persists for thirty to forty-five minutes, and can be tested by pricking the injected area with the tip of a sterile needle.

MEDICATIONS FOR SLEEP OR SEDATION (TRANQUILIZERS)

Conventional sleeping medications should not be taken at altitudes above 10,000 feet (3,000 m). Under the influence of these drugs, respirations can be slowed to such an extent that the blood oxygen level falls drastically, aggravating the symptoms of acute mountain sickness. Acetazolamide is the drug of choice for promoting sleep at higher elevations.

Sleep-promoting medications may be useful for individuals who have difficulty sleeping the first night or two away from the comfort of a warm, soft bed, but they should not be taken routinely.

MEDICATIONS

Benzodiazepines

The benzodiazepines are a group of drugs with almost identical pharmacologic properties, but chlordiazepoxide (Librium®) and diazepam (Valium®) are most commonly used as tranquilizers, and flurazepam (Dalmane®) is most commonly used for promoting sleep. Diazepam (Valium®) also is used to relieve muscle spasm, particularly in the back muscles.

The benzodiazepines are safe, although questions have been raised about triazolam (Halcion®). Lethal overdose is rare unless some other drug, usually alcohol, is taken along with very large quantities of the benzodiazepine.

Precautions

Unusual drowsiness may persist the day following ingestion of any of these drugs.

Like the strong analgesics, benzodiazepines depress brain function and should not be given to individuals with head injuries or central nervous system disease.

Benzodiazepines potentiate the depressive effects of alcohol.

Persistent insomnia may be the result of a psychiatric disorder and should be treated only by a physician.

Dose

To induce sleep, take flurazepam (Dalmane®), 15 or 30 mg, orally at bedtime. Diazepam (Valium®), 5 to 10 mg, is equally effective. Triazolam (Halcion®), 0.125 to 0.25 mg, is also just as effective and, because it is shorter acting, is less prone to produce morning drowsiness. However, triazolam has been reported to cause paradoxical excitation, confusion, depression, and amnesia, particularly in elderly and debilitated individuals, more often than other benzodiazepines. Only the smallest effective dose should be administered.

For sedation or as a tranquilizer: chlordiazepoxide (Librium®) or diazepam (Valium®), 5 to 10 mg orally two to four times per day.

As a muscle relaxant: diazepam (Valium®), 5 to 10 mg orally two to four times per day.

Other Medications

Diphenhydramine (Benadryl®) is an antihistamine but is approved by the FDA for use as a sleeping medication, particularly for elderly individuals who may become excited after taking barbiturates.

Other medications capable of inducing sleep have significant disadvantages or would rarely be needed or available in wilderness situations. Barbiturates are not as safe as the benzodiazepines and are particularly dangerous when combined with alcohol. They produce greater cerebral depression and have a greater tendency to cause a "hangover" characterized by lassitude and somnolence.

Chloral hydrate has been widely used in hospitals but is not convenient for wilderness use because it is a liquid. Glutethimide (Doriden®) and methaqualone (Sopor® and others) are not as effective as the benzodiazepines for legitimate uses and have been abused so extensively that they have fallen into disrepute. Glutethimide has the singular disadvantage of not being removable by dialysis so that an overdose can not be effectively treated.

ANTIMICROBIAL AGENTS

The antimicrobial agents include antibiotics and sulfonamides, which are used to treat established infections, and antiseptics such as povidone-iodine, which kill microorganisms on contact.

Bacteria are classified according to their reaction with the gram stain—gram-positive or gram-negative; according to their shape—cocci (spheres), bacilli (rods), or spirochetes (spirals); and according to their ability to grow in the presence of oxygen—aerobic if they can grow with oxygen present or anaerobic if they can not. This classification is used in the discussion that follows.

The Penicillins

Penicillin, the first antibiotic to be discovered, is still widely used and is effective treatment for many common infections. Chemical modifications to penicillin have produced a family of compounds, "the penicillins." Penicillins actively kill bacteria (are bactericidal); some antibiotics just keep them from multiplying (are bacteriostatic). Organisms usually susceptible to penicillins include streptococci, which cause "strep" throat, cellulitis, and impetigo; *Streptococcus pneumoniae,* which causes conjunctivitis, pneumonia, and middle ear infections; *Neisseria meningitidis,* which causes meningitis; and the spirochete that causes syphilis.

As antibiotic use has increased over the years, some organisms have become resistant to penicillins. In the developed world, for example, staphylococci, which cause boils, abscesses, and wound infections, are usually resistant. Penicillins, including ampicillin and amoxicillin, are no longer expected to be effective against the organisms likely to cause gastrointestinal infections such as traveler's diarrhea, dysentery, or typhoid fever.

Phenoxymethyl penicillin (penicillin V) is the penicillin most suitable for oral administration because it resists destruction by acid in the stomach. Aqueous crystalline penicillin G is usually used for intravenous therapy. Procaine penicillin G is used for intramuscular treatment because it is less painful and persists longer than aqueous penicillin. Benzathine penicillin G is also administered intramuscularly. It is absorbed much more slowly, lasts much longer, albeit at lower blood concentrations, and is rarely used to treat infections other than syphilis.

Some bacteria produce an enzyme called penicillinase that destroys penicillin. Penicillinase-resistant penicillins that are effective against such organisms include orally administered cloxacillin and dicloxacillin. Nafcillin is the intravenous penicillinase-resistant penicillin of choice.

Infections should be treated with penicillin only if the causative organism is known to be susceptible.

Precautions

The penicillins are usually very safe, but allergic reactions occur in about ten percent of the patients receiving them. Most of these reactions consist of skin rashes, a low fever, or other minor problems, but a few individuals develop severe anaphylactic reactions that may be lethal within minutes. (See chapter 20, "Allergies.")

Anyone who has suffered anaphylaxis to any of the penicillins must never be treated with any of them again because a potentially lethal reaction can occur. A history of previous minor allergic reactions is not predictive of such a life-threatening event, but for individuals who have had minor reactions, penicillins should be avoided.

If signs of anaphylaxis develop in a patient receiving a penicillin, the drug should be discontinued immediately. The patient should be warned of his allergy to penicillin and must tell his physician and anyone who subsequently cares for him. He should wear a bracelet or a tag that warns of his allergy. Participants with allergies to penicillin on a wilderness outing should inform other members of the party and must make preparations in advance to have other antibiotics available.

Dose

Phenoxymethyl penicillin V: 250 to 500 mg orally every six hours.

Procaine penicillin G: (Wycillin®) 0.6 to 4.8 million units intramuscularly once or twice daily.

Aqueous crystalline penicillin G: 10 to 20 million units per day intravenously in equal doses every two to four hours.

Ampicillin: 500 to 1,000 mg orally every six hours.

Amoxicillin: 250 to 500 mg orally every six hours.

Dicloxacillin: 250 to 500 mg orally every six hours.

Nafcillin: 1.5 to 2.0 g intravenously or intramuscularly every two to six hours.

Amoxicillin/Clavulanate

This combination of drugs, sold under the name Augmentin®, combines amoxicillin, a broad-spectrum penicillin analog, and clavulanic acid. The acid inactivates a wide variety of beta-lactamases by blocking active sites of theses enzymes, which are transmitted by plasmids and are responsible for bacterial resistance to the penicillins and cephalosporins.

Precautions

The principal risk associated with administration of this drug is allergic reactions, which have occasionally been fatal. Anyone who has had an allergic reaction to any of the penicillins or cephalosporins should not receive amoxicillin/clavulanate.

Dose

One 500 mg tablet every twelve hours or one 250 mg tablet every eight hours. (Note: the 500 mg and the 250 mg tablets both contain 125 mg of clavulanic acid, so two 250 mg tablets can not be substituted for one 500 mg tablet.)

The Cephalosporins

The cephalosporins are a group of antibiotics chemically and therapeutically similar to the penicillins. The organisms against which the first-generation cephalosporins and the penicillins are effective are virtually the same. Second- and third-generation cephalosporins are effective against a wider spectrum of organisms. However, the cephalosporins are considerably more expensive than the penicillins.

Cephradine (Anspor® and Velosef®), cephalexin (Keflex®), and cefazolin (Kefzol® and Ancef®) are first-generation cephalosporins used to treat staphylococcal and streptococcal skin and soft-tissue infections and urinary tract infections. Cephradine and cephalexin can be administered orally; cefazolin is administered intramuscularly or intravenously. Cefotetan (Cefotan®) is a second-generation cephalosporin that is usually administered intravenously and can be a useful alternative to either clindamycin or chloramphenicol for treating anaerobic bacterial infections such as peritonitis. Ceftriaxone (Rocephin®) is a third-generation cephalosporin administered intramuscularly and intravenously that is particularly useful for treating meningitis.

Precautions

Ten percent of the individuals allergic to penicillin are also allergic to the cephalosporins. Anyone who has had a severe reaction to penicillin, particularly an anaphylactic reaction, should not be treated with cephalosporins.

In general, the cephalosporins enter the cerebrospinal fluid poorly and, except for ceftriaxone, should not be used for treating meningitis.

Dose

Cephradine (Anspor®, Velosef®) and cephalexin (Keflex®): 500 mg orally every six hours.
Cefazolin (Kefzol®, Ancef®): 500 to 1,000 mg (1 g) every eight hours intramuscularly or intravenously.
Cefotetan (Cefotan®): 500 to 3,000 mg (3 g) every twelve hours intramuscularly or intravenously.
Ceftriaxone (Rocephin®): 1,000 to 2,000 mg (1 to 2 g) every twelve or twenty-four hours intramuscularly or intravenously.

The Macrolides: Erythromycin, Azithromycin, and Clarithromycin

The macrolides are generally effective against pneumococci, streptococci, mycoplasma, and most staphylococci. The oldest, and least expensive, is erythromycin. Because of the frequency of nausea with erythromycin, azithromycin (Zithromax®) and clarithromycin (Biaxin®) are sometimes preferred. They are used primarily to treat soft-tissue infections in individuals who are allergic to penicillin. As a penicillin substitute, they would not be first-choice agents for severe staphylococcal infections. These agents are also useful in treating the most common causes of pneumonia.

Precautions
Very few adverse reactions to macrolides occur; those that do appear to be mild.

Dose
Erythromycin: 500 mg orally every six hours.
Azithromycin (Zithromax®): 250 to 500 mg orally once daily.
Clarithromycin (Biaxin®): 250 to 500 mg twice daily.

Clindamycin
Clindamycin is another antibiotic with antibacterial effects similar to penicillin and is a suitable substitute for individuals allergic to penicillin. In addition, clindamycin is effective against staphylococci and a number of anaerobic organisms, particularly *Bacteroides fragilis,* one of the most common of the anaerobic organisms that cause peritonitis.

Precautions
Two to twenty percent of patients being treated with clindamycin develop diarrhea. Usually the diarrhea is mild, and treatment can be continued. However, rare individuals develop a life-threatening colitis from overgrowth of toxin-producing bacteria in the colon. Copious fluids and electrolytes are lost, and large amounts of blood and mucus appear in the stools. Clindamycin must be stopped at once if this type of diarrhea appears, the lost fluids must be restored (intravenously if necessary), and metronidazole should be given orally every eight hours for ten days.

Dose
300 mg orally every six hours; 300 to 600 mg intramuscularly or intravenously every eight hours.

The Aminoglycosides
The aminoglycosides are a group of antibiotics that include streptomycin, tobramycin, neomycin, and gentamicin. Streptomycin is now used only for tuberculosis or bubonic plague. Neomycin use is limited to topical preparations such as ophthalmic ointments. Tobramycin and gentamicin are effective against a large number of gram-negative bacilli and are used for severe infections such as peritonitis. Due to their toxicity, these antibiotics should not be used for relatively minor infections. They are ineffective against anaerobic bacteria and gram-positive organisms such as streptococci.

Precautions
The aminoglycosides are excreted by the kidneys and can produce damage to those organs. Patients with renal disease should not receive aminoglycosides or should receive them in smaller doses.

The aminoglycosides can cause damage to the inner ear and the auditory and vestibular nerves, resulting in deafness, ringing or buzzing in the ears, loss of balance, or vertigo.

The aminoglycosides should not be injected directly into a body cavity or be given rapidly by vein. Respiratory arrest due to a form of nerve block can result.

In general, only a physician familiar with their use and toxicity should administer aminoglycosides.

Dose
Gentamicin and tobramycin: 1.7 mg/kg of body weight intramuscularly, followed by 1 mg/kg of body weight every eight hours.

The Tetracyclines

The tetracyclines (Achromycin® and others) and doxycycline (Vibramycin®) are effective treatment for infections produced by a broad spectrum of organisms that includes rickettsia and some viruslike organisms, as well as a large number of gram-positive and gram-negative bacteria. However, the tetracyclines are bacteriostatic drugs, and a number of more effective agents have replaced them for the treatment of many infections. Currently, the disorders for which tetracyclines are the antibiotic of choice are certain mycoplasmal and rickettsial infections, urinary tract infections caused by susceptible gram-negative organisms, and cholera.

Precautions

Tetracycline therapy may cause mild diarrhea due to the suppression of normal intestinal bacteria. The diarrhea is rarely severe and usually ends when the drug has been stopped.

Nausea and vomiting sometimes occur in patients receiving tetracyclines.

All tetracyclines increase sensitivity to ultraviolet light and predispose individuals receiving them to severe sunburn.

Tetracycline can permanently stain the dental enamel in young children. It should not be administered to children and pregnant women whenever other agents are available.

Tetracyclines are poorly absorbed from the stomach when given with milk or other dairy products, with antacids, or with bismuth (Pepto-Bismol®). They should be given one hour before or two hours after meals.

Dose

Tetracycline: 250 to 500 mg orally every six hours.
Doxycycline: 100 mg orally every twelve hours.

Chloramphenicol

Chloramphenicol (Chloromycetin®) is a potent antibiotic with such a wide spectrum of antibacterial activity that it could be one of the most valuable antibacterial agents but for one flaw. In about one of every 25,000 to 50,000 patients receiving this drug, lethal bone marrow suppression occurs. This reaction can not be predicted. Some investigators claim that the death rate due to adverse reactions to chloramphenicol is no greater than the death rate caused by reactions to penicillin. Nonetheless, administration of chloramphenicol is usually limited to a few specific life-threatening conditions that include:

- ▾ Bacterial meningitis in patients allergic to penicillin and ceftriaxone, or when only oral therapy can be given
- ▾ Severe anaerobic infections for which clindamycin is not effective
- ▾ Infections by gram-negative bacilli that do not respond to other antibiotics
- ▾ Severe rickettsial infections

Precautions

In view of the severe bone marrow depression that can result from chloramphenicol therapy, its use should be limited to those rare situations for which it is specifically indicated.

Dose

250 to 1,000 mg (1 g) or 12.5 mg/kg of body weight, orally or intravenously, every six hours.

The Quinolones: Levofloxacin, Ciprofloxacin, and Ofloxacin

Levofloxacin (Levaquin®), ciprofloxacin (Cipro®), and ofloxacin (Floxin®) are quinolones, antimicrobial agents effective against a broad range of bacteria. They are particularly useful for urinary tract and gastrointestinal infections. Levofloxacin is useful for treating pneumonia. Ciprofloxacin and ofloxacin are useful for gonorrhea.

Precautions

In animal studies, high doses given to immature animals produced permanent cartilage damage. Therefore, quinolones should not be administered to children or pregnant women. However, in emergencies ciprofloxacin has been given to children with no adverse results.

Dose

Levofloxacin (Levaquin®): 500 mg orally once or twice daily.
Ciprofloxacin (Cipro®): 500 mg orally every twelve hours, preferably two hours after eating.
Ofloxacin (Floxin®): 200 to 400 mg orally every twelve hours.

Polymyxin B, Bacitracin, and Neomycin Ophthalmic Mixture and Topical Ointment

This antibiotic mixture (Neosporin®) is available as an ophthalmic ointment, as an ophthalmic solution (drops), and as a topical skin ointment. It is used to treat conjunctivitis caused by a wide variety of organisms and to prevent skin infections.

Precautions

Some individuals are allergic to one or more of the components of this mixture and should not be treated with it.

The ointment produced for use on skin is called simply Neosporin® Ointment and should never be put in the eye because it may contain minor impurities that could be irritating or injurious to the eye.

The antibiotics used in this preparation are valuable for treating and preventing infections only in locations where the agents can not be absorbed by the body. They must never be taken internally.

Dose

For eye infections, a small amount of the ointment or one or two drops of the solution should be instilled behind the lower lid every three to four hours.

Trimethoprim-Sulfamethoxazole

Trimethoprim-sulfamethoxazole (Bactrim®, Septra®, TMP-SMX, or "trimethoprim-sulfa") is a combination of two agents, one of which is a sulfonamide. Sulfonamides are useful for treating many gastrointestinal and urinary tract infections because they can be administered in preparations that produce high concentrations of the drugs in these organs. Additionally, some organisms resistant to antibiotics are readily destroyed by sulfonamides.

Precautions

Sulfonamides in general are not very soluble in water and tend to precipitate in the urine, in effect forming small kidney stones that can cause significant damage. In order to prevent such damage, patients receiving these drugs must consume large quantities of fluids to maintain a high urinary volume (at least one to one and one-half liters per day).

Some patients are allergic to sulfonamides and should not be treated with them.

Individuals with glucose-6-phosphatase deficiency should not take sulfonamides. (This disorder, which must be diagnosed by a physician, usually causes mild anemia and is aggravated by certain drugs, particularly some sulfonamides.)

Sulfonamides cross the placenta, are excreted in milk, and can have harmful effects on a fetus or newborn. Only a physician should administer them during the last months pregnancy and to nursing mothers.

Dose

160 mg of trimethoprim and 800 mg of sulfamethoxazole (one double-strength tablet) orally every six to twelve hours.

Silver Sulfadiazine Cream

Silver sulfadiazine cream is a sulfonamide in an ointment (Silvadene®, SSD Cream®, and others) that is applied to burns to help control bacterial infections. It is effective against a wide variety of organisms, particularly the organisms that most commonly infect burns.

Precautions

Because silver sulfadiazine is a sulfonamide, the precautions described for trimethoprim-sulfamethoxazole should be observed.

Dose

A thin layer of the cream should be applied sterilely to the burn twice a day if the burn is exposed. Dressings covering a burn should not be removed just to apply the cream if no evidence of infection is present.

Metronidazole

Metronidazole (Flagyl® and others) is a drug used to treat a variety of parasitic infestations and bacterial infections. Its principal use in wilderness circumstances would be for treating giardiasis and amebiasis.

Precautions

Alcoholic beverages taken during therapy with metronidazole can cause severe vomiting and should be avoided while the drug is being taken and for one day afterward.

Metronidazole should not be administered during the first trimester of pregnancy and should be given only by a physician to anyone with concomitant disease, particularly liver, blood, or neurologic disorders.

Metronidazole should not be given to children except to treat amebiasis.

Dose

For giardiasis: 250 mg orally three times a day for five to ten days.

For diarrhea associated with antibiotic therapy: 250 mg three times a day for a person weighing less than 150 lb (70 kg) and 500 mg three times a day for larger individuals.

For amebiasis: 750 mg orally three times a day for five to ten days.

Chloroquine

Chloroquine is highly effective for both prevention and treatment for chloroquine-sensitive malaria. Unfortunately, chloroquine-resistant falciparum malaria is widespread. As a result, mefloquine is the prophylactic agent of choice for travel to most malarious areas. Chloroquine is also effective to some extent in the treatment of amebiasis.

Precautions

In the dosages used for preventing or treating malaria, chloroquine has few serious side effects. Therapeutic doses may cause minor gastrointestinal disturbances. Skin rashes or itching occasionally occur. However, these symptoms often do not require interruption of therapy or prophylaxis and rapidly disappear when administration is ended.

Dose

0.5 g orally once weekly on the same day of the week, starting two weeks before entering a malaria-endemic area and continuing for five weeks after leaving.

Mefloquine

Mefloquine (Lariam®) is administered for preventing or treating chloroquine-resistant falciparum malaria.

Precautions

Individuals allergic to mefloquine or related agents, particularly quinine or quinidine, should not take this drug.

Because dizziness occasionally follows mefloquine ingestion, individuals taking it must be careful with activities such as driving a car, piloting an aircraft, or using machinery in which injury could occur. Psychiatric reactions such as anxiety, depression, restlessness, hallucinations, or confusion occur rarely with mefloquine, and the drug should be stopped if these appear. Persons with significant, preexisting psychiatric illness, particularly those on psychiatric medication, should take mefloquine with caution.

Animal studies have shown serious complications from mefloquine taken during pregnancy. There are no studies of the safety of mefloquine in pregnant humans. The drug should only be taken by pregnant women if the potential benefits justify the potential risk to the fetus.

Dose

250 mg once weekly beginning one week before entering an area in which chloroquine-resistant falciparum malaria is known to exist, and continuing for four weeks after leaving the area.

Atovaquone and Proguanil (Malarone®)

Malarone® is a combination of the antimalarial agents atovaquone and proguanil that is given to prevent *Plasmodium falciparum* malaria in areas where chloroquine resistance has been reported. It is also useful for the treatment of acute, uncomplicated *P. falciparum* malaria. Although there are no adequate, well-controlled studies of atovaquone and proguanil in pregnant women, Malarone® may be used if the potential benefit justifies the potential risk to the fetus.

Dose

Prophylactic treatment with one tablet daily started one or two days before entering a malaria-endemic area and continued daily during the stay and for seven days after return.

Benzalkonium Chloride

Benzalkonium chloride (Zephiran®) is a cationic quaternary ammonium surface-acting agent that is a highly effective antiseptic. Aqueous solutions of benzalkonium and povidone iodine are the only agents readily available that are capable of killing bacteria in the depths of a wound without killing or seriously damaging the tissues.

Precautions

When used as intended, benzalkonium chloride has very little toxic effect. However, serious results, including collapse, coma, and death, can result if the solution is ingested.

Alcoholic solutions (tinctures) as well as aqueous solutions are available, but the aqueous solutions are more suitable for wound antisepsis and do not burn or sting, as does the tincture.

Solutions of benzalkonium must be kept in glass bottles, a definite problem in wilderness situations.

Dose

Benzalkonium chloride is used as a 1:750 solution for disinfecting intact skin before needle puncture or for cleaning minor wounds. For washing out deep or dirty wounds, the solution should be diluted with disinfected water to about 1:3,000, and copious quantities should be used, particularly for bites inflicted by a possibly rabid animal.

Povidone-Iodine

Povidone-iodine, an iodophor and a loose complex of iodine with polyvinylpyrrolidone, was patented in 1956 and subsequently has become widely available as a ten percent solution under the trade names Betadine®, Povidine®, Pharmadine®, and others. These preparations offer two significant advantages for wilderness use: they can be kept in polyethylene containers instead of glass, and they are effective disinfectants in dilute solutions so that less must be carried.

Povidone-iodine retains the strong bactericidal activity of iodine but eliminates many of the disadvantages, such as skin irritation, staining of the skin, and some of the odor of iodine. A 1:100 dilution of a ten percent solution has been found to have much greater bactericidal action than the original stock solution, and 1:1,000 dilutions are almost equally effective.

Precautions

Rare individuals are allergic to iodine; a chronic skin rash is the usual manifestation. Such individuals should not use povidone-iodine.

Povidone-iodine has been recommended for water disinfection, but no substantiating data have been provided. The 1:10,000 dilution that would result has been found to have no significant antimicrobial activity. At the present time, these agents can not be considered reliable for water disinfection.

Dose

For skin disinfection before injections, the undiluted solution is suitable and convenient. For rinsing a larger wound, the original solution should be diluted several hundred times and the wound thoroughly rinsed with large quantities of the solution, particularly following the bite of a possibly rabid animal.

MEDICATIONS AFFECTING THE HEART, BLOOD VESSELS, AND RESPIRATORY SYSTEM

Acetazolamide

Acetazolamide (Diamox®) inhibits the enzyme carbonic anhydrase, which catalyses the reversible combination of carbon dioxide with water to form carbonic acid. This drug promotes renal bicarbonate excretion and tends to reduce the respiratory alkalosis (increase in blood pH) resulting from carbon dioxide loss at altitude by faster and deeper breathing.

Acetazolamide reduces the severity of acute mountain sickness symptoms in individuals who must ascend from sea level to 12,000 to 14,000 feet (3,700 to 4,300 m) without adequate time for acclimatization. It may not eliminate such symptoms entirely. In addition, acetazolamide promotes acclimatization.

A significant effect on high altitude pulmonary edema has not been demonstrated.

Perhaps the greatest benefit from acetazolamide is relief of sleep problems at altitude. Elimination of episodes of severe hypoxia during sleep may be responsible for better tolerance of altitude during waking hours.

Precautions

Acetazolamide is a sulfonamide, although it does not have any antibacterial actions. Persons allergic to sulfonamides may be allergic to this drug.

Persons with liver or kidney disease should not be treated with acetazolamide, and the drug should not be given during the last months of pregnancy or to nursing mothers.

Some individuals develop tingling sensations in the lips, fingers or hands, toes or feet, or occasionally other areas, blurring of vision, and alterations of taste when taking this drug. These sensations disappear when the medication is stopped.

Dose

To prevent acute mountain sickness: 250 mg orally every twelve hours starting one to two days before ascent and continuing for three to five days after arrival.

To promote sleep at high altitude: 125 to 250 mg orally at bedtime.

Dexamethasone

Dexamethasone (Decadron® and others), a synthetic glucocorticoid, is a potent steroid that is used to treat a variety of disorders, but its value in the wilderness is quite limited. The ability of this agent to reduce the edema associated with the spread of malignant tumors from other organs to the brain led to therapeutic trials for high altitude cerebral edema. In the wilderness, its value is largely limited to the treatment of severe acute mountain sickness and high altitude cerebral edema.

Dexamethasone is as effective as acetazolamide for treating acute mountain sickness. However, it does not promote acclimatization. Symptoms of acute mountain sickness relieved by dexamethasone therapy recur when treatment is stopped. Dexamethasone is recommended only when preventive measures have been neglected or have been impossible, such as in emergency rescue situations, and symptoms have developed. However, recreational skiers susceptible to acute mountain sickness at altitudes of 8,000 to 10,000 feet commonly take dexamethasone instead of acetazolamide because they want to enjoy carbonated beverages, principally beer.

Precautions

Significant side effects from dexamethasone administered for the short time periods required to evacuate individuals with acute mountain sickness or high altitude cerebral edema—evacuation should be the principal of therapy—are essentially nonexistent. The primary risk is relying on dexamethasone alone and not evacuating the affected individual to a lower altitude.

Prolonged therapy with dexamethasone is associated with major side effects, but such prolonged therapy should never be needed for altitude problems. Skiers should not take dexamethasone for more than five or six days.

Dose

4 mg orally or intramuscularly (if the individual is unconscious) every six hours.

Nifedipine

Nifedipine (Procardia® and Adalat®) is a member of a class of drugs, the calcium channel blockers, used primarily to treat hypertension and coronary artery disease. Because this drug lowers pulmonary artery pressure, it has been given to some individuals with high altitude pulmonary edema. In studies of individuals with unusual susceptibility to high altitude pulmonary edema, nifedipine reduced the incidence of that disorder. However, its usefulness in other persons has not been established.

Precautions

Nifedipine administered for the time required to evacuate an individual with high altitude pulmonary edema would produce few side effects. However, the therapy for high altitude pulmonary edema is descent to lower altitude. Oxygen may be helpful and should be administered during descent. Nifedipine alone can not substitute for those measures.

Dose

30 mg orally three times a day.

Nitroglycerin

Nitroglycerin relaxes the walls of small blood vessels, permitting them to dilate and increase the flow of blood. This compound (which is the explosive) is most commonly used to treat angina pectoris (severe chest pain associated with inadequacy of the blood supply to the heart) but dilates all small arteries and can be used to increase the blood flow to other organs or tissues. As the result of dilatation of cerebral arteries, throbbing headaches frequently follow the use of nitroglycerin.

Precautions

The most serious side effect of nitroglycerin therapy is a drop in blood pressure due to the dilatation of blood vessels. Fainting or, worse, aggravation of the cardiac damage could result. Therefore, a patient receiving this drug must be closely attended. He should lie down with his head lowered if symptoms of faintness or dizziness appear.

The tablets should be kept in their original brown bottle and should not be kept longer than six months after purchase because they begin to lose their potency. Cotton wads should not be kept in the bottle, which must be kept tightly stoppered.

Dose

0.4 mg (1/150 grain) or 0.8 mg sublingually at the onset of an attack. If the pain persists, additional tablets may be taken at fifteen- or thirty-minute intervals for a total of four tablets during one hour. The tablets may be chewed but must not be swallowed. About three minutes is required for the medication to take effect.

Digoxin

Digoxin is one of the digitalis preparations, which are the oldest and most valuable drugs available for the treatment of a variety of heart disorders. Digitalis strengthens the contraction of the heart muscle, permitting more effective cardiac function for patients in heart failure. Digitalis preparations also help restore normal cardiac rhythm for patients with many types of abnormal rhythms. (These drugs are not beneficial and may be quite harmful for persons with normal hearts.)

Precautions

Loss of appetite, nausea or vomiting, and slowing of the heart rate to less than sixty beats per minute are indications of digoxin toxicity. If such signs appear in a patient receiving this drug, the dose must be reduced but not stopped.

Digoxin must be given with great care to anyone who has taken any digitalis preparation within the previous week. These drugs are excreted slowly over a period of several days or longer. An overdose could result if treatment were restarted shortly after it had been discontinued.

A number of digitalis preparations, such as digitoxin, have similar names. These preparations must not be confused because the therapeutic doses are significantly different.

Dose

Initially: 0.25 mg orally every two hours for a total of 1.5 mg.
Maintenance: 0.25 mg orally once daily at the same time of day.

Epinephrine

Epinephrine (adrenalin) is a hormone secreted by the medulla of the adrenal gland. It is used to treat spasm of the bronchi due to anaphylactic shock or severe asthma, or to relieve the spasm and respiratory obstruction of laryngeal edema. Adrenalin is effective when injected or when applied directly to the involved tissues. It is destroyed by the acid and digestive enzymes in the stomach and is ineffective when administered orally.

Precautions

Epinephrine must be administered very slowly and carefully to elderly individuals or to persons with heart disease of any kind, high blood pressure, thyroid disease, or diabetes. It also should not be given to persons in shock from blood loss. Epinephrine is a powerful cardiac stimulant; its effect on individuals with cardiac disorders could be lethal.

Repeat injections of epinephrine should not be given until the obvious effects of a previous injection have disappeared. An overdose of epinephrine could cause severe problems for persons with normal hearts.

The epinephrine preparation must be discarded without being used if it has turned brown or contains a precipitate. However, outdated preparation in which such changes have not occurred can still be safely administered.

Dose

Subcutaneously: 0.3 cc to 0.5 cc of a 1:1,000 solution (3 to 5 mg) every fifteen to thirty minutes.

Inhalation: Prepared aerosols contain different amounts of epinephrine, but most will deliver 3 to 5 mg with two careful, deep inhalations.

Aminophylline

Aminophylline is closely related to caffeine chemically and pharmacologically but does not have as much stimulating effect on the central nervous system. This drug is used to treat asthma because it relaxes the bronchial walls and permits the bronchi to dilate, relieving respiratory difficulty. At high altitudes, aminophylline can prevent interruption of sleep by Cheyne-Stokes respirations, but acetazolamide is preferable for that purpose.

Precautions

Aminophylline in therapeutic doses has few toxic effects.

Dose

500 mg (suppository) inserted well up into the rectum.

DECONGESTANTS

These agents cause the blood vessels in the nasal mucosa to contract, reducing their volume but also reducing the amount of fluid collected in the tissue (edema) around the vessels. Decongestants shrink the swollen mucosa of the nose for patients with colds, hay fever, or sinusitis. Importantly, these drugs not only relieve obstruction to the passage of air, they also promote drainage from the small canals opening into the sinuses.

Phenylephrine

Phenylephrine hydrochloride, a widely used decongestant and well known as Neo-Synephrine®, has been found to increase the incidence of cerebrovascular accidents (strokes). It has been replaced in most decongestants (and in most drugstores), including the proprietary product cited above.

Oxymetazoline

Oxymetazoline, a decongestant that is equally effective and much longer acting than phenylephrine, lasts up to twelve hours after a single application. (Because the onset of its action is slower, some individuals have gained the impression that oxymetazoline is not as effective as phenylephrine.) A 0.05

percent solution is contained in a number of preparations such as Afrin® and Dristan® long-acting nasal spray, but some drugstore chains sell identical preparations under their own label at a price forty to fifty percent below that of the established brands.

Administration of the nasal spray should be repeated ten minutes after the first application. Initially the spray only reaches the mucosa over the more prominent structures in the nasal cavity. Not until this portion of the mucosa has been shrunken can a subsequent application extend into the recesses where the small canals draining the sinuses open.

Precautions

After the effects of the nasal spray have worn off, swelling of the nasal mucosa and airway obstruction recur. Such "rebound" symptoms are often worse than the initial symptoms. With each subsequent application, the duration of the spray's effects tends to become shorter. For this reason, use of the spray perhaps should be limited to the hours when decongestant action is needed to promote restful sleep. An oral decongestant should be used in conjunction with the spray to obtain more complete and longer-lasting results. Rebound following oxymetazoline does not seem to be as severe as that following shorter-acting decongestants.

Dose

One or two sprays in each nostril every twelve hours.

Pseudoephedrine

Pseudoephedrine (Sudafed® and others) is a systemic decongestant. The drug acts through the nerves supplying the blood vessels in the mucosa of the upper respiratory tract, causing those vessels to contract. Excess fluid in the mucosa (edema) is reduced, the mucosa shrinks to normal thickness, and obstruction to the passage of air is relieved. This drug also shrinks the mucosa lining the small canals that drain the sinuses and the eustachian tubes that drain the middle ears, allowing air or fluid to move through these structures and helping to avoid aerotitis media, aerosinusitis, and infectious sinusitis.

Precautions

Only a physician should give pseudoephedrine to individuals with high blood pressure, heart disease, thyroid disease, or diabetes.

Pseudoephedrine acts as a mild stimulant and makes some individuals restless or jumpy, which can inhibit restful sleep. Reducing the dose of the drug by only taking part of a tablet usually relieves these side effects.

Dose

60 mg orally every six to eight hours.

Triprolidine with Pseudoephedrine

This combination of an antihistamine with a systemic decongestant (Actifed® and others) is one of the most popular for controlling the symptoms of allergic reactions such as hay fever or for colds.

Precautions

The precautions that must be observed are the same as those for both the antihistamines and pseudoephedrine.

Dose

One tablet every eight hours.

ANTIHISTAMINES

Antihistamines are a group of drugs that block the effects of histamine, a substance released during allergic and inflammatory reactions and considered responsible for many symptoms of allergy. In addition, some of these agents can prevent or reduce symptoms of motion sickness.

Precautions

All antihistamines have a tendency to cause drowsiness, although individual susceptibility varies. Some more recently developed agents produce much less drowsiness, but even those drugs are not completely free of this side effect. They are currently available only by prescription. Anyone who has taken an antihistamine must be very careful about engaging in activities for which drowsiness could be a hazard, particularly driving a car.

Dose

Depends upon the preparation being used.

Dimenhydrinate, Meclizine, and Cyclizine

Dimenhydrinate (Dramamine®), meclizine (Bonine® and Antivert®), and cyclizine (Marezine®) are antihistamines used primarily to control motion sickness. All should be taken about one hour before embarking on a trip. All are fairly effective against allergies.

Precautions

All antihistamines have a tendency to cause drowsiness, although individual susceptibility varies. Anyone who has taken an antihistamine must be very careful about engaging in activities for which drowsiness could be a hazard, particularly driving a car.

Dose

Dimenhydrinate: 50 mg orally every four hours.
Meclizine: 25 to 50 mg orally every four hours.
Cyclizine: 50 mg orally every four to six hours.

MEDICATIONS FOR GASTROINTESTINAL DISORDERS

Paregoric

Paregoric (camphorated tincture of opium) is a mixture of several compounds, the most important of which is morphine. This mixture is used to control diarrhea through the immobilizing action of opium derivatives on the lower gastrointestinal tract.

Precautions

The problems related to using any drug to control diarrhea are discussed in chapter 12, "Gastrointestinal Disorders."

Paregoric is classified as a controlled substance because it contains opium. Addiction to paregoric does occur rarely but not from reasonable use.

Dose

One teaspoon (5 cc) orally every two hours or after each bowel movement.

Diphenoxylate with Atropine

Diphenoxylate with atropine (Lomotil®) is a combination of two compounds that is used to control diarrhea through slowing of intestinal mobility.

Precautions

The most important complications resulting from the administration of diphenoxylate are those from using any drug to control diarrhea.

This drug is chemically very similar to meperidine, although lacking its analgesic and euphoric properties. Addiction is at least theoretically possible, and diphenoxylate is classified as a controlled substance.

Dose

Two tablets four times a day is the maximum recommended dose. Smaller amounts should be used if they are effective.

Loperamide

Loperamide (Imodium®) helps control diarrhea by reducing intestinal mobility. The suspension and capsules are now available over the counter.

Precautions

The most important complications associated with the administration of loperamide are those resulting from using any drug to control diarrhea.

Dose

Two 2 mg capsules followed by one 2 mg capsule after each unformed stool, not to exceed eight capsules in any twenty-four-hour period.

Prochlorperazine and Promethazine

Prochlorperazine (Compazine®) was one of the first tranquilizers and is quite similar to chlorpromazine (Thorazine®), which is better known. Although these agents were major therapeutic advances, more effective drugs have largely replaced them, and the principal use of prochlorperazine currently is treating severe nausea and vomiting.

Promethazine (Phenergan®) is a chemically closely related drug that also has significant antihistamine activity. However, its most prominent use is treating severe nausea and vomiting.

Individuals who are vomiting repeatedly often are unable to retain oral medications, and rectal suppositories must be substituted.

Precautions

Prochlorperazine and promethazine must not be given to individuals who are comatose or whose consciousness is significantly impaired.

Only a physician should give either of these agents to children younger than two years old. In wilderness situations, prochlorperazine probably should not be given to preteenage children.

Dose

Prochlorperazine: 5 to 10 mg orally three or four times a day as needed; 25 mg rectally (suppository) every twelve hours as needed.

Promethazine: 25 mg rectally (suppository) every four to six hours as needed.

Antacids

Antacids are preparations that contain combinations of aluminum hydroxide, calcium carbonate, magnesium carbonate, magnesium hydroxide, and magnesium trisilicate. They are administered to neutralize acids in the stomach in the treatment of peptic ulcers and for relief of symptoms of indigestion. Some of the preparations are flavored. Alkets®, Titralac®, Robalate®, Alka-Seltzer®,

Alka-2®, Amphojel®, Gaviscom®, Gelusil®, Maalox®, WinGel®, Rolaids®, and Tums® are well-known antacids.

Precautions

Magnesium-containing antacids sometimes produce a mild diarrhea, but this side effect rarely requires treatment or interruption of therapy. These drugs are absorbed from the gastrointestinal tract in minimal amounts, if at all, and have no effects on the rest of the body. They are of no value in preventing acute mountain sickness.

Antacids should not be taken indiscriminately over long periods of time. Prolonged consumption of antacids and calcium-containing foods such as milk can lead to calcium deposits in the kidneys and impaired renal function.

Dose

The dose depends upon the preparation being used but usually consists of one or two tablets as often as required for the pain or distress of an ulcer or indigestion.

Antispasmodics

Antispasmodics reduce the amount of acid produced by the stomach and reduce peristaltic activity, both of which are desirable in the treatment of indigestion, peptic ulcer, and acute pancreatitis. Some of the better-known antispasmodics are Donnatal®, Pamine®, Pro-Banthine®, and tincture of belladonna. Many others of equal effectiveness are available.

Precautions

Antispasmodics produce blurring of vision and dryness of the mouth as their most common side effects. Following ingestion of one of these drugs, a person might not be able to participate in activities requiring visual acuity, such as driving a car.

Individuals with a history of glaucoma should not be treated with these drugs. Blurring of vision by antispasmodics results from dilatation of the pupil and immobilization of the muscles that focus the eyes. Dilatation of the pupils in this manner can seriously aggravate glaucoma, a condition characterized by increased intraocular pressure.

Some antispasmodics have a significant constipating effect and should not be used alone. A generous fluid intake and the use of antacids that have a laxative action, as most do, counteracts this tendency.

These drugs also have a tendency to immobilize the urinary bladder, resulting in urinary retention that requires urethral catheterization. Although this complication would be rare in wilderness users, therapy may have to be discontinued for several days and then resumed at a lower dose if it occurs.

Dose

The dose depends upon the preparation being used. The drugs are usually given one-half hour before meals and at bedtime. A double dose may be given at bedtime if the patient awakens at night due to ulcer pain.

Preparations for intramuscular injection are available for treating patients with acute pancreatitis for whom oral therapy is undesirable.

H₂ Blockers

Several agents, one of which is histamine, or "H_2," stimulate the cells that secrete acid in the stomach. The H_2 blockers inhibit the secretion of acid in the stomach by blocking the sites at which histamine attaches to the walls of the acid-secreting cells. These agents were first introduced in 1976 and were a major advance in the treatment of peptic ulcers, drastically decreasing the need for surgical treatment of this disorder. Most of these agents are now available over the counter and include Pepcid®, Zantac®, and Tagamet®.

MEDICATIONS

Sucralfate

Sucralfate (Carafate®) helps peptic ulcers to heal (and helps prevent new ulcers) by, in essence, forming a film that coats the surface of the ulcer and keeps out gastric acid and digestive enzymes. This agent is absorbed from the gastrointestinal tract in only minuscule amounts.

Precautions

Because sucralfate is not absorbed, it is quite safe, and no contraindications have been established.

Dose

1 g orally four times a day on an empty stomach; after ulcer symptoms have disappeared, the dosage can be reduced to 1 g twice a day.

Misoprostil

Misoprostil (Cytotec®) is a synthetic prostaglandin E_1 analog that inhibits the secretion of gastric acid, but it also stimulates the secretion of mucus and bicarbonate, which help protect the gastric and duodenal mucosa from the erosive actions of acid and digestive enzymes. It is principally used to prevent ulcers in individuals receiving NSAIDs—of which aspirin is the most common.

Precautions

Misoprostil must not be used during pregnancy because it frequently causes abortions. In a wilderness situation, the resulting bleeding and other problems could be disastrous. The safety of this drug for nursing mothers and children has not been established.

Dose

100 to 200 µg orally four times a day, with meals and at bedtime.

Proton Pump Inhibitors

Proton pump inhibitors, of which the best known is omeprazole (Prilosec®), block secretion by the acid-producing cells of the stomach. These agents are the most effective yet developed for treating peptic ulcer and gastroesophageal reflux (heartburn). No contraindications exist, although the safety of the drug during pregnancy and in children has not been established. No significant side effects occur during administration for the short intervals that would typify wilderness outings. A physician's prescription is required for these drugs.

Dose

Omeprazole: one 20 mg sustained-release capsule daily, swallowed whole before meals or at bedtime.

B

THERAPEUTIC PROCEDURES

The injuries for which the following procedures are therapeutic have been discussed in the chapters of this text. Some of these procedures are rarely used. Others, such as intramuscular injections, are used quite commonly, particularly in expedition circumstances.

ADMINISTERING MEDICATIONS

Oral Medications

The oral route is the easiest, most convenient, and safest method for administering drugs. It has two major disadvantages: the time required for a drug to be absorbed and variations in the rate and completeness of absorption. Acid and enzymes in the stomach completely inactivate some therapeutic agents, and they must be given by another route.

Individuals who are not fully conscious may aspirate oral medications and must never receive them.

Oral therapy is much less effective for a person who is nauseous or vomiting. Even if the drugs are not expelled, emptying of the stomach is greatly retarded, and the onset of action by the agent is delayed because orally administered drugs are usually absorbed only in the small intestine.

With the exception of agents that are irritating to the stomach, such as aspirin or ibuprofen, oral medications should be taken at least one-half hour before meals. The stomach empties more slowly and irregularly when it is filled with food, which delays onset of the drug's actions. Food interferes with the absorption of some medications.

Intramuscular Injections

The intramuscular route for administering drugs avoids the vagaries of intestinal absorption but is associated with several hazards. The most significant is the risk of an overdose. An excessive dose or the wrong drug given orally can be partially retrieved by making the person vomit. No such "safety valve" is available for medications that have been injected.

Intramuscular injections are associated with a slight risk of injecting the drug directly into a blood vessel inside the muscle, which would produce higher and more toxic blood concentrations of the agent than the slower absorption from a true intramuscular site.

Intramuscular injections are usually not absorbed well by individuals who are in shock or are hypothermic. If several injections of an agent were given and the medication was not absorbed until the person recovered, all would be absorbed at once, producing an overdose and possibly serious toxicity.

The needle used for an intramuscular injection may injure nerves, blood vessels, or other structures if the site for the injection is not carefully chosen (Fig. B-1).

The most common complication of intramuscular injections is an infection produced by bacteria introduced with the needle. Although the needle may be free of bacteria, the skin through which it passes can not be completely sterilized. Thorough cleansing of the skin and avoiding needle contamination usually limit the quantity of bacteria introduced to a number that the body's defenses can destroy.

The following steps should be followed in administering any therapeutic agent intramuscularly:

1. The skin over the injection site should be cleaned with soap and water, swabbed with alcohol (or a disinfectant such as Betadine®), and permitted to dry.
2. The label on the drug container should be read closely to ensure that the proper medication in the correct dose is being administered.

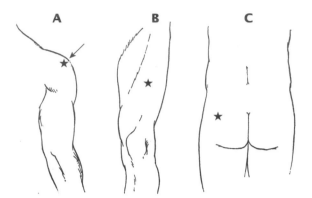

FIGURE B-1. Sites for the administration of intramuscular injections (A, shoulder; B, thigh; C, buttock)

3. A syringe of appropriate size should be fitted with a twenty-five-gauge needle.
4. The rubber top of the vial through which the needle is to be inserted should be swabbed with alcohol or a disinfectant.
5. The drug should be extracted by inverting the vial, inserting the needle through the rubber top, injecting a volume of air equal to the volume of fluid to be removed, and withdrawing the medication. While the needle is still in the vial, air bubbles or excess medication should be expressed from the syringe.
6. The label on the container must be reexamined to ensure that no mistakes have occurred. Such errors are far easier to prevent than to correct.
7. Without touching the injection site, a mound of skin and muscle should be pinched up so that the needle does not strike the underlying bone, and the needle should be inserted with a jab.
8. Before injecting the medication, the plunger of the syringe must be pulled back to make certain the needle is not in a blood vessel. If blood is pulled back into the syringe, the needle must be removed and inserted into a different location.
9. The contents of the syringe should be injected slowly to minimize discomfort, but the needle should be withdrawn quickly.

Subcutaneous Injections

Subcutaneous injections are absorbed more slowly than intramuscular injections, which is an advantage with a few agents, such as epinephrine. The technique for subcutaneous injections is the same as that for intramuscular injections, but the needle should be inserted at an angle so that it stays in the subcutaneous fat and does not enter the muscle. Injections can be made wherever a significant amount of fat is present beneath the skin.

Intravenous Medications

Intravenous drug administration is required in a few medical emergencies, may be the only effective way to administer drugs to individuals who are in shock, and is the most effective method to treat some severe infections because higher blood concentrations of a therapeutic agent can be attained. Additionally, a more constant blood concentration of the drug can be maintained without the swings associated with intermittent intramuscular or oral administration.

However, intravenous injections may be hazardous because high drug concentrations in the blood can develop quite rapidly. If a medication is injected too rapidly, severe complications—even death—

can result. As with intramuscular injections, once an agent has been injected intravenously the drug can not be recovered—no "safety valve" is available. If the person has an allergic reaction to the drug, little can be done to reverse the process. Such injections must be given only when necessary, and specified rates of injection must be closely observed.

The technique for administering intravenous medications over a long period of time is the same as that for intravenous fluid administration. Intravenous antibiotics are usually administered by injecting the antibiotic directly into a bottle of intravenous fluids. Drugs also may be injected through a special port on the tubing.

If the injections are intermittent, as are the periodic injections of morphine to provide analgesia for a person in shock, the large veins located in the fold of the arm at the elbow should be used. Preparation of the injection and the injection site should be the same as that for intramuscular injections. After the needle has been inserted into a vein, a small amount of blood should be withdrawn to dilute the drug and make certain the needle is in the proper location. Subsequently, the drug should be injected slowly, but continuously, over a period of two to three minutes.

Intravenous Fluid Therapy

Intravenous fluid therapy is required to replace normal and abnormal fluid losses for individuals who are not able to take fluids orally, to administer blood or plasma following a severe hemorrhage, and for the intravenous administration of some medications.

Currently, catheters are used in most U.S. medical centers for the administration of intravenous fluids because they rarely puncture the vein walls after they have been inserted, as do sharp needle tips, and they do not become dislodged as easily.

The technique for administering fluids intravenously is simple. Individuals planning outings to wilderness areas where intravenous fluids might be required should learn the technique beforehand from an experienced nurse or intravenous technician.

Although minor details in the way intravenous fluids are administered by different individuals vary, the basic technique is as follows:

1. The protective cap should be removed from the container of fluids to be administered, the tubing on the dispensing apparatus should be clamped below the drip chamber, and the apparatus should be inserted into the proper opening. The drip chamber, a small reservoir that keeps air bubbles from being carried into the subject's vein by the fluid, should be half filled by being squeezed repeatedly. (Compressing the drip chamber forces air out of the tubing between the chamber and the fluid container. When the pressure is released, the chamber expands and draws fluid back into the space previously occupied by air.) After the chamber is half full, the tubing should be filled by briefly releasing the clamp. The container (with its tubing) should be suspended two to three feet above the body of the person who is to receive the fluids.

2. The person should be placed in a supine position, and a tourniquet that blocks venous but not arterial blood flow should be placed around the upper arm. (The pulse must be palpable at the wrist.) The subject should open and close his fist several times to engorge the superficial veins with blood. Letting the arm hang down for a few minutes or covering it with a warm, moist towel helps make the veins more prominent if they are small or obscured by subcutaneous fat.

3. A large, prominent vein in the lower arm, preferably on the inner, flat surface, should be selected, and the overlying skin should be cleaned with soap and water and swabbed with alcohol or a disinfectant. After the skin has dried, the subject's arm should be held in one hand with the thumb stretching the skin over the vein into which the catheter is to be inserted. (Intravenous catheters consist of an outer thin sheath—the catheter—that has a hub into which the intravenous tubing is inserted, and an inner metal needle that protrudes

FIGURE B-2. Technique for inserting a needle for intravenous therapy

beyond the tip of the catheter and has a handle but no hub.) The apparatus should be held almost parallel with the vein with the bevel of the needle upward (Fig. B-2). The needle should be inserted through the skin, into the vein, and threaded up the vein for about one inch. A slight "give" can be felt as the vein is entered and blood flows back into the needle.

4. After the needle has been threaded into the vein, the hub of the catheter should be grasped securely to ensure that it is not pulled out, and the needle should be extracted. The end of the intravenous tubing should be inserted into the hub of the catheter, the clamp on the tubing should be released, and the tourniquet should be removed from the subject's arm.

5. Once the fluids are flowing satisfactorily, the catheter should be anchored with tape, and the last eight to ten inches of tubing should be formed into an S or U and taped to the person's arm. Such loops absorb any accidental pulls on the apparatus and prevent dislodging the catheter. If the individual is not fully conscious or is thrashing about, his arm should be anchored in some manner while fluids are being given.

6. Usually the clamp on the tubing should be partially closed so that the fluid is flowing at about 200 cc per hour (approximately 50 drops per minute). However, plasma administration following a severe hemorrhage or fluid replacement for disorders such as cholera often have to be made at much faster rates. Occasionally, fluids must be given at more than one site in order to achieve the needed speed of administration. (Intravenous lines and the rate at which they are running must be checked at least every hour.)

7. Swelling at the site of the catheter indicates that the vein has been punctured and fluids are infiltrating into the tissue. The catheter must be withdrawn, discarded, and another catheter inserted at another site. No effort should be made to reinsert the catheter in the original vein until all swelling has disappeared, which requires several hours. The swelling usually produces little or no discomfort and requires no specific treatment. Such events are much less common when fluids are given through a catheter than when fluids are administered through a needle.

8. If the fluid fails to flow when the tubing is unclamped, the catheter may be obstructed. Changing its position slightly may move the tip away from the wall of the vein and restart the flow. Squeezing the tubing may force out small clots or plugs of tissue blocking the catheter. If the tourniquet on the upper arm has not been removed, or a similar venous obstruction (by tight clothing, for instance) is present, the fluid can not flow. Occasionally such measures are

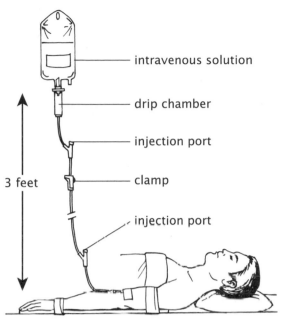

intravenous solution

drip chamber

injection port

3 feet

clamp

injection port

FIGURE B-3. Apparatus for administration of intravenous fluids

not successful in starting or restarting flow, the catheter must be withdrawn, and a new catheter must be inserted at another site.

9. When more than one container of fluids is to be given, a dispensing apparatus can be inserted into the second container, the tubing filled as described, and a large needle placed on its tip (Fig. B-3). The tubing should be clamped and the needle inserted into an injection port in the tubing to the first container. When the first container has emptied, its tubing should be clamped above the injection port, and the clamp on the second tubing should be released. The tubing from the first container can then be inserted into a third container of fluids if one is to be administered. This technique eliminates the need to clamp the tubing to the subject precisely as the last fluid runs out of the first container but before the drip chamber empties, and frantically trying to insert the dispenser into a second container before blood clots in the catheter and obstructs it.

10. If intravenous fluids are expected to be needed for several days, they can be administered slowly to keep the catheter open for fluid administration the following day. (At a rate of 100 cc per hour, or about 25 drops per minute, about twenty-four hours would be required to administer 2,500 cc of fluid.) After forty-eight to seventy-two hours, the catheter should be removed and another catheter inserted at another site if it is still needed.

11. The veins used for intravenous fluid therapy usually clot after the catheter is withdrawn and are not suitable for subsequent use. In situations where intravenous fluid therapy at more than one site is anticipated, the first catheters should be placed near the person's wrists and subsequent catheters placed higher up the arms as the veins become obstructed.

12. The veins on the back of the hands should not be used for intravenous therapy if other sites are available because this area is quite sensitive. However, for individuals who are in shock or hypothermic, or who are obese, particularly if they have darkly pigmented skin, such veins may be the only ones that can be found.

13. Occasionally, veins for intravenous therapy are impossible to access, particularly in obese people or individuals who are in shock, hypothermic, or severely dehydrated. In an emergency, fluids can be administered by inserting the needle beneath the skin of the back, abdomen, or upper thighs and letting the fluid infiltrate the subcutaneous space. Absorption from such sites is erratic, and administration may produce some discomfort, but when fluids are needed, this route is better than not giving fluids at all. Medications should not be administered in this manner.

NASOGASTRIC INTUBATION

Nasogastric intubation is a highly desirable—almost essential—element in the care of individuals with intestinal paralysis (paralytic ileus) or obstruction. All of the serious disorders associated with severe, acute abdominal pain produce such paralysis; the effects are most severe with intestinal obstruction or disorders causing peritonitis.

Large quantities of air are swallowed with food or liquids, including saliva. Gas is always present in the gastrointestinal tract, and swallowed air is the source of most of it. If the stomach is paralyzed, its contents—including gas—can not be expelled into the intestine, and it quickly becomes ballooned with air. The distended stomach impinges on the diaphragm and interferes with respiration; it also presses on the veins in the abdomen and impedes the return of blood from the lower body to the heart.

Large quantities of fluids—digestive juices, partially digested food, and other liquids that have been consumed—pool in the paralyzed stomach with the air and eventually lead to vomiting. Loss of the fluids and electrolytes can produce or aggravate dehydration, and pneumonia or respiratory obstruction may result if the vomit is aspirated.

A tube inserted through the nose and esophagus into the stomach permits the air that is swallowed to escape and prevents most of these problems. The tube is uncomfortable because it causes a sore throat, but it usually does not cause gagging or related symptoms.

The use of nasogastric suction is not without hazard because fluids are removed from the stomach as well as air. If these fluids are not replaced intravenously with a balanced salt solution or saline, salt and water depletion inevitably result. If fluids for intravenous therapy are not available, the nasogastric tube should be used only to remove air that has collected. After the air has escaped, the tube should be clamped and only reopened when significant quantities of air have reaccumulated

The technique for nasogastric intubation is as follows:

1. The tube, at least a size eighteen French, should be chilled and the tip lubricated with a bland jelly, mineral oil, or at least water before it is inserted.
2. The subject should be sitting up and should have cold water, crushed ice, or snow to swallow.
3. The tube should be inserted through one nostril, along the floor of the nasal cavity, to the back of the throat. Then the person should be instructed to swallow. As he swallows, the tube should be thrust further so the tongue and muscles of the throat can guide it into the esophagus. Several attempts are usually necessary. When the tube does enter the esophagus, the individual should be told to keep swallowing. With each swallow, the tube should be thrust further down until a length equal to the distance from the person's nose to his stomach (which should have been previously marked) has been inserted.
4. After the tube is in place, a small amount of air should be injected through it with a large syringe or bulb syringe. If the tube is in the stomach, bubbling sounds made by the injected air can be clearly heard. If the tube has coiled in the back of the person's throat or turned on itself in his esophagus and has not entered the stomach, such sounds are not heard, and the tube must be partially withdrawn and reinserted.
5. Rarely, the tube may enter the trachea, causing the individual to cough and sometimes to be unable to talk. If the tube is withdrawn promptly, no harm is done, but he may be understandably reluctant to undergo further attempts at intubation.

6. After the tube is in place, it must be taped to the person's nose or forehead to prevent its being expelled or swallowed entirely. Air and fluid in the stomach can be withdrawn with a syringe equipped with an attachment to fit the tubing. After the stomach is emptied, the tube should be attached to a suction apparatus constructed by suspending a jar filled with water several feet above the subject's body. (A lower bottle can collect the drainage.)

7. Nasogastric tubes have a tendency to become obstructed by mucus or particles of food. Therefore, the tube should be flushed with a small amount of a salt solution (or water if a salt solution is not available) every two hours. (The fluid used to irrigate the tube must be subtracted from the total volume lost through the tube when calculating the subject's fluid requirements.)

8. The total volume of fluid lost through the nasogastric tube must be carefully measured and recorded. All of the fluid lost in this manner should be replaced intravenously with a balanced salt solution or saline.

URETHRAL CATHETERIZATION

Following prolonged periods of unconsciousness or after severe trauma, particularly injuries in which the lower portion of the body is paralyzed, the urinary bladder may be severely distended. Due to stretching of the bladder muscles and pressure against the opening of the bladder, the individual may be unable to void. As his bladder becomes more distended, it becomes painful. To relieve the distention a catheter must be inserted into the bladder through the urethra. The discomfort from this procedure is surprisingly small, usually much less than that from a distended bladder.

Urethral catheterization is rarely required for females, whose much shorter urethra offers far less resistance to voiding. If urethral catheterization is needed for a female, it must be carried out by someone with enough knowledge of female anatomy to correctly identify the urethral opening.

Rarely, an individual with a distended bladder repeatedly voids a small amount but does not completely empty his bladder. For such individuals, distention requires longer to develop but can become much more severe because it is less obvious. Since the individual is voiding, the primary symptom is the severe discomfort from the distended bladder.

Usually a period of approximately eight to ten hours is required for the bladder to become distended. Urethral catheterization can often be avoided if the person can be induced to void before that much time has elapsed. Having him stand up and walk around for a few minutes or placing his hand in warm water is frequently helpful in achieving his goal.

The greatest risk from urethral catheterization is infection, but meticulous care to avoid contamination of the catheter greatly reduces this hazard.

The following procedure should be followed for urethral catheterization:

1. Everything needed must be assembled before the procedure is begun. Any break to obtain a forgotten item invites contamination and infection. The required supplies consist of a sterile urinary catheter (size sixteen or eighteen French), sterile rubber or plastic gloves or sterile instruments to handle the catheter, sterile lubricating ointment, and alcohol swabs. A sterile towel on which to place the items is a great convenience and helps avoid contamination. The sterile wrapper from the gloves may be an appropriate substitute. A receptacle to collect the urine should also be on hand, particularly if the volume of urine must be measured.

2. The glans must be cleaned with alcohol, a disinfectant, or just soap and water, and the catheter must be removed from its container without being contaminated. The circumstances and assistance available should determine which is done first, but the glans should not touch any nonsterile objects after it has been cleaned. For women, the labia should be spread and the opening of the urethra and surrounding mucosa should be cleansed in a similar manner. The labia must not be allowed to close until the catheter has been inserted into the bladder.

3. A small amount of a sterile lubricant should be applied to the catheter tip, and, with the

individual in the supine position, the catheter should be inserted into the urethra and gently threaded upward until urine begins to flow from the open end. In men, this maneuver is facilitated if the penis is pulled upward to straighten the urethra and eliminate any folds in the mucosa lining this passage. After the urine has ceased to flow, the catheter should be gently withdrawn.

4. Most individuals require only a single catheterization and are subsequently able to void without difficulty. However, subjects with paralysis of the lower portion of their bodies usually have to be catheterized every eight hours to prevent overdistention of the bladder and possible renal injury. For such persons, an indwelling (Foley) catheter should be inserted. This type of catheter has a small balloon just below the tip. After the catheter has been inserted, this balloon can be inflated by injecting fluid with a syringe and needle into the nipple provided for this purpose on the external end of the catheter. The balloon must be deflated by clipping off the end of this nipple before the catheter is withdrawn. However, a catheter of this kind can usually be left in place for three to five days. To reduce the risk of infection, the subject may be given one of the antimicrobial drugs recommended for urinary bladder infections.

TUBE THORACOSTOMY

Tube thoracostomy is a severely hazardous procedure. The possible complications include infection, puncture of the heart or a major blood vessel, laceration of the lung, or even penetration of the diaphragm and laceration of the liver or spleen, all of which would probably be disastrous in a wilderness situation. This procedure must only be attempted when the following conditions can be met:

▾ The subject is dying as the result of impaired respiratory function due to air or fluid in the chest, which would almost always be the result of traumatic injury.

▾ All of the required equipment is available: flutter valve, trochar or means for inserting the tube, and the necessary tubing. A local anesthetic and means for preventing infection are also desirable.

▾ A physician has instructed the person performing the procedure.

In spite of the hazards it presents, this procedure, properly performed, may be lifesaving for individuals with a tension pneumothorax, particularly at high altitudes. Tube thoracostomy should be performed as follows:

1. If possible, the subject should be sitting up with his arms forward, propped in this position if necessary. If he can not sit up, he should have his head and chest higher than the rest of his body, and the side of the chest in which the tube is to be inserted should be uppermost.

2. If the person's condition allows time, the attendant should scrub his hands and arms with soap or Betadine® and a brush for ten minutes—by the clock!

3. A wide area of the individual's chest above the nipple on the injured side should be similarly scrubbed. Subsequently this area should be swabbed with iodine followed by alcohol or Betadine®, or just alcohol if nothing else is available.

4. If sterile rubber gloves are available, they should be put on after the attendant's hands have been scrubbed and the subject's chest has been scrubbed and swabbed with an antiseptic.

5. The rib at the same level as the nipple or at its upper margin should be identified. A point just lateral to the nipple (just beyond the edge of the breast for females) and at the upper margin of the rib should be selected for the thoracostomy.

6. The point selected can be anesthetized by infiltration with a local anesthetic (lidocaine). The infiltration should extend down to the rib and over its upper border.

7. A flutter valve (Heimlich valve) should be attached to one end of the chest tubing before the thoracostomy is begun. The valve must be checked to be certain it is not attached backward.

8a. If a trochar is available, a small nick about one-quarter inch (6 mm) in length should be made

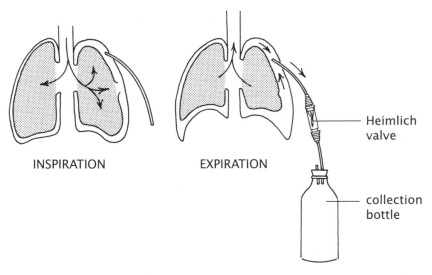

INSPIRATION   EXPIRATION

Heimlich valve

collection bottle

FIGURE B-4. Pulmonary function with a pneumothorax treated by tube thoracostomy[1]

in the skin with a sterile scalpel blade to facilitate its insertion. The trochar should be pushed firmly through the chest wall until it stops against the rib. Then the tip should be moved upward slightly until it passes over the top of the rib, thus avoiding the blood vessels that course along the bottom of every rib. The chest wall is one and one-half to two and one-half inches (4 to 6.5 cm) thick, depending upon the individual's muscularity and the amount of fat present.

8b. If a trochar is not available, a one inch (2.5 cm) incision should be made with a sterile scalpel and carried down to the rib. The bleeding that accompanies this incision can safely be ignored. The rib should be palpated with a sterile finger to ensure that its upper margin is located.

9a. After the trochar passes over the top of the rib, it should be pushed into the chest cavity. A gush of air or fluid should be encountered as the pleura is entered. The tubing with flutter valve attached should be passed through the trochar so that two to three inches of tubing extend beyond the trochar into the chest. While holding the tubing to make sure it is not pulled out, the trochar should be withdrawn. (Leaking of air around the tubing is prevented by the muscles and other tissues of the chest wall.)

9b. With a pair of forceps or with a scalpel—carefully—the muscle above the rib and the underlying pleura should be punctured. A gush of air or blood should be encountered. Puncturing the pleura is usually painful in spite of the local anesthetic, and the subject may require reassurance. A sterile finger can briefly palpate the inner surface of the pleura to ensure that the chest has been entered. Then the tubing should be inserted, using the finger in the incision to guide it into position with about two inches extending into the pleural cavity.

10. Usually the subject experiences marked relief of his respiratory difficulties immediately. If he does not, the tube should be checked to make certain it has been inserted to the proper depth and is not obstructed.

11. The tube should be anchored to the chest wall with tape so that it can not be pulled out or forced farther into the chest. A sterile bandage should be placed around the opening in the chest wall.

12. After the tube is in place, air and perhaps a little blood can be seen to pass through the valve whenever the person coughs. With severe lung injuries, such emissions can be seen during quiet respiration. The valve should collapse during inspiration to prevent air being sucked into the chest.

13. If a large amount of fluid or blood is being lost through the tube, a sterile receptacle of some type should be attached to the end away from the person's body, preferably with a second length of tubing, in order to measure the volume of the loss and prevent soiling the subject's clothing, sleeping bag, or other items (Fig. B-4).

14. Most individuals must be evacuated with the tube in place. However, small lung punctures usually seal within one to four days, at which time air no longer flutters the valve on the end of the chest tube. When no evidence of air has been seen for six hours or more, the tube can be clamped, and the subject watched closely for several hours to determine whether respiratory distress returns. If he remains in satisfactory condition, the tube should be left clamped for twenty-four to forty-eight hours. If no air passes from the tube when the clamp is released at the end of this time, the tubing may be withdrawn to reduce the risk of infection. If bubbles are seen, the entire procedure should be repeated forty-eight hours later. The individual must be closely attended during the time the tube is clamped so that the clamp can be released if respiratory difficulty develops.

INSTRUMENT STERILIZATION

Sterilization of instruments before they can be used is sometimes necessary. At sea level, boiling in water for fifteen minutes provides adequate sterilization, but equipment must be available for removing the items from the water without contaminating them. At higher elevations the boiling temperature of water is lower and the time required for sterilization is prolonged, but the additional time required is not easily determined. Boiling in a pressure cooker for fifteen minutes under fifteen pounds of pressure should be adequate at almost any altitude.

Scalpels, forceps, scissors, and similar metal instruments can be sterilized by washing them thoroughly, dipping them in alcohol, and lighting the alcohol. The instruments must be permitted to cool before they are used. (Blowing on the items to cool them produces contamination with bacteria from the nose and mouth.)

Regardless of the manner in which they have been sterilized, needles and syringes used for one individual must never be used to administer injections to another. The methods of sterilization in the field are too uncertain and the risk of transmitting hepatitis or more dangerous infections is too great to chance in this manner. Most needles and syringes currently available are disposable—designed to be used only once and then discarded. Supplies of this type should be secured for wilderness outings. Items such as forceps and scalpels are also available in sterile, disposable kits that are convenient and relatively inexpensive.

Dressings and instruments should be wrapped in paper and autoclaved. Items protected in this manner remain sterile for several months if they are undisturbed and stay dry. If the items become wet, sterility is lost.

REFERENCES

1. Johnson J and Kirby C: *Surgery of the Chest,* 3rd ed. Year Book Medical Publishers, Inc., 1964. (Adapted and used by permission.)

C

MEDICAL SUPPLIES

No wilderness party can be completely prepared for every medical problem. Only the materials needed to care for common medical problems can be carried. The materials needed for severe accidents or major illnesses should be available at a base camp or similar central location.

No two individuals, whether physicians or not, can agree about the items that should be included in a wilderness medical kit. *(Because opinions vary so widely, and often are so deeply entrenched, serious consideration has been given to eliminating this portion of the text. —Ed.)* The following lists contain materials likely to be needed for acute medical disorders. "Personal Medical Supplies" are items that probably should be carried by everyone on almost any outing. "Outing Medical Supplies" are items that should be available in popular wilderness areas and on expeditions to remote areas. (Obviously, larger parties can carry a larger quantity and a greater variety of medical supplies.) The "Airdrop Medical Kit" suggests items that could be available by airdrop or similar means to victims of major accidents and possibly should be carried by major expeditions. Physicians should be consulted about the dosages and quantities of the items to be included.

Medications for preexisting disorders, such as diabetes or asthma, must be supplied by the individuals with such conditions.

Personal Medical Supplies

        Acetaminophen, ibuprofen, or aspirin—50 or more
        Aspirin or acetaminophen and codeine—20 to 30
        Meperidine, 100 mg tablets—10 or more
             or
        Morphine, 10 or 15 mg tablets—10 or more
        Adhesive pads (Band-Aids®), large—10 or more
        Sterile gauze pads, four-inch squares—6 or more
        Porous adhesive tape, two-inch width—1 roll
        Moleskin, four-inch squares—4 to 6
        Elastic bandage, three-inch width—1 or 2
        Triangular bandage—2 or 3
        Tweezers—1 per party
        Sunscreen—generous supply
        Wound antiseptic such as Betadine®—2 to 4 ounces
             or
        Betadine® Swabs—5 to 20
        Personal medications—as needed

Outing Medical Kit
Medications (oral except where specified)
ANALGESICS
        Aspirin and/or acetaminophen and/or ibuprofen
        Codeine (with aspirin or acetaminophen)
        Morphine (oral and injectable)

or
Meperidine (oral and injectable)
Dibucaine ointment

ANTIMICROBIAL PREPARATIONS
Penicillins—phenoxymethyl penicillin, ampicillin (oral and intramuscular), cloxacillin
Ciprofloxacin
Tetracycline
Trimethoprim-sulfamethoxazole
Neosporin® ophthalmic drops
Substitutes for members allergic to penicillin or sulfonamides
Antimalarials appropriate for area
Wound antiseptic(s)

GASTROINTESTINAL MEDICATIONS
One or more antacids
One or more motion-sickness agents
One or more laxatives
One or more antidiarrheal agents
One or more H_2 blockers

CARDIAC AND RESPIRATORY AGENTS
A systemic decongestant
A local decongestant spray, preferably long-acting
Epinephrine
Alupent Inhaler® or equivalent
Acetazolamide
Dexamethasone

OTHERS
One or more antihistamines
One or more sedatives or tranquilizers
Sunscreens

Bandages and dressings
Sterile gauze pads
Nonadherent gauze pads
Spenco Second Skin®
Bandaging materials such as Kling
    Adhesive strips (Band-Aids®)
Butterfly strips
Sterile absorbent cotton
Cotton swabs (Q-Tips®)
Eye pads
Triangular bandages
Adhesive tape, two inch (porous)
Hypoallergenic tape
Elastic bandages, two or three inch
Moleskin

Equipment
>Surgical forceps and tweezers
>Magnifying glass
>Penlight
>Scissors
>Scalpel with blades
>Syringes and needles
>Oral thermometer
>Stethoscope
>Sphygmomanometer
>Plastic oral airway(s)
>Tracheostomy device
>Tongue blades
>Inflatable lower leg splint
>Traction splint
>Hot water bottle(s)
>Sawyer snake venom extractor
>Cervical collar

Items in personal medical kits

Airdrop Medical Kit
Items in outing medical kit
INTRAVENOUS FLUIDS (PLASTIC CONTAINERS)
>Balanced salt solution
>Five or ten percent glucose

TUBING AND NEEDLES FOR ADMINISTRATION
INTRAVENOUS ANTIBIOTICS

Oxygen bottles, masks, valves, and tubing
Equipment for therapeutic procedures
>Sterile gloves, lidocaine, syringes, and needles
>Trochar, tubing, and valves for thoracostomy
>Tubes, bottles, and syringes for nasogastric intubation
>Catheters and lubricant for urethral catheterization

Leg and arm splints
Additional medications for known medical problems
Rescue gear
>Rewarming gear
>Rock-climbing and ice-climbing gear
>Collapsible or wheel-equipped stretchers

Camping gear
>Sleeping bags
>Tents
>Clothing

Food and potable water
Two-way radio

LEGAL AND ETHICAL CONSIDERATIONS

PRINCIPAL CONTRIBUTORS:
Forrest C. Wilkerson, Attorney-at-Law (Legal Considerations)
Charles S. Houston, M.D. (Ethical Considerations)

In a society ruled by a judiciary that at times seems to consider its members responsible for everyone but themselves, outdoor enthusiasts must be aware of the legal problems that can arise from wilderness activities. Laws for dealing with many common problems, particularly death in the wilderness, have already been codified and are briefly addressed in the first portion of this discussion.

However, answers for many other problems are not so easily determined. A philosophical consideration of these issues is provided in the second portion.

LEGAL CONSIDERATIONS

Few participants in wilderness activities would hesitate to provide medical care or to assist with the evacuation of an ill or injured individual, whether a member of their party or another. None of the following should raise doubts about that ethical—not legal—obligation. However, persons who do elect to render medical aid to others do have certain legal responsibilities, as well as definite legal rights.

The following are general principles of the applicable laws in the United States and Canada. However, each state, province, and nation makes its own laws, and they vary considerably. Anyone involved with such legal problems must obtain specific information about the law in the geographic area with which he is concerned.

Personal Liability

Almost no country has laws that require anyone to help a stranger in distress. An outdoorsman can decline to provide medical assistance to anyone with legal impunity. Any obligation that exists in wilderness circumstances is ethical or traditional, not legal.

In contrast, a legal obligation to provide medical care or other assistance does exist if the individual has negligently caused the injury.

If medical assistance is provided, even though not required by law, it must be given reasonably and carefully. The diligence that would be exercised by an ordinarily prudent person under similar circumstances must be exercised. Anyone providing medical care is legally liable for harming the injured person if the injury could have been avoided by reasonable care. Additionally, more severe injuries or diseases are recognized to require closer attention and more extensive and sophisticated treatment.

The need for wilderness users to be familiar with first aid is well recognized. An outdoorsman could be held liable for injuries resulting from lack of familiarity with techniques generally known to others, particularly if he had indicated in some manner beforehand that he had such knowledge. A physician is held to a higher standard. He must conduct himself as an ordinarily prudent doctor of medicine.

The circumstances in which assistance is rendered are also significant. The care legally required is that which is reasonable under the circumstances. The law takes into account the location of the victim, hazards for the person rendering aid, the equipment available, and the physical condition of the parties.

Finally, although a legal basis for claims sometimes does exist, lawsuits arising from voluntary medical assistance are rare. Few claims have followed voluntary assistance for individuals involved in wilderness accidents or illnesses.

Establishing Death

The problem of establishing that a person is dead is primarily medical, not legal. A death certificate signed by a physician is the customary method. If a physician is not available, a statement by persons who have actually seen the body and checked it for life usually suffices. If the body can not be found or recovered following an accident such as a drowning or an avalanche, the statement of someone who witnessed the accident is ordinarily adequate. If no one saw the accident, death may still be established satisfactorily by circumstantial evidence, such as abandoned equipment, a deserted automobile or campsite, or the last statements of the deceased.

However, when such evidence can not be found, and only the disappearance of the missing person into a wilderness area can be documented, particularly if the wilderness area is one from which he could escape without difficulty, death might be impossible to establish. In such instances enough time must pass for legal "presumption" of death, usually seven years.

Disposal of the Body

The next of kin and local law enforcement agencies both have a legal interest in the body. The next of kin has the right to determine the disposal of the body (usually cremation or burial), where this shall be done, and what religious ceremony or other customs are to be followed. Law enforcement agencies must determine the manner of death to ensure that no crime has been committed and no public health hazard exists, and they must ensure that disposal of the body does not offend public sensibilities.

The next of kin and the law enforcement officials may decide to leave a body in a remote, inaccessible location. Following a wilderness death, the members of a party are not legally obligated to retrieve or even to find the body.

Estate and Life Insurance

Death occurring in the wilderness, even if the body is not recoverable, does not pose insurmountable problems in the administration of an estate or the settlement of life insurance claims. For administration of the estate, death must be proven, but the testimony of persons who actually saw the body is usually sufficient to establish the fact of death. If the deceased had life insurance, proof of death is a necessary condition for the payment of benefits. In general, proof of death that is adequate for administration of the estate is sufficient for life insurance.

A different problem is associated with insurance that had a double indemnity clause that pays twice the face amount of insurance if death is accidental. Often an exact cause of death must be ascertained. For example, after a fall the question of whether death resulted from a heart attack that precipitated the fall might be raised. If a heart attack caused the fall but injuries incurred in the fall killed the person, death usually would be considered accidental and the double indemnity provision would apply. If the individual died before the fall as the result of a heart attack, death would not have been accidental and the double indemnity provision would not apply. Deciding which occurred may be impossible. For automobile accident deaths in which the victim has a heart attack and then crashes his car, double indemnity is commonly paid because injuries from the wreck can not be proven not to have caused the victim's death. (Many individuals survive heart attacks.)

The best method for answering such questions is to carefully examine the accident site and the victims, thoroughly question all witnesses to the accident, and write down the details as soon as possible. The body still may have to be evacuated for an autopsy to establish the cause of death.

ETHICAL CONSIDERATIONS

With hundreds of thousands—even millions—of persons of all ages and abilities going to altitudes that may present hazards for their health, an inevitable question arises: who is responsible for their safety? The obvious, and overly simple, answer is the individual, which is correct in the final analysis. Anyone who decides to go in harm's way should do so with foreknowledge and with reasonable preparation and understanding.

Risk is an important part of life. Testing limits fuels growth. Challenge has led humans to use fire, to traverse oceans and deserts, to climb the highest mountains, and to journey into space. The risk-free life may not be worth living, but those who take risks and expect to survive must plan ahead and prepare as well as possible.

Consider the naive individual who seeks a simple adventure—perhaps a visit to a mountain resort, where he will ride a chairlift up a mountain. He has a right to expect the chair not to fall. If it does fall, he (or his next of kin) blames the owner or operator. But if our "adventurer" develops altitude illness and must be hospitalized—perhaps even dies—who is at fault? Failure to know in advance that he might get sick should no longer be an excuse after all that has been written on the subject. Failure to seek help is more the fault of the individual than anyone else, but absence of an adequate medical facility may be blamed on the owner of the resort. Hundreds of damage suits for such errors have been filed. Some are justified; many are not.

When a climber goes with a few friends to an alpine peak and falls, or is stranded by storm or illness, where should he turn for help? In areas where thousands of climbers are active, local authorities have established systems staffed by highly skilled professionals who can provide rapid rescue, often saving lives. Who should pay the costs for such systems and for expensive rescues? Who is responsible when a rescuer is injured or killed? If the outcome is not what might reasonably be expected, should the victim have recourse? If the ski patrol responds too slowly, or is inept, is someone liable under law?

Such questions arise over and over again, and precedents are set every day, most blaming the agency that has directly or indirectly been paid for a service used by the victim. Courts seem increasingly to discount the fact that the individual has voluntarily placed himself at risk, and instead blame the party with "deep pockets."

The highest and most difficult mountains pose more serious and complex issues, and these are changing rapidly. Fifty years ago, those who went to remote mountains knew they were completely on their own. Radio contact was difficult or impossible, rescues would take many days or weeks, and the party expected to rely on its own strength.

In the last few decades this has changed. Many more people, both experienced and inexperienced, are undertaking major climbs and explorations. Radio communications or instant worldwide telephone contacts make possible consultations and rescues that previously were out of the question. Helicopters may pluck individuals from high places that are difficult or impossible for rescue teams to reach on foot. Who is responsible for such services? If they are unavailable, is someone to blame?

More and more novice climbers are paying large sums to be taken up great mountains. Explicit or implied is the responsibility of the contractor to safeguard the customer. Failure to have made adequate plans for likely contingencies is an appropriate reason for litigation, but how extensive and detailed should the contingency plans be? Should a physician with specific responsibility for the health of the clients be included in the party? How elaborate should the medical equipment be? Should it include aids such as a hyperbaric bag or medical oxygen? Should equipment to communicate with others and within the party be required? Should the availability of helicopter rescue be part of the preparations? Who is to pay for these and other, more extreme situations?

Most recently, the capacity of any professional, however experienced, to guide a party or individual above 22,000 feet (6,700 m), the so-called Death Zone, has been challenged. Who is responsible if not the contractor? What safeguards should be taken in advance? A medical certificate? If so, from whom, and at what level of expertise? A waiver of liability (that may not be recognized by a court)? Should clients purchase their own insurance? Be required to satisfy criteria for ability and experience? Should persons contracting to guide others be certified? If so, by whom, and by what standards?

Throughout the history of mountaineering, climbers have come to the aid of others, usually strangers, in emergency situations. That has been inherent in the brotherhood of climbing. Is there a real obligation or only a traditional ethic? What risks should an individual or party be expected to take in an effort to rescue another? What if the rescuer further injures the victim? What if a party ignores cries for help from a stranger in a crisis of the stranger's own making?

Many property owners deny access to tempting cliffs and mountains for fear of lawsuits. Recently, some protective arrangements have been made for individual owners of attractive sites, and such restrictions are improving, but they are yet to be tested in court.

Not only are these thorny issues, they are being made even more complex by the great number of persons going into danger and the flood of lawsuits, both justified and frivolous. Little help in solving them can be expected from a judicial industry that absorbs as much as half of the money that changes hands as a result of such proceedings.

GLOSSARY

Abrasion: A wound of the skin—and sometimes the underlying tissue—caused by scraping or rubbing.

Abscess: A localized collection of pus caused by infection and inflammation that destroy tissue. (Pimples and boils are small abscesses in the skin.)

Acidosis: An abnormally acidic condition of the blood that may be produced by a metabolic disorder such as diabetes mellitus or by severe accidental hypothermia.

Acute: 1. Appearing after or persisting for a relatively brief period of time. (Does not indicate a specific time interval but a short period of time in relation to the condition for which it is used. An acute onset would be minutes for some disorders, weeks for others.) 2. Requiring immediate or urgent attention.

Aerosinusitis: A painful condition of the paranasal sinuses produced by a rapid increase in external pressure (due to water submersion or a rapid descent from altitude) while the openings into the sinuses are closed and the pressure within the sinuses remains lower than external pressure.

Aerotitis: A painful condition of the middle ear similar to aerosinusitis but produced by pressure changes while the eustachian tube is closed.

Airway: Passages through which air enters and leaves the lungs.

Analgesia: Relief of pain.

Analgesic: A medication that relieves pain.

Anemia: A reduced number of red blood cells in the circulating blood.

Angina pectoris: Crushing or squeezing chest pain caused by a reduction in coronary artery blood flow due to arteriosclerosis.

Arrhythmia: An abnormal rhythm, usually referring to the heartbeat.

Arteriosclerosis: A disease of arteries characterized by deposits of material that narrows the lumens (most significantly) and also stiffens or "hardens" the walls.

Aspirate: To inspire (air is aspirated into the lungs); to draw in by suction (fluid is aspirated into a syringe).

Asthma: A disorder, typically allergic in origin, characterized by respiratory difficulty and caused by spasm of the muscle in small bronchioles that narrows their lumens.

Avulsion: An injury in which tissue is torn away or forcibly separated.

Bleb: A large blister.

Boil: An abscess located in the skin and subcutaneous tissue.

Bronchi: Air passages between the trachea and the smaller bronchioles.

Bronchioles: Air passages between the bronchi and the alveoli, the smallest saclike units of the lung.

Bronchitis: Inflammation of the bronchi and bronchioles, most often resulting from infection but also caused by cold injuries or burns of the bronchial mucosa.

Cardiac: Pertaining to the heart.

Cardiac output: Volume of blood pumped by the heart over a specific period of time, usually one minute.

Carrier: A person who is immune to an infection but transmits it to others by carrying the organisms within his body.

Catheter: A tube introduced into an internal organ or structure; a urethral or urinary catheter is passed into the urinary bladder.

Central nervous system: The brain and spinal cord.

Cerebral: Pertaining to the brain.

Cervical: Pertaining to the neck.

Cholera: An infection characterized by watery diarrhea so profuse that death from dehydration can result in less than a day.

Chronic: Appearing after or persisting for a relatively long time; opposite of acute.

CNS: Central nervous system

Coma: A state of total unconsciousness.

Comatose: Totally unconscious.

Conjunctiva: Thin membrane that covers the white, visible surface of the eye and the inner surfaces of the eyelids.

Contusion: A bruise.

Convulsion: A series of intense, paroxysmal muscular contractions, commonly involving the entire body.

Crepitant: Producing crackling sounds or having a crackling sensation.

Cricothyroid: Area between the thyroid cartilage (Adam's apple) and the large cartilaginous ring (cricoid cartilage) just below.

Cricothyroidostomy: A surgical opening in the cricothyroid membrane that allows air to enter the trachea; created when the airway above that site is obstructed.

Cyanosis: A purple or bluish discoloration of the lips, nails, and skin that typically results from reduced oxygen in the blood.

Cystitis: An inflammatory disorder of the urinary bladder.

Debridement: Removal of foreign material and dead tissue from a wound.

Dehydration: Loss of excessive quantities of (body) water.

Delirium: A state of temporary mental confusion and clouded consciousness characterized by anxiety, tremors, hallucinations, delusions, and incoherence.

Diabetes mellitus: A disorder of glucose metabolism that results in increased urinary output, glucose (sugar) in the urine, a tendency to develop severe infections, and other disorders, including accelerated arteriosclerosis and renal failure.

Diagnose: To distinguish one disease or injury from another; to identify an illness or injury.

Diagnosis: Identification of an illness or injury.

Dissociation: Separation of related psychologic activities into autonomously functioning units, as in the generation of multiple personalities (abnormal), or shutting out the emotional aspects of an injury scene while concentrating on the measures necessary to carry out a rescue (normal).

Dysentery: A bacterial infection of the gastrointestinal tract that results in diarrhea, mucus and pus in the stools, and fever.

Dysmenorrhea: Painful cramps associated with menstruation.

Dyspnea: Abnormal shortness of breath; awareness of the need to breathe.

Edema: An abnormal collection of fluid within body tissue; pulmonary edema is fluid within the lungs.

Electrocardiogram: A recording of the electrical activity of the heart.

Electrolyte: One of the four major ions (sodium, potassium, chloride, and bicarbonate) in serum.

Embolism: Sudden obstruction of a blood vessel by an embolus, often resulting in death of the tissue supplied by that vessel.

Embolus: A clot or similar tissue carried by the blood stream from a peripheral site, such as a leg vein, through larger, more proximal vessels and the heart, until it is forced into a smaller artery, usually in the lung.

Encephalitis: An infection of the brain, most commonly caused by a virus, and often spread by mosquitoes.

Endemic: Peculiar to or prevailing in or among a (specified) country or people.

Epididymitis: An infection of the epididymis, the structure in which sperm collect before being transported to the seminal vesicles.

Epilepsy: A neurologic disorder characterized by repeated convulsions.

Epizootic: An infectious epidemic in animals.

Extrasystole: An abnormal cardiac rhythm in which a normally beating heart suddenly contracts after a shorter interval than usual; sometimes called "skipped beats."

Extravasate: To force a material such as blood out of its normal channel (a blood vessel) into surrounding tissue.

Exudate: Any substance, most commonly inflammatory cells and protein, that passes through blood vessel walls in living tissue and can be removed or extracted; most frequently associated with inflammation.

Fascia: A sheet or membrane of fibrous tissue investing muscles or various other structures.

Fever: A higher than normal body temperature, most commonly the result of infection but also caused by other disorders.

Fibrillation: An abnormal cardiac rhythm in which cardiac muscle fibers contract independently of each other instead of in synchrony. When only the atrium is involved, the cardiac rhythm is completely irregular. If the ventricle is involved, the condition can be lethal if not corrected within minutes because cardiac output falls to very low levels.

Flaccid: Completely lacking in muscle tone; totally relaxed.

Flatus: Gas or air expelled from the intestines.

Gangrene: Death of a part of the body, such as an arm or leg, usually the result of an inadequate blood supply but sometimes due to infection.

Gasp reflex: Involuntary tendency to gasp or inspire when suddenly immersed in cold water.

Generalized: Spread throughout the body; opposite of localized.

Glomerulonephritis: A renal disorder characterized by reduced renal function, low urinary volumes, and protein in the urine.

Gonorrhea: A sexually transmitted infection that typically produces painful urethral inflammation and a discharge in men but often produces no symptoms at all in women.

Hallucination: A sound, sight, or other sensation perceived as real in the absence of an actually existing object or source.

Heart failure: Inability of the heart to pump out all of the blood returned to it that causes fluid to pool (edema) in the peripheral tissues or lungs, depending upon which ventricle is failing.

Heart valves: Valves that maintain the forward flow of blood within the heart.

Heimlich maneuver: A maneuver for dislodging obstructing material, usually aspirated food, from the larynx or trachea.

Hematoma: A mass formed by clotted blood within tissue.

Hematuria: Blood (intact red blood cells) in the urine.

Hemoglobinuria: Hemoglobin in the urine, a reflection of disorders distinctly different from those that cause hematuria.

Hemorrhoids: Enlarged veins beneath the skin of the anus.

Hydrated: Containing water. (Normally hydrated means containing a normal amount of water.)

Hypertension: High blood pressure.

Hyperthermia: A higher than normal body temperature.

Hypoglycemia: A lower than normal concentration of glucose (sugar) in the blood.

Hypothermia: A lower than normal body temperature.

Hypoxia: Presence of a lower than normal quantity of oxygen; can refer to body tissues, blood, or the atmosphere.

Immunization: Production of an immune condition by administration of an agent that stimulates a protective response.

Incubation period: Period of time between infection by microorganisms and the onset of detectable signs or symptoms.

Infarct: Death of tissue caused by arterial obstruction or dead tissue resulting from arterial obstruction.

Intramuscular: Within muscle; the site for injection of a medication.

Intravenous: Within a vein; the site for injection of a medication or fluids.

Intubate: To place a tube into a passage such as the trachea, usually to keep the passage open.

Jaundice: Accumulation of bile pigments in the blood, usually resulting from liver disease, that produces yellow discoloration of the skin and eyes.

Ketosis: Accumulation of ketones in the blood, most commonly as the result of diabetes or starvation.

Laceration: A traumatic injury characterized by cutting or tearing.

Larynx: Upper part of the trachea; "voice box."

Lumen: Open passage within a tubular organ such as intestine or a blood vessel.

Lymph nodes: Collections of tissue that trap bacteria and debris and help retard the spread of infection or other disease processes.

Macerate: To reduce to a soft mass by soaking; to digest.

Malaise: A generalized feeling of discomfort or indisposition; feeling ill.

Malaria: A parasitic infectious disorder characterized by cyclic chills, fever and sweating, that is transmitted through the bite of female *Anopheles* mosquitoes.

Meningitis: Inflammation of the thin membranes that surround the brain and spinal cord, usually as the result of infection.

Metabolism: Processes in living organisms that use energy to construct compounds from assimilated materials, or break down such materials to release energy.

NSAIDs: Nonsteroidal anti-inflammatory drugs.

Necrosis: Death of tissue as the result of disease.

Neurologic: Of or pertaining to the nervous system.

Nontraumatic: Not caused by or associated with physical injury.

Nutrient: Any component of food that aids growth, development, or replacement of tissues.

Osmosis: Diffusion of water through a semipermeable membrane.

Osmotic pressure: Hydrostatic pressure created by diffusion through a semipermeable membrane.

Palpate: To feel or examine by touch.

Palpation: Examining by touch.

Palpitation: A rapid or irregular heartbeat of which a person is aware.

Paralytic ileus: Paralysis of the intestine that produces functional obstruction; most often caused by peritonitis.

Paresthesias: Abnormal sensations, commonly tingling or buzzing; sensations felt when a limb "goes to sleep."

Paroxysmal tachycardia: An abnormal cardiac rhythm characterized by a heartbeat that is quite fast but entirely regular.

Pathogenic: Producing disease.

Penicillinase: An enzyme produce by some bacteria that inactivates penicillin and produces resistance to that drug.

Peptic ulcer: A crater in the mucosa of the stomach or duodenum produced by the combined digestive action of gastric acid and digestive enzymes.

Peritonitis: Inflammation of the thin membrane lining the abdominal cavity that results from infection or irritation by intestinal contents or blood.

Pharyngitis: Inflammation of the pharynx, the space behind the mouth and nose; a "sore throat."

Pleurisy: Inflammation of the pleura, the thin membrane that covers the lung and the chest wall.

Pneumonia: Infection of the lung.

Prognosis: A prediction or conclusion regarding the course and termination of a disease or injury.

Prone: Lying flat in a face-down position.

Prophylaxis: Preventive treatment for disease.

Proteinuria: Protein in the urine.

Pulmonary: Of or pertaining to the lungs.

Puncture wound: A wound, usually produced by an object such as a nail or thorn, that is deep but has a narrow, constricted opening.

Purulent: Consisting of or containing pus.

Pustule: A pimple or small boil.

Pyelonephritis: An infection of the kidney.

Radial pulse: Pulse felt at the wrist on the thumb side routinely used to determine heart rate.

Radiation of pain: Sensation of pain experienced in an area other than the anatomical site of the injury or disease where it is produced.

Rebound tenderness: Pain produced by releasing pressure with the fingers on the abdomen and allowing the abdominal wall to rebound; almost always an indication of an intra-abdominal condition that requires surgical treatment.

Renal: Pertaining to the kidneys.

Resorb: To reabsorb.

Respiratory: Pertaining to the lungs or their function.

Resuscitate: To revive; to restore to life or consciousness.

Rheumatic fever: An inflammatory disorder associated with streptococcal infections in which the valves of the heart are damaged, often irreversibly.

Roughage: Food that is high in fiber and adds bulk to the gastrointestinal contents.

Salpingitis: An inflammatory disorder, usually infectious, that involves the fallopian tubes and may mimic appendicitis and other intra-abdominal disorders that require surgical therapy.

Shock: A condition characterized by low blood pressure, fast but weak pulse, pallor, "cold sweats," and mental impairment that commonly results from trauma or other disorders that produce severe bleeding.

Signs: Physical evidence of disease discovered by examination.

Sinus: A mucosa-lined space in the bones of the skull.

Sinusitis: An infection of one of the sinuses in the skull.

Soft tissue: Nonosseous tissues of the body. (The joint ligaments and internal organs usually are not included.)

Somnolence: Oppressive drowsiness or sleepiness.

Spasm: An involuntary muscular contraction, usually painful.

Sphygmomanometer: A device for measuring blood pressure.

Spinal canal: Canal within the vertebral column through which the spinal cord passes.

Sprain: An injury characterized by incomplete rupture of the supporting ligaments around a joint.

Stethoscope: A device that aids listening to body sounds, particularly those of the heart and lungs.

Strain: An injury characterized by stretching, with or without mild tearing, of a muscle or tendon.

Stress: An emotionally or physically disruptive or disquieting event or condition.

Stroke: Death of brain tissue caused by hemorrhage or arterial obstruction.

Subacute: Appearing after or persisting for a period of time that is intermediate between acute and chronic in duration. (See Acute.)

Subcutaneous: Beneath the skin.

Subdural: Beneath the dura, the fibrotic membrane covering the brain; most commonly used in reference to a hematoma.

Supine: Lying flat in a face-up position.

Suture: 1. To unite parts by stitching; to sew together the edges of lacerated tissue. 2. The joints between the bones of the skull.

Symptom: Any abnormal function, sensation, or experience that indicates the presence of disease.

Syncope: A brief episode of unconsciousness, usually not associated with a significant illness; fainting.

Syndrome: A group of signs and symptoms that occur together and comprise a disease entity.

Synergism: Two or more agents acting in combination to produce an effect greater than the sum of their independent effects.

Syphilis: A sexually transmitted infection that may produce no early symptoms but can be devastating years later if untreated.

Tachycardia: An abnormally fast heart rate.

Thoracostomy: A surgical procedure that creates an opening into the chest.

Thrombophlebitis: Thrombosis within veins that produces inflammation and pain.

Thrombosis: Clotting of blood, typically within a blood vessel, that does not follow an identifiable traumatic injury.

Torsion: Twisting an organ or tissue in such a manner that the flow of blood to the tissue is obstructed.

Toxic: Having a poisonous or noxious effect.

Toxin: A noxious or poisonous substance.

Trachea: Large air passage between the mouth or nose and the bronchi and lungs.

Tracheostomy: An opening in the trachea through which air can flow; produced to bypass an obstruction above that site.

Trauma: 1. A physical force that injures the body; an injury produced by physical force. 2. Any external force that produces injury, including emotional trauma.

Traumatic: Of or pertaining to trauma.

Tuberculosis: A chronic infection, most often pulmonary, characterized by extensive tissue destruction and death if untreated.

Varicose veins: Dilated, tortuous veins, most commonly in the legs

Vascular: Of or pertaining to blood vessels.

Vertigo: A feeling that one's self or one's environment is whirling around; not synonymous with dizziness.

INDEX